AMERICA IN THE TWENTIES AND THIRTIES

D1002882

Also by Sean Dennis Cashman

Prohibition: The Lie of the Land (THE FREE PRESS)

America in the Gilded Age (NEW YORK UNIVERSITY PRESS)

America in the Age of the Titans: The Progressive Era and World War I
(NEW YORK UNIVERSITY PRESS)

America, Roosevelt, and World War II (NEW YORK UNIVERSITY PRESS)

AMERICA IN THE TWENTIES AND THIRTIES

The Olympian Age of Franklin Delano Roosevelt

SEAN DENNIS CASHMAN

NEW YORK UNIVERSITY PRESS

NEW YORK & LONDON

Library of Congress Cataloging-in-Publication Data
Cashman, Sean Dennis.
America in the twenties and thirties.
Bibliography: p.
Includes index.
1. United States—Civilization—1918–1945.
2. Roosevelt, Franklin D. (Franklin Delano), 1882–1945.
I. Title.
E169.1.C297   1988   973.91   88-5278
ISBN 0-8147-1412-9 (alk. paper)
ISBN 0-8147-1413-7 (pbk.)

New York University Press books are Smyth-sewn and
printed on permanent and durable acid-free paper.

Book design by Ken Venezio

For Colin Morris

CONTENTS

ILLUSTRATIONS

PREFACE AND
ACKNOWLEDGMENTS

THIS BOOK is intended as an interdisciplinary history of the
United States in the period 1920–1941, ending with the Japanese attack on Pearl Harbor. It charts the course of domestic
politics and foreign policies, and tells something of the stories of
industrial and economic, social and cultural history. These were
crucial years for the United States, in which profound developments occurred in politics, transportation and communication,
culture, and world affairs. The achievements of the New Deal of
1933–1939 and the lost generation of artists were set against the
dramatic backdrop of the Great Depression, the advent of World
War II, and revolutions of Left and Right in Europe and Asia.

The book is a work of synthesis, based partly on primary
sources, partly on recent scholarship. It is a companion volume to
America in the Age of the Titans, covering the Progressive Era and
World War I in the period 1901–20. The book aims at a clear
presentation of essential facts and a synthesis of academic interpretations, and places some emphasis on the personalities of the
principal actors.

I began this book in August 1984 at the invitation of Colin Jones, who, throughout its composition, offered constructive advice about structure and detail. My initial research was facilitated by two travel grants provided by the University of Manchester, England. The support and encouragement of my former colleagues in the Department of American Studies there, notably Professor Peter Marshall, were most appreciated. The book was completed in 1987 at New York University when I was visiting professor in history, having been invited to teach there by Professors Carl Prince and David Reimers.

The book was written concurrently with *America in the Age of the Titans* but took longer to complete. Toward the end of final revisions in summer 1987 I was invited by Dr. Peter Diamandopoulos, president of Adelphi University, Garden City, Long Island, to apply for the post of dean of arts and sciences there. The interesting sequences of interviews at Adelphi and the appointment capped what had been a most stimulating year and the loyal faculty and administrators at Adelphi gave me warm support in the various stages of production.

To some people, three years would seem a long, to others, a short, time to write a book such as this. In fact, this period brought to fruition years of studying and teaching the period, beginning with my D.Phil. thesis at Oxford and continuing at the University of Manchester, England, in a series of interdisciplinary courses with my esteemed colleague, Godfrey Kearns. Thus, this is a book I had started to write in my mind several times before being given the opportunity to do so for publication. While wanting to give appropriate weight to political history, both Colin Jones and I also wanted to emphasize major developments in social and cultural history, including inventions, transportation, and the arts. Even so, the history is not complete. It does not treat such important subjects as philosophy, education, and sports, and only touches upon music. To ensure thorough presentation of black history, I have reviewed the period 1865–1920 as well as the 1920s and 1930s.

Without the assistance and participation of several friends and colleagues, my task would have been far harder. Iain Halliday undertook preliminary work, locating material, synthesizing previous scholarship, and writing drafts on various subjects, including Los Angeles as a metropolis, and the arts. The extent and variety of his work were much appreciated. Daniel Couzens both found material and prepared draft sections on the subjects of radio and music. Chris Hasson provided an account of workers and labor organizations. Chris Harries read widely in the field of black history, made a judicious choice of texts for me to study, and provided an outline of black history. In every case, my friends' help prepared the ground for what had to be done. Dr. Daniel Cornford, formerly of the Universities of California at Santa Barbara and San Francisco, and of Manchester, and an expert on labor history, read the chapter on labor. He had vigorous arguments to make about what extra scholarship was required. I also owe much to the encouragement of my mother, Margaret Cashman, and my good friend, Kenneth McArthur throughout the period writing this book.

The illustrations were found in the Museum of Modern Art, the Whitney Museum of American Art, and, principally, in the Prints and Photographs Division of the Library of Congress. Ms. Mary Ison, head of the reference section, and Ms. Maja Felaco were most helpful in advising on the selection of illustrations. Mrs. Eileen Grimes of Manchester typed most of the manuscript and typing was completed by Mrs. Lee Plaut of Adelphi University. At Manchester Ms. Caroline Sutton typed most of the voluminous correspondence. The index was devised by Robert Madison.

INTRODUCTION

COMPOSER AND lyricist Kurt Weill once observed that, for every generation, there was a special part of the world about which fantasies were conceived—for Shakespeare and his circle it was Italy; for Mozart and his contemporaries it was Turkey. For twentieth-century artists it was the United States, and during a precise period at that—1920–1941—now remembered as great years in the development of American society.

Politically, the period came to be dominated by one man, Franklin Delano Roosevelt, elected president for an unprecedented four terms and who served for over twelve years in office (1933–1945). As surely as Zeus had led a new race of Olympian gods who superseded the defunct titans of Greek mythology, in America FDR led his cabinet colleagues and political allies alike in a program of wide-ranging federal reforms, using progressive ideas to reorder government in the wake of half a century of industrial and economic expansion achieved by the titans of American industry and politics. Yet in the early 1920s Roosevelt's career, having begun so promisingly as assistant secretary to the navy (1913–1920), went into eclipse following a profound personal tragedy.

In the early 1920s downtown Chicago was dominated by a medley of skyscrapers, turning the city center into a series of vertical, manmade canyons. The Chicago Tribune Tower (left) of Raymond Hood and John Mead Howells (1925) was a Gothic creation crowned by a circle of buttresses, while the tower of the white Wrigley Building (right) by Graham, Anderson, Probst, and White (1921) was inspired by the Giralda (the Moorish tower) in Seville, Spain. (Library of Congress).

Paradoxically, what was a disastrous presidential campaign by Democratic nominee James B. Cox, governor of Ohio, in 1920 was, on balance at least, a *succès d'estime* for Roosevelt, his vice-presidential running mate. For FDR had made himself nationally widely known and personally liked. Nevertheless, when Warren Harding and Calvin Coolidge were elected president and vice-president, Roosevelt was out of public life for the first time in ten years. The Republican landslide seemed a rejection of the progressive spirit as much as a rejection of Wilsonian liberalism at home and abroad. Roosevelt retreated into the legal profession. Yet he continued to manage a variety of social, political, and charitable activities, many of which generated public appearances and guaranteed press copy. He set his sights on winning nomination and election as senator for New York in 1922. He supported the way the Republicans resolved the fiasco of the Senate's rejection of the Treaty of Versailles and League of Nations by making, first, a separate peace with Germany and, second, by organizing the Washington Naval Conference of 1921–1922.

Roosevelt and his family—his wife, Eleanor, and their four sons and one daughter, Anna—spent their summer vacation of 1921 off Campobello, New Brunswick. On Wednesday, August 10, 1921, they alighted from their yacht, the *Vireo,* to help put out a forest fire on one of the islands. "Late in the afternoon we brought it under control," he remembered. "Our eyes were bleary with smoke; we were begrimed, smarting with spark burns, exhausted." Then, to relieve tension, they raced across the island at Campobello and ended the day by taking a swim in the frigid sea off the Bay of Fundy. "I didn't feel the usual reaction, the glow I'd expected. When I reached the house the mail was in, with several newspapers I hadn't seen. I sat reading for a while, too tired even to dress. I'd never felt quite that way before." He went to bed before supper was over. The next day brought the crisis to a head. "When I swung out of bed my left leg lagged but I managed to move about and to shave. I tried to persuade myself that the trouble with my leg was muscular, that it would disappear as I used it. But presently it refused to work, and then the other." He had a temperature of 102°.

On Friday morning, August 12, he could not stand and by the evening could not even move his legs. A specialist diagnosed paralysis caused by a blood clot and prescribed massage, a remedy performed resolutely by Eleanor Roosevelt and confidant Louis Howe. His uncle, Franklin A. Delano, consulted various specialists who suspected poliomyelitis and this was confirmed by Boston specialist Dr. Robert W. Lovett on August 25. Although his political career was already formidable, Roosevelt was still only thirty-nine. Thus he was cut down, literally, in his prime. Frank-

lin and Eleanor wanted to stay in public life and they were indomitable. Louis Howe kept the terrible news of Roosevelt's illness
out of the newspapers until August 27, by which time it was truly
possible to declare he was recovering. Thus Howe deliberately
created and nurtured the impression that there was nothing fundamentally wrong—essential if FDR were to resume his political
career. In an instant the social butterfly in Roosevelt was extin-
guished and with it the opportunities for political advance by
display. In its place was a cocoon, an invalid confined to bed or
wheelchair and sometimes encased in plaster.

The worst was not really over. In January 1922 his knee mus-
cles began to tighten, drawing his legs up behind him. His physi-
cian, Dr. Draper's, remedy was to put both legs in plaster casts
and use wedges driven farther each day, to stretch the tendons
back. In February steel braces were fitted from hips to feet and,
by maneuvering himself from his hips and moving, FDR could
give an impression that he was walking, albeit clumsily, although
he had no balance at all and no power in his legs. Through
arduous exercise, he built up his upper body and transformed his
shape from slim to stocky.

Eleanor Roosevelt told historian and biographer Frank Freidel
in an interview in 1952 that Franklin's polio strengthened his
already formidable self-control. Because he had to choose a particular course of treatment and stick to it for one or two years, he
recognized the advantage of deciding upon a political policy and
abiding by it. Many politicians, having made a decision over
which they have no further control, remain worried lest it is not
the right one. However, FDR developed a capacity to free his
mind from worry about things he could not change. Thus in the
Great Depression and World War II alike he was free to concentrate on what he could usefully do.

The man who could not walk found limitless fortitude, stamina, and political skill. It was he who, as president, would drive
the nation forward in the Great Depression and World War II,
while, at the same time, being able to identify with, and be
identified with, the forgotten man at the base of the economic
pyramid.

1

DRIVING AMBITION
The Continuing Revolutions in Transportation

IN 1922 photographer Paul Strand began to take photographs of working parts of his motion picture camera and, fascinated, went on to photograph such other machines as drills and lathes, commenting on the beauty of their forms and workmanship and proclaiming them as one part of a new Trinity: "God the Machine, Materialistic Empiricism the Son, and Science the Holy Ghost." For the United States the period 1920–1941 could not be described in classical terms as an age of such precious metals as gold, silver, or bronze. However, it was one in which much of American civilization owed its forms to the industrial metals steel and aluminum, and to the mineral oil. It was, indeed, an age of *machinery: m*otor cars, *a*irplanes, *c*ameras, *h*ydroelectric power, internal combustion engines, *n*ewspaper printing presses, *e*lectrical engines, *r*adio, and *y*arns of artificial fibers.

In their *Art and the Machine* (1936) critics Sheldon and Martha Cheyney claimed how the "age of machine-implemented culture

Plymouth automobile assembly line. By mass production, standardization, and interchangeable parts, Ford and other auto manufacturers brought motor cars within reach of their workers' pockets, not only increasing the revolution in transportation but also preempting any claim of socialism that American capitalism divorced workers from the results of their labor. (Library of Congress).

had begun." In "The Americanization of Art" for a machine-age exhibition catalog of 1927, constructionist Louis Lozowick stressed how "The history of America is a history of stubborn and ceaseless effort to harness the forces of nature . . . of gigantic engineering feats and colossal mechanical construction." Here was an inspiration for art, the raw material of industrial function, structure, and standardization that could be discerned in the "rigid geometry of the American city: in the verticals of its smoke stacks, in the parallels of its car tracks, the squareness of its streets, the cubes of its factories, the arcs of its bridges, the cylinders of its gas tanks." Such mathematical order, indeed, organization, invited the "plastic structure" of art to capture the "flowing rhythm of modern America" in an idiomatic American art.

Despite the dramatic economic profile of each decade—superficial prosperity in the 1920s, the agonies of the Great Depression in the 1930s, followed by the miracle of recovery and growth in 1940s—many Americans understood that this was a period with its different industrial and social strands drawn together by science and technology, with ever-faster communication and an ever more diverse range of consumer products. As historian Richard Guy Wilson explains in the 1986 catalog for the exhibition, *The Machine Age in America 1918–1941*, "The machine age meant actual machines such as giant turbines and new machine materials such as Bakelite, Formica, chrome, aluminum, and stainless steel. The machine age meant new processes—mass production, 'Fordism'—factories, great corporations, and new ways of hiring. . . . The machine age encompassed the vast new skyscraper city, with its transportation systems compacted one on top of the other, and the new horizon city composed of filling stations, drive-ins, and superhighways."

The ever-increasing number of new inventions had led to the creation of a new vocabulary to describe them. In 1888 a group of academics undertook to make a dictionary in ten volumes of all the words in English. The project was to last forty years. As they labored, the world moved ahead of them. Thus, in 1893, while they were still on letter A, appendicitis came into common use but too late for inclusion. When they got past letter C the cinema came into being and the lexicographers decided to include it among the Ks as kinema. Over 400 words beginning with C were also too late for inclusion. By the time the project was complete in April 1928 about one new word had entered the language for every old one. A supplementary volume was already necessary. Whereas in the nineteenth century there were only two colors of stocking—black and white—now there were forty-three. The 1929 edition of *Webster's International Dictionary* found over 3,000 words had come into being in the period 1909–27. Of the 299 words beginning with letter A, 221 (two-thirds) were in the fields of science, medicine, and invention, and 82 of those were in aviation; 7 were in machinery. Only 1 was in art—atonality.

The heroes of America's advanced, increasingly technological society were Henry Ford and Charles A. Lindbergh, Jr. In 1920 one car in two throughout the world was a Ford Tin Lizzie. Pioneer car manufacturer Henry Ford had transformed the society into which he was born through an astute combination of advanced technology and paternalist management. A more authentic folk hero than Ford was Charles Lindbergh, whose solo $33\frac{1}{2}$-hour transatlantic flight from New York to Paris in May 1927 also combined new technical expertise with the traditional pioneer spirit. On his return New York brought down a storm of ticker tape to celebrate an achievement in which all Americans could take pride.

The Transportation Revolution of the 1920s and 1930s

Whatever the contribution to society of such men as Lindbergh, it was the automobile that shaped the new machine society and its culture most decisively. It was not only an agent of mobility but also a potent symbol of a new order. The scale of the continuing revolution in transportation achieved by cars between the world wars is suggested by the following statistics. In 1920 1,905,500 passenger cars were produced; in 1930, 2,787,400. In 1920 there were, altogether, 7.5 million cars on America's roads; in 1930 26.5 million—or one car for every five Americans. In 1940 3,717,300 cars were sold in the United States. The rise in the number of miles traveled was equally dramatic—from 1921 with 55,027 miles per vehicle to 1930 with 206,320 miles per vehicle and then 1940 with 302,188 miles per vehicle. In the 1920s private intercity motor car traffic soon exceeded rail traffic and by 1930 it was six times greater. Very soon cars were not only a convenience but also a necessity for mind as well as body. When Sinclair Lewis came to satirize the small-town world of a middle-aged real estate man in *Babbitt* (1922), he observed, "To George F. Babbitt, as to most prosperous citizens of Zenith, his motor-car was poetry and tragedy, love and heroism. The office was his pirate ship but the car his perilous excursion ashore." By the 1920s the automobile was automatically linked in most minds to the glamorous world of the happiness of pursuit created by advertising and to upward social mobility.

André Siegfried in *America Comes of Age* (1927) asserted how "it is quite common to find a working-class family in which the father has his own car, and the grown-up sons have one apiece as well." The wife of an unemployed worker in *Middletown* told the Lynds, "I'll never cut on gas! I'd go without a meal before I'd cut down on using the car." In fact, less than half of blue-collar families owned automobiles. In his article, "Affluence for Whom?" for *Labor History* of Winter 1983, Keith Stricker concludes that there were probably 16.77 million cars for 36.10 million consumer units (families and individuals) and thus about 46 percent of the units had cars. An automobile was not a sign of affluence when a used car could be bought for $60 outright or for a deposit of $5 and delayed purchase by monthly instalments of $5. Of course, Americans were more likely to have cars than Europeans and the urban family probably had about a fifty-fifty chance of owning a car. Many automobiles belonged to companies; some families had more than one car; and many single people had cars. Some cars were scrapped during the year; some cars belonged to farms.

By the mid-1920s the automobile industry was dominant in the American economy and had made tributaries of such other American industries as petroleum (using 90 percent of petroleum products), rubber (using 80 percent), steel (20 percent), glass (75 percent), and machine tools (25 percent). Socially, the automobile increased opportunities for leisure and recreation, bridging town and country, affording escape and seclusion from small town morality, and generally shaping the view of an ever more mobile population to an urban perspective.

The Big Three: Ford, GM, and Chrysler

Just after World War I Henry Ford dominated automobile manufacture, both nationally and internationally, although on the domestic scene he would face increasingly serious competition from General Motors. In fact, the 1920s saw the full emergence of two

New lamps for old. Shopworn Democratic standard-bearer William Jennings Bryan and Henry Ford, the mechanical genius whose name was synonymous with the new age of machines, in a publicity photo to promote Ford's peace ship in 1915. Ironically, Ford came to detest many new values of the society he himself had done more to transform than any other individual and set about recreating a tribute to a bygone rural Arcadia in his Dearborn museum, while fundamentalist Bryan, who was usually taken as a symbol of bygone agrarian protest, became in the 1920s a front man for a Florida real estate company dedicated to creating an idyllic leisure retreat for the affluent. (Library of Congress).

other giant auto companies, General Motors (GM) and the Chrysler Corporation, to take their place at the side of Ford as the Big Three companies among automobile manufacturers.

Among other leading producers General Motors, founded in 1908 by William Durant, was originally intended to become a combine of other companies. As initially formed, it included the companies of Buick, Cadillac, Oldsmobile, and Oakland, and several lesser firms. By a series of rapid financial combinations, acquisitions, and mergers, Durant created a network of suppliers, assembly plants, and distributors. However, following an unexpected decline in sales, in 1910 Durant was forced out of General Motors. He then acquired Chevrolet and, supported by Pierre Du Pont and John Julius Raskob and the wealth of the Du Pont family, he recaptured control of General Motors in 1915. (The Du Ponts were an American family of French descent with a fortune originally based in textiles, chemicals, and explosives. Their concerns were incorporated in 1902 by Henry Algernon Du Pont. His three cousins, Thomas Colman, Alfred Irénée, and Pierre Samuel Du Pont, served as directors.)

By the end of World War I William C. Durant was planning construction of plants and facilities on such a vast scale that he required extra funds not only from the Du Ponts but also their British associates, the Nobels, and the House of Morgan. Indeed, it was only the outsize contribution of this powerful trio that saved General Motors from bankruptcy in the postwar recession. However, when William Durant tried to maintain the price of General Motors above its current market rate, he was forced to retire for the second, and last, time.

Henry Ford dealt with a postwar recession by cutting prices, insisting on rigorous economies throughout his company, and obliging suppliers and dealers to help him out; the suppliers by selling parts more cheaply, the dealers by accepting additional stocks that they could not sell immediately. Moreover, Ford attempted vertical integration, control of all processes from start to finish, acquiring raw materials and transportation to achieve an even flow from source to production to distribution. His aim was a giant and incessant conveyor belt for the universal car. Ford's new plant on River Rouge became a prime example of modern, integrated production, in which Ford produced nearly all parts for the Model T and even made his own glass and steel. Although it was a superb achievement as technology and industrial integration, the Rouge plant was less successful as a business venture since it was inflexible and run on high fixed costs. The complex had been created to make a product that was already fifteen years old. Even minor changes could only be introduced at great expense. Ford's difficulties arose not only out of his failure to recognize changing customer demands and their implications for marketing, but also the swift success with which General Motors managers exploited the new situation.

Pierre Du Pont replaced Durant as president of General Motors and began to reorganize the corporation's administration and finances, and to revise its policies in production and marketing. Pierre Du Pont took his cue from Alfred P. Sloan, Jr., president of one of the firms acquired by Durant in 1916, and allowed such operating divisions as car, truck, parts, and accessories to retain their own autonomy. Thus the division managers continued to control their own production, marketing, purchasing, and engineering—as they had under Durant. However, what was new in the Du Pont-Sloan system was a new general office, comprising general executives and advisory staff specialists, to assure planning, coordination, and overall control.

First, Du Pont and Sloan (who then succeeded Du Pont as president in 1923) defined the roles of various executives in the general office and senior division managers in order to clarify authority and communications. Second, they arranged for the continuous collection and circulation of statistics to disclose the performances of the operating divisions and, indeed, the entire corporation. In time, much of this information and the decisions it inspired came to depend on market forecasts about production, costs, prices, and employment. It served as a yardstick for measuring performance.

General Motors led the way in improved mechanics and design. When automobile pioneer Charles K. Kettering became general manager of General Motors' research laboratories (1925–1947), he directed research on improving diesel engines and the development of a nontoxic and noninflammable refrigerant. He also devised and conducted research into higher octane gasoline, adding tetraethyl lead. Cars became more comfortable; until the 1920s most new automobiles were open cars but by 1929 the great majority were closed models. In order to entice consumers, General Motors' marketing included the development of an extensive range of models, an annual model, massive advertising, schemes to allow customers to trade in their old car in part payment for a new one, and regular and systematic analyses of the market. However, by using some of the same parts and supplies for their different models, General Motors hoped to retain one major advantage over the Ford system—economy of scale. Thus, between them, Pierre Du Pont and Alfred Sloan, by their rational innovations, boosted General Motors' share of total sales from 12.7 percent of the market in 1921 to 43.9 percent in 1931 and 47.5 percent in 1940. General Motors created a new, decentralized form of management at the precise time that Henry Ford was ridiculing systematic management while drawing the threads of control of his own company more tightly into his own autocratic hands.

The Chrysler Corporation was formed out of the failing Maxwell Motor Company in 1925 by Walter P. Chrysler who introduced his own design of car, featuring a high compression engine. He also acquired the Dodge Brothers Manufacturing Company in 1928 and produced the Plymouth, a successful model that allowed Chrysler to compete with Ford and General Motors, thereby becoming one of the Big Three car manufacturers. In 1929 Chevrolet introduced the six-cylinder engine and set a pattern for future development wherein auto manufacturers concentrated on engineering improvements, suspension, engines, and overall design.

Thus the American automobile market was to be dominated by the Big Three producers. Independent manufacturers could only survive if they produced automobiles for a narrow, specialized market, such as motor cars for the affluent. However, in general they either declined, went out of business, or were absorbed by the Big Three.

Early automobiles were designed in the fashion of horse-drawn carriages and, as late as the 1920s, they continued the basic feature of clearly separated parts in their overall design. However, in the course of the 1920s manufacturers were made forcibly aware of the significance of body styling, especially after the introduction of closed cars, which increased their share of the market from 10 percent in 1919 to 85 percent in 1927. The most significant designer was Harley Earl of General Motors. Coming from a background of custom-body building in Los Angeles and, having specialized in creating unique designs for individual Hollywood film stars, Earl knew how to create the widest range in styles from the same essential design and to provide even greater sophistication by subtle changes in body, attachments, and color within different price ranges. By 1928 designer Norman Bel Geddes refined the conventional angular design of cars into a rounder, more harmonious form in a design that was never put into production by manufacturer Graham Page but which influenced others' work.

Walter P. Chrysler had his top engineers, Fred Zeder, Owen Skelton, George McCain, and Barl Breer, and outside designers William Earnshaw and H. V. Hendersson, produce a streamlined automobile, the *Airflow*, for 1934 and in successive years. It had a torpedo-like body, bullet-shaped headlamps, slanted windshields, and curved window covers. The overall shape was a parabolic curve, like the then fashionable teardrop. However, such striking changes in the front of the vehicle were less significant than Chrysler's visible alterations to the body, with the engine placed farther forward and lower between the two front wheels—rather than in its usual position behind the front axle—and a lower frame seating passengers between front and rear axle, and all in a steel body welded to a steel frame. The interiors used chrome tubing for the seats and marbled rubber for the floor. Here was one of the most beautiful of all designs of the machine age, complete with a long, low-slung look decorated with a triad of horizontal speed lines to accentuate the car's purpose.

Cars conveyed more than their passengers. They could carry packages containing alcohol and did so in the period of national prohibition of alcohol. They certainly carried change—the conventions of the countryside were challenged by those of the city. They provided means and opportunity for sexual freedom impossible in a static society. In the Lynds' study *Middletown* one judge referred to the car as "a house of prostitution on wheels." Because they were used so much by bootleggers and gangsters, automobiles were never dissociated from criminal activities in the public mind. "Don't shoot, I'm not a bootlegger," was the caption popular among car owners in Michigan, and prohibited there by the attorney general in 1929. Whereas at the beginning of the 1920s automobiles represented an alternative to alcohol, at its end they symbolized booze and beer running and everything that was

Charles Sheeler, *River Rouge Plant,* (1932), 20″ × 24⅛″. (Photo by Geoffrey Clements; Collection of Whitney Museum of American Art, New York). In 1927 the Ford Motor Company commissioned precisionist artist Charles Sheeler to take a series of photographs of its River Rouge Plant, the first factory capable of manufacturing a complete automobile on one site. The definitive collection of thirty-two photographs and thirteen paintings, drawings, and prints were a celebration of the modern factory and its products in which all is sleek and immaculate.

subversive of national prohibition of alcohol. In addition, they provided an unfortunate comparison with liquor: how a potentially lethal invention could be controlled and made comparatively safe.

In *Responsible Drinking* (1930) Robert Brinkley compared the ill effects of alcohol with those of the automobile. He concluded that morals had withstood centuries of drinking but had broken down after two decades of driving. Driving was intoxicating. Cars had facilitated crime. Driving was habit-forming. Millions of people would hardly be able to use their legs again. However, the temperance movement had concentrated on the prohibition of alcohol. It had remained unconcerned by the social upheaval caused by the car. Of course, cars were part and parcel of contemporary social and economic life. They were controlled by careful drivers and compulsory insurance policies, by legislation and licenses. Could not liquor be regulated in the same way? The penalties of the automobile included urban congestion, road accidents, and gasoline pollution.

The motor vehicle facilitated the growth of suburbia, but, it must also be noted, the specific needs of the motor vehicle itself began to change the look of urban America. As traffic jams began to occur increasingly in the 1920s, citizen protest prompted the organization of local safety councils and encouraged cities to enact ordinances limiting speeds and parking and to erect traffic lights to control movement. In 1922 New York introduced the first manually operated traffic lights that were soon developed into an automatic system by Philadelphia and Cleveland. In Boston the parking charge was first invented, but not until 1932 did the parking meter make its debut in Oklahoma City. The first shopping center with adjoining parking lot opened in Kansas City in 1924 and in 1929 the first ramp garage was in use in Detroit. These are all important, but by now overly familiar elements in the makeup of the contemporary urban scene in America.

Detroit, in common with other cities engaged in production, had, and still has, a special relationship with the automobile. The motor capital grew by 126 percent during the decade 1910-1920, a ratio second only to that of Akron, the tire capital, at 173 percent. Los Angeles and Houston, both centers of oil production, experienced such phenomenal rates of growth in the 1920s and beyond when the automobile was exploited to its fullest potential.

The motor vehicle revolution led to ever-wider use of trucks for goods and buses for passengers as well as of private motor cars. Trucks carried mail, farm produce and livestock, and manufactured goods. In 1899 the Post Office began to experiment with delivery of mail by truck in some cities. In 1904 only 700 trucks were sold but most auto manufacturers added a truck line to their regular production and by 1918 over half a million were in use. In particular, trucking expanded in the 1930s. There were 4.5 million registered trucks in 1940, a seventh of all vehicles. Unemployed truck drivers bought trucks on credit to establish a tiny one-man business, carrying furniture, animals, and farm produce. Truck operators were not regulated until 1935.

Americans soon became aware of the convenience and cleanliness of buses, especially for intracity journeys. The first buses were simply elongated passenger cars with a stronger chassis and extra seats. The prototype of modern buses was designed and created by Frank and William Fageol, a bus close to the ground with a low step at the entrance and a lower center of gravity. A subsequent model placed the engine under the floor so that the entire inner space of the body was available for passengers. Hundreds of small bus companies competed for passengers and by 1930 there were enough good roads for intercity bus services to become firmly established. In that year about a fifth of all intercity commercial travel was by bus.

Buses had considerable advantages over railroads for shorter journeys because they could vary routes and were cheaper than trains requiring tracks and stations. America's (eventual) 3 million miles of roads and highways gave car, bus, and truck a flexibility that railroads simply could not provide. The smaller size and seating capacity of buses also allowed greater variety of service. Needless to say, both trucks and buses were dependent on improved roads and more of them. During the 1930s the number of registered buses rose by 80 percent. In 1930 buses were providing about 25 percent more passenger miles than intercity railroads. In 1940 they supplied about 40 percent more. During the 1930s bus fares were about 10 percent cheaper than railroad fares, a factor in the sharp reduction in rail fares during the depression.

Changing Strategies of the Big Three Auto Manufacturers

However, whatever public demand for automobiles in the 1920s and 1930s, it was greatly exceeded by the potential supply. Manufacturers could make far more cars and trucks than they could sell. By the mid-1920s most Americans who could afford a motor car had bought one and the market for automobiles was a replacement market. Thus the automobile industry moved from initial growth to a competitive stage between the different manufacturers. The market was saturated and thus marketing, rather than sheet production, became the prime concern of manufacturers. As Alfred Dupont Chandler, Jr., explains in *Giant Enterprise* (1964), "Marketing now became a greater challenge than production. The underlying marketing problem was no longer to sell an individual his first car but to get the man who already owned one to buy a new car. And management became a greater challenge than finance. Effective coordination, appraisal, and planning were essential if costs were to be kept down and the market was not to be oversold." While General Motors forged ahead with its new methods of management and marketing, Henry Ford stubbornly persisted in his shopworn strategy. Thus his share of the market fell steadily from 55.7 percent in 1921 to 24.9 percent in 1931, and then to 18.9 percent in 1940.

We might say the cause of Ford's tragedy was his success. Having shaped American society for the 1920s in a most decisive fashion, he failed to move with the times. He failed to appreciate the dynamic character of the mass market for cars that he himself had done so much to create. He refused to let Edsel, his only son and the national president of the company, exercise any real control over his creation. His tyranny damaged Edsel's health and, at times, came close to destroying the firm. In his "Sketch for a Portrait of Henry Ford," poet William Carlos Williams refers to Ford, somewhat laconically, as "a tin bucket," full of "heavy sludge," and "steel grit." The bucket with the dent swings round at ever-faster speed and its handle soon "gives way and the bucket is propelled through space. . . ."

The Ford family drama was a topsy-turvy version of *King Lear* in which the father conspired against his son and drove him to an early grave. The outwardly loyal Harry Bennett modeled his professional character on the type of man played by James Cagney in the movies. He was a fixer who got things done, such as taking care of the mother of Henry's illegitimate son and hiring strong-arm gorillas to beat up union leader Walter Reuther. "If Mr. Ford told me to blacken out the sun tomorrow," remarked Bennett, "I might have trouble fixing it. But you'd see a hundred thousand sons-of-bitches coming through the Rouge gates in the morning all wearing dark glasses." Bennett created an illegal private police force, the "outside squads," closer to fascist black shirts than anything else. Ford repeatedly humiliated Edsel, always backing Bennett in disputes. Thus Edsel, forced to endure endless frustration, developed "Ford Stomach," the illness and anxiety experienced by men on the shop floor and caused by relentless adherence to timetables on the assembly line. Edsel died of an ulcer and cancer at the age of forty-nine.

Henry Ford kept the Model T in production for too long. In his *Ford* (1986), Robert Lacey sums up Ford's propensity for managerial autocracy as "Absolute control plus divided attention equals a recipe for disaster." Ford belatedly learnt that the new mass society he had helped shape would not just select goods on the basis of cost. It expected efficiency and choice of style. The new society of mass consumption was also a new society of mass communications in which radio, movies, and advertising stirred aspirant needs and desires in people all the way from New York to San Francisco. Because of his limited design, Ford was excluded from the world of upward social mobility and he simply did not realize how deep was the need for individual fulfillment. The common man did not want to stay common. Ford's loyalty to the Model T was not simply a matter of personal pride. He did not want to foreclose a line that had long been popular and, more importantly, he did not really want to have to close down his workshops while they were being reequipped and thereby lose markets to his competitors in the interim before he did introduce a new car.

However, the Ford company was part of a capitalist system in which the weakest competitor went to the wall. No matter how false were the new values that led the public to move from the cheap Model T, because it was cheap, simple, black, and ugly, to other models, no matter how far Ford wanted to rely on internal company strength, he was eventually forced to respond to the public crisis of confidence in his car. When profits declined dramatically, he decided to extinguish the Model T in 1927, close his plants, and reequip them for an improved model, the Model A. Ford's strategy was essentially a retreat. Yet, having done all this, in 1929, the first full year of the Model A, Ford took only 31.3 percent of the market while General Motors retained 32.3 percent. Moreover, their profits were rising. In 1928 General Motors reported a profit of $296.25 million—one of the largest ever by an American corporation to that time. During the period 1927–1937, including eight years of the Great Depression, General Motors took an average profit of $173.2 million, while Ford took an average annual loss of $1.4 million. The depression hit Ford at an especially awkward time when he was constructing a large new plant, River Rouge, and needed to buy back shareholders' stock to raise the capital. He survived the depression but his period of near monopoly control had passed.

Ford clung to a forlorn belief that his company was more efficient than was General Motors. Ironically, he believed his company recognized ability in younger men more quickly than they did in General Motors—ironically, because many of his executives left him for General Motors in the 1930s. The best of the renegades included William S. Knudsen in production and Norval Hawkins in sales. In the Ford company authority became concentrated among a few unscrupulous and hardheaded favorites. However, Ford's old-fashioned views on the way to administer a modern business were less damaging than his refusal, or inability, to recognize his competitor's superior innovations in marketing.

The General Motors' executive committee and international sales committee tried to increase their share of the market by steadily improving the performance and regularly changing the design of their cars. Charles Kettering and his research staff concentrated on improving such things as axles, transmissions, and crankshafts in order to make their cars easier and more comfortable to drive. Harley Earl and his styling section made the cars' design and colors most attractive. General Motors cultivated good relations with local dealers and showed acute understanding of the dealers' changing needs in the depression, raising the dealers' margin of profit on new cars to 24 percent, encouraging them to

The United States prepared for the postwar boom in automobile sales and their promise of suburban life with such compelling symbols as this 1945–1946 model of the Nash Ambassador Six. (Library of Congress).

apply modern accounting procedures, and, above all, trying to prevent them from becoming overstocked.

Chrysler adopted General Motors' strategy. By concentrating on the inexpensive Plymouth, Walter P. Chrysler had 25.4 percent of the market in 1937, compared with Ford's 21.4 percent, and in 1940, 23.7 percent, compared with Ford's 18.9 percent. Despite the introduction of the Ford V-8 in 1934, Ford's sales continued to fall and the company lost an average of $1.4 million per year in the period 1931–1941. By the mid-1940s the Ford company might have gone bankrupt but for the wartime spending of the government of Franklin Roosevelt that he despised. Apart from some production triumphs in World War II, Ford's later career was marred by bitter conflicts with management and labor alike. The Henry Ford of $5 a day could not understand that right. However, in the course of the 1920s builders introduced a three-lane highway in which the central lane was to be used for turning and passing in both directions. Alternative titles were motorway, freeway, parkway, turnpike, expressway, and, even, limited way.

The freeway was distinguished by multiple traffic lanes and a central median strip. It moved across the natural landscape of the countryside and the man-made cityscape, such as the Pulaski Skyway over Jersey City or the Outer Drive around Chicago, both constructed in the 1930s.

The parkway's most distinctive features were its limited access and being placed in a carefully designed landscape. The leading parkway designer of the period was Gilmore D. Clarke. However, the first automotive parkway was the Bronx River Parkway, authorized by the New York State Assembly in 1907, and constructed in the period 1919–1923 from the North Bronx to White Plains in Westchester County. It set the pattern for future parkways, with an initial road of four lanes, two in each direction, occasionally separating to enfold hillocks and copses but generally following the undulating meander of the Bronx River. Wherever it was not possible to demolish signs or intrusive buildings, trees were planted to mask them. Encouraged by the success of the Bronx River Parkway, the Westchester County Park Commission began to construct various other parkways, partly to convert the recreational areas of Westchester County and partly to provide more convenient access to New York City. Thus, in the period 1923–1933 the commission had eighty-eight miles of parkways and ten miles of freeways constructed. The leading designer, Gilmore D. Clarke, went on to a successful career as the designer of the Taconic State, the Long Island, New York City, and George Washington Memorial parkways.

By 1936 the Bureau of Public Roads had spent almost $2 billion altogether on the construction and improvement of 324,000 miles of federal highways. The idea of highways and freeways penetrating yet accommodating the natural landscape of rivers, hills, and valleys, and of piercing cities and towns, and the ways they were achieved were major accomplishments of the 1920s and 1930s. Swiss architectural historian Siegfried Giedion was enraptured by

America's numerous highways and observed in his *Space, Time and Architecture* (1941) how "Full realization is given to the driver and freedom to the machine. Riding up and down the long sweeping grades produces an exhilarating dual feeling, one of being connected with the soil and yet of hovering just above it, a feeling which is nothing else so much as sliding swiftly on skis through untouched snow down the sides of high mountains."

· It was World War II, with its special needs of transporting workers, war materiel, and supplies of food and manufactured goods across great stretches of country, that provided a major impetus to the extension and renewal of the American highway system. Perhaps the most notable highway project was the Alaskan Highway (Alcan). Construction began on March 12, 1942, and was completed by December 1 that year. Alcan extended 1,523 miles from Davison Creek, British Columbia, through Canada and the Yukon Territory to Fairbanks, Alaska. Conceived as a military supply route, it cost $138 million to build and was opened to tourists in summer 1948.

Service Stations

The most widely known form of architecture inspired by the automobile was the gas, or service station. Different oil companies established different sorts of structures to promote their own special images. The Texas Star and Mobil flying horse were recognized nationwide atop clean, efficiently run buildings. Holabird and Roth designed prototype stations for Texaco's distributors with flat, overhanging roofs atop distinctive glass boxes. Gulf also achieved prototype stations with a large display room but with curved glass, horizontal strips and fins, and a setback towered entrance. The prototype building for Standard Oil by Alfred Clauss and George Daub of Philadelphia, with distinctive porcelain panels in red, white, and blue, was sufficiently festive to appeal to organizers Philip Johnson and Henry-Russell Hitchcock who included it in the Museum of Modern Art International Style exhibit of February and March 1932.

The most successful and widely known standardized service stations were prototypes designed for Texaco in 1936 by Walter

Dorwin Teague as part of Texaco's assertive marketing campaign. Along with the prototype stations, with large display windows, a canopy with fins, and crowned by the giant Texaco Star, came a new advertising campaign promoting the premier gasoline "for those who want the best," and clean rest rooms checked by an inspection team. By 1940 500 Texaco stations had been built based on Teague's original design.

Aviation

For a time flying and airplane development stumbled after World War I but then, toward the end of the 1920s, they gathered momentum once again, thanks to new research, both public and private. In 1926 the Guggenheim Foundation established a special fund that provided grants of $3 million altogether, partly to promote aeronautical knowledge, partly to help extend the boundaries of aeronautical science, partly to encourage commercial and civil aviation and assist the development of planes and equipment, and partly to encourage wider use of airplanes. By the time the fund was liquidated in 1930, it had achieved many of its objectives.

By the mid-1920s it was clear that a market for new aircraft was emerging. Thus government administrators realized that there was a need for a firm governmental hand, exercising some control and coordination, both to ensure safety and to avoid the sort of unbridled chaos that had marked the years of railroad construction. Accordingly, the administration of President Calvin Coolidge (1923–1929) created a board to plan a national aviation policy. In turn, their recommendations were incorporated into the Air Commerce Act of 1926, the Navy Five-Year Aircraft Program of 1926, and the Army Five-Year Program.

American passenger airlines grew out of the Post Office service. Firstly, it was the airmail service that laid out an extensive route system. Then, in 1925, distribution of airmail was contracted out to private companies who were encouraged to carry passengers in order to part-subsidize the operation. Finally, legislation was enacted to connect a number of major cities through the transcontinental mail routes. The first regular passenger service, based on the mail system, opened on April 4, 1927, between Boston and New York.

Lindbergh's Solo Flight Across the Atlantic

Two epochal flights demonstrated the potential of planes as a means of mass, rapid transportation: Louis Blériot's record flight across the English Channel of July 25, 1909; and Charles A. Lindbergh, Jr.'s, solo flight across the Atlantic Ocean on May 20–21, 1927. (In 1919 two English pilots, Alcock and Brown, first flew across the Atlantic from Newfoundland to Ireland.)

Charles A. Lindbergh, Jr., son of a Minnesota congressman but born in Detroit in 1902, was of Swedish extraction. He grew up in Detroit and Washington, and attended the University of Wisconsin as well as flying schools in Lincoln, Nebraska, and the army in Texas. In 1926 he served as an airmail pilot on the run from St. Louis to Chicago. His nonstop transatlantic flight, promoted by a press competition, turned Lindbergh into a folk hero whose receptions in various European and American cities were turned into victory tours. As Anne Michaelis explained in a poem, "Lindbergh,"

> Alone, yet never lonely,
> Serene, beyond mischance,
> The world was his, his only,
> When Lindbergh flew to France.

A crucial factor to explain Lindbergh's amazing popularity was due to the timing of his solo flight. The uncomfortable barnstorming warplanes, hastily converted for peacetime use, were getting older and some were being taken out of service. Lindbergh demonstrated the amazing potential of flight as a rival to conventional modes of travel. He revitalized public interest in aviation at a time when aircraft research and development had become somewhat stagnant. His timing was in tune with the rising expectations of the few people who chose to travel by air. They wanted newer, more comfortable planes, and the airlines had to respond to their passengers because they were competing with such longer established modes of travel as railroads, ships,

Charles A. Lindbergh, Jr., the attractive, gangling pioneer aviator whose solo transatlantic flight of May 1927 not only demonstrated the enduring American traditions of rugged determination and technical skills in new fields but also revived flagging public interest in aviation. (Library of Congress).

and automobiles, all of which were more comfortable and accessible.

People ascribed Lindbergh's heroism to his personality and praised his Swedish self-containment, his mechanical precision, and even his commercial ambition. His personality was taken as a representation of the restraints associated with aviation. Man's ability to fly depended on a balanced combination of disciplines that were the exact opposite of carefree. Lindbergh liked to give an impression of casualness, prompting the *Times* of London to call him "the flying fool." In fact, his numerous achievements depended on meticulous preparation and care.

He was soon regarded as an expert in the comparatively new field of aviation and became a technical adviser for Transcontinental Air Transport and Pan Am and personally pioneered some of their routes. He received the Medal of Honor.

Other epochal flights suggested expanding horizons of achievement in the air. C. C. Champion set an early record for altitude by flying 37,995 feet above Washington (1927); Bert Hinkler flew solo from London to Australia (1928); and Commander Bird flew over the South Pole (1929). In the 1930s daring aviators attempted flights around the world. Lindbergh flew to Shanghai, China; Amelia Earhart made two attempts at crossing the world in 1937; Howard Hughes tried to do so in 1938. Other feats included intercontinental races, such as the MacRobertson International Race from England to Australia in 1934. Although it was won by a British plane, American planes came second and third and thus the race introduced the DC-3 and Boeing 247D to a wider public, prompting European airlines to buy these American models. The Schneider Cup revived racing in closed courses, notably the USA National Air Races in Cleveland.

Castles in the Air — The Big Four and Pan Am

Civil aviation developed out of a central American need. In a country as large as the United States with as scattered a population and large cities, people were quick to appreciate the speed and convenience of air travel, compared with more traditional forms. Increasing passenger expectations coincided with the advent of new, improved planes. Moreover, the mail service had already established a network of routes and flight paths, with lighted beacons providing necessary signals to guide airplanes. Once again, people saw air travel as a way of rising above the restrictions of national territory and of opening up new relationships across the world. British investigative journalist Anthony Sampson comments in *Empires of the Sky* (1984) "But the pilots and entrepreneurs soon discovered that they could not fly without their governments' support, and that even within their own country they could not make their airlines pay without subsidies or the mail contracts which governments awarded. In every country the soaring ambition of the aviators and their financiers came up against the controls and military designs of their governments."

By 1930 the United States had four major airlines, all launched on the model of shipping lines: Bill Boeing and engine makers Pratt and Whitney had formed the United Aircraft and Transportation Corporation, later United Air Lines; the Aviation Corporation, founded by railroad magnate W. A. Harriman in 1929, eventually developed into American Airlines; and entrepreneur C. M. Keys, chairman of the Curtiss airplane company, was a pivotal figure in the creation of North American Airlines, predecessor of Eastern Airlines, and TAT, later TWA. By 1930 these four airlines—United, Eastern, TWA, and American—had all established transcontinental routes, their prime catchment area for the next half century. Altogether, 73 million passenger miles were flown in 1930, the first year of air hostesses, part attendant, part waitress, and part nurse, to serve passengers. In 1938 the Big Four were joined by Continental Airlines, founded in Denver by Robert Six.

The airlines also had their tycoons—Cyrus Smith (American), Bill Patterson (United), Eddie Rickenbacker (Eastern), and Jack Frye (TWA)—each obsessed with the challenge of creating networks and opening up the continent. The airline pioneers competed furiously with one another but retained a spirit of friendly rivalry like barroom gamblers. After all, they were bound together by their mutual obsession and the novel experience of flight that had captured public imagination in less than a generation. Their competition for landing rights and the need to find

A new age of transportation dawned with the advent of ever larger airplanes. The Florida Flyer arrives at Newark airport, New Jersey, in 1934. (Library of Congress).

refueling stages led to the further development of Fort Worth, St. Louis, and Kansas City. Aviation was largely untouched by the depression. Dozens of companies, large and small, with hundreds of planes flew ever more passengers and carried increasing loads of mail in the 1930s. Between 1930 and 1940 air passenger traffic multiplied twelve times to just over a billion passenger miles in 1940, while airfreight traffic more than tripled in volume. In 1934, for the first time, over a million airline tickets were sold in a single year.

Many of the minute airports that served as refueling stages were truly isolated places—quite different from frontier railroad stations of the previous century. F. Scott Fitzgerald described the type in his last, unfinished novel, *The Last Tycoon*.

I suppose there has been nothing like airports since the days of the stage-stops—nothing quite as lonely, as sombre-silent. The old red-brick depots were built right into the towns they marked—people didn't get off at those isolated stations unless they lived there. But airports lead you way back in history like oases, like the stops on the great trade routes. The sight of air travellers strolling in ones or twos into midnight airports will draw a small crowd any night up to them. The young people look at the planes, the older ones look at the passengers with a watchful incredulity.

During the 1920s commercial airplanes carried between twelve and fifteen passengers, sometimes more. However, in the 1930s overall airplane design greatly improved the associated technology of engines, propellers, movable wing surfaces (or flaps), and retractable undercarriages, and this allowed for larger planes, carrying between thirty and forty passengers, the first economically viable transport aircraft.

The depression and World War II provided a turning point for commercial aviation. This was most obvious in the early 1930s when airlines began to benefit from earlier research, both governmental and private, and an ever growing corps of young, and optimistic aeronautical scientists and engineers, committed to the development of commercial airplanes. By 1932 aircraft design was far superior to that of the planes of World War I. In a word, it was streamlined. New airplanes were internally braced, low-strung monoplanes, built entirely of metal. They had such improved features as air-cooled engines, controllable pitch propellers, retractable undercarriages, and insulated and sound-proofed compartments for pilots and passengers. Although later developments included such features as jet engines, more powerful propeller engines, and much larger capacity, the all-metal monoplane of the very early 1930s has provided the essential prototype for all later civil aircraft design.

In 1932 Donald Douglas sold TWA several DC-2 planes. They carried fourteen passengers at 170 mph. From 1936 his new all-metal DC-3, powered by two 900 horsepower Wright cyclone motors, became the most popular model on all major airlines and was known as "the Model T of aircraft." It carried twenty-one passengers and revolutionized air travel on account of its safety and reliability. The DC-3 combined maximum economy, safety, and speed and carried twenty-one passengers. It was the first passenger plane to make a profit without benefit of an airmail route subsidy. The DC-3 flew a route from New York to Los Angeles, a journey lasting twenty-four hours, including eighteen hours in the air, with three or four stops for refueling.

Canada was one of the few developed countries without a scheduled national air service and until the late 1930s American airlines carried Canadians across their country. The Canadian government founded Trans-Canada Airlines but the new air networks crossed the frontier with the United States along the forty-ninth parallel and began to erode Canada's separate economy irreversibly.

Modern aircraft design in the United States was stimulated by the arrival of German immigrants Max Munk and Theodore von Karman, the creation of the Daniel Guggenheim Fund for the Promotion of Aeronautics in 1926, and research by the National Advisory Committee for Aeronautics (NACA).

In the late twenties and thirties the appearance of airplanes was much enhanced by a number of technological improvements such as the powerful and elegant radical engineering of Pratt and Whitney, and Curtis-Wright. Cantilevered wings, better braced and attached to the fuselage than the old flat wings attached by external wires and struts, allowed designers to achieve more streamlined designs overall. Thus John K. Northrop's Vega of 1927 for Lockheed and his Sirius of 1929 set new standards of design, while providing superior machines as to range and speed for pioneers Lindbergh, Amelia Earhart, and Wiley Post. In 1931 Russian immigrant Igor Sikorsky designed and built the first Clippers for Pan Am. Following closely, Glen Martin's flying boats, such as the M-130W China Clipper of 1934, demonstrated a new integral aircraft design, notably in the way the wings rose naturally from the body.

Industrial designers contributed to improved interiors. For the never realized Air Liner Number 4 Norman Bel Geddes and Otto Koller provided the plane's interior design with all the accoutrements of a luxury ocean liner. In Martin's China Clippers, as modified by Worthen Paxxon and Frances Waite Geddes, there was a lounge with sofas that converted into sleeping berths at night. As further modified by Henry Dreyfuss and Howard Ketcham, the Pan Am Clippers gained an exotic reputation as the airline extended its operations into Latin America and the Orient.

The most significant developments in aviation design were the almost simultaneous achievement of the 247 by Boeing and the DC-1 by Douglas. The Boeing 247 flew its maiden flight on February 8, 1933; the Douglas DC-1 first flew on July 1, 1933. The Boeing was an all-metal monoplane with two short-cowled radial engines and retractable landing gear that could carry ten passengers from coast to coast in twenty hours, including seven stops for refueling en route. The DC-1, designed by Donald Douglas to replace the discredited Fokker trimotor planes, was also superior to the Boeing 247. It drew on innovations by Jack Northrop to provide an all-metal, multicullar wing mounted beneath the fuselage. By the time of its third revision, the DC-3 of 1935–1936, it could accommodate twenty-eight passengers. The streamlined fuselage was constructed of special lightweight aluminum, riveted to the frame and polished to perfection. Its flowing appearance and sterling performance alike captured public imagination as it reduced the transcontinental journey to fifteen hours, thereby stimulating passenger sales and relieving airlines from dependence on federal mail contracts. In time, companies right across the world adopted DC-2 and DC-3 airplanes that became standard everywhere.

In the early 1930s there were only about 200,000 passengers traveling by air in the United States and Europe each year. Fatalities were high with one passenger killed in an accident for every 8 million passenger miles traveled. By the end of the 1930s, when several million passengers were traveling each year, there was one fatality for every 100 million passenger miles traveled.

Transatlantic flight was most significant, heralding a new era of travel to follow in the years after World War II. Between 1932 and 1937 transatlantic flights were by airships, such as the *Graf Zeppelin* and the *Hindenburg,* flying between Frankfurt, Germany, and Lakehurst, New Jersey. The day of the airship was brief, brought to an abrupt end by the crash and explosion of the *Hindenburg* at Lakehurst in 1937.

The first of the forty-seater Handley Page airliners ready for delivery to Britain's Imperial Airways—the first aircraft designed for passenger comfort, providing a drawing room with eighteen seats (here), a cocktail bar, a saloon with twenty seats, a chart room, and a wireless cabin. (Photo by Underwood and Underwood; Library of Congress).

The flying boat was then the staple carrier for intercontinental flights until 1938 when it was replaced by the Boeing 314 clipper widely adopted in 1939, the year transatlantic flights began. The major intercontinental carrier was Pan American World Airways, founded in 1928 and originally operating a route from Florida to Cuba. By 1938 and 1939, under its dynamic president Juan Trippe, it was running passenger services on routes to South America, across the Pacific to Manila in the Philippines, and to England. Pan Am introduced a new Martin M-130 four engine on its Pacific routes in 1935. That year Imperial and Pan Am began a series of pioneer transatlantic flights. In August 1939 they started a regular transatlantic service with inflight refueling by flying boats. The service was interrupted by World War II and, at first, Pam Am clippers could only land in Ireland. Nevertheless, the North Atlantic Return Ferry introduced a year-round service, eventually run by BOAC. Commercial aviation was disrupted by the war and military attention shifted to the use of airplanes. Nevertheless, the destructive experience of war stimulated substantial developments in airplane design and construction and these benefited civil as well as military aviation. The state of military transport aviation shaped commercial aviation in the immediate postwar years, providing the world with flying boats for civil transportation.

As with every new form of manufacturing and commerce introduced since the American Civil War, air transportation posed special problems for government regulation. At first the Department of Commerce assigned routes, awarded pilot certificates and licenses, and determined standards of safety through its Aeronautics branch. However, the system was rocked by scandal and airmail contracts were canceled in 1934 after the discovery of a number of illegal arrangements. In 1934 Senator Hugo Black of Alabama led sensational hearings to investigate how former postmaster general Walter Brown had awarded airmail contracts. Jim Farley, the new postmaster general, accused Brown of conspiracy and collusion. Indeed, airline chiefs were brought to testify about their relations with the man who had helped create their airlines. Although they were opening up a continent all over again and encouraging mankind to review its horizons, airline companies had an early reputation as buccaneers. To the public it seemed here was a new race of robber barons.

President Franklin D. Roosevelt (1933–1945) distrusted the Big Four and Pan Am but, when he tried to find an alternative to commercial airlines, he failed. He canceled all domestic airmail contracts and called in the army to fly the mail, but army pilots could not handle the quantity or the routes and ten of them were killed. FDR had to reinstate the airline contracts. First, the government introduced a temporary airmail law to return mail delivery to the private sector. The bill provided for the appointment of a Federal Aviation Commission (FAC) to study the general situation and make recommendations for the future organization of aviation. Its views were implemented in the Civil Aeronautic Act of 1938, creating a Civil Aeronautics Authority (CAA), within the Department of Commerce. In 1940 the CAA became the licensing and regulating body for civil aviators and a Civil Aeronautics Board (CAB) was created under the secretary of commerce to control the economic organization of airlines and determine standards of safety. The new board continued a system of so-called controlled competition by which airlines sought routes from government to be approved by the president. In practice, the Big Four, who were not well established, were awarded "grandfather rights," that is, permanent certificates on domestic routes, while Pan Am continued to enjoy its foreign monopoly.

However, FDR did achieve a critical change when he separated manufacturing companies, such as Boeing and United, from owning or controlling airlines. This fundamental shift in policy encouraged the airlines to pick and choose between manufacturers, thereby stimulating competition and increasing the pace of advances in technology. On the West Coast such aircraft companies as Boeing, Douglas, and Lockheed competed for airline custom until just before, and during World War II, when orders for military planes became even more lucrative.

World Fairs

It was not only the art, industry, and gadgets of the machine age that were on the agenda for transformation but also the general environment. This was a special feature of two world's fairs, the Century of Progress Fair, Chicago, in 1933–1934, and the World of Tomorrow Fair, New York, 1939–1940, both of which boasted pavilions devoted to new worlds. In Chicago visitors could see a General Motors assembly line devised by Albert Kahn, while in New York they could view *Democracity* by Henry Dreyfuss and thereby enter a future made by machines. *Democracity* was a model city within the Persiphere, a round building of 200 feet in diameter wherein people passed through the Trylon, 700 feet tall, and finally descended a ramp, the Helicline to the ground.

The way science and technology were enriching American civilization was a theme dear to the National Research Council (NRC), funded by big business and supported by university scholars. The NRC was instrumental in the Century of Progress and World of Tomorrow expositions in Chicago and New York. In particular, the Chicago exposition was regarded as a showcase for "the transformation of life through the ministrations of sciences." An official slogan was "Science Finds—Industry Applies—Man Conforms." The buildings provided visitors with a progress from primitive machine shops of the 1830s to the mass production lines of Ford and General Motors of the 1930s, while the structures themselves were designed to exploit metallic sheafs, electric cascades, and suspended roots. The New York World's Fair offered visitors a similarly idealistic vision of tomorrow's world. As its president, Grover Whalen, commented, "a glimpse of the community of the future—a future conditioned by science." Albert Einstein, the preeminent physicist whose name was synonymous with scientific advance, acted as front man to an Advisory Committee on Sciences. His most popular contribution was the movie, *The City*, directed by Ralph Steiner and Willard Van Dyke and with a score by Aaron Copland, as a celebration of greenbelt towns. Pavilions dedicated to business were designed to look like laboratories of the future.

The most significant was *Futurama* designed by Norman Bel Geddes as part of the General Motors Pavilion. Visitors entered through a gigantic curved wall painted like an automobile in a silver metalic finish and thence proceeded to a large, darkened auditorium which they crossed aboard a rubber-tired train on a route to simulate an air trip across the United States of 1960. They saw miniature automobiles, orchards, and fields encased by glass, and a modern metropolis composed of skyscrapers. The final destination was a full-size version of a street intersection they had just passed over in model form and now containing the latest products from General Motors. The message was clear. Technology and machines were not the essential problem for America in the Great Depression but, rather, the solution.

FDR opens the New York World's Fair of 1939, the last great demonstration of the peaceful potential of the new machine age before its destructive forces were unleashed by World War II. (Photo by courtesy of Charles Ober).

2

THE 1920s
An American Dream That
Became a Nightmare

THE ROARING TWENTIES, a gangster film released in 1939, shows how the world of entertainment has romanticized the history of the 1920s and made icons of the gangster, the tycoon, the movie star, and the flapper. Legend has it that America was suddenly different at the end of World War I, with the controversy over the League of Nations, the Great Red Scare, the commercial use of radio, the scoring of jazz, the imposition of national prohibition, the introduction of woman suffrage, the campaign for normalcy, and immigration restriction. The historical boundaries of the decade were clearly defined by these events and, at its close, by the Wall Street Crash of 1929.

Because our view of the 1920s has been colored by its various portrayals on screen, by the boom in advertising, and the chaos and license associated with prohibition, it has been tempting for historians to take the Age of Ballyhoo at its word and describe it as a period of newfound prosperity, with high earnings for work-

An emancipated flapper, a nymphet with bobbed hair, outsize necklace, short shift, and unfurled stockings, teaches an old dog how to dance the Charleston in John Held's cover design for *Life* of February 18, 1926. Held was one of the most admired cartoonists of the Jazz Age, noted for his deft satires of its high jinks, especially in illustrations to stories by F. Scott Fitzgerald. (Library of Congress).

ers and low rates of unemployment. Moreover, the stark contrast with widespread destitution in the Great Depression has lent point to the metaphor of prosperity rolling merrily down Main Street until 1929. It seemed there was a genuine shift in consumer spending to such durables as automobiles and domestic appliances. Thus Jim Potter in *The American Economy between the World Wars* (1974) speaks for many historians when he argues how "the bread and butter problems of survival of earlier decades were now replaced for a majority by the pursuit of happiness in the form of the traditional minority pursuits of wine, women and song."

Aggregate statistics on production, income, and consumption are, indeed, impressive. The real Gross National Product (GNP) rose by 39 percent between 1919 and 1929, and real per capita GNP by 20 percent in the same period, while personal disposable income rose by 30 percent. Appliances flooded the market, and general personal consumption increased. According to Harold G. Vatter in "Has There Been a Twentieth-Century Consumer Durables Revolution?" in the *Journal of Economic History* for March 1967, whereas between 1909 and 1918 the annual sale of durables to consumers was, on average $4.29 billion, between 1919 and 1929 it was, on average $7.06 billion, an increase of 65 percent.

The revolution in consumption was most apparent in the home. The percentage of households with inside flush lavatories rose from 20 to 51 percent between 1920 and 1930. The number of homes with radios rose from zero to 40 percent over the same decade. There were equally significant increases, but on a smaller scale, in the percentage of homes with vacuum cleaners, rising from 9 to 30 percent; of washing machines from 8 to 24 percent; and of mechanical refrigerators from 1 to 8 percent. (These are the conclusion of Stanley Lebergott in *The American Economy: Income, Wealth, and Want* [1976].) The proliferation of relatively cheap electrical and mechanical devices for cooking and cleaning eased the physical chores of housekeeping. Moreover, more houses relied on canned and frozen foods to provide their basic diet.

As a result of technological changes, the capacity of electric generating stations rose from 22 million horsepower to 43 million between 1922 and 1930. These changes included a better design of machinery that reduced the cost of generating power, improvements in the means of transmission of power over long distances, and interconnection between separate stations to make the distribution of power more even between localities. Thus, whereas in 1920 35 percent of the population lived in homes lit by electricity, by 1924 over 50 percent did so, and by 1930 68 percent. Moreover, whereas in 1910 there was one telephone for every 14½ people, in 1920 there was one for every 8½ people.

It is scarcely surprising that such developments should have produced a new generation of salesmen and advertising executives to carry various products to middle America. The successful salesman, like the sports star, was meant to exude magnetism and vitality. Sinclair Lewis's fictional real estate salesman, George F. Babbitt, referred to the ideal salesman as "the real He-man, the fellow with Zip and Bang," the fellows who have "hair on their chests and smiles in their eyes and adding machines in their offices."

The new emphasis on material things is clearly illustrated by changing understanding of the verb "to sell." Dictionaries up to the 1930s confined its meaning to transfer goods for a price. Yet what this exchange suggested had expanded. Sell had invaded the worlds of the mind and the spirit. To convert someone to a new belief you would "sell him the idea," to impress him favorably you would "sell yourself to him." Thus a missionary would "sell religion to unbelievers." A statesmen who would have "gone to the people" on the issue of secession in the 1860s, or "educated the people" on gold and silver in the 1890s, would, in the 1910s, "sell the League of Nations to the country." If he was successful, he would have made a good deal, congratulate himself that he had "put it over."

The traditional view of widespread prosperity in the 1920s based on consumption has been offset by exhaustive studies, such as the Brookings Institution's *America's Capacity to Consume* (1934) that emphasized the poverty of most Americans in the 1920s. Irving Bernstein in *The Lean Years: A History of the American Worker, 1920–1933* (1966) concluded that the 1920s were golden "only for a privileged segment of the population" and, among others, Robert Ozanne in *Wages in Practice and Theory* (1968) has shown how wage increases in the 1920s were relatively small. On the whole, labor historians have admitted that the distribution of income became more unequal and that certain industries (and, indeed, regions) failed in a period of general affluence. The sick industries included farming, coal mining, textiles, railroads, shipping and shipbuilding, and shoe and leather production. Geographically, the Northeast, Mid Atlantic, and Pacific states were the most prosperous regions. Least prosperous were the agricultural states of the South and the Northwest. Moreover, the distribution of wealth throughout society was most uneven and this provided the prime source of social tension. The top 1 percent of the population earned almost 15 percent of all earned incomes. In 1926 207 people paid taxes on incomes of $1 million or more—the highest number then recorded. Corporate net profits rose in the decade by 76 percent. The Brookings Institution report showed how unequal was consumption. It found that in 1929 the highest 24 percent of all spending units made 50 percent of all purchases; the highest 20 percent made 50 percent of all expenditure on housing; and the top 20 percent made 36 percent of all purchases of food and 50 percent of all expenditure on such items as health, education, and recreation.

The United States was facing profound economic problems beside those of postwar conversion. However, their nature was imperfectly understood by government and people. Although the war had apparently strengthened American industry, its economic structure was now seriously warped. For one thing, the war had expanded and speeded up industrial capacity, firstly to supply Europe and, later, to supply the United States. In 1920 exports had reached $8.25 billion, an increase of 4 percent over 1919 and of 333 percent over 1913. The cost of imports was about $5.75 billion, an increase of 35 percent over 1919 and almost 300 percent over 1913. However, America's capacity to produce was far beyond its capacity to consume during peacetime or to export abroad once other nations had resumed their normal production. As the economic crisis hit various industries in the period 1919–1921, many firms in business and farms went bankrupt but manufacturers survived by curtailing production and laying off men. Perhaps 4.75 million men altogether were out of work in 1919. The upshot of industrial confusion was labor strife and strikes. The first in the long series of strikes and lockouts was a strike of dock workers in New York from January 9, 1919, followed by strikes of dress- and waistmakers, shipworkers, engineers, and firemen, culminating in the Great Steel Strike, beginning on September 22, 1919.

To make matters worse, there were also "strikes" by consumers, protesting the high cost of living. In 1918 the index of retail food prices was 168.3; in 1920, it was 203.4. The government reacted to the buyers' strike by fixing maximum prices for bread, milk, and coal. In Washington Congress forbade increases in rents and state and city governments followed suit. Manufacturers gradually reduced their prices and in 1922 the retail price index fell to 141.6 as America entered a recession.

The Narrow Gate: Immigration Restriction

A prime source of social tension was ethnic rivalry. Forty years of continuous immigration on a massive scale had made the United States the most heterogeneous nation ever. In 1920 the population was 105,710,620 people in the continental United States and 12,279,997 in its overseas possessions. Of this population, 58.5 percent were children of white native parents; 7.0 percent of mixed native and foreign parentage; 15.5 percent of foreign parents; 10.5 percent were black Americans; and 13.75 percent were first-generation immigrants. Following the Great Red Scare of 1917–1921 and the rout of Woodrow Wilson's foreign policy over the League of Nations, the country became suspicious, even hostile, to all things foreign, including immigration. The war had revealed how close were the sympathies of millions of American citizens to their countries of origin. Their double loyalty led to charges of "hyphenated Americanism." In his forlorn defense of the Treaty of Versailles, Wilson maintained "Hyphens are the knives that are being stuck into this document."

Racism was now corroborated more than ever before by pseudoscientific analyses. Thus in *The Passing of the Great Race* (1916) Madison Grant maintained that it was race that determined the quality of civilization and that only Aryans had built great cultures. "The man of the old stock," opined Grant, "is being crowded by these foreigners, just as he is today being literally driven off the streets of New York City by the swarms of Polish Jews. These immigrants adopt the language of the native American, they wear his clothes, they steal his name and they are beginning to take his women, but they seldom adopt his religion or understand his ideals. . . . " Lothrop Stoddard in *The Rising Tide of Color* (1920) and Professor Edwin East of Harvard warned how the white races were being overwhelmed by more fertile colored races. Perhaps the most influential diatribes of all were articles by Kenneth Roberts for the *Saturday Evening Post* in which he urged a revision of immigration laws to permit fewer Polish Jews, whom he described as "human parasites," to enter the United States.

By February 1921 Ellis Island, the immigrant reception center, was jammed by the number of immigrants seeking entry and the immigration authorities diverted ships to Boston to loosen the bottle neck. Congress was panic-stricken and precipitately passed an emergency measure to restrict immigration. It passed the House in a few hours without the vote being recorded and was adopted by the Senate shortly afterward by 78 votes to 1. This first immigration act, the Emergency Quota Act, signed by President Warren Harding on May 19, 1921, was intended as an interim measure.

It decreed that no more than 357,000 immigrants could be admitted to the United States in one year. This figure was about a third of the annual totals in the years before World War I. Moreover, the fixed number was broken down into a series of national quotas. Each quota represented 3 percent of the immigrants from any particular country in the United States in 1910. Thus the new, restricted immigration was to be based on a mix of old and new immigrant groups. The act was intended to last for one year only but it was subsequently extended until 1924. In those three years Congress discovered that the assigned quotas were at variance with the proposed ceiling and that far more immigrants than it intended were entering the United States. In 1924 the total number was more than 700,000. Furthermore, the act failed to discriminate against immigrants from southern and eastern Europe as much as its advocates wanted.

The definitive act of 1924, the National Origins Act, cut the maximum figure to 164,000 by pushing the base year for the quota proportions to 1890 and cutting the annual quota for each nationality to 2 percent. The year 1890 was chosen as being six years before the new immigration exceeded the old. During congressional debates congressmen reviled and ridiculed the new immigrants of the great cities, especially New York, to whom they imputed every contemporary evil. "On the one side," claimed Congressman Jasper Napoleon Tincher of Kansas, a farmer and stock raiser, "is beer, bolshevism, unassimilating settlements and perhaps many flags—on the other side is constitutional government; one flag, stars and stripes. . . . "

The 1924 act stated that after 1927 the annual quota for each nationality was not to be computed from the number of foreign-born in the United States at any given time but from "the number of inhabitants of 1920 whose origin by birth *or ancestry*" could be attributed to a specific national area. The secretaries of state, commerce, and labor had the invidious task of fixing national origins. However they found "national origins" so difficult to define that they postponed this part of the law until 1929.

The act of 1924 had other special features. Quotas established in 1921 applied only to Europe, the Near East, Africa, and Australia and New Zealand. There were no restrictions for countries in the western hemisphere. However, arrangements for certain Asian countries, notably Japan, ensured the virtual exclusion of Japanese immigrants. While each restricted nation was allowed a minimum of 100 immigrants per year, Japan was pointedly insulted by the declaration, "No alien ineligible to citizenship shall be admitted to the United States." Secretary of State Charles Evans Hughes (1921–1925) tried to persuade Congress that this provision was a wanton insult to a supersensitive nation with whom the United States was seeking naval limitations at Washington. However, Congress, itself sensitive to anti-Japanese opinion on the Pacific coast, would not be deterred. Moreover, the Supreme Court decided in the case of *Ozawa* v. *The United States* (1923) that people of Japanese birth were ineligible for naturalization. The intention and effect of the law was crystal clear. By its callous disregard of human rights, Congress was providing Japanese militants with an additional reason for hating the United States.

In short, the effect of the act of 1924 was to hold immigration from 1925 to 1930 to an annual average of 300,000. In the 1930s the combined effect of the act and the Great Depression held immigration down to an annual average of about 50,000. People in other countries complained when families were kept apart by the new measures, with wives denied permission to join their husbands in America. An interesting side effect of the new laws and different from those intended by their sponsors was increased immigration to the United States by people of Hispanic and Indian origin from Mexico and Puerto Rico and of French origin from Canada.

In addition to reactionary xenophobes, the laws were welcomed by progressives, liberals, and many ordinary folk who felt that many of the problems of American society could be solved, only if the composition of society remained static. Moreover, organized labor, led by the AFL, favored such restriction. So prevalent was the feeling and the traditional thinking behind it, that while the quotas and ceiling were relaxed in succeeding decades, the principles behind them were not overturned until the Immigration Act of 1965.

The law finally took effect in 1929, establishing a total limit of 153,714, excluding the Western Hemisphere and Asia. Britain was allowed an annual quota of 65,361 immigrants, whereas Italy was allowed only 5,803, Poland, 6,524, and Russia, 2,784 immigrants. In response to demands, under President Herbert Hoover's administration the State Department instructed American consuls to refuse to issue visas to prospective immigrants who did not have $50 in cash, the amount deemed essential to be self-supporting. Ironically, the new immigrants, accused of trying to subvert American values and institutions, had not been able to exercise sufficient political influence to get the act defeated in Congress.

Another source of social tension was the widening division between town and country. For the first time the number of people living in towns — communities of 2,500 or more — exceeded those

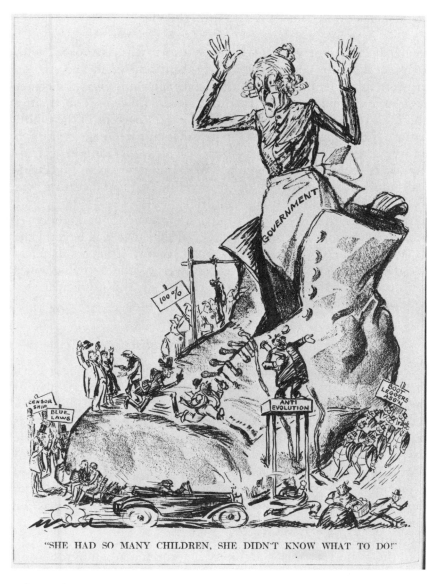

"SHE HAD SO MANY CHILDREN, SHE DIDN'T KNOW WHAT TO DO!"

"She Had So Many Children, She Didn't Know What To Do." A cartoon of the federal government overwhelmed by the social problems of the 1920s, ranging from prohibition and gangsterism to sexual permissiveness and its critics, fundamentalism, and racism. The resulting social conflicts took such forms as intolerant extremism and antisocial self-indulgence. (Library of Congress).

living in the countryside (51.4 percent in towns, compared with 48.6 percent in the countryside). Sixty-eight cities contained 100,000 or more inhabitants, and each of these major cities was the center of a larger population. By 1930 there were ninety-six such cities and their total population accounted for 44.6 percent of the whole nation. This reflected the ever increasing shift from agriculture to industry since for every forty-six people now working in agriculture there were fifty-four engaged in manufacturing and mechanical industries. Moreover, the gross value of manufacturing was almost three times that of agriculture.

American cities offered their inhabitants a variety of experience, whether for work, recreation, or social life, that was beyond the capacity of the countryside and small towns. Country dwellers dreaded the encroaching political power of the growing cities with their jazz and bootlegging, racketeering and municipal corruption, and their diverse mix of ethnic groups.

Los Angeles as Metropolis

In the period from 1920 it was Los Angeles rather than New York or Chicago that provided the essential model and spatial plan of the typical twentieth-century American city. This was the new metropolis dominated by the automobile. In 1920 Los Angeles was the tenth largest city in the nation with a population of some 577,000 people, about the same size as Pittsburgh. On the eve of World War II that figure had increased to 2,785,000 with the real explosion coming during the war and afterward so that, by 1970, the population was 9,475,000 and the metropolitan area was the third largest manufacturing center in the United States after Chicago and New York.

In the same way that geography determined Washington's and Chicago's growth and success as cities, so it did with Los Angeles. Waves of migration to California and the Southwest ensured the city's expansion, while new resources and industries fueled its economic growth. For Chicago, it had been railroads, prairie farms, the forests of Michigan and Wisconsin, and iron ore from Lake Superior that had made of the city a center for transportation, food processing, lumber, steel, and machinery. A warm and sunny climate, the presence of oil, and airlines were turning Los Angeles into a capital of petroleum refining, of national distribution of fruit and vegetables, of motion picture production, and the focal point of the aircraft, aerospace, and war research industries. During the 1920s and 1930s a combination of factors led to the city's expansion: irrigated agriculture, oil discoveries, the motion picture boom, and waves of midwestern and Texan immigrants seeking work, fortune and, possibly, fame. Oil revenues contributed to the cost of the construction of an ocean port at Long Beach, and rail connections to the East and the Southwest were laid. These improvements in transportation made Los Angeles a preferred site for warehouses and the branch plants of national corporations. In the 1920s both Ford and Goodyear built Pacific plants in the city and were followed by many other firms.

However, one element of manufacturing remained underdeveloped in Los Angeles until the 1940s. The city's factories were very isolated, being some 2,000 miles from the western edge of the midwestern manufacturing belt at St. Louis, Missouri. Thus metalworking and general machinery did not feature as part of the city's industrial potential until the great and unusual demand for aircraft during World War II resulted in the birth of an aerospace industry and all its concomitant manufacturing capabilities.

A special feature of Los Angeles is that, in being quintessentially a city of the twentieth century, it has a very special land use and transportation structure in comparison with older cities such as Chicago and New York. It has a low density of settlement, the majority of its inhabitants move about with ease, and it is not dominated by a single downtown area. Los Angeles is an amorphous metropolis. Although, like other cities, it does have slum tenements and apartment buildings, it is characterized by the single-family dwelling unit. There are three main reasons for this predominance of the single house, and none of them can be traced back to the schemes of town planners: the culturally-induced predilection of certain Americans for detached homes; the need and the business opportunity involved in supplying water and transportation for burgeoning land development; and, perhaps, most important of all, the freedom and sheer pleasure bestowed by the automobile.

In the early years of the twentieth century some three out of four newcomers to Los Angeles were white, native-born Americans from eastern cities and midwestern farms and towns. Both white city dwellers and farmers alike brought with them the tradition of the detached single-family home. Fulfilling this demand meant the creation of suburbia and the provision of water and public transport. Speculators were not slow to provide these services and they built a complex of interurban streetcars that had some lines stretching from twenty to thirty-five miles out from the city center. The widespread use of the automobile in the 1920s encouraged the trend toward diffusion and, in fact, increased the extent of suburbia to massive proportions. The automobile allowed developers to build housing beyond walking distance from the interurban streetcars. Eventually and inevitably, the interurban lines began to lose money from competition with automobiles and then, when traffic jams in downtown Los Angeles became intolerable, the municipality called for the construction of the city's famed rapid-transit system to alleviate traffic, revitalize the street railways, and save the downtown area from congestion. It is interesting to note that the citizens of Los Angeles, unlike the citizens of many other cities in the 1920s, voted against proposals for a subway system. In their view, their city was new and open plan and bore no relation to the cramped conditions of other, older, cities that could not do without underground transportation.

Whatever their virtues as places for residence and recreation, it was the vices of the cities, real or imaginary, that exercised country folk in the 1920s. As English radio producer Daniel Snowman explains, during the 1920s America was in the midst of a whole series of transitions, "No longer rural, but not yet dominated by either industry or the white-collar professions; no longer overwhelmingly Anglo-Saxon or Protestant but not yet resigned to becoming a genuinely pluralistic society." One result was continuous conflict between the new urban civilization and traditional rural values. At stake was social, political, and religious tolerance. The darker side of the decade surfaced with alarming frequency as if to demonstrate that society could not accommodate all its conflicts. As Daniel Snowman says, "These manifestations took two major forms: intolerant extremism and anti-social self-indulgence." The accompanying table shows how the political and social phenomena of the decade may be distributed into these categories.

Intolerance	*Indulgence*
National Prohibition	
Senate rejection of the League of Nations	Ohio gang in Washington
	Veterans' Bureau Scandals
Great Red Scare and Palmer Raids	Teapot Dome Scandal
Sacco-Vanzetti Case	Florida land boom
Revival of the Ku Klux Klan	Mellon tax proposals
Immigration restriction	Gangsterism and racketeering
Fordney-McCumber Tariff System of foreign debt repayments	Sexual license
	Great Bull Market
Case of *Adkins* v. *Children's Hospital*	
Scopes Trial	
1928 presidential election	

Sacco and Vanzetti

The case of Italian immigrants and anarchists Nicola Sacco and Bartolomeo Vanzetti reflects this. The central crime in the case was the theft of a $16,000 payroll of the Slater and Morrill shoe factories in the industrial town of South Braintree, twelve miles south of Boston, on April 15, 1920. During the robbery, the paymaster Frederick A. Parmenter, and his guard, Alessandro Berardelli, were shot and killed by two thieves who made their getaway in a stolen car with other bandits. Twenty days later cobbler Nicola Sacco and fish peddler Bartolomeo Vanzetti were arrested although they both had alibis.

The evidence that convicted Sacco and Vanzetti before the Norfolk County Superior Court at Dedham on July 14, 1921, concerned identification, ballistics, and consciousness of guilt. The district attorney, Frederick A. Katzmann, was a skilled counsel who ruthlessly exploited the defendants' poor command of English to goad and slight them, making it seem to the jury that their imperfectly expressed explanations were deliberate malice against the United States. Katzmann also appealed to the biased jury's basest emotions and he was abetted by the incompetent and malicious judge, Webster Thayer. Popular anecdotes have him referring to the accused as "dagoes" and "anarchist bastards."

The case quickly became a sensation at home and abroad. What roused Americans of all classes was not so much whether Sacco and Vanzetti were guilty but whether they should live or die, and what determined people's attitudes was, primarily, their own social perspective. The general public, what we might today call Middle America, demanded death.

The American friends of Sacco and Vanzetti organized themselves to save their heroes. The Sacco-Vanzetti Defense Committee was led by a succession of ordinary working-class men, notably Aldino Felicani and Gardner Jackson, ready to risk social ostracism on behalf of the class war. Over the years it distributed over 200,000 pieces of printed material, including an irregular *Official Bulletin,* published between December 1925 and September 1930. Its aim was to exploit every reasonable line of action to reverse the conviction and use it until a better came along.

Over the period 1921–1925 Judge Webster Thayer staunchly resisted various requests for a new trial that were advanced on various grounds of which the most persuasive was the inconclusive nature of the ballistic evidence. At one point a convicted murderer, Celestino F. Medeiros (or Madeiros), confessed to the South Braintree robbery and murder by way of a note to Sacco on November 18, 1925. So shocked were the staff of the Boston *Herald,* previously hostile to the defense, when Thayer denied a new trial after the Medeiros confession, that the newspaper reversed its attitude. Its chief editorial writer, F. Lauriston Bullard, wrote his famous leader "We Submit" that won him a Pulitzer prize. In particular, Bullard found Thayer's innuendos distressing. Medeiros's confession ought to be tested in court for "the criterion here is not what a judge may think about it but what a jury might think about it."

Like later members of ethnic minorities in prison, Sacco and Vanzetti were educated and radicalized by their experiences, becoming proficient in English and, in Vanzetti's case, skilled in social analysis. When their line of defense was exhausted, they were brought again before Judge Thayer on April 9, 1927, and made moving pleas asserting their innocence and the prejudice of the judge before being condemned to death. Vanzetti told Judge Thayer

I would not wish to a dog or to a snake, to the most low or misfortunate creature of the earth—I would not wish to any of them what I have had to suffer for things that I am not guilty of. But my conviction is that I have suffered for things that I am guilty of. I am suffering because I am a radical and indeed I am a radical; I have suffered because I was an Italian, and indeed I am an Italian; I have suffered more for my family and for my beloved than for myself; but I am so convinced to be right that if you could execute me two times, and if I could be reborn two other times, I would live again to do what I have done already.

Sacco and Vanzetti were electrocuted shortly after midnight on August 22, 1927. Medeiros died with them. Their funeral procession in Boston on August 28 became a riot between family mourners, 50,000 spectators, and police in which women marchers and innocent onlookers were attacked and beaten without provocation. There were also demonstrations elsewhere, notably in Chicago and Seattle, attended by IWW members. However, mass public grief did not atone for the shame felt by artists, radicals, and intellectuals. Novelist John Dos Passos declared that, from the moment of their execution, America was two nations and Sacco and Vanzetti had been victims in the struggle for supremacy. As graphic designer Ben Shahn observed later, the case was a searing experience for American artists—like "living through another crucifixion"—and a most formative one.

The tensions between Left and Right, young and old, town and country that had been exacerbated by the Sacco-Vanzetti case extended to other matters—serious, frivolous, and bizarre.

The New Woman and the Cult of Youth

Among the supposedly new features of society after World War I were the new woman, symbolized by the flapper, and the ascendancy of youth. Indeed, a milestone of political history was reached when the Senate voted for woman suffrage by fifty-six votes to twenty-five on June 14, 1919, and the Nineteenth Amendment was submitted to the states. Tennessee was the thirty-sixth state to pass the amendment on August 18, 1920, and it was declared duly ratified by Secretary of State Bainbridge Colby (1920–1921) on August 26. It was estimated that the Woman's Suffrage amendment would add 9.5 million women voters to the existing electorate of 17.5 million men. In the event, women stayed away from the polls in 1920 and 1924 and, when they did vote, they were no better informed than men.

Moreover, as historian Carl Degler has remarked, "Suffrage, once achieved, had almost no observable effect upon the position of women." Thus the majority of American women were still treated as an underprivileged minority, less equal as individuals and as citizens. A logical extension of NAWSA's (the National American Woman Suffrage Association's) suffrage program would have been a new campaign for another constitutional amendment to remove all legal discrimination as regards such matters as jury service, property rights, child custody, and protection for working women. This was the route that Alice Paul, the dominant voice in the National Women's party, chose to follow, calling for a constitutional amendment providing that "equality of rights under the law shall not be denied or abridged by the United States or by a State on account of sex." This is sometimes called the ERA (Equal Rights Amendment).

However, the majority of former suffragists considered the ERA a betrayal of all they had fought for because it would nullify existing special protective laws for women. "The cry Equality, Equality, where Nature has created inequality," declared Florence Kelley of the National Consumers' League, "is as stupid and as deadly as the cry Peace, Peace, where there is no Peace." To give up protective legislation for working women who had so little protection would be to subject them even more to men. The proposed amendment would open a Pandora's box of divisive litigation and no one would be able to predict the consequences. Thus, when the Supreme Court declared, in the case of *Adkins* v. *Children's Hospital,* decided by a vote of five to three on April 9, 1923, that a minimum wage law for women in Massachusetts was unconstitutional because it infringed the rights of management, it divided the two arms of the women's movement. The National Women's party regarded it as a victory for equal rights, while most women's, labor, and liberal associations denounced it as a regressive decision, breaching the precedent of *Muller* v. *Oregon* (1908).

A singular demonstration of the emergence of the new woman in society was the cult of the flapper. The term "flapper" was first used in England and introduced by H. L. Mencken to the United States in 1915. A girl who flapped had not yet attained full maturity and her flapper dresses were intended to transform juvenile, angular figures into an aesthetic ideal. Her hairstyle was a Ponjola bob, as first worn in the United States by dancer Irene Castle during the war. Her dresses were short, tight, and somewhat plain with a low waist; her stockings were silk or rayon and flesh colored and could be rolled below the knee or taken off in hot weather. According to John C. Fügel in *The Psychology of Clothes* (1930), the whole effect carried the eye from body to limbs to emphasize the long lines of arms and legs. The so-called boyish figure and face were still ultrafeminine in the excessive use of makeup and provocative display of leg.

Moreover, flapper styles were not restricted to adolescent girls. Even the Sears Roebuck catalog deliberately aimed at women in Middle America, drew on the fashions of New York society and *Vogue* magazine, offering modish designs at moderate prices. Thus F. Scott Fitzgerald noted how the flapper was passé by 1923 when other age groups began to copy her style. Such simple clothes as the flappers wore could be produced for almost any figure, saving time and money on fitting and alterations, and were manufactured in great quantities. As Elizabeth Sage observes in *A Study of Costume* (1926),

With the entrance of women into the business world the demand came for comfortable dress which did not hamper the wearer in any way, and would hold its own no matter in what situation its owner found herself. It must have lasting qualities as well, for the business woman like the business man must not be bothered with constant repairs. It must be easy to put on. The designers set to work and the one-piece slip on gown was the result.

Mass production not only led to uniformity and simplicity but also to greater variety by way of textures, styles, and colors and to more types of clothes for different occasions—professional, formal, and casual. Thus it dawned on the rag trade that women grew up to wear certain dress sizes, seven of which would fit half of the women in the whole country.

Critics of the flapper were more disturbed by her aggressive modernity than her sexuality and they were more perplexed by the fact that she represented only the most overt changes in the presentation and, indeed, life-styles of many American women. Samuel Byrne, editor of the *Observer* of Pittsburgh, was one who tackled this theme in June 1922.

There has been a change for the worse during the past year in feminine dress, dancing, manners, and general moral standards. The causes are the lack of an adequate sense of responsibility in the parents or guardians of girls, a decline in personal religion, a failure to realize the serious ethical consequences of immodesty in girls' dress, a dulling of moral susceptibilities, an inability to grasp the significance of the higher things in human life, and, last, but not least, the absence of sufficient courage and determination to resist the dictates of what is known as Fashion when these are opposed to decency.

The gist of such articles was that modesty and morality were somehow indivisible from traditional female presentation. Once one was relaxed, all was lost in the other. Contemporary dress and modern behavior were attacked together by middle-aged, middle-class women who clung to certain nineteenth-century values of their class in which marriage was seen as the price men paid for sex and sex the price women paid for marriage. The new woman who showed off her body and enjoyed sex before marriage was threatening traditional American values.

Society was paying greater attention to the young than ever before, partly out of respect for the thousands of youths lost in the war. Another influence in this respect was current psychological thinking that individuals must be nurtured while they are young, before their habits are set. A third factor was the growing significance of machines, primarily the automobile, that could be handled most dexterously by young people. A fourth factor in the new emphasis on youth was that social changes gave youth economic independence and, following close behind, moral and intellectual independence. Whatever his age, any youth who had taken part in the war emerged as a mature man, licensed to behave as the superior of those who had not taken part.

Moreover, the proportion of high school graduates among all seventeen-year-olds increased from 16.3 percent in 1920 to 27.5 percent in 1929. A minority of middle-class folk could keep their children in education for longer, not only sending them to college for an undergraduate course but also, sometimes, supporting them through a postgraduate program. Thus children finished school at age seventeen, graduated, perhaps, as late as twenty-three, and completed a Ph.D. by the time they were thirty. Thus the number of students in higher education rose by about 50,000 each year. In 1926 one out of every eight young Americans between the ages of eighteen and twenty-one was in college. This was four or five times the number achieved by other developed countries. Perhaps standards for undergraduate programs became more lax as curriculae widened. The reverse was true of graduate schools that made high demands in the fields of medicine, law, and engineering, and, in the case of Ph.D. programs, most rigorous ones. Universities cultivated research students and their teachers began to concentrate more on research and scholarship, throwing undergraduates more on their own initiative.

Thus youth received unprecedented opportunities for advancement and fulfillment and began to display greater defiance of traditional values. The natural arrogance of youth and the new opportunities for its display afforded by society reversed traditional patterns of behavior. Youth, rather than maturity, provided the model for others. This was certainly the case on the dance floor, in the beauty parlor, and the sports field. When it came to clothes, manners, and fashions, mature folk strove to act like their children and sometimes their grandchildren. Indeed, to an unusual extent, American culture in the 1920s was prefigurative, with adults learning from the younger generation of adolescent girls, creative writers and artists, intelligentsia, and students.

In this climate it is not surprising that sexual fulfillment and orgasm were no longer taboo subjects. Lesser writers, taking advantage of the trail of sexual discovery blazed by such varied and distinguished authors as Sherwood Anderson, John Dos Passos, and Theodore Dreiser, made a great deal of money out of books about sex. Warner Fabian in *Flaming Youth* and *Unforbidden Fruit* titillated his readers with what journalist Mark Sullivan calls an "apotheosis of pruriency." James Branch Cabell achieved special notoriety when his *Jurgen* was suppressed after its publication in 1920. The heroine of Victor Marguerite's *The Bachelor Girl* was a hostess in Paris who treated her guests to the ultimate in hospitality. To appeal to the smart set, sex had either to take place in exotic locations, filled with eastern promise, or amidst opulent but neurotic cafe society, as portrayed by Ben Hecht, Carl Van Vechten, and Maxwell Bodenheim. Poet Edna St. Vincent Millay expressed the Greenwich Village cult of bohemian freedom in a much quoted stanza.

> My candle burns at both ends;
> It will not last the night;
> But ah, my foes, and oh, my friends,
> It gives a lovely light.

The Roaring Twenties

There was a revolution in the world of communications as the expanding mass media of newspapers and magazines, radio, and cinema began to shape popular culture toward an increasingly urban point of view. Thus the presentation of fashions, sports, entertainment, and a minimum of political reporting were becoming increasingly standardized, giving society a similar view of itself all the way from New York to San Francisco and from Chicago to New Orleans. The cults associated with movie stars and sports heroes gave America certain well-focused images of itself, its fashions, and its customs.

In 1919 the first tabloid newspaper, the New York *Daily News,* was published. It set a pattern and encouraged a vogue for a new form of journalism copied, in New York, by Bernard Macfadden's *Evening Graphic* and William Randolph Hearst's *Daily Mirror,* and, in Chicago, by the *Daily Illustrated Times.* The *Daily*

News eventually had the largest circulation of any American paper. It carried more photographs and cartoons than news and comment, and more advertisements than either. Indeed, its copy was devoted more to gossip than to news and more to entertainment than information, what one critic called "more sex than sense."

All the tabloids came to specialize in crime stories, divorce reports, national disasters, sports, strip cartoons, and personal columns offering readers advice on sex and marriage. All these subjects provided plenty of opportunity for titillation. What was missing was serious news on politics, economics, and social issues, and critical reviews of the arts. The tabloids encouraged a new form of the literature of exposure, sometimes called "keyhole journalism," providing intimate detail (or conjecture) of the secret lives of people in show business, sports, and high society. The new reporters became masters of innuendo and their doyen was Walter Winchell. Originally from the Lower East Side, Winchell had finished school at sixth grade, pretended he had only once read a book, and dismissed intellectuals by describing a philosopher as "somebody who knows all the platitudes and copies things that are clever out of books."

As well as celebrating heroes like Ford and Lindbergh, papers sensationalized sordid dramas. The Hearst chain was the most adept in exploiting sex and crime to the utmost. The murderess Ruth Snyder achieved posthumous notoriety by being photographed during her execution. The *Daily News* regaled its apparently gourmet readers about how she was going "to cook, *and sizzle,* AND FRY!" in the electric chair.

In 1922 ten magazines each claimed a paid circulation of over 2.5 million and another twelve claimed a circulation of over 1 million. The majority were pulp magazines, printed on cheap wood-pulp paper, and devoted mainly to lowbrow detective, western, or movie fiction. Some specialized in true confessions of fits of wrongdoing followed by bouts of repentance. Compared with the magazines of the early Progressive Era, magazines of the 1920s carried far fewer serious articles and devoted more space to sports, fashion, and leisure activities. Whereas in the 1900s biographical articles were about politicans and businessmen, in the 1920s and 1930s they were about sportsmen, movie stars, and radio personalities.

Most notable of the new magazines was *Time* magazine, founded in 1923 with Henry Luce as its first editor. From the start, it tried to make politics a popular subject without trivializing the issues and personalities, except when they called for it. In the 1930s it experimented with a missionary style of film newsreel, *The March of Time,* intended not only to inform the public about major political issues but also to shape their opinions.

Entertainment played a significant part in social life. It reduced tensions and helped maintain equilibrium between the divisions in society. The trivial games crazes of the 1920s—Mah Jongg in 1922, crossword puzzles in 1924, golf every year—all had their part to play. More important still were spectator sports, especially team sports as devices to maintain social equilibrium. The player expended his emotional energy in physical competition; the spectator sublimated his in adulation of a favorite star. In football Harold E. ("Red") Grange of Illinois enjoyed a meteoric but ephemeral career. According to the *New York Times* of October 19, 1924, 67,000 people watched him and the University of Illinois team beat Michigan in the Illinois Memorial Stadium. Of all the games, baseball was the most celebrated. Of all the sports' starts, the most idolized was George Herman ("Babe") Ruth, first of the Boston Sox and, after 1920, of the New York Yankees. In 1920 a man died of excitement when he saw Babe Ruth hit a ball into the bleachers. In the season of 1921 Ruth hit fifty-nine home runs and he maintained his superiority over other players throughout the decade.

The financial incentive for stars, promoters, and managers, as well as newspaper reporters and radio commentators, was unprecedented. The public's capacity for vicarious satisfaction reached a peak in attendance at the two boxing matches between Jack Dempsey and Gene Tunney in Philadelphia in 1926 and Chicago in 1927, both of which Tunney won on points. For the first match, 120,000 people paid almost $2 million; for the second, 145,000 paid $2.5 million. The Chicago amphitheater, Soldiers' Field, was so enormous that two-thirds of the audience on the

Dempsey and Firpo by George Bellows (1924), 5″ × 63¼″. (Geoffrey Clements Photography; Collection of Whitney Museum of American Art, New York). Boxing contests allowed spectators to sublimate ethnic loyalties in enthusiasm for the skill and prowess of a new generation of champions. Assigned to cover the September 3, 1923, fight between Jack Dempsey and Luis Firpo of Argentina for the *New York Evening Journal,* Bellows chose the episode in the first round when Firpo knocked Dempsey through the ropes into Bellows's own lap. Dempsey climbed back into the ring and, in the second round, knocked Firpo out. For the painting Bellows modestly moved himself to the extreme left.

periphery did not know who had won; almost 50 million people listening to commentator Graham McNamee on radio did and eleven of them died of excitement during the bout. As a recent analyst, Elliot J. Gorn, observes, "Spectacles like the Dempsey-Tunney fights were (now) part of a larger fantasy world of popular idols, status symbols and leisure time pleasures which offered

Americans vicarious release from an oppressively rationalized society."

Gorn shows how Dempsey and Tunney both represented different but central social values and their two prize fights helped exorcize social tensions and contradictions. James Joseph ("Gene") Tunney was the son of an Irish-American working-class family in Greenwich Village who served in the marines during the war from which he emerged as light-heavyweight champion of the AEF, hence the "fighting marine." He was tall, blond, and handsome and his poise, physical grace, and strength were a tribute to his professional commitment to clean living and arduous training. Despite sixty fights, he was unscarred and this was because he was a defensive fighter who parried blows rather than dealt them out until in time he wore down stronger opponents. When Henry Ford attributed his own commercial success to managerial intelligence, mixing speed, power, and accuracy with economy, system, and community, he was using exactly the vocabulary sports commentators used to describe Tunney's fighting style. Like Ford and Lindbergh, Tunney owed his tremendous success to his fusion of Puritan restraint, heroic individualism, and technical skill. Thus the fighting marine was a mixture of manager and hero, embodying the spirit that had tamed a wilderness and conquered its inhabitants.

In comparison, William Harrison ("Jack") Dempsey excited both tremendous adulation and vicious hate. He was the ninth of thirteen children of a luckless Colorado miner, a young tough who drifted through the violent copper mining camps of Utah and Colorado, part laborer and part hobo, dividing his youth between the pits and the ring. His vicious fighting style when he won the championship against Jess Willard in 1919 earned him the title of the "Manassa Mauler." Furthermore, he was associated with an unsavory collection of hangers on, including gamblers and gangsters, and, for a time, it seemed he was more interested in living off his reputation than in defending his title. Thus, established and upwardly mobile Americans could not adopt him as a mascot of American virtues as they could Gene Tunney. Nevertheless, he appealed to working-class men across the country who saw him as an unreclaimed outlaw. Dempsey was a long representative of what Elliot J. Gorn calls the "deep subterranean well of discontent" and he and his cronies "projected a fantasy of unreconstructed virility and independence" against the threat of depersonalization in modern society.

Like radio, movies, and other forms of mass culture, sports helped persuade a nation divided by race, class, and ethnicity that it had a common identity. For white- and blue-collar workers alike, bored with their work, but with more money to spend on entertainment than ever before, sports not only represented escape from routine but also celebrated physical skill, courage, and endurance.

The Roaring Twenties is also celebrated for its high jinks, absurd activities, such as marathon dances, in which people engaged as a means of frenetic escape or to attain momentary publicity. The idea of marathon dances began in Britain and became popular in New York after Alma Cummings established a new world record of twenty-seven hours in New York on March 31, 1923. On April 19 a new record of ninety hours was set at Cleveland. Physical collapse was common enough and, occasionally, dancers died from overexertion.

America Dry: The Tragicomedy of Prohibition

During the twenties national prohibition was the most avidly discussed subject in American society. It was a subject of far more interest than foreign affairs or party politics and indissoluble from fashion, entertainment, and crime. What, when, why, and how people drank were questions affording limitless speculation. Drys believed that drinking among poor people was reduced; that there was a decline in absenteeism from, and inefficiency at, work; that people spent more money on food, clothing, and shelter; and that everyone shared more evenly in the general prosperity of society. Wets charged that drinking became more fashionable than ever; that prohibition and its excesses led to a decline in social behavior; that an immoderate law could not be enforced; that it led to greater corruption in city government and an increase in gangsterism and racketerering. To this day historians argue about how successful was the reform.

Not only was the task of keeping America dry impossible for the federal government, especially after 1923, but also the Anti-Saloon League did not have the sort of structure and techniques to cope with the new situation. According to K. Austin Kerr in *Organized for Prohibition* (1985), the League was organized to achieve prohibition legislation, but not organized for prohibition observance. All it had was a facade of power that it used insidiously in politics in the early 1920s. It was divided into two factions. One, led by its charismatic but megalomaniac counsel Wayne Wheeler wanted ever stricter enforcement laws and control of appointments to law enforcement agencies. The other faction, led by Ernest Cherrington, wanted to leave enforcement to government and concentrate on educating the public through its giant press at the American Issue Company in Westerville, Ohio.

Enforcement of the Eighteenth Amendment, which took effect on January 16, 1920, was provided by the National Prohibition Enforcement Act of October 27, 1919, devised by Wayne Wheeler of the Anti-Saloon League but named after Andrew Volstead of Minnesota who presented it in the House. An "intoxicating liquor" was defined as one with a two-hundredth part of alcohol or 0.5 percent. It did not, of course, define the amount of alcohol that it would take to make someone drunk. Yet the definition of an intoxicating beverage as 0.5 percent of alcohol surprised some people who had previously supported prohibition. They had assumed that, as was the case in many dry states, only distilled spirits would be banned. Thus it was the Volstead Act, rather than the Eighteenth Amendment, that proscribed beer and wine as well as distilled spirits. However, farmers were still allowed their sweet cider.

Some wets did agree with drys that the amount of liquor people drank decreased substantially. In the period 1911 to 1914 the average annual amount was 1.69 gallons per head. In the period of wartime restrictions, 1918 to 1919, the amount decreased to 0.97. At the outset of national prohibition in 1921 to 1922, there was a further decrease to 0.73 gallons. Only in the later years, from 1927 to 1930, did the amount rise again to 1.14 gallons. These are the figures of Clark Warburton, writing in the early 1930s for volume twelve of the *Encyclopedia of Social Sciences*.

Although these statistics were moderate, drys considered them too generous about the amount of alcohol consumed. The most enduring legend associated with prohibition—the one that has captured public imagination—is that of the abuse of law. To begin with, the illicit supply of beer, wine, and spirits was a mere trickle. Later, from 1923 onward, it became a torrent. The principal ways of obtaining alcohol were by smuggling, by bootlegging, by homebrewing and moonshining, and by misappropriating wine intended for medicine or church services.

In early 1920 a new phrase was coined to describe the smuggling of liquor—"rum running." Smuggling provided the surest way of getting liquor of high quality into the United States. The total frontier was 18,700 miles, made up of approximately 12,000 miles of coast, 3,700 miles of land borders, and 3,000 miles of lake and river front. Alcohol was smuggled into the United States from Canada, Mexico, and the West Indies, and from ships outside the three miles of territorial waters around the coast, the so-called "Rum Row." Smuggling did not long remain a matter of individuals against the state; it became big business. In New York Arnold Rothstein saw how to smelt gold from the amber hue of whiskey. Rothstein was parodied by F. Scott Fitzgerald as Meyer Wolfsheim, an unctuous bootlegger in *The Great Gatsby*. He was supposed to have bribed eight players of the Chicago White Sox baseball team $100,000 to play badly and lose the first games in the 1919 World Series. The story broke, to the embarrassment of the White Sox and subsequent losses for Rothstein and his partners. According to legend, he tried to organize a national syndicate of crime based on sectional cooperation between different gangs. Rothstein created a central buying office to procure alcohol for wholesale and retail from Canada, the West Indies, and even England and Scotland. By 1927 the syndicate, known variously as the Big Seven and the Seven Group, enjoyed a monopoly of liquor traffic on the North Atlantic coast from Boston to Baltimore. It was to be the prototype of national syndicates based on any illicit trade. According to Rothstein's principles, the success of the syndicate depended on cooperation between the different ethnic groups—Italian, Irish, Jewish—rather than internecine competition.

A novel situation now existed for brewers who still wanted to make and sell real beer. Brewers who had the capital, the product, and the expertise began to cooperate with gangsters who provided them with distribution and protection. More than anything else it was the invention of the beer truck that led to the inception of nationwide criminal syndicates in the prohibition years. Unlike wine and spirits, beer was a bulky commodity. It could not be manufactured or transported in secret and it was only profitable when sold in large quantities. Therefore, beer peddlers required considerable resources: a fleet of trucks; weapons, ammunition, and hit men to ward off competitors; funds to bribe police and authorities to ignore the obvious evidence of brewing and distribution *en masse*. Only large and brutal gangs would supply what was required.

In Chicago the brewer Joseph Stenson and his three brothers collaborated with the gangsters Terry Druggan, Frankie Lake, and Johnny Torrio in the operation of five breweries. From 1925 Torrio's successor, Al ("Scarface") Capone, became the most flamboyant, the most widely publicized, and most notorious gangster of the era for his brutal control of gangland territories in Chicago. In Detroit the Purple Gang was a loose coalition of two different Jewish groups, the Oakland Sugar House Gang of Harry Altman, Harry Keywell, and others and the original Purple Gang of Harry Fleisher, Henry Shore, and others. It was similar in other cities. In Boston Charles Solomon, in Philadelphia Max Hoff, in Denver Joseph Roma, and in Cleveland the Mayfield Road Mob peddled beer and carved out gangland territories for its distribution. Moreover, since gangsters provided a front as directors of the brewery they also took the fall—legal liability when something went wrong.

Speakeasies were illegal bars during national prohibition. The term was first used to describe an unlicensed saloon in 1889 and, according to H. L. Mencken, originated in Ireland as "speak softly shop." Whereas before prohibition traditional saloons were often situated at the corner of the block, speakeasies were located in a basement, a back room, or an upstairs apartment. Speakeasies were accredited with three social revolutions. They introduced women, other than prostitutes, to bars. They led to uneasy alliances between the proprietors and gangsters who protected them from police harassment. In general, they sold raw liquor at high prices and were common scenes of fights, raids, and unlicensed behavior. Furthermore, they led to the establishment of night-clubs that survived the repeal of national prohibition in 1933.

Clients of speakeasies and nightclubs delighted in a new mixed drink. The cocktail was a concoction of wine or spirits mixed with fruit juice or soda. Three hundred varieties of cocktail had existed before national prohibition, including the mint julep and the scotch highball. The mix now masked the foul taste of recon-verted industrial alcohol. Thus, cocktails first punished the palate with a bizarre taste before the alcohol went on to pollute the stomach.

The significance of prohibition for Chicago lies partly in the flamboyance of Al Capone, partly in the excesses of his crimes, and partly in the nature of the Chicago underworld. Prohibition was being imposed in the United States at a time when the Italians, a comparatively new immigrant group, were making their bid for full acculturation in the city and for some political control of their environment. That new environment was largely determined by syndicated crime, hitherto the preserve of Jewish and Irish groups who fought back against the mixed South Side Gang of Capone with its Italians, Jews, and Poles.

The notorious climax of Chicago's gang warfare was the St. Valentine's Day Massacre of February 14, 1929, when seven members of the North Side Gang were mown down by machine-gun fire in a warehouse at 2122 North Clark Street. Like other assassinations of the period, the murders served a double func-tion, satisfying the requirements of a blood feud and preparing for some sort of consolidation of crime to which these gangsters would be an impediment. Capone, it seemed, ruled with impu-nity but without remorse. He certainly was not afraid of official retribution. Between 1927 and 1930 there were at least 227 gang-land killings in Chicago. However, in that time, only two gang-sters were tried and convicted of murder.

Nevertheless, the wars did not last forever; self-preservation was as keen an instinct as vendetta. Then there was a truce of sorts. Probably the first national summit of organized crime in

The most popular among all prohibition agents were Izzy (Einstein) and Moe (Smith) whose dexterity in disguise earned them an unequaled record of entrapping unsuspecting bootleggers and speakeasy operators. Apparently, going to work was never a drag in costumes as dazzling and disingenuous as these. (Library of Congress).

the United States took place at the Hotel Statler, Cleveland, on December 5, 1928, when twenty-seven gang leaders from Chicago, St. Louis, Buffalo, New York City, Gary, Newark, and Tampa met to discuss the national distribution of whiskey and future criminal syndicates of Sicilians and Sicilian-Americans. A second conference, at the President Hotel, Atlantic City, New Jersey, from May 13 to May 16, 1929, was open not only to Sicilian and Italian but also Jewish and Irish gangsters. The Sicilian monopoly had been broken. The conclave was representative of crime throughout the nation. It is possible that the conference established territories in a loose federation of criminal syndicates across the nation. By the power of might the local boss who proved himself most efficient became head of his territory: gangs were to unite and forbear feuds. Mafia historian Fred Cook believes that a multimillion dollar fund was established from a pool of resources to be used for bribery of politicians and public officers on a massive scale. It was also decided that L'Unione Siciliana, a fraternal organization of Sicilian immigrants that had been penetrated by criminal elements as a nucleus for an American mafia, would be reorganized from head to foot.

Prohibition was supposed to be enforced by a federal agency, called the Prohibition Unit until March 3, 1927, and, thereafter, known as the Prohibition Bureau. The Unit had none of the prerequisites for making a success of its job: good salaries to make graft superfluous; continuity of personnel; cooperation from government and the general public. Throughout the twenties the annual appropriation from Congress was modest—an average of $8.8 million. Of course, deprived of its excise taxes during prohibition, the federal government had less revenue to spend on enforcement of liquor laws. The total number of agents in the Prohibition Unit varied between 1,500 and 2,300 men and the entire staff was never more than 4,500. The rate of pay was between $1,200 and $2,000 a year in 1920 and about $2,300 a year in 1930. In the first eleven years of the service 17,972 appointments were made but there were 11,982 resignations and 1,608 dismissals for various corrupt practices.

It was, perhaps, the failure of courts to maintain prohibition that most discredited the new law. First offenses usually carried fines of not more than $1,000 or six months' imprisonment; later offenses usually carried fines of between $200 and $2,000 and imprisonment of between one month and five years. The Jones Act of 1929, which made violations a felony, provided maximum penalties of a $10,000 fine, or five years' imprisonment, or both, for the first offense. However, the national average of fines remained $130 and the average prison sentence was 140 days. In some parts of the country prosecutors and judges were so hostile to prohibition that true enforcement was not possible. Sometimes juries refused to convict bootleggers. The number of prohibition cases was much more than the judicial system could accommodate. In 1920 federal courts tried 5,095 prohibition cases out of a total of 34,230 criminal cases altogether. During the twenties the number of prohibition cases went up fifteenfold. In 1929 federal courts tried 75,298 prohibition cases alone.

It had been in rural areas that the prohibition movement had first tested its strength. Once rural isolation was ended by the invasion of press, automobiles, and movies, rural prejudice could not long survive. City papers, now regularly critical of prohibition, were becoming the press of all the states. Between 1925 and 1930 rural subscriptions to city papers doubled. As prohibition historian Andrew Sinclair suggests, "The automobile became so much the representative of the new way of life that its use in nullifying national prohibition was inevitable." Cars and beer trucks carried the precious commodity of alcohol. Whereas at the beginning of the decade automobiles represented an alternative to alcohol, at its end they symbolized booze and beer running and everything that was subversive of prohibition.

From the ranks of doctors, lawyers, businessmen, and labor a new association emerged against national prohibition. This was the Association Against the Prohibition Amendment (AAPA) founded by Captain William H. Stayton on November 12, 1918, and formally incorporated on December 31, 1920. Stayton was an elderly man who had served in the navy, practiced at the bar, and was working in Washington for the Navy League, a lobby for increased naval defenses. His political experiences had left him profoundly disillusioned with the federal government on account of what he considered its inappropriate interference in the lives of individuals.

The size of AAPA membership fluctuated but by 1926 it may have stood at 726,000. Stayton cultivated affluent businessmen who could easily afford to cover the considerable expenses of a political lobby. Among early members were Stuyvesant Fish, president of the Illinois Central Railroad, and Charles H. Sabin, president of Guaranty Trust Company of New York, a Morgan bank. Most important among later recruits were General Motors executives John Julius Raskob and the three Du Pont brothers of Wilmington, Delaware, (Pierre, Irénée, and Lammot). In their paternalistic outlook, prohibition reform was a mission, a question of social responsibility.

Alcoholism and alcohol abuse were serious problems for American society. While national prohibition may have dried up the United States more than the legend propagated by gangster movies from 1930 onward would have us believe, it was not working at all properly by the end of the decade and was yielding new problems of gangsterism and racketeering. The tragedy was not simply that prohibition failed but that, because of the way it failed, politicians abandoned serious attempts to discuss federal control of stimulants, drugs, hallucinogens, and alcohol lest they appear foolish. A new legend developed that outright bans on cigarettes, spirits, and marijuana were bound to backfire on those who had introduced them. Hence the underlying problems of addiction and their putative solutions remained untreated. While politicians prevaricated, America remained amused and aghast at the failure of the countryside to put the clock back with the reform that became a folly.

The tragicomedy of prohibition was a setback for such Protestant churches as the Baptists, Methodists, and Presbyterians, all of whom had supported the dry crusade. In any case, Protestantism was having great difficulties as people spent more and more leisure time in various secular pursuits. In 1927 the *Christian Century* reported how the evangelical churches had lost over half a million members in twelve months. The exceptions were fringe movements that attracted a wide variety of fanatics. In the East

Dr. Frank Buchman, originally a Lutheran minister from North Dakota, enticed the wealthy to religious house parties where his initiates, including graduates from Ivy League colleges, attended group confessions. Buchmanism, sometimes known as the Oxford Movement or Moral Rearmament, invited members to seek "God guidance," after a personal "washing out" of sins, by a daily period of spiritual silence.

The Revival of the Ku Klux Klan

The reaction to modernism was strongest in the South. In popular legend the South was a place forgotten by time and marooned in ignorance. Columnist H. L. Mencken's contempt and loathing for the South know no bounds. The South was "the bunghole of the United States, a cesspool of Baptists, a miasma of Methodism, snake-charmers, phoney real-estate operators, and syphilitic evangelists."

A more informed but equally hostile attack against the South was launched by William Henry Skaggs, formerly of Alabama but later of New York. In *The Southern Oligarchy* of 1924 he produced a vitriolic catalog of its numerous evils: political corruption, illiteracy, peonage, racism, lynching, and various abuses by landlords. Less bitter but equally perceptive was the interpretation provided by Columbia professor Frank Tannenbaum in a slim collection of essays, also of 1924, *Darker Phases of the South*. In order to preserve its much vaunted racial purity, the South had segregated its Anglo-Saxons so effectively that it had buried them in mill villages. The white plague of the South was cotton. The exploitation of cotton accounted for soil erosion, the poor state of race relations, and for poverty, ignorance, and peonage.

One potent expression of primitive fear was the revival of the Ku Klux Klan. The second Klan, the "Invisible Empire, Knights of the Ku Klux Klan, Inc.," lasted from 1915 to 1944. It was as secret, violent, and subversive as the Reconstruction Klan and was ultrapatriotic, nativistic, and moralistic. Its revival was the work of William J. ("Colonel") Simmons of Alabama, a former Methodist circuit preacher who specialized in organizing fraternities. He chose Stone Mountain, Georgia, sixteen miles from Atlanta, as the venue for a special Klan launching ceremony on October 26, 1915. He told Congress later that it was there at midnight, "bathed in the sacred glow of the fiery cross, the invisible empire was called from its slumber of half a century to take up a new task." This was a week before the Atlanta run of D. W. Griffith's film, *The Birth of a Nation*.

The revived Klan's catchment area was not simply the South but, more particularly, the Southwest (especially Texas), the Midwest (especially Indiana, Ohio, and Oklahoma), and Far West (especially Oregon and California). The elaborate rituals and secret signs of the Invisible Empire appealed to a rural populace, bombarded with propaganda against the Germans in the war, but cheated of its prey at the end. In 1920 there were no more than 50,000 members but the Klan provided an outlet for nativist hysteria.

Whereas the impressive-looking Simmons was an ineffectual dreamer, two of his disciples, Edward Young Clarke and Mrs. Elizabeth ("Bessie") Tyler, were born organizers. They were canny enough to appreciate the commercial opportunities of a secret organization collecting high initiation fees. By July 1921 Clarke had sent 214 organizers, or Kleagles, across the country to recruit initiates. Estimates vary but it was said that Clarke had converted at least 90,000 people to the hooded order within fifteen months. In 1923 total Klan income was $3 million. Business also boomed for southern manufacturers involved with the Klan. The Gate City Manufacturing Company of Atlanta, Georgia, was designated sole manufacturer of Klan regalia. Each white robe, worn with a pointed cap to resemble a ghost of the Confederate dead, cost $6.50.

From being a somewhat simple-minded fraternal organization in its early days the Klan became openly racist from 1920 onward. It started to represent itself as a defender of white against black, Gentile against Jew, and Protestant against Catholic. Bessie Tyler told New York newspapermen that to be for the white race meant to be against all others. Clarke proposed sterilizing black Americans. Simmons declared that never in the history of the world had a "mongrel civilization" survived: his goal was "one-hundred-per-cent Americanism." Opposition to Catholicism was not based primarily on differences in theology but, rather, ethnicity. As we know, in the main Catholics were new immigrants. Their religion was taken as a symbol of the cultural differences between the new immigration and the old. Simmons warned the Junior Order of United American Mechanics in Atlanta on April 30, 1922, that, far from being a melting pot, America was "a garbage can! . . . When the hordes of aliens walk to the ballot box and their votes outnumber yours, then that alien horde has got you by the throat."

The Klan also appealed to those new inhabitants of towns and cities who had assumed an urban hide but who retained their rural outlook. John M. Mecklin explained the attraction of the Klan for the small-town hick adrift in the big city,

He is tossed about in the hurly-burly of our industrial and so-called democratic society. Under the stress and strain of social competition he is made to realize his essential mediocrity. Yet according to traditional democratic doctrine he is born free and equal to his fellow who is outdistancing him in the race. Here is a large and powerful organization offering to solace his sense of defeat by dubbing him a knight of the Invisible Empire . . . the chosen conservator of American ideals, the keeper of the morals of the community.

Thus the Klan afforded recreation and fraternity to its inmates. In the small towns its rituals relieved the boredom of everyday routine and the mass initiation of new members was a popular entertainment in southern communities.

However, Klan leaders could no more redress the grievances of their members than they could undo the Industrial Revolution or American immigration. Instead, they indulged in bribery, intimidation, and torture by flogging, branding, and acid burning, and even in mutilation and murder. Discontented former Klansmen exposed the Klan and its atrocities to the New York press that syndicated their tales across the country. The New York *World* ran a series of well-documented, alarmist, and sensational articles from September 6 to 26, 1921, laying bare the Klan's history and aims. The intention was, in part, to depress Klan membership. In fact, the articles had the opposite effect: they gave it wide publicity and encouraged membership in the North and East.

The Klan continued on its foul path of murder and mayhem

and established a pattern of man's inhumanity to man in every state that it defiled by its presence. A historian of the Klan, David Chalmers, rates the number of victims of assault in the 1920s at well over a thousand in Oklahoma and Texas, at over a hundred in each of Alabama, Georgia, and Florida, and at scores in the other Klan states. The victims were usually errant whites.

The most notorious and gross of Klan atrocities were the Mer Rouge murders in Louisiana. In Morehouse Parish, Louisiana, two men who criticized the Klan, planter's son Watt Daniels and garage mechanic Tom Richards, were kidnapped and murdered on August 24, 1922. They were killed by being run over by a large road-grading tractor that crushed and splintered their bodies. Then they were dismembered and their mutilated corpses were deposited in Lake Lafourche, whence the pieces rose in December. An open hearing lasted from January 5 to 25, 1923, during which the state called over fifty witnesses, including Klansmen. However, it could not prove who had murdered the young men.

The Klan was not only a simple-minded fraternity engaged in cruel terrorist outrages but it was also a force to be reckoned with in politics. In 1922 and 1923 the Klan helped elect governors in Oregon and Georgia, congressmen in several states, and local officials throughout the country. In 1924 it helped elect governors in Maine, Ohio, Colorado, and Louisiana. It elected senators for Texas in 1922 and for Oklahoma in 1924. Warren Harding belonged to the Klan and disgraced the White House by being inducted there.

From 1921 to 1923 the internal feuds of the Klan were well publicized in a series of court cases, most notoriously the attempt by Dallas dentist Hiram Wesley Evans to oust Colonel Simmons. It was proved in court that Simmons alone held the copyright to the Klan's name, charter, constitution, and regalia. A later, but apocryphal, story has Hiram Evans giving Simmons some heartfelt advice about Klan costume. "Why don't you throw in the towel?" he asked. Simmons replied, "Because I need it to wrap round my head."

However, the eventual usurpation of Hiram Evans was not the end of the Klan's troubles. In Indiana David C. ("Steve") Stephenson, the kingmaker who had engineered Evans's coup, built up the Klan as a mass organization that could form the basis of a political machine. Unfortunately, his self-indulgence got the better of his political acumen. First, he saved the office of state superintendent of public instruction that his opponents had wanted to abolish. Then, he expected the incumbent, plump spinster Madge Oberholtzer, to repay him with sex. He had her hustled aboard a train bound for Chicago and forced himself on her. The next day she took bichloride of mercury tablets, a poison that caused her agony. Stephenson had to let Madge return home to her parents where she subsequently died. Her father charged him with second degree murder and, after a sensational trial, Stephenson was found guilty and sentenced to life imprisonment in the penitentiary in Michigan City. What happened to the Klan after 1924 was less disintegration than decomposition. The *Washington Post* of July 6, 1929, estimated that there were only 82,000 Klansmen left. On November 3, 1930, it said the number had dwindled further to 35,000. This was partly on account of public disgust at Klan atrocities and feuds but more because the initial causes — postwar xenophobia and inner city frustration-had been dissipated and the onset of the depression had engulfed all other social problems. The Klan had no answer for this calamity.

The Scopes Trial

The conflict between old and new, countryside and town, extended to religion and reached another climax with the Scopes trial of 1925, centered on the conflict between modernism and Darwin's theory of evolution on the one hand and religious fundamentalism, the literal interpretation of the Bible, on the other.

The Scopes trial represented, in the words of George I. Schwartz and Philip W. Bishops, "the last significant attempt to discredit Darwin's theory by those who sincerely believed that the Biblical story of the creation of man was a complete explanation of the origin of species." For that very reason it roused intense feelings among fundamentalists and evolutionists. Thus the Scopes trial was, to Carlyle Marney, "a seizure, a paroxysm, a grand colic in the bowel of the American folk-religion." Walter Lippmann ex-

753

The Scopes trial of 1925 in which John Scopes was convicted of teaching evolution in contradiction to the state laws of Tennessee that required all teaching about Creation to conform literally to the myths of Genesis. Scopes was defended by Clarence Darrow, standing in front of the table, whose eloquent arguments educated America about the merits of Darwin's theory of natural selection. John Scopes is seated immediately behind Darrow. (Library of Congress).

plained the social significance of the case, "The campaign in certain localities to forbid the teaching of 'Darwinism' is an attempt to stem the tide of the metropolitan spirit, to erect a spiritual tariff against an alien rationalism which threatens to dissolve the mores of the village civilization."

While man's scientific knowledge was increasing, his understanding of himself and his place in the universe failed to keep pace. As to southerners, it is tempting to say that their understanding was actually shrinking. Indeed, the South was over-

whelmed by what seemed the inconceivable nature of new scien-
tifiic discoveries and the complexities and contradictions of the
new urban and industrial civilization. Education in the South was
largely controlled by the church with each major denomination
providing at least one university or college in every state. The
curriculums were out of date, emphasizing only religion and the
classics. There was not a single top-quality university in the entire
South. The disciplines of science and engineering were somewhat
neglected and libraries were inadequate. Proponents of fundamentalism celebrated common ignorance. Hal Kimberly, a Georgia
assemblyman, thought that all that was worth knowing was contained in only three books. "Read the Bible. It teaches you how
to act. Read the hymn book. It contains the finest poetry ever
written. Read the almanac. It shows you how to figure out what
the weather will be. There isn't another book that is necessary for
anyone to read, and therefore I am opposed to all libraries."

The state of Tennessee had contributed to the debate between
fundamentalism and Darwinism in 1925 by passing the Butler law
against the teaching of evolution in public schools. Quite simply,
the law proscribed the teaching of "any theory that denies the
story of the Divine Creation of man as taught in the Bible, and to
teach instead that man has descended from a lower order of
animals." Few state politicians cared about it one way or the
other.

It was not the law's proponents but its enemies who decided to
bring a test case to court and try and get it repealed. In Dayton,
Tennessee, George W. Rappelyea, a manager of iron and coal
mines, persuaded John Scopes, a young biology teacher, to provide the American Civil Liberties Union (ACLU) with a test case.
All he had to do was to teach evolution and get arrested. In New
York Roger Baldwin announced, "We shall take the Scopes case
to the United States Supreme Court if necessary to establish that
a teacher may tell the truth without being thrown in jail." The
ACLU launched a defense appeal fund that eventually raised $11
million.

Both sides wanted to attract maximum publicity by getting
celebrities to take part. William Jennings Bryan, now a front man
for Florida Realtors, announced on May 13 that he had accepted

an invitation by the World's Christian Fundamentals Association (WCFA) to prosecute the case. "We cannot afford to have a system of education that destroys the religious faith of our children," he declared. "There are about 5,000 scientists, and probably half of them are atheists, in the United States. Are we going to allow them to run our schools? We are not." According to John Scopes himself, Bryan's entry into the case threw a monkey wrench into the gears of the ACLU. They had to field a defense counsel of equal weight. This was to be Clarence Darrow, "attorney for the damned." Darrow had never prosecuted anyone; he was a tireless advocate of free speech, nonviolent resistance, and the rights of the individual against the collective power of the state.

Public interest in the Scopes trial was so great that it received wider press coverage than had any previous trial. Moreover, the trial set a precedent by being the first trial ever broadcast. Judge Raulston boasted, "My gavel will be heard around the world." A heatwave struck Dayton on the very first day of the sessions, July 10, making the tiny overcrowded courtroom almost unendurably hot and serving to heighten tension.

The state's position was that if Scopes had taught that man was descended from animals he implicitly denied the story of Creation as told in Genesis. The case for the defense rested on three grounds: that the Butler Act was unconstitutional because it violated freedom of religion by making the Bible the test of truth; that it was unreasonable, given modern knowledge of evolution; and that it was indefinite because people interpreted the Bible differently. In the course of his argument Darrow tried to show that the Bible, taken literally, was a maze of contradictions. But if it was interpreted with insight and intelligence the story of Creation in Genesis was quite compatible with the theory of evolution. The implications of his argument were that truth is inimical to any closed order because it threatens basic assumptions. Judge Raulston allowed defense attorney Arthur Garfield Hays to read transcripts from seven distinguished scientists that explained the prehistory of the world. They gave special emphasis to the relationship between homo sapiens and other animals and their evidence was supported by scientific data. The defense also drew on testimony from four theologians who discussed interpretations of the Bible and the relationship of religion to science. Although the judge prevented the defense from presenting such statements in their entirety to the jury, he could not stop the syndicated press carrying them verbatim across the country. Thus was America taught about evolution and biblical scholarship.

It was because all other avenues had been closed to him that Darrow eventually decided to call Bryan for cross examination. How was it estimated that Noah's flood happened in 4004 B.C.?

"I never made a calculation," said Bryan.

"A calculation from what?"

"I could not say."

"From the generations of man?" asked Darrow.

"I would not want to say that."

"What do you think?"

"I do not think about things I don't think about."

"Do you think about things you do think about?"

"Well, sometimes."

The crux came with a simple question that devastated Bryan.

"Do you think the earth was made in six days?"

"Not six days of twenty-four hours."

The crowd gasped. When he realized his error, Bryan jumped to his feet, purple with rage, and exclaimed, "I am simply trying to protect the word of God against the greatest atheist or agnostic in the United States." At last, Bryan had compromised Genesis with evolution, had made himself ridiculous, and destroyed the prosecution's case.

The next day Darrow made the most of the situation by inviting the judge to instruct the jury to find John Scopes guilty. He wanted the case to go to the State Supreme Court. Accordingly, the jury found Scopes guilty on July 21. Nothing could hide the fact that Bryan was crushed and broken. However, though he was an ardent prohibitionist, Bryan was a glutton for food. His eating was as hearty as ever and on July 26, 1925, he died of apoplexy in his sleep. Thus Bryan had, appropriately enough, gone with the wind.

The Tennessee Supreme Court heard the appeal at Nashville and finally announced its decision on January 14, 1927. It upheld the Butler Act but it reversed the original judgment of a technical (but uncontested) issue of the fine of $100. The victory of fundamentalism led to its defeat. Everywhere there was an argument about evolution became a prime market for books on the subject. Universal Pictures recognized this and in 1931 produced a 42-minute movie about evolution, *The Mystery of Life,* in which Darrow appeared to appreciative audiences and good reviews.

3

THE INCOMPLETE
POLITICS OF THE
REPUBLICAN ASCENDANCY

THE PROBLEMS associated with economic dislocation, labor strife, and radical agitation in 1919 and 1920 were clear indications that many of the mechanisms regulating society were not working. On May 14, 1920, Senator Warren Gamaliel Harding of Ohio explained his understanding of America's needs. "America's present need is not heroics, but healing; not nostrums, but normalcy; not revolution, but restoration; not agitation, but adjustment; not surgery, but serenity; not the dramatic, but the dispassionate; not experiment, but equipoise; not submergence in internationality, but sustainment in triumphant nationality. . . ."

"Normalcy" could mean all sorts of things, except what Harding intended. The American norm was not relaxed stability but social mobility, economic development, political agitation, and cultural experiment. Such restlessness was in part the result of the fact that American society lacked a homogeneous social structure. Nevertheless, Harding inadvertently expressed a social truth, that a society perplexed by deep problems is not likely to try and cure them, least the remedy prove more painful than the disease and prejudice the comfortable lot of its more privileged members.

As the decade advanced it became clear that America's undoubted social problems would be ignored by both main parties. Novelty of fashion, entertainment, and invention were prized while radical dissent and fundamental criticism were derided or suppressed. When Fitzgerald observed "it was characteristic of the Jazz Age that it had no interest in politics at all," he was not only referring explicity to the low popular vote in the presidential elections of 1920 and 1924, when less than half the electorate (respectively 49.3 percent and 49.1 percent) went to the polls, but also implicitly to public unwillingness to address politics to social ills.

The Available Man

Harding was the tool of an ambitious corporation lawyer, Harry Daugherty. When Daugherty first met Harding in 1900 at a small-town hotel in Richwood, Ohio, he was struck by Harding's perfect physical proportions, his natural grace, and his resonant voice. Thus he was supposed to have said, "Gee, what a president he'd make." What Daugherty meant was that Harding would make a good-looking candidate and that, once in office, he would fulfill a popular conception of a president. He had been editor of the Marion *Star,* then lieutenant governor of Ohio, before becoming a senator. Superficially, he had all the necessary experience of high office to make him a suitable candidate. Moreover, he was genial. After the high-minded autocratic style of Woodrow Wilson, congressmen yearned for an amenable, amiable president who was one of themselves.

The Republican National Convention of 1920 met in Chicago but it was in the dark recesses of the original smoke-filled room in the Blackstone Hotel that the key decision was made to nominate Harding. The men from the smoke-filled room of the Blackstone Hotel had already agreed that, to balance their conservative candidate, the best man for vice-president would be Senator Irvine Lenroot of Wisconsin. However, no sooner had Lenroot

This mawkish photograph of President Calvin Coolidge (center) surrounded by members of his cabinet, including Secretary of State Charles Evans Hughes (seated second from left) and Secretary of the Treasury Andrew Mellon (seated third from right), beneath a memorial photograph of the late Warren Harding, was taken in 1923 to emphasize Republican solidarity and an orderly succession. However, it is difficult to tell who are living and who are dead among such glum waxworks. (Library of Congress).

been proposed to the delegates in Chicago than Wallace McCamant, delegate from Oregon, climbed on his chair, and put forward the name of Governor Calvin Coolidge of Massachusetts, popular hero of the Boston police strike. Immediately the stenographer at the convention recorded "an outburst of applause of short duration but of great report." Coolidge's nomination by 674½ votes out of 984 was recorded "with tumultuous applause and cheers"—the only spontaneous event in the entire convention.

Meeting at San Francisco, the Democrats nominated Governor James M. Cox of Ohio, a small city editor and publisher and former congressman. As governor, he had championed progressive legislation, especially in the field of workmen's compensation acts, and thus brought to an end the spate of lawsuits instigated by injured employees against their employers. His running mate was Assistant Secretary of the Navy Franklin D. Roosevelt.

Like McKinley in 1896, Harding chose to conduct the campaign from the comfort and convenience of his own front porch in Marion, Ohio. The centerpiece of Cox's campaign was a twenty-nine-day whistle-stop tour of eighteen states west of the Mississippi from which he garnered not one electoral vote. He could not believe the country's indifference to the League of Nations. As Franklin K. Lane, once secretary of the interior under Wilson, remarked, "Cox will be defeated not by those who dislike him but by those who dislike Wilson."

In the election Harding took 16,143,407 popular votes (60.4 percent) to Cox's 9,130,328 (34.2 percent). The Socialist, Eugene V. Debs, took 919,799 votes (3.4 percent). Thus Harding carried 37 states, and 404 votes in the electoral college to Cox's 11 states and 127 votes. The election returns were broadcast for the first time by the pioneer radio station KDKA in Pittsburgh. The result was taken as an overwhelming repudiation of Wilsonian liberalism at home and abroad. The United States was now committed to twelve years of Republican ascendancy.

As president, Harding (1921–1923) proved an amiable simpleton manipulated by sinister forces. It was said that, whereas George Washington could not tell a lie, Warren Harding could not tell a liar. Thus he took into office with him his old small-town friends, the Ohio gang, principally Harry Daugherty who became attorney general. From the Senate he took with him John W. Weeks as secretary of war, Harry S. New as postmaster general, and most sinister of all, Senator Albert B. Fall of New Mexico. After Republican elders dissuaded him from appointing the devious and unsuitable Fall as secretary of state, he moved him to the interior, an appointment that the Senate, for once, and to its subsequent shame, confirmed without the formality of referring it to a committee. Also out of misplaced sentiment, Harding appointed Edwin N. Denby as secretary of the navy. A former congressman, he had enlisted as a private in the Marine Corps in 1914 (although he was already forty-seven) and subsequently had risen to the rank of major. Harding made the unscrupulous Colonel Charles R. Forbes, whom he had met casually while on vacation in Honolulu, head of the Veterans Bureau. In fact, Forbes was a self-seeking opportunist who had won round Mrs. Harding. To a man, they shrank from the irksomeness of their jobs.

Half way through his cabinet selection, Harding got the urge to raise its stature and appointed Charles Evans Hughes secretary of state, Herbert Hoover secretary of commerce, Henry C. Wallace secretary of agriculture, and Andrew W. Mellon secretary of the treasury. Mellon, who owed his fortune to aluminum steel, was obliged to resign directorships in sixty corporations before his appointment was confirmed. It was to be said of Mellon that three presidents served under him.

Harding could move from particular acts of kindness to generous acts of political skill. In order to settle the continuing steel dispute, Harding invited forty-one steel magnates to the White House in 1922 when he persuaded them that twelve hours was too long and arduous a period for a regular working shift. Thus on August 2, 1923, Judge E. H. Gary, head of U. S. Steel, announced the abolition of the twelve-hour day and on August 13 the plant at Gary, Indiana, was put on an eight-hour day, setting a precedent followed by the entire industry.

Harding repeatedly announced his commitment to economy in government. The Budget and Accountancy Act of June 20, 1921, provided for the establishment of the Budget Bureau in the Treasury, with powers to revise, reduce, or increase the estimates of the various departments. Its intention was to put each on a business basis by making it accountable to one section. In addition, the act tried to compel Congress to keep its appropriations within limits set by budget offices. Harding appointed Chicago banker Charles Gates Dawes to the new post of budget director.

Dawes was one of the most striking political personalities of the age. He first made his mark on public opinion when he gave evidence to Congress as to whether the Democrats had indulged in war profiteering. (During the war he had been head of the supply procurement division in France). "Damn it all," he told the committee, "the business of an army is to win the war not to quibble around with a lot of cheap buying. Hell and Maria, we weren't trying to keep a set of books, we were trying to win the war." Throughout his subsequent career he remained "Hell and Maria" Dawes to the public. He was also the only vice-president and ambassador (to Britain) who wrote popular songs, such as "It's All in the Game."

Business wanted the Republicans to lower taxes, raise tariffs, and provide government subsidies without imposing restrictions on business practice, except for the curbing of labor. They achieved much of what they wanted. Secretary of the Treasury Mellon accordingly urged Congress to repeal the wartime excess profits tax outright and reduce the maximum surtax on incomes above $66,000 from 65 percent to 40 percent. To compensate the Treasury for the losses, he proposed a wider distribution of indirect tax on the less wealthy by doubling the stamp tax on documents, imposing a tax of 2 cents on postcards and bank checks, and introducing a federal license tax on cars. Accordingly, in the Revenue Act of November 23, 1921, Congress removed the excess profits tax and revised the maximum surtax to 50 percent. The specious justification for the relief of the rich was that burdensome taxes on wealth inhibited creative investment. If government continued to cream off the cat's share of profits, then business would not take the risks necessary for industrial and commercial expansion.

To propitiate the less affluent, the tax threshold for heads of families with $5,000 or less was raised from $2,000 to $2,500, and the exemption for each dependent was raised from $200 to $400. Nuisance taxes were abolished. The tax on the net profits of corporations was set at 12.5 percent, instead of 10 percent. In general, government policies were deflationary and served to curb business expansion. The federal government collected about $4 billion in annual revenue and spent just over $3 billion. It used the surplus to liquidate the national debt, that fell from about $24 billion in 1920 to about $16 billion ten years later. Prosperity returned. Unemployment, having reached a peak of 5.73 million in 1921, began to decline and settled at about 2.5 million. Those in work found that their purchasing power, if not their actual wage, was rising.

The greatest ally of business at the courts of Harding and his successor, Calvin Coolidge, was Secretary of Commerce Herbert Hoover, a constructive critic of business practices. He deployed the bureaus of standards and of foreign and domestic commerce to research ways of eliminating waste and gave wide publicity to their findings. In 1928 Hoover's Committee on Economic Trends reported how per capita production had improved by 35 percent in the 1920s. Herbert Hoover actively encouraged the formation of trade associations along the lines of the oldest, the United States Brewers Association, founded in 1862, and the National Association of Manufacturers of 1895. These associations funded central agencies that collated and distributed information on such matters as prices, production, credit, insurance, and relations between employers and employees for the benefit of their member corporations and individual stockholders. In addition, they funded lobbies to advance or retard legislation, according to the special interests of their interest group. Under Hoover's benevolent eyes they grew in number and influence.

Conservative business interests wanted to restrain government from using its right to regulate business according to formidable powers vested in the ICC (Interstate Commerce Commission) by the Hepburn Act of 1906, the Federal Reserve Board of 1913, the Federal Trade Commission of 1914, and the Federal Power Commission of 1920. For whatever reason, business was usually successful.

Let us look at just one industry, the generation of electric power, and the way its particular commission, the Federal Power Commission, operated. The production of electric power was greatly expanded during the 1920s and its distribution became available to ever more people. This was achieved by means of technological improvements and interconnections between different companies. However, these changes were initially most expensive and only the strongest companies could afford them. The route to strength was amalgamation. In 1926 there were over 1,000 mergers in public utilities. Many involved municipal plants that were sold out to private companies. Public utility magnates wanted to eliminate public ownership. By 1930 ten "groups of systems" controlled three-quarters of the nation's electric power. They sold to industry at lower prices than those charged to domestic consumers, lest industry should invest in its own plants. However, the price charged to domestic consumers also fell and the rate of domestic consumption went up.

It was the duty of the Federal Power Commission to supervise the manufacture and distribution of electric power. The act of 1920 gave the commission power to grant licenses for the construction of new plants, regulate rates of currents across state borders, require uniform systems of accounting from the companies, and decide on the issue of new securities. Because the commission initially comprised the secretaries of war, agriculture, and the interior, it assumed the political complexion of the new administration.

Senator George W. Norris of Nebraska, exasperated by the way Harding and Coolidge, by conservative appointments, had helped destroy the new federal system of regulatory commissions, wrote a scathing attack on Republican policies that both *Collier's Weekly* and the *Forum* refused to print. It finally appeared in the *Nation* of September 16, 1925. Norris's chief conclusion was that Republican policies had "set the country back more than twenty-five years." With heavy sarcasm he noted, "It is an indirect but positive repeal of Congressional enactments, which no administration, however powerful, would dare to bring about by any direct means. It is the nullification of federal law by a process of boring from within. If trusts, combinations, and big business are to run the government, why not permit them to do it directly rather than through this expensive machinery which was originally honestly established for the protection of the people of the country against monopoly and control?" In the light of such comments, historian John D. Hicks concludes how "In a sense, the slanting of government during the 1920s to support whatever stand the dominant business interests wanted was far more scandalous than the merely political depravity for which the Harding regime was noted."

Both industry and agriculture demanded a protective tariff against cheap foreign produce and persuaded Congress to pass the Fordney-McCumber tariff of September 21, 1922. However, it passed Congress on party lines only after acrimonious debate in which the Senate proposed some 2,082 amendments to the original House bill. The underlying and overwhelming sentiment was that the American producer must have the advantage in the American market. It was especially aimed at such products of Germany and Japan as silk and rayon, china, cutlery, and toys.

In one respect, the Fordney-McCumber tariff was an improvement on its predecessors since it provided for a more efficient administration of tariff regulations, based on a systematic classification of products. Moreover, on the advice of the commission, the president could raise or lower duties by up to 50 percent on specific items in order to achieve parity between American and foreign costs. However, of thirty-seven changes under Harding and Coolidge, thirty-two were upwards. The five decreases were picayune; on millfeeds, bobwhite quail, paintbrush handles, cresylic acid, and phenol. Whatever the incidental benefits to certain industrialists, the new tariff harmed American agriculture and industry in the long run.

The Sheppard-Towner Act of 1921 provided for maternal and infant health care under the charge of the Children's Bureau in the Department of Labor. It was intended to provide a basis for future development, a basis necessary for the kind of welfare state most Western European countries have instituted. However, yielding to pressure from the American Medical Association, Congress refused to renew the act in 1929. Critic and historian Linda Gordon remarks of their decision how "the demise" of the act "marked America's turn away from a permanent governmental responsibility for the health and welfare of its citizens."

The most famous acts of the Harding administration were the notorious misuses of federal resources and public monies. At the Veterans Bureau Forbes proved an energetic organizer who diverted the massive congressional appropriation of $36 million for medical care of injured veterans and the construction of hospitals to fradulent contractors and to himself. Hearing of the extent of Forbes's misdeeds, Harding and Daugherty arranged that he should first go abroad and then resign. The Senate started an investigation. However, while Forbes was away, his legal assistant, Charles F. Cramer, shot himself dead in his bathroom.

It became an open secret that the surest way of advancing sinister interests was to bend the ear of the unscrupulous attorney general and the easiest way to do that was through Daugherty's protégé, Jess Smith. One of their ruses to make money was to sell bootleg liquor impounded by the prohibition authorities and held in a house at 1625 K Street whence it was sold illegally and at great profit. William J. Burns ran the Department of Justice for Daugherty as a private protection racket. In particular, his agent Gaston B. Means, was supposed to have taken $7 million altogether from bootleggers who bought pardons for their convictions. The money was left in a goldfish bowl before being turned over to the Department of Justice. Unfortunately, the gullible and greedy Smith did not have the sort of cast-iron constitution required of those involved in political intrigue and shady deals while they are continuously in the public gaze. Smith could not stand the strain and he, too, committed suicide by shooting himself.

Harding was deeply worried by mounting evidence of misconduct by the Ohio gang. Quite simply, he was out of his depth as president and knew it. "My God, this is a hell of a place for a man like me to be," he said. He threw himself with ever greater abandon into his hobbies of golf during the day and poker at night.

Harding's health was certainly not up to the arduous tour to the West and Alaska that he undertook in late June 1923. Speaking at cities en route exhausted him and he died in San Francisco on August 2. Some of his doctors concluded that he had suffered a heart attack and was developing bronchial phneumonia. There was nothing odd in a man of Harding's age and soft constitution dying from apoplexy. For years he had overindulged himself in food, drink, and finally worry. Yet he was greatly mourned and the long train journey of the casket of the dead president from San Francisco to Washington, the lying in state at the Capitol, and the final journey to Marion, Ohio, provided a splendid opportunity for public display of hysteria and grief.

Vice-President Calvin Coolidge was staying at his family's farmhouse in Plymouth, Vermont, when he was awakened at 2:00 A.M. on August 3, with the news of Harding's death. His father, who was a public notary, then administered the oath of office to his son in the sitting room. "What was your first thought when you heard that Harding had died?" portrait painter Charles Hopkins asked of Coolidge later. "I thought I could swing it."

The contrast between the two presidents could hardly have been more marked. Where Harding was the available man, Coolidge (1923–1929) was a puritan in Babylon. Harding was large and handsome while Coolidge was shriveled and insignificant. Where Harding had been genial and well liked, Coolidge was aloof and austere. Someone said that he spoke so little that each time he did open his mouth, a moth flew out. However, his reputation for silence is belied by numerous anecdotes that suggest a mordant wit. Of a Baptist preacher who ate very little before a revival meeting because, he said, abstinence improved his preaching, Coolidge remarked after the sermon, "Might as well have et." To the society woman who said to him at dinner, "I made a bet that I could get more than two words out of you," he said curtly, "You lose." "What is your hobby?" "Holding office."

Teapot Dome Scandal

In April 1922 an obscure citizen of Wyoming complained to Senator John B. Kendrick that certain oil lands, usually known as Teapot Dome on account of the unusual shape of one hill, and intended to supply the navy, were being secretly and wrongfully leased by Secretary of the Interior Albert B. Fall to a private corporation, Mammoth Oil Company, owned principally by one Harry F. Sinclair. Under pressure from the Senate, the Department of the Interior admitted that not only had Teapot Dome been leased to the Sinclair Company but that it was also about to lease the Elk Hills reserve in California to the Pan-American Petroleum and Transportation Company of which the head was

"Nonsense, if it gets too deep, you can easily pull me out!" cries the very fat lady of excessive government spending to the emaciated taxpayer as she drags him from the shallows of deficit to the larger waves of debt in this 1920s cartoon by Herbert Johnson. (Library of Congress).

Edward L. Doheny. The explanation was that the oil was being drained from these reserves by wells on adjoining lands and that, within a few years, government reserves would be exhausted.

However, Senator Robert La Follette of Wisconsin was not satisfied and persuaded the Committee on Public Lands to instigate a formal investigation through a special committee chaired by Senator Thomas J. Walsh of Montana. Walsh was an Irish-American Catholic of penetrating mind, restrained manner, and inexhaustible energy who labored assiduously over the oil scandals for the next eighteen months. At the public hearings beginning on October 25, 1923, the weight of technical evidence was that leasing of oil reserves to anticipate drainage at the edges was quite unjustified. The oil supply was intended for the navy and it had been most irregular of Secretary of the Navy Edwin Denby to allow Secretary of the Interior Fall to issue leases to commercial companies. Although Coolidge was willing to stand by the hapless secretary of the navy, Denby could not endure the situation, and resigned.

At first, Walsh had next to no evidence against his suspects (Fall, Denby, Doheny, and Sinclair), but the process of inquisition began to arouse attention from various people who wanted to settle old scores with Fall. From their accounts it transpired Fall had moved from penury to opulence within two years and now had considerable ranch lands in New Mexico. It became evident that Doheny had "loaned" Fall $100,000 to improve his ranch. Thus Fall stood condemned: he was an experienced politician who, while he held public office, had received $100,000 from a man to whom, it his official capacity, he was about to grant a valuable lease. Moreover, he had lied about the money.

Because of Daugherty's involvement with the oil scandal, the Senate preferred to have charges against Fall and Doheny brought by a special counsel independent of the Department of Justice. For this task Coolidge chose Owen J. Roberts, a Republican lawyer from Philadelphia, and Atlee W. Pomerone, a former Democratic senator from Ohio.

The various trials of Fall, Sinclair, and Doheny on several charges of conspiracy and fraud resulted in the surprising acquittal of Doheny and Fall for fraud (December 16, 1926), and of Fall and Sinclair (April 21, 1928). However, Fall was convicted for having accepted a bribe (October 25, 1929), sentenced to a year's imprisonment, and fined $100.000. Thus was Fall the first cabinet officer of the United States to go to jail. Paradoxically, Doheny was acquitted in March 1930 on a charge of bribing Fall. Harry F. Sinclair, who refused to give the Walsh committee straight answers, was cited for contempt by the Senate, and tried and convicted in the criminal courts. He was sentenced to pay a fine of $1,000 and spend three months in jail. Later, when he was charged with Fall of having conspired to defraud the government, it was discovered that he employed detectives to shadow the jury and he was sentenced to another six months in jail.

Public confidence in public officers was visibly shaken. Accordingly, to remedy the damage, Coolidge and the new attorney general, Harlan Fiske Stone, attempted to improve the watchdog of public activities, the Bureau of Investigations, originally founded as an investigative branch of the Department of Justice in July 1908. In 1924 Stone had it reorganized under a new director, J. Edgar Hoover, who remained its head until his death in 1972. The title Federal Bureau of Investigations (FBI) was adopted in July 1935. It was the bureau's task to investigate crimes and undertake domestic intelligence activities and in 1930 it began to collate and publicize reports on crime from various police forces, subsequently published as *Uniform Crime Reports.*

Hoover had already worked in the Justice Department for seven years, notably as a special agent in the Enemy Aliens Bureau. His special gifts had been most apparent during the Great Red Scare of 1917–1921, particularly in 1919 when he became special assistant to the attorney general, A. Mitchell Palmer. While Palmer was a zealot of exaggerated ambitions whose enthusiasm was rewarded with legendary authorship of the Palmer Raids, it was Hoover who masterminded the kangaroo courts and deportations of radicals and subversives, real or imagined.

In his biography *Secrecy and Power* (1987), Richard Gid Powers notes that, since it was anti-Communist fervor that brought Hoover to power, it was anti-Communism that defined his political career. His central principle was continuous opposition to all who threatened the authority of lawful government especially "communists, subversives, and pseudo-liberals." In the 1930s he established a counterintelligence program or Cointelpro against the Communist party, penetrating and exposing its cadres. He investigated and harried suspects to the point of breaking the law. In his own manifesto against Communists, *Masters of Deceit* (1958), Hoover relished a stereotype of evil radicals based on popular images from science fiction, comic books, and detective novels. Hoover's values were those of his childhood and youth in Washington at the turn of the century—provincial white morality.

In private Hoover admitted mistakes. His public image was of unswerving certainty of purpose. According to an apocryphal story, once he announced the death of an agent in a shootout who was, in fact, only wounded, other FBI agents drew straws to select which of them should visit the hospital to turn Hoover's announcement into reality. He liked his typist to leave wide margins so that he could add personal comments to memos. Once he wrote at the side of a narrow margin, "Watch the borders," thereby prompting agents to put bureau offices near Canada and Mexico on full alert.

He was deeply jealous of individual agents who scored personal successes. Thus when Melvin Purvis received due credit for the entrapment and summary execution of outlaws John Dillinger and Pretty Boy Floyd, Hoover despatched inspectors to Purvis's office in Chicago who wrote adverse reports about him. Thus pressured, Purvis resigned in 1935. He found himself unable to get a job elsewhere, whether in movies or among the Senate staff. Purvis never realised who his real enemy was and remained obsessively loyal to Hoover. In 1960, he shot himself. As a final insult, Hoover decided not to sent a letter of condolence to the bereaved family of his unknowing victim.

The Progressive Revival and the Election of 1924

The test of the reformed federal government came with the presidential election of 1924. On the first ballot at the Republican National Convention, Coolidge won the nomination in Cleveland in June by courting Republican regulars, thus earning Borah's public support. "Give him a chance to make good. I think he is an able man." Behind the scenes Coolidge wooed business, with whom he was popular, and succeeded in giving them even greater control of the party. The Republican campaign slogan was "Keep Cool and Keep Coolidge," emphasizing Cal's imperturbable serenity. Asked by a reporter if he had a statement to make about the campaign, he answered, "No." Asked, "Can you tell us something about the world situation?" he answered, "No." "Anything about prohibition?" "No—Now remember, don't quote me."

However, the Democrats' principal problem was the association of many leading politicians with the revived Ku Klux Klan. The Klan had two principal objectives at the Democratic National Convention of 1924. It wanted to help William Gibbs McAdoo win the presidential nomination and it was determined to prevent the party from condemning it by name. This first objectives would involve trouncing McAdoo's rivals, wet Governor Alfred E. Smith of New York and dry Senator Oscar N. Underwood of Alabama, both of whom were declared opponents of the Klan. In pursuit of its goals, the Klan had participated in the Democratic state conventions in Arkansas, Oklahoma, Texas, and elsewhere. As a result, perhaps 80 percent of delegates from Arkansas and Texas were at least sympathetic to the Klan if not actual knights. Indeed, the New York *World* estimated that about 300 delegates to the national convention were Klansmen.

The convention met on June 24, 1924, in the sweltering auditorium of Madison Square Garden, New York. When he rose on the second day to nominate Oscar Underwood for president, Alabama delegate Forney Johnson first called on the convention to take a stand against secret un-American organizations such as the Ku Klux Klan. This attack brought the issue into the open. It sharply divided delegates in northern states from those in the South. As the controversy became ever more heated, it transpired that a majority of delegates did not intend to condemn the Klan.

For the Democrats the decision was a disaster. It embittered the convention and prevented the nomination of either of their leading candidates. John W. Davis, a Wall Street lawyer from West Virginia, was a compromise candidate nominated after 103 ballots cast over seventeen riotous days. The total number of votes cast at the convention would be 1,098. The convention, broadcast by radio, divided Democrats across the country on a scale unknown since the Civil War and unsurpassed until 1968. "How true was Grant's exclamation," observed Hiram Johnson to his family, "that the Democratic party could be relied upon at the right time to do the wrong thing!"

The Republicans' indifference to reform and the Democrats' incapacity led to the rise of alternative groups pledged to reform. The most widely known leader of the reform movement was Senator Robert M. La Follette of Wisconsin, briefly unpopular for his opposition to American intervention in the war, but now, through his speeches, reaching a wider audience than just the state readers of his own *La Follette's Magazine*. Almost his equal in influence was Senator George W. Norris of Nebraska, tireless champion of public rights against the interests of monopolies, especially the utility empires. Other progressives included Senators Edwin F. Ladd and Lynn J. Frazier of North Dakota, Burton K. Wheeler of Montana, Magnus Johnson and Henrik Shipstead of Minnesota, and Smith W. Brookhart of Iowa. Outside the Senate they included Congressman Fiorello La Guardia of New York (later mayor), John R. Commons of the University of Wisconsin, Felix Frankfurter of the Harvard Law School, and journalists William Allen White of the Emporia *Gazette* and Chester H. Rowell of the San Francisco *Chronicle*. They were all disaffected with the Republican party.

Accordingly, these progressives now organized themselves into three different political groups: the American Labor party of 1919, based on trade unions; the Committee of Forty-eight, composed of old Bull-Moose progressives—those who had supported Theodore Roosevelt for president in 1912—and led by J.A.H. Hopkins, a New Jersey insurance broker, who finally formed a Farmer-Labor party in 1920; and the Conference for Progressive Political Action (CPPA), based on railroad brotherhoods and formed in Chicago in February 1922. Their projected reforms included the abolition of the electoral college and the use of direct primaries for all elective officers, including the presidency, the rapid convening of new Congresses, and the exclusion of special privilege interests from government.

Encouraged by the problems of both main parties, the CPPA held a national convention in Cleveland in July 1924 that was attended by 600 delegates from labor unions, farmers' organizations, and the Socialist party. At the insistence of Robert La Follette, they decided not to form a third party and thus jeopardize the seats of many sympathetic progressives in Congress who held seats as nominal Democrats or Republicans. Instead, they would concentrate on the presidential contest, nominating La Follette with Democratic Senator Burton K. Wheeler of Montana as his running mate.

The progressive plank declared that "the great issue" was "the control of government and industry by private monopoly," that had "crushed competition" and "stifled private initiative and independent enterprise" in pursuit of "extortionate profits." How-ever, progressives were reluctant to accept the socialist remedy of government ownership of industry. Thus, their platform reiter-ated the nineteenth-century remedies of the Populists against great monopolies. However, they did advocate the right of organized labor to collective bargaining, urged the abolition of the use of injunctions in labor disputes, favored a constitutional amendment to restrict the use of judicial veto (by which federal courts could declare laws void), proposed ten-year terms for federal judges, and suggested a revision of the Treaty of Versailles.

In the election Coolidge took 15,718,211 popular votes, ex-ceeding the combined total of Davis's 8,385, 283 and La Follette's 4,831,289. Thus Coolidge had 54.0 percent of the popular vote while Davis had 28.8 percent and La Follette 16.6 percent. La Follette carried only his home state, Wisconsin, while Coolidge had thirty-five states, giving him 382 votes in the electoral col-lege, and Davis, with twelve states, had 136 votes. The Coolidge landslide also gave the Republicans control of Congress. In the House there were now 247 Republicans to 183 Democrats and 2 Farmer-Laborites and 2 Socialists; in the Senate there were 56 Republicans to 39 Democrats and 1 Farmer-Laborite.

On the surface, it seemed that La Follette had been beaten badly. Yet his campaign had made a considerable impact on politics. He scared bosses in both parties by coming second in eleven states (California, Idaho, Iowa, Minnesota, Montana, Ne-vada, North Dakota, South Dakota, Oregon, Washington, and Wyoming). In thirteen others he took enough votes so that Cool-idge carried them by pluralities rather than outright majorities. Those dissatisfied with the Republicans were as likely to vote for La Follette, who was liberal, as for Davis, who was not. Thus, leading Democrats concluded that if the Democrats were ever to win again, they would have to field liberal candidates with liberal programs.

Despite the setback, La Follette tried to stir the CPPA for the midterm congressional elections of 1926. However, the AFL would not continue to work with a third party and, without its consid-erable support, the CPPA dissolved. However, before this hap-pened La Follette died of a heart attack on June 18, 1925, and was succeeded in the Senate by his son, Robert M. La Follette, Jr., who took his seat as a Republican.

A Puritan in Babylon

Supported by comfortable Republican majorities, Secretary of the Treasury Andrew Mellon could now get his preferred tax proposals enacted. The Revenue Act of 1926 repealed gift taxes outright and reduced minimum surtaxes and estate taxes from 40 to 20 percent, raising only corporation tax from 12 to 12½ percent. In 1928 this was again reduced to 12 percent. These various revisions were a boon to the truly rich. A man with an income of $1 million now paid less than $200,000 in income tax, compared with $600,000 before the alteration. According to Harvey O'Connor in *Mellon's Millions* (1933) the annual amount released by the new tax schedules to the Mellons for extra investment was about $350 million.

In the late 1920s all seemed well with the economy on the surface. American capitalism enjoyed a boom: between 1925 and 1929 the number of factories had increased from 183,877 to 206,663 and the value of their production for the domestic market rose from $34 billion to $37.78 billion. The Federal Reserve index of industrial production had risen from 67 in 1921 to 100 in 1925, and then 126 in June 1929. However, there were cracks in the economic plates just below the surface. Economic growth in the early twenties was most notable in construction and the automobile industry. From 1925 onward both were in decline. New residential construction earned $5 billion in 1925 but only $3 billion in 1929. Automobile production continued to grow in these years but at a much slower rate and this in turn reduced the production of steel, rubber, glass, and its other tributary industries. By 1929 it was clear that all of these were dangerously overextended. Since there was no new industry to supersede the auto industry as the pivot of the industrial economy, it was inevitable that a serious recession would ensue.

In agriculture the crisis was chronic. From 1921 onward American farmers paid the inevitable price for capacity production during the war. Once the war was over, Europe had less need of American grain. In consequence, the steady supply of bumper harvests in the United States amounted to gross overproduction. The impending disaster for American agriculture in the 1930s is best suggested by the fall in the value of farm products from $21.4 billion in 1919 to $11.8 billion in 1929. Other statistics confirm the depressing trend. Farm tenancy increased from 38.1 percent of farms in 1920 to 42.4 percent in 1930. The percentage of farms mortgaged also rose from 37.2 percent in 1920 to 42 percent in 1930.

In Congress farmers were supported by an active pressure group that was predominantly Republican in character and usually known as the farm bloc. It was the guiding force behind farm legislation of the decade designed to ease agricultural problems. The Packers and Stockyards Act of 1921 gave the Department of Agriculture considerable powers over the meat-packing industry and broke the big meatpackers' monopoly over the stockyards. The Grain Futures Act eliminated much of the fraud and grain speculation in the grain exchanges. The Capper-Volstead Act of 1922 released farm cooperatives from the antitrust laws. Most active in the farm bloc was Senator George W. Norris who proposed a revolutionary scheme whereby government warehouses would store the surplus, public corporations would buy it, and government agencies would sell and transport it abroad. Instead, Congress passed the Agriculture Credits Act of 1923, aimed principally at livestock farming and which allowed the farmer to borrow money, using his crop as collateral, postponing its sale, and storing it for periods lasting from six months to three years until prices were more favorable.

Two midwestern industrialists also succeeded in getting Congress to act. George N. Peek and General Hugh S. Johnson had first worked together in the War Industries Board and in the twenties led the Moline Plow Company of Moline, Illinois, which, like other farm servicing industries, was under great financial pressure. Peek and Johnson realized that the essential problem was that farmers had to buy their equipment in a domestic market in which industry was protected by high tariffs but that they had to sell their produce in a world market that was not so protected. What agriculture needed, surely, was for some form of parity or equality between its purchasing power and that of industry, a "fair exchange value." This could be achieved if agriculture could regulate its supply of produce to meet the domestic demand. This would involve dumping the surplus abroad at current world prices, and maintaining high prices for produce sold at home by a tariff. The losses sustained by the government on produce sold cheaply abroad would be compensated by special equalization fees to be paid by the farmers.

The Peek-Johnson scheme was first proposed in Congress in 1924 by Senator Charles L. McNary of Oregon (a wheat state) and Congressman Gilbert N. Haugen of Iowa (a corn state). Despite support from business as well as farm organizations, and by Secretary of Agriculture Henry C. Wallace, it was defeated in the House on June 3, 1924, by eastern Republicans acting on instructions from Coolidge. However, the farm bloc then proposed a measure with wider coverage of such crops as cotton, tobacco, and rice. In this way they enticed support from southern Democrats and their second bill was passed by Congress in 1927. It listed only six basic commodities (cotton, wheat, corn, rice, hogs, and tobacco) and proposed a Federal Farm Board of twelve members, one for each Federal Land Bank District, to administer the scheme. The Board could raise domestic prices to the level of the official tariff on each item. The equalization fee was not to be assessed on the farmers but on the processing, transportation, and sale of crops. Coolidge vetoed the bill in 1927 and again in 1928 when it was passed a second time by Congress. On neither occasion could the farm bloc find the necessary two-thirds majority to override the veto. Nevertheless, the parity scheme and other plans for agriculture united farmers and farm organizations as had no previous movement.

Lean years for farmers were also hard for the industries that served the farm. One indication is that rural banks failed in this period and so, too, did other banks. In the prosperous year of 1928 as many as 549 banks failed: in 1929, 640 did so. Here were sure signs of an economy deep in trouble.

The Bitter Harvest of 1928

The most exciting and divisive political event of the 1920s was the presidential election of 1928 when the wet, Democratic, and

Catholic governor of New York, Al Smith, stood against the dry, Republican, and Quaker secretary of commerce, Herbert Hoover. At the outset it looked as if the 1928 election would be fought on the economic problems of agriculture. However, in the end the campaign was the climax of the conflict between rural America with its allegiance to proven values and urban America with its masses committed to social and political experiments. It also represented the climax of fifty years' debate about prohibition in which nativist pride, religious prejudice, legal pedantry, and political bigotry were the determining factors.

Al Smith was the son of poor Irish Catholics and had started work in Fulton Street Fish Market, New York, when he was twelve. As a loyal Tammany man who was also a progressive reformer, he rose in the Democratic party and served four terms as governor of New York between 1919 and 1929. His prestige was taken as an illustration of "Americanism," the philosophy that merit determined success in a pluralistic society. Smith was now preeminent in the Democratic party. From 1926 onward there was open public debate about the suitability of a Catholic for the presidency and discussion as to whether Smith would break the "unwritten law" that no Catholic could ever become president. There was a general misapprehension that a Catholic president would put the duties of church before state, involve America in entangling alliances, and subvert democracy. In 1926 Catholics accounted for 15.97 percent of the total population. (When Kennedy ran for the presidency in 1960 they accounted for 23.2 percent.) However, of the remaining 84.03 percent in 1926, only 27.36 percent belonged to Protestant churches and only 3.50 percent attended Jewish synagogues: 53.17 percent had no religious affiliation. The statistics, however, belied the incipient religious intolerance of the age.

Ironically, Smith, a city slicker if ever there was one, was to be promoted as champion of the downtrodden farmers and, not surprisingly, repudiated by them on account of his religion, his background, and his opposition to prohibition. Smith compounded his problems by taking advice from a "golfing cabinet" of nouveaux riches industrialists, including General Motors executive John J. Raskob, whom he made his campaign manager.

Unsuccessful Democratic presidential candidate Al Smith puts his case on the radio in 1928. Radio was a medium that cruelly exposed his regional limitations of voice and political style, thereby underlying his Tammany origins, his association with the new immigrants, and his opposition to prohibition, all of which were as objectionable to hidebound rural America as was his Catholicism. (Library of Congress).

Smith hoped to convince the public that the Democrats did have the support of big business. However, Raskob alienated the party on account of his own well-publicized Catholicism, and, as a leading member of the Association Against the Prohibition Amendment (AAPA), his wetness. Nevertheless, Raskob spent at least $5.3 million on Smith's campaign, a record to that time.

After his nomination as Republican candidate, Herbert Hoover promised a federal commission to investigate prohibition, which he referred to as "a great social and economic experiment, noble in motive and far-reaching in purpose." His words were reduced by others to "noble experiment"—offensive to both wets and drys. But his proposal undermined Smith's appeal to all wets who could now vote for Hoover on the assumption that he would first investigate and then change the law.

Smith's main strategy was a whistle-stop tour of the country but he was harassed in the South, West, and Midwest by the Ku Klux Klan. In 1928 it was still a vibrant force and, against Smith, it received covert support from various Protestant churches led by Methodist Bishop James A. Cannon, Jr., of the Anti-Saloon League. Cannon diverted Democratic monies to a campaign against the party nominee (and also into his own pocket). He undertook extensive campaign tours deliberately inciting religious hatred.

The vivacious Smith could not be persuaded to stand still before a radio microphone and the effect of his voice, with its pronounced East Side accent, moving in and out of earshot, was grotesque and his words unintelligible to many in the South and West. By comparison, Hoover, who was known as a dull speaker, disciplined himself to talk directly into the microphone, have his shyness mistaken for modesty, and give a general impression of midwestern sobriety.

There was a heavy turnout at the polls with 67.5 percent of voters casting their ballots. Smith won the largest popular vote given to any Democrat to that time, 15,016,169 (40.7 percent). Hoover took 21,391,993 (58.2 percent). He had 444 votes in the electoral college to Smith's 87. Six southern states went Republican (Florida, Kentucky, North Carolina, Tennessee, Texas, Virginia). But industrial Massachusetts and Rhode Island went Democrat for the first time since the Civil War. Although Smith lost Pennsylvania, Illinois, and Wisconsin, he narrowed the Republican lead there.

Never again would the Democrats count on the Solid South but, instead, search out new catchment areas. Thus the electoral significance of the South would diminish. Smith, moreover, inaugurated a trend that was to make the Democrats the future majority party of the nation. In the twelve most populous cities the Democrats had a majority of 38,000 whereas the Republican majorities there had been 1,638,000 in 1920 and 1,252,000 in 1924. The Republican hold on these cities was broken by Smith who, thus, cleared the path for Franklin D. Roosevelt's victory in 1932. More women voted than before and Catholic women gave their votes to Smith. As for Congress, the Republicans took 267 seats in the House, against 163 for the Democrats and 1 for the Farmer-

Laborites, and now had 56 seats in the Senate against 39 for the Democrats and 1 for the Farmer-Laborites. In the gubernatorial contests the Republicans won 30 and the Democrats 18.

Smith's consolation prize was the result of another of Raskob's pet schemes. Raskob wanted New York to have its own equivalent of the Eiffel Tower. On August 29, 1929, Al Smith, now president of the Empire State, Inc., announced that the organization would build the world's tallest skyscraper. It would be 1,200 feet high, with 102 stories of offices for 25,000 people. It would stand on Fifth Avenue at Thirty-Fourth Street and the Waldorf-Astoria Hotel would be demolished to make room for it. The Empire State Building was to be a physical representation of the inevitable triumph of modernism.

On the eve of his retirement from the presidency, Calvin Coolidge's old neighbors in Vermont gave him a farewell present of a handmade rake. At the presentation ceremony the orator described the sterling qualities of the hickory wood from which it was made. "Hickory, like the president, is sturdy, strong, resilient, unbroken." Coolidge turned the rake over and remarked quite simply, "Ash." For the last time, Coolidge had exercised his special talent for unwitting irony in his choice of the right word. The decade of invention, intolerance, and indulgence was about to come to an end.

4

SNOW IN HARVEST
The Onset of the Great
Depression

WE MIGHT characterize the 1920s as an American dream that
became a nightmare. Despite the publicity about progress
and prosperity, it seemed that, in economic terms, society was
digging its own grave, its citizens the victims of an inadequate
economic mechanism. American prosperity in the 1920s stood on
brittle glass. However, in 1929 the mirror cracked when the
economy was shattered by the Wall Street Crash. The crisis for
the old order had been brewing for many years and the climax
lasted three months—September, October, and November of
1929. The consequences continued for a decade afterward as the
Great Depression spread its shadow over the land.

Heedless of the basic flaws in the American economic system,
those with money to invest did so eagerly and greedily in the
1920s. For, as historian William E. Leuchtenburg explains, "The
prosperity of the 1920s produced the contagious feeling that
everyone was meant to get rich." Thus well before the Wall Street

Crash of 1929 there was the Florida Land Boom of the mid-twenties, an episode that had all the hallmarks of a classic speculation bubble.

No single individual was responsible for the Wall Street Crash. No single individual was the architect of the babel of speculation that preceded it. Thousands of people contributed freely to the debacle. In the early twenties stock prices were low; in the mid-twenties they began to rise. The main index for these years is provided by the *New York Times* industrial averages, an aggregate of twenty-five leading industrial stocks. Between May 1924 and December 1925 the *Times* averages rose from 106 to 181. By December 1927 the *Times* averages were 245, a gain of sixty-nine points in the year.

The rise was partly a response to a British decision about the exchange rate that had widespresd repercussions. In 1925 Winston Churchill, chancellor of the exchequer, returned Britain formally to the gold standard, making the pound sterling the equivalent of £1 = $4.86. He did so for mistaken reasons of prestige and failed to recognize the subtle but disastrous effects of overvaluation. The American response was decisive. In August 1927 the Federal Reserve System lowered the rediscount rate from 4 percent to 3.5 percent. It did this partly to discourage the flow of gold from Europe to the United States, partly to encourage the flow of European imports and thus help certain European countries stabilize their currencies, and partly to stimulate American business. Unfortunately, the Federal Reserve overstimulated the stock market.

The great bull market began in earnest on Saturday, March 3, 1928. For instance, General Motors rose from 140 to 144 that day and in the next week crossed the psychologically significant figure of 150. There was a specific explanation. Since Henry Ford had discontinued the Model T in 1927 and reequipped his plants for the Model A, production of Ford cars would obviously be somewhat impeded. Thus General Motors would gain customers at Ford's expense. One indication that trading was at astonishing, unprecedented levels was the fact that day after day the stock ticker, unable to cope with the demand, was late: on June 12 it was almost two hours late in recording prices on the floor.

Fifth Avenue at 42nd Street, New York, 1933, dominated by the Empire State Building (1931), the most famous skyscraper in the world, designed by Shreve, Lamb, and Harmon with most skillful massing to make optimum use of the city's zoning laws and with a facade of limestone, granite, aluminum, and nickel capped by a crown of setbacks and a rounded tower. It both dominates the landscape and merges into it. Close by is the New York Public Library (1897–1911) by Carrere and Hastings, a modest, neoclassical building. (Photo by Irving Underhill; Library of Congress).

The ecstasy of speculation sent American investors in the 1920s into a wonderland where all had won and all must have prizes. The great Wall Street stockbroking firms opened an increasing number of branch offices across the country. Where there had been about 500 branch offices in 1919, in October 1928 there were 1,192. Business was not confined to the New York Stock Exchange, that accounted for only about 61 percent of transactions; the stock markets of Boston, Chicago, and San Francisco were also most active.

Few bankers urged caution. One who did so was Paul M. Warburg of the International Acceptance Bank who was reported by the *Commercial and Financial Chronicle* of March 9, 1929, as calling for a stronger Federal Reserve policy and predicted that, if the exuberant bonanza of unrestricted speculation was not stopped, then there would eventually be a disastrous collapse. A minority of journalists never lost touch with reality. Poor's *Weekly Business and Investment Letter* referred to the "great common-stock delusion." Both the *Commercial and Financial Chronicle* and the *New York Times* warned that a day of reckoning would come.

Of course, very few people were actually buying and selling stocks and shares. In 1929, when the total population of the United States was 121,767,000, the member firms of twenty-nine exchanges had no more than 1,548,707 clients altogether. And of these, 1,371,920 were clients of member firms of the New York Stock Exchange. Those involved in the precarious and potentially damaging marginal trading were only slightly more than 50,000. Thus, as J. K. Galbraith emphasizes, "The striking thing about the stock market speculation of 1929 was not the massiveness of the participation. Rather it was the way it became central to the culture." It was as if by foolhardy, spendthrift actions, a whole society was digging its own economic grave, a victim of its own inadequate economic mechanism. Such foolhardiness was to bring snow in harvest.

The economy had already entered a depression ahead of the stock market. Industrial production peaked in June 1929, when the Federal Reserve index stood at 126. Thereafter, it began to decline. By October, the Federal Reserve index of industrial production was 117. Thus economist Thomas Wilson later maintained that the ensuing fall in the stock market was reflecting a change that had already occurred in industry, rather than the other way round.

A few shareowners, suspicious of market fluctuations, quietly sold stock at advantageous prices. In time everyone began selling as much as possible. Real panic set in on the morning of "Black Thursday," October 24, 1929, when 12,894,650 shares changed hands in a vicious spiral of deflation. In the mad scramble to sell people were ready to part with shares for next to nothing. Among visitors to the New York Stock Exchange that day was Winston Churchill who might have rued his decision to return Britain to the gold standard four years earlier. To the *New York Herald Tribune* of October 25, 1929, Wall Street on Black Thursday was like a carnival with huge crowds in a holiday mood surging around the narrow streets of the financial centers and with hotels nearby overflowing with brokers' men. The atmosphere was most tense with enraged brokers vandalizing stock tickers and (largely unsubstantiated) rumors of others having jumped from windows. But it was prices that were falling through the floor.

At noon organized support rallied at 23 Wall Street, the offices of J. P. Morgan and Company. Led by Thomas W. Lamont, the senior partner of the House of Morgan, a pool of six bankers was formed to save the situation. Nevertheless, "Black Tuesday," October 29, 1929, was the bitter climax of everything that had gone wrong before. The amount of trading and the fall in prices was greater than ever. Altogether, 16,410,030 sales took place and the *Times* averages fell 43 points, wiping out all the gains of the previous twelve months. The worst losses were sustained by overvalued investment trusts. Goldman, Sachs Trading Corporation fell from 60 to 35; Blue Ridge fell from 10 to 3. The collapse of the stock market was greeted with blunt vulgarity by the weekly stage paper, *Variety*. Its headline of October 30, 1929, was "WALL STREET LAYS AN EGG."

The period of great bankruptcies began. The first major casualty of the crash outside New York was the Foshay enterprises of Minneapolis, a floundering utilities company, supposedly worth $20 million but already deeply in debt. The Wall Street Crash had eliminated potential investors who might have rallied to it. Now their savings had been wiped out. The market continued to fall inevitably until Wednesday, November 13, 1929. The *Times* averages then stood at 224, compared with 542 in early September. Altogether stocks and shares had lost $40 billion in the autumn of 1929.

The crisis continued along its remorseless and inevitable path of economic disintegration. Despite temporary gains in early 1930, the stock market continued to fall until July 8, 1932, when the *Times* averages were 58, as compared with 224 at their low ebb on November 13, 1929.

Causes and Consequences of the Wall Street Crash

The Wall Street Crash exposed the underlying instability of the American economic system — the overexpansion of industry and the farm surpluses, the unequal distribution of wealth, and the weak banking structure. In *The Great Crash — 1929* (1954) J. K. Galbraith emphasizes five principal weaknesses of an unsound economy. The first was the bad distribution of income. The top 5 percent of the population took a third of all personal income. This inequality meant that the survival of the economy depended on a very high level of investment by the wealthy few, or a high level of luxury spending, or both. Since there was a limit to the amount of food, housing, and clothing the rich could consume they must either spend their money on luxuries or investment. However, both luxury and investment spending were subject to a variety of changing circumstances. They could not remain steady.

A second unsound feature was the bad corporate structure. The most damaging weakness was the great, and comparatively recent, infrastructure of holding companies and investment trusts. Holding companies controlled a majority of shares in production companies, especially in the fields of railroads, public utilities, and entertainment. Even in economic crises holding companies insisted on their dividends, whatever the essential economic needs of the operating (that is the productive) companies from which they derived their great wealth. Thus the operating companies had to give priority to paying dividends rather than being able to invest in new plants or improved machinery that might have led to higher production. The system kept the operating companies weak and fueled deflation.

A third feature was the inherently weak banking structure of the United States with an excessive number of independent banks. In the first six months of 1929 as many as 346 banks with average deposits of $115 million failed. This was a tyranny of the weak. When one bank failed, others froze their assets, thus inviting investors to ask for their money back. In turn, such public pressure led to the collapse of ever more banks. Thus isolated instances of bank mismanagement led to a chain reaction in which neighboring banks collapsed like a row of dominoes. When a depression hit employment and people withdrew their savings, bank failures proliferated.

A fourth feature was the imbalance of trade. As we have observed, the United States became a creditor nation in the course of World War I. However, afterward the surplus of exports over imports, which had once paid for European loans, continued. High tariffs restricted imports and this factor impeded the ability of other countries to repay their loans. During the twenties they tried to meet their payments in gold while at the same time the United States was increasing its loans to foreign countries. Congress impeded further repayment of foreign loans by trade when it passed the Hawley-Smoot tariff, signed by Hoover on June 17, 1930, that raised tariff levels quite decisively. The upshot was a sharp reduction in trade and general default on repayment.

The fifth feature was the poor state of economic intelligence. The people running the economic machinery simply did not fully understand the system they were operating. Official dependence on outdated clichés—such as maintaining the gold standard, balancing the budget, and opposing inflation—all posed insuperable barriers to an early solution to the crisis. Moreover, it was harmful to the economy as a whole for the people in charge to equate the national interest with the special interests of the businesses they served.

Nevertheless, the greater fell with the lesser. Charles E. Mitchell of the House of Morgan, Ivan Kreuger, the Swedish Match

King, and officials of the Union Industrial Bank of Flint, Michigan, were among financiers found out for various forms of sharp practice.

Another crook who was made a scapegoat was Samuel Insull of Chicago. Insull was an English immigrant whom Thomas Edison had employed successively as secretary, assistant, and then general manager. At the turn of the century he was head of Edison's offices in Chicago and in 1908 formed the Commonwealth Edison Company, a $30 million corporation consolidating the Edison companies around Chicago, of which he became president. Insull's speciality was combining small power companies into ever larger units with improved facilities for generating electric power and then distributing it. He was a director of eighty-five companies, chairman of sixty-five boards, and president of another eleven. He owed his fabulous wealth to a conglomerate of 150 utility companies, serving 3.25 million people, and employing 50,000. It was valued at $3 billion. Unfortunately, he had a sinister side, his mania for creating pyramids of holding companies that were no better than a chaotic financial jumble. He refused to take account of the fact that a fall in profits of the operating companies, fundamental to the whole system, would reduce the unstable tiers to rubble. In early 1932 his empire collapsed, partly because it was overextended and overcapitalized and partly on account of fraud. The value of its stock fell to 4 percent of its 1931 level and two of Insull's investment trusts were declared bankrupt. In July 1932, having been indicted by a Cook County grand jury for outrageous debts of $60 million, Insull fled to Europe. He moved from Paris to Rome and, finally, to Athens because Greece had no extradition treaty with the United States. When an extradition treaty was signed in November 1932, he escaped to Turkey disguised as a women. He was eventually returned to the United States and stood trial. However, he was found not guilty as a result of a major loophole in the law: holding companies were not subject to regulation.

The causes of the Wall Street Crash were complex. The results were plain for all to see. The tawdry affluence of the twenties went out like a light.

The Years of the Locust

After the seven fat years of prosperity of 1922–1929, America entered a devastating and extended economic depression that lasted longer than seven lean years. The worst period was the notorious "Years of the Locust" of 1929–1932. Industry foundered. Instead of expanding, railroads and utilities contracted. Their new capital issues of bonds and stocks fell from $10 billion in 1929 to $1 billion in 1932. In 1932 the physical production of industry was 54 percent of what it had been in 1929. The automobile industry was working at a fifth of its previous capacity in 1929. By 1932 steel production was only operating at 12 percent of capacity and railroad freight was half of what it had been in 1929. The Gross National Product fell from $103.1 billion in 1929 to $58 billion in 1932, that is, a fall per captia from $847 in 1929 to $465 in 1932.

The story in agriculture was much the same. Capital investment in agriculture fell gradually from $79 billion in 1919 to $58 billion in 1929 and then precipitately to $38 billion in 1932. Realized gross income from farming fell from $13.9 million in 1929 to $6.4 million in 1932. The decline was most severe in basic export crops such as wheat, cotton, and tobacco.

At first industries tried to conserve their failing resources and faltering organization by such devices as cutting the working week or reducing wages. U.S. Steel became the first major corporation to reduce wages on September 22, 1931, when it announced a cut of 10 percent. It was followed by General Motors, Bethlehem Steel, and other corporations.

As sales continued to fall and the depression showed no signs of improving, business and industry cut costs further by discharging some of their work force. Those who were out of work could not afford to buy goods. This led to a vicious spiral of deflation. Sales fell yet again, leading to ever more layoffs and the further contraction of purchasing power. It was a vicious circle affecting farmers and industrial workers alike. Neither could afford to buy the products of the other. The problem was double-headed: chronic overproduction and perennial underconsumption, both at the same time.

The most profound consequence was unemployment on a massive, unprecedented scale. As historian William E. Leuchtenburg observes, the statistics of unemployment read like casualty figures in the great battles of the world war. In the three years following the crash an average of 100,000 workers were being discharged every week. According to the Bureau of Labor Statistics of the U.S. Department of Labor, published on June 29, 1945, there were 1.49 million unemployed in 1929 and this number increased gradually over the months to 11.9 million in 1932. This represented a percentage rise from 3.1 percent of the civilian labor force in 1929 to 24.0 percent in 1932. Other sources, such as the National Industrial Conference Board, the AFL, and the Labor Research Association (LRA), disputed these figures. The LRA said that the true number was 16.78 million.

Such unemployment was not shared evenly across the regions or between social and ethnic groups. By 1932 a million were unemployed in New York and so were 660,000 others in Chicago. In Cleveland 50 percent of the labor force was idle, in Akron 60 percent, and in Toledo 80 percent. In an article, "Negroes Out of Work," of April 22, 1931, the *Nation* showed that black unemployment was four to six times as high as white, particularly in industrial towns. In the depression blacks were displaced by whites in the lowly occupations of waiters, hotel workers, and elevator operators. In the specially created jobs in public works there was also positive discrimination against blacks.

The Protestant work ethic died hard. Millions who lost their jobs blamed themselves for their misfortune. A generation raised on the belief that hard work inevitably led to success could not come to terms with collective failure. Poverty was shameful and, to the middle class, something that had to be concealed from their friends and neighbors. Your neighbor opposite may have looked like an executive but, perhaps, when he left home each morning, he subsequently changed his suit to go begging, work in construction, or sell shoelaces or apples on street corners. Perhaps he spent his days looking for work.

Mass unemployment had grave consequences for marriage and

A breadline of haunted, hungry men waits for a meal in a soup kitchen supported by private charity alongside Bryant Park, 42nd Street, close to the New York Public Library in this classic depression photograph of February 1932. (Library of Congress).

birth rates and for immigration. With no prospect of employment young people either postponed marriage or, if they were already married, postponed having children. In 1929 there were 1.23 million marriages, in 1932, 982,000. In 1929 the birth rate was 21.2 per 1,000 population; in 1932 it was 19.5 per 1,000. In 1932 emigration exceeded immigration: 35,576 immigrants arrived and 103,000 emigrants left.

However, the most obvious consequence of mass unemployment was that those who could afford neither rent nor mortgage payments were put out of house and home. Masses of unemployed and destitute folks set up squalid camps on the edges of cities. These grotesque suburbs were a mixture of tents made from old sacking and shacks built with corrugated iron and even cardboard. They were called Hoovervilles. Their inhabitants depended on charity to stay alive. If that was not forthcoming, they combed the streets looking for garbage in the gutter and trash in the cans to find something to eat. Author Thomas Wolfe described such scenes in New York as "homeless men who prowled in the vicinity of restaurants, lifting the lids of garbage cans and searching around inside for morsels of rotten food."

Soup kitchens were provided by missions, churches, and hospitals, by the Salvation Army and, in Chicago, by Al Capone. The fare was meager, the portions diminutive. Thomas Minehan, a graduate student at the University of Minnesota, studied breadlines at close quarters. Everywhere he saw the prominent ribs, concave abdomens, and emaciated limbs that were the hallmarks of malnutrition.

The extent of the problem of human misery and want is indicated by a survey of *Fortune* magazine, in September 1932. *Fortune* estimated that 34 million men, women, and children, that is 28 percent of the total population, were without any income at all. (This estimate did not include America's 11 million farm dwellers, who represented 25 percent of the population trying to live off the land.) Private charity accounted for only 6 percent of the funds altogether spent on the poor in 1932. Public welfare was unequal to the other 94 percent. Municipal income came from taxes on real estate, all grossly overappraised. When local taxes fell 20 or 30 percent behind payment, cities cut their costs by reducing such services as maintaining roads and clearing snow.

It was extremely hard for people to get on a relief roll. Before an applicant could be considered, he had to sell all his possessions, including his home, cancel all his insurance policies and become literally destitute. The social stigma attached to relief discouraged all but the most needy. Ten states deprived the recipients of relief of their constitutional right to vote. Some churches barred families who received welfare from attending services. *Fortune* also disclosed in September 1932 that only 25 percent of duly qualified families were getting some form of relief. Unmarried people and couples without children were often excluded.

Schools, their children and teachers, suffered most on account of the improvidence or incapacity of local government to meet the depression. At the outset teachers' pay was cut to finance welfare. As the school population grew, classes became ever more overcrowded, textbooks dirtier and more dog-eared. At last schoolteachers were even denied their pay. In 1932 a million children were not being educated because of lack of funds. In Dayton, Ohio, schools were open but three days a week. In Arkansas more than 300 schools were shut for ten months of the year.

Before 1932 no state had a program for unemployment insurance. In 1929 only eleven states provided old age pensions. The total sum paid was $220,000. In 1931 there were 3.8 million one-parent families headed by a woman and only 19,280 of these families received any form of state aid. The average monthly award varied from $4.33 in Arkansas to $69.31 in Massachusetts. The Massachusetts award was the highest in any of the states but, even so, the yearly total was only $832, well below the sum of $2,000 that economists considered sufficient to supply an average family with basic necessities.

New York State was the first to accept state responsibility for relief on a massive scale. Here the influence of Governor Franklin D. Roosevelt was decisive. During the winter of 1930–1931 he had the State Department of Social Welfare and the State Charities Aid Association undertake a joint study of unemployment and relief. Their report insisted that the greater part of relief must come from public, and not private, funds. The Assembly, dominated by the Republicans, was reluctant and Roosevelt used a well-planned radio campaign to focus public opinion on the need for state aid. Thus he put pressure on the Assembly. It established a Temporary Emergency Relief Administration (TERA) to help city and county governments solve the problem of relief. The first administrator was a New York social worker, Harry Hopkins.

Men, women, and children who could find no sustenance at home simply took to the roads—more particularly the railroads where they became nonpaying, unwanted, stowaway passengers. By 1932 there were between one and two million roaming the states on freight cars. The transients or vagrants were a mix of hoboes, dispossessed farmers and sharecroppers, unemployed school leavers, and unemployable middle-class executives. Newton D. Baker told the *New York Times* of May 4, 1932, how

Every group in society is represented in their ranks from the college graduate to the child who has never seen the inside of the schoolhouse. Expectant mothers, sick babies, young childless couples, grim-faced middle-aged dislodged from lifetime jobs—on they go, an index of insecurity in a country used to the unexpected. We think of nomads of the Desert—now we have nomads of the Depression.

Novelist Thomas Wolfe contrasted the wretched plight of the dispossessed at night in New York with the shimmering skyscrapers of commerce nearby. To him these were towering symbols of indifference and man's inhumanity to man. Above and beyond the public toilets frequented by vagrants were

the giant hackles of Manhattan shining coldly in the cruel brightness of the winter night. The Woolworth Building was not fifty yards away, and a little farther down were the silver spires and needles of Wall Street, great fortresses of stone and steel that housed enormous banks. The blind injustice of this . . . seemed the most brutal part of the whole experience, for there . . . in the cold moonlight, only a few blocks away from this abyss of human wretchedness and misery, blazed the pinnacles of power where a large section of the entire world's wealth was locked in mighty vaults.

His point was that an economic system that tolerated exploitation to the extent of widespread unemployment and pitiful destitution could surely not survive indefinitely. People expected federal intervention, that is, specifically, presidential action, to raise the Great Depression.

Herbert Hoover brought a variety of talents and experience, both political and commercial, to the presidency in 1929 but, when he left office in March 1933, he was condemned as inefficient and inhumane. An apocryphal story has Hoover walking along the street with Andrew Mellon whom he asked for a nickel to make a phone call to a friend. "Here's a dime," replied the secretary of the treasury. "Call up both of them."

Hoover's cardinal sin was that he failed to raise the Great Depression. It is a popular, but erroneous, misconception that he did nothing about it. Critic Robert S. McElvaine observes, "He was a man of principle but his inflexibility proved his undoing in the face of economic collapse." He believed that his ideas about politics and economics were unassailable because they had been forged in, and tempered by, long experience. He recognized that enterprises such as public utilities entailed common interests and carried public responsibility. Accordingly, they must be regulated by government acting on behalf of its citizens. Nevertheless, government had no right to interfere with a free market economy. The American system had achieved the highest standard of living in the world precisely because the power of the federal government was limited. The economy allowed equality of opportunity and encouraged individual initiative. In his *1933: Characters in Crisis,* Herbert Feis, then an economic adviser in the State Department, recalls "Hoover was not an insensitive nor inhumane man; quite the contrary. But he could not grasp or would not face the grim realities which called for deviations from principles and practices that he deemed essential to American greatness and freedom."

However, Hoover was sensitive to growing areas of discontent against his own party. One such was in the very seedbed of Republicanism, the farm belt of the Midwest and Great Plains, from which the party had garnered seven presidents. Farmers already caught in the grip of agricultural recession resented the domination of their party by eastern interests. Since the farm belt would always play a pivotal role in the outcome of elections, Hoover recognised that he must improve the farmers' lot. He had first called the Seventy-First Congress into a special session before the crash in April 1929 to consider the pressing problems of agriculture.

Hoover would not countenance legislation on the lines of the McNary-Haugen proposals. Therefore, the Agricultural Marketing Act of June 1929 was intended to provide the farmers with a form of self-help. The act established a Federal Farm Board with funds of $500 million that it was to use to create farmers' marketing cooperatives and so-called "stabilization corporations." The stabilization corporations were assigned the task of storing and then disposing of surplus in order to help stabilize farm prices. What the farm boards could not do was restrict production, and excessive production in 1931 and 1932 resulted in huge surpluses and, thus, prices fell through the floor.

Moreover, the board clearly had no power to control the worldwide agricultural depression. As the European depression deepened, Europe reduced its imports of American produce even further while trying to sell its own surplus grain on the world market. The consequences of excessive surplus at home and abroad were devastating. The price of wheat fell from an average of $1.04 a bushel in 1929 to 67 cents in 1930 and then to between 30 cents and 39 cents in 1932. These prices were well below the cost of production. A system of voluntary cooperatives could not handle problems on this scale. The Farm Board appealed to Congress to restrict acreage and production.

Hoover's attempts to bring relief by raising the tariff on farm produce were also futile. Apart from sugar and butter, fruit and wool, very few imports were in competition with American agriculture. Tariff legislation had traditionally become a subject for barter between different interest groups in Congress. The Hawley-Smoot Act, which became law on June 17, 1930, was a classic instance of this. The average rates on all duties rose to new heights. The Fordney-McCumber tariff of 1922 had set the previous record with average duties of 33 percent. But it was surpassed by the Hawley-Smoot tariff in which the average duty was

40 percent. While affording some relief to diary and meat products, the new tariff was of no general use to agriculture. In turn, Britain and Germany abandoned free trade and set up economic barriers of their own. Other nations soon followed suit. International trade, already impeded by the depression, was thus further reduced.

Hoover met the problem of unemployment partly by calling on local government and private welfare agencies to provide extra employment and partly by extending the amount of public works undertaken by the federal government. He secured additional appropriations from Congress for public works from $250 million in 1929 to $410 million in 1930 and, thereafter, by stages to $726 million in 1932. However, individual welfare schemes were undernourished and quite inadequate for the needs of the time. There was more to welfare work than just forming committees. The Federal Home Loan Bank Act of July 1932 was intended to save mortgages by easing credit. It established a series of Federal Home Loan Banks to ease the problems of loan associations, insurance companies, and other organizations involved in mortgages. However, since the maximum loan was only to 50 percent of the value of the property, the measure was largely ineffective.

The most significant recovery measure of the early depression was the Reconstruction Finance Corporation (RFC). The RFC was based on the War Finance Corporation of the war and chartered by Congress on January 22, 1932, to lend funds of $500 million to banks and railroads, construction companies and various lending associations, especially those in danger of bankruptcy. This was the agency that funded projects such as the Golden Gate Bridge in San Francisco and the Mississippi River Bridge in New Orleans. But its support of certain banks made it an easy target for criticism. The first president of the RFC was noted banker Charles Gates Dawes, author of the Dawes plan on reparations and former vice-president under Coolidge. Shortly after Dawes retired from the RFC and returned to the Central Republic Bank of Chicago, the RFC awarded his bank a loan of $90 million, a sum almost as great as its supposed deposits.

However, the mood of the dispossessed changed dramatically in 1931 and 1932. Hitherto, the depression had astonished a generation who accepted the legend of the richest nation in the world without understanding how the dream could turn sour. The government faced truculent, disruptive action by farmers and war veterans.

It was the countryside that stirred itself first. The first signs of unrest came in isolated incidents of violence born of incredible frustration at the turn of events. Such was the Cow War, in which Iowa dairy farmers resisted the state's compulsory TB tests on cattle. Farmers armed with clubs and staves turned on state deputies appointed to oversee the tests and were only quelled by the intervention of the state militia equipped with tear gas.

Various farm groups organized themselves as the Farmers' Holiday Association. It eventually fell under the charismatic leadership of Milo Reno who had first proposed a farm strike in 1927. This would have involved farmers refusing to market their produce in order to make the towns and cities aware of their problems and bring about a rise in prices. They turned their slogan into a jingle:

> Let's call a "Farmers' Holiday"
> A Holiday let's hold
> We'll eat our wheat and ham and eggs
> And let them eat their gold.

The use of the term "Holiday" in place of "strike" was intended as a sardonic parody of the way banks closed their doors on bank holidays to customers they could not serve.

Farmers who could not meet their mortgage payments lost their farms in foreclosures. The dramatic increase in the number of farms being sold in the early depression is suggested in statistics released by the U.S. Department of Agriculture Bureau of Agricultural Economics. In 1929 58.0 farms in every 1,000 changed hands and of these 19.5 were forced sales; in 1932 76.6 farms in every 1,000 changed hands and 41.7 of these sales were forced. Thus did years of work count for nothing and a generation of farmers was dispossessed. Their grievances at such injustice took more serious and constructive forms. In early 1933 as many as seventy auctions of farm property took place in which the friends and neighbors of the dispossessed thwarted the auctioneers by

As president, Herbert Hoover (1929–1933) failed to fulfill his reputation as "the Great Engineer" who had fed Europe and America in World War I and sustained business as secretary of commerce in the 1920s. (Photo by Harris and Ewing of 1928; Library of Congress).

bidding a few cents for the items on sale and then returning them to their original owner. Such auctions were called "penny auctions" or "Sears Roebuck Sales." One farm in Haskins, Ohio, with a mortgage debt of $800 was acquired for $1.90. When such tactics did not work and an outsider took the farm he might be intimidated by an empty noose placed on a tree or with threats. After a spate of penny auctions, John A. Simpson, president of the National Farmers Union, warned the Senate Committee on Agriculture in January 1933, "The biggest and finest crop of revolutions you ever saw is sprouting all over the country right now." Edward A. O'Neal III, president of the American Farm Federation, said, "Unless something is done for the American farmer we'll have revolution in the countryside in less than twelve months." Because of mounting pressure Governors Charles Bryan of Nebraska and Floyd Olson of Minnesota signed state bills declaring a moratorium on farm mortgages.

War veterans provided a greater show of discontent. In 1924 Congress had voted a pension or bonus to war veterans. This was in the form of adjusted compensation certificates redeemable in 1945. In the early years of the depression veterans called for immediate payment when the money could be put to more effective use for personal relief, financial investment, or material support for their families. In Portland, Oregon, they elected Walter W. Waters, a former sergeant and cannery superintendent, to organize a march to the Capitol to dramatize their plight. This was the Bonus Expeditionary Force (BEF) that attracted thousands of veterans and transients as it moved across the country in the spring and summer of 1932. Other groups from different regions also began streaming into Washington, many with their wives and children. By mid-June there were between 15,000 and 20,000 bonus marchers in the city. They took up residence in various Hoovervilles. Their main camp was in southeast Washington on the other side of the Anacostia River across the Eleventh Street Bridge.

Roused by the bonus marchers' desperate plight, the House, on June 15, by a vote of 226 to 175, passed an enabling bill proposed by Congressman Wright Patman of Texas. It would have allowed immediate payment of the bonus. The estimated cost was $2.4

A detachment of 700 men from the Far West among the bonus army encampment on the east side of the Capitol in Washington, D.C., vowing they will remain there until Congress enacts a special bonus law to provide veterans with their pensions immediately. (Photo by Underwood and Underwood of July 13, 1932; Library of Congress).

billion. However, the bill was rejected by the Senate on June 17. Some veterans agreed to leave, using loans for travel home provided by the government and to be deducted from the payment in 1945. Others refused to budge. Their truculent mood disturbed both President Hoover and the commissioners of the District of Columbia whose anxiety increased when Congress adjourned.

On the night of June 17 some bonus marchers had begun to occupy a group of derelict red brick buildings on Pennsylvania Avenue. The occupation had the tacit support of the District police superintendent, Pelham D. Glassford, a retired brigadier who sympathized with the veterans and had food and blankets distributed to them. The squatters along Pennsylvania Avenue within three blocks of the Capitol itself were a humiliating eyesore to the Hoover administration because their presence exposed the inadequacy of the federal government. The authorities feared that the uninvited guests were harbingers of a revolution. For the first time since 1918 the White House gates were chained, barricades were erected around the executive mansion, and traffic was not allowed within a block. Secretary of War Patrick Hurley was determined to use any incident as a pretext for dislodging the marchers. One such occurred on July 28, 1932.

The evacuation of a small building on the corner of 3rd Street and Pennsylvania Avenue deteriorated into a full-scale riot. This was sufficient excuse for Hurley to summon federal troops under General Douglas MacArthur who, despite counsel of moderation from his aide, Major Dwight D. Eisenhower, proceeded to disperse the bonus marchers with infantry, cavalry, and tanks. The veterans were driven back across the Eleventh Street Bridge into the main camp at Anacostia Flats. The tents, shacks, and packing crates of the camp in which the bonus marchers were sheltered were all set on fire. The entire camp was razed to the ground. Two babies died of tear gas. A soldier deliberately ran a bayonet through the leg of a seven-year-old boy, Eugene King, who was trying to rescue his pet rabbit. As night fell women and children were ferried to Salvation Army hostels. Men with battered heads and eyes streaming from tear gas were carried off to the hospital by ambulance. The routed marchers were officially barred from Maryland and Virginia although police escorted a few stragglers through Maryland to Pennsylvania whence they were herded in turn by state police to Ohio. And so from state to state the weary band was dispersed. By the fall they were indistinguishable from the rest of America's huge transient population.

It was clear that by his actions, a mixture of arrogance, insensitivity, and cowardice, compounded by MacArthur's excesses, that Hoover had committed a gross political blunder that was to cost him dear. It was as if he were stage-managing his own defeat in the election of 1932.

The Rise of Franklin Delano Roosevelt

The Republican National Convention assembled in Chicago on June 14, 1932, and renominated Hoover dutifully but without any enthusiasm. The platform repeated the time-honored commitment to the gold standard, protection of the tariff, and traditional government economies whilst supporting the farmers' cooperative efforts to control agricultural production. On the issue of prohibition it was neither wet nor dry but moist, favoring resubmission of the Eighteenth Amendment to the states.

Hoover and the Republican party were most uneasy about what lay ahead. By 1932 the impact of the Great Depression was causing an irreversible shift in the political loyalty of millions. This was especially apparent among farmers, blacks, and the middle class. Thus, after decades of status as a party of honorable opposition, the Democrats were about to emerge as the natural party of government. In part, this was because the persuasive lobby of wets committed to the repeal of prohibition helped transform it after the resounding defeat of 1928. Opposition to national prohibition played a decisive part in the election of 1932 and its aftermath.

The role played by Democratic national chairman and General Motors executive John Julius Raskob in remodeling the party was pivotal. It had been Raskob's ambition to transform the Democratic party into "an organization which parallels, as nearly as conditions will permit, a first rate business enterprise operating all the time; spending money effectively and meeting the real issues at hand." Raskob recognized that the recipe for sustained electoral success was continuous work. Accordingly, in 1929 he put Jouett Shouse of Kansas, a former congressman, and Charles Michelson, former Washington correspondent for the New York *World,* in charge of publicity. Within two years he had created a permanent, professional national organization, the first of its kind and a model for the future.

The leading contender for the Democratic presidential nomination in 1932 was Governor Franklin D. Roosevelt of New York.

FDR's background, upbringing, and early political career barely suggest that he could become the greatest president of the United States in the twentieth century. He was born on January 30, 1882, in Hyde Park, New York, the only son of an elderly father and youthful mother. They were a wealthy Hudson River family of Anglo-Dutch extraction. Thus FDR received a privileged education. He entered Harvard in 1900 and finished his undergraduate courses in three years. In 1904 he went to Columbia University Law School and in 1905 married a fifth cousin, Anna Eleanor Roosevelt, who was given away by her uncle, President Theodore Roosevelt. In time the couple had four sons and a daughter. After passing the New York State bar examinations, FDR entered a Wall Street law firm as a junior clerk, but his political ambitions were already set on the presidency. In 1910 he was elected state senator for the Democrats and at Albany he led an insurgent group against Tammany Hall.

In 1913 President Woodrow Wilson brought him into his administration as assistant secretary of the navy—like Theodore Roosevelt before him—and he made himself popular with admirals, cultivated labor and business, but found himself in open disagreement with his superior, Secretary of the Navy Josephus Daniels, and Woodrow Wilson himself, over such matters as naval expenditures and rearmament. However, he was reconciled with Tammany Hall when he worked for Al Smith in 1918 during Smith's campaign for governor of New York. Thus in 1920 FDR was nominated for the vice-presidency as a candidate acceptable to Wilsonian, independent, and Tammany Democrats alike. He even gained by the rout of the Democrats that year because he had the advantage of national exposure without carrying any responsibility for the defeat.

At this point greater tragedy struck him when in 1921 he contracted poliomyelitis. It was incorrectly diagnosed and treated at first and it left him permanently paralyzed from the waist down. Against the wishes of his always indulgent and interfering mother but supported by his energetic wife and his closest confidant, political reporter Louis M. Howe, he concentrated first on gaining physical strength and then resumed his political career. Urged by Smith and supported by Raskob, he became Democratic candidate for governor of New York in 1928 when Al Smith ran for the presidency, winning by 25,000 votes whereas Smith, himself, lost the state.

As governor, Roosevelt treated the traditional problems of industrial monopolies and the new ones of the depression. He achieved cheaper electric power, both through the promotion of public power and more effective regulation of private utility companies. He met the two problems of unemployment and conservation by putting unemployed young men to work on land reclamation and tree-planting throughout the state. In short, no governor worked harder to ease the depression.

In a speech of April 7, 1932, Roosevelt declared that the country faced a more grave emergency than in 1917. He compared the Hoover administration to Napoleon at Waterloo who had staked too much on his overextended cavalry and forgotten his infantry. Thus the administration had forgotten "the infantry of our economic army." "These unhappy times call for the building of plans that rest upon the forgotten, the unrecognized but the indispensable units of economic power, . . . that put their faith once more in the forgotten man at the bottom of the economic pyramid." Precisely because of his illness, the wealthy Roosevelt could identify with the forgotten man and, by virtue of the way he had fought his illness to resume a political career, he became a symbol of the will to triumph over terrible adversity.

However, to political pundits, Roosevelt seemed to offer little beyond his illustrious name. He was much criticized by conservatives and radicals alike. Underlying all the censure, sometimes implicit and sometimes spoken, was the notion that here was simply another Hoover. This was a theme common to the Scripps-Howard chain of newspapers and to the *Nation*. Walter Lippmann opined of Roosevelt in the *New York Herald Tribune* of January 8, 1932, "He is a pleasant man who, without any important qualifications for the office, would very much like to be President."

Roosevelt entered the Democratic National Convention, which met in Chicago on June 27, 1932, with a large majority of delegates pledged to support him. However, his majority fell substantially short of the two-thirds necessary at that time to secure a presidential nomination. Roosevelt's nomination on the fourth ballot came as a result of the intercession of Joseph P. Kennedy of Boston with William Randolph Hearst. The newspaper magnate effectively controlled the California delegation, nominally led by William Gibbs McAdoo. Hearst was in his mansion at San Simeon, California. Kennedy called him by phone. Unless Hearst released the California votes, Roosevelt's nomination would be blocked. It would be the deadlock of 1924 all over again. Either Al Smith or Newton D. Baker would claim the prize. Hearst detested Smith for impeding his own political ambitions after the war. He distrusted Baker because he was a champion of the League of Nations and Hearst was an inveterate isolationist. On July 1, William Gibbs McAdoo, anticipating the withdrawal of Mississippi from Roosevelt's side, announced that California "did not come here to deadlock this convention, or to engage in another desolating contest like that of 1924." He then gave all forty-four votes of California to Roosevelt. Thus was he revenged on Al Smith for having been denied the nomination in 1924. Illinois, Indiana, and Maryland came round to Roosevelt. At the end of the fourth ballot he had 945 votes.

Only Smith from his hotel remained obdurate and refused to allow his delegates to release their votes to make the nomination unanimous. Not only was he resentful of Roosevelt's success as governor but also embittered by the way Roosevelt struck bargains with his former allies in order to secure the nomination. As H. L. Mencken observed, Smith looked on Roosevelt as a cuckoo who had seized his nest.

Until 1932 it was the custom for nominees to deliver their acceptance speeches weeks later from their homes. This was what Hoover did in Washington on August 11. However, Roosevelt broke all precedents. He arranged to fly to Chicago immediately

General Douglas MacArthur, army chief of staff, personally supervised the breaking up of the bonus camps, razing them to the ground, and finally dispersing the exhausted veterans and their families—a maneuver that contributed to the further decline of Hoover in public esteem. (Photo by Underwood and Underwood of July 29, 1932; Library of Congress).

to address the convention that had nominated him. The decision to fly was itself a novelty when commercial flights were infrequent. Roosevelt proved he was good copy across the nation as well as in his state. In his address of July 2 he declared: "I pledge you, I pledge myself, to a new deal for the American people. Let us all here constitute ourselves prophets of a new order of competence and of courage. This is more than a political campaign; it is a call to arms. Give me your help, not to win votes alone, but to win in this crusade to restore America to its own people." The next day a cartoon by Rollin Kirby was reproduced in papers across the country. It showed a farmer looking at an airplane in the sky. The plane bore the inscription "New Deal." The phrase, coined by Judge Samuel Rosenman of New York, was a hybrid of Theodore Roosevelt's "Square Deal" and Woodrow Wilson's "New Freedom." To boost public morale Roosevelt's campaign song, now played everywhere, was the optimistic "Happy Days Are Here Again."

The Democratic platform of 1932 not only favored repeal of the Eighteenth Amendment but also proposed loans to the states for unemployment relief, approved the principle of old age insurance to be achieved by state laws, and advocated control of surplus crops whilst paying lip service to the orthodox wisdom of a balanced budget and a hard currency.

Roosevelt replaced John J. Raskob as chairman of the Democratic National Committee with Jim Farley, secretary of the New York Democratic Committee. Farley was an Irish Catholic who had never belonged to Tammany Hall. Unlike Raskob, he had the common touch. He neither drank nor smoked. Yet he was a wet and enough of a celebrity in his own right as a salesman of construction materials to advertise Lucky Strike cigarettes for the American Tobacco Company. Raskob's appointee as publicity agent, Charles Michelson, released a barrage of publicity for FDR and against Hoover. Roosevelt's academic advisers, the Brain Trust, led by Professors Raymond Moley, Rexford G. Tugwell, and Adolf A. Berle, Jr., of Columbia University, and General Hugh S. Johnson, provided well-researched data and effective briefs for Roosevelt to draw on.

Roosevelt's strategy was to concentrate on the West. New

York he knew he could hold and the South was not likely to treat him the way it had Al Smith in 1928. In order to entice the farm vote, he toured the West and Midwest extensively, securing support from maverick Republicans and old Progressives, such as George W. Norris, Henry C. Wallace, Basil Manly, and Judson King. Radio was even more important in the campaign than it had been in 1928. Hoover's sententiousness was no match for Roosevelt's uncanny ability to project exuberance, compassion, and humor. Indeed, his personality transcended the campaign.

In the election of November 8, 1932, Roosevelt received 22,809,638 votes, 57.4 percent of the total, against Hoover's 15,758,901, 39.7 percent. In the electoral college he had 472 votes to Hoover's 59. He carried all but six states, a larger victory than any Democrat before him. Norman Thomas, the Socialist candidate, received only 881,951 votes and William Z. Foster, the Communist candidate, took only 102,785. Both failed to exploit and gain from widespread unrest and discontent. In Congress the Democrats had 310 seats in the House and the Republicans had 117. In the Senate the Democrats had 60 seats, the Republicans 35.

Both observers and participants alike thought prohibition had been decisive in the outcome of the election. The *New York Times* of November 10, 1932, calculated that the forthcoming Seventy-third Congress would have 342 wet congressmen and 61 wet senators. Eleven states had held referenda on prohibition during the elections. In nine states the electorate voted to repeal state laws on prohibition. In Connecticut and Wyoming sizable majorities petitioned Congress for repeal of national prohibition. As the historian of repeal, David Kyvig, observes, the juxtaposition of three things: the election of 1932; the repeal movement; and the Great Depression produced an electoral result that seemed absolutely clear. People wanted a change of government; the repeal of prohibition; and new economic policies.

Hunger and Thirst

National prohibition was being made a scapegoat for the Great Depression. Arguments against prohibition were neither more nor less true than before the Wall Street Crash but its repeal was effectively urged by those who thought here was a panacea for the country's economic ills. Hence, hunger was a better advocate than thirst. It was far more eloquent against prohibition than any speech or sentence. As historian John D. Hicks explains, "It was the psychology of depression that made people change their minds. In prosperous times voters could tolerate the inefficiency of prohibition, make jokes about it, let it ride. But with the advent of depression its every fault was magnified, and the best jokes turned stale. The people were in a mood for change. Zealots who had promised the millennium as a result of prohibition, and had delivered bootleggers and racketeers instead, were in a class with politicians who had promised prosperity and delivered adversity. It was about time to wipe the slate clean and start over."

The AAPA decided to provide the public with more substantial evidence of the failure of prohibition than it had received hitherto. It created departments of research and information under John G. Gebhart, a New York social worker. His task was to collate information and publicize the ills of prohibition. Between April 1928 and January 1931 his department distributed over a million copies of thirteen pamphlets.

The AAPA's series of well-researched pamphlets brought public recognition of the need for a full-scale and reliable government enquiry into prohibition. In office, Herbert Hoover expanded his original plan for a national investigation into prohibition. Under the chairmanship of George W. Wickersham, who had served under Taft as attorney general, the eleven commissioners met for nineteen months from May 28, 1929. The commission elicited advice from experts, both academic and professional, on such subjects as crime and courts, police and prisons, and juvenile delinquency. The vast majority of people writing to, and appearing before, the commission told members in no uncertain terms that prohibition was not working and that it should be repealed.

The Wickersham Commission issued its final report on January 7, 1931. Although as many as seven members of the commission were openly critical of prohibition, all but one signed a final summary endorsing it. The contradiction between the individual reports declaring for reform and the shared summary declaring for further trial that had been forced on the commission by Hoover caused an uproar in the press. For example, Franklin P. Adams ridiculed the commission in a famous satirical verse for the *New York World* in February 1931:

> Prohibition is an awful flop.
> We like it.
> It can't stop what it's meant to stop.
> We like it.
> It's left a trail of graft and slime,
> It don't prohibit worth a dime,
> It's filled our land with vice and crime.
> Nevertheless, we're for it.

Hitherto, it had been generally assumed by both sides that women supported the Eighteenth Amendment. In fact, women were just as sensitive to the scandal of prohibition as men and became equally militant in their opposition to it. Their opposition in a new lobby, the Women's Organization for National Prohibition Reform (WONPR), was decisive in the movement for repeal. The WONPR was the creation of Pauline Morton Sabin, wife of Charles H. Sabin, president of Guaranty Trust, a Morgan bank. He was also treasurer of the AAPA. Not only did she persuade New York socialites Mrs. Coffin Van Rensselaer, Mrs. Caspar Whitney, and others, to join her, but she also enlisted upper-class women in the regions, all with time on their hands and a flair for publicity. Joining the WONPR became the fashionable thing to do. A "Sabin woman" could be received anywhere. On May 28, 1929, twenty-four such socialites from eleven states met at Chicago's fashionable Drake Hotel to launch the WONPR. Chicago was chosen rather than New York because its widely publicized crime problem was indissoluble from prohibition.

At the WONPR's first national convention, held in Cleveland in 1930, the Sabin women declared for outright repeal of prohibition. Pauline Sabin attached great importance to a huge membership. She understood that protest movements could succeed only if they continued to grow. As chairman, she worked assiduously from a small office in New York, writing articles, enrolling members, and making speeches. In April 1931 the WONPR claimed 300,000 members altogether and in 1932 it claimed 600,000 members in forty-one state branches.

Once the election was over and leading politicians had accepted the result as a clear indication that the public wanted repeal, events moved quickly. Repeal was necessarily the first step to raise the depression. Thus, where Congress would act ahead of Roosevelt's inauguration, and act decisively, was in the matter of prohibition. Republican Senator John J. Blaine of Wisconsin drafted a new constitutional amendment to be ratified by state legislatures. It proposed three things: an end to national prohibition; that the federal government retain the right to protect dry states against the importation of liquor; and that Congress should have concurrent power with the states to forbid the return of the saloon. On February 16, 1933, Senator Joseph T. Robinson, Democratic majority leader, led a group of senators who revised the Blaine measure to provide for ratification by specially elected state conventions, and removed the provision to prevent the return of the saloon. Thus they gave the Twenty-First Amendment its definitive form. The new amendment repealed the Eighteenth Amendment while prohibiting the importation of intoxicating liquor into states that forbade it. Moreover, the amendment was to be subject to ratification by state conventions within seven years. In this final form the resolution was approved by the Senate by 63 votes to 23 on February 16, 1933. On February 20, 1933, it was passed by the House by a vote of 289 votes to 121.

On April 10, 1933, the first state convention to vote for repeal was held in Michigan at Lansing. Of the one hundred delegates elected to consider ratification of the Twenty-First Amendment on April 3 only one was a dry. As convention followed convention it became clear that even such traditionally dry states as Alabama, Arkansas, and Tennessee now favored repeal. It was rare for the wet majority to fall below 60 percent. Of the total popular vote, 15 million, or 72.9 percent, favored repeal.

The federal government precipitated repeal by anticipating it. One of Roosevelt's first acts, after taking office on March 4, 1933, was to request a special session of Congress on March 13 to revise the Volstead Act, pending repeal of prohibition, to allow beer of 3.2 percent alcohol. Among his arguments was the need for additional federal revenue that could be raised by a tax on beer. Thus beer became legal under new federal dispensation on April 7, 1933. It was freely consumed on that day in Washington and in nineteen states. It was so scarce in New York that the stock joke was that people longed for prohibition so that they could get a drink. A week later an Associated Press release claimed that the federal government had already taken $4 million in license fees and taxes on barrels of beer. A Federal Alcohol Control Administration was established by FDR under the National Recovery Administration on December 4, 1933.

Best Cellars

Unfortunately, the repeal of prohibition was not the end of the story for criminal syndicates.

Deep public outrage at the scope of criminal activities was, nevertheless, somewhat appeased by the entrapment and conviction in 1931 of the most outrageous criminal, Al Capone. He was caught not for his most notorious crimes but, on the orders of Hoover and Mellon, for income tax evasion, thereby bypassing his known suborning of Chicago's officers and police. He was found guilty and sentenced to a total of eleven years' imprisonment, fined $50,000, and charged $30,000 in costs—a record for tax avoidance to that time. Capone was imprisoned first in the Atlanta Penitentiary and later in the newly opened prison at Alcatraz where he eventually slid into madness, a victim of neurosyphilis. As actress and screenwriter Mae West observed, "There are no withholding taxes on the wages of sin."

However, the elimination of Capone was a comparatively minor achievement given the scale of underworld activities as a whole. The Wall Street Crash was as crucial an event to the underworld as to the rest of society. During the depression gangsters' clients, shorn of their former affluence, could no longer afford their special services. Because of recession the gangs were once more in competition with one another. Rivalries that had become submerged in the revelry of the twenties once more burst into the open. Especially notorious was the feud between Giuseppe ("Joe the Boss") Masseria and Salvatore Maranzano in New York.

The settlement of their so-called Castellammarese War of 1930–1931 was synonymous with the institution of a Mafia on a national scale.

The pivotal players in New York were Salvatore Lucania and Meyer Lansky. Lucania belonged to the new generation of Italians and Sicilans who formed alliances based on common interests with men from different ethnic groups. His right hand man was Francesco Castiglia, or Frank Costello, of Calabria and his closest ally was Meyer Lansky, a Jew. An exceptional mathematician, Lansky began his career in organized crime as an automobile mechanic who provided gangs with fleets of souped-up trucks and cars before he entered the bootlegging industry. Lansky and Lucania were protégés of Arnold Rothstein and members of the Big Seven group from its inception. When Rothstein was killed in 1928 over a gambling debt, they became his heirs and continued to run a syndicate based on a mix of ethnic groups—Italians, Jews, and Poles. Ranged against them were Sicilian gangs, such as those of Masseria and Maranzano, that prided themselves on their elite ethnic composition.

Lansky and Lucania (Lucky Luciano as he was now called after returning from a one-way ride) stirred up trouble between Masseria and Maranzano, allowing Maranzano a temporary victory. Some historians date the founding of the American Mafia to Maranzano's decisions implemented at a secret meeting of unknown date. He instituted criminal governace by a chain of command from a supreme boss of all bosses, to family bosses, and underbosses. In order to anticipate wasteful feuds families would be apportioned regional areas. Mafia historian Gaia Servadio lists the cities that were to become the new centers of syndicate crime: Boston, Buffalo, Chicago, Cleveland, Detroit, Kansas City, Los Angeles, Newark, New Orleans, Philadelphia, Pittsburgh, San Francisco, Miami, and Las Vegas. Havana in Cuba would remain open to all. New York City would be divided among five families: the old Masseria gang now led by Frank Costello and Salvatore Luciano with Vito Genovese; the old Reina gang led by Tom Gagliano with Thomas Lucchese; the Maranzano gang divided into two families, one led by Joseph Profaci and the other by Joe Bonanno;

and in Brooklyn a coalition of Philip and Vincent Mangano with Albert Anastasia.

However, the war was not yet over. On September 11, 1931, four men pretending to be income tax inspectors entered Maranzano's Park Avenue office and killed him in a most brutal fashion. Maranzano's death was a sensation in the popular press that carried lurid accounts of scores of murders of "Mustache Petes," old style bosses, across the country on September 10, 1931. However, all that Lansky and Luciano needed to do was to cut off the head of the big fish in order to bring the lesser fry into line. Lansky was twenty-nine and Luciano was thirty-four when they stood at the threshold of supreme criminal power. They succeeded in part because they did not seek the title *capo di tutti capo*.

Under Luciano the syndicate, or Mafia, exploded its traditional boundaries of recruitment. Between 1931 and 1934 it began to take in so-called full Italians, that is Italians and Italian–Americans whose parents were both Italian. Lucky realized that the Wall Street Crash that had brought incipient tensions in the underworld to a head would, in the long run, also provide it with greater stability. It gave gangsters a golden opportunity to compensate themselves against future losses in the inevitable demise of prohibition. They could now enter legitimate business with honest citizens who had lost their assets. They alone could provide funds for needy businessmen. For instance, in 1931 Frank Costello formed an association with the Mills Novelty Company of Chicago, the largest manufacturers of slot machines. With a partner, Dandy Phil Kastel of New Orleans, he established a whole series of companies such as the Tru-Mint, the Village Candy, and the Monroe Candy companies. Their machines were placed in bars, candy and cigar stores, and stationery shops across the country.

With the aid of another of Rothstein's men, Frank Erickson, they developed a network of illegal off(race)track betting among small shopkeepers and their customers in the ghettos. Shopkeepers were paid $150 a week for handling the bets—the sum had been finely calculated by syndicate accountants from an average of gains, losses, and expenses. These bookkeeping businesses were safe from the police who were bribed to turn a blind eye to them. For those days when horses were not running they developed the numbers racket, a means of allowing punters the opportunity to bet a few cents on the random selection of a three digit figure, anything from 000 to 999. The numbers racket was first tried in Harlem in 1925 among poor blacks whom their white predators thought too immature to see how slim were the chances of winning. A craze developed and spread. Thousands of people were required to run the system across the country and all shared in the profits on a percentage basis.

The Chicago conclave of 1931 was not the end of the matter. Over the next three years subsequent meetings were held in Cleveland, Chicago, and New York. Representatives from syndicates in New York, Chicago, Cleveland, Minneapolis, Boston, Philadelphia, Miami, New Orleans, and New Jersey sometimes met in the new Waldorf Astoria Hotel, New York City. It was one of the homes of Lucky, now a businessman, Charles Ross. On the advice of Aaron Shapiro, a Fifth Avenue lawyer, this criminal syndicate took the National Recovery Administration of June 16, 1933, as its model with a commission governing the operation and development of the principal syndicates. It seemed happy days were here to stay.

Of course, it is never truly so. For almost sixty years the Crash of 1929 held a special place in economic history and folklore and had almost assumed the enjoyable status of myth. It did seem that the controls and safeguards introduced in the 1930s by the federal government served to control the vagaries of the stock market and forestall another such crash. However, in 1987 the dramatic fall of share prices on "Black Monday," October 19, quite eclipsed the single-day record of "Black Tuesday," October 29, 1929, and spread ominous chills across world markets about the continuous perils of prosperity.

5

HAPPY DAYS ARE HERE AGAIN
Franklin D. Roosevelt and the Early New Deal

Roosevelt and the Bank Crisis

IN EARLY 1933 the depression continued along its relentless path. Industrial production foundered, unemployment mounted, farm mortgage foreclosures became more common than ever, banks failed, and state authorities could not meet their relief obligations. One obstacle in the way of positive executive action was the rather long period of four months between the presidential election on November 8 and inauguration on March 4. This had long been a quadrennial problem for American politics. Accordingly, to remedy matters, the Twentieth Amendment had already been proposed by Senator George W. Norris of Nebraska and passed by Congress on March 3, 1932. It eliminated the so-called "lame duck" session of an old Congress by requiring the new Congress to meet on January 3 following the election. It also brought forward the date of the presidential inauguration from March 4 to January 20. However, the Twentieth Amendment was not ratified until February 1933 and thus would not take effect until 1935 and 1937.

In the meantime, there was a stultifying loss of confidence between election and inauguration. Herbert Hoover tried to arrange for a smooth transition by attempting a dialogue with Roosevelt. He tried to extract assurances from FDR that he would comply with his ideas on tariffs and taxes, currency and the budget, if only for the sake of public confidence. But Roosevelt was a past master at parrying suggestions that implied commitment to any previous policy.

A series of bank failures, most notably in February 1933, made the collapse of Hoover's intended dialogue most unfortunate. As we have observed, the weak American banking system was a prime cause of the Great Depression. Bank failures were something of a chronic feature of American economic life during the early thirties. There had been 1,345 in 1930, 2,298 in 1931, and 1,456 in 1932. By 1932 and 1933 the American banking system was in a state of acute crisis.

The crisis deepened in October 1932 when the governor of Nevada anticipated the failure of an important banking chain by closing the state banks in a bank holiday. Then at midnight on February 14, 1933, Governor William A. Comstock of Michigan issued a proclamation closing all 550 banks in the state for eight days. The crisis had been precipitated by a run on the Union Guardian Trust Company of Detroit. The Michigan bank holiday led to panic across various states and a whole series of bank holidays. In a speakeasy in New York a man in his cups asked the bartender how many states had declared bank holidays. "Thirty-eight," was the answer. "Ah!" said the customer. "That ratifies the depression!"

One important side effect of these closures was the flow of gold reserves from the Federal Reserve System and banks in New York City both to support the deposits of banks across the country and at the demand of panic-stricken foreign investors. Thus, in just over two months, from January to early March 1933, the nation's gold reserves fell from over $1.3 billion to $400 million. By early 1933 America's 18,569 banks had only about $6 billion altogether in cash to meet $41 billion in deposits. In the two days before the

Franklin Delano Roosevelt, the greatest president of the twentieth century, achieved the highest office in the United States despite his crippling condition of poliomyelitis. Identifying himself with the forgotten man at the base of the economic pyramid, he led the New Deal, a comprehensive program of legislation designed to raise the Great Depression and remedy basic inequalities in the structure of American society, before directing America's military and domestic strategies in World War II to bring the United States to a summit of global power. This publicity still for the presidential election of 1932 was said to be FDR's favorite photograph. (Library of Congress).

inauguration clients withdrew $500 million from banks across the country. Increasingly, the bank crisis made people of all classes recognize the imperative need for decisive executive action, even modified dictatorship. Walter Lippmann declared in his "Today and Tomorrow" column for the *Tribune* of February 17, 1933, that, "The danger we have to fear is not that Congress will give Franklin D. Roosevelt too much power, but that it will deny him the powers he needs."

Roosevelt stage-managed his own inauguration on March 4, 1933, with impeccable flair that captured the imagination of the entire country. Hence, Miguel Covarrubias painted the regal scene for *Vanity Fair* in the classical manner of David's *Coronation of Napoleon,* a brooding monument of ensemble. Instead of simply saying, "I do," after Chief Justice Charles Evans Hughes had read out the oath of office, Roosevelt repeated the full text. He then embarked on a stirring inaugural speech. "Let me first assert my firm belief that the only thing we have to fear is fear itself— nameless, unreasoning, unjustified terror which paralyzes needed efforts to convert retreat into advance." These ringing words resounded across the nation. No phrase had been borrowed. As the radio broadcast continued, listeners far and near were stopped in their tracks. "I shall ask the Congress for the one remaining instrument to meet the crisis—broad Executive power to wage a war against the emergency, as great as the power that would be given me if we were in fact invaded by a foreign foe." Hoover looked askance.

Roosevelt's portentous text was delivered with such impeccable diction that the audience far and wide all but tasted his words. In his narrative history, *Since Yesterday* (1939), Frederick Lewis Allen summed up the impression made by FDR on the vast radio audience thus:

You can turn off the radio now. You have heard what you wanted to hear. This man sounds no longer cautious, evasive. For he has seen that a tortured and bewildered people want to throw overboard the old and welcome something new; that they are sick of waiting, they want some-body who will *fight* this Depression for them and with them; they want leadership, the thrill of bold decision. And not only in his words but in the challenge of the very accents of his voice he has promised them what they want.

The bank crisis and FDR's determination to meet it demonstrate just how decisive would be his new start. On Sunday, March 5, Roosevelt summoned Congress into extraordinary session on Thursday, March 9, to consider the bank crisis. Taking advantage of legislation from the war that gave the president wide executive authority in case of a bank emergency, he then declared a four-day national bank holiday on Monday, March 6. He thus prevented further panic withdrawals and gold hoarding, whilst allowing time for Treasury officials to devise emergency draft legislation. During the bank holiday people improvised a temporary extra currency, a mix of barter and credit, stamps and streetcar tokens, Mexican pesos, and Canadian dollars.

The Bureau of Engraving and Printing acquired 375 extra workers and they worked round the clock printing bale after bale of money and using the outdated dies plates of 1929 since there was no time to have new ones engraved. Nevertheless, the various measures that were about to be taken to rescue the banks had already been discussed by Hoover's cabinet and advisers. However, because Hoover was irresolute and reluctant to close the banks by presidential proclamation, he failed to act on his colleagues' advice. However, FDR would act where Hoover would not and, to ensure the strategy was a success. he retained Hoover's men at the Treasury, notably Arthur Ballantine, undersecretary, and Floyd Awalt, acting comptroller of the currency.

On March 9 a special session of Congress approved the Emergency Banking Relief Act. In the House the debate lasted only forty minutes. The act provided aid for hard-pressed but solvent banks. The RFC could buy the preferred stock of banks, giving them additional operating funds from the Federal Reserve Banks. On April 19, 1933, Roosevelt forbade the hoarding and exporting of gold. He decided to do this to preempt the revival in Congress of the discredited idea of coining silver to achieve inflation. Banks examined and approved by government assessors could reopen immediately. Those that required further examination—about a quarter—could pay out only part of their deposits. After a few days banks that had previously accounted for 90 percent of all deposits were allowed to reopen.

On March 12 Roosevelt gave his first radio address, or fireside chat, as president. His aim was to make the emergency action intelligible to all and his gentle but invigorating words also encouraged reinvestment. By April over $1 billion in currency had been returned to bank deposits. The crisis was over. In the words of Frederick Lewis Allen, "The New Deal had made a brilliant beginning."

The name of Franklin Delano Roosevelt was to become synonymous with twelve years of assertive leadership, and a major extension of executive powr. This was even implied by the way Roosevelt was known simply by his initials, FDR, with their suggestion of an enclosed word FEDERAL. FDR was the only president to be elected four times and his second election in 1936 set a record for overwhelming victory. Roosevelt's enigmatic personality was the most teasing of any twentieth-century American leader, part patriarch, part child. To his allies he appeared exuberant, charming, and generous. His inviting manner often gave his visitors the impression he agreed with their recommendations and there is little doubt that, like all other leaders, but in his own special way, he used ambiguity as a political tool to rouse support or silence criticism. To his enemies he seemed a duplicitous and vindictive megalomaniac. Despite his patrician education, his experiences in practical politics and his courageous fight to overcome the crippling limitations of his paralysis combined to make him compassionate toward those with physical, social, and psychological disabilities.

He was not an intellectual. Indeed, he was not widely read. He did not have a particularly original mind nor was he capable of sustained analysis. However, he was creative in the imaginative use he could make of the superior talents of others and in the constructive use he could make of apparently conflicting ideas. "A second class intellect—but a first class temperament" was Oliver Wendell Holmes's comment on FDR. His intuitive, flexible approach allowed him to combine both new and old ideas, to retain what worked and to discard what did not. Before making his decisions he sought divers opinions and weighed the myriad questions of public interest and political consequence. His reorganization of the executive was an outstanding administrative achievement. Indeed, contemporary Washington was largely his creation. Thus, as his director of the budget observed, he was "a real artist in government."

Roosevelt transformed the presidency not only beyond its abject position in the years of the Republican ascendancy but also beyond the last formidable resurrection of the office achieved by Theodore Roosevelt and Woodrow Wilson in the progressive period. He dispatched messages to Congress along with draft legislation, and put pressure on committee chairmen and other key figures in Congress through letters and meetings. Thus, by the end of the thirties, Congress expected presidential initiatives. It looked for guidance from the administration from whom it expected a regular program of proposed legislation.

Furthermore, FDR dominated the front pages of newspapers as had no other president before and as none has done since. By his unsurpassed number of 998 press conferences, by getting his aides to answer all letters, which totaled between 5,000 and 8,000 each working day and, most of all, by his 28 radio broadcasts, called "fireside chats" by CBS manager Harry C. Butcher, FDR made himself the most accessible president since Theodore Roosevelt. Roosevelt's fireside chats were, in themselves, models of directness and simplicity, and imbued with his warmth and courage. Indeed, all his speeches and his performance of them showed grace and finish. Roosevelt was in his element with the press, sharpening his political talents and developing his special techniques in conversation, a mix of humor, seriousness, sincerity— and evasion.

Roosevelt's career before and during his presidency was much advanced by the distinctive support of his wife, Eleanor. Theirs was an astonishing political collaboration. She had had the advantage of being Theodore Roosevelt's niece but the disadvantages of being orphaned by the time she was nine and of growing up tall and awkward with protruding teeth. Yet her amazing energy, initiative, and social conscience stirred her to work for social improvement, and, in so doing, find fulfillment. Where FDR was crippled, she was mobile and she moved across the country and reported what she found back to him. But if theirs was a professionally harmonious business relationship, his longest romantic relationship was with Eleanor's part-time social secretary, Lucy Mercer Rutherford, with whom he had started an affair as early as 1913.

Being first lady was, at first, a liberating experience for Eleanor Roosevelt as she delivered lectures, visited slums, and talked to the people. Her column, *My Day,* was syndicated in 135 newspapers and she also wrote a question-and-answer column for the *Woman's House Companion.* In addition, she broadcast on radio twice a week, being sponsored by such products as Sweetheart toilet soap and Simmons mattresses, and she gave her fee to the American Friends Service Committee. But in time she found her role frustrating. Whereas she was committed to various radical and cooperative projects, she could not carry FDR with her. To her critics, her good works were ill-judged and improper interferences. Nevertheless, she enhanced the status of professional women by conferring awards on those whose research had led to social improvement like Alice Hamilton, Harvard expert on industrial toxicology. Throughout her life her constant companion was inner loneliness—the price she paid for professional fulfillment.

The New Dealers and Their Policies

Any examination of the various policies of the New Deal suggests that it was experimental, inconsistent, and diverse. One reason for this is the varied characters and qualities of the New Dealers. Roosevelt's cabinet appointments were a mix of the conventional and the progressive. Secretary of State Cordell Hull, formerly senator from Tennessee, was a typical southern conservative, except on the tariff, which he wanted to reduce, and on international affairs, on which he was, perhaps, more of an expert than anyone else of his generation. Already sixty-one in 1933, he served until 1944—longer than any other secretary of state. In time FDR proved himself closer to the undersecretary, Sumner Welles, than he did to Cordell Hull.

Migrant Mother by Dorothea Lange is one of the classic icons of the Great Depression. Dorothea Lange (1895–1965) of New York began to work as a professional photographer in San Francisco after the theft of her money forced her to abandon a planned trip around the world. Along with thousands of others, this portrait of a modern madonna was taken to publicize Farm Security Administration programs to relieve rural poverty. The young mother of thirty-two was living in a tent with her family in a camp for migrant farm workers in Nipomo, California, in February 1936. They had just sold the car tires to buy food. (Library of Congress).

The most distinctive appointments were those of Harold L. Ickes, Frances Perkins, and Henry A. Wallace. Harold L. Ickes of Chicago, who became secretary of the interior, was a progressive Republican turned Democrat. His lawyer's training gave him instant understanding of corruption in office and his progressive zeal led him to weed it out. He had a fiery temper and liked to be known as "the old curmudgeon." However, he proved a most cautious administrator. Behind his back FDR called him "Donald Duck." Frances Perkins, the first woman in any cabinet, had been a social worker who had served with Smith and FDR at Albany, and now became secretary of labor. Her colleagues disliked her assertiveness and sharp tongue. Yet in Congress Perkins made firm and valuable allies of Senator Robert F. Wagner of New York and Congressman David J. Lewis of Maryland. However, the staid leaders of the AFL disliked her simply because she was a woman. Henry A. Wallace, secretary of agriculture, was the son of Henry C. Wallace, secretary of agriculture under Harding and Coolidge. The son had deserted the Republicans for Al Smith in 1928 and for FDR in 1932. Once in office, he moved decisively into the great problems of agriculture. His solutions were pragmatic and ingenious.

Another innovation was the extensive use of a brains trust, or brain trust, a group of academic advisers somewhat like those used by Theodore Roosevelt and Woodrow Wilson. But FDR broadened the basis of selection, expanded its role, and gave wider publicity to his brains trust to the point of institutionalizing it. From Columbia University Roosevelt used Professors Raymond Moley, Adolf A. Berle, Jr., and Rexford G. Tugwell. These various academics were not just confined to the sidelines as advisers without power. Thus, Raymond Moley was assistant secretary of state in 1933, and Rexford G. Tugwell was assistant secretary of agriculture in 1933 and undersecretary in 1934–1937. Thus were intellectuals transformed into practical experts.

Roosevelt also employed General Hugh ("Ironpants") Johnson, originally of the Army and the Moline Plow Company, who helped write speeches and draft agricultural and business legislation before becoming head of the National Recovery Administration. Lawyers Thomas A. Corcoran and Benjamin

Cohen of Harvard drafted legislation that was "lawyer-proof," including the Securities Exchange Act of 1934. They were eventually superseded as presidential assistants by social worker Harry L. Hopkins who came from New York to head the Federal Emergency Relief Administration in 1933 and then served as administrator of the Works Progress Administration (1935–1938), secretary of commerce (1938–1940), and administrator of Lend-Lease in 1941. It was said of Hopkins that he had the purity of Saint Francis of Assisi combined with the shrewdness of a race-course tout.

Because of the expanded role it allotted to the federal government and the unprecedented volume of legislation, the New Deal encouraged the growth of the legal profession. More lawyers were needed to frame laws, to work as government administrators, and to advise and act for firms and private citizens. Thus, as Jerold S. Auerbach suggests, the New Deal "enabled a new professional elite to ascend to power," a privileged class drawn from those social and ethnic backgrounds that had hitherto excluded them from the white, Anglo-Saxon Protestant legal establishment. Thus "Between 1933 and 1941 professional power in the public arena shifted from a corporate elite, served by Wall Street lawyers, to a legal elite, dominated by New Deal lawyers."

Among the bright young lawyers who came to the capital to work for the New Deal were Dean Acheson, who became, for a brief time, undersecretary of the Treasury; J. W. Fulbright, who worked in the Department of Justice; Hubert Humphrey, who worked as a relief administrator; and Henry Fowler, who worked in the TVA (Tennessee Valley Authority). The Department of Agriculture attracted a formidable array of such talents, including Thurman Arnold, Abe Fortas, Adlai Stevenson, Lee Pressman, and Alger Hiss. Being lawyers, they were obsessed with process. Their obsession with mechanism was a prime factor behind the New Deal's opportunism, its predilection for compromise, and its readiness to accept the existing balance of power between competing interest groups.

The New Dealers were genuinely reform minded and confident they could improve society by reshaping it. To this end they combined the experience of national planning in World War I; the

urban social reforms of Progressives at the turn of the century;
the Populists' aims for agriculture and finance of the 1890s. Ralph
F. de Bedts distinguishes four principal schools of thought among
the New Dealers. Conservatives, such as Jesse Jones and Lewis
Douglas, adhered to traditional laissez-faire economics, accepting
only a limited amount of government interference to reflate the
economy by way of public works, and maintaining the gold
standard at all costs. Their arguments were opposed by the infla-
tionists, successors to the Populists, who wanted monetary inflation and who were willing to use silver as legal tender and alter
the gold content of the dollar. Not surprisingly, this school of
thought was centered in silver states and represented by Senators
Burton K. Wheeler of Montana and Key Pittman of Nevada. A
third school of Progressives favored trust-busting as a means of
breaking up the overwhelming influence of giant corporations for
the sake of the economic health of the whole nation. These
Wilsonians included Louis D. Brandeis of the Supreme Court and
Felix Frankfurter of the Harvard Law School.

The most influential New Dealers we could term economic
planners. They advocated central, planned intervention by the
federal government in the economy, based on the academic rea-
soning of economic progressives like Herbert Croly and Thorstein
Veblen. However, even this fourth group was divided between
conservatives, who wanted to see a partnership between business
and government with business in the lead, and reformers, who
wanted the federal government to regulate business on lines subsequently suggested by English economist John Maynard Keynes.
According to this school, not only was a balanced budget unnecessary but it might also stand in the way of recovery. By trying
to balance the books orthodox accountants were further constrict-
ing demand and helping to intensify the depression they were
trying to raise. The way out of the depression was in debt,
carefully calculated government spending on public works to
create employment in bad times and, thereafter, nicely calculated
government taxation in good times. Thus the government would
act as a stimulating or retarding factor according to circumstances. Among the economic planners, the conservatives were

led by Raymond Moley and Hugh Johnson and the reformers by Adolf A. Berle, Jr., and Rexford G. Tugwell.

One of Roosevelt's prime political skills was his ability to synthesize different ideas. Roosevelt tried to secure the utmost from his team by treating the individuals within it as rivals who were thus obliged to compete with one another and become ever more productive. Thus FDR found the optimum solution to any problem by creating a trial by combat between different theories. Not only did the New Deal attempt to raise the depression with programs for relief and public works but Roosevelt was also concerned about malfunctioning in the American political and economic system as a whole. He was motivated to correct inequalities that the system seemed to perpetuate.

The emphases of the New Deal changed considerably in the period 1933–1938. Thus, for convenience, historians distinguish between the "first" New Deal of 1933–1935, which was primarily devoted to recovery and relief, and the "second" New Deal of 1935–1938, which was aimed at a wide reform of the economic system, by long-term measures to pass on the benefits of modern technology to farmers and consumers whilst providing safeguards against any future depressions. However, there were elements of the "first" New Deal in the "second," and vice versa. But the major emphasis in both is evident. Some historians, such as Barry D. Karl, also distinguish a "third" New Deal in the legislation of 1937 and 1938 that was intended to introduce national planning but foundered in the stormy sea of adversary politics.

The First Hundred Days and the Early New Deal

Because the Democrats had said next to nothing in the election about the need for national economic planning, the impact of the first hundred days was overwhelming. Part of Roosevelt's extraordinary political success in getting his legislation through Congress lay in the new situation. After the twelve years of Republican ascendancy, the new Congress was overwhelmingly Democratic and its freshmen were eager to respond to bold initiatives.

Contemporary revelations by an investigating subcommittee of the Senate Finance Committee had made the public aware of how great was the need for reforms in banking, securities, and the stock market. Under the skillful chairmanship of Democratic Senator Duncan U. Fletcher of Florida and the penetrating and tenacious counsel, Ferdinand Pecora, it exposed exactly how bankers had appropriated funds for their own use and also evaded income tax. The Pecora committee constituted what Frederick Lewis Allen calls "a sort of protracted coroner's inquest upon American finance." Its procession of unwilling witnesses disclosed "a sorry story of public irresponsibility and private greed" that was "spread upon the front pages of the newspapers." Perhaps the most notorious case was that of Charles E. Mitchell.

Great public outrage and the New Dealers' response to these revelations led to the Glass-Steagall Banking Act of June 1933. It separated commercial banks from their investment affiliates so that they could not use either their depositors' funds or the resources of the Federal Reserve for speculation. It also gave the Federal Reserve more control over its tributary, or member, banks. Moreover, it established the Federal Deposit Insurance Corporation (FDIC), which insured clients' deposits up to $2,500 initially, and, later in 1935, up to $5,000, $10,000 in 1950, and subsequently, $15,000. This particular proposal was deeply resented by the American Banking Association, who claimed it was governmental interference. Here the New Deal's support from western and southern banking interests was decisive in getting the act passed.

The Truth-in-Securities Act of 1933 and the Securities Exchange Act of 1934 were inspired by further discourses of the Pecora committee that J. P. Morgan, Jr., had a select list of friends to whom the House of Morgan offered stocks below the market price. They included conservative Democrats Bernard Baruch, John Julius Raskob, and William Gibbs McAdoo, and Republicans Calvin Coolidge and Owen J. Roberts. The drama of the investigations was given wit and point when, during the course of J. P. Morgan's testimony, a circus promoter managed to put a midget on Morgan's knee. Here was capitalism, both large and small, for all America to see. Another discovery was that "pools" had operated to bring about rapid rises in particular stocks, usually by spreading false reports of their value or by intense buying and selling activities. In such ways, a pool created a public appetite for the stock of Radio Corporation of America (RCA), through the agency of the brokers M. J. Meehan and Co. It succeeded in increasing the value of RCA stock from 79 to 109 in seven days, after which the participants sold out to capitalize on their good fortune. Such discoveries led the public to seek protection for investors as well as depositors. Such was the background to two important pieces of stock market legislation.

The Truth-in-Securities Act of 1933 required brokers to furnish complete information to prospective investors as to the true value of securities. Moreover, it held the underwriter and corporate officer responsible for the truthfulness of the stock's registration and the arrangements under which it was sold. The Securities Exchange Act of 1934 established the Securities Exchange Commission (SEC) as a nonpartisan agency to oversee and regulate the activities of all stock exchanges and to prevent fraud and manipulation. Outraged by threat of government surveillance, leaders of the New York Stock Exchange, which accounted for more than 90 percent of national securities trading, threatened to move the exchange to Canada if the bill were passed. But the overwhelming evidence of past malpractice convinced public and Congress alike that the measure was essential. The subsequent trial and imprisonment of Richard Whitney, president of the New York Stock Exchange, for embezzlement in 1938 confirmed public opinion of this. Those who opposed the legislation at first were later convinced that it afforded banking and securities much-needed government protection. On the advice of Raymond Moley, FDR appointed speculator Joseph Kennedy to head the SEC. Moley reasoned that, precisely because Kennedy was a speculator, he knew all the loopholes in the law, and would, therefore, be best equipped to plug them. Perhaps this was why his appointment roused the implacable, but impotent, fury of Wall Street. Kennedy's fortune was so large that he could afford to act against the interest of a speculator clan of which he was a member.

Roosevelt understood that the core of the economic crisis in 1933 was the very low level of prices. The clear remedy was to reverse the process, first by restoring confidence in the banks (which had been recently achieved), and second, by increasing the amount of currency in circulation.

On March 6, 1933, Roosevelt prohibited the redemption of currency in gold coin. On April 5 he issued an executive order whereby gold (coin, certificates, and bullion) had to be delivered to the Federal Reserve in exchange for an equivalent amount in currency or coin. Two weeks later the Treasury announced that it would no longer grant licenses for the export of gold. These several measures had the effect of taking the United States off the gold standard at home while still retaining gold to support its currency and allowing government payments abroad in gold. Lewis Douglas, director of the budget, was aghast at the very idea of taking the dollar off the gold standard. Roosevelt's action, he said, would mean "the end of Western civilization." However, on April 23, 1933, Will Rogers reminded his readers just how irrelevant was all the talk of undermining civilization by abandoning hard money. "The best way to tell when each of us went off the gold is to figure back how many years it was since we had any." Indeed, more informed conservatives than Lewis Douglas, led by such bankers as Charles Gates Dawes, Russell Leffingwell, and J. P. Morgan, Jr., approved FDR's policy of devaluation wholeheartedly.

Roosevelt's policy still left open the possibility that creditors could require debtors to repay loans in gold, instead of currency, and thus they would gain an advantage. Therefore, in June 1933 Congress passed a joint resolution that voided clauses in loan contracts requiring payment in gold. The joint resolution was upheld by the Supreme Court in 1935. The overriding intention behind these various measures was to bring down the value of the dollar on foreign exchanges while raising prices at home. By May 1933 the international value of the dollar had fallen to $0.85 in gold, meaning that other countries could buy 15 percent more American goods than before. At home wholesale prices also showed a slight increase. This success placed FDR in a quandary during the London Economic Conference attended by Secretary of State Cordell Hull in June and July. Delegates from other countries wanted a general stabilization of currencies, including the dollar,

The New Deal goes to war. Fontana Dam, completed in 1944, was built to generate electricity for the U.S. defense effort during World War II. Built on the Little Tennessee River in western North Carolina, Fontana is the highest dam east of the Rocky Mountains. Its three turbine-generator units can produce 238,500 kilowatts of electricity. (Tennessee Valley Authority).

but Roosevelt could not agree to that when the falling value of the dollar was revitalizing the American economy. Thus, for the sake of immediate economic benefits at home, FDR refused American support for any multilateral monetary policy, thereby causing considerable embarrassment to Cordell Hull in London, torpedoing the whole conference, and incurring hostility from Western Europe.

However, the policy of allowing the dollar simply to float in the exchange market produced neither the right level of exchange abroad nor economic recovery at home. Hence, on the advice of the brain trust, FDR decided to bid up the price of gold. The secretary of the treasury, William H. Woodin, was ill at this time and the undersecretary, Dean Acheson, was utterly opposed to the idea. Thus he was obliged to resign and was succeeded by Henry Morgenthau, Jr. On October 22, 1933, FDR announced that the RFC would buy gold on government account above world market price (initially at $31.36 an ounce). The price of gold was fixed by FDR and his advisers each morning. Once Roosevelt increased the price by 21 cents an ounce simply because he liked the number 21. As the price for gold rose, so the value of the dollar declined. In January 1934 the ratio stood at $34.45 = 1 ounce of gold (in comparison with March 1933 when it had stood at $20.67 = 1 ounce of gold). In effect, the dollar had been devalued by 40 percent. This was what Al Smith called a "baloney dollar."

FDR now decided to stabilize things. In the Gold Reserve Act of January 30, 1934, Congress set the price of gold at $35 an ounce. However, the silver lobby was sufficiently influential to oblige FDR and Congress to accept a Silver Purchase Act of June 1934, requiring the Treasury to buy silver both at home and abroad until a quarter of all United States monetary stocks was in silver or until the market price of silver had reached $1.29 an ounce. This quite unnecessary piece of legislation was no more than a bribe to a powerful special interest group. It seemed every cloud had a silver lining.

For its chief strike against the depression the government proposed a special agency, the National Recovery Administration (NRA). The National Industrial Recovery Act was passed by Congress on June 16, 1933 (the last of the first hundred days). It tried to achieve planning and cooperation between the three sectors of business, labor, and government. Industry received government support in its aims to reduce cutthroat competition and unfair practices and, in return, made certain concessions to labor that were thought to be in the national interest and would promote recovery. Title I of the act declared a state of national emergency and suspended some antitrust laws. It established the National Recovery Administration (NRA), required government and industry to draw up codes of practice as to business competition, and hours and wages. Public hearings would be held before the NRA to determine that the interests of business, labor, and government (as the guardian of consumer and general interests) were being observed in individual industries. After approval by the president, individual codes of practice, agreed at the hearings, would become legally binding and, thereafter, action under the code would be exempt from the antitrust laws. Section 7a declared that employees could join unions, appoint officers, and were entitled to collective bargaining. Thus the act accepted the existence of giant corporations and, to protect the public from abuse, relied solely on cooperation between business and government.

Title II authorized the president to create an emergency Public Works Administration (PWA) with $3.3 billion for "pump priming" expenditures on such public works as highways, dams, schools, and federal buildings. The PWA was put in charge of Secretary of the Interior Harold L. Ickes. General Hugh S. Johnson was given control of the NRA.

Johnson was a troubleshooter of diverse experience and considerable initiative. At the very outset he predicted for the *New York Times* of June 17, 1933, just how chequered would be the career of the NRA in an extraordinary mix of metaphors, "It will be red fire at first and dead cats afterwards. This is just like mounting the guillotine on the infinitesimal gamble that the ax won't work." Within three weeks Johnson had persuaded the heads of the textile industry to agree to the first set of NRA codes. Finally, 557 basic codes were approved, encompassing every sort of business from bottle caps to brassieres and burlesque theaters. To expedite proceedings, Johnson devised a blanket code, known as the President's Reemployment Agreement, that allowed small businesses to subscribe to the main tenets of the NRA on hours and conditions of work and wages without the inconvenience of lengthy hearings. In this way he hoped to increase employment and purchasing power quickly. Those who conformed were entitled to display an emblem, the Blue Eagle, underneath which was inscribed the motto, "We Do Our Part." To achieve maximum publicity Johnson also organized rallies and parades with songs and dances.

However, the NRA aroused widespread dissatisfaction. Consumers said the NRA had led to a steep rise in prices ahead of wages. Labor said Section 7a was inadequate for its needs and that, anyway, it could be circumvented by unscrupulous employers. Small businesses said the codes were drafted by big business in its own interests. Moreover, they did not have the resources to comply with the sort of far-reaching regulations devised for large firms. In particular, they could not always afford the minimum wages prescribed by the codes. Although it held the trump cards, big business was increasingly alarmed at the prospect of increased government regulation and the gains of organized labor. It regarded the NRA as the thin end of a most unwelcome wedge.

Unexpectedly, opposition to the NRA grew in other quarters. On March 7, 1934, Congress established the National Recovery Review Board under criminal lawyer Clarence Darrow to study monopolistic tendencies in the codes. Its report emphasized that the NRA encouraged the monopoly tactics of big business. Public respect for the NRA was damaged further when a dry cleaner was sent to jail in New Jersey for pressing trousers for less than the regular code price. Furthermore, FDR realized that Johnson, whom he admired, was something of a liability for his outspoken comments in the face of so much criticism. When the press discovered his liking for alcohol and love for his secretary, he justified her high salary by saying "she was more than a stenographer" and when they reported that he complained, "Boys you're hitting below the belt." FDR replaced him with Donald Richberg, and then relaxed some of the codes.

The final blow came on May 27, 1935, when the Supreme Court, in the case of *Schechter Poultry Corporation* v. *The United States,* invalidated the NRA. The *Schechter* case concerned an appeal by operators of a slaughterhouse against conviction for having broken the code of fair competition agreed by the live poultry industry in New York City. The Court unanimously declared that the NRA was unconstitutional on two grounds. First, Congress had delegated its powers to the executive in violation of the constitutional principles of separation of power. Second, it had wrongly laid down federal regulation of intrastate commerce as well as of interstate activities. FDR was outraged and told his press conference of May 31, 1935, "We have been relegated to the horse-and-buggy definition of interstate commerce." This bitter climax to mounting public censure of the NRA masked the fact that the NRA had to face almost insurmountable obstacles.

Years later Moley and Tugwell thought the *Schechter* decision against the NRA was a turning point for the New Deal. FDR was deeply disillusioned and abandoned his early idealism. Instead of another umbrella reform, Roosevelt decided to extract the NRA's good features, such as collective bargaining, maximum hours, and minimum wages, and enact them separately.

Agricultural recovery was just as complex a problem as industrial recovery. Moreover, its solution was even more urgent since the ills of agriculture had led to violence in some parts of the Midwest. There were two principal problems: the increasing number of mortgage foreclosures on farms; and the fact that farm purchasing power, in terms of the industrial goods farmers had to buy, was at its lowest level ever. Thus FDR proposed another series of emergency measures. On March 27, 1933, he centralized those agencies dealing with agricultural credit in the Farm Credit Administration. In April 1933 Congress passed the Emergency Farm Mortgage Act to fund emergency loans for farmers in immediate danger of losing their farms and, subsequently, short-term loans for livestock farmers. The Frazier-Lemke Farm Bankruptcy Act of June 1934 enabled farmers to recover farms previously lost when mortgages had been foreclosed and it allowed them to do so on terms prescribed by a federal court with interest set at only 1 percent.

As to long-term measures, there was the same variety of opinions about agriculture as there had been on industrial recovery. FDR and Secretary of Agriculture Henry A. Wallace conferred with farm leaders to consolidate various ideas in the Agriculture Adjustment Act of May 12, 1933. The new supervising agency was the Agricultural Adjustment Administration (AAA) that declared the following were staple crops: wheat, corn, cotton, tobacco, rice, milk, hogs—and, later, added livestock and sugar. Individual farmers made an agreement by which, in exchange for acres taken out of cultivation, they were given benefit payments. The money to finance the program came from a tax levied on processors of staple foods who passed on the tax to consumers by way of higher prices. George N. Peek became head of the AAA and, through his agents, he persuaded cotton farmers to plow under 10 million acres, a quarter of the crop, in return for benefit payments. The AAA also bought 6 million piglets that were slaughtered and processed to feed the unemployed. Thus was plenty destroyed in the midst of want. Public outcry on behalf of the slaughtered piglets vented itself in abuse of AAA officials. Few, including the farmers, understood the underlying principles behind government policy. Cotton farmers plowed under a quarter of the crop in exchange for benefits but overfertilized the remaining land so that the 1933 crop actually surpassed the 1932 crop of 13 million bales by 45,000 bales. In response to this counterproductive activity, Congress passed the Bankhead Cotton Control Act of 1934 that set production quotas for cotton and placed a prohibitive tax on all cotton sold in excess of the quota. The Kerr-Smith Tobacco Act of June 1934 introduced the same sort of restrictions on tobacco farmers.

To solve the problems of farm tenancy, the Resettlement Administration, established in April 1935 under Rexford G. Tugwell, tried to move farmers from poor land to new cooperative communities but without much success. In the Bankhead-Jones Farm Tenant Act of July 1937 Congress tried to raise farm tenants and sharecroppers to the status of owners. It established the Farm Security Administration that allowed tenants to borrow money at 3 percent interest to purchase land. Over a three-year period it made available small rehabilitation loans of an average of $350 each to 750,000 tenant farmers.

The achievements of the AAA were considerable. In 1933 10.4 million acres were taken out of production; in 1934, 35.7 million acres; and in 1935 30.3 million acres. Partly because of these policies of crop limitation and partly because of serious droughts, farm prices rose. A bushel of wheat fetched, on average, only 33 cents in 1933, but, thereafter, the price rose gradually to 88 cents in 1938. In sum, total farm income rose from $4.5 billion in 1932 to $6.9 billion in 1935. Thus farmers were a third better off financially by 1935 than they had been in 1932.

Above all, the AAA was also a creation of considerable political significance since it allowed FDR and the New Dealers to put into practice their central conception of balance between the various sections of the economic community and to persuade urban congressmen that a revitalized economy could not be built upon a declining agriculture.

Dam the Flowing Tide

The reform that became synonymous with the New Deal in the early days was the Tennessee Valley Authority. It combined agricultural and industrial blows at the depression. The valleys of southern Alleghenies were a poverty-stricken area, their soils washed away by a fatal combination of exploitive hillside farming, heavy rainfalls, and frequent flooding. Conservationists wanted a coordinated strategy to preserve the region from itself. In 1908 Theodore Roosevelt sent Congress a report of the Inland Waterways Commission that proposed a coordinated approach to the problems. By the National Defense Act of 1916, Woodrow Wilson intended the building of an Alabama nitrate plant at Muscle Shoals to avoid dependence on foreign sources of energy, especially in wartime. However, the plants were not finished until the end of the war. Sensing their future industrial potential, in 1921 Henry Ford offered the secretary of war an annual rental of $1.5 million for the facilities to produce electric power and to manufacture nitrates for use as fertilizers. However, the plants had cost $80 million to build and, thus, progressive Senator George W. Norris of Nebraska, chairman of the Senate Agriculture Committee, successfully opposed this fraudulent offer on the grounds that it was a gross act of exploitation of community resources. Norris's own bill to make the Muscle Shoals project the center of a vast water and regional power project was vetoed by Coolidge in 1928 and then by Hoover in 1929. In contrast, FDR supported the idea.

On April 10, 1933, having conferred with Norris, FDR asked Congress to create the Tennessee Valley Authority (TVA), which was achieved in an act passed on May 18, 1933. Under the terms of the act, the TVA was to complete and extend the Muscle Shoals project, creating a new 650-mile inland waterway to connect the South with the Great Lakes, the Ohio River, and the

Missouri and Mississippi river systems. The TVA was to construct new dams and improve existing ones, to control floods, to generate cheap hydroelectric power, to manufacture fertilizers, to check erosion, and to provide reforestation. It had the right to fix the resale rates of power it generated—"the yardstick"—by which the rates of competing private utility companies could also be elevated. In general, under a board of three directors, it was to promote the economic and social welfare of people in seven states, extending for an area of 80,000 square miles with a population of 2 million.

The waterway allowed the importation of sorely needed automobiles, iron, cement, and gas to the region via barges. The TVA invented new fertilizers, showed farmers how to conserve moisture in the soil, and how to use contour plowing and cover crops. Thus, farm income in Tennessee improved by 200 percent in the period 1929–49, compared with a national average improvement of 170 percent during the same time. The TVA encouraged wider and greater use of electricity and the penetration of industry into the region to benefit from cheap hydroelectric power. By the early 1940s the TVA's average annual consumption of electricity was 1,180 kilowatt-hours per person at the rate of 2 cents per hour, compared with a national average of 850 kilowatt-hours per person, at the rate of 4 cents an hour.

The TVA statute of incorporation put the manufacture and distribution of electricity into a secondary role as a byproduct. This was partly because the New Dealers expected the private power companies to complain of unfair competition to the Supreme Court. Thus they forced the Court to find that the actual wording of the act would not allow it to decide against the TVA. In the cases of *Ashwander* v. *TVA* of February 1936 and *Tennessee Electric Power Company* v. *TVA* of January 1939 the Court upheld the constitutionality of the TVA and its right to sell electricity. The leader of the concerted attack by nineteen private companies against the TVA was Wendell L. Willkie, president of Commonwealth and Southern, who then sold the entire facilities of the Tennessee Electric Power Company to the TVA for $78.6 million, a rather high price.

The concept of the yardstick provoked greater controversy. It was impossible to distinguish between the cost of actually producing electricity from such necessary safety precautions as dam maintenance and flood control. In later years, the TVA provided power for the entire aluminum industry and also for the development of the atomic bomb. It led to the creation of new areas of recreation for tourists. Most significant, it advanced the opportunities for an entire region, an impressive, if overdue, experiment in social renewal.

The great dams of the 1930s were as formidable a contribution to the world of American machines as were the suspension bridges. Not only did such creations as the Hoover, Grand Coulee, and Tennessee Valley Authority dams provide irrigation, prevent flooding, generate electricity, and allow more land to be farmed but they also, in turn, transformed the living conditions of millions, while ushering in a new era of hydroelectric power. The creation of such huge multifunctional dams captured the imagination of all classes and generations who lived through the Great Depression and who recognized in this one striking feature of the New Deal a benevolent achievement of governmental planning. They also recognized that here was a potent symbol of man's ability to control the environment and harness the forces of nature for the improvement of society.

Although the United States had enjoyed the benefits of such dams as the Arrowrock, Idaho, (1912–1916) and the Deadwood, Idaho, (1929–1930), it was in the 1930s that the country entered a formative period of dam building, commencing with the Hoover Dam, Boulder City, Nevada (1930–1936). This dam, situated over the Colorado River in the hostile, torrid desert, thirty miles from Las Vegas, gave rise to Boulder City, a dormitory and service town for its numerous engineers, 5,000 construction workers, and their families. At the time of completion, at over 726 feet and with 3.40 million cubic yards of concrete, it was the highest and largest dam in the world with the largest reservoir, Lake Mead, with 28,53 million acre feet of water. It also had the largest power capacity. Continuous construction by day and night was undertaken in daunting circumstances, with summer temperatures on and under the site of between 120° and 140° and winter temperatures below 20° with such hazards as blustery winds.

There was also the mighty Colorado River that threatened to engulf the entire project, and workers imperiled by natural and machine-made hazards as they swung along canyon walls to strip away rock. The excitement and drama of construction were captured by photographer Ben Glaha for the Bureau of Reclamation.

Before actual construction, it was necessary to divert the Colorado River through man-made tunnels, erecting temporary cofferdams to block the river, and finally, excavating the site. These were monumental feats of engineering and only afterward could dam and power plant be constructed. There were other, major, technical problems. If the concrete used for retaining was simply poured down, it would have taken about a hundred years to cool and harden and it would then have shrunk so much as to crack the entire edifice. The solution was to pour individual slabs of concrete and hasten their cooling by circulating refrigerated water through them by means of tubes, thereby cooling each section in seventy-two hours.

As to the appearance of the dam, the engineers used consultant architect Gordon B. Kaufmann of Los Angeles to provide a facade that would arise naturally from the landscape and yet dominate it by means of setbacks, surmounted by winged bronze monuments designed by Oskar J. W. Hansen, and a powerhouse designed in an orthodox streamlined fashion.

The Hoover Dam set the pattern for the eight dams of the Tennessee Valley Authority constructed in the period 1933–1941 that also included such construction villages as Norris, Tennessee, named after the progressive senator for Nebraska who had championed the scheme. The Norris Freeway was a two-lane, limited-access road linking dam and town to Knoxville. Not only did civil engineer Arthur E. Morgan want the best possible technical engineering for construction but he also wanted the best possible social engineering for the construction workers and their families and not just some hastily erected shanty town that would become a desolate ghost town as soon as the immediate project was completed. Architectural historian Richard Guy Wilson observes in *The Machine Age in America* (1986) how "TVA architecture— the dams, powerhouses, locks, visitors centers, and mounted buildings—exhibits a common aesthetic, the attempt to monumentalize and emphasize machine iconography. Simple forms, great sheer surfaces where possible, the particularization of details, and the machines themselves—whether Gantry Cranes at Kentucky Dam, 1938–41, or the turbines at the Pickwick Landing Dam, 1934–1938—make the dams more than functional engineering; they became works of great art."

Relief

A central aim of the New Deal in its early days was to provide relief on a scale never previously attempted. What had most deterred the Hoover administration from a vast program of federal relief was the cost involved. The federal government simply did not have sufficient revenue. And it was clear that, while the orthodox wisdom of a balanced budget remained government policy, nothing could be done.

Unlike his predecessor, FDR was willing to depart from the conventional wisdom to relieve widespread distress. The first significant relief measure was aimed at young people between the ages of eighteen and twenty-five, a proportion of the unemployed that was quite disproportionate to the actual numbers of the group. The Civilian Conservation Corps Reforestation Relief Act of March 31, 1933, created the very first New Deal agency, and the one that most bore the imprint of FDR and his earlier reforestation projects in New York State. The Civilian Conservation Corps (CCC), managed jointly by the departments of Labor and the Interior, organized projects of reforestation, soil conservation, building firebreaks and forest lookout towers, and constructing recreational facilities in national parks. FDR was singularly impressed by the organizational skills of General Douglas MacArthur and Colonel George C. Marshall. Between 1933 and 1942 more than 2 million young men served in the agency, usually for periods of about nine months. Their pay was $30 per month, plus board and lodging, and $25 was sent to the youths' families in order to spread relief and purchasing power.

To provide relief for the urban unemployed the Federal Emergency Relief Act of May 12, 1933, established the Federal

Emergency Relief Administration (FERA) under Harry L. Hopkins. It divided its appropriation of $500 million evenly between the states, providing $1 for every $3 spent by the local authorities, with the remaining half going outright to the poorest states for direct relief.

The Public Works Administration of July 1933, established under Title II of the National Industrial Recovery Act (NIRA) and placed under the supervision of Secretary of the Interior Ickes, was intended to revitalize industry by creating public works to stimulate the need for capital goods. However, Ickes proved so cautious in dispensing the allocation of $3.3 billion that the PWA did very little to stimulate recovery or provide relief. FDR, somewhat disturbed by this and acting on the advice of Harry Hopkins, took $400 million of PWA money and created a new, temporary agency, the Civil Works Administration (CWA) in November 1933 and asked Hopkins to run it. It was this that led directly to the rise of Hopkins within the New Deal and his eventual ascendancy over all of FDR's other advisers. The CWA put more than 4 million people to work in the winter of 1933–1934 in various makeshift projects, but it drew opposition from both Republicans and Democrats and FDR closed it in early 1934. FERA was then given extra funds and thus increased its family allowance payments to $35 per month by July 1935. However, the PWA became a major achievement, creating schools, bridges, dams, sewers, post offices, and court houses.

To prevent foreclosure of domestic mortgages, Congress, by the Home Owners Refinancing Act of May 13, 1933, created the Home Owners Loan Corporation. It rescued urban home mortgages by refinancing the loans at lower rates of interest over longer periods of time. In June 1934 Congress established the Federal Housing Administration (FHA), a system of federal mortgage insurance, permitted to insure up to 80 percent, and later, 90 percent of newly constructed homes costing $6,000 or less at low rates of interest payable over long periods. Thus, it also tried to revive the stagnant construction industry. Moreover, it made home ownership possible for many who would otherwise never have had the opportunity to buy their own house.

Such extensive spending on relief increased the federal debt from $19.5 billion in early 1933 to $22.5 billion in late 1933. Once various state, municipal, and other resources had been depleted and the federal government assumed greater burdens, it rose to $28.7 billion in 1935 and then, in 1937, to $36.4 billion. Thereafter, its rise was the direct result of military expenditures. Later, when the debt reached astronomical heights, there was much less criticism of deficit financing than in the early days, when its levels were modest. Thus objections were not really about the actual size of the debt so much as the way the money was spent.

As business gradually revived in 1933, there was talk of a Roosevelt market. The Federal Reserve Board's adjusted index figure for industrial production rose from 59 in March 1933 to 100 in July 1933 (compared with the 1929 high of 125). However, there followed a setback. In August the index fell from 100 to 91 and by November it had receded further to 72. Not until December 1933 did it recover its position at 101. This fall was damaging psychologically. People had expected much of the New Deal and the NRA in particular, and their disappointment was keen. For this and other reasons, FDR and his cabinet were well aware that their emergency legislation had still not brought recovery and that more fundamental reforms were necessary. Thus did FDR's own progressivism become more sharply defined and more readily implemented.

The humanitarianism of the New Deal deeply touched the electorate, which rewarded the administration in the midterm congressional elections with an unprecedented Democratic majority. The Republicans lost twenty-six out of thirty-five contested seats in the Senate and the Democratic majority in the House was increased to 318 against 99 Republicans and 11 others, who normally voted with the Democrats. In the state elections only seven states survived the Democratic landslide. The midterm elections proved conclusively that the political balance had shifted from the Republicans to the Democrats. Congress would now have a far more liberal complexion than ever before and the new congressmen were increasingly impatient of compromise legislation. Moreover, the problems of the depression would actually get more complex and demand more radical solutions than anything yet attempted.

The Dust Bowl

The coming of the New Deal may have brought happy days to Washington but elsewhere it was still hard times. In certain regions the depression had actually deepened. Perhaps the greatest terrors were reserved for the inhabitants of the Dust Bowl, the states of North and South Dakota, Montana, western Kansas, eastern Colorado, Oklahoma, and northern Texas. Here, an inhospitable climate and harsh geography were transformed by human mismanagement into a graveyard for the American dream of agrarian opportunity.

Once the Great American Desert was settled with improved methods of farming, it was exploited by overplowing with John Deere plows that cut below the topsoil and by overgrazing. During World War I tractors for large-scale machine farming were used to expand crop production in order to supply America and Europe with more grain, principally wheat. What remained of the steppe grass and sod covering that protected the Great Plains was ruthlessly plowed away. This was a triumph of factory methods over the farm and the process continued its relentless, exploitive way during the twenties. At first, years of exceptional, heavy rain hid the true significance of human mismanagement. However, in dry years, the topsoil simply blew away. As the tragedy unfolded, the government began to count the cost. The National Resources Board estimated in 1934 that 35 million acres of previously arable land had been destroyed, that the soil of another 125 million acres had been exhausted or removed, and that another 100 million acres of land were threatened. By this time the Dust Bowl comprised 756 counties in 19 states.

The extent of the tragedy drew a wealth of commentary. In an article, "Saga of Drought," for *Commonwealth* of September 14, 1934, Charles Morrow Wilson recorded a common enough scene in a series of staccato statements, each with the precision of a telegram message.

Southwest is parched. Temperature above 100 in shade for forty-three successive days. Missouri Pacific Railway hauling tankcars of water for

Farmer and Sons Walking in the Face of a Dust Storm, 1936, by Arthur Rothstein. Rothstein was the first photographer to join the Farm Security Administration project. In this photograph he had father and older son pose carefully, leaning against the wind as they walked in front of a shed, partly submerged by dust, and had the smaller son hold back, covering his face with his hands. Thus Rothstein dramatized their poverty at the mercy of the elements. (Library of Congress).

use of livestock. First time in history. Sam Nance, farmer near Ardmore, Oklahoma, shoots 143 head of cattle to save them from starving. Cotton crop one-half normal. Apples, peaches, small fruits 30 percent normal. Livestock congesting packing centers. Beef selling on foot as low as $.01 a pound. Pasturage exhausted. States too broke to grant drought aid. United States adjudges 81 counties for primary emergency relief; 119 for secondary. Arkansas river four feet below normal record. Town and city reservoirs failing. Churches praying for rain in many parts of Arkansas, Oklahoma and Texas.

Chronic agricultural problems were then worsened by a series of great windstorms of which the first began in South Dakota on

November 11, 1933, and spread its pall as far south as Texas. This was the great black blizzard. In her article, "Dust," for the *New Republic* of May 1, 1935, commentator Avis D. Carlson described what it was like to be caught in a dust storm.

The impact is like a shovelful of fine sand flung against the face. People caught in their own yards grope for the doorstep. Cars come to a standstill, for no light in the world can penetrate that swirling murk.

Dust masks are snatched from pockets and cupboards. But masks do not protect the mouth. Grit cracks between the teeth, the dust taste lies bitter on the tongue, grime is harsh between the lips. . . .

In time the fury subsides. If the wind has spent itself, the dust will fall silently for hours. If the wind has settled into a good steady blow, the air will be thick for days. During those days as much of living as possible will be moved to the basement, while pounds and pounds of dust sift into the house. It is something, however, to have the house stop rocking and mumbling.

Then, after years of praying for rain, settlers and townsfolk had their requests answered with a terrible vengeance. When the rains came they did not stop. The *New York Times* of January 23, 1937, reported how floods had made 150,000 homeless in twelve states. Conditions were worst in Indiana, Kentucky, Ohio, and Tennessee. Refugees sheltered from snow and sleet in box cars, public buildings, churches, and tents. *Time* magazine of February 8, 1937, recorded how the Ohio River "looked like a shoreless yellow sea studded here and there with tree tops and half submerged buildings. To people crouching on house roofs, it was an immeasurable amount of ugly yellow water surging higher and higher hours without end. . . ." Finally, perhaps half a million people were made homeless. In all, floods and windstorms claimed 3,678 lives in the mid-thirties.

In national terms drought and flood achieved what the federal limitation on crops could not. They eliminated surplus. For the hapless individuals involved, it was utterly disastrous. Thousands upon thousands of farms failed. When their owners could not meet their mortgage payments, the banks foreclosed them. The U.S. Department of Agriculture Bureau of Agricultural Economics estimated that in 1933 93.6 farms in every 1,000 changed hands and 54.1 of these sales were forced or somehow related to defaults. This was the greatest number of farm transfers in the 1930s, but every year the number was in the low 70s or high 60s per 1,000 farms, until 1939 when it fell to 63.8 sales per 1,000 farms.

Most farmers who lost their farms did so because they got into a bottomless pit of debt to banks, insurance companies, or private investors. Some were held by the government for nonpayment of taxes. In 1934 the National Resources Board estimated that almost 30 percent of the value of farm land in the West and Midwest was owned by government agencies or private creditors. In the Great Depression as many as 42 percent of farmers were tenants, compared with only 25 percent in 1880. Moreover, in 1935 less than two-thirds of tenant farmers had lived on their land for more than a year. Tenancy had various disadvantages. Tenants were much less likely to settle than owners and they did not share owners' special concern for land and equipment. The whole agricultural system encouraged restless mobility down the socioeconomic scale.

By its policies, the New Deal's agricultural agency, the AAA, encouraged the process. A farm owner who was being subsidized for growing less could afford to evict his tenants or sharecroppers, live off the federal check, buy tractors and other labor-saving implements, and then hire labor by the day instead of throughout the year. The displacement of agricultural workers was most noticeable in cotton production. In 1930–1937 sales of farm tractors in ten cotton states rose by 90 percent. Whereas the actual number of farms increased in the rest of the country, in the southern and southwestern states it actually declined. Paul S. Taylor, who studied two cotton producing counties in Texas, observed on the sharp decline in the number of farms, "commonly, the landlord who purchases a tractor throws two 160-acre farms operated by tenants into an operating unit and lets both tenants go. Sometimes the rate of displacement is greater, rising to 8, 10, and even 15 families of tenants."

One consequence common to both industrial and agricultural depressions was that millions of people were uprooted. The thirties was a decade of great migrations. Some states lost population —Vermont, the Dakotas, Kansas, Nebraska, and Oklahoma. The largest migrations were from the South and the Appalachians to the industrial centers of Ohio, Illinois, Indiana, and Michigan. However, it was states with warm climates that were most likely to be attractive to migrants—Arizona, California, and Florida. Indeed, the general movement to the Pacific was, eventually, to make California the most populous state.

One sort of migration was more famous than another of the others. In 1934 and 1935 Okies, dispossessed farmers, not only from Oklahoma but also Arkansas, Texas, and elsewhere, began to cross into California, looking for work as fruit pickers. They traveled in old jalopies along U.S. Highway 30 through the Idaho hills and along Highway 66 across New Mexico and Arizona.

The most famous record of the Okies' migration was provided by John Steinbeck in his best-selling novel, *The Grapes of Wrath* (1939). Steinbeck recorded the early movement of the migrant families who, ironically, could only ensure the survival of their individual members by splitting up. He followed the declining fortunes of a fictitious family, the Joads, whose miseries are caused by the intransigence of banks, the indifference of government, and their own incapacity to adjust to a changing world.

However, the mass migration was not welcome to residents of California who dreaded the sudden influx of destitute Okies and the social dislocation it would cause. A billboard on the Nevada-California border of 1935 proclaimed "Okies Go Home: No Relief Available in California." Once they were actually in California the Okies found themselves in desperate competition for work with such other itinerant families as evicted sharecroppers from Alabama, tenant farmers from Arkansas, and perennial vagabonds. In no time at all the California labor market for fruit pickers and other menial agricultural work became glutted. Thus, in the words of Frederick Lewis Allen, "to the vast majority of the refugees the promised land proved to be a place of new and cruel tragedy."

6

STORMY WEATHER
The Later New Deal

Thunder from Right and Left

ONCE BIG business discerned the beginnings of recovery, it began to vent unreasonable diatribes on "that man in the White House" and his progressive measures. Whereas to his admirers, FDR was leading the country through a period of momentous reforms, to his critics, he was fomenting class rivalry, undermining the American system of free enterprise, and trying to undermine the Constitution. Marquis W. Childs analyzed the hatred FDR aroused in an article, "They Hate Roosevelt," for *Harper's* of May 1936. He described this hatred as a passion and an irrational fury that permeates "the whole upper stratum of American society." Among the lackeys of the plutocracy it became something of a status symbol to revile Roosevelt in the most scurrilous terms. There were bitter jokes such as the one about the eminent psychiatrist summoned prematurely to Heaven to treat God "because He has delusions of grandeur—He thinks He is Franklin D. Roosevelt."

It was said of Roosevelt by his enemies that he was a traitor to his class. What they meant was that, since Roosevelt came from an upper-class Hudson River family, it should have been his intention to protect the old plutocracy. However, instead of rewarding industrial entrepreneurs and landowners for their contribution to American society, the New Deal made relief to the indigent poor a priority. This, according to the orthodox wisdom, was tantamount to encouraging idleness among the workshy, as well as going against the Protestant work ethic and the American myth of rags to riches.

More significantly, the dominant plutocracy objected to the fact that relief payments, programs of public works, and an expanded bureaucracy to administer them could only be paid for by increased taxation on themselves. This came most decisively in the Revenue Act of 1936 that imposed higher taxes on gifts and estates, on corporate incomes and high personal incomes. What they most resented, therefore, was not the theory but paying for the relief. In addition, the plutocracy resented legislation that curbed their own financial activities, in such measures as the Glass-Steagall Banking Act and the Truth-in-Securities Act, both in 1933, and the Securities Exchange Act of 1934.

Of course, far from being a traitor to his class, Roosevelt was its savior. Government supervision of banking and the stock market not only ensured prevention of the worst abuses of the 1920s but also provided an implicit government seal of approval of the way finances, both high and low, checking and speculative, were conducted. Moreover, those despised later measures of social reform, such as the Social Security and Wagner acts of 1935, and the more equable distribution of wealth achieved by other acts, undercut the appeal of revolutionary movements that sought to overturn the entire capitalistic system. Thus FDR and the New Dealers reformed the system in order to preserve it. The essence of the New Deal was a conservative treatment of radical problems.

However, at the time the plutocracy could not see the wood for the trees. In August 1934 business leaders, including former ardent supporters of FDR in 1932 in the former AAPA, constituted themselves the American Liberty League, determined to

"Who's Afraid of the Big, Bad Wolf?" The wise little pig who built his house of bricks, unlike the foolish pigs who built theirs of straw or hay, has the pleasure of seeing the big, bad wolf descend the chimney only to get a roasting in the stewpot over the hearth. The situation and song in Walt Disney's classic cartoon movie were taken as symbols of the United States' cheerful determination to defy and beat the ravenous wolves of the Great Depression at home and cataclysmic wars in Europe and Asia overseas. (Walt Disney Productions; RKO Pictures; Museum of Modern Art Film Stills Archive).

encompass his destruction. It was bipartisan but led by John Julius Raskob, and R. R. M. Carpenter, brother-in-law to the Du Ponts and vice-president of the Du Pont Corporation. The new league could count on other big guns of business and their considerable financial resources. It adopted the same membership and had the same influence as had its predecessor, the AAPA, attracting such capitalists as newspaper magnate William Randolph Hearst, the three Du Pont brothers, Sewell L. Avery of Montgomery Ward, and Colby M. Chester, president of General Foods. They orchestrated press campaigns criticizing FDR's dictatorial methods, the invasion of individual freedoms by the New Deal, and the allegedly communistic legislation in support of labor unions. R. R. M. Carpenter was supposed to have told Raskob with much indignation, "five Negroes on my place refused to work this spring, saying that they had an easy job with the government," and, "a cook on my houseboat quit because the government was paying him $1 an hour as a painter."

There was also thunder from the Left. In California novelist Upton Sinclair had published a campaign document, *I, Governor of California and How I Ended Poverty*, in 1933, which sold about a million copies and encouraged the growth of an insurgency movement, EPIC (End Poverty in California). Its program was a mix of state socialism and rural cooperatives, in which unemployed people were to be allowed to produce work on cooperative farms or factories leased by the state. They would be paid in scrip that could be used only to buy food or goods produced by the cooperatives. Upton Sinclair won the support of novelist Theodore Dreiser, poet Archibald MacLeish, and lawyer Clarence Darrow. He roused Democrats in the state party and took the nomination for governor from party favorite George Creel in the primary election of August 1934 with a far greater majority than the incumbent governor, Frank Merriam, achieved in the Republican party.

Sinclair's campaign provoked concerted opposition from conservatives of both parties and the federal government allied together in an attempt to defeat him. It drew on the resources of Hollywood, which produced fake newsreels showing jobless hordes swarming across the state lines to become expensive wards of California. As a result of their nicely timed and well-orchestrated campaign, Merriam trounced Sinclair by 260,000 votes in the election and another 303,000 votes went to a third-party candidate.

More troublesome to FDR was Dr. Francis E. Townsend, a retired medical doctor, originally from Illinois but now living in Long Beach, California, where he had worked as assistant county health officer until forced to retire in 1933 at the age of sixty-six with less than $200 in savings and no other means of earning his living. He proposed old age pensions for people retired at sixty who would receive $200 per month, provided they took on no extra work and spent the entire sum within the month in the United States. The Townsend plan was to be financed (initially) by a 2 percent tax on all business transactions. This was later amended to direct income tax on corporations and individuals. The Townsend scheme appealed to millions across the country whose plight and feelings of hopelessness were similar to his own. Moreover, Townsend claimed that the retirement of people over sixty would create vast job opportunities for the young unemployed and that the introduction of monthly pensions would further stimulate the economy by creating a demand for goods and services that would, in turn, generate more jobs.

Townsend took on a partner, Robert E. Clements, an energetic Texas realtor of thirty-nine, and together they incorporated Old Age Revolving Pensions, Ltd., on January 1, 1934, dispatching literature to all and sundry. Having launched Townsend Clubs across the country and built up a membership of 1.5 million, they started publishing a newspaper, the *Townsend National Weekly,* and began lobbying Congress with a series of mass petitions. As a result of their campaign, Congressman John S. McGroarty of California, who owed his election to the support of local Townsend Clubs, introduced a pension bill into the House in early 1935. It was opposed by the administration as expensive and impractical.

By far the most aggressive and noisome criticisms of the New Deal came from Senator Huey Long of Louisiana and Father Charles Coughlin of Michigan. Drawing on the residue of the old Populist movement in the South and Midwest, they both launched effective crusades against the encroaching power of the federal government. Alan Brinkley, a recent historian of the Long and Coughlin movements, observes in his *Voices of Protest* (1982) how the two leaders used their eloquence to evoke and express a dissident ideology. They affirmed values and institutions threatened by modern developments and offered their followers promise of a fairer society in which traditional values and institutions would be protected. They ascribed current social and economic problems to a selective list of scapegoats, principally the unseen interests of Wall Street, and they promised to prevent any further expansion of government.

Senator Huey P. Long, the self-styled "Kingfish" of Louisiana, was an amazing phenomenon even among southern demagogues. He combined genuine compassion for the dispossessed with ruthless political ambition. Born in 1893 into an extremely poor area of Louisiana, Winn Parish, where his father rose from obscurity to owning the town bank, Huey Long first went to work as a door-to-door salesman. After studying at the Tulane University Law School for only eight months, he learned enough to pass a bar examination and began to practice law. In 1918, at the age of twenty-five, he was elected to the State Railroad Commission, the only political office for which he was then eligible. Thereafter, he steadily advanced his political career to become governor in 1928.

Huey Long was tall but graceless, with tousled brown hair and pudgy jowls, but, although he moved like an oaf, he had an impish, pert face and his whole personality was unruly and mischievous, suggesting his inner impatience and driving ambition. Indeed, his whole persona appealed to the rural population but was most threatening to the atrophied society of Baton Rouge and its oligarchy of planters, merchants, and industrialists.

Within three years of taking office he had abolished state poll taxes, declared a moratorium on debts, and excused the poor from property taxes. In 1928 Louisiana had only 300 miles of paved highways and 3 bridges. By 1933 it had 3,754 miles of paved highways, 40 bridges, and almost 4,000 miles of gravel farm roads. Moreover, as well as organizing a campaign to eliminate adult illiteracy, Long transformed Louisiana State University from a provincial college into a major institution. The new public buildings he commissioned, including the state capitol, governor's mansion, and New Orleans airport, not only satisfied Long's personal vanity and outsize ego but also provided extra work and boosted public morale.

According to state law, Long could not run for governor again in 1932 and thus he ran, instead, for the U.S. Senate in 1930, won, but delayed taking his seat until 1932 when he could install a stooge, Oscar K. Allen, as governor in his place. However, he continued to participate in front of, as well as behind, the scenes of state politics by taking charge of debates in the assembly and ordering the representatives to pass his proposed measures. On one day in November 1934 the state senate passed forty-four bills in only two hours, that is, one every three minutes. In this way and by selective use of bribery, torture, and intimidation, Long made himself dictator in his state.

Although he was an adept self-publicist, sometimes his boorishness was counterproductive. A trivial incident in August 1933 caused Long excessive embarrassment. It arose out of the flamboyant behaviorism he had now adopted. When he got drunk at a party at the Sands Point Casino, Long Island, New York, he tried to relieve himself in the men's room through the legs of a man already using a urinal. History does not say whether he was every inch a king—only that he was rewarded with a black and bloody eye for his cheek. "Kingfish to Crawfish" was the comment of the *New Republic*. A journalist in New Orleans inquired if it were true that Long had accepted an engagement to appear in a freak show at Coney Island for $1,000 per night.

Huey Long's own plan for national recovery was "Share Our Wealth," which he announced on the radio on February 23, 1934. It called for a wide redistribution of wealth among the lower economic groups. This was to be achieved by liquidating all personal fortunes above $3 million and providing every family with $4,000 or $5,000 to buy a house, an automobile, and a radio. The program also prescribed old age pensions, a bonus for veterans, minimum wages, and a free college education at government expense for young people of tested intelligence. To promote his point of view Huey Long issued pamphlets, made effective speeches, and promoted a song extolling the virtues of his scheme. The "Share Our Wealth" scheme was crude and, in its present form, impracticable, but it expressed a self-evident truth about just how unfair was the uneven distribution of wealth. Thus it was also a modestly successful political movement from which Long could advance his presidential ambitions.

FDR was exasperated by Long's attempt to appropriate control of the New Deal and his colossal rudeness. At a White House meeting Long kept his hat on, only removing it to tap the crip-

The effervescent Huey Long, first governor and, later, senator of Louisiana, where he reigned as the self-styled Kingfish, was a dangerous foil for FDR, partly because his "Share Our Wealth" campaign threatened to undermine the appeal of New Deal economic policies, partly because he could divide the Democratic party in the South. (Library of Congress).

pled president on the knees to emphasize his points. FDR took his revenge by distributing federal patronage to Long's political enemies in Louisiana.

Another thorn in FDR's side was Father Charles E. Coughlin, the radio priest. He was of Irish-American descent, Canadian birth, and had first come to the United States in the 1920s to Royal Oak, Michigan, near Detroit. He soon borrowed $79,000 from the archdiocese of Detroit to build a brown-shingled church of St. Therese, the Little Flower of Jesus, seating 600 people. In July 1926 the new church was threatened by a huge burning cross planted on the front lawn by the local Ku Klux Klan, who, it will be recalled, were opposed to Catholics and immigrants.

Despite this act of intimidation and because Coughlin's various efforts at fund-raising were still producing the revenue necessary to run the church, he persuaded Leo Fitzpatrick, manager of the local radio station, WJR, to let him broadcast his appeals on the air. From his first broadcast on October 17, 1926, he was an immediate success. Wallace Stegner recalls in *The Aspirin Age,* Isabel Leighton's 1949 collection of impressionistic synopses of the age, how Coughlin had "a voice of such mellow richness, such manly, heart-warming confidential intimacy, such emotional and ingratiating charm, that anyone turning past it on the radio dial almost automatically returned to hear it again." His voice was a vessel that could be filled or drained at will. It was "without doubt one of the great speaking voices of the twentieth century." The strength of his personality was such that by 1930 he was able to mount regular Sunday evening broadcasts, "The Golden Hour of the Little Flower," for seventeen CBS stations.

His early radio addresses were essentially religious, interpretations of the Bible. From 1930 onward they became almost exclusively political in content. The reason was not hard to find. After the Wall Street Crash, Detroit, which was almost entirely dependent on the automobile industry, had the highest unemployment rate of any large American city. The most common criticisms leveled at Coughlin were that he was an upstart priest interfering in politics. The CBS network was most sensitive to these charges and, fearful of offending the federal government, in April 1931 they refused to renew his contract. Not daunted, Coughlin went back to WJR in Detroit and arranged individual contracts with eleven private stations in the East and Midwest. By the end of 1934 more than thirty stations were broadcasting his addresses. By 1934 Coughlin was so popular that he was receiving more mail than FDR—sometimes over a million letters a week, requiring 150 clerks to process them.

The Charity Crucifixion Tower, his new granite and marble church, stood seven stories high and was decorated with a huge, bas-relief figure of Christ, illuminated by spotlights at night. At the side of the tower were a gasoline station, "Shrine Super-Service," and a Little Flower hot dog stand. Thus it was fair game for journalistic ridicule. *Time* magazine declared on April 10,

1933, that the "Charity Crucifixion Tower reminds many De-troiters of a silo" and called the architect "Silo Charlie."

Like Huey Long, Coughlin was an early supporter of FDR whom he used to call "Boss." Unlike Long, he had no personal political ambitions but he was disturbed by the failure of the early New Deal to move quickly to the Left. Coughlin's prescriptions for raising the depression were two: reform the currency and reorder the financial institutions. Silver donations had made Coughlin the greatest owner of silver, which he described as "the Gentile metal." He advocated the coinage of silver in a new dollar containing 75 percent gold and 25 percent silver, in order to increase the amount of money in circulation and thus increase purchasing power and stimulate the economy. In late 1934 and early 1935 Coughlin moved further to the Left, calling for the abolition of the privately controlled Federal Reserve System and the creation of a national bank to be controlled by popularly elected representatives. To achieve these reforms Coughlin orga-nized the National Union for Social Justice in 1935. It was said the prospective constituency was 8.5 million people

The dissident ideology propounded by Coughlin and Long drew from a traditional idea that individuals should be able to control their own destiny and not have it controlled by some faceless bureaucracy serving the financial interests of unseen cor-porations. It was concentrated wealth that had come close to destroying the community in the great bull market and the Wall Street Crash. The community could be revitalized by a new economic order with decentralized government, limited owner-ship of property, and controlled capitalism. Yet, ironically, it was the radio, itself a means of greater centralization, that made it possible for Coughlin and Long to propound their arguments for decentralization.

Since neither Long nor Coughlin could achieve a working rela-tionship with the New Deal, they turned to their newly created organizations with extra broadcasts, recruiting drives, and public speaking engagements wherever the authorities would permit them an audience. The Long organization spread from the South along the states bordering the Atlantic coast as far north as Connecticut and had footholds in Pennsylvania, Missouri, Wisconsin, and

Indiana. However, it was naturally stronger in the West than the Midwest, with California the most receptive state outside the South. The National Union for Social Justice spread from the Midwest to New England and the northeastern seaboard generally.

Coughlin and Long were formidable enough separately. Together, they could organize a huge constituency and they were being drawn together by their supporters, so closely did public opinion associate one with the other. Furthermore, various organizations, such as the Farmer-Labor Party and the Farmers' Holiday Association, and the Townsend Clubs, were united in what they saw as the common aim of the Long and Coughlin movements—"SHARE OUR WEALTH."

The electoral threat of Huey Long and the Share Our Wealth movement to FDR disappeared on September 9, 1935, when Long was fatally wounded inside the Louisiana State Capitol. Long's assassin, Dr. Carl Austin Weiss, who was immediately gunned down by Long's bodyguards, was the son-in-law of Judge Benjamin Pavy, a political enemy to the Kingfish. With Long gone, his movement split into two bitter factions and soon fell apart.

There was yet more thunder on the Left. Governor Floyd B. Olson of Minnesota was the dynamic leader of a Farmer-Labor party, whose platform proposed fundamental economic reforms, including state appropriation of idle factories to put the unemployed to work, state ownership of public utilities, a moratorium on farm mortgage foreclosures, exemption of low-income families from property taxes, and a government bank. However, while his administration accomplished environmental legislation and some regulation of public utilities, it proved less radical than his election promises. In 1936 he died of cancer at the early age of forty-five.

In Wisconsin Robert La Follette's sons, the unassuming Robert, Jr. ("Young Bob") and the extrovert Philip, dissatisfied with the pace of the New Deal, founded a new Progressive party in May 1934 and were elected as senator and governor, respectively, that year, while seven Progressive candidates were elected to the House of Representatives. They were supported by the League for Independent Political Action, an insurgent movement of eastern intellectuals that included John Dewey, Lewis Mumford, and Archibald MacLeish. This group favored a third party to unite leading midwestern movements, including its own creation of 1933, the Farmer-Labor Political Federation (FLPF).

Disenchantment with the old machines was also seen in New York City in 1933 where Republican Fiorello H. La Guardia was elected mayor after the Democratic machine of Tammany Hall was shown, in a sensational investigation, to have corrupted municipal politics. In office, La Guardia instituted a series of welfare programs on the lines of the New Deal. He was supported by the American Labor party that helped his reelection in 1937 and contributed to FDR's own electoral victory of 1936.

These various activities, commonly known as "Thunder on the Left," were, collectively, a significant factor in pushing the New Deal itself farther to the Left. FDR drew off their fire by kindling it for his own blazing reforms. Social security drew much of its momentum from Dr. Townsend's plan and the Revenue Act and the Holding Company Act were largely inspired by FDR's determination to refute Huey Long's charge that he was the creature of the utility corporations. Of yet more fundamental and ironic significance was the fact that FDR turned criticism of the New Deal from the Left to generate even wider public support for his policies. Historian Robert H. Walker puts it this way: "Franklin D. Roosevelt made visible use of the popular fear of violent revolution in gaining acceptance for a politico-economic program which many Americans might otherwise have regarded as itself unacceptably radical." Indeed, when Congress met for its second session on January 4, 1935, FDR asked for a "second New Deal" of sweeping reforms: security against illness, old age, and unemployment; slum clearance; and a program of works for the unemployed.

The New Deal at Flood Tide

Perhaps the most significant legislative achievement of early 1935 was the expansion of federal relief. By early 1935 perhaps as many as 5.5 million people were in receipt of relief; if their dependents were also included, then the total was 20.5 million, 17 percent of the total population. If those who were only in work because they were working for government relief projects are included, then it is clear the government was supporting over 20 percent of its citizens.

These statistics were not welcome to the New Dealers. Both FDR and Hopkins shared the traditional American view that relief by itself undermined character. Therefore, FDR and Hopkins wanted the 3.5 million people who were out of work but able-bodied and skilled to be given work through federal monies rather than a dole. Accordingly, the Emergency Relief Employment Act was designed to meet this special requirement. It passed the House by 317 votes to 70 and the Senate by 67 votes to 13 to be signed by FDR on April 8, 1935.

The Emergency Relief Appropriation Act established new agencies, notably the Works Progress Administration (WPA), for its purposes. (The following account is, like that for other legislation in this chapter, closely based on Ralph de Bedts's interpretation in *Recent American History*.) The Works Progress Administration, which changed its name in 1939 to Works Projects Administration, was awarded an appropriation of $5 billion, the largest in American history. It led to open conflict between Ickes and Hopkins. Ickes wanted to concentrate on recovery rather than relief and gave support to large public works projects to aid industry through expenditure on capital goods. This would ensure recovery in the long run. Hopkins, however, wanted to put as many people as possible into truly productive jobs and thus rely on their spending their wages to help business revive. He was supposed to have said, "People don't eat in the long run," and his approach to problems won him control of the WPA. Wages were somewhat above the dole but lower than wages in private industry. This led to opposition from liberals who wanted to raise wages and the compromise was to give the president "discretionary control" to raise wages. In 1936 the average wage was $52.4 per month. The average number of people employed by the WPA at any one time was 2 million—although by 1941 altogether 8 million, or 20 percent of the workforce, had at some time or other worked for the WPA. The WPA could not enter all fields.

It could not compete with private business and, because of costs, it could not engage in home construction.

Nevertheless, it built 12,000 playgrounds, 1,000 airport landing fields, 8,000 school buildings and hospitals, and, by instruction, publishing, and libraries, waged a campaign against adult illiteracy. It was, argues William Manchester, the WPA that transformed America's cities, creating the potential for additional transport, access, and other facilities. In New York it cut the Lincoln Tunnel linking Manhattan and New Jersey and built the Triborough Bridge linking Manhattan and Long Island. In Washington it created the mall and the Federal Trade Commission. In Dallas it laid Dealey Plaza; in California it built the Camarillo Mental Hospital; in Kentucky, the Fort Knox gold depository. Moreover, during this period federal appropriations for the armed services were minuscule in comparison with the need. Thus the contribution of the WPA to the maintenance of army posts and naval stations ensured their physical survival. Furthermore, the WPA provided the nucleus for, first, the wartime and, second, the postwar industrial expansion of business.

The WPA was under continuous attack from various quarters, including militant unionists (both within and without the WPA). Conservatives returned to traditional criticisms that federal relief undermined the Protestant work ethic, that many WPA projects were of dubious value in themselves and were being used for party political advantage. This last criticism was met by Congress that passed the Hatch Act in August 1939 forbidding federal employees (except officials at higher levels of policy making) from taking part in politics. The WPA aimed to create work for young people in its subsidary, the National Youth Administration (NYA), administered by Aubrey Williams, which gave priority to those who had graduated from high school and tried to persuade as many as possible to remain in education and stay out of the labor market. By 1941 it had employed about 1.5 million young people, favoring college students whom it paid between $10 and $20 per month.

Despite the expansion of federal relief in the early part of the year, it seemed to many of his supporters that FDR was becoming indecisive in 1935 until May when the U.S. Chamber of

Commerce announced it would not cooperate any longer with the New Deal and when the Supreme Court declared the NRA unconstitutional in the case of *Schechter Poultry Corporation* v. *The United States* on May 27, 1935. FDR reacted vigorously to both setbacks, denouncing both capitalists and the court in vehement tones and presenting to Congress in June 1935 five important new pieces of legislation. All were sweeping reform measures urged by liberals and progressives alike. These measures were the heart of the Second Hundred Days.

The first of these, the Wagner-Connery National Labor Relations Act, had originally been introduced by Senator Robert Wagner of New York. It was aimed at the many company unions set up to undermine labor's attempts to organize independently. FDR and Frances Perkins originally opposed the bill and they gave it their enthusiastic support only after it had passed the Senate by 63 votes to 12 on May 16, 1935, and after the Supreme Court had invalidated the NRA in the *Schechter* case eleven days later. FDR was not, at first, committed to the bill, yet his later support ensured that it passed the House by a large majority before he signed the Wagner Act on July 5, 1935. Workers were guaranteed the right to collective bargaining through unions of their own choice and the union chosen by the majority became the bargaining voice for all. The bill, moreover, established a three-member National Labor Relations Board (NLRB), headed by Professor J. Warren Madden of Pittsburgh, to supervise its enforcement, if necessary, by holding elections. Thus did the company union become illegal. Employers were forbidden to resort to "unfair practices," such as discrimination against union members or refusal to accept collective bargaining with union representatives.

The NLRB's wide powers aroused considerable controversy. Employers could maintain they had fired workers for inefficiency, whereas those workers would insist that their discharge was really owing to their union activities. The AFL and its craft unions claimed that the board was too partial to the Committee for Industrial Organization (CIO) and its industrial unions. Fifty-eight lawyers associated with the American Liberty League confidently predicted that the act would be adjudged unconstitutional and advised employers not to comply with it but, instead, to seek injunctions against it from sympathetic courts. However, in 1937 the Supreme Court upheld the new law in a series of decisions of which the most celebrated was *NLRB* v. *Jones and Laughlin Steel Corporation,* declaring that workers had a fundamental right to organize through unions. In 1938 the court went further by ending the legal abuse of injunctions to prevent strikes.

The Wagner Act was one of the most important acts in the history of American labor, aiding the rise of "big labor" as part of New Deal strategy to balance the component parts of society. It was said that it averted 869 threatened strikes in its first five years. Thus did the New Deal's policy to labor accomplish what Milton Derber of the Institute of Labor and Industrial Relations regards as "a fundamental restructuring of the industrial relations system." Whereas the immediate effects supported labor and made possible the unionization of those industries engaged in mass production, the result in the long term was to give to the federal government the pivotal role of arbitrator between labor and management, an arbitrator who decided upon and enforced the rules. By widening the scope of its social responsibility in providing minimum standards of pay at work and social security payments for unemployment and illness, the federal government encouraged the active participation of organized labor in the theater of national politics, especially within the Democratic party.

The second of FDR's five proposals became the Social Security Act. Only a few states provided old age pensions, and all were inadequate. Only Wisconsin had laws governing unemployment compensation. Thus the Social Security Act, in large measure stimulated by thunder from the Left, was a departure from all previous practice. However, knowledge of Townsend's more excessive demands prompted congressmen, who might otherwise have been reluctant, to find FDR's more modest proposals palatable by comparison. The bill moved easily through Congress, passing the House by 372 votes to 33 and the Senate by 76 votes to 6, and became law on August 15, 1935.

The Social Security Act provided an unemployment insurance plan and old age and survivors' pensions. Unemployment insurance was to be administered by the states and not the federal government. A federal unemployment tax was imposed on all

Mexican migrant fieldworker, on edge of frozen peafield, Imperial Valley, California, in March 1937 by Dorothea Lange. Both Dorothea Lange's first husband, painter Maynard Dixon, and her second, economist Paul S. Taylor, encouraged her work and, with Taylor, she recorded the plight of migrant farm workers for the Farm Security Administration. Herself a childhood victim of poliomyelitis, she, too, identified with the forgotten man. (Library of Congress).

employees. In order to encourage the states to keep their side of the bargain and pass enabling legislation, Congress provided that employers would be allowed a credit of up to 90 percent of the tax for contributions made to state unemployment compensation funds. In the end, all the states had passed the requisite legislation within two years. The act covered 27 million people but excluded many in agriculture, domestic service, and those working for small employers. In 1938 maximum payments were $18 per week, but much less in the South, and the national average was less than

$11. Payments extended for sixteen weeks only. The old age pension portion of the act created a federal annuity system to be financed by equal contributions from employer and employee, beginning at 1 percent of wages and increasing gradually. Payments were to begin in 1940. Fewer than 50 million people were covered by the original act and those reaching age 65 were to receive a pension in proportion to their contributions. Retired workers would receive a minimum of $10 and a maximum of $85 per month. Both sums were later raised. Frances Perkins said in her account of the Roosevelt years that FDR took greater satisfaction in the Social Security Act of 1935 than in anything else he achieved on the domestic front. The Social Security Act was a major landmark of social reform that made social security a basic function of the government.

Roosevelt's third proposal was the Banking Act of August 23, 1935, which was intended to give the federal government control of such matters in banking as reserve requirements and rediscount rates. Marriner S. Eccles of Utah, governor of the Federal Reserve Board, believed Wall Street exercised too much power in national finance and determined to revise the Federal Reserve Act of 1913, despite well-orchestrated opposition from the banking community led by Senator Carter Glass of Virginia, who resented any revision to the 1913 act that he himself had partly drafted. The result was a compromise between the Glass and Eccles points of view.

In future each Federal Reserve Bank elected its own head but he had to be approved by the board of governors of the Federal Reserve System (FRS). Thus was the Federal Reserve System made subject to more centralized control, moving the capital of banking from New York to Washington. Decisions on reserve requirements and discount rates were given to the board of governors. Moreover, the Open Market Committee of the FRS, which controlled open market operations in government securities, was put under a policy-making committee over which the central board had majority control, instead of being subordinated to the member banks and in a purely advisory capacity. All large state banks seeking the benefit of the new federal deposit insurance (achieved earlier in 1933) were now required to join the FRS and accept its jurisdiction. Thus, despite compromise, the act set a precedent in removing control of the nation's finances from private banking and placing it with the federal government.

The fourth measure, the Public Utility Holding Company Act of August 1935, was passed despite unprecedented lobbying against it by the giant public utility companies. However, not only Congress and FDR but also public opinion were convinced of the need to reform a whole set of abuses. Stocks issued were often overvalued or fradulent; sometimes public utility companies bribed legislators to advance or block legislation in their interest; the rates paid to holding company investors were usually excessive in order to support the top-heavy structure of the system. All of this was widely known. Therefore, Roosevelt and his allies wanted the dissolution of utilities holding companies in order to protect consumers against excessive rates and prevent unhealthy concentrations of economic power. The act was proposed by Congressman Sam Rayburn of Texas and Senator Burton K. Wheeler of Montana.

The act ordered the liquidation of holding companies more than two times removed from their operating companies (instead of all holding companies more than once removed from the operating companies, which the administration wanted). All utilities combines had to register with the Securities Exchange Commission (SEC), and this body could decide which holding companies could survive, that is, whether or not they were one or two times beyond the operating companies. If it thought any holding companies were not in the public interest it could order their elimination. In addition, the SEC was given control over all financial transactions and stock issuance of the utilities companies, which had to register with it. Some companies refused to register but the Supreme Court upheld the act and the great utilities companies were broken up within three years. The most significant achievement of the act was to stop the issue of fradulent utilities stocks.

An additional agency created at this time was the Rural Electrification Administration (REA) of May 1935, established to build generating plants and power lines in rural areas since only 10 percent of American farm families had electricity. Under the

Rural Electrification Act of 1936, farmers were encouraged to take advantage of REA loans at low rates of interest and form their own cooperatives in order to build their own plants. This encouraged private power companies to build power lines into remote rural areas, previously considered unprofitable. Thus, by 1941 40 percent of farms received electricity and, by 1950, 90 percent.

The Revenue Act of 1935 or Wealth Tax Act was greeted with more abuse than any of the Seventy-Fourth Congress's other laws. Newspaper magnate William Randolph Hearst called it "Soak the Successful" Act. FDR, undeterred, wanted to encourage a wider distribution of wealth and, also, reduce the need for deficit financing. Hitherto, tax on the wealthy was minimal. A man with an income of $16,000 paid only $1,000 in tax. In his message to Congress of June 19, 1935, recommending a revision of the tax system, FDR said, "Social unrest and a deepening sense of unfairness are dangers to our national life we must minimize by rigorous methods. People know that vast personal incomes come not only through the effort or ability or luck of those who receive them, but also because of the opportunity for advantage which Government itself contributes. Therefore the duty rests upon the Government itself to restrict such incomes by high taxes."

The new act set higher taxes on gifts and estates, raised corporate income taxes, and imposed an excess profits tax on profits above 15 percent. Moreover, it placed surtaxes on personal taxable income above $50,000, according to a graduated scale from 31 percent at the starting figure of $50,000 to a maximum of 75 percent on net incomes over $5 million. In addition, the act taxed undistributed corporation profits. The new tax law did not achieve the ambitious changes desired by its advocates and feared by its enemies. However, it did make the system of taxation far more equitable, although the monopoly of wealth by the top 1 percent remained substantially intact.

Congress also enacted ad hoc legislation in reaction to the scuttling of the NRA by the Supreme Court. Thus, the Guffey-Snyder Act of 1935 created a National Bituminous Coal Commission to supervise production quotas and prices, hours and wages. Because it guaranteed collective bargaining and attempted to set uniform wages and hours it, too, was set aside by the Supreme Court. Congress, therefore, replaced it with the Guffey-Vinson Act of 1937 that reproduced all the original terms of 1935, except for this last one concerning uniform hours and wages. Congress also passed the Connally Act of 1935 on the shipment of oil; the Alcohol Control Act of 1935, which reintroduced the NRA liquor code and placed its supervision under the Treasury; the Robinson-Patman Act of 1936 against favoritism through differential pricing; and the Miller-Tydings Act of 1937, allowing establishment of fair-trade minimum retail prices by manufacturers.

Most substantive was the Motor Carrier Act of 1935 that brought all interstate passenger bus and trucking lines under ICC control. The act also produced a model code based on the railroad code. This prohibited rate discrimination, provided maximum hours for labor, and allowed the ICC to review stock issues and proposals for mergers. A supplementary Transportation Act of 1940 made domestic water carriers and truck companies subject to the same requirements. In 1936 Congress passed the Patman bonus bill, giving war veterans immediate payment of their "bonus" instead of in 1945, something FDR had previously opposed but on which he had now changed his mind.

Once the Supreme Court had declared the AAA unconstitutional in January 1936, Congress devised an alternative, the Soil Conservation and Domestic Allotment Act of 1936, to continue arrangements by which the federal government paid subsidies to farmers who curtailed production. The Merchant Marine Act of 1936 created a maritime commission (headed by Joseph P. Kennedy) to plan trade routes, labor policies, and shipbuilding programs. Moreover, in order to discourage the practice of employing foreigners in order to depress wages, it required that three-quarters of ships' crews were American. The commission was also to build up an auxiliary merchant fleet in case of war.

The Election of 1936

Both sides agreed that the election of 1936 would be a battle of momentous significance. Democrats believed victory was theirs and were most concerned that it should be large enough to carry on the momentum of the most recent New Deal legislation. The Republicans were apprehensive. They welcomed any Democratic defectors and, to stave off a rout, counted on the undoubted fact that millions of people were still unemployed. It was Republican strategy to field a candidate who would alienate neither conservatives nor progressives. Thus Governor Alfred M. Landon of Kansas became the sole contender. He was a progressive from the Midwest who was not associated in any way with the discredited administration of Herbert Hoover. He was duly nominated in Cleveland on June 11, 1936. To journalist Walter Lippmann, Landon was "a dull and uninspired fellow, an ignorant man." Landon was called the Kansas Coolidge by Henry Ford, an epithet that drew an effective riposte from FDR who remarked that the Kansas sunflower was yellow, had a black heart, and always died before November.

After his inevitable renomination on June 12, 1936, FDR compared his critics to "a nice old gentleman" rescued from drowning by a friend in 1933 but who subsequently complained that, though his life had been saved, his fine silk hat had been lost in the misadventure. He returned to his effective distinction between politics and government that he had first made in 1932. FDR admitted "Governments can err, Presidents do make mistakes, but the immortal Dante tells us that divine justice weighs the sins of the cold-blooded and the sins of the warm-hearted in different scales." For, "Better the occasional faults of a Government that lives in a spirit of charity than the constant omission of a Government frozen in the ice of its own indifference." Moreover, "Government in a modern civilization has certain inescapable obligations to its citizens, among which are protection of the family and the home, the establishment of a democracy of opportunity, and aid to those overtaken by disaster. . . . There is a mysterious cycle in human events. To some generations much is given. Of others much is expected. This generation of Americans has a rendezvous with destiny."

The Democrats had to contend with more than their Republican rivals. After the assassination of Huey Long in 1935, Father Coughlin had to carry the double constituency by himself and, finding it difficult to channel the emotional momentum he had helped generate, preferred to draw on a new political ally, Congressman William ("Liberty Bill") Lemke of North Dakota, in a newly formed Union party, to which Gerald L. K. Smith and Dr. Townsend also committed themselves. Lemke became their presidential candidate. He was a shrill speaker who sported outsize clothes, a gray cloth cap, and a glass eye. From the outset relations between these allies were most tense and the ill-fated alliance fell victim to petty jealousies. At the climactic national convention of the Townsend Clubs, held in Cleveland in mid-July 1936, Coughlin, removing his coat and collar, decided to exceed Gerald Smith in his vicious abuse of FDR, to the great embarrassment of the pitifully small delegation of 5,000. His vituperation knew no bounds. "The great betrayer and liar, Franklin D. Roosevelt, who promised to drive the money changers from the temple, has succeeded (only) in driving the farmers from their homesteads and the citizens from their homes in the cities. . . . I ask you to purge the man who claims to be a Democrat from the Democratic Party, and I mean Franklin Double-Crossing Roosevelt." The greater were Coughlin's attacks on FDR, the larger was the desertion of his followers. His constituency declined to a lunatic fringe of Irish-Catholic fanatics.

Political pundits, with the evidence of public opinion polls adverse to FDR, thought that Landon had a fair chance of winning. It was certainly possible to argue that the election of Roosevelt in 1932 was a freak of circumstance and that the New Deal had failed to raise the depression. According to the Bureau of Labor Statistics (BLS), unemployment was 8.59 million whereas the Labor Research Association (LRA) claimed it was 12.61 million. Moreover, prominent Democrats were withdrawing their support from the New Deal. Taking its cue from press censure, the *Literary Digest* predicted that Landon would take 32 states with 370 electoral votes and that Roosevelt would take only 16 states and 161 electoral votes. However, Dr. George Gallup used different methods for his newly formed American Institute of Public Opinion and predicted a Roosevelt landslide of 477 electoral votes against 42 for Landon.

Not content with relying on the record of the New Deal, FDR went on the attack with a whistle-stop tour. The tenor of FDR's

remarks are suggested by his final campaign speech of October
31, in Madison Square Garden, when he said:

For twelve years this nation was afflicted with hear-nothing, see-noth-
ing, do-nothing government. The nation looked to the government but
the government looked away. Nine mocking years with the golden calf
and three long years of the scourge! Nine crazy years at the ticker and
three long years in the breadlines! Nine mad years of mirage and three
long years of despair! Powerful influences strive today to restore that
kind of government, with its doctrine that that government is best
which is most indifferent. . . .

Never before in our history have these forces been so united against
one candidate as they stand today. They are unanimous in their hatred
for me—and I welcome their hatred.

He concluded with open defiance of the plutocracy, in a ringing
remark thrown out with ecstatic arrogance.

I should like to have it said of my first administration that in it the forces
of selfishness and of lust for power met their match. I should like to
have it said of my second administration that in it these forces met their
master.

In the event, FDR won every state except Maine and Vermont,
just as his campaign manager, Jim Farley, had predicted. He took
27,752,869 votes to Landon's 16,674,665. Thus was Roosevelt the
first Democrat in eighty years to be elected president by a popular
majority, taking 60.8 percent of the total to Landon's 36.5 percent. In the electoral college he had 523 votes to Landon's 8. The
Union party took only 882,479 votes, the Socialists, 187,720
votes, and the Communists, 80,159 votes. Roosevelt's victory
thus set standards for all future elections and his popular vote was
not exceeded until Lyndon Johnson's 61.1 percent in 1964.

The credibility of the *Literary Digest* evaporated overnight. It
had used outdated methods in its poll, taking the opinions of
telephone subscribers, both present and former, who had yet to
recover from the depression and were still blaming government
for their misfortune. The sales of the *Literary Digest* declined and
it soon sold out to *Time* magazine.

The overwhelming Democratic victory created a preponder-
ance of Democrats in the House of almost three to one. In the

Senate 75 out of 96 members were now Democrats; only 16 were Republicans. In the state elections Democrats took 26 of 33 contested elections, including Kansas, Landon's own state.

For a brief time Roosevelt was carried away by his sweeping electoral victory and in his arrogance he momentarily lost his remarkable capacity for knowing what was politically feasible and what was not. Thus the great mandate of 1936 led to unexpected pitfalls for FDR in 1937.

The Storm over the Supreme Court

At his second inauguration, instead of expounding on the New Deal's achievements, Roosevelt struck a new militant note: "In this nation I see tens of millions of its citizens—a substantial part of its whole population—who at this very moment are denied the greater part of what the very lowest standards of today call the necessities of life. . . . I see one third of a nation ill-housed, ill-clad, ill-nourished." Indeed, according to a report by the National Resources Planning Board, *Security, Work, and Relief Policies* (1942), in 1936 18.3 million families, 60 million people altogether, received less than $1,000 per year. Excluding those who received relief, the average family income was $1,348 and this had to support a father, mother, and one or two children in a rented house or apartment. As William Manchester remarks, "The inconvenience and economies of the Depression had been institutionalized." Roosevelt's second inaugural speech became one of the most quoted and has been frequently referred to by analysts to suggest increasing New Deal commitment to end poverty. But, ironically, the problems of "one third of a nation" were to receive considerably less attention in Roosevelt's second term than in his first.

In his first address to the new Congress Roosevelt tried to expose the causes of much of the failure of existing institutions to accommodate themselves to the new requirements of government. In particular, he commented on the Supreme Court's reluctance to accept the New Deal. During the depression the Court had consistently voted—usually by a majority of five to four—against state laws seeking new economic remedies for the depres-

sion. In 1935 and 1936 the Court brought much New Deal legislation to an abrupt stop on the grounds that Congress was
delegating its power to the president. The extent of the problem
is simply illustrated. In the previous 140 years the Supreme Court
had nullified only sixty laws. In 1935 and 1936 it invalidated
eleven. Moreover, FDR, at the end of his first term, became the
first president ever to serve a full four-year term without being
able to make a single Court appointment.

In 1933 the Supreme Court had been an extremely conservative
body although the other senior branches of government clearly
wanted a change. Four of the justices were archconservative:
James McReynolds, Willis Van Devanter, Pierce Butler, and George
Sutherland. Of these, McReynolds, in his mid-seventies, was
considered one of Woodrow Wilson's mistaken appointments,
while Van Devanter, at seventy-six, was so infirm that he could
not even complete his share of the clerical work of the Court,
writing out its decisions, which, therefore, had to be undertaken
by his colleagues. All of the conservative justices held that private
property was sacrosanct and that an economic policy of laissez
faire was the only right course in the depression.

The liberal justices were Benjamin Cardozo, Harlan Fiske Stone,
and Louis D. Brandeis. Both Cardozo and Brandeis were Jewish
and all were committed to civil rights. Brandeis, the oldest justice, brought to judicial problems a new emphasis upon facts,
statistics, and a pragmatic approach to social problems. His decisions and those of Cardozo and Stone implied that government
and laws must change with the times. The remaining two justices
are sometimes called "the swing men." They were Owen Roberts, who had prosecuted the Teapot Dome Scandal in the 1920s,
and Chief Justice Charles Evans Hughes, former governor of
New York and former secretary of state. Hughes tried to keep
the peace between all the factions. While lacking the compassion
of the liberals, Hughes was a rare mix of statesman and jurist
whose austere, Jove-like presence commanded respect and awe.
In the end he moved his politics from right to left.

The first adverse decision came in January 1935 in *Panama
Refining Co.* v. *Ryan*. This was a case about Section 9c of the
National Industrial Recovery Act that allowed the president, un-

der certain circumstances, to prohibit the transportation of oil across state lines. By a vote of 8 to 1 the Court declared Section 9c unconstitutional because it was incomplete: it established neither guidelines for, nor restrictions upon, presidential authority. The Court was also hostile to any modest redistribution of wealth. In the case of *Railroad Retirement Board* v. *Alton Railroad,* also in 1935, by a vote of 5 to 4, the Court declared unconstitutional a railway retirement act on the grounds that the Constitution did not provide for the compulsory institution of railway pensions, which were a misuse of the property of the employers.

The most notorious adverse decisions were those of Black Monday—May 27, 1935. The Court found the Frazier-Lemke Farm Mortgage Act unconstitutional, ruled that the removal of Federal Trade Commissioner William E. Humphrey was a matter for Congress and not the president, and, as we know, in *Schechter* v. *The United States,* found the NIRA unconstitutional because it interfered with interstate commerce. It should be emphasized that the adverse decision in the *Schechter* case was unanimous. The liberals sided with the conservatives. Sensing the significance of this decision, the *Daily Express* of London opined: "America Stunned: Roosevelt's two years' work killed in twenty minutes." In January 1936 the Court went further and ruled 6 to 3 against the AAA in *United States* v. *Butler et al.* By 5 to 4 it ruled against the Municipal Bankruptcy Act (requested by cities across the country). By 5 to 4 it found in *Carter* v. *Carter Coal Company* against the Guffey-Snyder Coal Conservation Act, an act specifically written after the NIRA decision in the *Schechter* case of the previous year. Al Smith jubilantly told a Liberty League dinner how the Supreme Court was "throwing out the alphabet three letters at a time."

Supreme Court rejection of the New Deal had reached epidemic proportions. Thus, as British political scientist John Lees declares, "The conjunction of a grave political and economic emergency, an assertive and popular President, and a strong-willed judiciary, provided in 1933 the ingredients for a constitutional conflict of major dimensions." Roosevelt and his supporters feared that the nonelected justices were preventing the duly elected branches of government from doing their job. The Court and its supporters feared that the will of the majority was being used by the president to make himself a dictator.

The president and his team had long considered how best to remedy matters. FDR favored the plan of Attorney General Homer S. Cummings, the court-packing bill S.1392, announced on February 5, 1937. Its premise was that Court personnel in general were deficient, particularly because too many judges were too old for the job. Therefore, FDR proposed that if a federal judge who had served ten years waited more than six months beyond the age of 70 to retire, then the president could appoint an additional justice—up to six on the Supreme Court and forty-four to lower federal courts. In his message FDR deliberately avoided any reference to the judges' widely publicized conservatism.

As far as increasing the actual number of justices to the Supreme Court was concerned, FDR had ample precedent since the number had been revised from six to ten and, finally, nine in the nineteenth century—and always for reasons of party politics. Moreover, his plan was based on one offered to Woodrow Wilson by his attorney general, James C. McReynolds, now the archconservative architect of court decisions against the New Deal. However, by disguising what was a blatant political stratagem as a means of restoring efficiency to the courts and using old age as a criterion, FDR had miscalculated. The oldest member of the Court, Louis D. Brandeis, at seventy-nine was the most liberal. Everyone knew it was not the age of other justices that was in question but their political opinions. Many distinguished congressmen over seventy also felt themselves threatened. It was frankly disingenuous to incubate such a profound change in secret, to tie reform of the Supreme Court to reform of the judiciary, to avoid admission of the differences between the Court and the New Deal, and to do all this so soon after an election in which the proposal had not even been mentioned.

Not only did the American Liberty League, the National Association of Manufacturers, the U.S. Chamber of Commerce, and the DAR campaign against the scheme, as expected, but also a host of local community associations, whose opposition was more disinterested. In his column of June 6, 1937, Walter Lippmann accused FDR of "proposing to create the necessary precedent, to

Cartoonist Clifford Berryman was as imaginative in exploring the comic possibilities of FDR as he had been with Theodore Roosevelt. This cartoon of March 9, 1937, shows how the Democratic donkey and the dove of peace scatter in dismay upon hearing Franklin Roosevelt's plan to pack the Supreme Court, a plan as offensive to FDR's allies as to his opponents. (Library of Congress).

establish the political framework for, and to destroy the safeguards against, a dictator." Previously loyal liberals, such as Senator Burton K. Wheeler of Montana, now joined with the opposition.

Nevertheless, the impasse between FDR and the Court was resolved and a serious crisis passed. First, Charles Evans Hughes wrote a letter to Wheeler in the Senate Judiciary Committee, which had been agreed by Willis Van Devanter (one of the conservatives) and Louis D. Brandeis (one of the liberals), showing that the Court was abreast of its work, and that an increase of judges would make for greater, not less, inefficiency. As Hughes explained, "There would be more judges to hear, more judges to confer, more judges to be convinced and decide. The present number of Justices is thought to be large enough so far as the prompt, adequate and efficient conduct of the work of the Court is concerned."

Second, the Court began to return decisions favorable to the New Deal. On March 29, 1937, in *West Coast Hotel Company v. Parrish,* by a majority of 5 to 4, it upheld a minimum wage law enacted by Washington State that was almost exactly the same as the one passed by New York State that it had nullified the year before. Public opinion preferred to believe the remark of a wit that "a switch in time saves nine." Apparently, Owen J. Roberts changed his mind realising that, unless the Court moved with the times, its influence would decline.

Third, in five decisions in April 1937 the Court allowed Congress control of interstate commerce, most notably in *NLRB v. Jones and Laughlin Steel Corporation.* In May in two decisions it upheld the Social Security Act by majorities of 5 to 4. Fourth, in May 1937, the physically senile Justice Van Devanter retired at long last, thus allowing FDR the opportunity to appoint a more liberal successor. As a result of these various events the more urgent reasons for reforming the Court evaporated.

FDR's worst tactical error in the whole episode was to insist on passage of the original court-packing bill even after the political need for it had disappeared. Thus he aroused deep antagonism in Congress. When the bill was eventually passed in August 1937 as the Judicial Reform Act, it was in emasculated form with no mention of the Supreme Court. However, FDR described the Court fight as "a lost battle which won a war." Between 1937 and 1940 FDR appointed liberals Hugo Black, Stanley Reed, Felix Frankfurter, William O. Douglas, and Frank Murphy to various vacancies on the Supreme Court. There was now a "Roosevelt Court," the most liberal since the mid-nineteenth century, committed to civil liberties, minority rights, and progressive legislation in general.

Ironically, the battle over the Supreme Court allowed many who had abandoned the New Deal earlier to move back into the mainstream of liberalism, claiming that they, rather than FDR, were the true heirs of progressivism. It was a small bloc of southern conservatives in Congress, led by Senator Carter Glass of Virginia, that first began to oppose the New Deal more forcibly. These men had begun to move away from the New Deal as early as 1935, but the storm over the Supreme Court gave them the excuse they needed to fight FDR openly.

The antagonisms aroused by the Court battle were fueled by the dissatisfaction of conservatives with the gains of labor, increased welfare and relief, and began to take on something of the character of the feud between town and country that had disfigured the 1920s. The conservatives were essentially from a background of rural politics themselves and from states in which rural politics were predominant. They opposed proposals for low-cost public housing, federal regulation of hours and wages, and legislation to achieve civil rights. What they feared was the advent of an interdependent, possibly collectivized, urban society. They saw increasing centralization in government without understanding the changes in growth of population and demands that underpinned it.

Roosevelt also suffered defections from the high ranks of the New Dealers such as Raymond Moley, General Hugh Johnson, and George Peek, all of whom distrusted the increased supremacy of government over labor, agriculture, and industry that they had, themselves, done so much to bring about. Among the former progressives who lost sympathy with the New Deal were Oswald Garrison Villard, Walter Lippmann, and Dorothy Thompson, all of whom were trenchant critics in journals and newspapers. They simply would not accept that increased centralization of government came out of ever greater public demands for governmental services or the need to regulate economic forces, partly to raise the standard of living for the most disadvantaged. They could not reconcile themselves to a system of national social security that was based on a degree of coercion by law. To these critics the New Deal was imposing a Servile State—the phrase borrowed from G. K. Chesterton. They made mistaken analogies between FDR and European dictators, and failed to appreciate that the totalitarian governments of Europe had come to power not because democratic governments had assumed too much power but, rather, because they had not done enough to support their principles.

The New Deal at Ebb Tide

Because of the furor over the court-packing scheme, FDR was unable to accomplish anything substantive of his ambitious program for the "one-third-of-a-nation" address. Nevertheless, in 1937 Congress acted on behalf of the destitute migrants of the Dust Bowl, the Okies.

The Bankhead-Jones Farm Tenant Act of July 1937 was a product of a government report, showing that family-owned farms were becoming something of the past as mortgages were foreclosed when crops failed. As we know, some families slid into tenancy and sharecropping, and the Okies and Arkies (migrants from Arkansas) took to the roads. The act created a Farm Security Administration (FSA) and incorporated it within the Resettlement Administration (RA) to help tenants and sharecroppers acquire farms from a special loan fund to provide for the purchase, refinancing, and rehabilitation of farms at low rates of interest. Thus, the FSA was to counteract the unfortunate side effects of the first AAA that contributed to dispossession when marginal lands were withdrawn from production in return for subsidies. The FSA also established thirty camps to provide temporary housing for thousands of destitute migratory families. In addition, it created medical and dental centers and funded cooperative aid for the purchase of heavy machinery by small farmers. Within ten years 40,000 families had bought their own farms through FSA loans and 900,000 families had borrowed a total of $800 million to rehabilitate their farms or, even, relocate them on more arable land.

One of the most impressive government documents of the depression years is not a book of statistics of the experience but the remarkable portfolio of photos taken by artists and photographers of the Farm Security Administration. Jack Delano, Carl Mydans, Walker Evans, Arthur Rothstein, John Vachon, and others, captured the plight and determination of impoverished America. Two of the group, Dorothea Lange and Ben Shahn, were especially gifted in encapsulating the desperate experience of migrants from the Dust Bowl and showing listlessness, despair, and helplessness in children, courage and stamina in their parents. Such prolific and talented artists provided the nation with graphic proof that the soil was exhausted, that the system had broken down, and that it was the urgent duty of the body politic to put things right.

The Wagner-Steagall National Housing Act of September 1, 1937, was designed to meet the problems of slum clearance and public housing. It established the United States Housing Authority (USHA) to act through public housing bureaus in large cities, loaning them sufficient money (up to 100 percent) at low rates of interest to build new homes. It was to be financed by issues of bonds. By 1941 160,000 units had been built for slum dwellers at an average rent of $12 or $15 per month.

The New Agriculture Adjustment Act of February 1938 was based on the so-called "ever normal granary" plan, storing surplus in fat years for distribution in lean years. It established how quotas in five basic staple crops—cotton, tobacco, wheat, corn, and rice—could be imposed by a two-thirds majority of farmers in a referendum. Those who adhered to the quota received subsidies based on prices of the favorable period of 1909–1914. In case of overproduction, the Commodity Credit Corporation could make storage loans up to 75 percent of parity price (later 85 percent). Thus, if the market price fell below that amount, then the farmer could store his crop in return for a loan at that level of 75 (or 85) percent. When the market price rose, then the farmer could repay the loan and sell the surplus. Because of the fierce droughts of previous years, crop insurance was made available to farmers. The premiums could be paid for either in wheat or its cash equivalent. A second new feature was the Food Stamp Plan under which farm surpluses were distributed through the Federal Surplus Commodities Corporation to persons on relief who received 50 cents of such produce free for every $1 they spent on other groceries. These relief payments, especially among the urban poor, helped reduce farm surplus, and increased the business of retail stores.

The last major law of the New Deal was the Fair Labor Standards Act of June 25, 1938, a most controversial measure that was only passed by Congress meeting in special session after numerous concessions by FDR and the New Dealers. It fixed minimum wages and maximum hours for all industries engaged in interstate commerce: it established a minimum wage of 25 cents per hour, with provisions for a gradual increase to 40 cents an hour; and it set maximum hours at forty-four hours per week, with a goal of forty hours within three years. Moreover, overtime work was to be paid at the rate of time-and-a-half. The act also set laws on child labor. It forbade interstate shipment of goods made either in whole or in part by children under sixteen. Further, children under eighteen could engage only in nonhazardous occupations. To supervise the new law a Wage and Hour Division was created in the Department of Labor with power to impose heavy fines for breach of regulations. As a result of the act, about 650,000 workers received wage rises and over 2 million had their hours of work reduced. Because of the need to secure the votes of grudging conservative congressmen, FDR accepted exemptions of benefit to their particular economic interests. Thus seamen, fishermen, domestics, and farm laborers were exempt from the provisions of the act. However, the bill outlawed child labor; it abolished the worst abuses of sweatshops; and it brought some protection to the three-quarters of working people not in organized labor.

The Food, Drug, and Cosmetics Act of 1938 expanded the Pure Food Act of 1906, giving the Department of Agriculture additional powers to control fraud by the manufacturers of foods and drugs. In particular, it required labels on bottles listing their contents. Nevertheless, Congress had not turned FDR's recommendations in his second inaugural address into positive legislative achievements and there followed an even more effective break on the New Deal than congressional intransigence.

Without question, the economy had shown signs of recovery from the worst of the depression in the period 1933–1936. The national income rose from little more than $42 billion in 1933 to $57 billion in 1935. Accordingly, the government began to plan for a balanced budget by 1939, gradually reducing its deficit. However, in August 1937 business fell back and there was a wave of selling on the stock market. In nine months in 1937–1938 the Federal Reserve Board's adjusted index of industrial production lost two-thirds of the gains it had made during the painful ascent of the New Deal years. It fell from 117 in August 1937 to 76 in May 1938. This was a faster collapse than in the devastating period 1929–1932. Farm prices fell by nearly 20 percent and, in the autumn, unemployment increased by more than 2 million. Harry Hopkins, Harold Ickes, and others argued for the continued injection of government funds into the economy, spending even to the point of deficit financing. Roosevelt reluctantly agreed. He was won round by stories of starvation in the South and extreme and widespread poverty in northern cities and, thus, asked Congress for a $3 billion program of relief and public works expenditures. By December 1938 this, and continuing New Deal programs, had halted the decline.

Believing that private business had failed to play its part in recovery, FDR also wanted increased surveillance of business monopolies. Therefore, Congress set up the Temporary National Economic Committee (1938–1941) under Senator Joseph O'Mahoney of Wyoming. It produced the most thorough study ever of American monopolies. But in 1941 its findings were overshadowed by foreign affairs.

The traditional regional division in the Democratic party, which the battle over the Supreme Court had widened, was confirmed by the failure of the Wagner–Van Nuys bill that would have made lynching a federal crime and allowed the families of lynch victims to sue the county in which the crime was committed. It was defeated by a southern filibuster. FDR, and his advisers, especially Hopkins and Ickes, were furious at the way southern Democrats used FDR's popularity to get themselves elected and, once in office, deserted the New Deal. Thus they tried to institute a purge of disloyal congressmen, such as Senators Millard F. Tydings of Maryland, "Cotton Ed" Smith of South Carolina, and Walter F. George of Georgia, in the midterm elections of 1938. FDR wanted

With her penetrating gaze fixed on the horizon, an indomitable grand-mother among the Okies looks ahead to the future. (Photo by Dorothea Lange; Library of Congress).

to oust these southern conservatives and to transform the Democratic party from a loose coalition of local and sectional interests, in which its congressmen conveniently blurred the issues when it suited them, into a tightly knit and cohesive bloc of definite, liberal views.

It is a political truism that for some men to live by principle others must live by compromise and when Roosevelt sought to overlook this and defy political reality, he was fighting a losing game. Not only was the strategy mistaken but also the tactics. Roosevelt tried and failed to have popular and influential Democrats dropped from the party ticket for the midterm elections of 1938. Thus Senators George, Smith, and Tydings survived FDR's attacks. Only Congressman John O'Connor of New York, albeit chairman of the powerful House Rules Committee, succumbed to Roosevelt's withdrawal of support and was defeated. He was nominated by the Republicans as their candidate but lost the election.

Moreover, in the midterm elections of 1938, the Republicans almost doubled their seats in the House from 88 to 169 against 261 Democrats—still a workable majority. In the Senate the results left sixty-nine Democrats against twenty-three Republicans. Nevertheless, the swing of public approval away from the New Deal could not be ignored. Thus in January 1939 no new reform measures were proposed. The political impulses that had allowed, even needed, the New Deal in the early 1930s were almost extinct. The New Dealers sought no more fundamental laws and the brief overwhelming ascendancy of the Democratic party was somewhat tarnished in many minds by the mistaken court packing scheme and by the comparative electoral setback of 1938. People were exhausted by adversary politics and both organized labor and business now preferred to follow a more moderate course in the interests of reducing class tension. Thus FDR's annual message on January 4, 1939, acknowledged the New Deal had come to an end.

However, the New Deal ended as it had begun with a demonstration that the greatest power of the federal government devolved from presidential initiative. FDR realized that if he, or any less energetic successor, were to survive the political strain of the presidency, then it would be necessary to institutionalize its administrative staff and reform the various agencies to make them more effective. However, his attempt to secure congressional approval for a reorganization bill had fallen foul of the soured atmosphere of 1938. The bill narrowly passed the Senate in March to be defeated by 204 votes to 196 in the House on April 8, 1938. Roosevelt's critics charged him with an attempt at Hitlerian despotism, a criticism fueled by Father Coughlin's unwanted return to political broadcasts in 1938, but many were really motivated by jealousy and malice.

FDR was neither defeated nor deterred and by Executive Order 8248 of September 8, 1939, he established the Executive Office of the President, staffed with six administrative assistants. Subsequently, the Council of Economic Advisers, the National Security Council, and the Central Intelligence Agency were moved into the Executive Office. In *The American Presidency* (1956) Clinton Rossiter concludes that this decision "converts the Presidency into an instrument of twentieth-century government; it gives the incumbent a sporting chance to stand the strain and fulfill his constitutional mandate as a one-man branch of our three-part government; it deflates even the most forceful arguments . . . for a plural executive; it assures us that the Presidency will survive the advent of the positive state. Executive Order 8248 may yet be judged to have saved the Presidency from paralysis and the Constitution from radical amendment."

The major legacy of the New Deal was that the operation of the national economy was made the responsibility of government in the interests of all its citizens and not just those of a particular class. Thus the federal government became an institution shared by all the people. For the first time they experienced its presence as it taxed hundred of thousands directly and distributed pensions and relief to millions. No longer was it a neutral arbiter between different branches or levels of government but, in the words of Felix Frankfurter, the "powerful promoter of society's welfare."

The state was personified by FDR whom millions regarded as a protector. In his *Being an American* (1948), Justice William O. Douglas remarked: "He was in a very special sense the people's President, because he made them feel that with him in the White House they shared the Presidency. The sense of sharing the Presidency gave even the most humble citizen a lively sense of belonging." Or, in the words of William E. Leuchtenburg in *Franklin D. Roosevelt and the New Deal* (1963), "Roosevelt's importance lay not in his talents as a campaigner or a manipulator. It lay rather in his ability to arouse the country and, more specifically, the men who served under him, by his breezy encouragement of experimentation, by his hopefulness, and—a word that would have embarrassed some of his lieutenants—by his idealism."

Historian Dexter Perkins has acutely observed, "The President . . . took his place at the head of the procession only when it was quite clear where the procession was going." The procession was, of course, the New Deal and public support for it, and, in one sense, FDR cannot be given credit for originality. The individual reforms of the New Deal were all variations upon earlier proposals, as Perkins also makes clear. The legislation of the New Deal grew out of the recent past.

While the New Deal achieved a more equitable society it left much undone. It left largely untouched the problems of tenant farmers, sharecroppers, migrant workers in agriculture and, among ethnic groups, blacks, Puerto Ricans, and Mexican-Americans. New Deal efforts in slum clearance were scarcely proportionate to the magnitude of the problem. Although FDR had called attention to one-third of a nation "ill-nourished, ill-clad, ill-housed" in 1937, only thirty years later Michael Harrington showed in *The Other America* that the proportion was almost as great.

It was especially frustrating for the most egalitarian New Dealers that their program bypassed black Americans, made only symbolic concessions to the status of women, and did little to improve the general standard of education. The New Deal was essentially devoted to economic and material recovery and thus civil rights between the sexes and the races were largely ignored. New Deal discrimination against blacks took various forms, such as banning them from construction work on the TVA, interpreting crop restriction policies of the AAA in such a way as to allow their eviction from farms, and pandering to the racist sentiments of federal administrators in the South. Even the Federal Housing Administration practiced discrimination. All of this was partly because FDR knew he dare not antagonize southern congressmen utterly and completely. But it was also because the New Deal was, as we have observed in its reform program, acting as an honest broker between different sections of the community and the greatest benefits were to be awarded to the best organized or politically influential groups.

The American political and economic system was strengthened by the New Deal but the depression and widespread unemployment remained. According to the minimal statistics of the U.S. Department of Labor, Bureau of Labor Statistics, unemployment rose from 1.49 million (3.1 percent of the labor force) in 1929 to 12.63 million (25.2 percent) in 1933. Thereafter, the level fell gradually until it was 7.27 million (13.8 percent) in 1937, only to rise to 8.84 million (16.5 percent) in 1939. As has been emphasized, these statistics were regarded as serious underestimates by the AFL, CIO, and LRA. Even the BLS admitted that wholesale prices remained well below their index number of 100 in 1926. Thus in 1929 prices were at 95.3 of the high level, falling successively to 65.9 in 1933, and rising gradually to 86.3 in 1937, and then declining to 77.1 in 1939. The Federal Reserve Board charted the physical volume of industrial production in these years according to an average of 100 for the years 1935–1939. In 1929 the index was 110. It was at its lowest in 1932 at 58. Thereafter, it rose to 113 in 1937, falling back to 88 in 1938, before rising to 108 in 1939. We can attribute some poverty to factors other than the unprecedented economic crisis, but they made the Great Depression more severe. One such factor was the increasing number of old people in the population. The number of people over sixty-five rose from 4.9 million in 1920 to 9 million in 1940, an increase from 4.6 percent to 6.9 percent. Another factor was the bitter climax of the long-term exploitation of the soil in certain areas that culminated in the Dust Bowl.

Given the unprecedented crisis it was surprising that the New Deal achieved as much as it did, rather than it left so many problems unsolved. In less than six years more significant changes were wrought by government than ever previously. Much of what the New Deal attempted but did not complete was halted by the war, by its own moderation and loss of momentum, and by the growth of opposition resulting from FDR's adversary politics of 1936 and 1937. Moreover, the New Deal fostered and encouraged widespread discussion about the values of society, the proper role and relationships of its various economic components —industry, business, agriculture, labor, and government—and just how mutually responsible and caring these groups in society should be to one another. In short, the New Deal educated the American people that industrial and social life must be a shared experience.

7

A HOUSE DIVIDED
Workers, Labor, and Ethnic Groups

Welfare Capitalism of the 1920s

THE GREAT Red Scare of 1917–1921 and the extinction of the postwar wave of strikes crippled the union movement for the next dozen years. During the course of the 1920s, the proportion of the nonagricultural labor force organized in unions declined from 18.6 percent to only 12 percent. The AFL scurried back into its shell of conservatism as the nation's factories and mills roared forward at an ever quickening pace. Employers, anxious to prevent another 1919, set about nurturing a sense of loyalty among their employees, and applied modern technology to the world of the worker.

Nevertheless, employers had come to the conclusion that they could get more out of their workers by cultivating their loyalty and dependence, rather than relying forever on the threat of wage cuts and unemployment. Housing, pension schemes, stock sharing, recreational services, health care, and educational benefits were offered to some workers who agreed not to join unions and avoided strike action. A 1919 Bureau of Labor Statistics special report on industrial welfare indicated a broad movement by management to stimulate corporate loyalty among employees. Of 431 establishments surveyed, 375 had begun some type of medical program and 265 reported having hospital facilities, 75 had pension plans, 80 had established disability benefit plans, and 152 had constructed recreation facilities for their workers. The selective nature of welfare capitalism was a point not lost on the president of International Harvester, Harold McCormick, who wrote in a letter to employees, "As you know, our Pension Plan is a purely voluntary expression of the company's desire to stand by the men who have stood by it." At least 6 million workers came to be covered by welfare programs in the 1920s, and a survey of 1926 found that half of the 1,500 largest American companies were operating comprehensive schemes.

It should be emphasized that, even at its peak, welfare capitalism covered only a minority of the work force, and often the schemes were somewhat piecemeal. The influence of welfare capitalism was felt strongest in company towns, where stringent rules already restricted workers' lives in and outside the plant. For example, strikers and their families in steel mill towns found that they were evicted from company-owned housing and denied access to the social clubs, libraries, and health clinics built by the corporation. The illusion of corporate paternalism was also developed in the form of "employee representation plans" and "works councils." Drawing on the arbitration guidelines established by the War Labor Board, companies offered workers the right to a formal grievance procedure within strictly defined limits. Between 1919 and 1924, some 490 firms established representation plans that served not only to redress petty complaints, but also to deflect and absorb more militant demands. "Given a channel for expression of legitimate grievances," writes economist Richard Edwards in *Contested Terrain* (1979), " 'loyal' workmen would not be driven into the ranks of the unions." Thus, company unions came to feature strongly in corporate publicity as a shining example of America's industrial democracy.

However, it was the change in the structure of the workplace

The calm and sobriety of prewar small town America is captured in this 1941 photograph of the business section of Taft, California, behind which loom the oil derricks of prosperity. (Wittemann Collection, Library of Congress).

that proved crucial in undermining the power of workers on the shopfloor. Companies set up personnel departments to remove decisions over hiring and firing from the foreman and commissioned scientific management studies to increase efficiency. Moreover, the administration of day-to-day factory life was put into the hands of a new army of professional managers.

Throughout the nineteenth and early twentieth centuries, attempts had been made to reduce the need for highly skilled labor by mechanizing the production process. For example, the Ford assembly line achieved enormous increases in productivity by transferring the decision as to the pace of work away from the worker, and into the hands of the manager who controlled the production line. "The delivery of work instead of leaving it to the workmen's initiative to find it" was how Henry Ford described it. With the new product in high demand, the Ford Motor Company's plants were able to produce 31,200 automobiles in 1925 with virtually the same machinery that had produced 25,000 cars in 1920.

Because of his scientific advances and his highly successful factory management, Henry Ford's schemes of employment were accepted by society at large. His $5 a day minimum wage for workers and his insistence on a high standard of social behavior from them were generally assumed to beneficial. However, minister and theologian Reinhold Niebuhr, who had a parish in Detroit, knew differently. He became a contributing editor of *Christian Century* in 1923 and, gleaning evidence from his parishioners, began a series of articles criticizing Ford. He showed that Ford's average annual wage was low and exposed other malpractices of the system. Ford's employees were broken by their work despite the $5 wage and the five-day week. Niebuhr knew that they were often dismissed in summary fashion in middle age, unfit for work elsewhere and emotionally dejected. Niebuhr found himself increasingly concentrating on welfare work for Ford's employees. After General Motors began to outsell him, in 1927 Ford discontinued production of the model T, closed his factories, modernized them, and then reopened them for his production of the new model A. In the interim period some 60,000 workers were unemployed. When the factories reopened, the former workers were engaged as new employees, starting again at $5 a day. Thus the new Ford car cost Ford's men at least $50 million in lost wages, not to mention the families broken up in the period of unemployment.

Reinhold Niebuhr believed certain factors in the capitalist system made this sort of injustice possible. One was the development of the city—a society without moral standards held together by a mechanical, productive process—and another was the selfishness inherent in human nature: "We are all responsible. We all want the things which the factory produces and none of us is sensitive enough to care how much in human values the efficiency of the modern factory costs." Thus Niebuhr concluded that the natural energy of man was harnessed to the inhuman drives of society. Men worked for a society that actually deprived them of the emotional benefits they thought came from it. Niebuhr did not merely criticize Ford and other industrialists but accused society as a whole for its indifference to human suffering. In *Does Civilization Need Religion?* (1927), he declared that the threat of depersonalization of the individual was inherent in modern industrial society and should be met by social reconstruction.

Problems of Labor

Even in the 1920s unemployment was much higher than was generally supposed and a continuous worry for most workers. However, estimates vary greatly. According to the *Historical Statistics of the United States* (1975), unemployment was 11.7 percent of the civilian labor force in 1921 and then fell to an average of 3.3 percent in the period 1923–1929, with the figure of 1.8 percent for 1926 being a modern peacetime record for the United States. Robert M. Cohen in "Labor Force and Unemployment in the 1920s and 1930s" for the *Review of Economics and Statistics* (1973) gives an average unemployment rate of 5.1 percent for 1923–1929. However, Paul H. Douglas, surveying only transportation, mining, building, and construction in *Real Wages in the United States, 1890–1926* (1930), provides an average of 12.95 percent in 1921–1926 and even the very best years of 1923, 1925, and 1926 average 8.1 percent.

The discrepancy is partly explained by the fact that those in work included many who wanted to work full-time but had only part-time employment. Without the sort of welfare support provided later, part-time work was hardship and made it more difficult to save for periods of total unemployment. As Caroline Manning noted in *The Immigrant Woman and Her Job* (1930), "due to the amount of part-time work during the past year or two, they have found it impossible to accumulate a financial reserve to fall back on when out of a job." In Muncie, Indiana, in 1924 43 percent of one sample of working-class families for the Lynds' *Middletown* (1929) lost at least a month of work and 24.2 percent lost three or more months of work. Thus, in the first nine months of 1929, average unemployment of these working-class families was 17.5 percent. A survey in Philadelphia by J. Frederick Dewhurst and Ernest A. Tupper, *Social and Economic Character of Unemploy-*

ment in Philadelphia (April 1929), showed 10.4 percent out of work because there was no work to be found (7.8 percent) or because of sickness, old age, and similar causes (2.6 percent). The analysts discussed 18.9 percent unemployed in industrial neighborhoods.

If many working-class families were poor in employment, unemployment plunged them into deep poverty. The wife of an unemployed roofer told Clinch Caulkins in *Some Folk's Won't Walk* (1930), "When my husband's working steady, I can just manage, but when he's out, things go back. First I stop on the damp wash, then on the food, and then the rent goes behind." Some families would rather almost starve than accept charity and one lived on nothing but bread and tea for six weeks. A father waited on a streetcorner at lunchtime "for fear if he came home he would be tempted to eat what they have been able to put on the table for the children." Those who suffered malnutrition were prone to such illnesses as pneumonia. Some people had nervous breakdowns or committed suicide by gassing themselves.

Despite the decline in European immigration, there was a glut of industrial workers after 1923. As the decade progressed, workers had a harder time finding jobs. The move of ever more people from countryside to city more than compensated for the abrupt end of immigration. It was an employers' market. Productivity increased and the increase was possible with the same number, or fewer, workers. Thus there were about the same numbers of industrial workers in 1928 and 1929 (respectively 8.1 million and 8.6 million) as there had been in 1919 and 1920 (8.6 million). Increased mechanization and reorganization of work displaced workers who might endure several months of unemployment before finding work again, as Isador Lubin shows in *The Absorption of the Unemployed by American Industry* (1929).

The mountains of paperwork generated by the modern corporation created a need for clerical workers, a need filled by women secretaries. The so-called feminization of the clerical labor force drew nearly 2.25 million women to work in offices by the end of the decade. Between 1910 and 1930, the proportion of women who worked in domestic service fell from a third of all women wage earners to a quarter. However, even with as many as 4 million women wage earners in the work force in 1930, the doors of organized labor remained difficult for them to prise open. Already largely excluded from the male-dominated internationals, a proposal by the Women's Trade Union League to organize separate federal locals for women was also rejected by the AFL. As a result, only 250,000 women belonged to unions at the end of the decade and half of them were in the garment industry. Moreover, the progressive principle of protecting women and children workers was rejected by the courts. In the case of *Adkins* v. *Children's Hospital,* decided by 5 votes to 3 on April 9, 1923, the Supreme Court invalidated an act of Congress setting a minimum wage for women and children in the District of Columbia. The majority found that the law was a price-fixing measure in violation of freedom of contract protected by the Fifth Amendment.

In the bituminous coal industry, the boom of the war years was followed by a crisis of overproduction, with domestic markets becoming glutted. Too many mines producing too much coal was the context in which miners struck in 1919 and 1922. The new president of the United Mine Workers (UMW), John L. Lewis, was forced to accept a settlement that preserved existing wage rates but gave no protection for jobs. Between 1920 and 1927, the number of miners working in the industry fell from over 700,000 to approximately 575,000. The UMW's losses in membership were even more spectacular, from a high of half a million bituminous coal members in 1921–1922, to, perhaps, 80,000 by mid-1928.

The problems of the coal industry had reached chronic proportions years before shareholders saw their surplus wealth crash on Wall Street in 1929. The continuous surplus of labor meant that a typical miner was working between 142 and 220 days a year, and often bringing home less than $2 a day, instead of the expected $7.50 union minimum. Miners and their families lived on diets of beans (euphemistically nicknamed "miners' strawberries"), gravy, and bread. Respiratory and intestinal diseases were widespread in mining communities. For those who complained too loudly about their impoverished existence, company officials were swift with the reminder that "there's a barefoot, hungry man outside waiting for your job."

Powerless to rescue the economy of coal, the UMW's president, John L. Lewis, concentrated on securing his grip on the union's internal organization. The son of Welsh immigrants who had settled in Iowa in the 1870s, John L. Lewis rose to become the most important and perplexing labor leader of the twentieth century. He assumed control of the miners' union in 1919, when a debilitated Frank Hayes was obliged to retire. Lewis was a big burly man with a luxurious lion's mane of hair, eyebrows like furry caterpillars, and a foghorn voice. His rhetoric mixed metaphors from the Bible, Homer, and Shakespeare, combining the commonplace and the grotesque to inspired effect. Of his own genius for self-publicity he once remarked, "He who tooteth not his own horn, the same shall not be tooted."

According to his biographers, Melvyn Dubofsky and Warren Van Tine, Lewis was a "man driven by ambition and perhaps eager to compensate for his lowly social origins by achieving parity with America's economic and political elite." Through a combination of subtle scheming, deceitful maneuvering, and ruthless opportunism, he accumulated power within the UMW as a model union autocrat. From this lofty position, Lewis also prospered as a bank president, investor, country-clubber, and dinner guest to leading businessmen and politicians. Yet, conversely, while he assimilated the values of business, John Lewis also maintained a deep commitment to the coal industry and to the organization of its workers. Forever the pragmatist, Lewis shifted his allegiances and demands as the contemporary political climate permitted. Thus, in the 1920s he remained passive while the membership of his union and the wages of miners plummeted. However, as the tide of events turned in 1932, the UMW leader became an advocate of militancy, demanding, first, governmental action to revive the economy, and, then, trade union action to mobilize the nation's industrial workers. Later, Lewis would stand alone among union leaders in resisting the government's efforts to manipulate the organized labor movement during World War II. Liberals regarded him as a politician of conscience and vision while to his conservative critics, he was proletarian evil incarnate.

John Lewis's career demonstrated how the political economy of

The gregarious and vociferous miners' leader, John Llewellyn Lewis
(left), a man of luxurious hair who led the movement for the ūnioni-
zation of unskilled and semiskilled industrial workers, eventually breaking with the AFL to form the Congress of Industrial Organizations.
(Photo by Underwood and Underwood; Library of Congress).

the period was more conducive to trade union autocracy than it was to working class militancy. Hard hit by open shop drives, and the depression that crippled some weaker industries, such as coal and textiles, union leaders often found that the only way to preserve their organizations at all was to centralize power and stamp out internal dissent. Gangsterism was also able to use union leadership struggles to creep into the labor movement. Meanwhile, conservative business unionists, such as William ("Big Bill") Hutcheson of the Carpenters, dominated the AFL's executive council, and held sway over the mild-mannered William Green who succeeded Samuel Gompers as president in 1924. Of Green, John L. Lewis later remarked, "Alas poor Green: I knew him well. He wishes to join in fluttering procrastination, the while intoning, 'O tempora, O mores!' "

AFL leaders stubbornly refused to pay attention to members' demands—let alone the 85 to 90 percent of unorganized workers —since the full power of American capitalism had a firm stranglehold around the neck of the labor movement. In an era that was marked by its low strike rate and falling union rolls, corporate paternalism could switch rapidly to overt repression if workers stepped too far out of line. Of 1,845 injunctions issued by federal courts to ban strike action in the period 1800 to 1930, almost half were issued in the 1920s. Indeed, the legal right of workers to bargain with their employers through labor unions remained in doubt right through to the 1930s.

In spite of the barrage of judicial and management attacks, the acquiescence of the rank and file was never absolute. On the shop floor, informal groups of workers continued to restrict output and undermine management's attempts to restructure the workplace. Elsewhere, workers made increasingly militant demands through works councils that occasionally took on a life of their own. Moreover, the scattering of radicals who had managed to escape the full force of the Great Red Scare also began to regroup and organize at grass roots level.

Throughout the 1920s, the Communist party, first founded in 1919 as the Workers' party, followed a strategy of boring from within the AFL unions. Led by the roving industrial organizer, William Z. Foster, the Communists attempted to capture the national movement for a Farmer-Labor party in 1922–1924, but their efforts were undermined by sectarianism and factionalism. They were more successful in trade union work, leading strikes in the textile and fur industries. However, communism was usually associated in the public mind with foreign ideologies and terrorist outrages and this was a liability in an age of increased nativism, making the task of converting English-speaking workers in the skilled trades difficult and often dangerous.

By 1928, when the newly emerged Soviet leader Josef Stalin called for a more revolutionary dual union line from the Communist party, many radicals had virtually abandoned hope of changing the AFL from the inside. However, Foster remained committed to trade union organizing and was displaced as party leader. Ironically, these disputes over strategy occurred just as a rank-and-file revolt was beginning within the UMW. John Brophy's "Save the Union" movement in 1927–1928 challenged Lewis's dominion, but Brophy was defeated in a characteristic display of diplomacy and brute force by the union president.

Theodore Draper's portrait of American communism in the 1920s in *The Roots of American Communism* is the work of an accomplished miniaturist. He rarely leaves the tiny smoke-filled rooms of New York and Moscow, disclosing the claustrophobic and obsessive world of the marginal communist movement of the 1920s ridden by intrigue and faction. Draper argues how three key events of the early 1920s transformed the Communist party's emulation of the Bolsheviks. The first was Lenin's pamphlet on "Left-Wing Infantilism" in which he criticized Western communists for failing to base themselves on mainstream labor organizations. Lenin's sensible argument moved Communists across the world to "a point of no return" in which, "For the first time, every Communist in the world was called on to change his mind in accordance with a change of line."

The second "fateful step" came when the Communist International, or Comintern, in Moscow was asked to choose and arbitrate between John Reed and Louis Fraina as representatives of two rival CPs in the United States. Thus, for the first (but not the last) time, American Communists, despite their bitter internal squabbles, wanted Moscow to arbitrate between them. "Even if there had been a greater willingness in Moscow to pursue a hands off policy, the Americans themselves would not have permitted it."

This led to the third fateful step. The Comintern imposed unity on the underground American CP and wanted it to work above ground. Ironically, "The first change of line was every other change of line in embryo. A rhythmic rotation from Communist sectarianism to Americanized opportunism was set in motion at the outset and has been going on ever since." Thus by 1922 American communism "was transformed from a new expression of American radicalism to the American appendage of a Russian revolutionary power."

In future, committed American radicals were to be blown about in gales of contrary doctrine.

Labor in the Great Depression

During the Great Depression of the 1930s many workers became deeply disillusioned and embittered by the apparent inability of government to ameliorate their suffering and the indifference of businessmen and industrialists to the harsh fate of the working class. Here it seemed was the crisis of capitalism that could lead to improvement by revolution.

Employers, struggling to regain their balance in the upheavals of the early 1930s, withdrew housing and health benefits, and slashed the size of their work forces. However, in discharging workers and turning whole families into scavenging transients, companies also lost the loyalty and confidence that welfare capitalism had been nurturing so carefully in the 1920s. Although some company welfare schemes continued to operate right the way through the depression, many workers became disenchanted and embittered by the apparent indifference or inability of industrialists and politicians to ameliorate their suffering. David Brody goes so far as to argue that "had not the Depression shattered the prevailing assumptions of welfare capitalism, the open shop might well have remained a permanent feature of American industrialism."

As coal miners were among the first major body of workers to experience the instability and arbitrariness of the American economy, it is not surprising that it was in the coal industry that labor unrest began to reemerge in the early 1930s, after a decade of relative calm. While the UMW was preoccupied with internal struggles over the leadership, miners in Kentucky, Ohio, western Pennsylvania, and West Virginia instigated a series of strikes, which, by 1933, accounted for 58 percent of all time lost to American industry.

Paralleling the insurgency in the mines, Communists, Socialists, and a new generation of radical activists, were helping to mobilize the mass of the urban unemployed whose needs had swamped the resources of private charities. Unemployed councils organized marches and rallies that often ended in violent confrontations with police. In March 1930 a demonstration by 35,000 people in New York's Union Square was dispersed when, according to the *New York Times,* "Hundreds of policemen and detectives, swinging night sticks, blackjacks and bare fists, rushed into the crowd, hitting out at all with whom they came into contact, chasing many across the street and into adjacent thoroughfares and rushing hundreds off their feet." In 1931 three people died during an anti-eviction struggle in Chicago, and a crowd of 60,000 people of mixed races marched on City Hall in protest over the incident.

The revival of the labor movement depended not just on the impact of the depression and the increase in local militancy, but also on the changed political context represented by the New Deal. Trade union experiences in the 1920s had shown how impossible was the task of unionization, if the government actively supported corporate repression of labor. The first piece of pro-labor legislation implemented by the administration of Franklin D. Roosevelt, as it desperately tried to stabilize the economy, was Section 7a of the National Industrial Recovery Act of 1933. This gave employees the right to bargain collectively through representatives of their own choice and without interference from employers. However, as the NIRA codes were to be hammered out within individual industries, and in the absence of adequate enforcement machinery, companies either ignored the act or reactivated "employee representation plans" and company unions. By

1935, nearly 2.5 million workers were covered by such plans, as compared with the 4.1 million members of trade unions. Although Section 7a lacked any concrete strength, it had a significant symbolic effect. It seemed as if the federal government, for the first time, was not only acknowledging but also legitimizing the right of workers to organize. However, the NIRA was declared unconstitutional by the Supreme Court in the *Schechter* case of May 27, 1935.

Senator Robert Wagner of New York and Congressman William Connery of Massachusetts then introduced a new bill, creating a National Labor Relations Board (NLRB), that established the right of workers to bargain collectively with management through various representatives chosen in elections supervised by the federal government. It also defined unfair labor practices. Congress passed it precipitately and it received Roosevelt's assent on July 5, 1935. Again, employers responded bitterly through repressive and obstructive actions, and successfully delayed the act in the courts for a further two years. However, American workers preceived the Wagner Act as a statement of support from president and federal government in line with their popular image of the New Deal. The Supreme Court finally upheld the Wagner Act in the case of *NLRB* v. *Jones and Laughlin Steel Company* on April 12, 1937, by 5 votes to 4.

Congress also helped labor by passing the Norris-La Guardia Anti-Injunction Act of 1932 that limited the use of court injunctions in industrial disputes; and in the Senate, the La Follette committee, as we have observed, was beginning to document scores of corporate violations of civil rights.

In 1938 Congress established a minimum wage of 25 cents an hour to rise to 40 cents within three years. However, to secure necessary support from southern Democrats, the sponsors agreed to exclude domestic workers and farm laborers and to allow regional wage differences. Sometimes such well-intentioned legislation had unfortunate results. For instance, in 1938 there were 8,000 Mexican-Americans working as pecan shellers in San Antonio, Texas. According to Selden Menefee and Orin C. Cassmore in *The Pecan Shellers of San Antonio* (1940), they were employed on a seasonal basis and earned 5 to 6 cents an hour, making a median wage of $2.73 in a working week of fifty-one hours. Their employers could not afford to pay them the minimum wage of 25 cents per hour without mechanizing their plants. Thus many closed down. When the plants were mechanized and reopened they employed, altogether, 3,000 shellers only, having fired another 5,000, the victims of technological change.

Again and again, it was the grass roots activity of militant cadres of workers that proved crucial in stirring individual workers into demanding their rights. Indeed, industrial workers began putting politicians and employers under mounting pressure to raise the depression. The number of workers involved in strikes rose from 324,210 in 1932 to 1.16 million in 1933. In 1934 working-class militancy reached a level not seen in the United States since 1919, as violent industrial conflicts paralyzed three major cities.

Striking electrical workers and members of the Unemployed League joined forces in Toledo, Ohio, to imprison 1,500 strikebreakers inside the city's Auto-Lite plant. A seven-hour battle between National Guardsmen and pickets followed, in which two strikers died and fifteen were wounded. In San Francisco, a strike by longshoremen extended to other workers and paralyzed the whole city when police shot dead two unarmed strikers on a picket line. Some 130,000 of the city's workers walked out in a display of solidarity that concerned the editors of the *Los Angeles Times* to the point of declaring "There is but one thing to be done —put down the revolt with any force necessary." The conservative leadership of the AFL was equally dismayed by the militancy of union members. William Green disowned the strike on July 18, 1934, and, three days later, the General Strike Committee voted for a return to work. Meanwhile, in Minneapolis on July 20, police fired into a crowd of striking teamsters, killing two and wounding more than fifty. Governor Floyd Olson of Minnesota placed the city under martial law, but, faced by the continued determination of the strikers and massive public outcry, was eventually forced to withdraw the troops. A national textile strike of the same year saw over 370,000 workers from Maine to Alabama stop work. In total, at least forty workers were killed in the industrial conflicts of 1934, and troops were called out in sixteen states.

Much of the trouble in the 1930s was caused by the companies' strong-arm strategies and provocative tactics. The La Follette Civil Liberties Committee learned in December 1934 that over 2,500 firms employed strikebreaking companies, of which the largest were Pearl Bergoff Service and the Pinkerton National Detective Agency. Both maintained a standing army, equipped with machine guns, tear gas, and clubs. They also hired spies to penetrate the work force and entrap radical agitators. Harassment of workers even extended to making them work at gunpoint. The Pittsburgh Coal Company kept machine guns aimed on employees in its coal pits. Chairman Richard B. Mellon explained to a congressional committee, "You cannot run the mines without them." Such operations were big business. The Pinkerton Agency earned about $2 million between 1933 and 1936, much of it from Detroit, center of the automobile industry.

Frances Fox Piven and Richard A. Cloward argue in *Poor People's Movements* (1977) that the most extraordinary feature of the increase in labor militancy was the spontaneity of many strikes, and the relatively small role of existing trade unions in promoting and directing local protest. Although many workers' battles were fought to win union recognition, if any union structure already existed, it usually remained on the sidelines. John L. Lewis and the UMW could claim little responsibility for the coal strikes during the period 1930–1933. Likewise, labor historian Jeremy Brecher notes in *Strike* (1979) that the flying squadrons of pickets that helped spread the 1934 textile strike across the country were "at first tolerated and perhaps encouraged by union officials, but as the squadrons led to confrontations, union officials tried to bring them to a halt." The relative militancy of particular groups of workers in particular industries often seemed to depend on small cadres of class-conscious radicals, ready to instigate confrontations. Communists, Trotskyists, and Musteites (followers of radical A. J. Muste) had been at the heart of the mobilization of strikers in Toledo, San Francisco, and Minneapolis in 1934. John L. Lewis observed on various tragedies of the period, "Labor, like Israel, has many sorrows. Its women keep their fallen and lament for the future of the race." From the point of view of labor, the most bitter cup was that most of the victims had died in vain. While local unions won recognition in the cities of Minneapolis, San Francisco, and Toledo, employers remained adamantly opposed to organized labor in the big industries—automobiles, steel, rubber, and textiles.

In the early thirties, according to the highest estimates, AFL membership rose from 2.96 million in 1930 to 3.04 million in 1934 and then 3.51 million in 1936. In that year there were, altogether, 4.1 million members of all trade unions. Provoked by the hardship of the depression, and spurred on by the actions of radicals and the rhetoric of New Dealers, militancy from the rank and file sent shock waves through the organized trade union movement. The AFL had consistently resisted attempts to extend its influence beyond craft-based organization because its leadership either disdained immigrant and nonwhite unskilled labor, or regarded the task of organizing in the mass-production industries as virtually impossible.

However, by the 1930s, the divisive influence of ethnic fragmentation was not as significant as it had once been. For example, in the steel industry, the proportion of European-born workers had declined from 50 percent in 1910 to 30 percent in 1930. These workers were also no longer confined to the least skilled and lowest paid work. More confident of their place in American society than their parents had been, the sons and daughters of immigrants were frequently in the vanguard of many of the period's industrial conflicts.

The AFL was hopelessly conservative. Its insistence on adhering to the craft form of unionism in the face of a total crisis for industry, labor, and the country was quite absurd and deeply angered new leaders like Lewis. Moreover, the AFL was ultraconservative on central political issues—being opposed to the whole notion of unemployment insurance. Indeed, many AFL leaders were Republicans—as was Lewis himself until the 1930s.

John L. Lewis now insisted that the AFL mount an intensive drive to bring millions of factory workers into union ranks. Lewis called for a new form of industrial union, whereby workers in such mass-production industries as construction and steel would have one union big enough to bargain with the giant corporations. At the convention in Atlantic City in October 1935 he led a formidable group of insurgents, including Sidney Hillman of the Amalgamated Clothing Workers, David Dubinsky of the International Ladies' Garment Workers, Thomas McMahon of the Textile Workers, and Charles Howard of the Typographers' Union. The confrontation between old and new schools of thought led to a fight on the platform between Lewis and "Big Bill" Hutcheson of the Carpenters in which Lewis punched Hutcheson, after Hutcheson had insulted a speaker from the rubber workers. He was carried out with blood streaming from his face. Lewis remarked later, "They fought me hip and thigh and right merrily did I return their blows." "With this historic punch," writes James Green, "Lewis signified the formal beginning of the industrial-union rebellion within the House of Labor and made himself the leading rebel."

Lewis and his allies soon met to form the Committee for Industrial Organization (CIO), ostensibly to work within the AFL to aid it in unionizing the basic industries. The AFL executive council ordered the CIO to disband and, when they refused, first suspended the ten renegade unions in August 1935 and, finally, in March 1937 expelled them. In splitting from the conservative main body of the AFL to form the CIO, Lewis and his followers had created a militant industrial union organization around which local militants could gather.

New militancy was characterized by a new tactic, the sit-down strike. On January 29, 1936, rubber workers in Akron, Ohio, laid down their tools and occupied the Firestone plant. Workers at the nearby Goodrich and Goodyear companies rapidly followed the example of the Firestone strikers by implementing labor's new-found weapon of the sit-down strike. Through plant occupations, workers used the techniques of nonviolent resistance to bring shame on their bosses and forced management to the negotiating table. As far as management was concerned, the sit-down strike was an outrage against private property, an underhand act of trespass in which Communists carpeted the shop floors with human bodies because they knew the company would not risk the

Edward Hopper, *New York Movie* (1939), oil on canvas, 32⅙″ × 40⅛″. (Collection, The Museum of Modern Art, New York). Edward Hopper captured the essential solitariness of people absorbed in their own thoughts, whether in crowded or desolate places in realistic works by arresting off-center composition, abrupt chiaroscuro of light and shade, and, sometimes, deliberate distortions of size. Here the ephemeral pleasures of well-heeled life on screen elude the contemplative usherette.

adverse publicity following the bloodshed of forcible removal or damage to its own plants and material. In Akron, the old AFL local was reorganized as the United Rubber Workers and affiliated with the new CIO.

Toward the end of 1936 the United Auto Workers sought a conference on collective bargaining with William S. Knudsen, executive vice-president of General Motors (GM). When he refused, men on the shop floors in Cleveland's Fisher Body Plant

No. 1 took spontaneous action on December 28 by sitting down and ignoring the moving assembly line belt. Their protest spread to Fisher Body Plant No. 2 in Flint, Michigan, and thence to Pontiac, Atlanta, Kansas City, and Detroit. Soon 484,711 men from sixty plants in fourteen states were involved. GM obtained an injunction ordering evacuation of the plants but it had no moral force once the press disclosed that the judge who issued the order was a major stockholder in General Motors.

On the eve of the General Motors sit-down strike, only a small proportion of workers were fully paid-up members of the United Auto Workers. However, once the strike began, many previously apathetic workers displayed very high levels of militancy and class consciousness. During the first eight months of 1937, the membership of the UAW increased from 88,000 to 400,000. At Flint, a psychologist declared that the strike created "a veritable revolution of personality" among the workers. One of the strikers, Bob Stinson, recalled that

Morale was very high at the time. It started out kinda ugly because the guys were afraid they [had] put their foot in it and all they was gonna do is lose their jobs. But as time went on, they begin to realize they could win this darn thing, 'cause we had a lot of outside people comin' in showin' their sympathy.

Whole communities rallied to the support of those on strike. Women workers and strikers' wives coordinated many of the demonstrations outside the plants, and organized a system of strike relief and food convoys. "I found a common understanding and unselfishness I'd never known in my life," said one woman. "I'm living for the first time with a definite goal. . . . Just being a woman isn't enough anymore. I want to be a human being with the right to think for myself."

The silence of Roosevelt, Secretary of Labor Frances Perkins, and other sympathetic New Dealers put extra pressure on Governor Frank Murphy of Michigan. A second court injunction obtained by GM lawyers threatened the sit-down strikers with prison sentences and a fine of $15 million if they did not give up by February 3, 1937. GM then chose its Chevrolet plant in Flint as the testing ground and Murphy called out the National Guard to surround the plant. John L. Lewis did not like the strike because it was a diversion from his campaign for union recognition in the steel industry. Yet he did not want to lose the car workers. Thus Lewis told Murphy he supported the strike and that he would order the men to disregard any order to evacuate the plant. "I shall walk up to the largest window in the plant, open it, divest myself of my outer raiment, remove my shirt and bare my bosom. Then, when you order your troops to fire, mine will be the first breast that those bullets will strike. And as my body falls from the window to the ground, you will listen to the voice of your grandfather as he whispers in your ear, 'Frank, are you sure you are doing the right thing?' " This was a telling touch. Murphy's grandfather had been hanged after an Irish uprising.

Murphy knew he could not abandon the strikers to the unmerciful GM company and, instead, insisted that food was delivered to them. Thus the UAW triumphed because of the tacit support of president, governor, and the conversion of Lewis, all of which broke the morale of General Motors. Through its strategy of a concerted attack on General Motors to immobilize its plants and only token demonstrations at Chrysler, Ford, Nash, and Packard, the UAW had divided and ruled. Instead of siding with GM, the other auto manufacturers simply took advantage of its embarrassment and exploited the market for their own automobiles. Thus by February 7 GM directors were forced to cut the dividend in half. After a crisis of forty-four days, William Knudsen agreed to the conference. All the other auto manufacturers recognized the UAW, except Ford, who held out until 1941, and they also signed agreements on grievance committees, seniority, a forty-hour week, and payment of time-and-a-half for overtime.

A prime target of the CIO in its drive to create and organize industrial unions was the steel industry. In June 1936 Phil Murray formed the Steel Workers Organizing Committee (SWOC), the first significant attempt at a steel union since the Homestead Strike of 1892. Not only did it entice thousands of workers out of company unions into its ranks but it also, with tacit government support, threatened and instituted costly strikes to force the steel companies to recognize it. The large steel companies, known as Big Steel and led by United States Steel, the corporation based on the original Carnegie companies, accepted SWOC. Myron Charles Taylor, chairman of the board of directors and chief executive, met Lewis by chance in the Mayflower Hotel, Washington, on January 9, 1937, and then and there arranged a series of private meetings with him to thrash out differences between Big Steel management and SWOC. The Carnegie-Illinois Steel Company signed a contract on March 2, 1937, and the other United States Steel subsidiaries followed with contracts granting union recognition, the forty-hour week, a 10 percent increase in wages, and overtime pay at the rate of time-and-a-half.

Because Big Steel had decided on a strategy of accommodation with the new union in the interests of harmony, it was widely expected that the remaining smaller companies, known collectively as Little Steel, would follow suit. However, three of them opposed SWOC. Republic Steel, Bethlehem Steel, and Youngstown Sheet and Tube resisted a new strike of 70,000 men in twenty-seven plants for union recognition in May 1937. They summoned their strikebreaking armies and threw them at striking workers.

On Memorial Day several thousand strikers and their families had assembled in prairie land east of Republic Steel's South Chicago plant. The mayor of Chicago had given his permission for a peaceful parade with marchers falling in behind banners with such notices as "Republic Steel violates Labor Dispute Act" and "Win With the CIO." Ahead of the marchers was a line of 500 Chicago police, all heavily armed. A police captain called out, "You dirty sons of bitches, this is as far as you go." Without any further warning, some of the police began attacking strikers' wives, pummeling their breasts with nightsticks. The strike leaders called out, "We got our legal rights to protect." "You got no rights" came the retort. Some workers threw a few empty soda pop bottles at the police and this was sufficient provocation to start a massacre, beginning with tear gas grenades and followed by gunfire. The police in South Chicago killed ten people and wounded ninety others outside the Republic Steel plant. The casualties were shot in the back as they fled in terror. Such conflicts became part of working class folklore—and art. In *An American Tragedy* (1937) Philip Evergood (1901–1973) dramatized workers and their families in a vicious clash with police against a background of a closed factory.

Subsequently, the Senate Civil Rights Subcommittee led by Robert La Follette, Jr., of Wisconsin began an investigation into the violation of the workers' civil rights and the shooting incidents. Their investigations disclosed that the Little Steel companies maintained illegal private armies and had extensive stores of munitions, including machine guns and tear gas. The adverse publicity was such that Little Steel was eventually compelled to recognize SWOC. Thus by 1941 over 600,000 workers had achieved union recognition in the very industry most bitterly opposed to labor organization.

In the course of 1937 a total of 4.7 million workers were involved in 4,740 strikes. For the first time in American history, all of the nation's key industries—steel, coal, auto, rubber, electricity—were affected by major industrial disputes. As historian William Manchester explains, labor violence was part of an American tradition. It was by violence that the United States had gained independence, conquered the West, and freed the slaves. Moreover, it was violence that "had raised working men up from the industrial cellar. Labor might forget that and turn conservative, but for liberals to deny other oppressed groups the right to revolt would prove impossible. Thus were the seeds of later anguish planted in innocence, even in idealism."

By the end of 1937 the new CIO unions claimed some 4 million members in 32 international unions and 600 independent locals. Genuine efforts were made to overcome differences in gender, nationality, and race. The number of women in unions tripled in the 1930s to stand at 800,000 in 1940. As to the activity of black and immigrant workers in this period, historian James Green says, "The CIO unions did not dissolve ethnic and racial group consciousness or end cultural antagonism, but they did give a highly divided workforce a basis for cooperation on issues of common concern."

In the lean years of the late 1930s, it was the AFL, revitalized by the challenge of its new rival, the CIO, that achieved the greatest increases in membership. Craft unions such as the Machinists, Teamsters, Electrical Workers, and Meat Cutters, began to organize vigorously on an industrial union basis, and proved more resilient against the recession and counteroffensive by employers. From October 1938 the CIO was known as the Congress of Industrial Organizations. In 1937, the first year of the two major unions, there were, according to official statistics, 3.18 million members of the AFL and 1.99 million members of the CIO. By 1940 there were 4.34 million members of the AFL and 2.15 million members of the CIO. That year there were 7.28 million trade union members of all unions.

The often confusing relationship between union leaders and the rank and file must always be set against the extremely vulnerable position of unions in America's major industries. It was the strike movement at grassroots level that was the prime force behind the creation of the CIO. Moreover, during several of the decade's major industrial struggles, CIO leaders were prepared to suppress or disown rank-and-file militancy (the sit-down strike, for example, was never officially endorsed), in return for union recognition from management. However, the opportunism and sporadic conservatism exhibited by Lewis and other union leaders often stemmed from a reluctance to encourage premature actions from workers that might lead a fledgling union into positions it could not effectively support. Nothing weakens a union so much as a lost strike. That is not to say that Lewis did not concern himself with monopolizing power as the archetypal union "boss"; and he often, in his own words, "put a lid on the strikers." However, as the Memorial Day Massacre had so violently demonstrated, working-class radicalism had limits even during the turmoil of depression America.

Radical Visions and American Dreams

Although Communists, Socialists, and other radicals had played a crucial role in the revival of the labor movement, their influence beyond grass roots organizations was negligible.

The Socialist party ceased to be an effective political force in the 1930s. The very fact of the depression makes even this surprising. However, it is not an exaggeration to say that New Deal legislation preempted many of the Socialists' proposals. Norman

Thomas, Socialist leader after the death of Debs in 1926, maintained for many years that the Socialist collapse was due to popular support for, and interest in, the New Deal. In his article, "Not So 'Turbulent Years' " (1979), Melvyn Dubofsky concludes that "By frightening the ruling class into conceding reforms and appealing to workers to vote as a solid bloc, Roosevelt simultaneously intensified class consciousness and stripped it of its radical potential." The Socialists might have gained by the great interest in social welfare but the party disintegrated and by the time of Pearl Harbor had become a diminutive sect. In the early days of the New Deal the Socialist party continued to rise to 23,600 members in May 1934, of whom 5,000 members were new in that year. However, this increased numerical support was lacking in financial substance. Ironically, as numbers went higher, financial support was a small fraction of that given in 1928 when membership was low. In 1932 only $26,000 in funds were raised from all sources whereas in 1928 the total of funds was $110,000. The Socialist party could have continued to profit in the 1930s but did not. The Socialists fell out among themselves and the opposing groups of militant youngsters and more conservative old guard became increasingly factious. Many of the younger Socialists, such as Paul Douglas, went to work in New Deal agencies while others, like David Dubinsky, rose to positions of leadership in organized labor and supported New Deal policies. They wanted to see their ideas of reform realized from positions of power.

There were other reasons for the decline of the Socialist party in the 1930s. One of Norman Thomas's biographers, Bernard K. Johnpoll in *Pacifist's Progress* (1970), mentions how new reform movements drew support from within the existing two-party system, primarily those of Fiorello La Guardia in New York and Upton Sinclair in California. Moreover, the Spanish Civil War diverted and divided radicals. There were, also, Trojan Horse activities of Trotskyites and other communist sects that were penetrating the Socialist party. Norman Thomas's own pacifism and isolationism alienated certain ethnic groups with European loyalties and, at the same time, antagonized radicals committed to reform in the United States. Thus the Socialist party was divided over domestic and foreign policies and its isolationist campaigns from 1938 onward resulted in a decline to only 1,141 members by January 1942. By then the Socialist party was nothing more than a minuscule sect.

The Communist party of America, while hardly larger than the Socialist party, with an estimated membership only 25,000 or 30,000, exercised much greater influence during the 1930s. American intellectuals, oblivious to the political brutalities of Stalin's dictatorship in the USSR, compared its supposed economic successes with the fumbling inability of the United States, the world's richest country, to treat mass poverty and unemployment. Some were active in the Communist party; others promoted socialist ideals in their writings.

In their *The American Communist Party, A Critical History: 1919–1957* (1957), Irving Howe and Lewis Coser believe that the key to understanding the CP from the 1930s was to see how it had been transformed in the 1920s into a totalitarian organization. Moreover, they tried to explain Stalinism in Russia with its cult of personality, show trials, and mass purges as one part of a general crisis for modern mass society.

Communism and its cruel caricature, Stalinism, derived not from a psychological malaise unique to or predominant among its adherents but from a general breakdown of society. . . . In a time of permanent crisis Stalinism seemed to provide a faith, to cry forth a challenge and make possible an ideal. . . . The tragedy of Stalinism arose when the quest for justice among its followers became indistinguishable from their loyalty to a profoundly unjust system of totalitarian domination.

The Communist party managed to broaden its appeal after 1935 through the Popular Front Against Fascism. However, by obediently, if reluctantly, following Moscow's alternating and ambiguous shifts in policy, communism in the United States was never able to hold sway in more than a few CIO locals and intellectual groups. This did not prevent many employers, union leaders, and right-wing politicians from claiming that the CIO was dominated by reds. John L. Lewis did allow Communists to recruit for the CIO, reckoning that they had the toughness and dedication to take on difficult tasks. One such, Len De Caux, became editor of

Many ethnic and religious communities retained their distinctive customs and appearances until, and beyond, World War II. A Mennonite couple at a public sale in Lititz, Pennsylvania, in November 1942, photographed by Marjory Collins for the Office of War Information. (Library of Congress).

CIO News, and another, Lee Pressman, served Lewis as chief counsel. By 1939 the United Electrical Union, the International Longshoremen and Warehouse Union, the Mine, Mill, and Smelter Union, the Fur Workers' Union, and the United Cannery Workers' Union were infiltrated by Communists, who had also penetrated certain sections of the Transport Workers' Union and Furniture Workers' Union. However, from 1939 onward Communist influence began to decline.

The antipathy of American political culture to left-wing radicalism encouraged the House Un-American Activities Committee —the body more commonly associated with the intolerance of the postwar McCarthy era—to begin its investigations and hearings as early as 1938.

During this period President Franklin Roosevelt's attitude toward labor was ambivalent and he certainly was not a pro-union politician. When the CIO revived an earlier slogan "The President Wants You To Organize" in 1936, FDR's administration considered (but declined) taking legal action against the unions. "The point was," as David Brody correctly asserts, "that workers believed it was true; they thought the president did want them to organize. Its underlying labor sympathy was the New Deal's special contribution to making the conditions for organizing America's industrial workers."

Another important contribution of the New Deal was, of course, the reshaping of national electoral politics. In alienating many sections of the business community, the Democratic party under FDR came to rely on the support of a coalition of working-class and labor groups. For example, in the 1936 election campaign, the Non-Partisan League was formed by AFL and CIO activists to mobilize working-class support for FDR. On the one hand, his reliance on union support pushed Roosevelt into adopting policies more sympathetic to labor. On the other, labor's fortunes, and the interests of its leaders, became increasingly tied to the success of the Democratic party. However, John L. Lewis resisted organized labor's growing dependence on the government. When the flow of pro-labor measures began to dry up after 1937, and the administration started to adopt an interventionist strategy toward the war in Europe, Lewis split first with the president, and, then, from the CIO. Lewis was concerned about increased collaboration between labor and government and, in retrospect, we can see that his fears were justified. However, instead of going on to form a labor party, which might have been the logical step to take, Lewis endorsed the Republicans in the 1940 election and stepped down from his position as CIO chief in favor of Phil

Murray of SWOC. The labor movement once again failed to translate its newfound numerical strength into an effective independent political organization.

The persistent difficulty of linking shop-floor militancy with electoral politics had been clearly evident during the CIO's local election campaigns in 1937. For example, in Akron, birthplace of the sit-down strike and possibly the most unionized city in the country, the CIO candidate for mayor was defeated by the Republicans because the working-class vote was split on issues of union strategy, growing public dissatisfaction with the New Deal, and claims that a radical city government would drive away business.

Thus, as America prepared for World War II, the labor movement was making divergent signals. In the twelve years to 1941, the number of workers organized in unions had almost tripled to stand at 8.41 million, or 27 percent of all industrial workers. For the first time in history, unions had made significant inroads into the mass production sector of the economy, and new legislation guaranteed the rights of workers to organize freely. However, in the wake of the upheavals and dramatic victories of the 1933–1937 period, unions struggled to maintain their newly won gains. Workers on the shop floor were asked to tone down their demands and stifle their militancy, as union leaders sought to build stable bridges between labor, management, and government. In the years to come, this strained relationship emerged as the key factor behind labor's ever shifting fortunes.

The Working Class on the Eve of the War

The United States was still largely a nation of small towns and rural communities in 1940. Of the 131,699,275 citizens listed in the census as living in the continental United States and the 118,933 living in overseas territories and dependencies, 74.4 million (56.5 percent) were designated as urban dwellers. However, as we know, urban meant only a community of 2,500 or more inhabitants. If we consider urban a community of far greater numbers, then a different picture emerges. Less than 50 percent of all Americans lived in cities with over 10,000 inhabitants; less than 40 percent lived in cities with over 25,000 inhabitants; and only 30 percent lived in cities with over 100,000. Thus in 1940 70 million people (55 percent) lived in places with fewer than 10,000 inhabitants. In other words, small towns were a dominant fact of American life.

Historian Richard Polenberg declares in *One Nation Divisible* (1980) that "American society on the eve of World War II was sharply divided along class, racial, and ethnic lines." He demonstrates the truth of his assertion about class and ethnicity in a penetrating analysis. His conclusion is also that of many sociologists who followed the Lynds' pioneering study, *Middletown,* with quasi-anthropological and scientific studies of such towns as Newburyport, Massachusetts, Indianola, Mississippi, and Morris, Illinois. "The social system of Yankee City (Newburyport) was dominated by a class order," said W. Lloyd Warner and Paul S. Lunt in *The Social Life of a Modern Community* (1941). The criteria for membership of the upper, middle, and lower classes and their various subsections differed little from place to place. Between 60 and 70 percent of people belonged to the lower-middle and upper-lower categories; about 15 percent belonged to the upper-middle classes; the remaining 15 to 25 percent were in the lower-lower class. Richard Polenberg sums up his interpretation of the class system in the declaration: "Class membership determined virtually every aspect of an individual's life: the subjects one studied in high school, the church one attended, the person one married, the clubs one joined, the magazines one read, the doctor one visited, the way one was treated by the law, and even the choice of an undertaker. Movement across class lines, if not impossible, was markedly infrequent."

Class was also, of course, largely determined by income. In 1939 factory workers earned, on average, about $1,250 a year. However, a highly skilled, experienced tool inspector in an automobile plant might earn as much as $1,600. An advertisement quoted a man who planned to retire on $150 a month, enjoying "life-long security and freedom to do as I please." Thus a salary of $2,500 would make one well-to-do. But only 4.2 percent of working people earned that much in 1939. Among the most highly paid group—urban men in full-time employment—only

11.8 percent earned as much as $2,500. Thus when public opinion polls asked people what they would consider a completely satisfactory income, over half of those who replied gave a sum less than $2,500. Annual earnings of more than $5,000 were way beyond what most people could imagine.

At the base of the economic pyramid were the underemployed, the seasonally employed, and the unemployed. The severe recession of 1938 probably led to an increase in unemployment from 7.5 million to over 11 million. Even in 1940, after the federal government had yet again expanded its programs of relief and national defense, unemployment was still about 9 million people. Furthermore, almost a quarter of the people in work worked less than nine months every year. Partial employment and unemployment account for some most revealing statistics. In 1939, if we exclude that 2.5 million people working on public relief, 58.5 percent of men and 78.3 percent of women were working for, or looking for work that paid, less than $1,000.

It was also people's social class that determined the quality of their medical care. The National Health Survey, a canvass of 740,000 families by the U.S. Public Health Service, published in *Public Health Reports* during 1940, disclosed that families with low incomes were sick longer and more often than better-off families but called doctors less often. In 1936 American families spent an average of $59 a year on medical care but poor families spent less than half that and wealthy families spent twice as much. Serious illness made people poorer. One in 250 heads of families earning $2,000 was permanently disabled but 1 in 20 heads of families on relief was physically unable to work. Moreover, dismal living conditions in themselves made people unhealthy. For example, a study in Cincinnati discovered that the high death rate from intestinal illnesses was centered in congested areas where houses lacked adequate sanitation.

The failure of the Wagner national health bill in 1939 and 1940 illustrated the failing fortunes of the New Deal. Not only had the Republicans made a strong showing in the midterm elections of 1938 and were determined to resist further social reforms but also vested interests lobbied congressmen to work against such legislation. The Wagner bill would have authorized federal aid for maternity and child care, public health services, and hospital construction. Furthermore, it proposed federal supervision of state efforts to implement compulsory insurance. Although the bill was intended to assist the indigent, those most in need of care but least able to afford it, the bill met with a hostile reception in Congress and FDR's indifference. The AMA opposed the bill because it thought the program threatened the relationship between doctor and patient and officials in the Public Health Service did not like the controversy the bill was causing. In the end, Roosevelt endorsed a limited proposal to build (but not maintain) "forty little hospitals" in poor, usually rural, areas at a cost of $50 million. The Senate approved the measure in 1940; the House never considered it.

Education was another gauge of social position. Just as quite small differences in income had a significant impact on standards of living, so minor differences in schooling had considerable repercussions on careers and prospects. In 1940 of the 74.8 million Americans who were twenty-five or older, only 2 in 5 had gone beyond eighth grade; only 1 in 4 had graduated from high school; only 1 in 10 had gone to college and only 1 in 20 had graduated from college. Nevertheless, a college education and degree were becoming recognized as the visa and passport to a career in the white-collar professions. Thus about 875,000 students were enrolled full-time in colleges in 1939. Half the graduates in the Wesleyan class of 1939 expected to make a career in business, medicine, law, or education. Yet the cost of college tuition, accommodation, and board ranged from $453 per annum at state colleges to $979 at private universities and was way beyond most people's pockets.

In 1940 11,419,000 residents, 8.5 percent of the population, had been born abroad. They included 1,624,000 people from Italy; 1,323,000 from Russia, Lithuania, and Rumania; 1,238,000 from Germany; 993,000 from Poland; 845,000 from Denmark, Norway, and Sweden; 678,000 from Ireland; and 163,000 from Greece. There were also 23 million second-generation white immigrants, born in the United States, one or both of whose parents were immigrants, and this accounted for 17.5 percent of the popula-

Not a finale to a Busby Berkeley musical but routine work for women, finishing transparent bomber noses for reconnaissance and fighter planes in the Douglas Aircraft plant in Long Beach, California, in 1942. (Library of Congress).

tion. Thus over one in four Americans was a first- or second-generation immigrant.

Immigrants and their children still accounted for the majority of the population in twenty large industrial cities, comprising two-thirds of the people in Cleveland, Ohio; three-quarters of the population in New York; and three-fifths of the people in Newark, New Jersey. There were large numbers of Finns in Montana, Norwegians in North Dakota, Germans in Wisconsin, and Czechs in Iowa. Immigrants, primarily French Canadians, constituted 40 percent of the population of Burlington, Vermont.

The census of 1940 discovered 377,000 residents who had been born in Mexico and were entitled to be in the United States. The true number, including illegal immigrants, was much larger. In political terms, these illegal immigrants were invisible. Because they were aliens, they could not work on public works projects and worked, whenever possible, in California in lettuce fields, in Texas in cotton fields, and in Michigan in beet fields. They tended to move about so much that they never comprised a significant political bloc. The rate of infant mortality among Mexican-Americans was twice the national average, while the death rate from tuberculosis was three or four times as great.

Mutual aid societies still had their halls, the centers of social life in ethnic communities, often with libraries or newspaper reading rooms, games rooms, and bars. There were also twenty-five fraternal associations for different ethnic groups, comprising almost 3 million members in 32,000 branches.

According to the census of 1940, English was not the mother tongue of almost 22 million people. There were not only foreign language newspapers and magazines but also foreign language bookstores, movie houses, and theaters. About 200 radio stations broadcast foreign language programs, providing, in the largest cities, almost a continuous series of programs in German, Polish, Yiddish, and other languages. They appealed primarily to older immigrants who could return to an aural world of once-familiar music, stories, and jokes. In North End, Boston, 85 percent of Italian immigrants listened regularly to such broadcasts—more than listened to programs in English.

Foreign languages were still widely used and helped foster ethnic identities. In 1940 237 foreign language periodicals were being published in New York; 96 in Chicago; 38 in Pittsburgh; 25 in Los Angeles; and 22 in Detroit. Richard Polenberg estimates that over 1,000 newspapers and periodicals with an aggregate circulation of almost 7 million were printed wholly or partly in a foreign language.

It would be easy to exaggerate the association of particular ethnic groups with certain occupations. Not all Jews worked in the rag trade but Maurice J. Karpf in *Jewish Community Organization in the United States* (1938) discovered that 10.7 percent of Jewish people in the New York telephone book worked in the needle trades, compared with 1.7 percent of those named Smith. Three-quarters of shoe repair and shoeshine shops in New York were owned by Italian Americans.

While older immigrant areas were disintegrating in major cities, certain ethnic groups were still associated with particular sections. Thus in New York City, the Italian community dominated the South Bronx; the Jews, Brownsville; the Germans, Yorkville; the Irish, Manhattanville. Even in small cities, such as Manchester, New Hampshire, there were ethnic quarters, notably Little Canada, Irish Acre, German town, and Norwegian village.

Indians and the New Deal

Anthropologists were beginning to appreciate the cohesive values of cultural heritage, rather than seeing different cultural values as somehow subversive of some idealized American way. Hence American Indians were becoming admired precisely for those characteristics that had, only a few years earlier, led to their being scorned as hopelessly primitive and, hence, inferior. These were their lack of individualism and sense of a progressive historical destiny and their emphasis on intuition and religious belief. Not surprisingly, Indians anxious to improve the quality of their life grew sick and tired of primitive characterizations of themselves as noble savages. When salon dilettante Mable Dodge Luhan tried to prevent the introduction of modern sanitation in the Taos Pueblo, one progressive Indian offered to exchange his primitive home for hers with all its modern conveniences.

Although the new anthropology was limited, it had its distinct political uses and was employed constructively by former New York social worker John Collier. In his autobiography, *From Every Zenith* (1963), John Collier expressed the impact Indian communities were having upon reformers:

The discovery that came to me, there, in that tiny group of a few hundred Indians, was of personality-forming institutions, even now unweakened, which had survived repeated and immense historical shocks, and which were going right on in the production of states of mind, attitudes of mind, earth-loyalties and human loyalties, amid a context of beauty which suffused all the life of the group. . . . It might be that only the Indians, among the peoples of this hemisphere at least, were still the possessors and users of the fundamental secret of human life—the secret of building great personality through the instrumentality of social institutions. And it might be, as well, that the Indian life would not survive.

In the 1920s John Collier challenged federal policy toward certain Indian communities, notably the Bursum bill that proposed to dispossess Pueblo Indians of certain land and water rights. Collier had developed a profound commitment to Indian culture that he saw as preferable to conventional American commercial values. He interpreted what he saw in the light of *Mutual Aid* by Kropotkin, an instance of how to endure by cooperative communal values rather than become engulfed by economic competition in the name of individual will.

In 1934 Collier became commissioner of Indian affairs in Roosevelt's administration, the very same year that Columbia University anthropologist Ruth Benedict's influential work, *Patterns of Culture,* was published. In her book, Ruth Benedict clearly preferred Pueblo culture with its emphasis on communal values to the somewhat possessive Northwest coast fishing cultures. Collier generalized from Benedict's hypotheses and from what he knew of the Pueblo Indians with their cohesive society. He then applied his generalizations to such different groups as the Plains Indians whose culture emphasized individual expression and who had adjusted to a system of individually owned farmland. Collier believed that previous federal policies had been misconceived. Whatever the motives, they had damaged Indian culture. Thus Collier wanted to remedy things.

Collier's wide-ranging proposals were enacted in a modified form in the Wheeler–Howard or Indian Reorganization Act of 1934. It applied to all states except Oklahoma and was, in time, accepted by 192 of 263 tribes who voted on it. The act had three principal aims: to bring an abrupt end to the discredited policy of allotment and continued white appropriation of Indian land; to establish a system of tribal government, providing Indians with some self-determination, "certain rights of home rule"; and to enhance the economic welfare of Indian reservations by creating a revolving credit fund and adding to Indian territory. In his pamphlet, *Modern Indians* (1982), David Murray concludes, "These were undoubtedly helpful and well-intentioned proposals, which in the end helped to ease the poverty and demoralization of many Indians, preserving their land-holdings and setting in motion the complex process of achieving a degree of self-determination." At the same time, the Wheeler-Howard Act proposed that the Bureau of Indian Affairs (BIA) should exercise a far more active role than hitherto according to the expertise of social scientists. The contradiction between the aim of granting the Indians greater autonomy while, at the same time, strengthening the hand of the BIA proved too much for Collier's new colonial policy.

Collier made enemies left and right. He knew that some of the Navahos' chronic economic problems were caused by continuous overgrazing by their sheep. In accordance with New Deal policy elsewhere, Collier's solution was to reduce the flock by slaughter. Whatever the merits of slaughter in terms of cost-effectiveness, to the Navaho it appeared a wanton act against their future security. The decision disclosed the gulf between the impersonal expertise of the administration and the cultural values of the Indians the administration was supposed to be preserving. Collier was essentially autocratic, insisting that the BIA was offering advice and that that advice must be heeded since the experts who gave it were bound to know best. In addition, Collier proved indifferent and, sometimes, downright hostile to Indian resistance to big corporations ready and anxious to extract precious minerals from their lands. Since he preferred land held by tribes to land held by individuals, Indians who wanted to adopt American economic values accused him of trying to send them "back to the blanket." Moreover, he was committed to reversing previous school policies. Instead of instilling white values in boarding schools, he wanted a return to traditional Indian values, a policy that some argued would produce young adults underequipped to cope with earning a living in contemporary America.

The sort of Indian government Collier wanted to establish was the form he considered most representative—an accountable democracy based on a constitution and elections by universal adult suffrage in which the winner was the candidate with the highest plurality. Many Indians considered this a white form of government not suited to Indian needs. Some would have no part in it. Consequently, it was those Indians who played the system and cooperated with federal policies who tended to get elected. They were also those who most conformed to white life-styles and were, often, of mixed race with less Indian blood than white. These "Indians" were sometimes called "progressives" and considered not truly representative. Thus traditional Indians still considered themselves ignored and dispossessed. Once again, the federal government's attempt to reform its Indian policy had resulted in a compromise that favored Indians who preferred assimilation. As Steve Talbot remarks in an article, "The Meaning of Wounded Knee, 1973," for Gerritt Huizer and Bruce Mannheim in *The Politics of Anthropology* (1979), "In essence the [Wheeler-Howard] Act marked a shift from the government's policy of direct rule of reservations as internal colonies to one of indirect rule, a shift from outright colonialism to a system of neo-colonialism."

From the beginning of 1942 Collier's program was being steadily deprived of money. Moreover, it fell victim to the slowly mounting political opposition to the New Deal and, in terms of the Indian problem, this took the form of yet another swing in federal policy. The conventional wisdom now believed that Indian communities should be awarded funds in order to facilitate the Indians' prompt acculturation as integrated American citizens. At the same time as this shift was occurring, many Indians were becoming more active politically. In 1944 they founded the National Congress of American Indians (NCAI), an organization that mixed national and tribal aspirations. Many of its leaders were tribal leaders also and after World War II the NCAI was sustained by the interest of former Indian servicemen (25,000 in all) who, like black Americans, had been radicalized by their wartime experiences. The NCAI, urged onward by younger, educated Indians, was to focus its efforts on legal cases and occupations to secure an extension or return of Indian lands from the whites.

8

WHAT DID I DO TO BE SO BLACK AND BLUE?
Black America

DISCRIMINATION AND harsh treatment of its black citizens was to become the most persistent social evil of America in the twentieth century. In an age when a central theme of art has been the oppression of the individual by the state, the plight of blacks was to be taken as a potent metaphor for imprisonment, whether social, physical, or psychological. Indeed, the black experience was a prime example of man's inhumanity to man. As novelist Richard Wright once observed in a much quoted remark, "The Negro is America's metaphor." Moreover, the black experience makes a stark comment on a central paradox of American history —how a nation composed of such diverse ethnic groups and beliefs could endure and survive. Thus novelist James Baldwin (1924–1987) declared, "The story of the Negro in America is the story of America, or, more precisely, it is the story of Americans."

Out of the total American population of 105,710,620 in 1920,

W. E. B. DuBois, noted black polemicist, photographed by C. M. Battey in 1918. After taking three degrees at Harvard, he became a professor of history at Atlanta University and began to devote himself to race relations and other black problems on which he adopted a militant position. He helped launch the Niagara movement for racial equality in 1905 and in 1910 he became director of publicity and research for the NAACP, a post he held for twenty-four years, during which he organized the Pan-African Congress (1919) before returning to Atlanta University as head of the department of sociology (1933–1944). (Library of Congress).

10,951,000 were blacks—about 10.5 percent of the whole. Eighty-five percent of them lived in the South—the eleven states of the old Confederacy and five others, Oklahoma and Kentucky to the west and Delaware, Maryland, West Virginia, and the District of Columbia to the north. Of the total population of 33,126,000 of this "Census South," 8,912,000 were blacks. Thus, whereas the ratio of blacks to whites across the country as a whole was, approximately, one in ten, in the South it was one in four. In two states, Mississippi and South Carolina, blacks predominated.

The abolition of slavery and the destruction of the rebel Confederacy in the Civil War (1861–1865) had led to the granting of equal social and political rights to blacks in the period of Reconstruction (1865–1877). The Thirteenth Amendment (1865) proscribed slavery. The first section of the Fourteenth Amendment (1866) defined American citizens as all those born or naturalized in the United States and enjoined states from abridging their rights to life, liberty, property, and process of law. The second section threatened to reduce proportionately the representation in Congress of any state denying the suffrage to adult males. Congress determined to protect black suffrage in the South by the Fifteenth Amendment (1869–1870) by which the right to vote was not to be denied "on account of race, color, or previous condition of servitude." Yet forty years later these rights had been assailed or eroded by white racists. The abject position of blacks was such that historian Rayford Logan in *The Betrayal of the Negro* (1954; 1969) described the turn of the century as "the nadir" of Afro-American history, notwithstanding the existence of slavery up to 1865.

The Nadir of Race Relations

The regular intimacy of contact under slavery was being superseded by a caste system with next to no sustained contact and resulted in an inexorable gulf between black and white. Although blacks were the largest of America's ethnic minorities, they were segregated in schooling, housing, and places of public accommodation, such as parks, theaters, hospitals, schools, libraries, courts, and even cemeteries. The variety and fluidity of access of the late nineteenth century were abandoned as state after state adopted rigid segregation in a series of so-called "Jim Crow" laws. ("Jim Crow" was the title of a minstrel song of 1830 that presented blacks as childlike and inferior.)

In *The Strange Career of Jim Crow* (1955; 1974) historian C. Vann Woodward argues that cast-iron segregation was a product of the late nineteenth and early twentieth centuries, and that the avalanche of Jim Crow laws began when poor white farmers came to power. Moreover, a new generation of black citizens had grown up who had never known slavery. Previously, aristocratic southerners had shown a paternalistic attitude to blacks, protecting them from some overt racist attacks by poor whites. They knew they did not need segregation laws to confirm their own privileged social position. Nevertheless, none of the states passed a single comprehensive segregation law. Instead, they proceeded piecemeal over a period of thirty to fifty years. Thus South Carolina segregated the races in successive stages, beginning with trains (1898) and moving to streetcars (1905), train depots and restaurants (1906), textile plants (1915 and 1916), circuses (1917), pool halls (1924), and beaches and recreation centers (1934). Georgia began with railroads and prisons (1891), and moved to sleeping cars (1899), and, finally, pool halls (1925), but refused to segregate places of public accommodation until 1954.

The South reacted against the natural tide of black resentment to its new restrictive policies with more repression. Mississippi was the first state effectively to disfranchise black citizens by a constitutional convention in 1890. It was followed by South Carolina in 1895, Louisiana in 1898, North Carolina (by an amendment) in 1900, Alabama in 1901, Virginia in 1901 and 1902, Georgia (by amendment) in 1908, and the new state of Oklahoma in 1910. Four more states achieved the same ends without revising their constitutions: Tennessee, Florida, Arkansas, and Texas.

Edgar Gardner Murphy, a humanitarian journalist, reported in *The Basis of Ascendancy* (1909) how extremists had moved "from an undiscriminating attack upon the Negro's ballot to a like attack upon his schools, his labor, his life—from the contention that no Negro shall vote to the contention that no Negro shall learn, that no Negro shall labor, and (by implication) that no Negro shall live." The result was an "all-absorbing autocracy of race," an "absolute identification of the stronger race with the very being of the state." Deploring the sorry state of affairs, Governor N. B. Broward of Florida told the state legislature in 1907 that "relations between the races are becoming strained and acute." In 1903 black analyst Charles W. Chestnutt said that "the rights of the Negroes are at a lower ebb than at any time during the thirty-five years of their freedom, and the race prejudice more intense and uncompromising."

As far as black history is concerned, we can interpret the period 1900–1941 as a journey over a giant suspension bridge across a turbulent river, the dark waters of racism. On near and far sides, the bridge is suspended between the poles of two very different Supreme Court decisions. The first is the notorious "separate but equal" ruling in *Plessy* v. *Ferguson* of 1896, symbol of the heinous institutional racism of the period 1890–1910; and the second is the ruling that separate is unequal of *Brown* v. *Board of Education* of 1954, the most momentous post–World War II court decision yet and a mighty symbol of the victories of the great civil rights movement of 1950–1970. The outlying buttresses of the bridge are provided by four of the most enduring civil rights or separatist groups that were formed in the period: the National Association for the Advancement of Colored People (NAACP) (1910), the Urban League (1911), the Nation of Islam (1931), and, in the 1940's, the Committee, later the Congress, for Racial Equality (CORE) (1943). The apex of the suspension bridge is provided by the great flowering of black cultural talent of the 1920s, known variously as the "Black" or "Negro" or "Harlem Renaissance." During these years four charismatic black leaders guided their followers across the bridge, albeit to different destinations: Booker T. Washington, W. E. B. DuBois, Marcus Garvey, and Asa Philip Randolph.

Moreover, certain of the phenomena that account for the way civil rights moved to the center of the political stage in the 1950s and then shifted emphasis to black power in the course of the 1960s were already present early in the century. These include: the Great Migration of blacks from countryside to city and from

South to North, making black problems known to the North and transforming blacks into a potentially potent political force to be courted by both parties and radical groups; increasing black literacy and awareness of the discrepancy between the ideals of the American Constitution and the blatant practice of racism, most notably in World War II; the development of nonviolent tactics to protest discrimination, initially by religious groups; various Supreme and lesser court hearings that provided forums for such eloquent black attorneys as Moorfield Storey, Walter F. White, and Thurgood Marshall to press for rulings on racial equality that exposed discrimination, established the legal principle of equality before the law, and legitimized the civil rights movement. Furthermore, the later tension between civil rights and black power was anticipated in the 1920s by the controversy between W. E. B. DuBois and A. Philip Randolph on one side and Marcus Garvey and his short-lived United Negro Improvement Association (UNIA) organization (1914) on the other.

Before 1900 black protest existed only in local groups, apart from a series of black conventions summoned to endorse presidential candidates. Nevertheless, state and local conventions debated the new laws on public accommodation and disfranchisement. Their protests were handicapped by black poverty, illiteracy, and fragmentation. Leaders found it almost impossible to develop black consciousness and unity on a scale to combat the considerable white forces arrayed against them, notably the adverse political climate, the indifference of the Supreme Court, and white intimidation and violence. Their political voice was silenced. There was no black congressman for twenty-seven years, between 1901, when George H. White of North Carolina left Congress, and 1928, when Oscar De Priest was elected for Chicago.

Booker T. Washington and W. E. B. DuBois

Since blacks were being displaced from their traditional trades and confined to menial jobs in the towns, those who did succeed in entering the worlds of business and the professions were obliged by white society to adopt its attitudes in order to retain their hard won position. Their undeclared leader was Booker T. Washington, head of Tuskegee Industrial Institute, Alabama. Washington was invited to speak at the opening of the Cotton States and International Exposition in Atlanta on September 18, 1895, by businessmen who recognized his remarkable powers of expression. His address was one of the most effective political speeches of the Gilded Age, a model fusion of substance and style.

In what was later called the Atlanta Compromise he abandoned the postwar ideal of racial equality in favor of increased economic opportunity for blacks. "The wisest among my race understand that the agitation of questions of social equality is the extremest folly and that progress in the enjoyment of all the privileges that will come to us must be the result of severe and constant struggle rather than of artificial forcing." He preached patience, proposed submission, and emphasized material progress. Those blacks who rejected the Atlanta Compromise, such as rising activist W. E. B. DuBois, considered it a capitulation to blatant racism. But Washington was telling white society exactly what it wanted to hear, that blacks accepted the Protestant work ethic. His most widely reported remark was a subtle metaphor about racial harmony: "In all things social we can be as separate as the fingers, yet one as the hand in all things essential to mutual progress."

Washington's emphasis on racial pride, economic progress, and industrial education encouraged white politicians and businessmen, such as steel tycoon Andrew Carnegie, to subsidize the black institutions he recommended. Through his close connections with business he was able to raise the funds necessary to create the National Negro Business League in 1900. Moreover, he used money not to advance black acquiescence but to fight segregation. Others sought a more open insistence on racial pride. In 1890 T. Thomas Fortune, a black journalist of New York, persuaded forty black protection leagues in cities across the country to join in a national body, the Afro-American League. Historian C. Vann Woodward assesses Washington's work thus: "Washington's life mission was to find a pragmatic compromise that would resolve the antagonisms, suspicions, and aspirations of 'all three classes directly concerned—the Southern white man, the Northern white man, and the Negro.' It proved, he admitted, 'a difficult and at times a puzzling task.' But he moved with consummate diplomacy, trading renunciation for concession and playing sentiment against interest."

The publication of *The Souls of Black Folk* by W. E. B. DuBois in 1903 solidified black protest around a new spokesman. William Edward Burghardt DuBois was born in Great Barrington, Massachusetts, in 1868, graduated from Fisk and Harvard, and attended the University of Berlin. After returning to America in 1894, he taught at Wilberforce University, Ohio, and Pennsylvania University, before becoming professor of sociology at Atlanta. Widely known for being a natty dresser, DuBois was also a creative writer who produced two novels, *The Quest of the Silver Fleece* (1900) and *The Dark Princess* (1928), and two volumes of essays and poems, *Dark Water* (1920) and *The Gift of Black Folk* (1924). One of DuBois's early supporters, James Weldon Johnson, said of *The Souls of Black Folk* that "it had a greater effect upon and within the Negro race than any single book published in the country since *Uncle Tom's Cabin.*" One of the essays was a withering attack on what DuBois considered Washington's acceptance of the heinous doctrine of black inferiority. DuBois insisted on an end to accommodation. "By every civilized and peaceful method we must strive for the rights which the world accords to men."

Deeply angered by Washington's counterrevolutionary tactics and intensely hostile to the strategy of accommodation, DuBois invited likeminded activists to a national conference at Fort Erie in July 1905 that established the Niagara movement. This was an elite cadre of about 400 college-educated professional people. The Niagara movement committed itself to continuing vocal protest against "the abridgment of political and civil rights and against inequality of educational opportunity." DuBois and others published the *Moon* and, later, the *Horizon* as unofficial journals of the movement. Nevertheless, the Niagara movement failed to establish itself as a distinctive national voice.

At a meeting in New York on May 31 and June 1, 1909, black and white radicals proposed a new national organization to protect the rights of blacks and a similar conference held in 1910 established the National Association for the Advancement of Colored People (NAACP) with its declared goal of "equal rights and opportunities for all." Under its first president, Moorfield Storey, the NAACP formed several hundred branches. Under the editorship of W.E.B. DuBois, the NAACP journal, the *Crisis,* reached a circulation of 100,000. DuBois's own column, "As the Crow Flies," attacked white racism. Together with the *Chicago Defender,* the *Pittsburgh Courier,* and the *Baltimore Afro American,* the *Crisis* made an ever-increasing spectrum of literate blacks aware of their national responsibilities and what the nation owed them.

The NAACP's distinctive strategy was litigation to challenge racist laws. For example, in 1917 the NAACP challenged a statute of Louisville, Kentucky, requiring "the use of separate blocks for residence, places of abode, and places of assembly by white and colored people respectively." Moorfield Storey took the case to the Supreme Court at a time when it was, in the terms of analyst Richard Kluger, peopled by men of Paleolithic perspective, notably Justices Willis van Devanter and James Clark McReynolds. Nevertheless, in the case of *Buchanan* v. *Warley* the Court unanimously, and surprisingly, decided on November 5, 1917, that "All citizens of the United States shall have the same right in every state and territory, as is enjoyed by white citizens thereof, to inherit, purchase, lease, sell, hold and convey real and personal property." However, the *Buchanan* decision resulted in a spate of private restrictive covenants under which residents agreed to sell or rent their property to individuals of one race only. The Court subsequently upheld this pernicious practice in *Corrigan* v. *Buckley* in 1926, maintaining that civil rights were not protected against discrimination by individuals.

The second-oldest surviving black organization, the Urban League, was founded in New York in 1911. It was primarily a social welfare organization assisting black migrants in finding work and accommodation and trying to relieve the worst excesses of black urban poverty. It, too, had a journal, *Opportunity,* founded in 1923, and, in the 1930s, the extreme circumstances of the depression allowed the organization the occasion for special pleas against economic as well as political oppression of black citizens. Of these first concerted attempts at black association, Harvard Sitkoff concludes in *A New Deal for Blacks* (1978), "The civil

For over thirty years, Paul Robeson proved himself among the most versatile of American artists, whether as college athlete, singer of spirituals, or a noble actor in plays by Shakespeare and Eugene O'Neill. In the film of O'Neill's *The Emperor Jones* he moved from cocky self-assurance to doubt and terror. However, throughout his successful career, Paul Robeson never lost touch with the dilemma of black Americans and he adopted increasingly radical political stands, culminating in his appeal for "Black Power" during the Little Rock crisis of 1957. (Musuem of Modern Art Film Stills Archive).

rights organizations of the early twentieth century lacked adequate finances, political leverage, the support of most blacks, influential white allies, and access to the major institutions shaping public opinion and policy."

Race discrimination, important in itself, had more momentous consequences because of the contemporary exodus of blacks from South to North. For the 1910s and 1920s were also the years of the Great Migration. The immediate reason for the exodus was the industrial requirements of World War I. Whites were being drawn increasingly into the armed services and newly created war industries. However, the war prevented European immigrants from coming to America and taking their place as laborers. Thus in 1915 agents for northern employers began recruiting black labor from the South. However, at least four times as many blacks went North on word of mouth than did so at the prompting of labor agents. The exodus was mainly spontaneous and largely unorganized; whatever the personal motives for individual moves, the collective motive was bad treatment in the South. The Great Migration was facilitated by railroad transportation and continued after the war was over. In sum, the South lost 323,000 black citizens in the 1910s and 615,000 in the 1920s—about 8.2 percent of its black population.

Carter G. Woodson recognized the significance of the phenomenon and founded the Association for the Study of Negro Life and History in September 1915 to review the momentous sociological changes in a regular publication, the *Journal of Negro History,* of which he was editor. In 1915 the association published Woodson's *A Century of Negro Migration* that described the exodus as "giving the Negro his best chance in the economic world out of which he must emerge a real man with power to secure his rights as an American citizen."

At home black leaders felt ambivalent toward American intervention. W. E. B. DuBois moved from opposing the war effort to support in June 1918 on the assumption that an Allied victory would yield blacks the right to vote, work, and live without continuous harassment. Other activists disagreed. The included Asa Philip Randolph and Chandler Owens, editors of the *Messenger,* a journal they had founded in 1915 as part of a strategy to recruit black hotel workers into a labor union.

A. Philip Randolph, born in Crescent City, Florida, would emerge as one of the most significant black leaders of the twentieth century. The son of James Randolph, an African Methodist Episcopal Church preacher, A. Philip moved to New York and joined the Socialist party in 1911. He was fired from successive jobs as an elevator operator, maintenance man, and waiter for having tried to start unions with his fellow workers. Roi Ottley describes him in *Black Odyssey* as "unique among Negro leaders in that he was neither preacher, educator, nor rabble rousing politician, but a labor organizer. Tall, dark, and brooding, Randolph impressed Negroes as being all soul." Along with fellow socialist Chandler Owens, Randolph condemned the war in the *Messenger* and traversed the country making speeches in opposition to it. He declared in the *Messenger,* "Lynching, Jim Crow, segregation, and discrimination in the armed forces and out, disfranchisement of millions of black souls in the South—all these things make your cry of making the world safe for democracy a sham, a mockery, a rape of decency, and a travesty of common justice." After an antiwar meeting in Cleveland in 1918 Randolph was arrested and jailed for a few days. In the antiradical hysteria following the war, the *Messenger* was banned from federal mails.

In the North black migrants were condemned by circumstances to a life in squalid tenement ghettos. They faced resentment and hostility from white workers who feared for their livelihood. In 1917 there were race riots in towns and on army bases. In July 1917 a savage race riot in East St. Louis killed between 40 and 200 blacks and drove almost 6,000 from their homes. The first year of peace, 1919, was the most violent in black history since Reconstruction: there were twenty-five race riots across the country.

With the death of prominent black spokesman Booker T. Washington in 1915 the initiative in the black political movement passed to the NAACP. Within ten years W. E. B. DuBois, editor of the NAACP journal, the *Crisis,* had made himself the leading black spokesman of the age. The NAACP's base was in the North but its principal officers were natives of the South—William Pickens, Robert W. Bagnall, Walter White, and James Weldon Johnson. Johnson had graduated from Atlanta University and was a distinguished novelist and poet who had served the State Department in Nicaragua and Venezuela. As secretary he expanded the NAACP's activities. In 1919 the association had 88,448 members distributed among 300 branches, of which 155 were in the South. This rapid increase in size since 1913 (when there had been only fourteen branches) laid the NAACP open to racist criticism that it had fueled postwar riots. This was ironic. The NAACP was an elite organization committed to legal protest against injustice. Nevertheless, it was determined that black citizens should be made aware of their civil rights.

DuBois was also the father of the Pan African movement with its belief in special cultural and political links between American blacks and Africa. Thus the NAACP supported the Pan African Congress in Paris in 1919 and lobbied statesmen at the peace conference for self-determination for African colonies. It was DuBois who recognized the connection between the struggles by African blacks for national independence from Europe and by American blacks for civil rights in the United States.

Southern senators, such as Walter F. George, John Sharp Williams, and James F. Byrnes, were utterly complacent in their faith that white supremacy was inviolable. On the surface, it seemed that statistical evidence was on their side. In the South only 21.1 percent of blacks worked outside of agriculture. Only 7 percent of blacks in towns had professional, managerial, or clerical occupations. Furthermore, blacks were still being systematically disenfranchised. In the South the real contest was not in the election itself but for the Democratic nomination. Thus the Democratic party prevented its black members from voting in primaries. It did this by state laws in eight states and by county or city laws in three others.

Texas was one of the states that decided to use the device of excluding blacks from Democratic primaries. However, Dr. A. L. Nixon, a black citizen of El Paso, supported by the NAACP, challenged the racist law in the case of *Nixon* v. *Herndon,* in which he was represented by Moorfield Storey, then aged eighty-two. The case reached the Supreme Court that ruled on March 7, 1927, that the Texas law violated the Fourteenth Amendment. The Texas state legislature decided to undermine the ruling by investing the state executive committees of the political parties with authority to decide who could, and who could not, vote. Thus the Democratic party committee restricted voting in primaries to "all white Democrats who are qualified under the constitution and laws of Texas." Dr. Nixon continued to press his, and the NAACP's, case and was now represented by attorney Nathan Margold, author of a report recommending the NAACP to oblige states to make black educational facilities equal to white. In the case of *Nixon v. Condon* the Supreme Court decided by 5 votes to 4 on May 2, 1932, that the power of executive committees to exclude blacks from primaries was a form of state power and, therefore, unconstitutional.

Within weeks the devious Texas Democrats had convened a state convention that declared that all white citizens could vote in primaries but blacks could not. When black Texan William Grovey tried to get a ballot for the Democratic primary election of July 1934, he was refused. Supported by black lawyers Carter Wesley and J. Alston Atkins, he fought the test case of *Grovey v. Townsend* to the Supreme Court, which, on April 1, 1935, unanimously ruled that the Texas Democratic party was within its rights because it was a private organization and not subject to the Fourteenth Amendment.

Sometimes blacks were allowed to vote in municipal elections, especially in Texas and Virginia. They played a decisive part in local elections in Louisville in 1920, Nashville in 1921, and Savannah in 1923. In Atlanta in 1921 and NAACP mobilized black voters to ensure the passage of a $4 million school bond of which $1 million was pledged to black schools. Some urban bosses elicited black support and repaid it in kind. In San Antonio, Texas, Charles Bellinger had a regular supply of black votes. Thus he controlled city elections in San Antonio from 1918 until 1935. In return, he provided blacks with schools and parks, a library and an auditorium, as well as paved streets and sewers.

Strange Fruit

Not content with holding blacks in social chains, vicious whites sometimes sought their lives. Many blacks were victims of lynch law, especially in the South where the trees of small towns bore strange fruit about once in every generation. The common charge was that the black victims of white lynch mobs had tried to rape white women. According to black surveys, there were over a thousand lynchings between 1900 and 1915. Moreover, as historian Harvard Sitkoff observes, "Petty brutality, lynchings, and pogroms against the Negro sections of towns occurred so frequently in the first decade of the twentieth century that they appeared commonplace, hardly newsworthy." American intervention in the war and its vicious propaganda to smash the Hun released a new tide of savagery. Between 1918 and 1927, according to NAACP officer Walter F. White in his *Rope and Faggot* (1929), 456 people were victims of lynch mobs. Of this number 416 were black, 11 were women and 3 of them were pregnant. Forty-two of the victims were burned alive, 16 were cremated after death, and 8 were either beaten to death or dismembered and cut to pieces.

Racist Winfield H. Collins defended this vile practice in a scurrilous book of 1918, *The Truth About Lynching:* "The white man in lynching a Negro does it as an indirect act of self-defense against the Negro criminal as a race." The practice of lynching was necessary "in order to hold in check the Negro in the South." Senator James F. Byrnes agreed. He told Congress that lynching was the surest way of defending white women from rape. Perversely turning the burden of guilt to the victims of lynching, he declared that "rape is responsible directly and indirectly for most of the lynching in America."

For some communities the act of lynching became what historian George Brown Tindall has called in *The Emergence of the New South* (1967) "a twentieth century auto-da-fé." It was an event for white men, women, and children to attend in order to relieve the boredom of small town life. They wanted entertainment and prolonging the torture of a hapless victim and taking bizarre photographs of the cruel scene gave them sadistic pleasure. A contributory factor in the epidemic of lynching was the depressed provincialism of isolated southern communities. According to historian James H. Chadbourn in *Lynching and the Law* (1933), a county given to lynching was "characterized in general by social and economic decadence." Its family incomes were well below average and 75 percent of its inhabitants were likely to belong to Southern Methodist and Baptist churches. Moreover, W. E. Wimpy of Georgia believed in an article for *Manufacturers' Record* of December 25, 1919, that the horrible practice could persist because the United States was divided into hundreds of minuscule sovereign governments. "These tiny kingdoms can kill their subjects like hogs if they want to, and under State rights they know there is no law on earth to prosecute them but their own law; no judge ever prosecutes himself."

The epidemic of lynchings allowed black leaders the opportunity to lance the boil of white hypocrisy and evasion. The NAACP assumed that if it publicized the outrages, mass public indignation would demand reform. Thus it organized public meetings, lobbied public officials, and stimulated press investigation. Walter F. White of Atlanta, appropriately enough, could pass for white. Thus he gained access to public officials in the South who held records of lynchings. Those officials who discovered he was black were more antagonized by his methods than they were by his disclosures.

The NAACP published its research findings as *Thirty Years of Lynching, 1889–1918*. The report was published to coincide with a national conference on the subject held in New York in May 1919. The review challenged popular stereotypes about lynching. In particular, it showed that fewer than one in six victims of lynching had even been accused of rape by their assailants. The conference called for a federal law against lynching.

In 1921 the NAACP established an office in Washington. Its aim was to lobby Congress in support of Congressman L. C. Dyer of St. Louis who had introduced an antilynching bill in 1919. The Dyer bill proposed to eliminate lynching by making counties in which the offence occurred responsible. If they failed to protect citizens or prisoners from mob rule and a lynching took place, then the county would be fined. The Dyer bill passed the House by 230 votes to 119 in 1922. However, it was defeated in the Senate because of a southern filibuster.

Although the Dyer bill failed in Congress, the publicity it earned helped reduce the extent of the evil. The South grew ashamed of lynching. Southern papers asserted that southern courts

Throughout the 1920s and 1930s the NAACP maintained a campaign against the notorious racist abuse of lynching, publishing terrifying photographs of hapless victims trapped by the merciless sadism of the most bigoted southern towns, ready to corrupt little children by scenes of torture and murder. (Library of Congress).

could handle the problem and punish aggressors without needing a federal law to show them how. According to the *Negro Year Book* (1932), whereas the total number of lynchings was eighty-three in 1919 it fell to sixteen in 1924. It rose to thirty in 1926 and then declined further to eleven in 1928. The NAACP did not work alone. In 1929 reporter Louis I. Jaffe of the Norfolk *Virginian Pilot* won an editorial prize for his campaign against lynching.

Another association working for improved race relations was the Commission on Interracial Cooperation (CIC). It was founded on April 9, 1919, by a group of whites and blacks in Atlanta, disturbed by the events of 1919. They gave priority to the special social needs of black soldiers and their families in the process of demobilization. The commission secured a grant from the National War Work Council and organized conferences to advise white and black social workers. The strategy was to persuade one white and one black social worker to act as liaison officers in each southern community. Their aim was to reduce social tensions. In 1920 there were 500 interracial committees and by 1923 there were about 800. The CIC was well aware of the extent of the problem as it uncovered "vast areas of interracial injustice and neglect that could not be cleared up in a few months or a few years."

After the first two years the CIC began to receive funds regularly from various Protestant churches and public foundations, and it instituted a campaign to redress black grievances. By this time Will W. Alexander, a former Methodist minister and YMCA worker from Nashville, had emerged as leader of the commission. His strategy was to get whites and blacks to cooperate with one another by sharing a common task of welfare. The CIC was supported by the NAACP, the black press, and the Methodist church and governors in seven states. It persuaded Governor Hugh M. Dorsey of Georgia to publish an account on April 22, 1921, of 135 atrocities against blacks in the previous two years. However, the CIC, fearing loss of funds from its white sponsors, failed to take a stand on the issue of desegregation.

Another social evil in the South was peonage, a sinister variant of contract labor. Peonage was illegal but it was common in labor camps throughout the South. Peons were immigrants enticed by fraudulent advertisements placed in labor agencies in the larger cities. They worked in the cotton belt from Texas to the Carolinas, the turpentine areas of Florida, Georgia, and Alabama, and on railroads, sawmills, and mines elsewhere. Unlike slaves, they had no value as investment. They were kept at subsistence level and only for as long as they could work. In 1921 John Williams killed eleven black workers at his farm near Covington, Georgia, rather than admit he was making them work out fines he had paid the county. Governor Hugh Dorsey disclosed over twenty cases of peonage in Georgia that year.

The New York *World* began a campaign against peonage. On November 24, 1929, the *World* published findings of Orlando Kay Armstrong, a former dean of journalism at the University of Florida. Armstrong exposed the abuse of forced labor in Florida. A state law of 1919 deemed that anyone who promised his labor in advance but failed to give it was guilty of a misdemeanour. The law could be used by unscrupulous bosses to misrepresent labor contracts and thus force men to work as peons against their will.

The New York *World* also revealed that the leasing of convict labor still persisted. It told the lurid story of Martin Tabert of North Dakota who was caught train hopping in Tallahassee and sent to a lumber camp where he was whipped to death. The camp doctor had tried to cover the traces of the malevolent whip master by saying the victim had died of malaria. The *World*'s exposure of the Tabert case prompted various investigations by Florida papers and an official investigation by the state legislature. As a result, convict leasing was eventually abolished.

However, fictional accounts of the penal system based on real life experience proved the most penetrating indictments of its excessive brutality. In 1932 two novels, *Georgia Nigger* by John L. Spivak and *I am a Fugitive from a (Georgia) Chain Gang* by Robert Elliot Burns, spoke more eloquently than official reports and aroused mass indignation.

The Garvey Movement

During the course of the 1920s feelings of alienation, outright rage, and, above all, despair among blacks encouraged extremism and division. One logical expression of this was emigration to

Africa, or repatriation, for blacks, as first proposed by sea captain Paul Cuffee in the 1810s and political separatist Touissaint L'Ouverture in the 1820s.

It was now Marcus Garvey who provided blacks with an avenue of escape from the Americas. Born in Jamaica in 1887, Marcus Moziah Garvey emigrated to London and worked there for several years as a printer. After his return to Jamaica, he led an unsuccessful printers' strike and lost his job. However, he was inspired by Booker T. Washington's autobiography, *Up From Slavery* (1901), to organize the Universal Negro Improvement and Conservation Association (later known as the UNIA), in August 1914. The aims of the new organization were to establish a universal cofraternity of blacks, civilize tribes in Africa, encourage race pride, and develop a "conscientious Christianity." Having been encouraged by Washington to visit Tuskegee, he arrived after Washington's death. Undeterred, he established the UNIA in Harlem, firstly among other West Indian immigrants. The organization reached its peak of membership in 1921 with between, perhaps, 1 million and 4 million supporters.

Garvey was a commanding and charismatic speaker who promoted the slogan "Africa for Africans at home and abroad" (a variant on a phrase first coined by Martin R. Delany in 1860), and exhorted his followers with "Up you mighty race, you can accomplish what you will." The UNIA established the Black Star Steamship Line to carry migrants across the Atlantic. It also petitioned the League of Nations to transfer the former German colonies in Africa, South West Africa and German East Africa, held as mandates by South Africa and Britain, respectively, to Garvey's control. In 1922 Garvey designated himself president of a new African republic. He organized a militia and created dukes of the Nile among his lieutenants. The panoply of grand titles and imperial uniforms soon seemed foolish. However, the UNIA was the first truly mass movement of black Americans, a predecessor of later black organizations, especially those advocating black power and black pride.

However, because Garvey criticized the lighter skinned integrationists and middle-class blacks of the NAACP for being ashamed of their ancestry, he himself drew withering attacks from such as

A. Philip Randolph, Chandler Owens, and W. E. B. DuBois. Randolph and Owens abused Garvey for concentrating on the issue of race and ignoring what they considered more important, the issue of class. The mutual attacks and recrimination were venomous in the extreme. DuBois described Garvey as "A little fat black man, ugly but with intelligent eyes and a big head." Garvey retorted, calling DuBois a racial monstrosity on account of his mixed African, French, and Dutch ancestry. He was "a lazy dependent mulatto." DuBois published his most virulent attack on Garvey in an editorial "A Lunatic or a Traitor" in the *Crisis* of May 1924, saying Garvey had convicted himself by his own "swaggering monkey shines." "Marcus Garvey is, without doubt, the most dangerous enemy of the Negro race in America and in the world. He is either a lunatic or a traitor."

In *Race First* (1976) Tony Martin comments,

What was most fascinating about the Garvey-DuBois struggle was that it was in a most real sense a continuation of the Washington-DuBois debate. The ideological questions raised were largely the same. Furthermore, Garvey was very self-consciously a disciple of Washington. Along with his admiration for Washington, Garvey had early imbibed a dislike for DuBois. He therefore saw himself as the heir to Washington's fight against DuBois and never missed an opportunity to compare the two, to the detriment of DuBois.

Garvey realized that Washington had accommodated himself to white racism but preferred to believe that, had he lived longer, Washington would have shifted emphasis from gradualism to black nationalism. He shared Washington's opposition to social equality, which he interpreted as free and unhindered social intercourse between the races. Moreover, unlike DuBois, Washington had preached and practiced self-reliance and formed a power base, independent of white influence.

Hostility between integrationists and separatists was so great as to split the UNIA convention in Harlem in 1922. James W. H. Eason, a Philadelphia minister and prominent member of the UNIA, quarreled violently with Garvey on the platform. He withdrew from the UNIA and set up a rival organization, the Universal Negro Alliance, pledged to concentrate on the problems of blacks in the United States. He was also due to testify against Garvey over various irregularities in the Black Star finances but was shot at a speaking engagement in New Orleans in January 1923. Two Jamaicans were indicted for attempted murder, Garvey's chief of police, William Shakespeare, and a patrolman, F. W. Dyer. However, Eason died before he could identify them and they were released. Outraged by this bizarre murder, the Committee of Eight, a group of black leaders, sent a letter to Attorney General Harry M. Daugherty, protesting about the length of time it was taking to bring Garvey to trial for irregularities in the funding of the Black Star Steamship Line. He was arrested on a charge of using the federal mails to defraud the public, convicted in 1923, and after his appeal failed, imprisoned in Atlanta in 1925. In December 1927 he was deported to Jamaica and died in obscurity in London in 1940.

The Garvey movement represented a new black consciousness in which millions of black citizens could sublimate their despair and disillusionment in the promise of a better and more fulfilled future. Most significantly, Garvey also convinced blacks that it was white racism and not black failings or inadequacy that was responsible for their poverty and sense of powerlessness. James Weldon Johnson of the NAACP commented how Garvey collected more money "than any other Negro organization had ever dreamed of." In a most prophetic statement, the *Amsterdam News* of November 30, 1927, declared how "Marcus Garvey made black people proud of their race. In a world where black is despised he taught them that black is beautiful."

The Harlem Renaissance

During the 1920s black consciousness in the North was being nourished by the Harlem Renaissance. Hitherto, even substantive achievements in literature, such as *The Litany of Atlanta* that DuBois wrote to commemorate the Atlanta Riot of 1906, were sporadic, hardly part of a movement. In contrast, the 1920s produced a wealth of black artistic and literary talent that paralleled similar achievements by whites. Both expressed the conflict of values in society between old and new, countryside and town, following

World War I and artists' alienation from small town bourgeois society.

Black arts now received extensive patronage from wealthy whites. The Great Migration that had swelled the black community of Harlem had also made it prosperous. Since New York was the artistic capital of the United States, it was in the interests of producers, publishers, and agents there to promote good art from those ethnic groups who could make a distinctive contribution. While Norman Mailer's perceptive and prophetic remarks of 1957 on "hipsters" and "the white negro" were still far into the future, the seeds of black influence on white fashions, customs, and articulation were already being sown. As writer Langston Hughes commented, "It was the period when the Negro was in vogue." In his *From Slavery to Freedom* (1947; 1967) historian John Hope Franklin explains how the black writers of the Harlem Renaissance expressed the social and economic grievances of blacks.

Despite his intense feelings of hate and hurt, [the black writer] possessed sufficient restraint and objectivity to use his materials artistically, but no less effectively. He was sufficiently in touch with the main currents of American literary development to adapt the accepted forms of his own materials, and therefore gain a wider acceptance. These two factors, the keener realization of injustice and the improvement of the capacity for expression, produced a crop of Negro writers who constituted the "Harlem Renaissance."

The pivotal figure was NAACP leader James Weldon Johnson, who both took part in and recorded the history of the Harlem Renaissance. Johnson produced his *Fifty Years and Other Poems* (1917), following it with a collection of others' work, *The Book of Negro Poetry* (1922), two books of Negro spirituals (1925 and 1926), a book of black sermons in verse, *God's Trombones* (1927), and an indictment of discrimination against black Gold Star mothers, entitled *Saint Peter Relates an Incident of the Resurrection Day* (1930). Johnson's considerable achievement was capped by the reissue of his 1912 *Autobiography of an Ex-colored Man* (1927) and two works that told the story of the Harlem Renaissance, *Black Manhattan* (1930) and *Along This Way* (1933).

Alain Locke of Philadelphia, who took a Ph.D. at Harvard and was the first black Rhodes scholar, published *The New Negro: An Interpretation* (1925), a collection of articles, essays, stories, and poems, first published in the *Survey Graphic*. His preface expressed boundless optimism about the future of black Americans, believing "The vital inner grip of prejudice has been broken" and "In the very process of being transported, the Negro is becoming transformed." "We are witnessing the resurrection of a people. . . ," a "rise from social disillusionment to race pride."

The first writer to capture a wide readership was Claude McKay, who immigrated from the West Indies in 1912 when he was twenty-one. After attending Tuskegee and the University of Kansas, McKay settled in Harlem and published poems in such magazines as the *Seven Arts,* the *Liberator,* and the *Messenger.* However, it was his *Harlem Shadows* (1922) that placed him in the fore of American poets with the plangent defiance of poems like "The Lynching," "If We Must Die," and "To The White Fiends." Therefore, he turned increasingly to prose, producing a novel of black life in New York, *Home to Harlem* (1928), an autobiography, *A Long Way From Home,* and a panoramic study of everyday black life in New York, *Harlem: Negro Metropolis.* The most cosmopolitan and prolific writer, Langston Hughes, was also the most wide-ranging and rebellious in terms of content and form. Thus he earned the nickname "Shakespeare in Harlem." He could move from the passionate defensive pride of race in *The Negro Speaks of Rivers* or mix noble expression in low-life settings in *Brass Spittoons.* His achievements in *Weary Blues* (1926) and *Fine Clothes to the Jew* (1927) were crowned by a novel, *Not Without Laughter* (1930), and *The Ways of White Folks* (1934), and his autobiography, *The Big Sea* (1940).

Other leading writers included Jean Toomer, Countee Culleen, Jennie Redmond Fauset, and Nella Larsen. NAACP antilynching campaigner Walter White was also an accomplished novelist who wrote *Fire in the Flint* (1924), a fast-moving tragedy of southern blacks, and *Flight* (1926), about a woman light enough to pass as white. In 1929 he wrote *Rope and Faggot: A Biography of Judge Lynch,* an acute summary of his research into the problem.

From 1910 onward black actors began to disappear from plays presented downtown and there soon developed a black theater in

Harlem in which black actors appeared before black audiences in both black and white roles. In April 1917 a group sponsored by Emily Hapgood appeared in three one-act plays by Ridgley Torrence at the Garden Theater, Madison Square Garden, that were widely reviewed by the white press. However, press concentration on America's formal entry into World War I immediately afterward obscured the achievement. In 1919 the black actor Charles Gilpin played Rev. William Custis in *Abraham Lincoln* by John Drinkwater and his performance reminded critics of the wealth of black acting talent.

Now white artists, writers, musicians, and dramatists began to draw on the black experience to explore the themes of rootlessness, restlessness, and alienation. One such was playwright Eugene O'Neill who was, like T. S. Eliot, greatly influenced by European expressionism and used modern psychology to analyse biblical and classical myths. In 1920 O'Neill's *The Emperor Jones* was produced in New York with Charles Gilpin as the deposed and ostracized dictator of a West Indies island who declines through persecution to a state of paranoia, all to the accompaniment of accelerating drums and within sets that symbolize his fears. Gilpin found the strain of having to use the term "nigger" again and again every night intense and he began to amend the text onstage and to drink heavily off it. Eventually, he was replaced by Paul Robeson. In *All God's Chillun Got Wings* (1924) O'Neill examined a marriage between a black husband and white wife. The scene at the close when the white actress must kiss the hand of the black actor caused a storm of protest when the play was published and led to threats against O'Neill.

In 1927 *Porgy,* a folk play by Dorothy and DuBose Heyward about the black community in Charleston, was presented by the Theater Guild with Rose McClendon and Frank Wilson. The greatest commercial success of the black legitimate theater was *The Green Pastures* (1930) by Marc Connelly. It retold the story of the Old Testament as if the playwright were Uncle Tom, and in which Richard B. Harrison played de Lawd.

Black performing artists had scored especial success as dancers, comedians, and singers in a variety of musical shows ever since Bert Williams and George Walker had brought their vaudeville

Richard Wright, author of *Native Son,* a moving novel of black consciousness that contains effective satire of whites, whether racist, liberal, or radical, and that set a new standard for black literature, providing a model followed by such diverse writers as Ralph Ellison and Alex Haley. (Carl Van Vechten Collection; Library of Congress).

act to New York in 1896. Black American music, whether jazz, blues, spirituals, or soul, has been among the most influential of all twentieth-century art forms across the world. These forms also shaped black music and its performers onstage in theaters. The writer-producer team of F. E. Miller, Aubrey Lyle, Eubie Blake, and Noble Sissle mounted the black revue *Shuffle Along* (1920), considered the most brilliant by any company to that time, and with a string of popular songs, including "I'm Just Wild About Harry" and "Love Will Find a Way." It established a vogue for black revues, such as Irving Miller's '*Liza,* Miller and Lyle's *Runnin' Wild,* and Blake and Sissle's *Chocolate Dandies,* which introduced Josephine Baker, (all 1923), and *Dixie to Broadway* (1924), which starred Florence Mills, "the little black mosquito," who also appeared in *Blackbirds* (1926).

Among white artists who painted black subjects were Mexican born Miguel Covarrubias and Winold Reiss who illustrated Alain Locke's *The New Negro.* Black artist Henry Ossawa Tanner enjoyed a reputation at the turn of the century that remained unsurpassed by his successors—Laura Wheeler Waring, who painted scenes from the lives of affluent blacks, and Edward A. Harleston, who concentrated on artisans.

With the coming of the depression, the initial flame that had fueled the Renaissance in Harlem began to flicker and the New York wits carried their torches to different parts of the country or Europe. Some new talents began to emerge and kept the spirit of the Renaissance alive until it should come into its second flowering at the end of the decade. Among these transitional writers was the anthropologist Zora Neal Hurston, a student of Franz Boas at Columbia, who collected a mass of folklore in the United States and from the Caribbean on which she would base scholarly articles and novels between 1931 and 1943.

The Great Depression

The Great Depression of the 1930s was a greater catastrophe for the black community than for the white. For those blacks who had a job, the average income during the depression in the South

was only $634 in cities and $566 in the countryside. Black sociologist Kelly Miller described the black American in 1932 as "the
surplus man, the last to be hired and the first to be fired." By
1933 50 percent of urban blacks could not find jobs of any kind
and most rural blacks could not sell their crops at a price that
would repay their costs. In the cities unemployed whites contested for menial work they would once have thought beneath
them and thus "negro jobs" disappeared as domestic service and
garbage collection suddenly became white occupations. Black
communities across the country were threatened by privation,
malnutrition, and even starvation. Not only did southern states
provide the lowest levels of unempolyment benefit and relief but
white officials also openly discriminated against blacks in admin-
istering them. Thus in Mississippi, where over half the population
was black, less than 9 percent of Afro-Americans received any
relief in 1932, compared with 14 percent of whites.

The Great Migration slowed down. Blacks were just as keen to
move from South to North as previously, not because they thought
they could find work more easily but because they heard relief
was administered more equitably in northern cities and that schools
there were better than in the South. However, the costs of transportation were beyond most blacks. Thus only 347,000 came
North in the course of the 1930s.

At first, the depression had a crippling effect on civil rights
organizations, reducing financial contributions from industry and
charitable foundations. At one point the *Crisis,* starved of funds
and subscriptions, was almost forced to close down. Faced with
the possibility of extinction, the NAACP, the Urban League, the
CIC, and other black groups agreed to pool their resources and
share the cost of lobbying operations. They formed a Joint Committee on National Recovery to supervise and coordinate various
programs. In the process the Urban League was transformed
from an organization responsible for a broad range of social services into a protest and lobbying group. However, the NAACP
expanded its activities to include cooperation with the CIO, lobbying Congress, and a small number of court cases, led by Charles
Houston, dean of Harvard Law School, William H. Hastie, and
Thurgood Marshall. Rather than challenge Jim Crow outright,

Houston began a painstaking assault on inequality in public accommodation.

The Great Depression also exacerbated racial tensions. The number of lynchings provides a barometer of race relations, rising from seven in 1921 to twenty-one in 1930 and twenty-eight in 1933. However, the NAACP campaign against lynching attracted widespread support although southern Senators repeatedly secured the defeat of antilynching bills. Lynching united the opposition of both black and white liberals, thereby swelling support for civil rights. The notorious murder of Claude Neal in Florida on October 23, 1934, was widely publicized in the NAACP pamphlet by Howard Kester, recounting how the mob vivisected its victim and hung his mutilated limbs from a tree outside a court house.

A bill proposed by Senators Edward Costigan of Colorado and Robert Wagner of New York called for the fining or jailing of state or local officials found delinquent, either in protecting black or white citizens from lynch mobs or in arresting and prosecuting violators of the law. Furthermore, it provided for a fine of $10,000 to be levied against the county in which the lynching took place. It was supported by governors of twelve states, including David Sholtz of Florida where Claude Neal had been murdered. Nevertheless, the Costigan bill was rejected in April 1935 after a filibuster of southern senators that lasted six days. However, many southern newspapers had now changed their minds and now favored legislation. Congressman Joseph A. Gavagan of New York proposed a new bill that passed the House in April 1937 by 277 votes to 120 after a terrible incident at Duck Hill, Mississippi, where a mob killed two blacks with a blowtorch. However, it was abandoned in the Senate on February 21, 1938, after a filibuster led by Senators Tom Connally of Texas and Theodore Bilbo of Mississippi.

The NAACP campaign had, as usual, been conducted by Walter White, who had become its executive secretary in 1930. White won nationwide recognition for his efforts, including the title of Man of the Year by *Time* magazine in January 1939. Perhaps because of all the adverse publicity, the number of lynchings gradually began to fall—from eighteen in 1935 to two in 1939.

Black Muslims

A number of black nationalist movements emerged during the 1930s, including the National Movement for the Establishment of a Forty-Ninth State, founded in Chicago in 1934 by Oscar Brown, Sr., and Bindley C. Cyrus. The most famous of such organizations was the Nation of Islam, popularly called the Black Muslims, and founded in Detroit circa 1931 by Wallace D. Fard (or Farrod Mohammed or Wali Forrod), a peddler of silks and raincoats of obscure origins, possibly black, possibly part Arab. The Black Muslims represented the most extreme reaction of black Americans to white racism.

Basing their beliefs on the Muslim religion and a version of the Koran, Black Muslims taught that all whites were devils, perverse creations of an evil scientist, Yakub, and that only blacks were the true children of Allah. Absurd? Well, as we have observed elsewhere, both the Jewish Torah and Christian Bible allow the book of Genesis not one but two different stories of the creation of the world and neither is consistent with subsequent scientific interpretations. Religions are conceived by men of faith rather than men of science and they enshrine myths, imaginative stories that help us understand the mysteries of human existence. The myth of the evil Yakub expresses a profound truth, the systematic exploitation of blacks by white society, notably in human slavery and, also, the ways society finds to justify and institutionalize white racism. Moreover, in the 1930s the myth became terrible prophecy. Thus in Germany the Nazis set out to perfect a master race of Aryans, to exterminate the Jews, and also dabbled in terrible sexual and scientific experiments on their victims in concentration camps. In the United States, scientists chose to study the degeneration of black sufferers of venereal disease by allowing them to survive but deteriorate without remedial treatment in the "Bad Blood" experiment at Tuskegee, chronicled by James Jones. The subjects were simply told they suffered from bad blood. Here in the 1930s were two instances of white science fulfilling the worst of contemporary black fears.

By 1933 the Black Muslims had established a temple, created a ritual, founded a University of Islam, and formed the Fruit of Islam, a bodyguard. The sect drew followers from other similar organizations, notably the Moorish Science Temple in Newark, New Jersey. This sect had been first founded in 1913 by Timothy Drew of North Carolina who subsequently opened temples in New York, Chicago, Detroit, and other major cities that were attended by an aggregate congregation of between 20,000 and 30,000.

By 1933 Fard had established a hierarchy in the Nation of Islam, notably his minister, Robert Poole of Georgia, known as Elijah Muhammad. When Fard disappeared mysteriously in 1934, Elijah Muhammad assumed control moving headquarters from Detroit to Chicago. During the 1930s membership stabilized around 10,000 but was damaged by the onset of war. Elijah Muhammad and some others were convicted of draft evasion and he was imprisoned from 1942 to 1946. During the war membership fell to below 1,000 with four temples in Detroit, Chicago, Milwaukee, and Washington, D.C. An obscure religious sect for almost thirty years, the Nation of Islam gained wide publicity in the late 1950s with the rise of its most charismatic leader, Malcolm X.

The cult of separatism had repercussions in the NAACP. In 1934 DuBois broke with the NAACP over his ideas for developing a separate state for blacks, a "Nation within a Nation." He averred that "if the economic and cultural salvation of the American Negro calls for an increase in segregation and prejudice, then that must come." DuBois was to return to the NAACP in 1944 and leave it once again four years later over another policy dispute. In the meantime, he had become a consultant to the United Nations and was more involved in the activities of the Communist party. These led to his indictment for subversion and subsequent acquittal and his unsuccessful campaign for election to the Senate on the American Labor ticket in 1950. Eventually convinced that Afro-Americans could not achieve justice in the United States, he emigrated to Africa and in 1962 he became a citizen of Ghana where he died in 1963 whilst engaged as director of a government-sponsored *Encyclopedia Africana*.

The Scottsboro Boys

Some blacks were attracted to communism because of its emphasis on economic and racial equality and its strategy of working-class solidarity. Radical interest in racial matters was furthered by white Communists, including James S. Allen, Herbert Aptheker, and Philip S. Foner who wrote about black culture and argued that racial prejudice must be erased. No single person represented the fusion of black protest and radicalism better than celebrated actor and singer Paul Robeson. He made no secret of his Communist sympathies, visited Russia in the 1930s, and praised the Soviet system for its apparent equality.

While it is true that blacks were potentially a fertile field for communism and perhaps 2,500 blacks belonged to the Communist party in the mid-1930s, black radicalism was essentially indigenous to the United States, uninterested in theory, especially foreign ideologies, and suspicious of Communist motives at home and abroad. The verdict of many was "It's enough to be black without being red, as well."

The Scottsboro incident of 1931 provided the Communists with the opportunity to rally black support. Here was something that had the hallmarks of a black variation of the *Sacco-Vanzetti* case of the 1920s.

The Scottsboro boys were nine black youths falsely accused of multiple rape on a freight train near Scottsboro, Alabama, on March 25, 1931, by two foul-mouthed white harlots, Victoria Price and Ruby Bates, who needed to explain their presence among the youths. The black youths, all aged between thirteen and twenty, were Charlie Weems, Ozie Powell, Clarence Norris, Olen Montgomery, Willie Roberson, Haywood Patterson, Eugene Williams, and Andrew and Leroy Wright. Viewed dispassionately, the allegations were none too likely. Willie Roberson was suffering from syphilis and gonorrhea and Olen Montgomery was blind in one eye. However, the sensational case touched an exposed nerve of race relations, sexual intercourse between black men and white women. The metaphor of imprisonment of white over black was here made physical, the unjust incarceration of innocent men.

At the first trial of Clarence Norris and Charlie Weems on March 30, 1931, two doctors gave medical evidence that the girls were not injured in any way consistent with rape. Nevertheless, in the hysterical atmosphere of Alabama in the 1930s all white juries doubtless felt they had no option but to convict blacks accused of raping white women and the only possible penalty was death. The sentence of electrocution was cheered by the crowd. At trials held later that week the other defendants were found guilty and also sentenced to death.

The publicity generated by the case, the speed of the trial, and the savage nature of the sentences, reached all parts of the country and led the Communist party to convene protests in Cleveland and New York. The International Labor Defense (ILD), a committee with close ties to the Communists, hired George W. Chamlee, a famous southern lawyer, to defend the youths. The way the Communists appropriated the case antagonized the NAACP and divided potential sources of support for the defense. Nevertheless such organizations as the American Civil Liberties Union (ACLU) and the Southern Commission on Interracial Cooperation (SCIC) sustained the defendants and helped save their lives through a long series of appeals before the state supreme court and the U.S. Supreme Court.

On March 24, 1932, the case reached the Alabama Supreme Court that sustained all the convictions but commuted the death penalty for Leroy Wright to imprisonment on account of his extreme youth. However, on November 7, 1932, the Supreme Court ruled in *Powell* v. *Alabama* that there must be a retrial on the basis that the prejudice of the all-white juries had denied the defendants due process of law as guaranteed by the Fourteenth Amendment.

At the first retrial (of Haywood Patterson), held at Decatur, Alabama, fifty miles west of Scottsboro, on March 27, 1933, ILD defense attorney Samuel Leibowitz failed to get any blacks elected to the jury but he had persuaded star witness Ruby Bates to appear for the defense and repudiate her earlier allegations of rape. The jury was obdurate and impervious to the new weight of evidence, again finding Haywood Patterson guilty and recommending the death penalty. The other defendants were also found guilty at their second trials and the Alabama Supreme Court set the date for their execution as August 31, 1934. Once again, the defense appealed to the Supreme Court. On April 1, 1935, in *Norris* v. *Alabama* the court duly and unanimously ruled that the exclusion of blacks from juries and grand juries was contrary to the Fourteenth Amendment.

The defense now drew its conflicting forces together and the ILD, NAACP, ACLU, and the League for Industrial Democracy created a special Scottsboro Defense Committee on December 19, 1935. However, for its part, the prosecution began to fall apart, ready to compromise with prison sentences for all but Norris. President Franklin D. Roosevelt tried to persuade Governor "Bibb" Graves of Alabama to parole the Scottsboro boys but Graves was under intense local pressure to resist him.

At this point the case was complicated by an incident on January 25, 1936, in which Ozie Powell, baited by the police, attacked a deputy, Edgar Blalock, in a car, slashing his throat, and was himself shot and seriously wounded in the head. He survived but with permanent brain damage. The prosecution now decided to concentrate on his crime of assault and overlooked the original allegation of rape. He was sentenced to twenty years' imprisonment.

By July 1937 the prosecution was ready to compromise, insisting on death for Clarence Norris, prison for four others (Charlie Weems, Ozie Powell, Andy Wright, and Haywood Patterson) and withdrawing the case against the remaining four (Olen Montgomery, Roy Wright, Willie Roberson, and Eugene Williams). Thus four defendants were released on evidence that had convicted four others. The *Times-Dispatch* of July 27, 1937, suggested that the dropping of charges against four "serves as a virtual clincher to the argument that all nine of the Negroes are innocent." The governor then commuted Norris's sentence to life imprisonment. State authorities began to release all the remaining defendants under various terms of parole between 1943 and 1950.

Another case that provided the Communists with an opportunity to entice blacks was that of Angelo Herndon, arrested for leading a demonstration in Atlanta in 1932, and charged on the basis of an old slave law with incitement to insurrection. He was sentenced to eighteen years' hard labor on a chain gang. The Supreme Court overturned the verdict in 1937 after a well-orchestrated campaign for Herndon's release.

By the mid-thirties organized labor was shifting its position with regard to blacks. In the early decade the AFL had refused to discuss discrimination. There were few black unions, apart from A. Philip Randolph's Brotherhood of Sleeping Car Porters (BSCP), founded on August 5, 1925. However, the upheaval in organized labor caused by the new demands of industrial workers, leading to the creation of the CIO and its subsequent secession from the AFL, and the determination of certain Communist organizers to inject the race issue into union affairs helped promote the black case. The communist National Textile Workers emphasized the need for racial equality, in contrast to the all-white exclusiveness of the United Textile Workers. Similarly, the Sharecropper Union in Alabama, the United Citrus Workers in Florida, and the Southern Tenant Farmers Union all practiced open membership. White institutions in general were showing themselves increasingly receptive to open discussion of race relations. Thus the Carnegie foundation sponsored Swedish sociologist Gunnar Myrdal to undertake the research and writing of his mammoth study of race, *An American Dilemma* (1937).

This subtle change in radical climate among better educated people began to have a marked effect on the attitudes of the political parties. In particular, blacks were becoming disaffected wth the Republicans. In 1932 Robert Vann, publisher of the *Courier,* the black newspaper with the largest circulation, wrote "My friends, go turn Lincoln's picture to the wall. That debt has been paid in full." Both the NAACP and the Urban League urged independent voting. Nevertheless, most blacks still voted for Hoover in 1932. Not until 1934 would they desert the Republicans in significant numbers.

New Deal or Cold Deck

The impact of the New Deal on the black community as a whole was, at best, indirect. The first major code of the National Recovery

Administration (NRA) for cotton textiles provided neither fewer hours nor higher pay for unskilled work, jobs that blacks normally occupied, and this differential treatment set a precedent for other textile codes. NRA codes in other industries, like steel and tobacco, specifically allowed lower wages for blacks than for whites. Where there was no legal discrimination, employers could still hire whites rather than blacks. In general, the shortcomings of the NRA toward blacks led to some calling it "Negroes Ruined Again."

Moreover, the administration of relief in the New Deal programs was decentralized and this allowed local and party officials to exercise their prejudices against black recipients. Of over 10,000 WPA supervisors in the South, only eleven were black. Not surprisingly, public assistance for blacks in the South was meager and difficult to obtain. White planters and landlords took advantage of the total or partial illiteracy of blacks and their economic dependence on them to prevent their AAA reduction checks from reaching them. When AAA procedure was changed to allow direct payments to tenants, certain landlords decided to dispense with tenants, whom they evicted, and collect the crop reduction bonuses themselves. Such dishonesty fueled discontent among both black and white sharecroppers who united in the biracial Southern Tenant Farmers Union. Later, the FSA encouraged black farmers to buy their own land.

However, by the time of the 1936 election a series of factors combined to aid the cause of civil rights. In 1934 Arthur Mitchell of Chicago became the first black Democratic congressman, having defeated the Republican Oscar De Priest. By 1936 the northern black vote was sizable enough to merit serious consideration by both major parties. The Republicans tried to present their presidential candidate, Alf Landon, as a defender of black rights in the party of Lincoln. Indeed, he had openly favored a law against lynching and a Republican pamphlet tried to take the credit for saving the Scottsboro boys from the electric chair.

However, the most striking changes occurred in the Democratic party: for the first time black delegates—thirty in all—attended the Democratic convention. Roosevelt chose a black minister to open the convention and had Arthur Mitchell deliver the first address, much to the disgust of southern representatives. Historian William Manchester comments ruefully, "In that year the black vote was still to be had for a prayer." Yet *Time* magazine accurately reported how, for the first time, the Democrats were making a serious bid for the black vote. Indeed, no other voting section shifted its allegiance so markedly: a Gallup poll disclosed that 76 percent of northern blacks voted for FDR. The Roosevelt coalition of farmers, workers, labor, intellectuals, and blacks was decisive in his landslide victory of 60.8 percent of the popular vote. Various black leaders interpreted this as the start of a new phase of black influence in politics. Earl Brown, a black political analyst, considered the black vote was now a key sector of the northern electorate. If the Democrats were to maintain, or the Republicans were to recapture, the black vote, they would have to offer blacks more in the industrial states.

Although southerners occupied half the chairs of congressional committees in every Congress throughout the New Deal, several leading administrators began to show an unprecedented concern for black rights. One of the most notable was Secretary of the Interior Harold Ickes who was also a former head of a Chicago chapter of the NAACP. However, it was Eleanor Roosevelt who was the most conspicuous New Dealer to demonstrate this new humanitarianism by her visits to Harlem, to black schools and projects, and her readiness to speak at black functions. She made the president accessible to black leaders, notably Walter White of the NAACP and Mary McLeod Bethune, president of the National Council of Negro Women, who were allowed interviews with FDR from 1936 onward—something that would have been unthinkable even three years earlier.

Roosevelt's personality and the extraordinary way he had overcome his poliomyelitis were likely to make him an attractive candidate to black voters. The warmth of his voice, the charisma of his style, and his uncanny ability to identify himself with human exploitation encouraged blacks, somewhat ironically, to think here was their stoutest champion since Lincoln.

Unlike previous presidents who had simply sought unofficial black advice, Roosevelt employed more blacks in office. Thus Mrs. Mary McLeod Bethune became director of the Division of

Negro Affairs in the NYA; William H. Hastie, dean of Howard University Law School, became first, assistant solicitor in the Department of the Interior, and, later, the first ever black federal judge; Robert C. Weaver also worked in the Interior and, later, in the Federal Housing Authority; Eugene K. Jones of the Urban League served as adviser on Negro Affairs in the Department of Commerce; Edgar Brown had a similar post in the CCC; and veteran social worker Lawrence A. Oxley was in charge of the Department of Labor's Division of Negro Labor. These and other such appointments were sufficiently numerous to earn the collective title of "Black Cabinet."

Furthermore, the expansion of the executive during the New Deal opened additional career opportunities for black, as for white, Americans. Whereas in 1932 the Civil Service employed fewer than 50,000 blacks, by 1941 it employed three times as many. The NYA under the liberal Aubrey Williams of Mississippi pursued a policy of appointing black state and local supervisors in those areas with a sizable black population. The NYA provided young blacks with funds to attend school from grammar schools to graduate schools.

These things stimulated greater political consciousness in black communities, especially in the South. Although only 5 percent of adult blacks voted in the South in 1940, others were forming a number of new voting organizations to try and persuade blacks to register to vote. For example, the Negro Voters League was formed in Raleigh, North Carolina, in 1931 and Committees on Negro Affairs were established in Charlotte, Durham, Greensboro, and Winston-Salem that together held a pro-Roosevelt rally in 1936.

Thus the political consciousness of blacks was being developed and they turned increasingly to the Democratic party. Toward the end of the 1930s Democratic candidates received as much as 85 percent of the vote in such black areas as Harlem in New York and the South Side of Chicago.

This phenomenon was to prove a decisive factor in Roosevelt's three campaigns for reelection. Of 15 major black wards in 9 cities, Roosevelt had carried only 4 in 1932. In 1936 he carried 9 and in 1940 all 15 wards elected him by large majorities. The

After a boxing exhibition at an air base in England, heavyweight champion Sgt. Joe Louis gets into the cockpit of a P-51 bomber and is advised about flying by pilot Col. George Peck. While the armed forces remained totally segregated during World War II, the irony of black servicemen separated from whites in a war widely publicized as a war against racism was not lost on a more militant generation of black activists. (Library of Congress).

marginal Democratic victory of 1944 was supplied by black votes in several states. For instance, in Michigan, which the Republicans had carried in 1940, the Democratic plurality of only 22,500 votes in the state as a whole was more than accounted for by the black Democratic vote in Detroit alone. In New Jersey black voters in 5 major cities provided Roosevelt with a plurality of almost 29,000 in a state that went Democratic by only 26,500.

However, the notorious poll tax, white primaries, and the maze of regulations about registration still thwarted black voting campaigns. In 1939 eight states used a poll tax of between $1 and $25 to disfranchise blacks (Alabama, Arkansas, Georgia, Mississippi, South Carolina, Tennessee, Texas, and Virginia). Moreover, four of these states (Alabama, Georgia, Mississippi, and Virginia) also enforced an annual liability (or fine) on every voter who failed to pay. All but South Carolina enforced payment for primary voting as well. Liberals joined forces with civil rights leaders to try and get such practices outlawed. Democratic Congressman Lee E. Geyer of California introduced a bill against poll taxes that passed the House in October 1941 but was blocked by southern senators in the upper house. The House voted various forms of anti-poll tax legislation in 1943, 1945, 1947, and 1949, only to see them all buried in Senate committees or blocked by filibusters.

There were advances for blacks in litigation. A series of constructive decisions by the Supreme Court during the 1930s paved the way for the major civil rights decisions of the postwar period. As the Supreme Court moved to the left, it changed the criteria for its decisions on civil rights showing decreased interest in the rights of property and an increased interest in the rights of the individual. This shift, too, stemmed from the upheaval of the New Deal. The Supreme Court greatly expanded the powers of the national government, reduced the principle of state's rights and, by implication, began to undermine the validity of political and social discrimination preserved by state governments.

In June 1935 Lloyd Lionel Gaines, a graduate of Lincoln University, the state-supported black college of Missouri, applied for a place at the law school of the University of Missouri, which was, then, all white. Although he was duly qualified, the university refused him admission and advised him either to apply to Lincoln (which had no law school) or to apply out of state. Gaines took legal action and the test case of *Missouri ex rel. Gaines* v. *Canada* was decided by the Supreme Court on December 12, 1938. By 7 votes to 2 the Court ruled against the state. In the words of Chief Justice Charles Evans Hughes, "A state denies equal protection of the laws to a black student when it refuses him admission to its all white law school, even though it volunteers to pay his tuition at any law school in an adjacent state. By providing a law school for whites but not for blacks the state has created a privilege which one race can enjoy but the other cannot." Equally significant was the Supreme Court's repudiation of southern subterfuges to deny blacks the vote. In the case of *Love* v. *Wilson,* on May 22, 1939, the Court finally ruled against the Oklahoma law replacing the grandfather clause the Court had nullified in *Guinn* v. *United States* (1915). It declared the replacement law as "a violation of the Fifteenth Amendment ban on racial discrimination in voting."

During the years of the Scottsboro trials a series of other cases provided unequivocal evidence that the absence of blacks from state juries was prima facie evidence of the denial of due process of law to blacks. For example, in *Brown* v. *Mississippi* the Court ruled on February 17, 1936, that use of torture to extract confessions from defendants was clear denial of due process of law.

When Harlan Stone succeeded the somewhat conservative Charles Evans Hughes as chief justice in 1941, NAACP attorney Thurgood Marshall became more optimistic about the outcome of civil rights cases. Stone's accession marked an even more decisive liberal shift in the court. It was also true that other recently appointed justices, Hugo Black (appointed 1937), Stanley Reed (1938), Frank Murphy (1940), and Robert Jackson (1941), had all served the New Deal and appreciated the significance of the black vote for the Democratic party.

On May 26, 1941, in *United States* v. *Classic* (a case arising out of corruption in white primaries in Louisiana and brought by white voters), the Court, by 5 votes to 3, awarded Congress the power to regulate primary elections, thereby reversing earlier decisions. This ruling gave NAACP attorneys William Hastie and Thurgood Marshall the confidence to use the *Classic* opinion as a basis for contesting all-white primaries in *Smith* v. *Allwright.* Marshall declared, "We must not be delayed by people who say, 'The time is not ripe,' nor should we proceed with caution for fear of destroying the status quo. People who deny us our civil rights should be brought to justice now." The Court decided on the *Smith* case on April 3, 1944, and ruled by 8 votes to 1 that actions by a political party to prevent blacks from voting in primaries were subject to the Fourteenth and Fifteenth Amendments. Whereas the impact of the Court's decisions on southern practices was negligible, its influence on the criteria for postwar decisions was vital.

Black Stars

Once again, the worlds of sports and entertainment attested to the continuing strength and vibrancy of black stars. Adolf Hitler's claims about Nordic supremacy were challenged by the great black American sprinter Jesse Owens of Ohio. At the 1936 Olympics in Berlin, German track officials deliberately handicapped Jesse Owens who, nevertheless, scored signal victories. Hitler made his disgust obvious by refusing to make the awards of gold medals himself and several other American athletes protested against the insult by refusing to accept their medals from Hitler. Two years later, heavyweight boxing champion Joe Louis, "the brown bomber," hammered home the point by pounding German boxer Max Schmelling (who had previously defeated him) to defeat at Madison Square Garden. By the time America went to war in 1941, Joe Louis had successfully defended his heavyweight title nine times. He was well aware of his social responsibilities. "I want to fight honest," he said, "so that the next colored boy can get the same break I got. If I act the fool, I'll let them down."

White society prized black singers and musicians for their range of emotional expression but denied them full recognition as citizens. When Benny Goodman, "King of Swing," employed black artist Teddy Wilson in his band, various hotel managers refused to allow Wilson to play with the band on dance floors. Duke Ellington and his band were allowed to perform at Loew's State Theater on Broadway but not at the Paramount or Strand. Singer Billie Holiday had to enter hotels by the back door. In Detroit a theater manager thought she looked too light and she was told to put on darker make-up. She remarked of a southern tour with Artie Shaw's band, "It got to the point where I hardly ever ate, slept, or went to the bathroom without having a major NAACP type production."

On one celebrated occasion white racism misfired and aided black pride. In 1939 black classical contralto Marian Anderson planned to give a concert at Constitution Hall on Easter Day. "A voice like yours," said conductor Arturo Toscanini to her, "comes but once in a century." Nevertheless, Marian Anderson encountered serious resistance. Her proposed auditorium was managed by the Daughters of the American Revolution (DAR). Journalist Mary Johnson, sensing a story, provoked the DAR president, Mrs. Henry M. Robert, Jr., into announcing that neither Marian Anderson nor any other black artist would ever be heard in Constitution Hall. Liberals were scandalized.

However, at the suggestion of Walter White, Harold Ickes gave permission to give the concert on the steps of the Lincoln Memorial, a far more prestigious and symbolic site. Eleanor Roosevelt resigned from the DAR and she and Ickes made sure that the front rows of the audience would comprise cabinet members, senators, congressmen, and Supreme Court justices. The widespread publicity ensured an audience of 75,000 who were engrossed by the contralto's power, range, and expression in a variety of songs from "America" to "Nobody Knows The Trouble I've Seen." Among the ensuing crush of people around Marian Anderson was a young black girl in her Easter best whose hands were already toughened by manual work. Walter White noticed her expression that seemed to say, "If Marian Anderson can do it, then I can, too."

Whereas the Great Depression and World War II inhibited certain cultural activities, they saw no lessening of black artistic achievement. The new poets included Melvin B. Tolson of Wiley College, who published a collection *Rendezvous with America* (1944), which included his most famous piece "Dark Symphony"; and Robert Hayden of the University of Michigan, whose first volume was *Heart-Shape in the Dust* (1940). Commentator Arna Bontemps produced *God Sends Sunday* (1931), and two historical novels, *Black Thunder* (1936) and *Drums at Dusk* (1939), before collaborating with Jack Conroy on *They Seek a City* (1945), an enthralling account of the urbanization of black Americans. George W. Lee described Memphis life in *Beale Street* (1934) and then brought out *River George* (1936), while Waters Turpin concentrated on the upper South of Maryland in *These Low Grounds*

(1937) and *O Canaan* (1939). Sculptor Augusta Savage was widely praised for her head of DuBois and her sculpture *Lift Every Voice and Sing,* exhibited at the New York World's Fair of 1939.

Chester Himes described racial tension and friction in a wartime industrial community, *If He Hollers, Let Him Go* (1945), which vividly evokes the confusions felt by blacks recently moved to industrial towns and their bitterness. In *Let Me Breathe Thunder* (1939) and *Blood on the Forge* William Attaway showed he could treat white as well as black characters and themes.

The most celebrated new talent of the second period was Richard Wright, who rapidly produced a collection of short stories, *Uncle Tom's Children* (1938), a folk history, *Twelve Million Black Voices* (1941), and his account of his Mississippi childhood, *Black Boy* (1945), as well as his most celebrated novel, *Native Son* (1940).

Native Son is about the social, psychological, and physical incarceration of the marginal man. Bigger Thomas, an unemployed black youth, is taken on as chauffeur by a supposedly liberal family, the Daltons, who are, in fact, the exploitive landlords of his slum home. He is compromised by their daughter, Mary, whose superficial gestures of friendship and equality confuse and terrify him so much that he smothers her by accident, and, frightened out of his wits, disposes of the body in a furnace. In the course of his getaway he brutally murders his black girlfriend, Bessie.

The story is told with a series of effective dramatic metaphors, beginning with the cornered rat Bigger kills in his home, continuing with Bigger's attempted escape across Chicago, where, like Eliza across the ice floes in *Uncle Tom's Cabin,* his very blackness is emphasised by the falling snow that renders the entire city a prison of whiteness, until it is Bigger himself who is trapped like a cornered rat. The language, images, and elaborate, surreal court scenes in which the political utterances of conservatives, liberals, and Communists are shown as stereotypes of sophistry—all are effectively treated to the literary equivalent of the dramatic and stark Soviet cinema posters of the period such as Grigory Rychkov's *The Tractor Drivers* (1939).

The genius of Wright's work is not only in the way he exposes the superficiality of white understanding but also, like William

Faulkner with the racially ambiguous Joe Christmas, how he makes articulate the hidden, confused emotions of his inarticulate hero by playing white rhetoric against black restraint and sullenness. The very title, *Native Son,* makes its own ironic comments, suggesting natives of Africa, children of the United States, who have an indigenous right to equal citizenship in the country of their ancestors and of their birth.

Black America on the Eve of World War II

In 1940 there were 12,866,000 black Americans, most of whom worked at unskilled and menial jobs with low pay. Only one in twenty black males worked in a white-collar profession (compared with one in three white males). Of every ten black women who worked, six worked as maids (compared with one in ten white women). Although twice as many blacks as whites worked on farms, a much smaller proportion farmed their own land.

Four times as many blacks as whites lived in houses with more than two people per room and only half as many blacks lived in houses with two rooms per person. The black mortality rate was almost twice that of whites. Thus in Washington, D.C., for example, the infant mortality rate among whites was 37 per 1,000 whereas for blacks it was 71 per 1,000. If they survived infancy, black citizens could expect to live, on average, twelve years less than whites. Of black citizens over twenty-five, one in ten had not completed a single year of school; only one in a hundred had graduated from college. Racism was still widespread and institutionalized. Thirty states proscribed marriage between blacks and whites. In the South not only did blacks have to use separate waiting rooms at bus and railroad stations, separate railroad cars, separate seating sections in movie theaters, separate churches and schools, separate restaurants and drinking fountains, but they also had to endure all manner of white refusals to allow them even a modicum of social respect. It was difficult, and most rare, for blacks to serve as police officers or become practicing lawyers. In the Deep South blacks were almost never employed as policemen. In 1940 the states of Mississippi, South Carolina, Louisiana, Georgia, and Alabama (states in which blacks made up over a third of the population) had not one black policeman between them. Nor did Arkansas and Virginia (where blacks accounted for a third of the population). There were only 4 black lawyers in Alabama, compared with 1,600 whites, and 6 in Mississippi, compared with 1,200 whites. Judges and court officials were invariably white. Blacks seldom served on juries. In consequence, blacks received odd, ill-balanced forms of justice. Thus courts tended to be lenient to blacks accused of committing crimes against other blacks but especially harsh to blacks accused of crimes against whites.

World War II and the Civil Rights Movement

World War II clarified attitudes toward race as government propaganda fashioned political ideology in an attempt to cover the contradictions of fighting a war against racism abroad while maintaining segregation at home. Thus the shortcomings of the American democratic system were tested to the limit. It was now all too easy for liberals and radicals alike to equate poll taxes and grandfather clauses, lynching, and the segregation of blacks in the United States with Hitler's persecution of Jews in the Third Reich. The *Crisis* published a photograph of a defense industry factory with a "whites only" notice outside and commented bitterly about aircraft made by whites, flown by whites, but paid for by blacks. "It sounds pretty foolish to be *against* park benches marked '*Jude*' in Berlin, but to be *for* park benches marked 'Colored' in Tallahassee, Florida."

The New Deal and Roosevelt's foreign policy rhetoric had roused black expectations of change but left them unsatisfied. With consummate, newfound political skills, black leaders were quick to exploit the situation. In January 1941, at a meeting that included Walter White, Mary McLeod Bethune, and Lester Grange (of the Urban League), A. Philip Randolph announced plans for a mass march on Washington to protest against discrimination in defense industries. Some commentators were skeptical of success. The Chicago *Defender* commented on February 8, 1941, "To get 10,000 Negroes assembled in one spot, under one banner, with justice, democracy, and work as their slogan would be the miracle of the century." However, Randolph was firmly convinced of black solidarity and believed he knew how to channel black indignation into constructive political action while preventing the Communists from exploiting the occasion. Indeed, Randolph's appeal transcended his immediate aims and touched a sensitive nerve in the black community at large. Across the country blacks formed committees to coordinate support and began organizing transportation to Washington. Thus encouraged, Randolph chose July 1 for the event.

Randolph's command and activities produced feelings of consternation bordering upon panic in Roosevelt's administration. It sought national unity and FDR did not want his plans for the war to be jeopardized by ethnic divisions at home. On June 18, 1941, Roosevelt met with Randolph and White and tried to separate bluff and realism in their tactics. "Walter, how many people will really march?" "No less than 100,000," replied White. Thus cornered, on June 25 Roosevelt issued Executive Order 8802, requiring that all employees, unions, and government agencies "concerned with vocational and training programs" must "provide for the full and equitable participation of all workers in defense industries without discrimination because of race, creed, color, or national origin." The march was called off. To enforce the order, FDR created a Fair Employment Practices Committee (FEPC).

The FEPC had no punitive powers and was even loath to penalize white violators. However, because it held hearings in public, many employers preferred to change their policies rather than risk unfavorable publicity. Nevertheless, the black press was jubilant and greeted Executive Order 8802 as a second emancipation proclamation. Unfortunately, the FEPC was scuttled by racists at the end of the war.

9

SOUNDS IMPOSSIBLE
The Golden Age of Radio

Radio in the 1920s

AFTER THE years of experiment and innovation in 1900–1920, radio broadcasting for the general public was born in the early 1920s and almost immediately expanded, first as a novelty, and then as a major recreation of the decade. The radio boom that started in 1921 should not be seen as an inevitable part of a cultural and technological tide. Indeed, it is often more significant how such tides have failed to roll on schedule. Despite the flood, the emergence of public broadcasting was not entirely relentless. The critical steps toward the birth of American broadcasting were taken between 1918 and 1922. Despite some calls in Congress for governmental control of radio, all private communication stations were returned to their original owners on March 1, 1920, while amateur enthusiasts had been allowed back on the air in the fall of 1919. The elite of radio's major interests believed radio would be used primarily for transoceanic and marine communiction and secondarily for long-distance telephone communications. Some wanted to mold the situation by an informal association between manufacturers and the federal government. Nevertheless, companies manufacturing radio parts believed that they must find a new market for their postwar surpluses. Almost immediately, the existing state of affairs in radio was challenged.

In March 1919, when Guglielmo Marconi was negotiating to buy the rights to the Alexanderson alternator from General Electric, the Marconi Company seemed to be the only possible customer and only possible winner of exclusive rights to this new, most powerful transmitter. However, such a monopoly control over American communication was deplored by the federal government, and particularly by the navy. Under Secretary of the Navy Franklin D. Roosevelt and other members of government gave encouragement to the General Electric representative, Owen D. Young, and the company's directors to revise the deal. General Electric would buy a controlling interest in American Marconi, anticipating and quieting any congressional objections about British Marconi having too great an influence. British Marconi agreed. As a manufacturer, General Electric was loath to run the American Marconi stations and, therefore, created the Radio Corporation of America (RCA). Eighty percent of its stock had to be American, with a government representative on the board of directors. The formation of RCA assured the United States of a new powerful position in world communication and satisfied the determination of Woodrow Wilson's administration to challenge and supersede Britain in this new field.

On July 1, 1920, General Electric, RCA, and AT & T ended a bitter dispute over patent rights by signing a broad patent pooling agreement. AT & T had purchased most of the rights to use the central device of the crystal radio set before the war. The deal with British Marconi meant that General Electric and RCA possessed the old American Marconi rights to the other two crucial parts of radio, the Alexanderson alternator and the vacuum tube. (The early history of radio discoveries and inventions was told in *America in the Age of the Titans,* chapter eight.) Consequently, production and use of the vacuum tube could begin in earnest. The patents pool was completed when the electrical manufacturer, Westinghouse, decided to join the other companies. So, by 1921, around 2,000 patents had been pooled. From the point of view of the giants, the infant radio industry was being nicely divided up. RCA would sell radio receivers that had been produced by General Electric and incorporated the latest in radio technology, the Armstrong patent for a supersensitive receiver, possessed by Westinghouse. AT & T could use radio telephone equipment for its business and produce transmitters. Thus in 1920 no one expected that the prime use of radio would be public broadcasting. When this was what happened, it soon shattered the comfort of the radio oligarchy.

On November 2, 1920, what would become the oldest and longest running station, KDKA, began broadcasting from Pittsburgh, announcing the Harding–Cox presidential election returns. As would be the case with the other pioneer stations, KDKA had begun as a successful amateur operation, 8XK, run by Dr. Frank Conrad, a Westinghouse engineer. It was when a Pittsburgh department store advertised radio sets to listen to 8XK that H. P. Davies, vice president of Westinghouse, decided to set up a radio station to promote sales of the company's receivers. Notably, this was before Westinghouse joined the patent pool and, so, was inclined to consider such an independent, innovatory tactic within its strategy. The first transmissions came, initially, from a rough shack and, then, a tent on top of a Westinghouse factory.

After KDKA came on the air, radio broadcasting seemed to grow but slowly in its first years. By January 1922 only thirty broadcasting stations had been licensed and by the end of the year only 100,000 radio sets had been purchased. In actual fact, there was a great deal of activity. Most radio sets were homemade and amateur licensed stations broadcast concerts, weather reports, lectures, and recorded music. By May 1922 the Board of Navigation in the Department of Commerce listed 218 such stations. The following spring, there were 556.

The breakthrough year for radio was 1922. Public interest across the world spurred inventors, engineers, and executives to create nationwide services. France began regular broadcasts from the Eiffel Tower, Paris; the first Soviet station began broadcasts from Moscow; Nederlandsche Radio Industrie began operations in Holland; and in England the BBC began life as the British Broadcasting Company. International agreement on copyright, wavelengths, and program exchanges were decided at a series of international conferences, beginning in Washington in 1927.

In the United States, even though amateurs seemed to lead the field in initiating public broadcasting, the full emergence of broadcasting was not a matter of independent, individual enterprise. The creation of KDKA showed the critical importance of corporate involvement. From September 1921, Westinghouse opened up a succession of stations. The other major companies were slow to enter broadcasting, mainly because they still thought the mainstay of their business lay in international communications. It was not until December 1922 that RCA created WDY in Roselle Park, New Jersey. General Electric had opened WGY in Schenectady (New York), KOA in Denver (Colorado), and KGO in Oakland (California). The domination of the patent pool members in broadcasting was evident when, in February 1923, of the 376 stations that the U.S. Department of Commerce listed, 222 were owned by General Electric, RCA, Westinghouse, or AT & T. Newspapers like the *Detroit News* (station WWJ) owned 69; educational institutions, 72 and department stores, 29. These early stations were largely publicity ventures, although churches and universities did use their stations for preaching, extension courses, and study programs. Broadcasters divided themselves into three groups—those selling radio sets, those seeking goodwill, and those seeking free advertising.

Since they were sidelines to other enterprises, the first radio stations were primitive and run on shoestring budgets. Many broadcasts were transmitted from hotel rooms because the main hotel was the tallest building in most cities. A studio simply consisted of a piano and a microphone or two. There was no volume control and mixing so that a broadcast of lusty opera singers with powerful voices large enough to fill a giant theater, could jeopardize the future of a station by blowing out expensive vacuum tubes. The early transmitters were often handmade and low-powered. A typical transmitter could take 100 watts. The mortality rate of pioneering stations was high. In 1922, 94 stations closed down while, over the spring and early summer months of 1923, another 150 stations folded.

Although many stations did cease broadcasting once some public interest in their novelty value faded, on the whole people were becoming addicted to radio. Ever more people exchanged their homemade crystal sets for readymade receivers. In 1923 between $30 and $45 million worth of radio sets were sold. In 1924 sales climbed to $100 million. Between 1922 and 1925 the industry produced and sold 4.1 million sets.

The success of broadcasting caused tension within the patent pool. AT & T challenged the casual way that early stations were subsidized by the companies. After setting up its own station, WEAF, in New York in the summer of 1922, AT & T declared that the pooling agreement had been contravened for it alone had the right to manufacture and sell transmitters for broadcasting. Moreover, AT & T held that it possessed exclusive right to sell time for advertising and to interconnect stations by telephone wire for network broadcasting. Thus the Telephone Groups of AT & T and Western Electric were ranged against the Radio Groups of RCA, General Electric, and Westinghouse. Most stations capitulated. Radio Group stations tried to create networks along the inferior telegraph wires of Western Union. The Radio Group fought back, successfully demanding that all manufacturers of radio sets had to acquire licenses from RCA in order to make any receiver part. Consequently, the bubble burst for the 748 radio manufacturers who had appeared between 1923 and 1926. In 1927 only 72 remained. In 1925 AT & T threatened to break the vital patents' pool. This tactic of confrontation led to a settlement of the dispute in 1926. AT & T received a monopoly of wire interconnections between stations while selling off WEAF to RCA and agreeing not to reenter broadcasting for eight years.

However, the attention of radio listeners was on the content of programs rather than the organization of radio broadcasting. The programming of early radio involved much experimentation but tended toward the broadcasting of variety shows consisting of music and comedy acts. A brief and distinct feature of early American radio was the extremely formal style of presentation of the various programs. Presenters were known only by their initials. Although they could not be seen by the public, they wore tuxedos and spoke from studios decorated like hotel dance floors with potted palm trees.

The airwaves of early radio were mainly given over to music. In the 1925 schedules of the major stations in New York, Kansas City, and Chicago, over 70 percent of airtime was devoted to performed music, of which 25 percent was dance music. Music was performed live. In 1922, Secretary of Commerce Herbert Hoover prohibited the broadcasting of phonograph records. He thought that, by broadcasting music from disks, stations would be cheating the public by giving them nothing more than they could enjoy without radio. Early wireless dance bands, many of which played live from hotal ballrooms, included the Vincent Copes Group and Coon Sanders Nighthawks. Many early radio stars were plucked out of the dying vaudeville theater circuit. Ukulele player and singer Wendell Woods Haze rose to become the first major radio personality and his marriage was even broadcast over the air in 1924. Such individual stars competed with the song and patter teams like the Happiness Boys and Tastee Loafers with whom stations filled their variety spots. By the late 1920s Broadway stars like Al Jolson and Eddie Cantor were making radio broadcasts. The staple diet of vaudeville songs was varied by stations like WLS of Chicago that broadcast country and western music. The highbrow audience was catered for by classical music played by symphony orchestras, thereby cultivating the respectable image of many stations.

Although early radio programming consisted mainly of light entertainment, stations produced programs featuring talks, discussions, and providing information. Following the precedent of KDKA, radio stations devoted themselves to large-scale election coverage, beginning with the 1924 election. The notorious Democratic National Convention in New York with all its unbridled chaos and apparently endless votes was widely heard and this partly accounted for the Democrats' temporary eclipse. Yet regular news bulletins were rare in the 1920s. Sometimes news items were used as fillers while stations owned by newspapers would mention a story only briefly in order to rouse interest and stimulate newspaper sales. Early stations specialized in covering sudden news events, for which radio was ideally suited, and caught the immediacy of the event. Since stations were also used to to monitor the maritime distress channel, shipwrecks provided special news items. Midwestern, landlocked stations provided weather reports for farmers and carried early storm warnings, though the Chicago station, WGN, distinguished itself with the $1,000 per day coverage of the Scopes trial in Dayton, Tennessee, somewhat in the manner of its election coverage. Although telephone and radio brought people more closely together, they also made separation more palatable through the aural illusion of intimacy. In radio alone audience participation was more possible then, for example, for an audience at a vaudeville theater. Interest was expressed in choice, firstly between turning on or off, later by selecting one program rather than another.

Many of the familiar types of programs were initiated in the first years. The U.S. Army began religious programs when it broadcast a church service in Washington, D.C., in August 1919. However, it was KDKA that made church services a regular feature in its schedule in 1921. In its broadcasts, radio technicians at the service were disguised, rather implausibly, as choirboys. Surprisingly, radio stations rarely broadcast sports programs. Boxing was among the first sports to be covered, with ringside reports from KDKA in 1921. The Dempsey-Tunney fights were especially successful as commercial ventures heard by 50 million listeners and causing mass hysteria. The World Series of baseball games was broadcast from 1923. There was little drama on the radio in the 1920s, although there were some experiments with the radio adaptation of successful Broadway shows.

The diversity of early radio programming lay in what might now seem unusual, the broadcasting of lectures on the widest possible variety of subjects. It is interesting that those stations owned by radio manufacturers broadcast lectures on the technical aspects of the new medium, lectures primarily aimed at radio enthusiasts whom such stations considered the nucelus of the new audience. Despite its popularity, listening to the radio was not yet an entirely passive affair because home audiences always required someone with technical expertise to adjust the various crystals, batteries, and tubes in the receivers. Radio hams vied with one another as to who could get the clearest reception and who could reach the most distant station, this was known as " 'DX'ing."

Starlet Clara Horton listens to a Hollywood concert on a radio set decorated with photos of stars Colleen Moore and Corinne Griffith. A publicity photograph of June 1, 1925, by Underwood and Underwood. (Library of Congress).

Local stations encouraged hams to indulge in this and helped by closing down at night.

The preeminence of the radio specialist came to an end with the refinement of the radio receiver. In the autumn of 1920 factory-made crystal radio sets like the Westinghouse "Aeriola Jr." became available. For a brief time there was a proliferation of small firms making their own sets or assembling those of Westinghouse and General Electric. By 1923 advertising in radio, as elsewhere, following the visible hand of marketing, was stressing brand name reliability, an indication of how much the public now realized that expensive radio sets were far preferable to cheap sets that gave very inferior reception. The competition for customers was beginning to decimate the numbers of small manufacturers, even though sales had risen from about 500,000 sets in 1923 to 2 million in 1925 and prices had doubled from the earlier average of $50.

Radio sets were intended to be simple to use and more attractive to look at, and to form the centerpiece of a family living room. By 1926 families could dispense with their numerous, heavy, and ugly batteries and plug their new sets directly into the mains. Volume, tuning, and the on-off switch were all controled from one knob. The early sets had used a bread board as a base for the mechanism, but in 1926 sets tended to be fitted inside mahogany cases. One result of the continuing national craze for radio was that by 1926 1 radio set had been sold for every 6 households. (In 1921 this ratio had stood at 1 in every 500.)

Ironically, as audiences grew, radio broadcasting in America was heading for a crisis. There were too many stations saturating the airwaves, and, consequently, reception was deteriorating. Given the very slender band allocated for broadcasting, a large city could only possess around 7 stations but there were, for example, as many as 20 in Los Angeles and 40 in Chicago. Some cities attempted a fair division of wavelengths and sharing of broadcasting time. The answer of those stations owned by major companies was to increase their power, thus fortifying their signal against interference. In 1924, David Sarnoff of RCA revealed plans for a number of superpower 50,000 watt stations. This solution brought only temporary respite for the other stations soon increased their wattage and the interference began again. As Edwin E. Slosson remarked in his article, "Voices in the Air," for the *New York Independent* of April 1922, "Broadcasting has turned the nation into a town meeting. But there is no chairman and no parliamentary law. This will bring about anarchy in the ether."

Radio seemed to be jeopardizing its recent successes. The situation begged for strict federal regulation. Yet, to a certain extent, the application of what little regulation existed had aggravated the problem. The Radio Act of 1912 was inadequte, having been ratified before broadcasting was even seriously contemplated. The act simply empowered the secretary of commerce to pass all applications for station licenses, regardless of available frequencies. The only criteria for ownership was American citizenship. Moreover, government officials repeatedly failed to foresee the overloading of the airwaves and, consequently, failed to execute forceful, realistic measures. Prior to the boom, one wavelength of 360 metres was allocated for broadcasting experiments. In December 1921 another wavelength of 485 metres was added. By the spring of 1922, the growing number of stations necessitated another wavelength, 400 metres. The outcome was the cramming of stations in each of the three wavelengths.

The mounting number of complaints about interference spurred on Secretary of Commerce Herbert Hoover to convene a conference on the subject of regulatory radio legislation. In February 1922 the conference recommended that government should allocate specific frequencies and other terms by which stations should operate. However, there was still no legislation by March 1923 and the interference had grown. A second conference made all the same recommendations as the first and further proposed a creation of three classes of stations—those requiring high power, medium power, or low power—and a five way regional division of radio. Herbert Hoover then introduced a new system of frequency assignments. Stations were alloted a specific wavelength within either an A or B band. Even so, there was still no legislation to supersede the 1912 Radio Act and Hoover had to call two more conferences in October 1924 and November 1925. Congress proved to be indifferent to the immediate need for legislation and passage of radio bills was slow.

Yet, after four years of discussion, the problem of interference remained unchanged. One senior government official involved with radio recalled the chaotic state of radio in 1925 as "interference between broadcasters on the same wave length became so bad at many points on the dial that the listener might suppose (how), instead of a receiving set, he had a peanut roaster with assorted whistles." Nevertheless, an Illinois Federal District Court, supported by the opinion of the attorney general, decided that the secretary of commerce possessed no legal powers to prevent the Zenith and other radio stations from jumping from their alloted wavelengths. This was a nonsense causing endless confusion, and the resulting uproar finally brought about legislation. The Radio Act of 1927 established the Federal Radio Commission to oversee the entire business of radio. As we shall observe, such regulation proved effective in the New Deal administration of President Franklin D. Roosevelt.

Advertising and the Networks—NBC and CBS

As radio stations became more than simply sideline operations, broadcasters became increasingly concerned about how to fund their programs. Among the stations this crucial issue competed with the concern for excessive interference and was discussed at the four inconclusive radio conferences. Radio executives did not immediately consider selling time for advertising to pay for programs. David Sarnoff, commercial manager of RCA, suggested a 2 percent tax on receiver sales. This was tried out only locally. One New York station envisaged an "invisible theater of the air" from which it tried to collect $20,000 in box office receipts. The plan failed. The AT & T station, WEAF, was the first to broadcast advertisements when a salesman extolled the virtues of living in Jackson Heights, in one of New York's earliest condominiums, for fifteen minutes on August 28, 1922. Tidewater Oil and American Express were among the first clients. The adoption of radio advertising did not become widespread immediately. Many stations were initially cautious about the concept, not least because of AT & T's policy of demanding royalties for the use of radio telephony for wire.

AT & T played a large role in initiating the modernization of American broadcasting when, in January 1923, the company inaugurated network broadcasting, connecting WNAC of Boston with WEAF of New York for the transmission of a saxophone solo. In March 1925 the inauguration ceremony of President Calvin Coolidge was relayed to twenty-four stations of which twenty were centered on WEAF.

Therefore, prior to 1926 the two prime characteristics of American broadcasting, toll advertising and network affiliation, had appeared. The settlement of the dispute between the Radio and Telephone Groups in 1926 rationalized radio and, subsequently, the widespread adoption of advertising and development of national radio networks began in earnest. Over the next seven years, radio broadcasting became a sophisticated industry, resembling the later arrangement of American broadcasting and finally shedding its amateur, experimental roots.

American radio would thus follow a very different path from radio in Britain, where the BBC followed the strict precepts about content, hours, sponsorship (by prepaid public license fees), and autocratic management laid down by the architect of British broadcasting, John Reith. So, the essential commercial nature of American broadcasting was formed and imposed within a decade. Moreover, it soon turned the listener into a consumer of radio rather than a customer.

As part of the 1926 settlement, RCA purchased the AT & T station, WEAF, that now became the nucleus of its new corporation, the National Broadcasting Company (NBC). On November 18, 1926, NBC began its network programming with a variety extravaganza transmitted from New York, Chicago, and Kansas City. Subsequently, NBC took over the RCA station, WJZ of New York, as the basis for a second network. The WEAF and WJZ networks became known as, respectively the Red and Blue networks. By 1928 NBC began regular coast-to-coast network programs and in 1933 was at the peak of its power. The company owned ten stations outright while another twenty-eight were affiliated to its Red network and another twenty-four to the Blue. A further thirty-six stations were nominally part of the NBC networks, having arranged to take network programming occasionally. These stations constituted fifteen percent of all stations in America. The domination of NBC was especially evident in those major cities where there were two NBC affiliates. The high status of NBC was made clear when, toward the end of 1933, it moved out of its Fifth Avenue offices and studios and into its new headquarters in the Rockefeller Center, deliberately entitled Radio City.

In 1927 the business manager of the Philadelphia Orchestra, Arthur Johnson, attempted to challenge the newly formed company, NBC, by setting up a rival network, United Independent Broadcasting, Inc. However, this venture seemed to offer only a paper threat to NBC, for AT & T refused to provide the new network with the vital telephone connections between stations because UIB lacked the necessary liquid capital. Yet, this "paper network" was the origin of the Columbia Broadcasting System (CBS), the future rival of NBC. Immediate financial disaster was averted when a merger was arranged with the ailing Victor Talking Machine Company. From their pooled resources, the network found enough cash to commence operations. The newly named Columbia Phonograph Broadcasting System went on the air in September 1927. The beginnings of CBS were marred by mishaps. The first night broadcast from the Metropolitan Opera, New York, was ruined by static electricity from an electric storm. In the first month, the network lost over $100,000, enough for the phonograph company to pull out of the merger. Thereafter, the survival of the infant network depended upon winning the support of several wealthy individuals. The owner of an affiliate station, Dr. Lear Levy, arranged for a millionaire sportsman, Jerome H. Louchheim, to buy control of UIB and provide it with enough money to keep the network running. However, at this time CBS was losing out to NBC in selling advertising time. Louchheim decided to drop what appeared to be an irreversibly bad investment.

In September 1928 the new owner of the network proved to be the savior of the company. UIB-CBS had run a successful series of advertisements for the Congress Cigar Company whose vice-president, William S. Paley, was so impressed that he and his family's firm bought a controlling interest in the network. Paley refashioned the company, consolidating the twin separate networks into one, buying a new flagship station, WABC of New York, and renegotiating the contract with the affiliates so that the company would pay a station $50 per hour, rather than a weekly $500 for ten hours, regardless of the actual time used. The company was rapidly revived so that, in 1933, the network encompassed ninety-one stations. Paley had first envisaged a career of selling cigars, but he remained chief executive of CBS until late 1977 and, so, a consistently influential figure in American broadcasting.

The development of the two national networks was a major

factor in the growth of advertising on radio. At last advertisers were impressed by how coast-to-coast coverage radio could penetrate nearly 70 percent of American homes. Radio advertisements allowed the sponsors to thrust themselves into people's homes directly. Harry P. Davis of Westinghouse declared that "broadcast advertising is modernity's medium of business expression. It made industry articulate. American businessmen, because of radio, are provided with a latch key to nearly every home in the United States."

Moreover, certain radio art forms were conceived and broadcast at this time, thereby establishing prototypes for situation comedies, dramas, and documentaries. The situation comedy, or sitcom, was one in which standard characters got themselves both into and out of several humorous situations in each episode. The first and most famous of these radio comedy dramas evolved from the minstrel double act of Freeman F. Gosden and Charles J. Correll, performed in blackface. Gosden and Correll were vaudevillians, who had performed their act at a local radio station in exchange for free meals from the hotel owner of the station, and were eventually hired by the *Chicago Tribune* station, WGN (World's Greatest Newspaper), to do over 600 performances of their *Sam 'n' Henry* act. The show was so successful that the pair were bought up by WGN's rival, WMAQ. Since WGN refused to allow the use of the original name the act was renamed *Amos 'n' Andy* and their adventures revolved around the Freshair Taxicab Company and the fraternal lodge of the Mystic Knights of the Sea. It was not until after the whole show was sold to the NBC-Blue network in the summer of 1929 that *Amos 'n' Andy* became a national phenomenon. It has been said that everybody listened to the evening shows and that cinema managers would delay the screening of films so that audiences could listen to *Amos 'n' Andy*.

The immense popularity of *Amos 'n' Andy* and other programs must have acted as a catalyst in convincing advertisers of the viability of radio advertising. Between 1928 and 1932 radio advertising rose from 2 percent of all expenditure on advertising to 11 percent, representing a growth from $20 million to $75 million. Originally, radio advertisements had been run during the day but by 1932 were broadcast throughout the day, particularly in the newly identified evening prime time. As a further indicator of its growth, radio advertising became a business in itself, supporting a range of managerial and publicity staff working for sponsors and networks. Local stations employed representatives to sell their time in major cities and thereby developed the national and regional business of quite small stations. For their part, large advertising agencies developed very close relationships with the major networks. At first, the agencies merely purchased time for their clients, but soon they began to create an attractive package of advertisements and programs. The networks welcomed this development because the production of national programs was proving to be expensive and complicated. So in 1931 and 1932 agencies controlled program selection and production. Moreover, advertising became more technically proficient and sophisticated, so that in the early 1930s advertisements no longer needed to be performed live but were prerecorded and mailed to many stations, allowing simultaneous nationwide sales campaigns.

At the Department of Commerce Herbert Hoover breathed a sigh of relief. He was sensitive to the controversies about audience changes and the clutter of radio advertising and pleased that the large companies upon whom he relied heavily for advice were taking the initiative and finding a solution. He also allowed the indiscriminate sale of wavelengths. As a result, radio became increasingly a matter of private property and the original concept of temporary licenses was abandoned. The outcome clearly belied Hoover's early statement that he would "establish public right over the ether roads." Thus some critics see the government selling out radio to private interests while concealing the truth about private ownership.

In 1931 36 percent of airtime was commercially sponsored. Paradoxically, the depression pushed networks and stations alike into devoting more airtime to advertising and made them increasingly dependent on its revenues. There was a period of considerable investment in expensive equipment to improve stations between 1927 and 1930. To make their signals clear and strong, the average wattage of stations was increasing so that, while in 1927 28 percent of stations managed to operate on 100 watts, only

3 percent did so in 1933. Moreover, the newly formed Federal Radio Commission demanded and successfully enforced higher standards of transmission, further increasing the expenditures of broadcasters. Understandably, then, broadcasters sought advertising revenue. The coincidence of the economic crisis and a need to fund such technical improvements and support ever more hours of programs meant that it became imperative to sell even more airtime for advertising. The central importance of advertising was apparent when networks and sponsors became interested in audience research, recognizing its value in organizing advertising. In 1929, Archibald M. Crossley formed the Cooperative Analysis of Broadcasting that served both networks.

Radio in the 1930s

During the depression the position of the two major networks was consolidated while many individual and small stations suffered or closed down. The income of the networks rose in the first years of the depression. The income of NBC climbed from $798,200 in 1929 to $2.16 million in 1930 and, then, to $2.66 million in 1931. In that year the income of CBS surpassed that of NBC, standing at $2.67 million, whereas, the previous year, the network had made only $985,400. However, income dramatically declined in the next year when the Great Depression deepened and businesses cut back their advertising budgets.

Small, local stations suffered more than the great networks. As local economies retrenched, interest in the new advertising medium was cut short. Yet, it should be emphasized that the majority of bankrupt stations had closed before the depression. The reorganization of the airwaves by the Federal Radio Commission and the trend toward more power and better equipment forced the small, often amateur, stations off the air. However, in general, radio survived and almost flourished during the first years of the depression. After their initial purchase of a radio set, people regarded listening to the wireless as free entertainment. At this time, the broadcasting industry met with a varied mix of success and failure rather than outright disaster or triumph. In 1931 333 stations reported profits while 180 were in deficit. In the early

1930s listening to the radio ceased to be a novelty or complex hobby and became an everyday, common habit. The audience was still growing, with half of urban families owning receivers and a growing number of rural listeners, for whom radio was the first affordable and available direct communication. The depression made the retailing of radio sets more of a buyer's market, with companies steadily lowering their prices so as to sell off their large stocks of unsold receivers. The average price of a radio set fell from $90 in 1930 to $47 in 1932.

This growing audience for radio enjoyed a developing range of programming, either paid for by business sponsors or wholly sustained by the stations or networks. At first, network programming was minimal, counting for only about three and a half hours of broadcasting every day in 1927. As advertising revenues increased and affiliate stations demanded ever more shows, network programs increased in number and spread from the original evening hours to fill up the daytime slots by 1933. This rush of programming proved a curtain raiser for the golden age of radio later in the decade. Many of the famous shows and many of the famous careers in broadcasting began during this period.

Music and variety remained the core of radio programming. The typical music program was of an orchestra or professional singer playing popular or light classical music. Such shows were usually sponsored, for example, by companies such as Michelin. Singers who became radio stars included Joseph M. White who performed as the "Silver Masked Tenor" and always wore his mask when he sang. Vocalist Bing Crosby began crooning on radio in 1931. More major firms preferred to sponsor and be associated with prestigious classical orchestras. Large variety shows were a staple of network programming that became noted for its more lavish production values. The first of these, the Fleischmann Yeast program, starring the singer Rudy Vallee, started in October 1929. Ed Sullivan, whose later television show would be particularly famous and successful, began hosting a variety show with more conversation than usual in 1931. As the depression devastated Broadway and many theaters closed, many stage stars and certainly many vaudeville players came into the new field of radio. Comedians George Burns and Gracie Allen formed a popular husband and wife comedy act in 1932. That same year, blackface singer Al Jolson, wit Jack Benny, and anarchic comedians the Marx Brothers made network shows. Even more than the networks, local stations found they could choose from a large pool of unemployed theatrical talent and offer payment of little more than food and shelter.

Radio drama began to grow into distinct and familiar forms. In 1929 the success of the serial, *The Rise of the Goldbergs,* a drama about the everyday life of a Jewish-American family, established the idea of a continuing cast in a different situation each week. Along with *Vic and Sadie* and *One Man's Family,* such serials aimed at women at home were the first soap operas, so-called because various soap powder companies sponsored them. Among the most popular and longest running were *Helen Trent* and *Ma Perkins.* Soap operas quickly developed a special formula for captivating and retaining a special consumer audience. In contrast with movies that were primarily concentrated on the male audience, radio soaps concentrated on women of all ages and, indeed, on people of both sexes who might feel themselves marooned in a home and required surrogate fictional families to engage their inner fantasies. The dominant character in a soap was usually a mother who had to help her family and friends resolve their problems and, indeed, the whole thrust of soaps remained matrifocal in the golden age of radio and the television era that followed. Later, soap operas devoted their story lines to the sexual needs of their heroines, while television situation comedies parodied this genre by ridiculing the periodic attempts of housewives Lucille Ball and Joan Davis to enter the professional worlds.

Radio of the 1930s began to thrill the listener and create more truly radio drama when *The Shadow* was first broadcast. Imaginative use of sound gave the show its eerie quality. The Shadow, a crimefighter called Lamont Cranston, was supposed to be able to "cloud men's minds" so that they could not see him and this effect was created by having Cranston speaking through a filter that made his voice sound distant and distorted. The program was also notable because Cranston was played for a time by Orson Welles, one of the supreme innovators of wireless. In *March of Time,* first broadcast in 1931, radio was used to disguise the fact that the reports of current events were, in fact, dramatized with actors who were excellent mimics. The White House complained so strongly about the verisimilitude of the soundalike for FDR that he was dropped. It is interesting to note that radio programs were beginning to use specific catchphrases. The Shadow would give a chilling laugh and say, "Crime does not pay . . . the Shadow knows!" Westbrook Van Voorhis of the *March of Time* would declare, "Time . . . marches on."

In the fall of 1930, the NBC-Blue network began to broadcast a fifteen-minute news program five times a week. Prior to this, news programs had been weekly, but this development at NBC-Blue started a trend toward regular news bulletins of hard journalism. The major radio news story of the late 1920s had been the solo transatlantic flight of Charles A. Lindbergh, Jr. In the early 1930s the prime news story was of the Lindbergh baby kidnapping in 1932. The success of the news bulletins about the case, which the networks and stations inserted into their evening schedule, and the huge interest in any coverage of the presidential election campaign suggested to many broadcasters that news could win large audiences. Yet the initial development of radio news immediately brought radio broadcasting into conflict with the newspapers. With radio cutting into their advertising revenue, newspapers became hostile toward radio, firstly, preventing the wire services, Associated Press, United Press, and International News Service, from supplying the fledgling newscasts and, secondly, beginning late in 1933, by ending all free listings of programs and demanding payment. Radio gave way to this pressure. For its news imformation, it was totally dependent on the wire services and the networks had to sign the Biltmore agreement (named after the New York hotel where it was drafted) which restricted radio to only two five-minute news broadcasts every day at 9:30 A.M. and 9 P.M. that could comment on, and interpret, only the news provided by a special news service, the Press-Radio Bureau. However, within a year, because so few stations subscribed to the Press-Radio Bureau and two of the wire services resumed their supply to radio, the agreement was abandoned. This paved the way for the fuller development of radio journalism later in the decade.

Radio news was overshadowed by renewed and expanded coverage of current affairs and shows outside conventional light entertainment, such as talk shows. The networks filled their daytime schedules with such programs. Walter Winchell hosted a popular gossip show on NBC-Blue in 1932. The U.S. Department of Agriculture cooperated in the running of *National Farm and Home Hour*. The most distinctive shows were the religious talk and comment programs, for example the Protestant *National Vespers* and *The Catholic Hour*. The broadcasts of Father Coughlin from the Shrine of the Little Flower in Royal Oak near Detroit for CBS were most controversial. Coughlin indulged in demagoguery on political and economic issues. He was one of the first and most effective radio speakers, with a magnificent sonorous voice, like a vessel that could be drained or changed at will with such varied and potent emotions as tenderness, anger, and pride.

In the late 1920s and early 1930s radio broadcasting entered a period of decisive development and consolidation thanks to greater organization throughout the industry. Alongside the influence of the networks, broadcasting was being influenced by more effective government regulation. The Federal Radio Commission started operating in March 1927. It had control over all interstate and foreign radio communications that came from the United States. Although prohibited from censoring broadcasts, the FRC could dictate the general operation of radio stations, their frequencies, power, and equipment. The FRC was given the necessary licensing powers to eradicate interference, but, at first, for only a year. Indeed, the FRC was really considered by Herbert Hoover and other officials as a part-time organization mainly to augment self-regulatory practices of the industry and adjudicate in disputes. So little consideration had been given to its everyday finances that the new agency had to beg office space for its meager staff from the Departments of Commerce and the Navy. On the other hand, the FRC was being put on probation. Congress was loath to give any new federal authority carte blanche freedom. Throughout its six-year history, the FRC depended upon Congress to renew its powers for yet another year.

In its first year the FRC began to tackle the congestion of the airwaves by widening the broadcasting band to between 550 kHz and 1500 kHz. After questioning stations about their operations, the FRC granted new, temporary licenses, specifying power, time limits, and frequencies. Some stations were closed down. Following renewal of its licensing authority in March 1928, the FRC found that Congress had complicated its task. The 1927 Radio Act had suggested that the FRC should keep radio coverage of the nation relatively equal between regions, but the new Davis amendment required the FRC to achieve such equality. This would mean challenging the obvious concentration of stations in the area of greatest population, the East Coast. Later that summer, the FRC closed down 109 stations that had caused serious disruption. Portable stations that functioned by moving around to find the best conditions for transmission were banned.

Subsequently, the FRC devised a new classification scheme whereby there would be eight "cleared" stations in each of the five regional zones that could transmit at the high power of 25,000 and, later, 50,000 watts so as to give the best reception for distant rural areas. Moreover, only one of these stations could be allowed to transmit at a time during the night, ensuring even better, long-distance reception. The other two classes were for thirty-five stations of no more than 1,000 watts and twenty-one low-power local stations in each zone. Finally, in 1929, the FRC was given licensing authority for an unspecified time. By 1930, interference was dramatically reduced. Thus, in the early 1930s, the FRC spent more time tackling the equalization issue, setting up a system of quotas. However, the imbalance of station numbers remained irreversible.

More significantly, the FRC became increasingly involved in legal and programming issues. In a number of legal cases that were concerned with broadcasting and heard in the federal courts, the FRC had its right to regulate, refuse to grant licenses, prevent transfer to station ownership, and act with discretionary powers, upheld. A good example of one of these precedent-setting cases would be the first, concerning a medical advice show on a Kansas station. In a popular "medicine question box" program, the station owner, Dr. John R. Brinkley, had peddled a quack remedy for sexual rejuvenation that consisted of goat glands. Brinkley's

During the 1920s radio served to extend people's horizons, sharpen their perceptions, and, like the automobile, carry the values of urban civilization to rural America. At first the machines had awkward ear pieces for each listener and many tangling wires. Here John Joseph Pershing and a group listen to a set. (Library of Congress).

license was not reissued and this decision was supported by a court in 1931.

In 1934 the FRC was replaced by the Federal Communications Commission. One of Roosevelt's first decisions in 1933 had been to appoint a committee to examine the role of government in regulating radio. This concluded that the FRC should become a permanent agency, concerned with the private, public, and governmental use of radio and of interstate telephone and telegraph communications. The Communications Act of 1934 created this agency. The establishment of the FCC represented the fruition of the FRC's aims. It also suggested future greater tension between the government and the broadcasting industry because, in the congressional hearings, the National Association of Broadcasters was extremely hostile to the idea of effective federal regulation.

The latter years of the 1930s represented a golden age for radio. Radio became increasingly accepted as an essential part of American life and, before competition from television materialized, it was the supreme form of home entertainment, offering a wide range of programs. Indeed, the success of radio struck severe blows at the record industry and even shook the dominance of the film industry. Those who had invested in radio in the 1920s now found their decision repaid by large profits.

The growth of the radio audience advanced at a rapid pace. Between 1935 and 1941 the number of houses that listened to the radio climbed from around 7 million to 28.5 million. By the end of the decade half the homes in America contained at least two radios and one could hear a radio playing, on average, for about five hours every day. It was evident that radio had made its way into American life by 1941 when 7.5 million American cars were fitted with radio. Moreover, the prices of radio sets continued to fall during this period, and inexpensive but reliable table radio sets became very popular. The trend in radio set manufacture was for a sharpening of competition between companies and, consequently, more aggressive salesmanship and price-cutting, rather than major technical developments. The result was that radio circuitry and parts became increasingly standardized and the factory process more streamlined. Even so, the considerable development of radio broadcasting before the war still left about 20 million rural Americans with only a partial radio service or no radio service at all.

After 1935, as the national economy began to improve moderately, radio broadcasting went through a period of renewed expansion. By 1941 there were 200 new radio stations. As an entire industry radio broadcasting employed 27,000 people in 1941, almost double the work force in 1935. Although many towns got their first radio station, coverage of the nation remained fundamentally imbalanced with, in 1936, 43 percent of all stations in areas with populations of 100,000 or more. With the repeal of the

Davis amendment in 1936, the licensing of urban stations dramatically increased. This period of growth threatened to lead to new waves of interference, and the government adopted a number of countermeasures. Some stations were restricted to transmitting only during allotted daytime periods. Others had to reduce the broadcasting power at night. The main method of limiting interference, which became common before World War II, was the installation of a directional antenna that concentrated transmission in one direction rather than another. By 1941 over 200 stations used this technique.

In 1939, to guarantee good reception over a large area, the Federal Communications Commission expanded the number of clear channel stations, creating a secondary class of 50,000 watt stations. Many attacked the clear channel stations for skimming off the cream of advertising revenue. However, rural politicians pointed out that high-powered stations provided remote, rural communities with their only radio service. This debate reached a climax in the late 1930s after WLW, a superpower 500,000 watt station, began broadcasting from Cincinnati in 1934. Its signal reached the whole of the Midwest and a sizable part of the South and East, thus offering a serious alternative to the dominance of the networks. Calling itself the "Nation's Station," WLW soon attracted a wealth of national and regional advertising. Yet, the domination of WLW was cut short by a Senate resolution in 1938 stating that 50,000 watts was enough power for an AM station to broadcast with. This decision set an upper limit that still applies. In 1939, then, WLW's license to broadcast at 500,000 watts was rescinded.

During the late 1930s the networks increased their domination of broadcasting in America. Some statistics seem to suggest otherwise though, for in 1939 the networks apparently only owned 4 percent of all stations. Yet, the majority of stations were small, local operations while the networks owned 25 percent of all clear channel, high-power stations and, through affiliation, controlled fifty of the remaining fifty-two clear channel stations.

With the addition of Mutual in 1934, the actual number of national networks grew to four in the 1930s: NBC-Red, NBC-

Blue, CBS, and Mutual. There were also twenty regional networks, of which six covered more than one state, for example, the Yankee Network of New England.

The newest national network, Mutual, was a cooperative venture between three 50,000 watt stations, WGN (Chicago), WOR (Newark and New York), WLW (Cincinnati), and WXYZ (Detroit). It was the affiliation of the New England Colonial Network and the Dan Lee Network on the West Coast in 1936 that transformed Mutual into a national network. CBS and NBC were never seriously threatened by the existence of Mutual, which was reduced to providing fillers for such stations.

Indeed, over this period CBS and NBC tightened their control over their affiliates, for example, binding stations to a five-year contract that the networks could end after the first year. Furthermore, once affiliated to a network, a station could not take programs from another network, unless their main supplier agreed. The networks had the option to appropriate broadcasting time at short notice and CBS could seize a whole day for its programs. Finally, stations could not refuse to air commercially sponsored network programs. Significantly, even the largest stations gave way to the demands of the networks because the major networks of NBC and CBS provided the most, and some of the best and cheapest, programs available.

Therefore, by 1940 radio broadcasting in America became centrally organized from the New York headquarters of the two major national networks. The relationship between radio and advertising reinforced the centralization of program planning and production. Radio advertising had continued to grow and agencies created not just the advertisements but also the programs, and combined them into "packages." Again, in this climate of economic depression, the valuable savings to be made from handing over such tasks to an advertising agency were attractive.

From the mid-thirties radio broadcasting had adopted a definite pattern in its dependence on advertising revenue that would continue into the television era. About 60 percent of the revenue from selling airtime went to the networks and their few stations. The remaining 40 percent was distributed among the other 700 stations. The networks and the agencies had identified the most profitable time slots for advertising: in the late morning and early afternoon for a large housewife audience and an evening prime time between about 7:00 P.M. and 11:00 P.M. Advertisers and networks were able to assess the habits and composition of the listening audience, thanks to the parallel development of audience research organizations. The original Cooperative Analysist of Broadcasting was joined by Clark-Hooper in 1934. These companies soon offered both ratings for individual programs and a breakdown of audiences into specific income groups and their geographic location. The final result of the development of advertising on radio and the networks was that, by 1941, two-thirds of all programs carried advertisements. In 1930 fewer than a third had done so. Moreover, from the new audience research data, advertising agencies, networks, and stations learnt and applied the important concept of audience flow, whereby a single program could increase the audience for the programs broadcast immediately before and after it. Therefore, broadcasters scheduled blocks of similar programs to build up the audiences for that time of day. Overall, then, broadcasting became a more sophisticated and, perhaps, then, a more stable business.

The oligarchy in broadcasting was not left undisturbed in the late 1930s and early 1940s. In March 1938 the FCC announced that it would be investigating whether the networks operated monopoly control over broadcasting. After hearing the testimonies of ninety-four witnesses and other evidence, a *Report on Chain Broadcasting* was issued on June 12, 1940. The proposed new regulations directly challenged the practices of the networks that had been developed over the previous ten years. Both the station and network would be contracted together for one year. An affiliate could use programs from other networks. The right of networks to demand options on large sections of station time would cease. An affiliate possessed the right to reject any network program. NBC would no longer be allowed to run two networks. Finally, the ownership of two stations within one market would be prohibited.

Both NBC and CBS fought the implementation of the rules in the federal courts in 1941. Mutual supported the new regulations, believing they would create greater competition. However, the

FCC repeatedly postponed the imposition of the new regulations, leaving the issue of network monopoly unresolved as the nation entered the war. Also, on the eve of World War II, the FCC began to investigate the desirability of newspapers to own nearly 30 percent of all stations.

Over the same time a dispute arose between the American Society of Composers, Authors and Publishers (ASCAP) and the broadcasters over the rates payable for use of music on the radio. ASCAP had increased its rates by 70 percent in 1937 and the broadcasters responded by creating their own licensing organization, Broadcast Music, Inc. From 1940, broadcasters tried to proceed without ASCAP music, for example, changing all of their program theme music. The dispute ended in 1941 with ASCAP agreeing to lower its rates.

A Golden Age

The period 1935–1941 is sometimes known as the golden age of radio, principally because of the programming. By this time radio stations were broadcasting for longer periods, many for eighteen hours or more a day. Thus there was a need for not just more but a greater diversity of programs. A survey in 1938 revealed that 53 percent of radio programs were music, 11 percent were talk shows, 9 percent drama, 9 percent news bulletins, 5 percent religious programs, 2 percent coverage of special events and, finally 2 percent miscellaneous subjects.

Music continued to dominate the schedules of all radio stations, but increasingly less music was performed live. From 1929 radio stations had begun to use electrical transcriptions, $33\frac{1}{3}$ rpm disks that played for about 15 minutes on each side and produced a better quality of sound than the 78 rpm records. Since these transcriptions were successful and offered listeners entertainment they could not buy for themselves, the FRC permitted this form of mechanical broadcasting. In 1938, 21 percent of programming was from electrical transcriptions and, in the following year, 573 stations were supplied with electrical transcriptions. Given the savings in wages for a singer, orchestra musicians, and technicians that were made, small local stations that were not part of a network depended upon such transcriptions to make up a good deal of their daily schedules.

The music of radio in the 1930s was predominantly big band music from the bands of Benny Goodman, Ozzie Nelson, Tommy Dorsey, Russ Morgan, and Sammy Kaye. This was the popular music of the decade, regularly playing on one of radio's top rated programs, *Your Hit Parade,* that began in 1935. Interestingly, nearly all of these famous bands had entered broadcasting and built up a following at local stations and, indeed, it seems generally the networks would acquire such existing bands rather than cultivate newcomers with original ideas and talent. Chicago radio stations were often the source of new programs.

Amateur talent shows were popular with audiences and broadcasters who used such shows as cheap filler material between their main programs. *Major Bowes and His Original Amateur Hour* was the leader of the pack, having started in 1934, discovered vocalist Frank Sinatra, and then moved to the NBC-Red network in 1935. The show regularly topped the ratings and was the ancestor of television's *The Gong Show,* so called because Major Bowes would strike his gong as a signal to eject inept performers. As in previous years, a growing number of network and station programs were variety shows with both comedy and music. Among the ex-vaudevillians to break into radio broadcasting successfully at this time was comic actor Bob Hope whose show began on CBS in 1935.

It was, perhaps, in the presentation of drama and news that radio in the late 1930s most excelled. The networks produced a steady stream of serious drama. In the main these were anthology series, consisting of adaptations from the theater, cinema, or literature, and some specially commissioned work. *Lux Radio Theater* presented hourlong radio verions of recently popular films. *Columbia Workshop,* starting in 1936 on CBS, was noted for its experimental drama.

Another CBS program, the *Mercury Theater on the Air,* which started in 1938, created a major sensation with one of radio's most famous events. Orson Welles led the Mercury Theater Company of Actors and on Sunday, October 30, 1938, broadcast his and Howard Koch's version of English novelist H. G. Wells's classic science fiction novel, *War of the Worlds*. This broadcast caused a mass panic in the eastern United States, and had thousands believing that Martians had actually invaded the Earth. The reasons for this were obvious and subtle. Wells and Koch changed the location and time of the first landing of the Martians in Wells's book from England at the turn of the century to New Jersey in the late 1930s. More significantly, the play took the form of a conventional radio broadcast that was repeatedly interrupted by news flashes of the invasion that became increasingly serious and, finally, terrifying. The earlier reports of a gas cloud sighted on Mars were rapidly followed by the landing of the Mars spacecraft, reports of casualties, the death of the radio reporter on the spot, and the evacuation of New York. Besides its verisimilitude, the program made an impact because of the curious patterns of program selection by radio audiences on Sunday nights. A majority of listeners preferred to miss the first minutes of the evening radio play on CBS so they could hear all of a popular ventriloquist show on NBC. They would turn over to CBS. Consequently, on that night many listeners missed the opening explanation of the program and believed here was a terrible news broadcast.

There were two other external factors that encouraged the spread of terror. First, from September 19 onward, the worst hurricane ever devastated the Atlantic seaboard, claiming houses, mansions, the land itself, and 700 lives. Second, Britain and France had reached the nadir of their notorious appeasement of German dictator Adolf Hitler and acquiesced in the dismemberment of Czechoslovakia in the Munich crisis, also in September 1938. Here was victory of an evil empire abroad and physical devastation at home that had profound psychological consequences for many Americans.

Although the work of Orson Welles and other radio dramatists is justly praised, it should be remembered the bulk of programming consisted of soap operas, situation comedies, and thrillers. By 1940 all of the networks broadcast about 75 hours per week of soap operas, the majority of which were commercially sponsored. These programs came in daily 15 minute episodes that were broadcast during the day and each began with a signature tune, a recapitulaton, or recap, of "what happened last time" and, then, plunged straight into the action. This genre was diversifying. For example, there were *Back Stage Wife* (the trials and tribulations of being the wife of a Broadway star), *Road of Life* (life in a hospital), and *Our Gal Sunday* (whose dilemma was encapsulated by the station blurb as, "Can this girl from a mining town in the West find happiness as the wife of a wealthy and titled Englishman?").

Adventure series became more sophisticated. *Gangbusters,* which started in 1935, was characterized by its opening cacophony of sirens, machine-gun fire, and marching feet. *Mr. Keen, Tracer of Lost Persons* and *Mr. District Attorney* were other popular mystery shows. Children were offered their own adventure serials, often about cowboys like Tom Mix or pilot heroes such as *Captain Midnight* and *Hop Harrigan.* In 1938, the already popular *Lone Ranger* was joined by the crime crusader, *The Green Hornet,* whom station WXYZ claimed was the masked cowboy's grand nephew. In his eradication of "public enemies that even the G-Men cannot catch," *The Green Hornet* was a show that epitomized the New Deal ethos of a moral and economic rearmament in the war against both depression and an imagined crime wave.

Half-hour situation comedies were also a developing staple of thirties radio. *Lil' Abner* began in 1939 and competed with, among other popular programs, Fanny Brice's portrayal of *Baby Snooks* who terrorized the lives of her father and baby brother, Robespierre.

Radio drama of all types proved to be incredibly popular in the late 1930s, with many shows heard by large and loyal audiences. It seemed that radio drama caught the imagination of Americans, not just because of its creative use of sound that was refreshingly different from the movies or theater, but because its drama depended upon the listeners' participation in visualizing settings and action fully. Indeed, programs in which listeners could actively participate were guaranteed to attract large audiences in the thirties. A very erudite show, *The University of Chicago Roundtable,* on NBC, in which faculty members and guests discussed current topics, was far more popular than conventional entertainment shows according to the ratings and participants received sizable mail from listeners requesting transcripts of the debates. *America's Town Meeting* on NBC took this format a step further by inviting members of a studio audience to express their opinions in a radio debate. Not surprisingly, then, quiz shows grew in popularity from about two hours of all programs a week in 1935 to 10 hours a week in 1941. One of the most popular shows was *Kay Kyser's Kollege of Musical Knowledge* and those other shows in which the audience tested its or an expert's general knowledge, for example *Dr. I.Q.* and *Information, Please!* In 1941 one of the most famous quiz shows, and one that involved almost an orgy of public participation, was *Truth or Consequences,* in which the failure of contestants to answer stupid questions led to the same contestants having to embarrass themselves by performing stupid stunts.

We might be inclined to interpret this willingness of Americans to participate in their radio listening as reflecting the belief, generally cultivated in the media, that Americans and their massive democratic institutions were, at long last, working together to vanquish unemployment and poverty. Since radio was free, and carried the propaganda of the New Deal, perhaps it was truly a populist media of the 1930s. Whatever the case, the diverse programs of the thirties bequeathed a crucial legacy, for they provided the original models for the standard programs of future television broadcasting, most obviously the situation comedy, quiz shows, soap operas, and anthology story series.

When considering the development of news programs before World War II, we might return to the broadcasting of *War of the Worlds* in 1938. The panic that the false newscasts caused indicated just how much Americans had begun to believe in what radio told them. Researchers have discovered that, as CBS told them the Earth had been invaded, listeners did not telephone their friends or other sources of news. Indeed, by 1940, for a majority of people, radio news had supplanted newspapers as the prime source of information. The growth of news on radio can be traced back to the collapse of the Biltmore agreement in 1935 when most of the major wire services broke the embargo on supplying radio. Most radio stations began news programs consisting mainly of local stories but also supplied with national news by a wire service. As their service expanded, the national networks broadcast more international news and, partly because this was such a good audience-puller, they also broadcast more major crime stories than did the newspapers.

Radio was unrivaled in providing fast and colorful reports direct from the scene of major and sudden events, especially natural or man-made disasters. An outstanding example of this was the explosion of the *Hindenburg* passenger airship as it docked at Lakehurst, New Jersey, in May 1937. Herb Morrison of the Chicago WLS station happened to be at Lakehurst and was able to make a disk recording of his and other eye witnesses' surprise and horror at watching the sudden inferno. Undoubtedly, broadcasters discovered that live, on the spot, reporting of such disasters attracted audiences by offering a vacarious thrill of being present at such tragedies. The coverage of the trial of Bruno Hauptmann for the murder of the Lindbergh baby in 1935 also enthralled listeners. It also led to new limits being imposed on radio journalism in the interests of justice and good taste. The courtroom bristled with microphones and Gabriel Heatter of Mutual acted as a host for the final, grisly, and live coast-to-coast radio presentation of the electrocution of the hapless Hauptmann. Consequently, the American Bar Association severely restricted radio coverage in courtrooms in the future.

Besides the overturning of the Biltmore agreement, the other factor behind the expansion of radio news in the late 1930s was how world events, especially the rise of Nazi Germany in Europe, became increasingly newsworthy. Paul White, news director of CBS, was instrumental in pioneering newscasts from foreign correspondents. In 1936, he arranged both the coverage of the abdication crisis in England, when King Edward VIII renounced the throne to marry American divorcée Wallis Simpson, and the outbreak of the Spanish Civil War with the rebellion of General Franco. In Spain H. V. Kaltenborn sent reports from a haystack sitting between the firing guns of both armies. So, at quite an early stage, it was understood that radio news was best when it was dramatically related. With the Anschluss or annexation of Austria, in 1938, White inaugurated a familiar device of radio journalism, having reporters based in several countries discuss current events as seen from their different vantage points. In the Munich crisis of 1938 when Hitler forced the partition of Czechoslovakia, NBC scooped the first glance at the terms of the Munich agreement only minutes after it was signed.

Even before America finally joined the Allies in fighting, World War II boosted news broadcasting. The figures for the number of hours in a year given over to news disclose how, whereas in 1937 news totalled 800 hours on all networks, in 1939 this had risen to 1,250 hours. In 1941 the number of hours of network news had nearly tripled to 3,450 hours.

During the 1930s radio also established itself as an integral part of the political process. The principal and most successful pioneer of political broadcasting was Franklin D. Roosevelt whose series of "Fireside Chats" had a tremendous effect on the American public. Altogether, there were only twenty-eight such chats and they were conducted as an informal conversation between the president and the citizen listening in his home. Moreover, these broadcasts were always made at prime listening time. Since the Republicans could not field a public speaker of Roosevelt's ability and presence, during the 1930s the GOP tended to experiment more with its party political broadcasts. In the 1936 campaign, besides using frequent radio commercials, the Republican party had Senator Arthur Vandenberg record a supposed debate with the president in which the answers of FDR to Vandenberg's questions were, in fact, excerpts from past speeches by Roosevelt. This tactic was banned by CBS on the grounds that it was misleading. To put their case to the public, the Republicans eventually produced an allegorical play detailing their electoral promises.

By 1940 the pivotal role of radio in politics was recognized when surveys suggested that most voters considered radio to be their first source of political news. Thus, in the battle for ratings and votes that Roosevelt's performance won in 1940, perhaps it was significant that Republican candidate Wendell Wilkie had seriously strained his voice early in the campaign. Moreover, on the night before the election, the Democrats marshaled together stars of stage, screen, and radio to lead a radio entertainment extravaganza and final party political broadcast.

FM

Technical advances continued, and transmission and reception were refined. Yet, even during the 1930s, the sound quality of radio was tinny and frequently disturbed by static electricity. However, there were significant new developments to correct this problem.

FM, or Frequency Modulation, radio was the answer, ensuring reception free of static electricity by canceling out the effect of atmospheric amplitude modulation by including similar modulation in the radio signal. Yet, most engineers felt that the best and easier solution to static was to muffle the static by increasing the transmitter power and force it down a narrower channel. FM became a practicable concept, thanks to the work carried out by Edwin Armstrong, who had been active in radio engineering before World War I. In the late 1930s, he reasoned that, for FM to succeed, it required a broader channel of 200 kHz, many times wider than the typical AM channel of 10 kHz (kilohertz). This band width produced excellent sound, free from interference made by electrical storms and other radio stations. In 1933, after the system was patented, Armstrong persuaded his friend, David Sarnoff of RCA, to finance experiments with FM. However, in 1935 FM transmission from the RCA aerials on top of the Empire State Building ceased; Armstrong left RCA and took the FM system with him because RCA would not support the necessary huge development costs, thereby making its massive investment in AM (amplitude modulation) obsolete. Such economic self-interest and skepticism of the major radio businesses would delay the commercial growth of FM in the 1930s. Eventually, after a year spent supporting his FM experiments with his personal fortune, Armstrong convinced John Shepherd, who owned the Yankee Network in New England, to set up an FM station. In fact, the first FM station was Armstrong's own experimental WZXMN in Alpine, licensed in 1938. Yankee began FM broadcasting from one station in 1939 and was followed by General Electric. FM receivers were manufactured and a fair number sold.

By 1940, FM radio was almost fully developed and ready for commercial operation. It offered the possibility of drastic changes in broadcasting, not least because the quality of the FM signal allowed a program to be relayed by radio transmission at an equal and even better quality than the usual, expensive AT&T connections to a network. In 1946, FM broadcasters went before the

FCC to lobby for commercial FM broadcasting. Significantly, the case for commercial FM broadcasting would only gradually edge forward, not just because of resistance from AM broadcasters but also because of resistance from the advocates of commercial television. Commercial FM radio began in 1941, using one of the available experimental television channels.

10

SEEING IS DECEIVING
Hollywood and the Movies

IN 1927 there were 17,000 movie theaters across the United States and in many towns the movie theater was the most impressive new building. In general movie theaters made the most of modern architecture as advertisement, emphasizing that, within their portals, was a fantasy world offering patrons escape from reality with such enticing attachments as crystalline towers and illuminated marquees. Movie production, exhibition, and attendance formed a continuous self-fulfilling cycle in which huge audiences required numerous, capacious theaters and enormous production from the great studios. It was this emphasis on quantity, rather than creative quality, that necessitated a production system based on studios working to industrial capacity. Hollywood studios were giant factories using the same organizational strategy to separate production into a series of parts in which each component unit would have its designated function. Thus writers of stories, screenplays, and subtitles worked in a specific section, while such activities as set construction, costume making, and technical services each had their alloted space also.

British character actor Boris Karloff lent the gangling monster of *Frankenstein* (1931) a touching pathos in the most famous screen version of Mary Shelley's early nineteenth-century novella that, as written by Garrett Font and Francis Edwards Faragoh and directed by James Whale, also borrowed material from Wegener's *The Golem*. The result was later described by the *New York Times* as "probably the most famous of all horror films and one of the best." (Museum of Modern Art Film Stills Archive).

When the great Hollywood studios converted to sound production, it was by expanding their facilities, adding such additional departments as sound mixing and dubbing, and music recording. The consequences were even more extensive as writing screenplays became more specialized and required division of labor into three areas: providing general treatments of original and adapted stories; breaking the scenario into a visual sequence, shot by shot; and writing the actual dialogue. Thus a film began as an idea or concept, based on original or adapted material, and moved through the studio system, department by logical department, from writing to design, production, and editing, with the same sort of momentum and ease as a Ford Model T car on the assembly line. Very few directors had the prestige to exercise a decisive influence on the shape of a script before production and on the finished version during cutting. Actual shooting lasted between fifteen and thirty days, depending on the complexity of production. It was the need to govern production according to a system that determined the finished artistic form of all films.

Each studio had a particular style of film. MGM mounted glossy musicals, melodramas, and comedies about high society, Warner Brothers specialized in thrillers, and Columbia was given to experiments in exposing political and social problems. Successful films thrived on proven formulas—star personalities, studio images, and manufactured dreams. All of this did not mean that Hollywood was efficient economically. The potential for economic disintegration was present in Hollywood before World War II. Perhaps this was what dramatist George Bernard Shaw recognized when he refused to sell Samuel Goldwyn the rights to film his plays: "The trouble, Mr. Goldwyn, is that you are only interested in art and I am only interested in money." Philip French, the historian of *The Movie Moguls* (1969), concluded that "Few of the studios were run in a way that approximated to any standard notion of business efficiency; their administration and accountancy were quite unlike those of large corporations." Beneath the surface of order and regulation producers, directors, and stars were confused by the Hollywood system and their own place in it. As English novelist J. B. Priestley said about Hollywood before World War II: "Its trade, which is in dreams at so many dollars per thousand feet, is managed by businessmen pretending to be artists and by artists pretending to be businessmen. In this queer atmosphere, nobody stays as he was; the artist begins to lose his art, and the businessman becomes temperamental and overbalanced."

The Director as Industrial Coordinator

The day of improvisation in filmmaking passed with pioneer director D. W. Griffith. As Hollywood studios became more like other production factories, the product became ever more stand-ardized. From being the principal auteur, the director became simply an executive responsible for drawing together the different contributions of screenplay writer, producer, actors, and techni-cians and overseeing a product from the middle to the finish. Individual films were considered but one unit in the studio's annual production of many.

Even leading directors were assigned all sorts of different ma-terial and expected to move easily from thriller to comedy to musical with the same impersonal determination as the studio. In the period 1930–1933 versatile director Mervyn Le Roy directed twenty-three films, including the very different crime thriller *Little Caesar,* the brutal social realism of *I Am a Fugitive From a Chain Gang,* and the backstage histrionics of *Gold Diggers of 1933.* In short, filmmaking had become another system of industrial production, like many others.

On the whole, Hollywood films of the 1920s were custom-made according to very tired formulas and this applied to the entire range of activities involved in making films and not only acting and directing. Whatever special gifts various technicians and designers may have possessed, they were restricted by the studios' insistence on conformity and repetition because conform-ity and repetition ensured mass production as regular as that of any other factory. Experiment was considered costly, time-con-suming, and dangerous because no one could predict the com-mercial outcome. Yet successful innovative films had always been copied by competing directors.

Hollywood's dependence on huge financial investment in the 1920s made such copying essential. Thus films conformed to a particular genre that would be made according to precedent. A few gifted directors, such as Erich von Stroheim and Ernst Lubitsch, could prise open the formula and introduce their own insights, developing character and situation by their own imaginative use of shots, crosscutting, and so forth.

The director most clearly influenced by the shift from artistic innovation to industrial production was Thomas Ince, who be-came the first film producer of any significance. Ince was most concerned to sustain audience interest by keeping the story moving. He cut as freely and felicitously as Griffith but only to this end. Ince also championed shooting film outdoors in the West, to capture the drama and excitement of cowboys and Indians pitted against one another on horses in motion and dwarfed by the towering canyons and endless deserts in the background. Unlike Griffith, Ince welcomed his elevation from director to producer and enjoyed supervising several films at once, ordering shooting according to a preplanned and detailed script. Thus Ince's directors were expected to make a finished product from a blueprint that specified dialogue, shooting, and production schedule exactly. Each was planned to ensure that the entire process of filming was cost-effective by assembling cast, crew, and equipment for the shortest time.

Ironically, Ince's career, like Griffith's, faded in the studio era he had helped introduce. Mogul Harry Aitken took Ince, Sennett, and Griffith from Mutual into a new company, the Triangle Film Corporation. Much was expected of the new company but it failed in 1919 when Sennett and Griffith failed to produce films that continued to attract audiences. Ince himself died mysteriously in 1924. It was rumored that he was pushed over a cliff after showing too great an interest in Marion Davies, mistress and protégée of William Randolph Hearst.

Another transitional artist was Douglas Fairbanks, swashbuckling hero of romantic comedies devised by Anita Loos and directed by her husband John Emerson. These comedies, made in the period 1915–1920, satirized the new film genres and American mores. They capitalized on Fairbanks's inability to underplay and turned his overacting into displays of athletic exhilaration, swinging from balconies and ceilings and across ravines. The films contrasted the dull routine of conventional life with wild, extrovert fantasy.

Censorship

From the very start movie makers found themselves attacked by prurient moralists for attempting to debase standards, supposedly encouraging laziness and sexual license. In the early 1920s the gulf between old-fashioned morality and cinematic permissiveness yawned wide. Films reflected growing urban values and became more suggestive and, indeed, realistic. Some implied that those who disobeyed the ten commandments still managed to live happily ever after.

Certain self-appointed guardians of public morality, lacking official justification for judgment, passed their own private censure on to their constituents. They included the Federal Motion Picture Council in America and the Women's Christian Temperance Union (WCTU). Their charges of undue license were based in part on covert anti-Semitism, implying that Jewish moguls were corrupting Christian morals.

Moral license on screen was accompanied by extramarital license off it. A series of widely publicized scandals involving Hollywood stars damaged the reputation of the entire industry because Hollywood had placed such emphasis on creating the star system. In September 1922 the mysterious death of call girl Virginia Rappe whilst at a party given by comedian Fatty Arbuckle in the St. Francis Hotel, San Francisco, led to Arbuckle's trial for involuntary manslaughter. He was acquitted at a second trial but not until revelations and, worse, innuendos that his great weight had ruptured Rappe's gall bladder, causing her death, ended Arbuckle's career before the camera. He worked in *Hollywood,* a bitter satire by James Cruze, and, thereafter, only worked behind the cameras directing films and using a new name. In 1923 English romantic actor Wallace Reid died prematurely and was pronounced a confirmed morphine addict. Hollywood had turned him into a habitual drug user by giving him morphine to help him continue acting whilst recovering from injuries sustained while filming. When director William Desmond Tanner (or Taylor) also died prematurely, rumors of his particular brew of sex and drugs tarnished the images of actresses Mabel Normand and Mary Miles Minter. It later transpired he was shot dead by Minter's mother.

Such scandals roused the indignation of Congress and it seemed Hollywood might even be threatened by federal censorship. It was this threat, above all, that prompted the movie moguls to create their own censor. They chose big-eared, buck-toothed Will Hays, former campaign manager to Warren Harding and current postmaster general. He was everything the wailing wall of Hollywood moguls was not—Gentile, Protestant, and Wasp. He became president of the Motion Picture Producers and Distributors of America (MPPDA), commonly known as the Hays Office. However, Hays was not content to provide a front of Christian decency in the lounge so that Hollywood could enjoy Babylonian license in the bedroom. The Arbuckle scandal and others convinced the tycoons that Hollywood would require a code of public morality for its films and a code of private morality for its stars. In practice this meant the imposition of small town morality. It was to be the same sort of imposition of intolerance on indulgence as prohibition. At a Hollywood ball they might "need nothing at all," but Hays would make them say goodbye to all that.

The Hays office code, correctly the Production Code, was drawn up by Martin Quigley, a Chicago publisher, and the Reverend Daniel A. Lord, S.J., of St. Louis University, in 1929. It was submitted to the West Coast Association of Producers of 1924 who, with the MPPDA, approved it in 1930. In 1934 the Code was made compulsory when a Catholic and former journalist, Joseph I. Breen, took charge of its administration. A fine of $25,000 was imposed on any member company of the MPPDA that released a film without Breen's seal of approval. The purpose of the Code was explained in a preamble: "No picture shall be produced which will lower the moral standards of those who see it. Hence the sympathy of the audience shall never be thrown to the side of crime, wrong-doing, evil or sin."

From such an opening the Code attempted to enforce morality by legislating what could and what could not be shown. However, not all of its provisions were ridiculous nor was its assumption that an audience "is most receptive of the actions and ideals presented by their most popular stars."

The Hays Code was not imposing an artificial convention by insisting that "the sanctity of marriage and the home shall be upheld." Yet most of the Code was given to prurient speculation on sex outside marriage: "Impure love must not be presented as *attractive* and *beautiful* . . . It must not be presented in such a way as to *arouse passion* or morbid curiosity on the part of the audience." All in all, the Code imposed a world picture on films that was quite inconsistent with adult experience. Yet it remained in effect for thirty-six years from 1930. Joseph Breen was its leading administrator and in 1953 he received an Academy Award for his "conscientious, open-minded and dignified management." Hollywood's observance of the Code was at best superficial and at worst hypocritical, a practice that turned vice into versa. The studios set out to titillate their public and they succeeded. Biblical subjects in particular lent themselves to explicit sexual display, for which director Cecil B. De Mille was especially notorious. His new religious look in décolleté gowns was always lo! and behold!

The Hays and Breen offices had not restricted themselves to morality. They were also in the business of political censorship. In 1937 Samuel Goldwyn submitted a screenplay by dramatist Lillian Hellman for *Dead End,* a gangster thriller, to Joseph Breen. Breen replied: "We would like to recommend . . . that you be less emphatic . . . in showing the contrast between conditions of the poor in tenements and those of the rich in apartment houses." Breen was less concerned with the rights of the poor than their smell. He did not want any emphasis on "the presence of filth or smelly garbage cans, or garbage floating in the river, into which the boys jump for a swim." His motives in suppressing these aspects of the script were, of course, pure. He was concerned with the social welfare of the working class: "This recommendation is made under the general heading of good and welfare because our reaction is that such scenes are likely to give offense." To whom they would give offense was not specified.

For all their impersonal emphasis on industrial efficiency in the interests of commerce, the great studios in their heyday responded to certain deep psychic needs in the American public. Almost all feature films in the studio years played on people's need to believe that human determination could triumph over adversity, such as the Great Depression. There was a concomitant corollary, that such benevolent human values as love, justice, and sincerity must inevitably succeed over selfishness, hypocrisy, and callousness, whether the story was domestic or political.

Hollywood in the 1920s

It was Erich von Stroheim and Cecil B. De Mille who were the natural successors of Griffith and Ince as innovator and showman in the 1920s. Gerald Mast perceptively satirizes the differences between them when he says, "Von Stroheim gave the public what he wanted, De Mille gave it what he thought it wanted. Von Stroheim was a ruthless realist committed to his art and his vision, De Mille was willing to throw any hokum into a film that was faddish or striking. Von Stroheim's films, despite their excesses and occasionally overstated moralizing, were controlled by the director's taste and intelligence; De Mille's films had everything but taste and intelligence."

Whereas both directors decided to capitalize on public obsession with infidelity among the idle rich, there is a world of difference between *Male and Female* by De Mille and *Blind Husbands* by von Stroheim, both of 1919. *Male and Female* is an extravagant, superficial, and meretricious examination of class attitudes toward sex, too much of which revolves around the cold miniature actress Gloria Swanson taking a bath. Ever conscious of the need to make a sensation, Gloria Swanson insisted that Cecil B. De Mille allow her to enter a lion's cage in *Male and Female*. At a preview of the completed film she overheard one member of the audience observe, "I wonder which one is stuffed."

However, von Stroheim's triangular melodrama, *Blind Husbands,* pares away excess incidents and trivia in order to expose the intensity of a neglected wife's desire for a German officer who courts her in front of her blind husband. Von Stroheim used detail expressively to evoke passion but his felicitous camera shots allowed him a range of subtle expressions. Like Griffith, von Stroheim was an expert at cutting and in creating authentic sets and costumes. However, von Stroheim's obsession with authenticity was costly in terms of money and time and he fell foul of Irving Thalberg who disliked his extravagance, his apparent inefficiency, and his disregard of studio bosses. Although von Stroheim's films were commercially successful and, in effect, subsidizing other productions, Thalberg dismissed him. Von Stroheim moved to Metro Pictures, another ailing studio he helped rescue before being sacked for a second time by Irving Thalberg.

At Metro von Stroheim worked first on a film version of the novel, *McTeague*, by Frank Norris and planned a thorough and literal interpretation with close attention to animal imagery and shot on location in San Francisco and Death Valley. The first version extended to forty-two reels, over three times as long as *Birth of a Nation*. When von Stroheim had cut it by more than half, to twenty reels, he refused to cut any further. Thalberg, now at Metro, fired him a second time. Thalberg then had resident studio scenarist June Mathis reduce the film further to ten reels, and ordered the destruction of all the excised sections. Despite the butchery, some of von Stroheim's personal vision survives. One of von Stroheim's most bitter climaxes comes when he shows how thirst for gold takes precedence over the natural human need for life-giving water in a desert with a man chained to his gold although his starving and parched body can only become food for vultures.

Von Stroheim was easy to hate and easier to fire, being extravagant and dictatorial. When he left Metro for Zukor he ran into all his old problems. Joseph Kennedy intended *Queen Kelly* as a celebration of his mistress Gloria Swanson but in von Stroheim's hands the film became ever more elaborate and sinister. Exasperated, Swanson had Kennedy finally pull the plug on Stroheim's career as a director by having the film abandoned in the midst of shooting just as sound was being introduced in the studios. Stroheim directed only one other film although he continued to act in various roles but always as a Prussian martinet, notably in Jean Renoir's *Grand Illusion* (1937) and Billy Wilder's *Sunset Boulevard* (1950). In this last film he played a dispossessed character whose tragic career in films echoed his own. He was the obsessed chauffeur of a faded and self-deluding star whom he had previously served as director and husband. Ironically, it was Gloria Swanson who played this part, inadequately but true to form.

Other significant directors of the 1920s included Henry King who made *Tol'able David;* James Cruze, who made *The Covered Wagon* (1923); Rex Ingram, who made *The Four Horsemen of the*

Apocalypse; Josef von Sternberg, *Salvation Hunters* and *Underworld;* John Ford, *The Iron Horse;* and King Vidor, *The Big Parade.* Among these other leading directors James Cruze was a master of satire, Rex Ingram was a specialist in composition, Josef von Sternberg excelled in the evocation of atmosphere, and John Ford began a very long career in westerns.

Documentary filmmaker Robert Flaherty made a naturalistic film of the everyday life of Eskimos in Hudson's Bay, *Nanook of the North* (1922). Flaherty was one of the few directors to enjoy true artistic freedom because he could film alone and on modest means. Nanook himself was quite uninhibited and lacking in any self-consciousness before the camera. Thus he lived his life for Flaherty whose artistic control of his means was such that concept and execution were one. Flaherty captured the beauty of immaculate frozen plains and also the rigors of the Eskimos' lives, their continuous struggle for food and shelter, complaisant and unaware that human life could be lived any other way.

Classic Comedies

The most enduring classics among silent films of the 1920s were the comedies. Among the newcomers were Stan Laurel and Oliver Hardy who were brought together by producer Hal Roach as a perfect comic fit of fat and thin. Their films were based on a visual anarchic convention akin to the musical convention of a slow-burning crescendo in a Rossini overture. Laurel and Hardy comedies were tight. If a Christmas tree catches in the doorway of a house, then tree, house, and parked cars nearby must all be destroyed as disaster follows calamity. In their acting Laurel and Hardy unfolded the spiteful child in the adult, reveling in the tyranny of the weak as tearful Stan undermines pompous Ollie's incompetent attempts to ride out hazardous situations.

When director Hal Roach chose Harold Lloyd as a leading man he wanted someone to combine the pathos of Chaplin with the zest of Fairbanks and the charm and zaniness of both. However, Lloyd's episodic comedies did not draw humor from character, simply from a series of potentially dangerous situations. In *High and Dizzy* (1921) he plays a newly qualified doctor who falls in

Chaplin's ascendancy as the preeminent comic genius of the silent screen was confirmed by such masterpieces as *The Gold Rush* (1925). In a celebrated sequence, desperately hungry, he cooked and ate an outsize boot, consuming it, sole and all, like a cordon bleu shellfish, and once again proving in his resourceful use of objects that versatility was the soul of wit. (Museum of Modern Art Film Stills Archive).

love with a somnambulist. The subsequent plot allowed Lloyd his trademark of a comedy of thrills when he has to protect the somnambulist walking on a perilous window ledge many stories above ground. When she moves back inside the building and locks the window behind her, it is he who is trapped and now performs a dazzling gymnastic routine of trips and stumbles that keep the audience on the edge of their seats in an original mix of perplexity and amusement. Lloyd's comedies were magic as pure sensation.

Buster Keaton came closest to equaling Chaplin's evocation of the tension between isolated individual and mechanized society and his exploration of the surface and undercurrent human relationships. Keaton specialized in a deadpan expression of a man resolutely determined to attain his goals, despite such monstrous obstacles as steamboat, hurricanes, locomotives, and whole tribes of savages. In *Daydreams* he eludes the police by hiding in the paddle wheel of a ferryboat that moves, forcing him to stay upright by walking without stopping, a metaphor for the sort of treadmill man must endure through life but cannot control.

Buster Keaton's masterpiece, *The General,* is cohesive from first to last, a comic epic about a railroad and the triumph of one man over others as well as such natural enemies as fire and water. The hero is clearly unequal to the task and the comedy is sustained by the disparity between human prowess and the natural forces he is pitted against. Keaton plays Johnny Gray, a confederate hero in the Civil War, who simply wants to run a train that the Union army wants to appropriate and use to wipe out his fellow Confederates. He is always saved by chance. A cannon aimed at him goes off only when the train has turned a corner, thus hitting the enemy straight in the flank instead. The film explains acts of heroism as absurd accidents—much the same point as was being made by the lost generation of war novelists.

Chaplin's *The Gold Rush* (1925) was an episodic film unified by Chaplin's continuous quest for physical wealth through gold and emotional security through love in a hostile, frozen world. The divertissements have become cinema classics. In an icy Alaskan cabin Charlie Chaplin cooks his shoe, carves it like best beef, salts it to taste, and chews it like a cordon bleu meal, twirling shoelaces like spaghetti, and sucking nails like chicken bones. In a dance hall he turns a spare rope into a belt unaware that a dog is tethered to the other end. The dog has to follow him around the dance floor, interrupting the other dancers, but when it darts after a stray cat, it is Charlie who has to run for his life. The consistent theme of the film is the way gold makes man inhuman, turning even conventional romantic leads, like the handsome lover, into callous cynics. When roommate Big Jim McKay becomes ravenous, he sees Charlie as a chicken to catch and eat. Though the sequence is hilarious, it is also disturbing because of its implied cannibalism. When their cabin teeters on the edge of a crumbling cliff the two friends turn enemies, with each trying to get out by scrambling over the other. Chaplin's choice of shots and his editing, while fully expressive, were unobtrusive, allowing mime to unfold story, situation, and humor as a continuous thread.

Sound

The talkies did not suddenly burst on the silver screen with the premiere of *The Jazz Singer* on October 5, 1927. The introduction of pictures with words was the result of three decades of experiment. The early film inventors had experimented with sound films, beginning with William Dickson in 1889. Leon Gaumont showed various films with synchronized sound in Paris after the turn of the century and German filmmaker Oscar Messter produced *The Green Forest* (1910) with synchronized sound.

The main problems were those of true synchronization between sound and picture, particularly when projected film was mechanically separate from recorded disk. However, German pioneers found a way of recording sound directly on film by using the principle of an oscilloscope, converting sound into beams of light recorded on the edge of the film strip next to the image. In the United States Lee de Forest perfected a similar process and also solved the second problem—amplification. A film had to be loud enough to reach (literally) thousands of people in the audience in huge theaters whose acoustics would carry according to capacity. De Forest had invented the audion tube in 1906—a vacuum tube that magnified sounds and relayed them through a speaker.

By 1923 de Forest was producing short films with synchronized sound. Moreover, in 1925 the Bell Telephone Company, through its research team at Western Electric, had produced a rival process of sound on disks, a system known as the Vitaphone. However, the Bell Company failed to persuade any Hollywood studio to use the Vitaphone. Producers were chary of an expensive and unproven innovation whose potential success would cause havoc in their, by now, more settled and more profitable business. The mere process of recording adequate sound alone would slow down film production. Furthermore, sound reproduction would be an extra economic imposition upon exhibitors who would have to acquire additional, expensive equipment and adapt their motion picture palaces accordingly.

Eventually, Bell and Western Electric offered the Vitaphone to Warners, an ailing company on the verge of bankruptcy. At first, Warners experimented with programs of short, sound films in 1926 and 1927 featuring Will Hays and various musicians. However, a rival, William Fox, began to make much the same sort of novelty programs, and, also, a newsreel with synchronized commentary. Fox was using his own separate system, Movietone. It had the sound recorded direct onto the filmstrip, something made possible by Theodore Case, who had pirated Lee de Forest's system. Thus Warners decided they had to bite the bullet and make a feature film with sound—*The Jazz Singer* with Al Jolson.

The artistic significance of *The Jazz Singer* was that it was the first film to use synchronized sound as the principal means of telling a dramatic story. In fact, the majority of the film was made as a silent with music added and synchronized. Only two sequences used synchronized speech, one building to a climax when Al Jolson sings *Mammy* to a theater audience. Whereas the silent sequences retained the fluidity of the better silent camera work, the sound sequences lacked movement and were dramatically inert, with the actors huddled close so that their voices could be captured by the microphones. Despite the visual plasticity of the silent sections and the static nature of the sound sequences, it was those very same sound sequences that provided the actors with greater opportunity to give voice and flesh to their characters.

Commercially, *The Jazz Singer* was an outstanding success whose very dimensions obliged the otherwise reluctant movie moguls to convert to sound if they wanted to retain their shaken hold of public taste. People wanted to hear as well as see films and Hollywood, desperate to please, converted wholesale to the new process.

However, talking pictures experienced various technical, artistic, and commercial problems. The camera, so fluent in silent films, was once again rooted to the spot so that the actors could be adequately recorded by the stationary microphone. Once again, filmmaking became an inferior means of recording theater performances. Now directors had to learn how to capture voice as well as face and master the requisite technical skills. Sound recording caught all noise and film cameras were notoriously audible with their incessant whirring. Thus, for a time, cameras were placed in a glass booth where they moved even less than before.

The introduction of sound led to reconsideration of the system developed over thirty years and a questioning of basic movie assumptions. Once again, filmmakers tried to find a parallel with the stage. They employed playwrights, stage actors, and theater directors and there was a brief period of misapplied stage principles. However, films could show any image while words were spoken. The synchronization of image and sound also allowed for disjunction of picture and sound in which a different image from an actor's face might be more effective than a literal presentation of a conversation. Moreover, movies could employ a greater range of sound effects than any play or opera—not only speech and natural sound effects, songs and musical accompaniment, but also distortion and subjective thoughts—all with perfect timing.

The whole process of conversion by studios and theaters was so expensive that they required massive injections of capital from banks. Thus did the movies become adjuncts to the great commercial banks who, incidentally and ironically, controlled the two major sound processes by Western Electric and RCA because these companies were themselves subdivisions of the Morgan and Rockefeller families. Thus the banks had created a sort of motion pictures version of the Dawes Plan for German reparations—one in which the studios had to borrow money from the banks to acquire equipment whose development the banks had themselves financed in the first place.

Sometimes the most illustrious artists of the silent era proved encumbrances in the age of sound. Foreign accents were inadmissible except in character parts. Native English speakers whose voices suggested rather different characters from their appearance —such as a handsome leading man with a high-pitched voice— might have been better off as mute artists (like Harpo Marx). The most famous of such casualties was John Gilbert, one of Greta Garbo's leading men, whose voice, as reproduced, seemed too fast and high. Different explanations have been given to account for his failure in sound, ranging from vocal inadequacy to technical sabotage on the orders of Louis B. Mayer.

Studios required very different material with effective dialogue. Not only did they import stage actors from Broadway but also established playwrights and novelists to provide scripts for them. Yet certain directors, notably the Russian Sergei Einstein, were convinced that film could absorb sound and Einstein made much of the symphonic possibilities of a film scene by engaging composer Sergei Prokofiev to enhance visual images with appropriate music.

Eventually came the invention of the camera blimp, a mask to cover its whirring sound while allowing it to film more freely. Director Rouben Mamoulian introduced the use of two microphones to record a scene, allowing for a final composite mix of their recording after balancing and regulating the volumes. The introduction of the boom, an instrument that allowed the microphone to move in earshot but out of sight just above the actor's head, allowed actors to move while speaking.

It was essential to transform sound into a positive asset to the entire artistic range of filmmaking. Innovative director Ernst Lubitsch exploited some of the possibilities of sound to support vision in his *The Love Parade* (1929) by having Maurice Chevalier make witty asides and a series of deliberate mistimed sound effects to jolt bride, groom, and congregation during a marriage ceremony. In *Trouble in Paradise* Lubitsch exploited sound as a means of innuendo by concentrating camera and microphone outside a room where a crucial scene of seduction is taking place. It was Lubitsch who first conceived the mix of rhythmic song and speeding train for *Monte Carlo* (1930) with both music and train getting faster as the song nears its climax.

The most imaginative use of sound and pictures was found by Walt Disney in his early animated cartoons. Walt Disney had moved to Hollywood from Kansas, where he had had a successful career as a commercial artist, in 1923. He and his animator, Ub Iwerks, soon mastered the technique of animated cartoons, but his adept use of sound made him preeminent in Hollywood.

Because he was not filming real people, Disney bypassed the restrictions of sound recording. Cartoon sound could always be added later and the fact that cartoons are fantastic, anyway, released sound (as well as vision) from immutable laws of realistic reproduction. The animals in a Disney cartoon could acquire human characteristics, and, indeed, act like people in the old films of Mack Sennett or Georges Méliès. Disney realised that sound and vision could be complementary in his *Steamboat Willie* (1928). When a goat devours a guitar and sheet music for the song *Turkey in the Straw* like so much grass, Mickey Mouse twists its tail, causing notes to stream from the goat's mouth as the soundtrack plays them aloud. Mickey Mouse then accompanies the tune with whatever tool he can turn into instruments of percussion—pots, pails, and washboard, along with squeaks and quacks from cat, pig, and duck—and finally, Mickey plays a cow's teeth like a xylophone.

Disney recognized similarities in superficially dissimilar sounds and pictures. The opening sequence of *The Skeleton Dance* (1929), the first of Walt Disney's *Silly Symphonies,* combines the eerie atmosphere of goblins at night, supported by owls hooting, bats flying, and wind whistling through percussion and a tense high note on a violin. Once the scene is set and the right atmosphere created, skeletons emerge from opened tombs and their jangling dances are underscored by appropriate rhythmic percussion.

Hollywood in the 1930s

The onset of the Great Depression hardly touched film prosperity. People needed entertainment and many could find the small change that was the price of admission to movie houses. However, the movies were hit by a temporary recession in 1933. The studios responded by rigorous economics and by eliciting some government assistance.

The studios now found it necessary to offer audiences two films for the price of one and double features became standard fare, as did novelty games such as Bingo and Screeno played for domestic prizes between screenings. Hollywood survived recessions in 1933 and 1938 and, thereafter, sailed through World War II on a flood of prosperity to its most profitable year ever in 1946.

While the studio system was successful in turning out films like an industrial factory turns out machines, it was much less successful in producing art of lasting value. Gerald Mast estimates that, of 7,500 feature films made in the heyday of the studio years of 1930–1945, perhaps only about 200 films made any lasting impression and survive as vital examples of the century's most potent performing art.

There were numerous parallels between the Elizabethan and Jacobean theater of 1576 to 1642, the primo ottocento of Italian opera of 1800–1851, and the great studio years of Hollywood. Each produced an art form—play, opera, feature film—that appealed to a wide audience. Each was performed by a repertory of artists supported by a company of writers, managers, costumiers, and designers. Each drew on artists who could adapt their technique and stage type to similar roles—whether prima donna, romantic tenor, tragic hero, comedian, or villain. Shakespeare had Richard Burbage and Will Kemp, Verdi had Gaetano Fraschini and Felice Varesi, and MGM had Clark Gable and Greta Garbo. Each form was steeped in its own conventions and clichés that a major creative genius could transform by his personal art. Moreover, much of the original material on which plays, operas, and films were based came from popular literature of the time. The Elizabethans enjoyed romances and histories by Holinshed and Plutarch; the Italians wanted the British romantics such as Byron and Scott and stories set in Tudor England; and film audiences wanted such literary masterpieces as *La Dame aux Camélias* and *Les Misérables* turned into films. It was a case of one art form helping perpetuate the myths and icons of another by lending them a new depth and perspective.

The studio system was responsible for choice of material and the style in which the finished film was made. Studio bosses assumed that a formula that was proven would work well again. This estimation of public taste and reliance on an established form accounts for the series of film cycles beginning with gangster movies in the early 1930s.

In 1932 gangster movies were the most popular of all film genres. Their vogue was greater than that of romances and musicals and far greater than that of westerns. As Dorothy Manners in *Motion Picture Classic* of June 1931 observed, "Gangsters . . . gun-

men . . . gamblers . . . hoodlums . . . heist guys . . . hold-ups
. . . 'baby-faced killers' . . . bandits . . . bullets . . . murders . . .
morgues . . . molls. Hollywood is going at the pace that 'kills' at
the box office! Of all the theme picture epidemics none has equaled
the intense rush of gangsters to the box office." It was Paramount
that first developed the genre and other studios—MGM, Fox, De
Mille Pictures, Columbia, and Universal—followed its example.
One studio, Warner Brothers, made the genre its specialty.

Gangster thrillers held a double fascination for the public. They
combined the realism of a social documentary with the emotional
power of a dream. They played on fears that American society
during prohibition and the economy during the depression were
unstable and foundering. Gilbert Seldes in *The Years of the Locust
—America 1929–1932* (1932) said the gangster film was particularly effective at representing aspirations and desires in the depression: "Rude manners, brutality, and action—contempt of authority, the theme of the bowl of cherries and the raspberry; and the
desire for work." Gangster protagonists projected an image of
energy and self-assurance that lent encouragement to the public.

Gangsters in early films were city cousins of western outlaws
like Billy the Kid and Jesse James who had supposedly robbed the
rich to help the poor. They were presented as good-natured hoodlums conspiring to overthrow corrupt officers. Outlaws stole
from banks and railroad companies rather than people, who were
the prey of politicians and public officials. Whereas the western
outlaw roamed the countryside—a horizontal world—and the
eastern gangster hustled in the cities—a vertical world—both
inhabited canyons. The outlaw lived in the natural environment
of mountains, cliffs, crevices; the gangster dwelt in the man-made
environment of skyscrapers, office blocks, and bonded warehouses. Vertical planes suggested impossible odds, a corrupt civilization curbing freedom, and complemented the protagonist's
rise and fall. Bootlegging in the movies made gangsters popular
in the cinema and in real life. Films such as *The Bootlegger's
Daughter* (1922), *Contraband* (1925), *Poison* (1924), *Four Walls* (1928),
and *Broadway* (1929) supplied audiences with the cheap thrill of
seeing services rendered and the satisfaction of knowing that though

Little Caesar (Edward G. Robinson) arrives at the Big Boy's place, an art deco mansion replete with Flemish tapestries, rococo furniture, crystal chandelier, and inlaid marble floor. Hollywood adopted a double standard in such gangster movies as *Little Caesar* (1930), ensuring that, while the screenplay emphasized that crime does not pay, it provided viewers with vicarious pleasure as they gaped at criminal opulence. (Museum of Modern Art Film Stills Archive).

the law was being flouted rough justice would be meted out to the criminals.

Underworld (1927), written by Ben Hecht for Paramount, was erroneously hailed as the first gangster film, because it was certainly the most successful example of the genre to that time critically and commercially. The director, Josef von Sternberg, skillfully evoked the atmosphere of a city at night. The gangsters' world was dark, with flashes of light from car headlights, matches, mirrors, and chandeliers. Gangster thrillers remained lugubrious, their very darkness implying a relationship between environment and crime.

Little Caesar (1930) and *Public Enemy* (1931) offered a summation of what had been achieved in the genre hitherto. However, their plots lack coordination between the different elements, and the characterization is crude. The huge public success of the films owed much to the atmosphere of the time they were released. Al Capone was at the height of his notoriety. Some knowledge of his career is essential for understanding the twists and turns of the plots. Contemporary audiences were familiar with the allusions and expected to interpret the inconsistencies of the stories accordingly. *Little Caesar* (1930), directed by Mervyn LeRoy from a novel by W. R. Burnett, is not about a big shot but a small time crook, Caesar Enrico Bandello (Edward G. Robinson), who begins by robbing a gas station and then goes East with his partner, Joe (Douglas Fairbanks, Jr.). *Public Enemy,* directed by William A. Wellman and based on a story *Beer and Blood* by John Bright, begins with a series of episodes to show how a boy brought up in the slums turns to crime as a means of escape. Tom Powers (James Cagney) and Matt Doyle (Edward Woods) graduate from petty crimes to warehouse robberies. On the run for killing a police officer, they become, first, truck drivers for a bootlegger (Robert Emmet O'Connor) and, then, partners with Nails Nathan (Leslie Fenton) in an operation to divert liquor from a bonded warehouse. When they become involved in gang war over disputed territory, Matt is killed. Tom attempts to wreak revenge on the rivals but is badly wounded outside their headquarters. His rivals manage to kidnap him from the hospital where he is recovering and then they deposit his corpse on the doorstep of his mothers' house.

According to John Spivak in *America Faces the Barricades* (1935), such characters as Rico in *Little Caesar,* Tom Powers in *Public Enemy,* and others were made to die as scapegoats for the depression. A capitalist system that could not bring about its recovery for over a decade required an excuse for its own shortcomings. Nevertheless, despite censorship codes and moral tags, gangster movies consistently projected their protagonists as energetic and egalitarian heroes. As Eugene Rosow finds in *Born to Lose* (1978),

"When the national mood was characterized by apathy, defeat, disorientation, and insecurity, movie gangsters were active; they knew what they wanted and they knew how to get it; they were self-reliant and unafraid in pursuit of their goals; and they projected a quality of forthrightness that stood in contrast to the hypocrisies of the Hoover regime and the media's coverage of the Depression."

The tradition of the American gangster film was founded on a paradox. The genre celebrates freedom of the individual in a nostalgic evocation of the underworld although the contemporary inception of a national criminal syndicate destroyed that freedom. The irony is that the myth was perpetrated by movie moguls who, within another American tradition, business monopoly, contributed to the growth of large corporations. Therefore, it is not surprising that, although gangster films have offered the public escape of a sort, they have never carried a universal message of freedom triumphing over tyranny with any conviction. An economic system that has enormous problems is not likely to seek their resolution by political means lest the process of solving them prove injurious to interested parties. Nor is it likely to encourage others to seek such a solution. Instead, studios offered audiences subtle propaganda in the guise of escapism. While real citizens were hard up in the depression, film characters were well-heeled. The elegance of studio sets and costumes, the inevitable poetic justice of plot answered a genuine need. They encouraged audiences to try and attain in their lives the affluence they saw on screen. If that failed, people could still share in the luxury of their favorite stars—but at a distance and only once or twice a week. When the Breen code insisted on a higher tone, Hollywood recast its mobsters as policemen and simply moved them across the street to the right side of the law. Thus conscience made heroes of James Cagney and Edward G. Robinson.

Another early genre was the journalist movies in which a tough-talking newspaper man covered the daring escapades of gangsters and police in such films as *Big News, The Front Page,* and *The Power of the Press.* The pivotal author was former pressman Ben Hecht of Chicago whose assertive dialogue conveyed the tough world of prisons, dives, and precincts as few others have done.

Hollywood had a commercially profitable but curious and uneasy relationship with the great American novelists of the period. It used Ernest Hemingway's stories, notably *A Farewell to Arms* (1932). It also used *To Have and Have Not* (1944), with the title, Humphrey Bogart and Lauren Bacall, but not much of the plot and, in two later versions, different titles. It was said Hemingway wrote *For Whom the Bell Tolls* specifically with Hollywood in mind and the film (1943) adjusted this account of an incident in the Spanish Civil War to fit the disparate talents of American Gary Cooper, Swedish Ingrid Bergman, and Greek Katina Paxinou. Hollywood also, and at different times, encouraged F. Scott Fitzgerald, William Faulkner, and John Dos Passos to work on genres quite unsuited to their considerable talents. Faulkner, master of southern surfaces, paradoxes, and psychological intensity, collaborated on the original version of Hemingway's *To Have and Have Not* (1944), Chandler's *The Big Sleep* (1946), and a ludicrous historical hokum *Land of the Pharoahs* as a vehicle for British regular Jack Hawkins and continuously aspirant star Joan Collins (1955). Not surprisingly, Faulkner's idea of working at home, rather than in the Hollywood studio office, was to return to his house in Mississippi. Sometimes, the choice of author was more apposite but, once again, studio insistence on industrial production and maintaining a roster of star names resulted in interesting combinations of original and screenplay writers. While Raymond Chandler was allowed to work on his own *The Big Sleep* and *The Lady in the Lake* (both 1946) and other Marlowe stories, he was also employed as a collaborator for James M. Cain's *Double Indemnity* (1944). Ben Hecht (1894–1964), who wrote authentic-sounding dialogue for press and hoodlums, was allowed to write his own screen version of his play *The Front Page* (1931), but moved through such different material as the trifling *Goldwyn Follies* (1938) and the screen version of Emily Brontë's passionate romance, *Wuthering Heights* (1939).

Sound made it possible to make musical films in which complex dance sequences were performed to complex music and rhythm. So potent was the appeal of music in films that most early talkies included song or song and dance routines often set in a nightclub, as in *The Lights of New York* and *The Blue Angel*.

However, very soon musicals became a fully fledged genre in their own right, whether based on Broadway shows or traditional musical comedies with such artists as Maurice Chevalier, Jeanette MacDonald, and Jack Buchanan. This form was succeeded by the backstage genre in which struggling artists triumphed against considerable odds. They included among their leading players such characters as the ingenue chorine suddenly promoted to leading lady who then becomes a star overnight, and a millionaire composer who is hiding his true identity (and wealth) so that he can rise by his creative genius alone. Director and choreographer Busby Berkeley devised a series of elephantine dance sequences with kaleidoscopic and acrobatic formations by countless dancers. Later musical films were dominated by the more intimate solo dancing of Fred Astaire whose preferred form was bourgeois comedies, supported by various comic artists, such as Edward Everett Horton, in well-routined performances and, usually, by his best dancing partner, the somewhat churlish actress, Ginger Rogers. America's leading theater composers—George and Ira Gershwin, Cole Porter, Richard Rodgers, and Jerome Kern—all provided special songs or complete scores for Hollywood's musical films of the 1930s. Other musicals were traditional operettas in Ruritanian costumes with casts led by Jeanette MacDonald and Deanna Durbin.

There were film series based on popular characters such as Chinese detective Charlie Chan and ingenuous youngster Andy Hardy, the role that established Mickey Rooney. Other films drew on a studio's ensemble of leading actors in complementary plots united by place *(Grand Hotel)* or time *(Dinner at Eight)* but without any true stylistic ensemble of playing together.

Film Comedy in the 1930s

Comedy remained a distinctive form and many of Hollywood's best films of the 1930s were comedies.

Chaplin retained his highly individual style because his pictures were so popular and commercially successful that he needed to make only superficial gestures to Hollywood's demands for talking pictures. Moreover, his visual style, based on straightforward, rather than inventive, camera work, which emphasized the subject rather than the way it was shot, was in accord with the typical talking picture and its conventions of even lighting, stationary camera, and straightforward exposition. In *Modern Times* (1936) Charlie is an industrial everyman at the mercy of the automated assembly line and cast adrift as security guard in the consumer paradise of an outsize department store. In *The Great Dictator* (1940), a comedy of mistaken identity and destiny, Chaplin played a forlorn Jewish barber who survives World War I and finds his country, Bacteria, overrun by the dictator Hynkel, and governed by a party ruling under the sign of the double cross. Chaplin daringly capitalized on the coincidental, if superficial, similarity between the appearance of his favorite tramp and the despot Adolf Hitler to play both roles with short-back-and-sides haircut and toothbrush mustache.

Director Ernst Lubitsch also graduated successfully from silent to sound films. His earlier hallmark had been expressive use of visual detail and now he used sound effects to the same ends. His most successful films relied on witty dialogue that exploited studio convention, notably *Design for Living* (1933), and *Ninotchka* (1939). In *Trouble in Paradise* (1932), a triangle about a master thief (Herbert Marshall) caught between his victim (Kay Francis) and his accomplice (Miriam Hopkins), Lubitsch cleverly exposed the difference between the glistening surface of cafe society and the mire of his characters' inner lives. Herbert Marshall and Kay Francis fall in love as they compulsively steal one another's personal items — watches, wallets, and jewelry. Lubitsch drew sparkling dialogue from Simon Raphaelson.

Frank Capra's comedies of manners were set in a United States of Main Streets and country roads with dialogue provided by Robert Riskin. Many were moralities in which a resilient innocent triumphed over social manipulators by winning over a girl who embodied false values. In *It Happened One Night* (1934) reporter Clark Gable encounters society girl Claudette Colbert as she pursues a worthless match. Together they discover the pleasures and penalties of long-distance travel. The tone of Capra's deliberately populist material was lightened by deft underplaying and characterization. In *Mr. Deeds Comes to Town* (1936) rural nouveau riche

Gary Cooper discovers that he must use his fortune to help the poor, rather than spend it selfishly on snob reporter Jean Arthur. In *Mr. Smith Goes to Washington* (1939) the problem is political, rather than financial, manipulation. In *You Can't Take It With You* (1938) an eccentric family are set against a world of elegance and sophistication.

The Marx Brothers represented the quintessence of American comic films—exaggerated physical types directed to draw the maximum effect from their personalities and spiced by acidulous verbal wit. The Marx Brothers' first film was a version of their successful stage show, *Cocoanuts* (1929). They set out to look and act outrageously—Groucho with heavy mustache, Chico with bulbous eyes, Harpo with frizzy hair and inane smiles. Their films used a conventional romantic story as excuse for gross behaviorism by the brothers. *Duck Soup* (1933), *A Night at the Opera* (1936), and *At the Circus* (1939) relied on audience amusement at a stage tradition being ridiculed by well-routined anarchy performed with split second timing. In *Go West* (1940) the trio stripped an entire train of its wood in order to fuel the locomotive.

Actress and screenwriter Mae West's dramatic persona was a parody of the predatory blonde, first as a mature woman who could still attract young men, later as a caricature of woman as part siren, part landscape, and part gorgon. In *Night After Night* (1932) her immortal answer to the remark of the hatcheck girl who admires her jewelry, "Goodness, what beautiful diamonds," was, "Goodness had nothing to do with it, dearie." Her throwaway remark, accompanied by a shrug and wiggle, defined her persona beyond a brief film career. Her success was certainly resented by the nominal star, George Raft, who recalled that Mae West "stole everything but the cameras." Mae West subsequently disclosed that she and George Raft had made love in a broom cupboard: "It was love on the run with half the buttons undone." It was astonishing, given her languid delivery, that she became a legend for a series of celebrated and salacious wisecracks, each delivered from the side of the mouth. Of her own plot for *I'm No Angel* (1933) she said, "It's all about a girl who lost her reputation but never missed it." Of her character, Tira, she remarked, "She's the kind of girl who climbed the ladder of success wrong by wrong." The butt of her satire was the golddigger, the predatory vamp whose hard character was delineated elsewhere by Joan Blondell and Jean Harlow. However, her stories conformed to prevailing values, pitting the shady lady against hypocritical forces of law and order and allowing her to elude punishment because her impulses were sympathetic. She was much restricted by the Breen office. In *Belle of the Nineties* (1934), when she sang "My Old Flame," she had to make clear why the fire was a smouldering ember by suggestive use of eyes and voice. The tepid lyrics by themselves do not even imply there was a flicker in the first place. Having dismissed a rival with a shove she ordered her maid (in a parody of "Give me a break"), "Beulah, peel me a grape."

Mae West's onetime partner in *My Little Chickadee* (1940), W. C. Fields, was a bibulous comedian with a sardonic wit to match his comic shape and gravelly voice. He had also moved from vaudeville to silent films. It was clear from this earlier period in silent comedies that Fields owed his success primarily to adept use of his ridiculous appearance of outsize tummy, luminous nose, and ludicrous historical costumes. Thus the funniness of Fields was essentially funny at its best in certain purely visual sequences, such as his awkward attempts at croquet in *Poppy* (1936) and his confusion with bent pool cues in *Six of a Kind* (1934). W. C. Fields cultivated a vulgar character of external gentility that barely concealed his boorish interior and inability to love. Yet his targets struck a responsive chord in film audiences who wanted to see mincing children and the sacred institution of marriage ridiculed by at least one comic master.

These films were based on dialogue, much of it effective screen dialogue convincingly caught by microphones. It was, indeed, dialogue, that dominated the way the films were made. Thus images were less important than speech. The dominance of speech over symbol determined that films would be shot in a straightforward manner that precluded imaginative or daring camera shots by way of odd angles, exaggerated close-ups, and special moving effects. Even lighting remained uniformly bright so as not to divert any attention from the artists' words to the atmosphere. Nevertheless, film lighting was more than purely functional and used to enhance the stars' appearances, highlighting their best features. Thus, in the 1930s, films followed the line established by Thomas Ince, concentrating on telling an interesting story clearly and concisely. Psychology and character motivation were shown by ritual—not by probing beneath the surface.

Of new developments increasing use of color was the most important. In the early cinema directors had used color tints for specific sequences. Some of the films of George Méliès were tinted by hand, frame by frame. Because sixteen pictures were projected every second, a film lasting only ten minutes would require 10,000 frames each painted separately. Some of the films of D. W. Griffith and Abel Gance were printed with color casts —blue for night scenes, red for passionate scenes, and yellow and green for others. Each of these directors was looking for a visual complement to the atmospheric music that accompanied the film in the cinema. Of course, the effect was not the same as color photography. In 1908 Charles Urban developed a color photographic process, Kinemacolor. It was opposed by the film trust and never used in the movies. However, the Technicolor Corporation, founded in 1917, was supported by the film industry. Technicolor perfected its process in 1933, using three strips of emulsion sensitive to blue, to red, and to yellow.

Yet Hollywood postponed its conversion to color. Black and white film was more responsive to different lights and afforded more subtlety of shade. It was easier to use and quicker to process. Besides, the financial priority was to complete the conversion to sound. Thus Hollywood reserved color for special effects, such as a Disney cartoon like *Snow White and the Seven Dwarfs* (1937) or a spectacle, such as Victor Fleming's *Gone with the Wind* (1939). Later, in World War II, color films were an occasional luxury. Priority was given to black and white films because they were easier and less costly to produce.

Walt Disney was best able to profit from color as could few others. While studios were wrestling with the vexed problems of needing color to make pictures more realistic, while needing to tone down the garish hues of color stock, Disney exploited vivid colors that could lend additional force, variety, and poignancy to

In his first full-length animated cartoon, *Snow White and the Seven Dwarfs* (1937), Walt Disney mixed elements from American and European art. The wicked queen was a glacial American society woman who transforms herself into a comical old hag from Central Europe; Snow White was a younger, prettier version of American adventuress Wallis Simpson, while her dwarfs looked European but sounded like Californian miners in the Gold Rush. (Walt Disney Productions; Museum of Modern Art Film Stills Archive).

his animated features. Moreover, subject, music, and color could all be reconciled as each shifted. Disney was free to manipulate color as the directors of feature films were not and he used color for his animals, Mickey Mouse and Donald Duck, and, as mentioned, in his first full-length film, *Snow White and the Seven Dwarfs* (1937).

Most fascinating was the mix of American and European styles of art. This is most clearly seen in the two personae of the wicked queen. At first, she is a cold glacial figure, clearly defined by the sort of ruthless American career woman often played by Joan Crawford—elegant, predatory, and modern. Later, when the queen takes a potion to transform herself into an old crone who will give Snow White the near-fatal apple, the artists' inspiration is clearly any old witch of European provenance who might find herself in Hansel and Gretel—gnarled, hunchbacked, and wart-encrusted. Snow White herself was like an improved version of Wallis Simpson, the American divorcée for whom King Edward VIII of Britain abdicated his throne. The dwarfs were European in a traditional visual sense but their vocal characterization and their immortal mining song, "Heigh ho!" were clearly all-American.

Disney's most grandiose feature film was *Fantasia* (1941), a sequence of cartoon shorts inspired by classical music played by the Philadelphia Orchestra conducted by Leopold Stokowski. Running for well over four hours, *Fantasia* set new standards for movies in color and sound and its imaginative concept has never been surpassed. While some of the choice and use of material was predictable—Beethoven's Pastoral Symphony set in a classical world of saccharine gods and centaurs, gamboling in an Arcadian landscape, and the insertion of Mickey Mouse as the Sorcerer's Apprentice—much was not. Disney and Stokowski turned a Bach prelude into a kaleidoscopic tone poem of rich orchestral sonorities and abstract designs; Stravinsky's then controversial ballet, *The Rite of Spring,* was turned into a history of evolution; the ballet, the *Dance of the Hours,* from Ponchielli's opera, *La Gioconda,* was turned into a parody of opera and ballet with outsize hippos performing dainty ballet steps in minuscule tutus until pursued for dear life by predatory alligators. Even the *Sorcerer's*

Apprentice allowed for a terrifying cascade of automated broom-sticks carrying so much water from the well that they threaten Mickey Mouse with drowning—a frightening symbol of mass production. Most successful was program music that deliberately calls for a picture—the *Nutcracker Suite* from Tchaikovsky's ballet and Mussorgsky's *Night on a Bare Mountain*—because here the material lent itself most easily to the sort of pictures at which Disney excelled—faeries, demons, and goblins cavorting amidst autumn leaves, mist, and fireworks. Most telling of all was the Chinese dance performed by waddling mushrooms. Yet here, too, the limitations of Disney's art were also disclosed, confining him to the same formula of faeries, goblins, and demons forever. However, Disney soon returned to conventional human repro-duction and emphasis on American regional values in his other feature films. *Bambi* (1942), about the growing pains of a deer, was free from the inhibitions of human characters and succeeded perfectly.

Face Value

The stars of the 1930s shone as brightly as those of the 1920s. There were even more of them and their screen personae were tailored and manicured to conform to enduring archetypes. Clark Gable was generally considered the decade's most handsome and desirable leading man, with large and widely spaced eyes, razor sharp moustache, and roguish charm, whether the parts called for a rough diamond or a sly wit. Swedish immigrant Greta Garbo was assigned a range of parts drawn from history and literary classics, notably Camille, Queen Christina of Sweden, and Anna Karenina. Her forte was to convey deep emotions by adroit use of a husky voice still bearing traces of a Scandinavian accent, a natural commanding presence, and deep commitment. Com-menting on her ability to capture psychological undercurrents, English critic Kenneth Tynan once remarked that what men saw in other women drunk, they saw in Garbo sober. English immi-grant and former Korda player Charles Laughton was used in a series of exaggerated, histrionic, not to say grotesque, parts, rang-ing from Captain Bligh in *Mutiny on the Bounty* to Quasimodo in

The Hunchback of Notre Dame. Exaggerated mannerisms were also a hallmark of Bette Davis, a miniature actress who tackled melodramas with the relish of an octopus caressing a shellfish. If the part did not call for period dress with flounces and frills, she provided them in her acting.

The most debonair leading man was Welsh immigrant and former acrobat Cary Grant, whose career in sophisticated roles requiring throwaway delivery of lines and a touch of menace beneath the offhand manner extended well over thirty years. The glacially arresting Joan Crawford was the archetypal career woman of ruthless determination willing to use or suppress her feminine charms as she continuously rose from rags to riches. Her character was best defined in the role of predatory tigress in *The Women.* Humphrey Bogart alternated roles on wrong and right sides of the law in much the same manner as James Cagney and Edward G. Robinson but with a keener wit, expressing bitter resentment of upper-crust indolence. In *Casablanca* he reminded former girlfriend Ingrid Bergman of their last meeting: "The Germans wore grey; you wore blue."

Hollywood performed truly special services to enhance the appearance of its leading players. Style and quality of makeup accentuated good features, stylish costumes redeemed awkward physical shapes, and becoming hairstyles, whether by hair curling, wigs, or toupees, capped what was intended to be a lustrous appearance. The homely appearance of Irving Thalberg's wife, Norma Shearer, was transformed by all means available. In the process of beautifying its players, Hollywood transformed an entire society's ideas of what was beautiful in the face. Close-ups were the essential means of capturing emotion and perfectly symmetrical or arresting features were essential for leading artists. Since sound films were based on dialogue, mouth and teeth were far more important on film than in life. Teeth had to be even, emphasized and, sometimes, brought forward cosmetically. Concentration on the mouth and lips in film generally not only accentuated these features in the players but in their audiences' expectations of what was desirable.

Hollywood makeup might be heavy but it could not be successful—unlike stage makeup—if it were crude. Thus the Hollywood studios' concentration on subtlety of eyeliners, eyelashes, accentuated cheekbones, and tight jaws was of considerable significance for the cosmetic industry as a whole, precisely because Hollywood raised people's expectations about their own appearance. Put crudely, this might mean that girls living on modest incomes might want to look like their favorite actresses. More profoundly, people appreciated the benefits of subtle makeup for themselves so that they could present themselves to best advantage. This was a revolution of sorts. Some of these changes, such as large and prominent teeth and slightly hollow cheeks, would have been thought unattractive and almost ugly in certain earlier societies. Initially, they did not amount to universal ideals of beauty but they were so persuasively and emphatically presented in film after film that they established basic criteria for beauty in a whole society.

With the advent of synthetic fabrics and mass-produced tailoring, the whole concept of fashion and style in dress had already changed profoundly. The lines of clothes became longer and more svelte. Moreover, slimness rather than curvature was promoted in advertising photographs. Because drawings and photographs are essentially two-dimensional, what was important was not so much that clothes looked well on the human figure in the round but on line drawings and photographs in print. Thus it was less important for a costume to look well on a person than for it to look elegant in print. Horizontal and vertical lines were far more important than depth. Not only the drawings but also the models who first displayed the clothes had to look well in photos and needed to be as slim and elongated, and, by implication, as two-dimensional as possible in order to show the two-dimensional designs off to greatest effect. Hollywood carried this cult further. People captured on film and, later, television, tended to look slightly heavier than in real life. Hence, it was most important for leading and romantic players to be slightly underweight if they were to look their best on film and have flesh impact—unless, of course, there was a deliberate point to their being fat (like Ollie Hardy and W. C. Fields) or with an odd shape that could be used in character parts (like Charles Laughton or Boris Karloff).

The emphasis on a certain artificial idea of what was handsome or beautiful enhanced the reputation of its players and ensured its image of physical perfection but often limited the dramatic quality of its principal product, the films. This can be seen in the partnership of German immigrants Josef von Sternberg and Marlene Dietrich. Josef von Sternberg directed several films with Marlene Dietrich rich in exotic atmospheres and in shimmering chiaroscuro of light and shade that make them seem significant in comparison to the anodyne lighting of other films. However, they are essentially empty, suffering from the same vapid plots and characterization as most other Hollywood films.

His second sound film, *The Blue Angel* (1930), was the most celebrated and probably the best Sternberg-Dietrich collaboration. It is a modern version of the Greek legend of Circe, a temptress who bewitches men who should know better and thus turns them into swine. It is also a tragedy of the downfall of the authoritarian but sterile schoolteacher, Professor Unrat, played by Emil Jannings, who is her principal victim. He follows her recklessly into a disastrous marriage and an ignominious end as night club cleaner and buffoon. His classroom is a cage but when he flies the coop, Lola-Lola uses him and casts him away like the cuckold she has made of him. Both Unrat's callous pupils and his indifferent night club coworkers fail to appreciate his human qualities. The students, in particular, are shown as incipient Nazis.

Von Sternberg's films after *The Blue Angel* became ever more elaborate and sumptuous, reaching an apogee in *The Scarlet Empress* (1934) with Dietrich as Catherine the Great and Harpo Marx as her discarded husband, Peter III. However, despite such powerful evocations of period atmosphere as the marriage ceremony between the timid ingenue princess from Germany and the half-crazed tsarevitch, von Sternberg's film rarely peers beneath the surface. This was a perennial problem in the whole series of baroque Sternberg-Dietrich collaborations, such as *Morocco* (1930), *Shanghai Express* (1932), and *The Devil Is a Woman* (1934). Too much was surrendered in the attempt to transform Marlene Dietrich into a timeless beauty of dazzlingly luminous appearance. Nothing she did dramatically had real thrust or emphasis. Her face was plasticized by cosmetic artists and lighting men and remained inexpressive rather than enigmatic or mysterious.

Directors in the 1930s

Despite the emphasis on glamor and surface, certain directors did emerge with strong personal visions during the 1930s.

John Ford had the same sentimental values as D. W. Griffith and he celebrated ordinary people and their homegrown institutions in films that were accessible as well as posing major symbols. In telling his stories Ford emphasized canyons, plains, and skies. However he minimised symbol and metaphor in order to propel exciting stories forward. The first film in which he revealed his strength was *The Informer,* about a traitor to the IRA during "the troubles" who pays physically and psychologically for his error. Not only did Ford have the considerable advantage of a strong screenplay by Dudley Nichols but also telling photography by Joseph Angst. Ford maximized the photography in a series of dissolves and blurred focuses to convey the tortured mental state of his antihero. Ford chose as his symbol of relentless pursuit by the betrayed revolutionaries a blind man, akin to Blind Pew in *Treasure Island,* whose black form, tapping its way along with a cane, follows Gypo, the traitor, wherever he goes. Blind justice as an avenging angel was an obvious enough symbol but it succeeded far more than von Sternberg's ornate symbols as a representation of internal and external guilt because it could also be taken literally.

Ford's most famous film, *Stagecoach* (1939), was successful enough to revive the fading fortunes of the western. This was somewhat ironic because the film was essentially a conventional interior drama of conversation and surfaces, capped by a crude chase between cowboys and Indians for the finale. The stagecoach was intended as a symbol of settled society on the move, a machine built to win the untamed west, although a railroad train would have been a more appropriate symbol. Its occupants were intended as a microcosm of society, with such archetypes as an outlaw and shady dance hall girl with hearts of gold, a young matron in need of being awoken to others' values, a drunken doctor who reforms, and a hypocritical banker who has stolen from his own bank but inveighs continuously against the errors

Twenty-six year old newcomer Orson Welles (upper left) dominated *Citizen Kane* (1941), his first film. Widely praised for skillful and evocative use of montage, dissolve, and sound, the film was a complex screen biography of a press tycoon, clearly based on William Randolph Hearst, and a lugubrious indictment of American pursuit of wealth and power at the expense of personal integrity. (RKO; Museum of Modern Art Film Stills Archive).

of his companions. The banker character might have been written and defined by Griffith, as might the prim busybodies who hound doctor and dance hall girl out of town at the start of the movie. Ford's special talents for emphasizing the interior strengths of little people were seen at their best in his film versions of John Steinbeck's novel, *The Grapes of Wrath* (1940). This protest work about the injustices that befall the dispossessed Oakies drew especially strong performances from Henry Fonda and Jane Darwell.

Howard Hawks made more active, and more violent films with an even stronger emphasis on plot than Ford. In this respect he was somewhat like Thomas Ince and also in his concentration on the difference between outer and inner strength. A routine Hawks film would focus on a strong man who discovers his vulnerability under pressure but survives, and a more fragile man who has surprising reserves of resilience to make him join his tougher companion, as happened in *The Criminal Code* (1931). Hawks's legacy was a series of dramatic thrillers in praise of macho men — *Scarface* (1932), *To Have and Have Not* (1944), and *The Big Sleep* (1948). All were shot with conventional studio paraphenalia, except for the westerns that convey the excitement of taming a wilderness.

British immigrant Alfred Hitchcock managed the transition from English to American filmmaking after 1939. His entire career was a tribute to the close relationship between American and British filmmaking after the introduction of sound. Hitchcock's films were apolitical and inevitably took place in the well-heeled world of cafe society, where smooth men wooed outwardly cool women. Gerald Mast suggests that Hitchcock's films took the form of mysteries with psychology or psychological dramas with mystery. The plots usually mixed drama and suspense with macabre comedy and revolved around international conspiracies or disturbed antiheroes. Hitchcock's films had murders committed in such public places as theaters, parks, and trains and they often culminated in improbable chases in famous locations that were dramatic enough in themselves. Hitchcock's special hallmarks were intense suspense, bathos, and irony, supported by deft cutting and sure command of detail, as in *The 39 Steps* (1935), *Rebecca* (1940), *Suspicion* (1941), and *Saboteur* (1942). In *The 39 Steps* a Scottish landlady discovers the film's first corpse and begins to scream while Hitchcock cuts to the whistle of a train moving toward Scotland, thereby superseding, while exaggerating, the natural scream.

Unlike other significant directors with several films that were artistically successful, Orson Welles's reputation rests primarily on three films: *Citizen Kane* (1941), *The Magnificent Ambersons* (1942), and *Chimes at Midnight* (1966), a screen adaptation of Shakespeare's history plays with Falstaff. Welles had been sought by RKO of Hollywood because of his successes in the theater with the Mercury Theater group. He chose for his first, and most famous project, *Citizen Kane,* a fictional biography suggested by the career of William Randolph Hearst. Welles was only twenty-six yet he acted in, directed, wrote, edited, and designed a film that was controversial on three levels—as a debunking biography; for its stylistic innovations and complexity; and as a sociological exposure of the hollowness of power politics. Welles devised and cunningly played with the most innovative camera work, managing to shoot close-up and distant scenes together and keep each in focus, with many scenes lit from behind, and with parodies of such newsreels as *The March of Time* to comment ironically on the passing of a celebrated man. The use of shadows and depth in *Citizen Kane* was partly the result of the use of new incandescent studio lighting (in contrast with the old carbon-arc lamps) and the use of high-speed panchromatic film that permitted a deeper field of vision. Welles's proven experience in radio was also much in evidence with a whole variety of sound effects.

The plot is a maze, leading to discovery of the significance of Charles Foster Kane, the great newspaper man's, last word, "Rosebud." It begins with the exterior of the mansion and moves step by step closer to the heart of the fallen man. Like a classical drama in five acts, the story begins with an exposition (the superficial newsreel). It is followed by a second act of development (the banker's version of Charles Foster Kane's youth). The third act is incident and crisis (the associate's account of Kane's business ventures and unfulfilled first marriage). The fourth act is the unraveling (the best-friend-turned-enemy's account of Kane's abandonment of principles and his failure to win political office, followed by his living entombment in a fantastic castle, Xanadu). The final act of catastrophe (the breaking up of Xanadu by workmen after Kane's death) ends with the destruction of his property, including the burning of a childhood sleigh, the "Rosebud." "Rosebud" represents all the life that has been drained away from the old tyrant, coming from innocence rather than maturity. As Robert Frost observed, "Rosebud" was the road not taken.

Welles's central probing question was why Charles Foster Kane's career began with such promise and ended in ignominy. Film historian Gerald Mast believes that the implied answer is a con-

Two stars who could not see into the future. *Dark Victory* (1940), directed by Edmund Goulding, had pouting socialite Bette Davis going resolutely blind to the sound of music and set a trend toward unhappy endings. Any irony in the title could not possibly have been foreseen by the star and her supporting player, young Ronald Reagan. (Museum of Modern Art Film Stills Archive).

demnation of certain American values—that love is a casualty in the relentless pursuit of wealth and power. Moreover, the film suggests that wealth and power are no compensation for a life without love. Kane believes in bulk buying, whether the commodity is newspapers, furnishings, or political votes. The public resists his hollow demonstrations of love and he fails to win high office. As an impresario he can train his second wife to become an opera singer but he cannot breathe talent into her poor voice and her career fails. Thus he confines the two of them in a loveless marriage amid a fantastic mausoleum of dead objects.

The parallels between the real tycoon William Randolph Hearst and Welles's creation, Charles Foster Kane; between Hearst's mistress and protégée and Kane's second wife; and between Hearst's

Californian mansion, San Simeon, and Kane's outlandish castle, Xanadu, in Florida, were not lost on any informed person. Not only did the Hollywood moguls find the satire upon Hearst too close for comfort as well as too explosive politically, but they were also disturbed by the film's failure at the box office. It was not what people wanted to see—a sombre melodrama that required audience concentration and openly criticized American goals, instead of a conventional, glossy story.

Whatever the film's merits as sociological comment, the whole is not equal to the sum of its parts. The nub of the story, the significance of "Rosebud," is dramatically uninteresting, not to say abstruse. Moreover, the characters are not fully developed because they are secondary to directorial inventiveness, including the breaking up of the screenplay into five separate synopses. *Citizen Kane* provided other directors with insights as to what could be achieved by montages, complex composition, and shots to the ceiling, but it reminded them not to neglect an audience's needs. While having no doubts about Welles's versatility, RKO was concerned about his failure to draw the crowds and thus began to restrict his control of his own work.

Welles's second film, *The Magnificent Ambersons* (1942), also explored the harmful effect that an egomaniac can wreak on family and friends and, once again, Welles employed some striking compositions in shadow and depth and effective montage sequences to show time passing and fortunes changing. Despite stylish acting, a conventional and somewhat implausible ending in which the callow young scion (Tim Holt) is transformed, and formulaic editing imposed on the film by the studio, the finished film was also a commercial failure. Welles now found Hollywood's gates closed to him, although he could prise them open briefly from time to time.

By the late 1930s it was clear to most informed members of the film community that Hollywood could not survive in the same form much longer. The very success of the great studio system was to be the cause of its downfall. The elephantine system could be hugely successful for a short time until initially undiscriminating audiences became satiated with a diet of similar products. Once this had happened, the studios were too immured in their

Thank Your Lucky Stars (1943) was typical of Hollywood's buoyant musical films during World War II in which all-star tuneful extravaganzas ended in a resounding finale. Here tinsel stars and planets glisten amid dry ice and a curtain call line up of Alexis Smith (center back) and (at front) Dennis Morgan, Joan Leslie, Eddie Cantor, and Dinah Shore. (Museum of Modern Art Film Stills Archive).

own industrial system to be able to respond quickly and decisively enough to the postwar challenges of television, the drift to the suburbs, and, with it, the increasing range of leisure pursuits on offer. In the meantime, the problem was postponed by the boom years of World War II in which the advent of television was itself postponed and audiences at home and abroad were so eager for entertainment that nearly all films, whether good, bad, or indifferent, did well at the box office.

Meanwhile, in 1938 the Department of Justice instituted an antitrust investigation into such restrictive practices in the film industry as block-booking, price-fixing, and pooling agreements between the theaters. Most notorious of all Hollywood's supposed abuses was the convention of a company producing and distributing its movies and also owning the cinemas where they were shown. This would reach a climax in 1948 when all the major companies agreed to give up the so-called restrictive practices. This allowed the "Little Three" studios (Universal, Columbia, and United Artists) to retire from the case because they owned few theaters. By 1952 all of the "Big Five" (Loew's, MGM, Paramount, Warner Brothers, and Twentieth Century Fox) had agreed to separate production and distribution from exhibition.

11

REQUIEM, BUT NO PEACE
The Lost Generation
and the Arts

"**Y**OU ARE all a lost generation," is the first of the two epigraphs to Ernest Hemingway's novel, *Fiesta,* or *The Sun Also Rises* (1926). The remark is accredited to Gertrude Stein and this pithy observation has remained as the unofficial title for the dominant literary generation of the 1920s, although Hemingway subsequently regretted using the phrase and Gertrude Stein denied ever having uttered it.

The writers of the lost generation were, strictly speaking, expatriates such as Hemingway himself, F. Scott Fitzgerald, Sherwood Anderson, and John Dos Passos, who all spent at least months, if not years, in Paris, but membership can be extended to include those writers who stayed at home and resisted the opportunity for exile with a comfortable bohemian life-style that Paris offered Americans owing to the strength of the dollar. However, in many ways, even those who stayed at home, such as Sinclair Lewis, Ring Lardner, and Eugene O'Neill, were in exile, internal exile. Writers were alienated by the culture of commerce that permeated the superficial, tawdry affluence of America in the 1920s.

The epithet "lost generation" has survived because it evokes the themes of alienation, disillusionment, and cynicism with tradition, religion, and even literature itself that dominated the literature of the 1920s. Yet in many ways these negative attitudes also helped consolidate the beginnings of modernism in America's written culture. The second epigraph to *The Sun Also Rises,* taken from Ecclesiastes, provides the novel with its title and is a poignant expression of Ernest Hemingway's outward pessimism and nihilism: "One generation passeth away, and another generation cometh; but the earth abideth for ever. . . . The sun also riseth, and the sun goeth down, and hasteth to the place where he arose."

Why was the lost generation so cynical, especially toward authority? They knew from their experience in World War I that governments were hardly likely to describe the harsh realities of modern warfare in concrete terms. Instead, official language described the war in terms of a chivalrous crusade, repeating such catchwords as "honor," "sacrifice," "country," such phrases as a "war to end all wars" and a "war to make the world safe for democracy," implying that the hosts of righteousness were doing battle for God against Evil. It was one thing to take up arms to save Anglo-Saxon civilization; it was quite another to endure the boredom and terror of trench warfare. World War I was, as Ernest Hemingway wrote, "the most colossal, murderous, mismanaged butchery that has ever taken place on earth. Any writer who said otherwise lied. So the writers either wrote propaganda, shut up, or fought."

The reality of the war could not be conveyed to those who had not taken part. A gap yawned between those (mainly young) men who had fought and their civilian elders who had not, the first true generation gap of the twentieth century. To the young who endured the war, the crimes of their elders must have seemed endless. Not only had they first blundered into war, but they had also lost a generation of young men and then lost the peace. All that remained intact was the machine—the machine of government as well as the divisions and the weapons of industrialized warfare. According to poet Ezra Pound, in one of the most quoted comments on the war, young men had died "For an old bitch gone in the teeth, / For a botched civilization."

One result was the sheer hatred by some artists and writers of all traditional forms of authority. Another was a search for a clean slate. In Europe these impulses led to the Dada movement that ridiculed bourgeois worship of great monuments of culture past and dead artists as divine creators. Thus the French artist Marcel Duchamp, an intermittent resident in the United States, painted a mustache and goatee beard on the Mona Lisa in *L.H.O.O.Q.* (1919), a title with letters chosen to make, in French, a lewd title meaning "She's got a hot ass."

Despite their criticisms of the way the war was waged, some of the novelists admitted to a sensual enjoyment of it. It was an initiation as Malcolm Cowley explained in *Exile's Return:* "The war created in young men a thirst for abstract danger, not suffered for a cause but courted for itself; if later they believed in the cause, it was partly in recognition of the danger it conferred on them." But this sentimental view and accumulative sense of nostalgia that pervades the war novels, "the wish to capture some remembered thing," had no practical value. The ambulance drivers, the young men betrayed by the war, were, truly, "a lost generation." "It was lost because its training had prepared it for another world than existed after the war and the war prepared it for nothing." Yet this generation had a unity and therefore a strength: "They were, in the first place, a generation and probably the first real one in the history of American letters. They came to maturity during a period of violent change, when the influence of time seemed temporarily more important than that of class or locality. Everywhere after the war people were fumbling for a word to express their feeling that youth had a different outlook."

The Impotent Hero

The Sun Also Rises by Ernest Hemingway (1898–1961) is one of the definitive documents of the lost generation and portrays a group of expatriates in Europe in all their futile dissipation and jaded cynicism. The central character of this novel, and its first-person narrator, is far from being a conventional hero. Indeed, Jake Barnes is the archetypal protagonist of the literature and the history of the twenties, the impotent hero. An injury sustained during World War I has emasculated him and condemns him to an unrequited and emotionally destructive love for nyphomaniac Lady Brett Ashley. She tells him at the end of the novel, "We could have had such a damned good time together." Jake responds with characteristic and emblematic cynicism, "Yes. Isn't it pretty to think so?" Men, we gather, pay for life by experience, or chance, or even money. It takes a relatively untarnished young man, the bullfighter, Pedro Romero, to get the better of violence by virtue of his profession. Brett renounces the young bullfighter, having contented herself by teasing Robert Cohn, the Jewish writer, as well as Mike Campbell (her fiancé), and Jake. For Jake himself there is no solace, either physical or mental, in his rejection. He had entered the war as a test of his manhood and it had destroyed his manhood. The novel owes some of its inspiration to T. S. Eliot's poem, *The Waste Land* (1922), which set the pattern and established the mood for the subject of disintegration in twentieth-century literature. Like Eliot's poem, Hemingway's novel reworks the legend of the Holy Grail. In Hemingway's version, Jake Barnes is both questing knight and fisher king with an incurable wound. The mythical cup and lance are life-size.

Jake Barnes must fight for balance. His fascination with bullfights represented a final attempt to get some meaning out of life —a life that has been displaced by the war and turned into a continuous hangover. The bullfight is, both for Jake Barnes and Ernest Hemingway, a palliative to their bewilderment. The matador creates and manipulates his danger; at least in the bullring, chance, the gods, and even governments have no say. "Purity of line" and "grace under pressure" are the responsibility of the individual in this environment. Malcolm Cowley says *Fiesta* captured the mood of a generation: "Young men tried to get as imperturbably drunk as the hero, young women of good families took a succession of lovers in the same heartbroken fashion as the heroine, [and] they all talked like Hemingway characters."

However, Hemingway presented himself as anything but an impotent hero and today his popular reputation as a writer depends to a large extent on the masculine mystique that surrounds his memory. In his youth he developed that passion for active outdoor pursuits, such as hunting and fishing, that was to mark his life and fiction deeply. After working briefly as a journalist in Kansas, eighteen-year-old Hemingway joined a volunteer ambulance unit in France before America entered World War I and then later transferred to the Italian infantry. In 1918 near the Austrian frontier he was severely wounded, an experience after which he "ceased to be hard-boiled," as he expressed it, and, having discovered his own vulnerability, set out to exorcise his own fear of death by confronting it himself or closely observing others in the process of confronting it. Hence, his obsession with violence and terror in boxing, bullfighting, safari, deep-sea fishing, war, and in his writing. Hemingway was a deeply competitive writer in the same way that he lived life as a competition against fear and the emotional void of the modern world. Hemingway's nihilism and his insistence on man's right to choose between stoicism or suicide—this last being the choice Hemingway himself, like his father before him, made in 1961—makes him a truly modern writer and links him to the many moderns who have pondered the human predicament and how to express it. Only illness and numerous physical accidents impeded (but did not end) his astonishing efficiency. It was as if the physical punishment he put his body through was some sort of boxing match with an invisible opponent.

Hemingway's style inspired an entire generation of writers with its directness and apparent simplicity. His first book, *In Our Time* (1925), was a collection of straightforward, attractive, and sometimes brutal short stories written from the expatriate viewpoint and intended to express Hemingway's vision of his home through the largely autobiographical figure of young Nick Adams. His next book *The Torrents of Spring* (1926), was an excursion into the realm of parody and is considered a comic masterpiece. In it Hemingway parodies Sherwood Anderson's novel *Dark Laughter* (1925) with its commonplace portrayal of blacks as the sensual and mystical children of nature who are ingenuously in possession of the secret of life. Hemingway also parodies himself in *The Torrents of Spring,* for the book eventually becomes a satire on the cult of masculinity in American society and American literature. *Fiesta* (or *The Sun Also Rises*) was published in the same year and thus Hemingway was established as a significant and promising young novelist. In 1929 *A Farewell to Arms*—a romantic tragedy of love and war based on the author's own experience during World War I—went a long way toward fulfilling his early promise by virtue of his, by now, characteristic close attention to structure.

Hemingway devised his writing strategies quite early in his career. When he wrote a short story, he would withhold mention of a central fact or problem. When he wrote a novel, he would place it clearly in geography and time. In either form, he devised sentences that carried an emotional impact not by claiming it outright but by giving the reader a crystal-clear understanding of the experience that caused the emotion. Although the last thing we think of Hemingway as being is Victorian, this was exactly the way Queen Victoria herself recorded her experiences in her numerous letters and journals—intense emotion expressed by precise representational facts. The most noted weapon in Hemingway's stylistic armory was his rigorous ability to compress meaning and emotion, giving his work tremendous authority and thrust. His clarity expressed his genius and, at first, made him widely appreciated as the most significant writer in English. In the 1920s his works were fresh, the stories moved quickly, and every page of clear prose seemed to pass a judgment on any excesses in all previous writing. The author's voice was ever present and always hostile to pretense. Thus Hemingway's words always disclosed his dislike of rhetoric and cant.

A Farewell to Arms is also the title of a poem to Queen Elizabeth I by George Peele. Its subject is the ephemeral, fading nature of young and physical pleasure in comparison with more lasting, sterling virtues:

> Beauty, strength, youth, are flowers but fading seen;
> Duty, faith, love, are roots, and ever green.

Hemingway turns this point to ironic and dramatic effect in his novel.

A Farewell to Arms opens with a heavily ironic passage that shows how individual death is absorbed into a bland and uncaring statistical estimate: "At the start of the winter came the permanent rain and with the rain came the cholera. But it was checked and in the end only seven thousand died of it in the army." Although this story of a romance between American medical officer Frederic Henry and English nurse Catherine Barkley, set against the dramatic background of the Italian front in World War I, is generally regarded as a typical antiwar novel, Hemingway's treatment of his characters and their response to the situation are complex and ambivalent. This is not some conventional story of a modern Romeo and Juliet torn apart by authority in World War I. While clearly indicting the entire conduct of the war and its slogans, Hemingway presents Frederic Henry as neither romantic nor idealist but, rather, as a callow youth who starts an affair with Catherine because this will be a more pleasant way of enjoying sex than going down to the officers' brothel. Catherine, having denied sex to her English fiancé who has been killed, is full of the pleasures of the body for Frederic Henry. Their attitude is entirely childish. At one point, when he is in hospital recovering from his injury, they worry that a lack of supply of wounded men in the war to the hospital will mean Catherine must be redeployed and their nocturnal trysts will come to an end. Sometimes he is irritated by her need to be told he loves her, for he does not care for the emotional complications of a lasting relationship that he, at first, finds difficult to sustain.

The only suitable reaction to the absurd chaos of war, as demonstrated in the chapters describing the retreat from Caporetto, is a personal retreat into oneself, making "a separate peace." The rhetoric of war is consciously rejected:

I was always embarrassed by the words sacred, glorious, and sacrifice and the expression in vain. We had heard them, sometimes standing in the rain . . . and I had seen nothing sacred, and the things that were glorious had no glory and the sacrifices were like the stockyards at Chicago if nothing was done with the meat except to bury it. There were many words that you could not stand to hear and finally only the names of places had dignity. . . . Abstract words such as glory, honor, courage, or hallow were obscene beside the concrete names of villages, the numbers of roads, the names of rivers, the numbers of regiments and the dates.

The result is not just an attitude to war but an attitude to life that Frederic Henry sums up in his description of ants falling off a log into a camp fire.

Eventually, hero and heroine feel impelled by their emotions to desert their posts. Yet it does conflict with Frederic Henry's sense of duty. And he suffers a judgment when both Catherine and his newborn son die, for presuming that he still has a world of his own imagination to retreat to. It is not only military arms but also the arms of the woman he loves that Frederic Henry must bid farewell to. The meek may only inherit the earth if the earth is left to them. One cannot exist peaceably in a world of violence. Some critics suggest Hemingway's characters can only fulfill themselves by sublimating their emotional energies in some act that ends in their death. Otherwise, they are faced with an alternative, emasculation. At the close of the book, during a shower of rain, Henry's feelings are more passionately expressed when he feels sentence has been passed on him for running away:

Poor little kid, I wished the hell I'd been choked like that. No I didn't. Still there would not be all this dying to go through. Now Catherine would die. . . . You never had time to learn. They threw you in and told you the rules and the first time they caught you off base they killed you.

In the army the simplest decisions are made for one, and in war, the greatest also. Hemingway moves from society to self in his concentration on the lonely, troubled hero. He is revolted by the phoney values of the world. He seems aware of the essential tragedy of man's existence. All he can do, like Frederic Henry when he walks from the hospital in the rain, is meet it with dignity and stoical endurance.

If we were to select one author as archetype of the lost generation in terms of both literary output and personal history, then F. Scott Fitzgerald would come closest. His first book, *This Side of Paradise,* appeared appropriately in 1920 at the beginning of the decade that has become irrevocably linked with his name and it

Novelist and short story writer F. Scott Fitzgerald, a key player among the lost generation, is highly regarded for the stylistic grace, emotional impact, and penetrating, psychological characterizations in his best works. In the 1930s, when the public mood shifted, it was no longer ready for the perceptions of a writer becoming increasingly alcoholic and tormented by the mental problems of a deranged wife. By the time Carl Van Vechten took this photograph on June 4, 1937, the glamor had worn thin. (Library of Congress).

immediately established his reputation as an acutely poignant and cynical commentator on the vagaries of his time. Critics and readers alike expected great things that were fulfilled neither by the publication of two selections of short stories, *Flappers and Philosophers* (1920) and *Tales of the Jazz Age* (1922), nor by the weak play, *The Vegetable* (1923), and his second novel, *The Beautiful and Damned* (1922). However, 1925 saw the publication of *The Great Gatsby,* a literary masterpiece and a powerful evocation of all that was rotten in the American dream in general and the dream decade of the 1920s in particular. The hero, Jay Gatsby, is a true romantic hero of his time who tragically expends vast amounts of time, energy, emotion, and money in his useless courtship of Daisy Buchanan, unfulfilled wife of the insensitive and adulterous Tom Buchanan. Yet no matter how tragic Gatsby is, his heroism is tainted by the fact that his money—the vital piece of charm he was lacking five years previously when Daisy first spurned him—has been acquired through illegal means, probably bootlegging.

Fitzgerald's heroes are measured less by their attempt to do things well than to do them stylishly. His heroes do not love a woman; they love youth and their inability to accept aging is accompanied by realization of their own romantic inadequacy. His composition of characters was plastic, a synthesis of half a dozen people. Thus, like the reader, he never saw Jay Gatsby clear himself, as he explains in a letter to John Peale Bishop of August 1925, because "he started as one man I knew and then changed into myself."

Jay Gatsby dominates the novel. The mystery of his past is carefully turned into suspense by effective use of gossip at parties. His adolescent romanticism is humorously obvious at the tea party and it is this innocent naivety that renders him vulnerable and eventually leads to his murder. The novel contains a whole series of aligned images—water, sport, couples, riches, class, family, and self-image—that reinforce the undercurrents of doubt and uncertainty. Thus sportswoman and snob Jordan Baker is fashioned in the image of a golf champion, a fact that makes her first attractive, then less so to the narrator, Nick Carraway, who eventually recognizes her sportsmanship as a jaunty but contemptuous charade played especially for a gullible public. Her cheating in a golf tournament is on a par, so to speak, with Tom Buchanan's cheating with Myrtle Wilson and then over the murder of Gatsby. They are both careless people who use their wealth and position to screen themselves from inconvenient reality. Gatsby needs wealth to court Daisy and will do anything to acquire it through Meyer Wolfsheim, the underworld gangster who supposedly fixed the World Series in 1919, prompting Nick to remark, "It never occurred to me that one man could start to play with the faith of fifty million people—with the single-mindedness of a burglar blowing a safe." The explicit link between sport and criminality underlines the irony of a nation childishly investing so much faith in a sporting fix. Fitzgerald can be a violent writer, notably in his account of Tom Buchanan's sportsman's physique as "a body capable of enormous leverage—a cruel body," and with a punch hard enough to break his mistress's nose in a single swipe at a party.

Nick Carraway is passionately attracted to Gatsby's glamor while being deeply aware of the tawdriness that underlies the tinsel. Nick attends Gatsby's parties and feels at ease with the elitist Buchanans. He shows both his general ignorance and inside knowledge about Gatsby but does not discover the whole truth about the millionaire's past as James Gatz until near the close of the novel. The novel emphasizes the power and glamor of money and the way it distorts people's emotions. Carraway makes much of his honesty but at the outset encapsulates the central theme of the novel by stating how his great uncle avoided danger by paying for a substitute to fight in his place in the American Civil War, then built up a profitable hardware business, and used the money to buy a cloak of respectability. It is Gatsby's tragedy that he enters the game too late and is proved maladroit.

It was, perhaps, inevitable that Fitzgerald should never attain such formal artistic perfection again in his career. Inevitable, partly because of the difficulty in repeating such a feat and partly because his personal life degenerated progressively into confusion and tragedy with his wife, Zelda, suffering from severe mental illness, his own declining financial resources, and a lack of confidence in his ability as a writer. Although Fitzgerald did what Gatsby had failed to do, earned enough money to win back the girl he loved but who wanted affluence, malign events turned the fairy story into a horror tale since Zelda slid into madness. She probably conspired against Fitzgerald and he proved himself unable to confront his problems. Thus his two collections of short stories, *All the Sad Young Men* (1926), *Taps at Reveille* (1935), and his novel, *Tender Is the Night* (1934), paled in comparison with *Gatsby* and were received without anything like the same enthusiasm.

Fitzgerald felt at a very low ebb in 1933 when his obsession with style condemned him to a literary treadmill of technical variations on a few themes. "We authors must repeat ourselves," he wrote in the *Saturday Evening Post* of March 4, 1933. "We have two or three great and moving experiences in our lives . . . then we learn our trade, well or less well, and we tell our two or three stories—each time in a new disguise—maybe ten times, maybe a hundred, as long as people will listen."

Tender Is the Night was planned as an epic novel with many diverse targets and, perhaps, its subjects could not be managed easily, certainly not neatly. One of the central themes is the demoralization of a promising American psychiatrist, Dick Diver, tempted and bought by the affluent family of a girl, Nicole, emotionally disturbed after being forced into incest with her father. He marries her and they prove sexually incompatible. Nicole, like a parasite, absorbs her husband's failing energies until she is completely cured and his true professional life is over. His youth spent, his charm evaporated, he has to eke out a broken life as an alcoholic doctor in small-town America. In a sense, the story is about Nicole's cure. In the case of Dick Diver, Fitzgerald's transformation of his character from one based on others to one based on himself was only half-completed. Since he had always emphasized primary personal emotion and had not concerned himself overmuch with narrative and conventional literary techniques, his work went wrong when he could not summon up the requisite personal emotion at will.

English critic Donald Monk explains how the strands of the plot snarl and tangle in both the first version, with its glittering beginning as seen by film starlet Rosemary Hoyt, heroine of *Daddy's Girl,* who provides "Rosemary's Angle" on the Divers at play on the Riviera, and the second, which is a straightforward chronological narrative. Fitzgerald, with his easy stylistic grace, found it difficult to distinguish between erotic love and familial love. However, attracted to the formidable women characters, Nicole and her sister, Baby Warren, and Rosemary and her mother, he found himself brooding on the corrosion of willpower, instead of analyzing it. It is the uncertain definition of a point of view that undermines the novel and the filaments of style are scattered in too many directions. *Tender Is the Night* is awash with images breaking surface but lacking direction. The themes of Nicole's cure and Dick's deterioration are supported by a series of transsexual mammary images, notably Nicole's dependence on him as "her dry suckling on his lean chest."

The moment of crisis never arrives. The plot of *Tender Is the Night* is predicated on a continuous postponement of a moment of dramatic truth until the need for it has passed. This is undoubtedly true to certain situations in real life but it leaves the reader dissatisfied. The final page contains what is perhaps the most understated and, therefore, brutal and dramatically effective, dismissal of any fictional hero in modern literature. *Tender Is the Night* does contain significant images of cars, notably the sharp persuasive image of a mountain-climbing car that is used to express Dick Diver's own predicament.

Mountain-climbing cars are built on a slant similar to the angle of a hat brim of a man who doesn't want to be recognised. As water gushed from the chamber under the car, Dick was impressed with the ingenuity of the whole idea—a complementary car was now taking on mountain water at the top and would pull the lightened car up by gravity, as soon as the breaks were released.

Dick's preoccupation with this unexceptional car is the natural response of an ambitious, ingenious man who wants to rise to the top without effort. The pulled-down hat brim reinforces Dick's future speculation as to how far relations can be stretched between doctor and patient. What is most telling is the explanation of mechanical balance and symbiosis, transference of mass and energy, that reverses Dick's dream of an easy climb and, ironically, implies how his strength will be poured into Nicole.

Fitzgerald died in Hollywood, alcoholic and exhausted from hackwork at the age of forty-four.

Unlike Fitzgerald, John Dos Passos (1896–1970), illegitimate son of a Portuguese immigrant lawyer and a southern woman, worked in Hollywood for just one year of his full and varied career. In 1934, in the midst of economic depression, Dos Passos found the big money in the Hollywood dream factory. The fact that he lasted only one year there was not surprising. Dos Passos's importance lies more in his uniquely personal contribution to the development of American literature than in his membership of any literary school. He spent the obligatory time in Europe, first as a member of the French, then the American, medical corps during World War I, and then, briefly, as a literary expatriate in Paris where he met writers such as Gertrude Stein, Hemingway, Fitzgerald, and Sherwood Anderson. Here the similarity ends. Although Dos Passos shared the lost generation's disillusionment with the postwar world, he was neither nihilistic nor disaffected and preferred to expend his energies in both writing books that closely expressed the problems of American society, and in supporting various political causes that he deemed crucial to the well-being of the nation's democracy.

His first book was *One Man's Initiation—1917* (1920), a clumsy but emotionally powerful war novel about an ambulance driver. This was followed by *Three Soldiers* (1921) that successfully explored the dislocating effects of war on three different character types. The inhuman qualities of the war are emphasised by images of metal. The attempt of the army in *Three Soldiers* to fashion tin soldiers out of young men of flesh and blood is indicated by the consistent use of words and phrases of metallic connotation in the sequence of chapter titles. Five of the total six have this connotation: "Making the Mold," "The Metal Cools," "Machines," "Rust," and "Under the Wheels." The men's debasement and initiation is also suggested by sexual experiences. The shock of first intercourse is tantamount to initiation into the war, and this is used in two ways. First, it provides a social comment on changing patterns of behavior by indicating the lapse of romantic ignorance before marriage. Second, the degradation of men before whores and the hypocritical military arrangements in procuring women but punishing men who contract disease, provide easy targets for criticism of the running of the war. However, it was the novel *Manhattan Transfer* (1925) that marked the emergence of both Dos Passos's mature style and his mature outlook on the world. It is a collective portrait of the vast and varied, but, to Dos Passos, diseased life of New York City, made up of scores of fictional episodes. Dos Passos used impressionism, expressionism, montage, simultaneity, reportage—all the new literary techniques that appeared for the most part in the twentieth century and can be conveniently labeled as literary modernism. His diverse style unfolding like a kaleidoscope facilitated his attempt to fill the role of novelist, in his opinion, "a sort of second-class historian of the age he lives in."

Time has shown that Dos Passos was in fact underrating his own talents as a novelist and historian. Since the trilogy of novels, *The Forty-Second Parallel* (1930), *1919* (1932), and *The Big Money* (1936), were collected under the title *U.S.A.* in 1938, he has proved that fiction can effectively and admirably fill the role of history, and has directly inspired in thematic and stylistic terms many leading contemporary novelists, including Norman Mailer and E. L. Doctorow, and the historian William Manchester. *U.S.A.* is an unparalleled epic—or rather, anti-epic, since this book is a criticism, not an exaltation, of American society—and covers the nation's history from the turn of the century to the end of the 1920s. It achieves this through devices such as "Newsreel" (reconstructions or news reporting), the "Camera Eye" (impressionistic visions analogous to the cinematographic viewpoint), and slanted biographies of leading historical figures such as Carnegie, Edison, Debs, and Frank Lloyd Wright, who represent the entire range of the political spectrum. The fictional and factual stories end in what Marcus Cunliffe has called "the defeat of the individual on every front." As the reader learns of the different fates of the characters he is meant to understand that most of them are destroyed within themselves by their experience in war. Man's heroism is measured not by his achievements but by the difficulties he overcomes. Thus Dos Passos shows his radicals, Mary French and Ben Compton, with whom he sympathizes, suffering more from their own limitations than the injustices of society. In fact, the three novels gain from their understated sense of irony —the ironies of fate by which acquaintanceships begin and end, and the ironies of history that bring bad deeds from good men, and reduce the well-meaning attempts of the wise to the ineffectual efforts of the incompetent.

Dos Passos was close to the Communist party during the 1920s and most of the 1930s although he never actually joined, and by 1939, with the publication of the novel, *Adventures of a Young Man* whose protagonist is betrayed by the Communists, he had moved firmly to the center of the political arena. His early political radicalism was the most obvious feature that distinguished him from the lost generation and it was a radicalism rooted in pure American soil: a concern for, and ultimate faith in, democratic values; an acute appreciation of the theories of the social scientist Thorstein Veblen; an open admiration for the heroes of the early American Left, Emma Goldman, Max Eastman, and the IWW. He looked on World War I as a giant conspiracy against humanity. To him, the war was part of a capitalist attack on the values and ideals of Jeffersonian democracy, a conspiracy that continued into the 1920s with the Great Red Scare, the persecution of labor and labor leaders, and the shooting of strikers. The plight of the Italian immigrant anarchists, Nicola Sacco and Bartolomeo Vanzetti, exemplified this attack. Dos Passos wrote a pamphlet, "Facing the Chair," on behalf of these two unfortunates. Immediately after their execution, Dos Passos went to work on *The Forty-Second Parallel,* the first of the *U.S.A.* trilogy.

Sherwood Anderson (1876–1941), too, was barely a member of the lost generation although, like Dos Passos, he shared some themes in common with Hemingway and Fitzgerald. Anderson's best-known work is *Winesburg, Ohio* (1919), a series of interrelated tales about the thwarted lives of small-town people, trapped in ignorance and intolerance, yet groping for life. In most of the tales there appears the figure of George Willard, a young newspaper reporter and, like Hemingway's Nick Adams, a surrogate for the author himself. Willard eventually rejects the town of Winesburg and sets off in search of the qualities and values of personal freedom, sexual vitality, lyric insight, and blood brotherhood that are in very short supply amongst the narrow-minded and suffocatingly conservative inhabitants of the small town. At the age of fifty-one Anderson returned to Winesburg, Virginia, having bought two weekly country newspapers and between 1927 and 1931 he wrote personal essays in the form of editorials, character sketches, and mood pieces. Anderson had his greatest successes in the short story rather than the novel and this was where his real talent lay. He once assessed himself as, "The minor author of a minor masterpiece." While this is essentially true, it fails to express the powerful influence that he had on other writers as Hemingway and Faulkner. Indeed, William Faulkner once called him, "The father of my generation of American writers and the tradition of American writing which our successors will carry on."

Jewish-American novels captured the essence of the immigrant experience because of their continuous unfolding of stories about an individual at odds with the world around him. For the heroes, and, one suspects, the authors, life is difficult, anyway, and the pressures of an urban, fragmented society upon individuals make it doubly so. Yet the novels are essentially optimistic, rather than pessimistic, since a central theme is that while life may be harsh, it is man's duty to try and understand his role in it and show understanding and compassion for the difficulties of his fellow men.

Ludwig Lewisohn, a German Jew, arrived in the United States in 1890 when he was seven. He came from a tradition of German Jews who had developed Reform Judaism. Lewisohn was dismayed to find how American society practiced subtle but hard forms of discrimination against even modern Jews. He described his disappointment in *Up Stream* (1922) and to maximum effect in his best work, *The Island Within* (1928). Lewisohn became convinced that the only way Jews could become well-adjusted was as individuals and for this they must revive their sense of a Jewish people.

The Island Within examines the psychological impact of anti-Jewish feeling on first- and second-generation American Jews. The novel moves from its opening in Europe to the United States. The hero, Arthur Levy, is initially confident that he is a true American, but gradually he becomes aware of differences between himself and other Americans because of their attitude toward him. The novel is set mainly in the very late nineteenth and early twentieth centuries, a period when Wasp society was resisting the rise of successive groups of Jews in American society. Lewisohn had great difficulty in obtaining a teaching post at university because he was Jewish. Much of *The Island Within* is based on Lewisohn's own experiences and his increasing awareness of Jewish consciousness. In the novel Arthur's Jewishness becomes the central factor in his life as he tries to reach out for the American ideal of equality for all. Eventually, he turns to the idea that Jews must preserve their sense of peoplehood, if they are to remain whole and not become self-hating through forlorn attempts at gaining access to gentile society.

Other second-generation Jewish immigrants were hit by discrimination and expressed the problems they experienced as marginal men while exploring the larger, social issues raised by prejudice. Some second-generation American Jews, especially in New York and Chicago, turned to a new orthodoxy to help them resolve such problems, the Communist party. Their contribution was significant and out of all proportion to their numerical membership, whether as organizers, activists, ideologues, or orators. In his pamphlet, "The Immigrant Experience in American Literature" (1982), Edward A. Abrahamson explains, "Whereas the writers of . . . the expatriate tradition had represented an educated, literate elite, able to travel abroad and experience an older, fuller, more confident culture, the writers who portrayed the immigrant experience marked a 'proletarianizing' influence which in some ways reflected more accurately what was happening in the United States itself."

Henry Roth was born in Galicia in 1906 and came to the United States as a small child with his mother to meet his father, the experience he draws on at the beginning of his novel, *Call It Sleep* (1934). He enjoyed some security in the Jewish section of the Lower East Side but lost it when the family subsequently moved to Harlem and he encountered anti-Semitism from Irish-Americans. In the Prologue Henry Roth describes the arrival of David Shearl and his mother, Genya, in New York, where they are met by his father, Albert. David is still wearing old-fashioned European clothes and his father, who cannot tolerate the idea of being thought a greenhorn, throws David's blue straw hat into the bay, a symbolic rejection of Europe. The entire scene of their arrival is presented as grim and despondent, rather than optimistic. Even the Statue of Liberty is perceived as something frightening. Liberty was evidently not a Jewish mother. The family live first in the Brownsville section of Brooklyn, later on the Lower East Side. Roth deliberately shifted the emphasis of his description of the Lower East Side to a harsher, cruder environment than the one he remembered. "In reality, I took the violent environment of Harlem—where we lived from 1914 to 1928—and projected it back onto the East Side."

To the boy, David, both his home and the streets outside are dangerous places—the streets because of the roaming gangs of gentile youths, his home because his father has become paranoid, uncertain whether David really is his son, and given to unpredictable bouts of irritation and bad temper. Roth shows tensions between various cultures, Irish and Jewish and Italian, and between two generations of American Jews. The father, Albert's, problems are largely caused by the need to come to terms with new urban society but compounded by his own awkward temperament.

The Impact of Freud

Eugene O'Neill (1888–1953) was the founding father of the modern American theater. O'Neill was the son of the actors James O'Neill (noted for his rendition of the Count of Monte Cristo) and Ellen Quinlan. Eugene O'Neill's early career was very checkered and included periods of acting, office work, gold prospecting, reporting, and, most significantly for his drama, a spell as a seaman. In 1912 he entered a sanitorium and, while recovering there from tuberculosis, he read the great dramatists of the world and began to write himself. In 1916 his first performed play, *Bound East for Cardiff,* was given its premiere at the Provincetown Players' new Playwrights' Theater in New York and thus dates the beginning of serious drama in the United States.

Eugene O'Neill with his wife, Carlotta. O'Neill's plays, with their obsessive characters and highly charged language, owed much to Sigmund Freud. The photograph is among hundreds of people in the worlds of literature, entertainment, and the arts between the 1930s and the 1960s by maverick writer and photographer Carl Van Vechten. (Library of Congress).

O'Neill was fascinated by the vagaries of human motivation and by mankind's self-destructive qualities, and he employed these themes with a pessimistic determinism that qualifies him for associate membership of the lost generation. He is also distinguished from the lost generation by virtue of his intellectual heritage that links him more with such heavyweight literary figures as James Joyce, T. S. Eliot, and August Strindberg, rather than Fitzgerald and Hemingway who never carried intellectual pretensions. The influence of Nietzsche in particular was to prove particularly relevant to O'Neill's work since—when combined with his natural American tendency toward individualistic concerns—it led him into exploration of the nature of self-reliance and heroic individualism in the face of social alienation, geographic isolation, and fervent competition.

There was another influence O'Neill never openly acknowledged. From the start the ideas of Viennese psychiatrist Sigmund Freud were received enthusiastically in America, but this enthusiasm hid the fact that these same ideas were also misperceived and abused by the vast majority of people. In books such as *The Interpretation of Dreams* (1900) and *The Psychopathology of Everyday Life* (1901) Freud explained the importance of the subconscious as a motivating factor in human behavior and provided certain guidelines for interpreting human motivation through analysis of our behavior and our dreams—the only element of our subconscious that we come into direct and knowing contact with. These new analytical techniques were, on the one hand, to prove indispensable to serious artists in their investigations into the mysteries of life and living and, on the other hand, proved extremely diverting and titillating to those who saw Freudian psychology as a means of escape from the inhibiting legacies of previous decades: sexual repression, patriotism, fundamentalist religion, and political idealism. Freud's ideas, apparently, licensed some people to throw these legacies out of the window. This was, of course, a complete distortion of the purposes to which Freud developed his theory. Freud was not an advocate of permissive behavior, but a dour, conservative, and deeply moralistic rationalist who disliked America. It was too brash and vulgar in comparison with the claustrophobic atmosphere and stuffy refinement of his native Vienna. A visit to America in 1909 to lecture at Clark University in Worcester, Massachusetts, did nothing to change his opinion.

Many popular writers produced a synthesis of his work that did nothing to endear America to Sigmund Freud. For example, André Tridon was prolific in his output of books that were a distillation of the more titillating ideas of Freud, Alfred Adler, and Carl Jung. Tridon took their ideas and stirred them enthusiastically as they boiled away in the pot. He was also capable of throwing in his own deeply considered psychological analysis of human behavior as seasoning to this psychological potpourri. Did you know, for example, that rice and old shoes at a wedding are obvious symbols of the semen and the female genitals? As cultural historian Robert Crunden summarizes Freud: "In his analyses of his patients' dreams and neuroses, he discovered what seemed to be an inherent conflict between the demands of human instinct, and the demands of society as a whole. The individual said, 'I want,' and society, from its broader experience, said, 'You can't.' " This was an argument tailor-made for those who hated the ideas of the previous decades and had seen them result in World War I.

Freud's ideas, long known to readers of classic drama—Shakespeare, Sophocles, Euripides, et al.—but now presented in a pseudo-scientific format had a profound impact on artists such as Eugene O'Neill. There are other numerous instances. In a letter to Ernest Hemingway of June 1934 F. Scott Fitzgerald found that "the purpose of a work of fiction is to appeal to the lingering after-effects in the reader's mind as differing from, say, the purpose of oratory or philosophy which respectively leave people in a fighting or a thoughtful mood." Fitzgerald agreed with one romantic tradition that insisted on the primacy of emotional intensity. "Almost everything I write in novels goes, for better or worse, into the subconscious of the reader." He told his daughter, Scottie, in a letter of 1936, "If you have anything to say, anything you feel nobody has ever said before, you have got to feel it so desperately that you will find some way to say it that nobody has ever found before, so that the thing you have got to say and the way of saying it blend as one matter—as indissolubly as if they were conceived together." Max Eastman, editor of *The Masses*, regarded Freud, correctly, not as a scientist "but an artist—a demonological poet—who insisted on peopling an underworld with masked demons who move about in the unlocal dark, controlling our thoughts and the action of our bodies." This was Freud's important contribution to art; he stimulated the artistic intellect and gave new depth to the possibilities for representation and analysis of human motivation.

In his play *The Emperor Jones* (1921), Eugene O'Neill expresses the psychology of his leading character through an experimental drama. This is a tale of a black Pullman porter who has managed to become dictator of a declining West Indian state. Jones suffers from "little formless fears" that are, in fact, in his subconscious, but that appear to him to be physical presences in the jungle that surrounds him. *All God's Chillun Got Wings* (1923) is a treatment of the problems of miscegenation and a diagnosis of how shock can provoke a regression to the mental state of childhood. It was expressed dramatically with the aid of a sophisticated stage set that contracted in size progressively throughout the play. *Desire Under the Elms* (1925) presented a variation on the theme of the Oedipus complex that O'Neill claimed was familiar to him from the original Greek source, rather than as distilled and refined through the mind of Sigmund Freud. *The Great God Brown* (1926) is a bitter examination of the personality masks that people use in their relationships with one another. *Marco Millions* (1928) was a satire on American commercialism transposed to Marco Polo's Venice. *Mourning Becomes Electra* (1931) had a rare psychological intensity, a play indebted to both Aeschylus and Freud, with Greek tragedy transposed to the life of the Mannon family of New England during the era of the American Civil War. O'Neill is undoubtedly America's greatest playwright and this is in no small part due to his understanding and exploitation of psychological factors.

Psychoanalysis became overwhelmingly popular and this affected not only sexual morality but the entire range of human consciousness. By advocating an alternative to society and economics as explanations for human behavior, the emphasis is thrown on the self apart from society. That "self" may be the subliminal-self or the id but it is still the self. Frederick Hoffmann writes that the literature of the 1920s shows ". . . many examples of the mind turning in upon itself, examining, explaining and excusing itself in psychological terms. Interest in self took the place and argued the futility of a sense of social responsibility." This preoccupation with oneself, separate from community and society, explains why politics and economics did not much interest the writers of the 1920s. Apparently, the way to keep psychologically healthy was to indulge one's libido and encourage one's flapper friends to do the same! Newspaper reporters offered instant psychological explanations for murder and divorce cases while columnists asked, "What are little boys made of? Oedipus Rex and

Infantile Sex." Margaret Mead's (1901–1979) book, *Coming of Age in Samoa* (1927), exploited this insatiable curiosity about sex under the guise of analytic anthropology. It quickly became the most surprising best-seller of the decade. However, by omitting Freud's biological determinism and arguing that a free society bred peace and harmony and well-adjusted adults, she offered a utopian adolescent vision that was enthusiastically embraced by the young.

From the start, Margaret Mead's *Coming of Age* was much criticized by more rigorous anthropologists for its lack of factual accuracy and poor discipline. *Coming of Age* may, or may not, be an academic fraud but it is a powerful fiction. Not only did Mead titillate her readers with old-fashioned romances about dusky natives having trysts under the palms but she wrote in most effective novelette style, inviting readers to compare their own repressed adolescence in provincial America with fulfilled sex on a fantasy island. Some of the subjects—rape, promiscuity, homosexuality—were, then, almost forbidden, but dangerous and thus exciting. Her master stroke was to focus on the adolescent girl in an age when society at home had made an icon of the adolescent girl as flapper. *Coming of Age* drew deep from American folklore and Mead hit a jackpot of sales. There are numerous signs in the book itself that her interpretation is at odds with the facts even she presents. The Samoan archipelago was not unspoilt. Already missionaries had imposed their will on certain sections; the economy was bound up with the United States and Europe; and Samoan natives who wanted greater education and social freedom were treated as social deviants. Now we are more likely to emphasize the text's significance as a bisexual's plea for greater toleration.

A more direct and equally popular representation of the nymphet as part siren, part ingenue, and part landscape was provided by Anita Loos (1894–1981) in *Gentlemen Prefer Blondes* (1925), Here the professional not-so-dumb blonde, Lorelei Lee, gives the reader her disingenuous protestations about her predatory intentions toward wealthy men in the form of a diary recording her single-minded devotion to orchids, champagne, and diamonds.

"Kissing your hand may make you feel good but a diamond bracelet lasts forever."

Journalists and Realists

Psychological treatment was not a prerequisite for literary success in America. Ring Lardner (1885–1933) established his name as a sports writer before the great success of his short stories brought him fame as a sardonic humorist and satirist. The best of his many collections of short stories are *How to Write Short Stories (with Samples)* (1924) and *The Love Nest and Other Stories* (1926). In these and later collections the stupidity and dullness of his protagonists, usually ordinary, working people, are analyzed with his usual pessimistic wit. In 1927 Lardner even turned his incisive wit on himself with the publication of his autobiography, *The Story of a Wonder Boy*. His use of the American vernacular brought him praise and gratitude from the most influential literary pundit of the time, H. L. Mencken (1880–1956).

Mencken himself, like Lardner, was hardly an intellectual. His formal education ended at high school and from then onward he immersed himself in the world of newspaper, magazine, and literary journalism. He attained his influence through his lively and daring editorships and criticisms that were often vehicles for his scathing wit. Mencken arrived at a fortuitous time in American history. The 1920s were peculiarly responsive to his iconoclasm that arose out of his feeling that American culture had become stultified by its rigid adherence to a particularly "Puritan" form of Christian morality and a foolishly persistent belief in egalitarianism.

The 1920s afforded Mencken plenty of opportunity to develop and express his iconoclasm through his editorship of the magazines *Smart Set* (1914–1923) and *American Mercury* (1924–1933). Moreover, Mencken was himself a prolific writer and, despite, or perhaps because of, his reliance on impressionism as a critical method, did his job with such gusto and panache that his name and his ideas spread far. However, the depression of the 1930s was certainly not a subject suited to Mencken's style. Indeed,

Mencken at first refused to believe in the depression's existence and dismissed it as "newspaper talk." He could not handle it and lost his readers.

Sinclair Lewis (1885–1951) was a writer who dealt with themes that were never far from mind whenever H. L. Mencken put his caustic pen to paper. Indeed, Lewis's most noted fictional character, George F. Babbitt, might be described as the prototype of Mencken's apocryphal human species, *Boobus Americanus*. Mencken and his followers applied this pejorative term dismissively to virtually everyone except themselves, but George Babbitt belonged to a race of Americans that require and deserve specific consideration.

Lewis himself was a journalist rather than a literary artist, and his fiction expresses this. However, he was the first American to be awarded the Nobel Prize for literature, an event that marked the apogee of his career in 1930. In his fiction Lewis used the tenets of realism as they had been worked out in the nineteenth century, even though in his Nobel acceptance speech he attacked the realist tradition as instigated by W. D. Howells. Nevertheless, he praised younger writers such as Ernest Hemingway and the ambitious and innovative Thomas Wolfe (1900–1938) whose *Look Homeward Angel* was published in 1928 and took literature into uncharted territory whither Lewis, with his conventional approach, was ill equipped to follow. However, this criticism cannot detract from the fact that, with *Babbitt* (1922), about a small-time, small-town real estate agent living in Zenith, Lewis created a classic American novel and a classic American character whose name has entered the English language.

The economic boom of the 1920s inevitably produced legions of Babbitts, middle-class aspirants who fulfilled their role as "boosters" in American society. Babbitt believes he is master of his own destiny; yet he is actually following the herd. Lewis's affectionate parody of popular slogans of optimism, health, and progress was uncannily prophetic of the fads of the decade and of consumerism and conformism long afterward. Lewis cannot be strictly classified as a member of the lost generation since his own reaction to the vulgar materialism and cultural impoverishment of the 1920s was ambivalent. For example, in *Babbitt* the force of his satire on the city of Zenith and its population of boosters is diminished by his recognition of the rebellious, individualistic impulses of George Babbitt, but what constitutes a loss for satire is a gain for the cause of psychological realism. Babbitt is saved from being utterly ridiculous by his friendship with Paul Riesling who encourages him to question the whole tribal structure. For a while, Babbitt becomes a rebel, violating social, political, and sexual taboos. However, Lewis does not permit any uplifting or revolutionary conclusion. Babbitt recognizes the heroism of strikers who openly display their "alien, red notions" but, nevertheless, he returns to his standardized, middle-class life. Sinclair Lewis creates a convincingly complex picture of the group pressure on an individual; yet Lewis manages to maintain, at the same time, a concentration on the idea of that individual's sense of being apart from society.

Sinclair Lewis drew entirely from everyday life, preparing his novels by recording names appropriate for particular characters from telephone directories, sketching precise maps of imagined towns, devising suitable backgrounds for his characters and defining their pets, garden plants, and favorite anecdotes—all in loose-leaf notebooks and usually before he began writing his novels.

At the end of a decade of prolific writing, including not only *Main Street* and *Babbitt* but also *Arrowsmith, Mantrap,* and *Elmer Gantry, The Man Who Knew Coolidge,* and *Dodsworth,* he was awarded the Nobel Prize for literature, an honor he had coveted and, indeed, lobbied for. When he received the award from King Gustav V of Sweden in December 1930 he turned his acceptance speech into a tirade on the poverty of American culture, prompting Calvin Coolidge to answer the storm of indignation at home with the dismissive remark, "No necessity exists for becoming excited." Lewis thought his career was over but his later, uneven, novels, *Ann Vickers, Work of Art,* and *It Can't Happen Here* were commercial successes and he became noted for playful wit, especially wordplay and wicked impersonation of John L. Lewis, FDR, Father Coughlin, and Huey Long. Fascinated by the theater, he collaborated with Lloyd Lewis on *Jayhawker* which played for only three weeks on Broadway in 1934, and he also adapted *It Can't Happen Here,* which opened to WPA productions in eighteen cities in 1936. Yet he had little understanding of the technical demands of the theater and sought advice on elementary matters from inexperienced actors in summer stock.

He met his second wife, journalist Dorothy Thompson, in Berlin where she was a newspaper correspondent for the *New York Evening Post* and the *Philadelphia Public Ledger*. Immediately, he sensed that this energetic, compassionate woman might help sustain him and proposed to her that very night and went on proposing until she accepted him a month later. Both were restless nomads and never settled on the farm they planned as a sort of country idyll. As Dorothy Thompson's career waxed, Lewis's waned and he hit the bottle more resolutely, rounding on his wife as some sort of malevolent Big Nurse. He complained he had to share a bed with world affairs and threatened to divorce her, naming Adolf Hitler as corespondent. When he was on the wagon, he would gnash his teeth at soirées dominated by her wit and insight as she held court to adoring young professionals. When someone said Dorothy Thompson should run for president in 1936, he retorted, "Fine. Then I can write 'My Day.'" When he argued with her, her response was to ridicule his arguments in a column, "Grouse for Breakfast."

The year that witnessed the publication of *Babbitt,* 1922, is a crucial one in the history of literature and intellectual activity including publications of T. S. Eliot's *Waste Land,* Joyce's *Ulysses,* and Walter Lippmann's *Public Opinion.* Moreover, in Italy the fascist dictator, Mussolini, came to power. In a preface to a collection of her essays published in 1936 Willa Cather (1873–1947) declared, "The world broke in two in 1922 or thereabouts, and the persons recalled in these sketches slide back into yesterdays seven thousand years." Cather was a novelist slow and meticulous in her prose style and her use of myth and symbol. Her early writing was much under the influence of Henry James, but with the publication of *Alexander's Bridge* in 1912 she began to find her own voice and was able to leave her job on the staff of the muckraking magazine, *McClure's,* and devote herself full time to fiction. Her most noted novels are *My Antonia* (1918), set amongst the immigrant farmers of Nebraska where she grew up, and *One of Ours* (1922) that won her the Pulitzer Prize. It tells the story of a young man's escape from an oppressive life on his family's mid-western farm to a vitalizing but, ultimately, fatal experience on the French battlefields of World War I. It was precisely the experience and the aftereffects of war that led Cather to make her apocalyptic statement about the year 1922. The writers of the lost generation would have agreed with her since their world was continually breaking in two, and, inevitably, like the unfortunate children they were, they were always left with the smaller piece.

American Poets

The poet T. S. Eliot would also have agreed with Willa Cather. In 1922 he published his seminal vision of a world materially and spiritually devastated by the experience of the war to end all wars. (He wrote *The Waste Land* while recovering from a devastating mental illness in 1915.) *The Waste Land* was recognized by Ezra Pound and other poets as a masterpiece of the modern movement when it was published. It was Pound who cut the first fifty-four lines from an opening line "First we had a couple of feelers down at Tom's place," with its obscure, suspicious double entendres, to the striking

> April is the cruellest month, breeding
> Lilacs out of the dead land, mixing
> Memory and desire, stirring
> Dull roots with spring rain,

with its echoes of Chaucer. It immediately established Eliot as the leading American poet of the day. No other poem in the English language provokes such extremes of feeling in critics and readers alike. Some see it as a poignant poetical rendition of what Eliot took to be the spiritual and moral plight of postwar Europe, while others see it as an obscure poem, pretentious in its classical allusions, and gratuitously pessimistic in tone. Eliot himself once— perhaps jocularly—dismissed *The Waste Land* as "just a piece of rhythmic grumbling." The poem certainly at first reads as a random series of symbolic images, but it is subtly and tenuously controlled throughout by a continuing narrative and an albeit inconstant narrator, Tiresias.

Eliot was born and raised in St. Louis, Missouri, but came from a Unitarian family whose roots were in New England. He graduated from Harvard in 1910 where he had been taught by the philosopher George Santayana, the linguist Irving Babbitt, and the literary historian Barrett Wendell. He first read Dante at Harvard, the poet who, in his own opinion, exerted the greatest permanent influence on his work. By 1911, at the age of twenty-three, he had completed *The Love Song of J. Alfred Prufrock,* a precocious poem with its vivid and sensuous images, its flexible tone, and its expressive rhythms.

In part, *Prufrock* is an investigation of Hell, defined as the pretentiousness of the women visitors to the gallery, the triviality of a life measured in coffee spoons, the uncertainty of toast and tea, and the fragmentary experiences of incoherent people. It is a "fog" and "yellow fog" that blots everything out and ensures one stays at home. Eliot's most assertive early poems are all set in the adolescent keys of unresolved self-doubt, self-absorbed hypersensitivity, and defensive, cold posturing. As critic M. L. Rosenthal has observed, *The Love Song of J. Alfred Prufrock* "positively sweats panic at the challenge of adult sexuality and of living up to one's ideal of what it is to be manly in any sort of heroic model."

In fact, various disclosures about Eliot's disastrous first marriage to Vivien Haigh-Wood that, perhaps, pushed him close to madness have recently threatened to overshadow Eliot's artistic achievement. Between his two happy periods—childhood and his second marriage to Valerie Eliot—Eliot drew from his personal anxieties and deep anguish and wrote his greatest poetry. *Rhapsody on a Windy Night* offers a squalid context of murky streets late at night, horror of sex with a prostitute who "hesitates towards you in the light of the door / Which opens on her like a grin," the moon depicted as a crackbrained old whore, and, at the close, a fear of waking into ordinary life. Such early works and those of other poets carry deep resonances because their adolescent terror is seen as a psychological complement to the gathering storm of World War I that was to shatter old forms of western civilization.

Irregular verse patterns, the procession of distorted, skeletal images with phallic symbols rendered sterile, add up to the shock of puberty, realization of death, and a vision of the macabre side of life.

After obtaining his B.A. and M.A., and embarking on his doctoral studies, T. S. Eliot settled in London in 1915 where, at first, he only just managed to scrape a precarious living by teaching, reviewing, and working for Lloyd's Bank. In 1927 he was confirmed in the Church of England and became a British citizen. Throughout his working life Eliot showed that human life was made up of an endless series of dying moments. The subject of T. S. Eliot's Ph.D. thesis, interrupted by the war, was English philosopher F. H. Bradley (1840–1924) and one of Bradley's prime concerns was the relationship between any given subject and the outside world that he regarded as one, existentially. To Eliot and Bradley our psychological perception of things was related to our geographical sense and this sense of identity varied according to our particular place at any given time. In the *Four Quartets* (1943) Eliot emphasized that culture was defined by place, by the way people were bound up in their environment and this included time. It seems that the culture of civilizations past has been turned into a chaotic jumble by the war. Accumulated knowledge cannot help us interpret the present nor see into the future. Nevertheless, we have to trust the universe because it is that, rather than our different cultures and languages, that binds us together. At its best, Eliot's poetry had an ability to make his readers feel the interaction of different experiences and realize that they, too, were in sum, a total of various complex internal and external factors. However, his plays, heavily imbued with Jacobean and Greek references but dramatically implausible, managed the astonishing feat of being both gross and coy at the same time.

Ezra Pound (1885–1972) was also an expatriate. He left America in 1908 for Europe and did not return until 1946 under tragic circumstances. If T. S. Eliot was the "invisible poet," then Ezra Pound was the "elusive poet," a scholar who remained suspicious of the tradition of English literature. Pound's M.A. was in Romanist literature. Throughout his career he did many translations of others' work and also worked such translations into his own poetry, such as the *Seafarer* (1912) that mimics the movement of an Anglo-Saxon line. After a period in Paris, Pound moved to Rapallo, Italy, where he remained until the end of World War II and where he composed the *Cantos*. In 1945 he was arrested for treason by U.S. army officers on the grounds of his previous public support of fascism. He was imprisoned in a cage in the open air and at his trial in 1946 found unfit to plead for reasons of insanity. He was confined in Elizabeth's Hospital for the Criminally Insane, Washington, D.C., until 1956 when pressure from other poets, such as Robert Frost, persuaded the authorities to release him. In the meantime, he had won the Bollinger Prize in 1949 for *Cantos* written in prison. Eliot saw Pound as a truly catalytic figure and called him "the animator of artistic activity in any milieu in which he found himself." In preference to the iambic pentameter, already discarded by Walt Whitman (1819–1892), Pound started to hammer out his own hard surface in a so-called imagist phase of 1912–1914. His work as a translator convinced him that, in translation, language was concerned with transmitting information and experience as clearly as possible and thus became neutral. He believed that, although the Americans had inherited the English language, they had not inherited the tradition and experience that that language was originally intended to convey. Thus he wanted to alter language (as in a translation), in order to carry the sense of breadth of American experience, stretching existing language to that end.

Pound had several obsessions of which only the poetical brought good, while the political and the racial brought only harm and tragedy. He was instrumental in the formation of the liberating theory of imagism that grew out of his obsession with the Japanese *haiku* or pictographic poetry. Imagism was the ultimate in economy and entailed using no superfluous word—no adjective, article, adverb, verb, or conjugation—that did not reveal something crucial to the reader. The most singular example of Pound's imagism is the poem "In a Station of the Metro," taken from the collection *Lustra* of 1915, and here reproduced in its minimal entirety:

> The apparition of these faces in the crowd;
> Petals on a wet, black bough.

Pound's explanation was that, "In a poem of this sort one is trying to record the precise instant when a thing outward and objective transforms itself, or darts into a thing inward and subjective."

As European editor between 1912 and 1919 of the "little" magazine, *Poetry,* owned by Harriet Monroe of Chicago, Pound was responsible for the publication of important works by such new authors as T. S. Eliot and Robert Frost. As English editor of the *Little Review* from 1917 to 1919, he placed James Joyce's *Ulysses* with one of its first publishers. Thus Pound was truly a catalyst in encouraging new literary talent and in helping to ensure the success of the little magazine movement that continues throughout the century as the major testing ground for avant-garde writers.

Pound the poet is remembered today for two works. First and foremost, by virtue of their sheer scale, are *The Cantos* (1925–1968) that, at almost a thousand pages, constitute Pound's attempt at creating a twentieth-century equivalent of Walt Whitman's masterpiece, *Leaves of Grass* (1855–1892). *The Cantos* are inconsistent in quality and too ambitious a project to have ever wholly succeeded. However, they do constitute a stunning compendium of poetical technique.

The finest section, "The Pisan Cantos," were written during his period of incarceration. (We must recall that in 1945, when he gave himself up to the American authorities in Italy, he was taken to the United States Army Disciplinary Training Center near Pisa and placed in a small cage made of airstrip landing mats above which an arc light burned throughout the night.) The first draft of "The Pisan Cantos" was written in this cage with a pencil stub in a children's notebook given him by a Jewish chaplain. He had no books except for Confucius and a poetry anthology he found in the lavatory. After he suffered his nervous breakdown, he was moved to a tent and allowed to use a typewriter. Yet he supplied the numerous and diverse details of history and literature from memory. He could do this because his quite incredible memory was aural rather than visual. He became impatient with his inability to type as fast as he could think and in his fury he hit blindly at the keys, causing them to jump all over the page and make erratic spacings, curious indentions, and odd dashes and capital letters that became punctuation. He usually kept two machines so that when one broke and had to be repaired he still had a spare. Pound's models for the *Cantos* were the epic poems of Homer and Dante that he transformed by echoes of Browning, Rosetti, and Whitman, and his experiments with collages of thirteen different languages, including Chinese. In fact, ten cantos (LII–LXI) are of early Chinese history, explaining how China prospered when a good emperor followed Confucian principles. Pound is also remembered for the poem, *Hugh Selwyn Mauberly* (1920) which, like *The Waste Land,* is a landmark in modern poetry. Pound and Eliot did what no poets had done before. They sacrificed their own authorial voice for the sake of their subject matter and left personae in the form of Mauberly and Tiresias, respectively, to face the aridity, the unreality, and the superficiality of postwar urban society.

Eliot and Pound's morbid vision of inner reality, their sense of human destiny moving down an irreversible death march, confirmed the deep pessimism about the human condition to the generation that attained maturity in the 1930s and 1940s and faced the horrors of World War II. As W. H. Auden later remarked, Eliot transmitted "the unmentionable odor of death" of our century. He also expressed a sense of a world out of kilter and out of control. Eliot "showed us a decisive image of ourselves in the mirror of a terrified age being quick-marched nowhere though still capable of making wonderful jokes about it all."

Hart Crane (1892–1932) is more important for what he set out to do rather than for what he actually achieved. Crane was a tragic figure, driven by compulsive and self-destructive alcoholic and sexual urges that culminated in a spectacular suicide. In 1932 he leaped into the sea on returning from Vera Cruz where he had hoped to write an epic poem on Montezuma and the Spanish conquest of Mexico. It is too easy to take a facile view of Crane and see him either as an amoral dissipate or as the romantically lonely scapegoat of an intolerant and brutal civilization. *The Bridge* (1930) is his longest and most important poem, modeled on *The Waste Land* in its form and intended as a kind of optimistic riposte to Eliot's negative view of the modern metropolis. *The Bridge,* like *The Waste Land* and *Ulysses,* follows a protagonist through the modern city. Crane's protagonist wakes in the morning, crosses over Brooklyn Bridge, wanders about the city, and then returns in the evening by the subway under the Hudson River. Crane tried to create an American mythology in this poem out of scraps of literature, history, and tradition with such figures as Columbus, Rip Van Winkle, the Wright Brothers, Walt Whitman, Edgar Allen Poe, Emily Dickinson, and Isadora Duncan. In the section entitled "Powhattan's Daughter" Pochahontas represents the American earth itself and its Red Indian heritage. However, it is the Brooklyn Bridge that is the unifying symbol of the poem, connecting the two halves of the city and, through the railroad that it carries, uniting the city with the country and the present to the past. This celebration of a great feat of engineering makes Crane an American representative of Futurism, an artistic movement expounded by the Italian Filippo Marinetti in 1909 when he called on art to exalt machines and imitate their motion.

Four poets who achieved their greatest successes and recognition after 1945 were active and influential during the first five decades of the twentieth century: Robert Frost (1874–1963), William Carlos Williams (1883–1963), Wallace Stevens (1879–1955), and E. E. Cummings (1894–1962).

Frost was a deeply ambiguous poet who hungered for success and created a larger-than-life popular image and an equally large supply of popular poetry that ensured him wide recognition yet hid his real nature. He is, perhaps, America's best-known poet, but his modernist awareness of the predicament of modern man goes largely unremarked by the many people who read his poetry. He made much of his crusty rural exterior and there was nothing abstruse about his work that was generally taken as a spontaneous, organic response to the wonders of nature. Nevertheless, as critic Richard Francis explains, his poems disclose a second, deeper meaning. When he urges a farmer not to mend a drystone wall separating his land from his neighbor's because territorial claims are not necessary in the natural world, he is really urging the paradox that territorial imperative is a perfectly natural response (in humans and in animals) to the environment. Similarly, taken superficially, his *Stopping by Woods on a Snowy Evening* is a traditional summation of the conflict between civilization and nature built up by an accumulation of images and a simple rhyme scheme. However, it is the horse, who wants to get back to the stable as quickly as possible, and escape possible dangers, whose response to descending night is far more natural than that of the self-indulgent man who wants to linger as long as possible to survey the scene. It is the horse that knows he and his master are better back in their social compact, that it is unnatural and dangerous to stay out late in the woods that afford him no gratification.

Birches is a poem about complex human needs, including sex, that children must learn by experience, in this case the boyish pleasure of finding the right balance by riding the branches of a birch tree as if to subdue them. Frost's simple titles are drawn from the natural world and imply love of the simple life of a golden age and the romantic tradition of Wordsworth. The *Oven-bird* does not simply die as do other birds but by enriching the life of a family it becomes part of the cycle of life.

Frost did not see nature as a sanctuary from the world of industry but he did believe that poetry, when successful, drew on deep roots of human consciousness and provided its readers with the means of resisting those forces in the world that erode human confidence and stability. As individuals we may be overwhelmed by events but we live again in poetry to celebrate the processes of self-expression. Thus, in part, poetry is about the human need to write poetry. In fact, Frost took his readers into the realms of irony and paradox.

William Carlos Williams was a doctor as well as a poet who found himself in a particularly advantageous position for writing of the American spirit since he saw it in sickness and in health tramping through his office in New Jersey for almost fifty years. Initially, his reputation existed only among other writers such as Ezra Pound and Hart Crane. Not until the publishing house New Directions started publishing his work in the late 1930s did he begin to attract a wider audience. Most of his first dozen books were printed privately or were subsidized. Williams always wrote in a mode based on the rhythms of the speaking voice, replete with idiomatic language, colloquialisms, and an intense interest in locale as both setting and subject. Indeed, his concentration on detail from everyday life and speech distances him from the elitist intellectualism of expatriates such as Eliot and Pound. This rejection of abstraction is succinctly expressed in his dictum, "No ideas but in things," that is, in turn, demonstrated in his poems whether they deal with, say, a red firetruck, or, "The Red Wheelbarrow." The four books of the poem *Paterson* (1946–1958) constitute his most celebrated and technically successful work with its epic exploration of the life of a man in the small city of the title.

Wallace Stevens was a man of deep contradictions. He was a most sensuous yet intellectual poet who spent most of his life working as an executive of the Hartford Life and Accident Insurance Company in Connecticut. He placed a very high value on poetry in particular and art in general, yet would only ever write in his spare time. Thematically, Stevens was at odds with most other American writers of the twentieth century who were deeply critical of their age. Instead of seeing dislocation and chaos in the destruction of old ways of life and living, he saw an opportunity for recreation that would be based on anarchic individualism, on an arrogant sense of self. Poetry would be a replacement for mankind's shattered faith in religion and God, but this poetry would be a highly personal process of subjective analysis of meaning. We are all poets, was Stevens's suggestion. The pity is that only very few of us have the gift of poetic expression. Stevens was optimistic in the way that he viewed his art as an antidote to meaninglessness: "Poetry is the Supreme Fiction," and the supreme fiction can cope with any chaos. His poetry and his poetic vision with its mystical overtones progressed from his first published collection of poetry, *Harmonium* (1923), through other collections, such as *The Man with the Blue Guitar* (1937) and *Notes Toward a Supreme Fiction* (1942).

E. E. Cummings should have belonged to the lost generation by virtue of the fact that he engaged in many of their prescribed pursuits—ambulance driving during World War I, expatriate living in Paris between 1921 and 1923, and pioneering experimentation with literary modernism. Yet, philosophically and stylistically, Cummings was a long way from the lost generation. He grew up in Cambridge, close to Harvard, where he later studied with distinction, and his Unitarian background provided him with a transcendental view of the world that permeates his poetry and contrasts starkly with the pessimism of the lost generation. During World War I Cummings was imprisoned in a French concentration camp because his companion, William Slater Brown, had written discontented letters to a German professor at Columbia University. Cummings was freed within three months, but only after his father had written to President Woodrow Wilson. As a direct result of this experience, he wrote *The Enormous Room* (1922), a prison journal that is full of comic invention, reportorial insight, and, even by virtue of its unconventional use of syntax, asserts a theme of humorous yet serious antiauthoritarianism.

Tulips and Chimneys was a large manuscript containing 152 of Cummings's poems that no publisher would accept. Only with the help of his ex-classmate John Dos Passos was he able in 1923 to publish a shortened version of the book containing sixty poems. In 1937 the original manuscript was issued in its entirety under its original title and it now stands as one of the classics of modernist literature. His poems caught the spirit of the jazz age through their great variety of tone, voice, and technique. Cummings was fascinated by the asyntactic language of Gertrude Stein (1874–1946) and the dismantled shapes of modernist painting. The new art made spontaneous perception the basis of expression and creation, just as in jazz music the soloist often departs from what is written. Cummings dismantled all the components of poetry and reassembled them: punctuation became a series of arbitrary signals sometimes used even as words. The function of nouns, pronouns, adverbs, and adjectives was often interchanged. Typography itself became a tool in the process of expressing what was essentially a lyric gift. His experiments are the direct literary equivalent of what happened in modern painting at this time. In fact, Cummings himself was also an accomplished and considered painter.

One playwright who benefitted from Gertrude Stein's ideas on language and form was Thornton Wilder (b. 1897), whose most famous play, *Our Town* (1936), is an American pastoral following a small regional community through a cycle of birth, marriage, and death and performed without scenery. This foolproof masterpiece is a gift for all amateur and professional companies, provided the players can assume their roles with sincerity and conviction. *The Skin of Our Teeth* (1942) is also somewhat experimental, following a representative family, the Antrobuses, through such cataclysmic events as Noah's Flood and Civil War and pitting traditional stereotypes, including prodigal son and obdurate father, and homely wife and lubricious mistress, against one another with satirical effect. Both these plays won Pulitzer Prizes and *The Skin of Our Teeth* became a preferred soubrette vehicle for Vivien Leigh.

Wilder was born in Wisconsin and grew up partly in Shanghai, where his father was consul general, before studying at Yale, the American Academy in Rome, and Princeton, and then teaching at Chicago University (1930–36). His first novel, *The Cabala* (1927), was inspired by his sojourn in Rome. In 1927 *The Bridge of San Luis Rey* established him as a leading novelist whose philosophic works of fate and chance owed much to the observations about civilization by Henry James and Marcel Proust before him. Wilder's imitative novels and plays carry deep philosophical undertones but his unerring consideration to keep readers and audiences continuously entertained prevent him from ever jolting them too greatly. If life is cyclical, then he argues, events will take their own course. Of his later pieces, the most enduring has proved to be *The Matchmaker* (1954), suggested by a Viennese tale but set in and around New York at the turn of the century and which provided the basis for the 1960s musical *Hello, Dolly!*

The cartoons and prose of James Thurber (1894–1961) for the *New Yorker,* in the days when it was edited by Harold Ross, were noted for a unique blend of precision, incisive wit, and provocative fantasy. Thurber's world was one of little men dominated by outsize wives (once presented as a woman becoming a house in a return-to-the-womb cartoon), as it might have been perceived by omniscient dogs. His work appeals to those readers whose sense of refinement and control is challenged by their own growing sense of anarchy and absurdity. His themes included the triumph of moral innocence in a society being transformed by the mass media, the cult of psychoanalysis, and sexual revolution. Among his sadly amusing short stories, the most famous, *The Secret Life of Walter Mitty,* carries an enduring myth—how a man over-powered by the demands of contemporary society makes up for his inadequacies by leading a combative, inner life in a series of imaginary, glamorous careers as crack pilot, leading medical con-sultant, and ace detective. In creating this secret world, later turned into a Hollywood vehicle for Danny Kaye (1947), Thurber appeals to all our interior dialogues between wish fulfillment and the dullness, apathy, and inertia of our daily routines. He drew upon life remembered from his eccentric family of Columbus, Ohio, and from his early careers as an aide in the American Embassy in Paris (1918–20) and as a journalist.

His keen-eyed vision of the world depended on acute observa-tion from limited means. In his own words, during his boyhood, "He fell down a great deal . . . because of a trick he had of walking into himself. His goldrimmed glasses forever needed straightening which gave him the appearance of a person who hears somebody calling but can't make out where the sound is coming from. Because of his badly focused lenses, he saw, not two of everything, but one and a half. Thus a four-wheeled wagon would not have eight wheels for him, but six." Thurber's disability of very poor sight worsened progressively over the years to the point of blindness just before his death.

Thurber's wit and wisdom yielded more anecdotes and telling remarks than Mae West. An irate telephone caller who has dialed the wrong digits, cuts the answering party with, "Well, if I Called the Wrong Number, Why Did You Answer the Phone?" A pa-tient man tells his date in an apartment lobby in a curious reversal of conventional sex roles, "You Wait Here and I'll Bring the Etchings Down." An outspoken guest exclaims to a scandalized couple whose son has just come into the room, "Why I Never Dreamed Your Union Had Been Blessed With Issue!" Many Thurber cartoons showed fantasy turned into reality as with the cross wife who rejoins to her husband, who has woken her up in bed, "All Right, Have It Your Way—You Heard a Seal Bark." And, of course, the seal is above the headboard. An artis-tic original, Thurber created an entire genre and became its master.

Music

Modernism was expressed even more clearly in music, especially in songs, than in poetry. Since music is one of the performing arts, successful music has to conform to a basic law of creative life: change and develop or stultify and die. The development of American music was astonishing. Jazz, with its broken cadences and strong rhythmic beat, constituted a radical departure from musical norms and was America's unique contribution to world modernism. The 1920s are often known as the jazz age, not because this was when jazz first appeared, but because this was the era in which jazz was first scored and made accessible to an audience beyond its roots in the culture of black Americans. Ironically enough, the most successful exponent of scored jazz music during the 1920s and beyond was a rotund band leader by the appropriate name of Paul Whiteman. It was Whiteman who in 1924 commissioned George Gershwin to write the first ever formal composition based on the elements of jazz. Whiteman's "semiclassical" orchestra gave *Rhapsody in Blue* a sensational premiere with Gershwin himself at the piano on February 12, 1924, at the Aeolian Hall, New York City.

During the twentieth century American popular music became a highly commercialized art form, a commodity mass-produced by a multinational music entertainment industry. The beginnings of this development can be traced back to changes that occurred in the first half of the century when, in addition, the substance of popular music was significantly affected by a stream of new music styles.

The foundation of the art and business of American popular music had been laid down in the last fifteen years of the nineteenth century when music publishing had become increasingly dominated by a number of companies based in New York and specifically located on 28th Street between Fifth Avenue and Broadway. This was Tin Pan Alley where companies like Thomas B. Harms, Inc., Willis Woodward, and Isidore Witmark typified a profitable business of writing and publishing popular songs on the basis of

A wartime audience of sailors on leave and their girlfriends enjoys swing music at O'Reilly's at Third Avenue and 54th Street, New York, on a Saturday night in February 1943. (Photograph for the Office of War Information by Marjory Collins; Library of Congress).

extensive market research. Songwriters were salaried employees rather than freelance artists while the market research was carried out by song pluggers, musicians who played drafts of new songs to selected audiences. In its harnessing of art to industry and commerce, the organization of Tin Pan Alley in 1900 was a forerunner for the studio system of Hollywood in later decades.

The music business in 1900 was one of selling sheet music to a piano-playing public. Publishers used the nationwide circuit of vaudeville venues to publicize their latest songs. Thus the importance of a close relationship between the music-makers and music-disseminators was established at an early stage. Undoubtedly, the later relationship between the recording industry and radio and television originated from this earlier business interdependency.

The musical talent and market research of Tin Pan Alley and vaudeville produced a succession of songs that were best-sellers and became firmly fixed in the emerging popular culture of the century: for example, "Give My Regards to Broadway" (George Cohan, 1904), "Shine on Harvest Moon" (Nora Bayers and Jack Norworth, 1908), "By the Light of the Silvery Moon" (Gus Edwards, 1909, and "When Irish Eyes are Smiling" (Ernest R. Ball, 1912). Songs from Tin Pan Alley developed a certain homogeneity. The general tone was sentimental and lyrics frequently referred to the city as a lively, colorful place or dealt with warm memories of a country childhood. Through market research these songs were responding to a common mood of the time, reflecting the fact that growing numbers of Americans were living and working in major cities. People were aware that they were cutting themselves off from a rural heritage and in the climate of progressivism were concerned about the standard of city life. Significantly, "popular music" would deviate from this diet of urban celebration and rural nostalgia only when America entered World War I and patriotic songs became popular. The way that the typical Tin Pan Alley song consisted of simple melodies, verses, and an emphasis on the repetition of the chorus helped to define the basic composition of the popular song in this century.

Even as Tin Pan Alley ruled, the first of a series of infusions of music from the black community was transforming the sound of all popular music. Between 1920 and 1941 the main influence was from jazz, but in the early 1900s it was ragtime and its success set the pattern for the introduction of jazz. Ragtime was a rigorous, vivid marriage of harmony and rhythm. It had emerged from the parlors of brothels because these were the only places where black pianists could play. The black classically trained composer, Scott Joplin, was its leading exponent, having written what was probably the first popular ragtime tune, "Maple Leaf Rag," in 1899. Joplin competed with other ragtime players like Jelly Roll Morton and Eubie Blake. The music of Scott Joplin was not, at first, written down and, indeed, musical notation could only give an approximate idea of his unconventional rhythms with their off-beat accents and varied timings.

Ragtime became popular because the simplicity of its tunes

meant that the large number of living-room pianists could play this form of music. Indeed, sheet music sales of ragtime made the first large profits for the music business in this century. "Maple Leaf Rag" sold over 1 million copies.

The best ragtime pieces involved a complex and energetic syncopation whereby beats in the music switch from being strong to weak and vice versa. Yet the majority of ragtime music was "junk rag," simply the playing of a string of catchy, jingling tunes at a breakneck speed. This reflected how, increasingly, rag became associated with player pianos. Its repetitive tunes were easy to punch out on the piano rolls. Moreover, junk rag was usually written by white men while the original black ragtime composers, like Joplin, often aspired to develop rag into a significant black art form.

Significantly, ragtime declined as the player piano was superseded by a superior means of mechanical recording and playback of music. Public enthusiasm for the gramophone broadened the appeal of popular music and transformed the place of music in society. In 1900 there were 100 companies in America manufacturing pianos, but the significant statistic of 1920 was that 100 million records were pressed in that year. (Thomas Edison had invented the phonograph in the 1870s and perfected it in 1888.) By 1920 the old cylinder system was replaced by the grooved disc and record players were being mass produced by Columbia and the Victor Talking Machine Company. When recorded on a disc, popular music became a true consumer item and industrial product. The ability to read music and play the piano were no longer prerequisites for a night of home entertainment. In the twenties the enjoyment of music became a more passive pleasure and the demand for records boomed. The scale of the popularity of gramophone records was such that serious composers like Aaron Copland not only commented upon it but also felt that their music should respond to this unleashing of popular culture. Furthermore, toward the end of the 1920s radio broadcasting and talkies provided additional forces for the popularization of music.

Therefore, jazz was drawn into the mainstream of American popular music at an opportune time. As befitted the free improvisation and rhythms associated with jazz, the popular music business in the 1920s became expansive, both artistically and commercially. The recording industry was relatively new and thus amenable to change. The demand for gramophone records required an expanded supply of popular music and one that was ever more diverse. Jazz music would eclipse the brief fashion for ragtime and have a greater influence on defining the style of popular music.

A new generation of popular music composers came to the fore in the twenties. Their music was distinguished by its use of jazz. The very public success of Irving Berlin, George Gershwin, and Cole Porter also indicated how the composers began to escape the anonymity associated with the successful Tin Pan Alley composers of the early 1900s. The popular composers of the 1920s displayed a common virtuosity in understanding jazz and synthesizing its qualities into the traditional form of the American popular song that they had learned from Tin Pan Alley. The work of these composers would set the scene for the 1930s and 1940s when they would further their reputations by working in Hollywood or continue to write for Broadway.

In 1893 the Balines, a family of Russian Jews, landed and made their home in New York. Their son, Irving, was then five years old. By his teens he was well known as a street singer and worked as a singing waiter for Pelham's cafe in Chinatown. In 1907 he published his first song, "Marie from Sunny Italy." It was through a printer's error on the title page of that song that he came to be known as Irving Berlin. Thus began the career of perhaps America's most successful popular composer. Although he lacked a formal music education and was unable to read music, Berlin eventually published 1,500 songs.

Soon after the publication of his first songs, Berlin made his stage debut and, subsequently, pursued a career of sometimes performing, but mainly writing for the musical variety theater of the day. In 1911, he contributed music and lyrics for *Alexander's Ragtime Band,* a show that was an international success. The 1914 revue, *Watch Your Step,* represented his first complete musical score and lyrics. As Broadway theaters began to boom, Berlin's own standing grew, for example, with his writing for the Ziegfeld Follies. By 1921 Berlin's position in popular entertainment was such that he felt he could build and run his own theater, the Music Box, upon which he staged his own revues. Consistently good box office returns proved Berlin correct. At the Music Box Berlin was not only making money, but also developing the stage musical into an increasingly sophisticated and versatile genre. For example, in 1925, Berlin collaborated with the Marx Brothers to write the first integrated musical comedy, *The Cocoanuts.*

Berlin was coming to prominence at a propitious time in the entertainment business. By the late twenties Hollywood studios were converting from silent to sound film production. The Broadway musical was immediately recognized as ideal subject matter for the new talkies. With their often lavish staging and chorus lines, Broadway musicals seemed almost to proclaim hosannas for the arrival of sound on screen. It was also less time-consuming to synchronize music and song in moving pictures than it was to synchronize speech. In addition, as Hollywood beckoned toward Broadway, the lights of Broadway were dimmed by the onset of the depression. Box office sales slumped and theaters and companies began to close.

Berlin was one of the many examples of Broadway talent attracted to Hollywood in the late twenties and early thirties. He would be one of the principal innovators of the film musical. In 1935 he wrote the score for *Top Hat,* a film that starred Fred Astaire and Ginger Rogers. Thereafter, Berlin wrote a succession of musical film hits, such as *The Gay Divorcée* (1937), *Holiday Inn* (1940), and *Annie Get Your Gun* (show 1945; film 1950), many based on his original theater shows. In the process he not only made his own fortune, but also helped to establish and further the careers of Bing Crosby, Fred Astaire, and Ethel Merman. His stage shows and films included songs that became popular classics, most notably "White Christmas" from *Holiday Inn* and "There's No Business like Show Business!" from *Annie Get Your Gun.*

The career of Irving Berlin is a case study in how popular music has developed in this century. After success on Broadway, Berlin's career truly took off once he became involved in the new mass mediums for music—motion pictures, radio broadcasting, and the phonograph industry. Indeed, Berlin is probably the greatest seller of gramophone records: his song "White Christmas" has sold 25 million copies of its original version and 100 million of other versions. Like later figures in popular music as diverse as Elvis Presley, the Beatles, and Bob Dylan, Berlin's success can also be attributed to his readiness and ability to adapt and synthesize the style and nuances of other musical influences. Berlin folded some of the distinctive characteristics of ragtime and jazz into his sentimental, money-spinning hit songs. Thus, Berlin's status in popular culture can be explained by a meshing of his own talent for artistic innovation (rather than invention) and the technical, commercial innovations (rather than inventions) occurring in America in the mid-twentieth century.

The music and lyrics of Cole Porter are characterized by a cool, urbane wit. This properly reflects the background and life-style of a composer whose grandfather had been a millionaire speculator. He was born in 1892 in Peru, Indiana, and studied at Yale (where he wrote football songs), Harvard Law School, and the Harvard Graduate School of Arts and Science. After serving in the American army in 1917–1918, Cole Porter led the life of a playboy, first in Europe and later in America. From an early age Cole Porter had been interested in music and by his teens was composing songs.

The success of the show *50 Million Frenchmen* in 1929 established him as a leading Broadway writer. The thirties were his most productive period. He wrote a string of stage successes, including *The Gay Divorcée* (1932), *Anything Goes* (1934), *Dubarry Was a Lady* (1939), and *Panama Hattie* (1940). Over the same time, Porter also wrote music for the movies. Of the songs he wrote for Hollywood between 1934 and 1940, many have become popular classics, for example "I Get a Kick out of You" (1934), "Begin the Beguine" (1936), and "I've Got You under My Skin" (1936). As significant as his melodies were his witty lyrics, especially in "Solomon," "My Heart Belongs to Daddy," "Miss Otis Regrets," and "Let's Do It."

George Gershwin spent his childhood in poverty on Manhattan's Lower East Side. However, there were, apparently, opportunities for the young George to listen to both jazz and concerts of classical music. George became interested in music and learnt

Versatile composer George Gershwin delighted audiences with music that mixed syncopated rhythms and lyrical melodies as he moved across the different forms of songs, piano concertos, orchestral tone poems, and opera. He combined the diverse strains of Afro-American, Latin-American, jazz, and popular music with the elegance of European operettas in a dazzling career cut short by his premature death at the age of thirty-eight. (Carl Van Vechten; Library of Congress).

piano from the age of twelve. Despite numerous music teachers, Gershwin never really mastered reading music, though he did become proficient in composing and orchestration. His teachers also introduced him to the work of a wide variety of composers. Indeed, his significance as a figure in popular music was his blending of classical music with the nuances and styles of popular music and jazz. Indeed, Gershwin sought out the latest, most idiosyncratic of contemporary American composers, such as Henry Lowell and Joseph Schillinger, and proceeded to learn their music philosophy.

Gershwin came to the attention of the public not with the publication of his first song "When You Want 'Em, You Can't Get 'Em," but the song "Swanee" that Al Jolson sang in *Sinbad* in 1918. The song was a best-seller on gramophone records and music sheets. With his reputation fully established, Gershwin wrote his first entire score, *La, La Lucille.* That Gershwin was committed to experimentation was evident when he pushed aside the composition of songs for other people's musicals and revues to concentrate on a short modern opera that he wrote in 1922, first called *Blue Monday* and, later, *135th Street.* Such an imaginative step caught the attention of Paul Whiteman, then probably the most famous bandleader, who commissioned Gershwin to write a symphony in a jazz style. This was *Rhapsody in Blue,* and usually considered Gershwin's first masterpiece.

In 1924 George persuaded his younger brother, Ira, to collaborate as a lyricist for future projects. *Lady Be Good* (1924) was their first big success, followed by *American in Paris* (1925), *Tip Toes* (1925), *Oh Kay* (1926), *Funny Face* (1927), *Strike Up the Band* (1927), and *Girl Crazy* (1930). George also wrote four film scores, including music for some Astaire musicals.

George Gershwin saw himself as more than the writer of light musical escapism and, with Ira, created, first, the political musical satire *Of Thee I Sing* in the early 1930s, and, in 1935, his other masterpiece, *Porgy and Bess.* For this opera Gershwin spent a summer on a South Carolinian island so as to research a black peasant community. *Porgy and Bess* was incorrectly termed a folk opera when, in fact, what the Gershwins did was take a traditional operatic format and mold it to suit the black characters and settings of DuBoise Heyward's brutal drama, bringing together the diverse musical styles of popular Tin Pan Alley music, jazz, and operatic arias. Despite mixed critical reaction and an, initially, cool public reception, the opera produced a number of popular songs: "Summertime," one of the most immortal of all twentieth-century melodies, "I Got Plenty o' Nuttin'," and "It Ain't Necessarily So," and the duet, "Bess, You Is My Woman Now." Tragically, George Gershwin died in 1937 of a brain tumor; Ira continued to write lyrics in partnership with, among others, Moss Hart, Jerome Kern, and Kurt Weill. George Gershwin wrote popular songs characterized by sweet melodies and repetitive refrains. His talent was limited, for often his long pieces include abrupt pauses. Yet all of his music was distinguished by its healthy cross-fertilization of musical influences, including elements of Jewish folk and synagogue music, and dynamic, jazz rhythms.

Richard Rodgers was born on Long Island in 1902. He studied at Columbia University where he wrote the music and lyrics for amateur musical productions. When he met Lorenz Hart in 1918, Rodgers found a collaborator who agreed with his complaint that too many songs relied on banal lyrics. With this in mind, the two men began their musical partnership.

Their first major success was a revue, *The Garrick Gaieties*. By the late twenties, Rodgers and Hart concentrated on musical dramas that dispensed with the song and dance format. *Chee-Chee* and *Present Arms,* written in 1928, were examples of this trend. After an unsuccessful time in Hollywood in the early part of the decade, they returned to Broadway, writing successes like *Babes in Arms,* a backstage musical about the aspirations of adolescent talents. This production demonstrated how much Rodgers and Hart had become two of the most versatile practitioners of the Broadway musical. The score was incredibly varied, with songs ranging from the lyrical "My Funny Valentine," through the sophisticated "The Lady is a Tramp," to the highly rhythmic "Johnny One Note."

On Your Toes satirized the conventions of backstage musicals and added an amusing sketch of Russian emigré ballet dancers, of whom there were many in the West in the 1920s and early 1930s, who affect an intensity of emotion they cannot sustain. The musical also burlesques such ballets as the Diaghilev-Bakst *Scshehera-zade* and its climax is a ballet that fuses jazz and American and Russian dance choreography, "Slaughter on Tenth Avenue." In 1940, the cynically realistic musical *Pal Joey* represented the final outcome of Rodgers and Hart's disgust with banal lyrics and story lines in Broadway musicals. It was not, in the first instance, a commercial success. Three years later Lorenz Hart was dead. Rodgers's partnership with Hart had produced works that advanced the art form of the American stage musical.

On joining forces with the lyricist Oscar Hammerstein II, Rodgers refined the art form even further, winning serious critical applause. *Oklahoma* (1943) was a yet more complete integration of song, dance, and drama. The conventions of the song and dance routine had gone, the chorus line replaced by ballets of square dance routines. Spurred on by Hammerstein, Rodgers discovered that he could successfully break from the cast-iron convention of a song having a recurring verse and chorus. Indeed, this early work of Rodgers and Hammerstein first suggested how the Broadway musical could mature into a dramatic whole and, finally, release itself from its crude revue antecedents. It began with an offstage serenade, "Oh, What a Beautiful Morning!" while Aunt Eller silently churned milk and, then, it moved through routines, setting cowboys and farmers, first, at odds and, then, as friends, through conventional love songs such as "Surrey with the Fringe on Top," and the love duet, "People Will Say We're in Love," to a rousing populist celebration, "Oklahoma!" Though more saccharine than the Rodgers-Hart shows, Rodgers and Hammerstein musicals always had a dark side, represented in *Oklahoma!* by the sinister, brooding Jed. In *Carousel* the principal character is an antihero, a wastrel, bully, and unsuccessful thief. In *South Pacific,* set on a Pacific island during the navy's campaign against Japan in World War II, the target was racial prejudice.

Although his most famous compositions use folk tunes to celebrate the American West, Aaron Copland came from a quite different background. He was born in 1900 into a Russian Jewish family living in Brooklyn, New York. Later he described his early life as drab and hard. Yet, after learning the piano from an elder sister, Copland strove to complete a full musical education through correspondence courses and one day become a composer. In 1921, he went to study music in France. When he returned to New York in 1924, his music was highly experimental. That same year the New York Symphony Orchestra performed his *Symphony for Organ and Orchestra* at Carnegie Hall. For the next ten years Copland continued to experiment, using jazz rhythms for his *Piano Concerto* of 1926 and later assuming a lean, spare musical style for works like *Piano Variations* (1930) and *Statements for Orchestra* (1933–1935), a work that showed the influence of Russian expatriate composer Igor Stravinsky.

Copland then made a critical decision. He has referred to the dissatisfaction that he felt at the time about the considerable distance that had developed between modern "classical" composers and the general public. Therefore, in the mid-1930s, Copland deliberately chose to enter the mainstream of popular taste and write modern pieces that would be accessible to the large audiences of radio, film, and gramophone recordings. Copland has said, "It made no sense to ignore them [radio, film, and gramophone records] and to continue writing as if they did not exist. I felt that it was worth the effort to see if I couldn't say what I had to say in the simplest possible terms."

Copland began to write a series of ballets about subjects that were particularly familiar to ordinary Americans. *Billy the Kid* (1938), *Rodeo* (1942), and *Appalachian Spring* (1944) for choreographer Martha Graham drew on American folk tunes and stories. In 1939, Copland wrote one of his first film scores for the screen version of John Steinbeck's *Of Mice and Men* (1939). As America was drawn into World War II, Copland responded by composing music pieces that examined the issue of warfare by very American references, for example his *Lincoln Portrait* of 1942. This was the most productive period of the composer's life and one in which he achieved international fame. The music itself was usually relaxed and expansive. One might see Copland's avoidance of artistic elitism as reflecting the preeminence of populism in American society and politics, the ideals of the New Deal policies, and the myths surrounding FDR's personality. Copland was active in the organization of concerts that were aimed at the ordinary, non-concertgoing people.

Ultimately, Copland wrote music tailored for an increasingly industrial and urban society. He exploited the latest methods of mass communication and incorporated a folksy jauntiness into his symphonies and ballets that perhaps satisfied a nostalgia for a simpler rural past that was thought to have disappeared recently. It was significant that his work was associated with the writings of novelist John Steinbeck and that the best of his music involves patterns of interweaving threads of precise, almost metallic, sounds and the freewheeling tunes of folk song and dance.

The creative achievements of popular composers who wrote for Broadway and Hollywood would have been much less had they not been able to fashion art from their subconscious, their cultural heritage, and their consciousness of the rich American tradition of performing and interpreting. In turn, the singers and musicians who performed the works of such composers as Gershwin, Porter, and Rodgers gave their music a color, vitality, and distinction that was special to the age.

European composers were fascinated by America's ascendancy in the machine age, but such works as Arthur Honegger's *Pacific 231* and Edgard Varèse's *Amériques* were rarely performed in the United States. Nevertheless, American composers did celebrate the machine age. Expatriate George Antheil wrote his *Ballet mécanique* in Paris. Frederick Shepard Converse wrote his *Flivver Ten Million* to honor the ten millionth Model T car and it was performed by the Boston Symphony Orchestra under conductor Serge Koussevitsky in 1927. The score had parts for a factory whistle, a Ford horn, and both wind and anvil machines. Jazz music also featured mechanical elements. John Alden Carpenter's jazz ballet, *Skyscrapers,* drew upon the frenzied sounds of the ever-restless modern city. In the ballet *Vanities* (1928) by Earl Carroll, one crucial sequence was a visit to a Ford plant choreographed by Busby Berkeley, whose later dance numbers in Hollywood musicals combined motorized stages and machinelike ensembles.

Musicians

In the 1920s the black blues singer and songwriter Bessie Smith was popularly acclaimed as the "Empress of the Blues." She had been born in 1898 in Chattanooga, Tennessee. Her early life was spent in the customary poverty of the black community of the South. Ma Rainey, who was, then, the most renowned blues singer, came across the young Bessie Smith and encouraged her to follow a professional singing career. When Clarence Williams, a black pianist and representative of Columbia Records, discovered Bessie Smith in 1923, she had already spent several years singing in Atlanta, Birmingham, and Memphis.

Bessie Smith was not the first singer to record blues music, since Mamie Smith had done so back in 1920. Yet, she did become the most successful blues recording artist of the time, making disks of 150 songs, often with the accompaniment of jazzmen like Louis Armstrong, Fletcher Henderson, and Benny Goodman. Her first recording session produced "Downhearted Blues" and her last, in 1933, "Down in the Dumps." Her recording success reflected how gramophone records were increasingly becoming consumer items in the 1920s. The earlier recordings of blues had been made for archival reasons, while Bessie Smith's records were best-sellers. Her first record, "Downhearted Blues," sold 780,000 copies in its first six months.

Bessie Smith also made innumerable live performances across the nation. Onstage she was a singer whose success was very much of the period of the national prohibition of alcohol. In New York she was a well-known figure at "Bufet Flats," high-class speakeasies where sexual encounters were also on the menu. A bold and confident artist who would frequently refuse to use a microphone in her live performances, Bessie Smith expressed both the hopes and frustrations of black Americans. She was associated with the so-called Harlem Renaissance that was at its peak in the 1920s. In 1929, Bessie starred in an all-black musical, *Pansy,* and film, *St. Louis Blues.*

However, by the early thirties, Bessie Smith's career was declining. The fashion for blues was over, record sales were greatly reduced on account of the depression, and she was now having to compete with a new generation of black women singers led by Ella Fitzgerald and Billie Holiday. It was while touring Mississippi in 1937 that Bessie Smith died of injuries caused by a car accident. Since she was refused immediate medical care from a

The vibrant singer Bessie Smith, "Empress of the Blues," whose soul-searching powers of communication melted musical hearts but not well enough to prevent her bleeding to death after a road accident when an ambulance refused to take her to a nearby hospital for whites only. (Photographed by Carl Van Vechten in 1936; Library of Congress).

nearby white hospital, it can be justly said that the Empress of the Blues was killed by Jim Crow—southern de jure segregation. Bessie Smith was both a success and casualty of the American recording industry's first attempt to exploit black music. By 1920 large numbers of blacks had migrated to the major cities, creating a market for what the record companies called euphemistically and inaccurately "race" records. Consequently, black musicians were signed up to make recordings and there was even a black-owned music label, Black Swan. When the economy collapsed in 1929, the purchase of records was one of the first luxuries to be cut. Suddenly, the remaining market for "race" records was killed off as the ailing record companies discarded their black recording artists.

In the twenties and thirties bandleaders and musicians Paul Whiteman and Benny Goodman were the leading popularizers of jazz music. Ironically, the success of such white men playing jazz paved the way for the general acceptance of black bandleaders and musicians such as Louis Armstrong playing the same music.

Paul Whiteman was born in Denver, Colorado, in 1890. His own instrument was the viola and, for a while, he led his band playing the violin. In the twenties his band became known as the premier dance band for the new, energetic styles of the Shimmy and Charleston. Benny Goodman had been born in Chicago in 1909. He learnt the clarinet at Hull House, the settlement house founded by Jane Addams. By the 1920s Goodman was a proficient enough musician to go out to Los Angeles to play with the Ben Pollack jazz band. His recording career began in 1926.

Whiteman promoted jazz as popular music by his employment of a succession of talented jazz soloists, most notably Bix Beiderbecke, Jack Teagarden, Eddie Lang, and Bunny Berigan. Moreover, it was Whiteman who encouraged George Gershwin to write *Rhapsody in Blue,* a work that Whiteman's orchestra was the first to perform in 1924. By 1930 much of the music that he and his orchestra played was strongly influenced by jazz. Thus in the early 1930s white bands were beginning to play jazz. Musicians had noted the success of the jazz-influenced music of Berlin, Gershwin, and Whiteman. Probably the first of the major white big bands was the Casa Loma Orchestra that became popular in

1930. As future big bands would do, the Casa Loma Orchestra performed a mix of slow and fast dance numbers. Moreover, their music was very much a youth phenomenon as the band was most popular on college campuses.

It was the orchestra that Goodman formed in New York in 1934 that spearheaded a new fashion for swing music and won him the title of "King of Swing." Swing is a form of popular jazz music with a pulsating, often fast, beat. The performance that Benny Goodman and his orchestra gave at the Palomar Ballroom, Los Angeles, has traditionally been seen as the birth of the swing era. The way that the orchestra had four saxophones playing parallel four-note chords epitomized the swing sound. It has been suggested that the term "swing" was coined by a BBC announcer sometime in the mid-1930s. Even as his orchestra encouraged the vogue for big band music, Goodman set up trio and later, quartet, ensembles that improvised in the traditional style and prefigured the future trend of modern, more idiosyncratic, jazz. In the 1940s, Goodman discontinued his orchestra and began to hire black musicians and eventually formed some of the first racially mixed popular jazz bands in America.

Unlike many of his contemporary musicians, Glenn Miller was not from New York or Chicago but was a midwesterner, born in 1904 in Iowa. After studying at the University of Colorado at Boulder, Glenn Miller, a talented trombonist, joined Ben Pollack's jazz band. By 1930 he was considered a seasoned professional musician, who did a great deal of freelance, session work. For a while Miller helped to organize bands for other people, working for the Dorsey brothers in 1934 and Ray Noble in 1935. Yet, eventually, Miller became eager to form his own orchestra and did so in 1938. At a time when radio broadcasting had become fully organized into two major networks and music programs dominated the airwaves, Miller rapidly won nationwide and, later, worldwide fame as a big band leader. In the 1930s Benny Goodman had broadened his appeal by film appearances. Similarly, Glenn Miller's reputation and record sales were boosted somewhat by his films, *Sun Valley Serenade* (1941) and *Orchestra Wives* (1942).

The appeal of Miller's big band music lay in the way that sweet, simple melodies and rhythms were played with disciplined orchestration. His band had an instantly recognizable saxophone sound. His music was not exactly jazz, since the usually improvised rhythms were tightly regulated. The success of Glenn Miller emphasized how much "sweet" swing dominated popular music by the late thirties. some of the biggest sellers of the decade were the Artie Shaw band playing Cole Porter's "Begin the Beguine" and Miller's own "In the Mood" and "A String of Pearls." Another emerging trend was the popularity of singers such as Frank Sinatra, Doris Day, Jo Stafford, and Perry Como who were employed to sing ballads in front of the band. It can be argued that Glenn Miller and the vogue for big bands represented the end result of a process whereby black music had been appropriated by whites and so made palatable for a larger, wealthier audience.

It was rather fitting that Americans became enamored with the big band sound and spectacle as the country moved toward entry into World War II. Miller's band and others were noted for their smart uniforms and an almost military marshaling of musicians to produce music. Glenn Miller joined the U.S. Air Force, eventually becoming a major and leader of the Air Force Big Band in Europe. Besides his musical talent, Glenn Miller is also remarkable for the posthumous intensity of his reputation. He disappeared on a flight between England and France in 1944. The considerable interest in Glenn Miller has been fueled not just by the mysterious circumstances of his death but also by the ability of gramophone recordings and films to provide a means of cultural immortality. Thus, Glen Miller and his music seem to epitomize the considerable degree to which American popular music had developed by 1945 largely as a function of the growth of mass communications and entertainment.

In 1933 John Lomax, a collector of folk songs, discovered an exceptional blues singer serving a sentence for murder in the Louisiana State Penitentiary. Huddie ("Leadbelly") Ledbetter was a black singer and guitarist who knew 500 blues songs by heart. After recording him for the Library of Congress, Lomax succeeded in having Ledbetter paroled. Ledbetter was regarded as one of the last great blues musicians, the principal custodian of its tradition. He had been born in Mooringsport, Louisiana, in 1885, learnt the twelve-string guitar at an early age, and had subsequently been the accompanist for a blues singer, Blind Lemon Jefferson. In the late 1930s and 1940s Ledbetter made many recordings, for example, "Honey I'm All Out and Down" and "Becky Deere, She Was a Gambling Gal." "Good Morning Blues" of 1940 was his most admired song. He died in 1949.

By 1945 the development of popular music as a major business was almost complete. The role of television in broadcasting popular music would be discovered after World War II. Jazz had been fully integrated into the mainstream of popular music and smooth, swing music prevailed. Yet, during the forties, there were signs pointing to the future appearance and impact of rock 'n' roll. The increase in industrial production for the war effort had accelerated the drawing in of large numbers of poor southern whites and blacks to work and live in the major cities of the USA. These groups brought not only unskilled labor into the cities but also their music. Rhythm and blues, a new style of blues singing with a faster, jazz beat, was increasingly enjoyed by urban blacks. It was also beginning to influence current popular music and was described as "novelty" music by whites who were amused by the furious speed of some songs. Ledbetter's "Goodnight Irene" was an example of novelty music. Significantly, such black music was enjoyed alongside the enthusiasm of poor southern whites for their "hillbilly," or country, music. This music involved both male and female singers with a backing of guitars, harmoniums, violins, and mandolins. Much of its particular style was derived from a tradition of church music. It was winning wider interest with its exposure on the radio and the success of performers like Gene Autry and Hank Williams, whose music bridged the hillbilly style and conventional popular music. Rock 'n' roll would be a blending of these emerging black and white music styles. Although it did not truly happen before 1945, it would require a white, country musician to cross over and play rhythm and blues for rock 'n' roll to begin to become marketable popular music.

In 1945 American popular music was on the verge of entering a new international phase. By virtue of its freedom from the devastation of war wrought in Europe and Asia, America was in a position to dominate the world not only politically and economically but also culturally. Gramophone recordings, radio, and movies had already cultivated a prewar interest in American popular music abroad. However, the stationing and advance of American troops in Europe had introduced a greater number of European countries to even more American music and, so, created a demand for more. Moreover, the European recording industry was shattered by the war and a low priority in the many programs for reconstruction, while the American music industry was intact.

Literature in the 1930s

Some leading writers of the 1930s shared the social concern that motivated many painters and there is a similar conflict between realism and grotesque perception. Nathanael West (c. 1902–1940), for example, wrote four short novels in his brief literary career that add up to one of the most telling criticisms of the United States ever produced. In West's view, the American dream was in fact a grotesque nightmare and his first novel, *The Dream Life of Balso Snell* (1931), is an examination of the subconscious mind that would have been impossible without Freud's innovative psychological theories. This novel is not typical of West's works in the sense that it is concerned with the disintegration of the isolated self, outside the social context, and constitutes a twisted and contemptuous expression of an individual's alienation. *Miss Lonelyhearts* (1933) provides us with an anonymous protagonist who cannot afford any such displays of private despair. He is the author and adviser for a newspaper agony column who is gradually overcome by the weight of genuine untreatable suffering, revealed in the letters he receives from his readers. His confused and often frantic attempts both to evade and to confront the enormity of pain and suffering end in failure and perturbing bathos when he is killed by one of his own readers as he runs toward him, arms outstretched, full of love. West's handling of his author's clients is deliberately poignant and grotesque, with an effective selection of animal imagery to undermine any sympathy the reader may have for their plight. *A Cool Million* is a more overtly social and political denunciation of America, with an innocent protagonist who is literally dismantled by American society in an uninhibited parody of the Horatio Alger myth of the Gilded Age in which the children's storyteller Horatio Alger propounded a myth of poor boys rising from rags to riches by dint of hard work and thrift. Lemuel Pitkin in *A Cool Million,* however, loses his teeth, an eye, a leg, and his scalp in the laissez-faire world and is then exploited by both communist and fascist organizations. *The Day of the Locust* (1939) is West's second masterpiece, and probably the best Hollywood novel in American literature. West himself worked in Hollywood on screenplays for the last five years of his life before he died tragically in a car crash in 1940, and this, his last novel, is peopled with bizarre and grotesque characters of the movie world. The book is replete throughout with suppressed violence and hatred that boil over in the last pages in an account of a mob riot at a film premiere.

Another author who was published during the thirties and specialized in reporting human grotesquery was William Faulkner (1897–1962). However, Faulkner, perhaps because of his southern heritage, focused on the family as an individual unit rather than society as a whole. Neither was Faulkner's work critical of humanity in the sense that, although he used a naturalistic style to emphasize such unattractive human qualities as brutality and violence, his work does balance this harsh view with an affirmation of positive human qualities and values that he listed in 1950 when he accepted the Nobel Prize for literature: "courage and honor and hope and pride and compassion and pity and sacrifice." This list might appear to indicate the work of a conservative and idealistic writer but Faulkner was, in fact, progressive and experimental in his style and use of form. In books such as *The Sound and the Fury* (1929), *As I Lay Dying* (1930), and *Absalom, Absalom!* (1936), he employed Joycean stream of consciousness, scrambled chronology, mythic and biblical parallels, and the manipulation within one book of seemingly disparate narrative lines.

In *The Sound and the Fury* Faulkner elaborates on typical southern stereotypes, such as a promiscuous girl, an idiot child, an unbalanced student, a sharp-witted cad—all scions of a dissolute southern family—and their harried, genteel hypochondriac mother and dependable black retainer, and plays most daringly with the material. The story is told by four characters, at first and most grippingly by Benjy, the idiot son, who cannot distinguish ideal-ized childhood past and more deprived adulthood present. Thus eight family characters across two generations share only four names. Here is an archetype of a stagnant family, a tale told by Macbeth's idiot, full of sound and fury but signifying nothing, living in the agrarian South, a place forgotten by time, its people marooned by ignorance. The most imaginative creation of *Light in August* (1932) is the central character, Joe Christmas, an orphan unsure whether he is black or white and reared by foster parents whose punishments he can cope with but whose occasional kind-ness he cannot. Years later, as a man living on the shady side of the law, he makes love to, and then, in a bizarre scene, kills, a white woman of some pronounced masculine traits. Here is the sort of gross murder perpetrated by numerous petty criminals in many different regions, who can only express themselves in inar-ticulate violence. However, in this instance, Faulkner unfolds the background, situation, and motive without any artistic distortion to dialogue or situation. The same novel carries forward the story of the life-giving, unmarried, and pregnant girl, Lena Grove, a Grecian urn who will give birth and be light in August. She is poor white trash but blessed with an outward-looking attitude to life that invites, and receives, all manner of help just when she requires it.

Faulkner's stark stories hint at long-hidden family secrets that have cast dark shadows over his characters. His world is violent, lurid even, but the somber scene is illuminated by biting shafts of humor and varied by the color and diversity of his characters. This is, perhaps, most apparent in his most monumental single novel, *Absalom, Absalom!* Thomas Sutpen tries to create a planta-tion and found a dynasty but his design founders on his own racial prejudice and his family's inability to love. The major crisis is the fratricide by one son of another (hence the allusion to King David's son, Absalom), rejected because he is part-colored. The dream of a dynasty is finally laid to ashes by the Civil War and, eventually, the line peters out in ignominy.

Carson McCullers (1917–1967) drew from her life in a small Georgia town and distilled the experiences in a series of unroman-tic romances set amid drab homes and burning summer heat.

Whatever the physical or psychological aspects of her characters, her central theme is love, fulfilled, forlorn, or thwarted. In *The Heart is a Lonely Hunter* (1940), the central character is a deaf mute, John Singer, whose compassionate nature encourages four other lonely people to try and communicate with him. *Reflections in a Golden Eye* (1941) portrays uncomfortable, ill-matched liaisons in a southern army camp. *Member of the Wedding* (1946) explores the emotional adjustment of an adolescent girl coming to terms with herself and her world. Besides Faulkner's epic novels, these were all miniatures in minor keys but keys that opened up wider doors and visions. Film versions of variable quality awaited a later, postwar, generation of artists and changed susceptibilities among cinema audiences.

The Civil War remained the most dramatic episode in American history and one for which there was an insatiable appetite among readers. Margaret Mitchell, the wife of an Atlanta advertising executive, provided exactly what they required in her mammoth novel, *Gone with the Wind* (1936), a novel it took her nine years to write. When Macmillan editor H. L. Latham met Margaret Mitchell in the lobby of his hotel in Atlanta in 1935 she was "a tiny woman sitting on a divan, and beside her the biggest manuscript I have ever seen, towering in two stacks almost up to her shoulders."

The story of how southern belle Scarlett O'Hara survives the Civil War and Reconstruction, how she rises above the barriers of poverty, caste, and sex amid the collapse of a civilization "gone with the wind," rises and prospers materially at a high emotional cost in a harsher, more demanding environment of the New South, was enthralling. It encapsulated a familiar American theme that riches can prove empty. Scarlett finally understands that her third husband, Rhett Butler, is her soul mate, once she has lost him. She remains indomitable.

Gone with the Wind sold 178,000 copies within its first three weeks of publication on June 30, 1936. This was, and remains, a unique accomplishment for an unknown author. It remained on best-seller lists for twenty-one consecutive months and by April 1938, when sales began to drop off, it had already sold 2 million copies. Fifty years later it had sold 25 million copies in twenty-seven langauges and thirty-seven countries and there were 185 official editions in print. Within a month of publication, movie rights had been sold to David Selznick for $50,000, a considerable sum in the 1930s. While the role of Rhett Butler was clearly attuned to the roguish charm of Clark Gable, search and competition for the coveted role of spitfire heroine Scarlett O'Hara was attended with the sort of publicity normally reserved for a presidential election. It was eventually resolved by the casting of little-known English actress Vivien Leigh. Numerous troubles followed, including a change of director when Gable and Leslie Howard (who played Ashley) found George Cukor too interested in the women's roles of Scarlett and Melanie (Olivia de Haviland) and he was replaced by Victor Fleming. The premiere at Loew's Grand in Atlanta on December 16, 1939, was a national event and the film set a special record, earning nine Hollywood Oscar awards, and for many years it was, at 231 minutes, the longest American film.

Rhett and Scarlett are not stock characters but engaging scoundrels of real depth and emotional intensity. Margaret Mitchell was dismissed as a hack writer but her account of the siege and arson of Atlanta and Scarlett's escape back to Tara along with Melanie and Prissy are most imaginatively handled and as a background to Scarlett's developing independence and her deepening, complex relationship with Rhett Butler. The story lives and is told in such a way as to retain, indeed, capture the reader's interest and imagination. The novel drew deep on American folklore, the myth of the Old South, and the sense of loss the continuing myth implies. The characters like Scarlett and Rhett who survive suffer the most tragic losses—both their loved ones and an imagined peace of mind. Critic Tom Wolfe explains *Gone with the Wind*'s continuing hold on the public: " . . . the idea of loss is also at the heart of the novel. A world irrevocably vanished, whether real or not, and Scarlett's personal losses—the ideal of Ashley, the reality of Rhett—evoke the losses in our own lives, those we comprehend as well as those we only sense."

Among the most popular form of American fiction was the so-called hard-boiled crime thriller, especially the works of Raymond Chandler (1888–1959), James M. Cain (1892–1977), and Dashiell Hammett (1894–1961). Their scintillating dialogue, spoken by deftly defined and truly urban characters, called for dramatization on screen and, indeed, this was recognized by the movie moguls who snapped up their properties for transformation by Hollywood.

Although Raymond Chandler was born into a Quaker family in Chicago, he went with his mother to England at the tender age of eight and was educated at Dulwich College, a traditional, private boarding school. After further education in France and Germany, he went to live in California in 1912, served in the army during World War I, and then worked for various oil companies. He did not begin writing until he was forty-four and between 1933 and 1939 published over twenty stories, usually for the *Black Mask,* a leading magazine of hard-boiled detective fiction. He moved his leading detective Philip Marlowe, the solitary, questing knight, through the neon landscape of Los Angeles in a series of darkly humorous cases, beginning with *The Big Sleep* (1939), *Farewell, My Lovely* (1940), *The High Window* (1942), and *The Lady in the Lake* (1943). In every case the killer was a leading lady, a modern Morgan Le Fay, who had, briefly, deceived the honorable Marlowe. Chandler wanted as charismatic, debonair, and tall a leading man as Cary Grant for Marlowe when Hollywood began to make screen versions of his works that were not especially faithful to the plots of the originals but which did capture their biting wit and the tense surfaces of characters under pressure with much to conceal. Instead, Hollywood fielded a series of actors adept at wisecracking to play the somewhat enigmatic Marlowe, notably Dick Powell and, later, James Garner, and, most definitively, the small Humphrey Bogart in *The Big Sleep* (1946).

Chandler's dialogue and recollections by Philip Marlowe are famous for their provocative wit. "She approached me with enough sex appeal to stampede a business men's lunch and tilted her head to finger a stray, but not very stray, tendril of softly glowing hair." Moose Malloy "was a big man but not more than six feet five inches tall and not wider than a beer truck. . . . Even on Central Avenue, not the quietest dressed street in the world, he looked about as inconspicuous as a tarantula on a slice of angel food." The isolated Marlowe has his fair share of sexual encounters as with the predatory and aptly named Mrs. Grayle of *Farewell, My Lovely*. "She fell softly across my lap and I bent down over her face and began to browse on it. She worked her eyelashes and made butterfly kisses on my cheeks. When I got to her mouth it was half open and burning and her tongue was a darting snake between her teeth." Yet, when it comes to sex, Chandler's hero, carrying the last name of Christopher Marlowe, a notorious Elizabethan playwright who led a double life as a government spy, promises more than he delivers. Like Dashiel Hammett's Sam Spade, Marlowe must remain a self-contained loner, untarnished by the tawdry world he moves through, and preserving his integrity from all forms of corruption.

In fact, Chandler's most persistant theme is the raw disorder of the great metropoles, especially Los Angeles with its garish neon signs and tawdry glitter amid downtown nightclubs, as well as the dark pavements of innumerable mean streets, shining with traces of midnight rain. His sympathetic and villainous characters alike are victims of the greed of the prevailing commercial order as well as their most lascivious (but implied) desires. The underside of the search for sexual or financial gratification is the unfulfilled barrenness of many California lives. Marlowe assesses some victims in *Farewell, My Lovely*.

I leafed through the bunch of shiny photographs of men and women in professional poses. The men had sharp foxy faces and racetrack clothes or eccentric clown-like makeup. Hoofers and comics from the filling station circuit. Not many of them would ever get west of Main Street. You would find them in tank town vaudeville acts, cleaned up, or down in the cheap burlesque houses, as dirty as the law allowed and once in a while just enough dirtier for a raid and a noisy police court trial, and then back in their shows again, grinning sadistically filthy and as rank as the smell of stale sweat. The women had good legs and displayed their inside curves more than Will Hays would have liked. But their faces were as thread-bare as a book-keeper's office cat. Blondes, brunettes, large cow-like eyes with a peasant dullness in them. Small sharp eyes with urchin greed in them.

James M. Cain, born in Annapolis, moved in his forties from work as a journalist and screenplay writer to become a novelist of lurid melodramas, beginning wtih *The Postman Always Rings Twice* (1934) and *Double Indemnity* (1936). His works abounded in sensation in realistic settings, featuring such infernal triangles as dissatisfied wife, discarded husband, and enraptured lover in both *The Postman* and *Double Indemnity;* a hetero-and homosexual triangle of Mexican-Indian prostitute, opera singer, and ambitious conductor in *Serenade* (1937); and an incestuous liaison in *The Butterfly* (1946). *The Postman Always Rings Twice* was, initially, banned in Boston and French writer Albert Camus later acknowledged its influence on his own writing. "No one has ever stopped in the middle of one of Jim Cain's books," claimed the *Saturday Evening Post* and it was almost true. The pace and brevity, the visceral excitement of illicit love, and calculated twists in the plot, contrive to sustain reader interest, in breathless narratives. His genre was violence in low-life settings—the same as the verismo opera composers whose works he had earlier studied as a singing student.

More credible, because less macabre and rooted in the social phenomenon of ever-increasing suburbanization was *Mildred Pierce* (1941), about the tortuous relationships between unfulfilled divorcée and restauranteuse Mildred, her little minx of a daughter whose singing career she sponsors, and various shiftless men. The women's roles were, apparently, tailormade for Joan Crawford and Ann Blyth in the film version, allowing la Crawford an artificial but credible display of maternal love on screen. Her public persona of gracious mother was utterly destroyed after her death in 1977 by the corrosive revelations of her adopted children. They told how, behind the scenes, she was a careless parent, almost psychopathic in her oscillations between hollow protestations of love and outbursts of sadistic cruelty.

After serving as a sergeant in World War I, which shattered his health, Dashiel Hammett worked as a private detective for a Pinkerton Agency in San Francisco, a career that provided him with material for his series of detective crime thrillers. In *Red Harvest* (1929), he first showed his ability to catch the cool tone of an American urban hero, a talent further developed in *The Dain Curse* (1929), and reaching fuller expression with the creation of wisecracking detective Sam Spade, first in *The Maltese Falcon* (1930). This effective crime thriller was filmed three times by Warners, of which the best account was the 1941 version with Humphrey Bogart as Sam Spade and a rogues' gallery led by Mary Astor, Sidney Greenstreet, and Peter Lorre, all at their most ghoulish.

Hammett modeled his most famous heroine, Nora, wife of Nick Charles, for *The Thin Man* (1932) on his longtime companion, playwright Lillian Hellman (1905–1985). New Orleans-born Hellman scored a *succès de scandale* with her murky play *The Children's Hour* (1934) with its undertones of sexual perversion in a girls' boarding school—a scandal that tarnishes the two principal teachers and tests their emotional resilience with tragic consequences. Her most commercially successful play, *The Little Foxes* (1939), showed an aristocratic Alabama family fall prey to the machinations of a malign trio of two unscrupulous brothers and their rapacious sister. While the melodrama requires a strong cast able to project various southern stereotypes and play well together as an ensemble, the part of Regina is a gift for any actress who can assume a series of feline characteristics and, alternately, cajole, wheedle, and dominate the other characters, sending out chills of biting frost. Tallulah Bankhead, who created the part with idiosyncratic drawl, hauteur, and mannerisms, was much copied by early interpreters of the role, notably Bette Davis in the film version (1941). Lillian Hellman's plays were notable for psychological insight, well-modulated violence, and the liberal attitudes of her most sympathetic characters. In her various memoirs, she later idealized herself as heroine, both in the 1930s as a Jew helping her friend, "Julia," save European Jewish refugees from the Nazis and in the 1950s for refusing to testify fully before the House Un-American Activities Committee and betray friends from the past whom she knew had previously supported various radical organizations or causes. Hammett fared less well and was imprisoned for being a former fellow traveler with the Communists. Subsequently, critic Mary McCarthy and Hellman's biographer doubted her veracity about crucial episodes. Far from being ennobling experiences, they believed that her escapades were largely products of her imagination.

Hammett also idealized Hellman as Nora Charles, the witty and sporting wife of urbane detective Nick Charles, in *The Thin Man* (1932). Although the thin man was the murderer's first victim, the name got attached to the detective, especially as played by William Powell in the first film (1934) and its five sequels (1937–1946). Nora was played by the witty Myrna Loy and her domestic scenes with William Powell were considered the first realistic portrayal on screen of an affectionate marriage of sophisticated people, like a modern Millamant and Mirabel from Congreve's *The Way of the World*.

Hollywood also turned the thirties' major regional novel into a plangent and commercially successful film. John Steinbeck (1902–1968) created his most celebrated novel, *The Grapes of Wrath*, in 1938. It is, indeed, a 1930s novel in terms of both subject matter and date of publication for it deals with the story of the "Okies," driven out of the dustbowl by a cruel combination of depression, drought, and inefficient use of the land. Steinbeck's book is an epic that uses alternate chapters and "interchapters" to follow the Joad family in particular and American society in general through the experience of dispossession and deracination. This technique of using a microcosmic and macrocosmic point of view proved both immediately effective in contributing to the novel's success and, eventually, influential in inspiring writers of another generation to use it once again. Like Faulkner, Steinbeck concentrates on the family and its significance although his message is perhaps more didactic. His main spokesperson is Ma Joad, "Use'ta be the fambly was fust. It ain't so now. It's anybody." While Steinbeck is clearly on the side of the dispossessed Okies, he is also critical of their ignorant methods of farming that had helped precipitate their tragedy and then Ma Joad's obsessive insistence on the family staying together, although it is only by the individuals going their separate ways that any of them has a chance of progress beyond mere survival. However, in this book Steinbeck's vision is just as modernist as, say, William Faulkner's, because, despite his use of realism to promote the cause of cooperation amongst human beings, the conclusion of *The Grapes of Wrath* remains ambiguous with young Rosasharn in a stable offering her milk that was intended for her stillborn child to a dying old man. The modernist point of view was essentially pessimistic in its sophistication and Steinbeck in this book was certainly not offering any optimism, beyond Rosasharn's later understanding that she must become more outward-looking and giving. At first we are shown the relationship between the family unit and "the people." The people is an older agrarian concept, from time immemorial linked to the land, while the family is a collection of individuals. However, the people, or prisoners, who tamed nature are now an anachronism in the world of modern farming. The concept of the people must be replaced by a new concept of "the group," itself an instrument of technology, just as the Joads need a truck to survive.

The success of Clifford Odets's (1906–63) play, *Waiting for Lefty* (1935), showed just how popular was the new social ethic of the 1930s. The play examines the personal dramas of a mixed group of taxi drivers debating whether to strike or not and ends with their united cry to strike. This shows Odets's recognition of the failure of a system in which self-interest supposedly produces prosperity for society as a whole. It seems that, for Odets, the creative individual of the 1920s is being replaced by the reforming group of the 1930s, a recognition that men had to work together for the common good in both public and private life and that the federal government had to intervene when individual initiative failed.

In 1937 Ernest Hemingway produced a novel with a measure of social awareness, *To Have and Have Not,* his only novel with an American setting, whose very title proclaims his awareness of injustice and inequality. The central theme of early Hemingway, man working out his salvation alone, is far less sure now. Harry Morgan says at one point, "I've got no boat, no cash, I got no education. . . . All I've got is my cojones to peddle," and yet his much-quoted, dying words are "One man alone ain't got no bloody f—ing chance." Morgan is without any orthodox social awareness. When Cuban revolutionary Emilio rants about the tyranny of imperalistic capitalism, Morgan shouts: "The hell with their revolutions. All I got to do is make a living for my family and I can't do that. Then he tells me about his revolution. The hell with his revolution." As critic Alfred Kazin notes: "The hero . . . is not, like most of Hemingway's heroes, an elaborately, self-conscious man against society; he is rather a mass-man, a man like any other, whose life has a beginning, a middle, and a significant end. Harry Morgan's voice is his excessive self-reliance, the pride in his own tough loneliness."

Ernest Hemingway developed his ideas on war and peace and social commitment in his novel about the Spanish Civil War, *For Whom the Bell Tolls* (1940), also the vehicle for a successful film. *For Whom the Bell Tolls* extends some of Hemingway's own philosophy, not least in the common involvement and responsibility of men indicated by the title. Yet the importance of the historical crisis of the war is minimized. The chief interest lies in the continuous presentation of sensory experience recorded as time passes, rather than in political commitment—something Hemingway had little interest in. The story tells of the successful attempt, at a fatal cost, of a group of loyalist guerrilla fighters to blow up a bridge in the Spanish Civil War of 1936–39. The Spanish conflict was extremely suitable for Hemingway's highly sophisticated style, and for his general purposes. It was contemporary; both sides felt themselves committed to an ideal; and the fighting was extremely bitter. Although the fighting was confined within Spain, the debate on the ethics of the war was universal; it became a true crusade for its intellectuals. The principal character of the novel, Robert Jordan, is an American university teacher for whom the attempt is also a working out of a personal destiny, the proving to himself that his life has significance. At the close of the novel, when he has been abandoned by his friends, he awaits immobile and wounded to be killed by the falangist guards. While waiting, he sifts true and false values to find a permanent meaning to life:

The anger and emptiness and the hate that had come with the let down after the bridge, when he had looked up from where he had lain, and crouching, seen Anselmo dead, were still all through him. In him, too, was despair from the sorrow that soldiers turn to hatred in order that they may continue to be soldiers. . . .

And then, not suddenly, as a physical release could have been (if the woman would have put her arms around him, say) but slowly and from his head he began to accept it and let the hate go out.

12

ARTISTIC LICENSE

IN HIS painting, *Watch,* of 1925, artist Gerard Murphy enlarged
the inside of a pocket watch, unfolding its labyrinthine mechanism and, thereby, showing how much everyday life in industrial society depends on precise regulation. The irony is that a
small mechanical timepiece not only dictates the workings of
larger human beings but also that the complex intricate system of
any industrial society is mastered by the machines invented to
serve it. Such a paradox was much appreciated by America's
artists, sculptors, and architects working between the world wars.

In "The New Condition of Literacy Phenomena" for the art
magazine, *Broom,* of April 1922, critic Jean Epstein claimed that,
in certain circumstances, machines became extensions of the self.
Thus, "spatial speed, mental speed, multiplication of intellectual
images, and the deformations of these images" were the essential
conditions of modernity. He projected a world in which technology dominated all human activity. In the 1920s and 1930s the
worlds of American painting and sculpture were riven by the sort
of conflicts between town and country that had characterized
American social and political history in the 1920s. The new machines continued to make as formative an impact on art as upon

everything else; realistic and regional art continued an often hostile dialogue with abstract art.

Whether their medium was painting, photography, or sculpture, American artists emphasized machines in their works. First, Alfred Stieglitz (1864–1946) documented such new artifacts as skycrapers, bridges, dynamos, and automobiles. Later, in the 1920s painters and sculptors explored geometric images that disclosed something of the speed and power of machines. By the 1930s the spread of machines into the countryside was so pervasive that artists began to consider interconnections between different areas of technology. While Walker Evans and Charles Demuth pondered the impact of the machine in the country, Charles Sheeler documented it as a total system. In his extensive mural for the Mining Industries Building of the West Virginia University at Morgantown (1940–1942) Robert Lepper (b. 1906) showed how coal and gas were first extracted and then transformed into energy before being distributed to industrial and domestic consumers. Thus his panorama of organic, mechanical, and biological forms related two instances of machine-age products in one locality to the scene nationwide. Sculptor John Storrs (1885–1956) etched the soaring form of skycrapers in a series of geometric, constructionist works that used such varied materials as polychromed stone, mirror glass, and metal strips and gave an impression of monumental forms most economically.

The Brooklyn Bridge assumed mythic significance in the art of John Marin (1870–1953), Louis Guglielmi (1906–56), and, most notably, Joseph Stella (1877–1946) who, through a series of remarkable paintings, showed the American public and critics that the bridge was a most potent symbol of their deepest aspirations. The most comprehensive of such works was his quintych of five panels, *The Voice of the City of New York Interpreted* (1920–1922), in which the outer panels of the Port of New York and the Brooklyn Bridge are succeeded by two inner panels of the "Great White Way of Broadway" and culminate in a central panel of Manhattan skyscrapers. Since automobiles represented speed, futurists chose to capture the movement of cars by using the elided, fragmented forms of cubism.

What was true of easel art was true of photography. In her

Charles Demuth, *I Saw the Figure 5 in Gold* (1925), 36″ × 29¾″. (The Metropolitan Museum of Art, The Alfred Stieglitz Collection, 1949). Demuth's "poster" painting, dedicated to his friend, poet William Carlos Williams, mixes words, arbitrary circles, a street lamp, and various distorted buildings in a mode that owes much to European cubists but yet remains essentially American.

Brooklyn Bridge, Water and Dock Streets, Brooklyn (1936) photographer Berenice Abbott (b. 1898) placed the bridge upper left between a disused warehouse in the foreground and the Manhattan skyline in the background, thereby implying the significance of technology in the transformation of New York. By the upward angle of *Manhattan Bridge: Looking Up* (1936), Abbott transformed its support into a monumental pylon, once again emphasizing technology as it was reforming society.

Yet artists continued to show an ambivalence to the machine, admiring its geometry and benevolent potential but recognizing its irrational and potentially destructive results. Because their art forms were many, and their images subtle, they could make ambiguous statements about the machine age, disclosing both myth and reality, good and evil inherent in modern technology. William Gropper (1897–1977) drew a series of pointed cartoons against the capitalist order. For the *Liberator* of 1922 he had a tailor entrapped in a sewing machine of utmost efficiency endure a caption "Work like hell and be happy." In *Hitchhiker* (1935) he had a forlorn angel of peace vainly trying to flag down a procession of Nazi tanks with an olive branch. Yet when he worked for the Department of Labor, Gropper chose to emphasize the heroism and prowess of American construction workers, building the Hoover Dam in *Construction of the Dam* (1937). Here men were fully in charge of their machines.

Overwhelmed by the array of motors and propellers on display at the *Salon d' Aviation,* Paris, in 1911, Marcel Duchamp observed to fellow artist Constantin Brancusi, "Painting is finished. Who can do anything better than this propeller? Can you?" In 1922 innovative photographer Alfred Stieglitz (1864–1946) had his colleagues attend a symposium on the subject "Can a photograph have the significance of art?" The discussion was published in *Manuscripts* for December 1922. Marcel Duchamp answered the question directly. "You know exactly what I think of photography. I would like to see it make people despise painting until something else will make photography unbearable." But photographers were not necessarily consistent for they shifted their emphasis. At the turn of the century reform-minded photographer Lewis W. Hine had followed in the honorable tradition of progressive journalist Jacob Riis in stark photographs documenting the drudgery of men, women, and children in inhospitable mills and factories across America. In his later years Hine celebrated the prowess of workers, notably those engaged in such fearless endeavors as the epic construction of the Empire State Building, most notably in his *Icarus* of 1931. In contrast, Margaret Bourke White concentrated on more formal studies. Her photographs of a textile mill at Amoskeag, New Hampshire, in 1932 emphasized just how efficient was American industry without hinting at the cost in human terms, implicitly approving the way things were being run, although she did protest against social conditions to the American Artists' Congress in 1935.

Not only did the machine widen the range of subject matter for all forms of art, providing them with new themes and powerful images, but it also introduced new materials and techniques. Twenty years after the public began to refer to a coterie of New York artists as the "Ash Can School," on account of their playful, quixotic treatment of urban scenes, Charles Burchfield (1893–1967) turned epithet into metaphor in his watercolor of a trash heap and weeds in a culvert entitled *Still Life—Scrap Iron* (1929). The junk of a machine age scattered over the countryside was a central image in a period when the town was overtaking the countryside.

Immigrant artists Marcel Duchamp (1887–1967) and Francis Picabia (1879–1953) were iconoclasts who were thrown into nihilism by their outrage at the carnage of World War I. Picabia's machine drawings for the Alfred Stieglitz review *291* emphasized the hard edges of machines and challenged the conventional academic wisdom as to what constituted a standard acceptable subject for a drawing or painting. In order to challenge the resolution and conviction of the Independents, the American artists who affected to adore his work, Duchamp, under the alias of "R. Mutt," a plumber, submitted a porcelain urinal entitled *Fountain,* for their exhibition of 1920. The Independents Committee was scandalized and rejected the exhibit: Duchamp resigned and proclaimed that it was the artist's selection of an object for display that turned it into an objet d'art. This, and this only, was the correct criterion for art. Because *Fountain* was, in fact, a machine for passing urine, it was obscene to a genteel art committee. The significances of the incident, sometimes known as the "Richard Mutt Case," was not the object itself but the happening, the way the urinal as sculpture tested public taste to the extreme. As Dickran Tashjian explains in *The Machine Age in America* (1986), "Duchamp had subverted deeply entrenched cultural norms for art by introducing an artifact from an industrial network into an art network involving studios, galleries, and exhibitions." In *Kora is Hell* (1920) poet William Carlos Williams claimed that Duchamp's *Fountain* was "a representative piece of American sculpture." To a credulous public, eager for titillation, Duchamp was now the "Buddha of the bathroom." Duchamp claimed how "The only works of art America has given are her plumbing and her bridges," thereby underscoring the irony of a situation already rich in irony whereby commonplace machine objects might be taken as serious works of art. The debate about what constitutes art continued to the end of the twentieth century and its comic possibilities were mercilessly exploited by Dada artists. In 1918 Morton Schamberg (1881–1918) joined a miter box and plumbing trap and entitled his sculpture-by-collage *God,* thus provocatively exposing the status awarded to sanitation in American society. It was in this context that realistic and regional art continued a hostile dialogue with abstract art.

Painting in the 1920s and 1930s

Stuart Davis (1894–1964) was a painter whose work was in many ways analogous to the poetry of E. E. Cummings. His mature style did not develop fully until he returned from study in Europe in 1929, but his inspiration came directly from the urban landscape of the twenties:

American wood and iron work of the past; Civil War and skyscraper architecture; the brilliant colors on gasoline stations; chainstore fronts, and taxicabs . . . electric signs; the landscape and boats of Gloucester, Mass.; 5 and 10 cent store kitchen utensils; movies and radio; Earl Hines hot piano and Negro jazz music in general.

Davis worked with all of these influences—often abstracting them in a stylized manner—to create colorful paintings that captured the commercial vigor of the decade. He was an individualist who avoided joining movements and was also one of the most articulate spokesmen for abstract painting while always describing himself as a realist painter. This may appear to be a contradiction in terms, but Davis often forcefully explained that his realism was not founded on naturalistic representation but consisted, again like an improvising jazz musician, of interpreting existing subject matter through an abstract style. Davis acknowledged the influence of jazz music on his paintings and the debt is quite evident in many of his works with their strong colors and sense of vigorous movement.

Another aspect of Davis's art worth noting is the fact that, together with the American school of painters known as the Precisionists, he was a precursor of the Pop artists. Some of Davis's work, such as his 1924 rendering of a packet of Odol disinfectant, brings to mind the icon of 1960s' pop art—Andy Warhol's representations of Campbell's soup cans. In the 1920s American painters first began to incorporate into their work the letters, words, and numerals that were becoming an integral part of the urban landscape. The social fabric was increasingly held together by a commercial culture that relied on signs, particularly advertisements, to get its message across. The Pop artists were to exploit this subject matter more fully in the 1950s and 1960s, but in the 1920s the Precisionists anticipated Pop artists with their highly stylized renderings of the urban and industrial scene. They took the commonplace and turned it into the monumental, as with Charles Demuth's (1883–1935) urgent, but splintered, representation of a fire truck moving in the city at night in *I Saw the Figure 5 in Gold,* inspired by a poem by his friend, William Carlos Williams, *The Great Figure.*

Together with Demuth, Charles Sheeler (1883–1965) was a leader of the Precisionists and between 1927 and 1930 he created a series of paintings based on the burgeoning automobile plants of Michigan. Sheeler was also a photographer and he developed a painting style that moved away from his early concern for French modernism and centered on a simple, almost photographic, realism. However, like Demuth, he was fascinated by the stark geometry of the new industrial plants and often his choice of subject matter in itself lent his paintings a quality of abstraction. *Classic Landscape* (1931), based on photographs of the Ford River Rouge Plant, for example, is, at first glance, a realistic representation of the Ford factory, but a closer look reveals that the factory is quite simply too clean to be a real one. The painting is even "too realistic" to be a photograph—it is without the atmospheric distortions of the camera that inevitably adorn photographs of industrial scenes taken at such long range. Sheeler's *Church Street El* of 1920 shows how realism can verge on abstraction. The buildings have been simplified to their geometric shapes. Sheeler's paintings bring to mind two other names that are sometimes used to describe the Precisionists—the Immaculates and the Cubist-Realists. It is strangely paradoxical that a painting can become too realistic by too much concentration on detail to seem real. The phenomenon has been exploited not only by the Precisionists, but in the 1970s and 1980s by the American Super-Realists, in particular Richard Estes.

The Precisionists never formed a movement in the strict sense of the word; they did not issue a manifesto, nor did they meet regularly. But they undoubtedly formed a movement in their shared concern for America's new industrial landscape. Demuth and Sheeler were two leading figures, but others included Preston Dickinson (1891–1930), Niles Spencer (1893–1952), Ralston Crawford (1906–78), and Georgia O'Keeffe (1887–1986).

However, O'Keeffe differed from these other artists by virtue of her application of precisionist principles to both industrial and organic forms. Her work is uniquely and unmistakably marked by the stamp of her forceful individualism, yet at the same time it is an absorbed synthesis of most of the progressive tendencies in American painting up to World War II. By the mid-twenties she was painting her famous studies of enlarged flowers, which, for all their rhythmic line movements, are essentially abstract compositions, reminiscent of Arthur Dove's free-form abstractions drawn from nature, Charles Demuth's crisp surfaces, and Charles Sheeler's sterile forms. Many critics have chosen to interpret her work in terms of stereotypical femininity, using such adjectives as "elegant," "pretty," and "typically feminine," in appreciations of her work. But a more significant explanation of her art is to be

Georgia O'Keeffe, *Lake George Window* (1920), oil on canvas, 40″ ×
30″. (Collection, The Museum of Modern Art, New York. Acquired
through the Richard D. Brixey Bequest). Here Georgia O'Keeffe has
isolated a shuttered window door from its surroundings and, by eliminating details that might disturb her immaculate presentation of form,
has heightened the overall visual impact.

found in a consideration of where she came from and the various influences she assimilated.

She was born near Sun Prairie, Wisconsin, in 1887 and spent her childhood in Virginia before moving to Texas. She retained a deep affinity with the enormous landscape of America's Midwest and West. Before meeting her future husband, Alfred Stieglitz, she had studied at Teachers' College, New York, with Arthur Dove (1880–1946), a teacher who based his instruction on an unorthodox source—the principles of design that he had discerned in Oriental art. He emphasized flat patterns and harmonious compositions that were to attract the interest of Stieglitz and his coterie when they were first shown O'Keeffe's work. O'Keeffe was influenced by other American painters who were drawing on European modernism for inspiration and technique but the most significant fact about O'Keeffe's painting is that she herself never actually studied in Europe. Not only did she create a synthesis of all the progressive tendencies in American painting but she also managed this without crossing the Atlantic to see at first hand the innovations of the European modernists. Her debt is to fellow Americans, not to Europeans. Gerald Murphy's (1888–1964) *Razor* of 1924 was noted at the time as being distinctively American in its choice and treatment of subject. The dash of colors and the stylized representation of three very American objects (safety razor, matchbox, and fountain pen) bring this painting even closer to Pop art than the work of the Precisionists.

Edward Hopper (1882–1967) was another painter who has been celebrated as a particularly American artist. Hopper, a realist who was not concerned with modernist styles, remarked, "To me, form, color and design are merely a means to an end, the tools I work with, and they do not interest me greatly for their own sake." Between 1906 and 1910 he made three journeys to Europe and spent most of his time in Paris. His strongest stylistic influence during these early years came from the French Impressionists and for a while he painted in a frankly Impressionist manner. However, American critics disliked these early works because they were too close to the art of Europe. After returning to America, Hopper abandoned his bright colors and adopted a more somber palette that was more in keeping with the subject matter he drew from his native country. Ironically, critics later charged Hopper with provincial nationalism in his painting.

Hopper's art has certainly come to epitomize the genre of American scene painting, but it is far from parochial or merely nationalistic. His early training in painting was at the New York School of Art and, although he studied under the traditionalist William Merritt Chase, it was Robert Henri, who joined the school in 1903, who was the greater influence. Henri passed on to Hopper the main drive of the Ash Can School—the desire to paint the life and sights around him. For Hopper this meant the city and the country. He painted both with a peculiarly individual vision.

Unlike the Ash Can School and early modernists, such as John Marin, when Hopper looked at the life around him in the American city he perceived not vitality but loneliness and melancholy. In contrast to the Precisionists, his canvases were often peopled, but rarely is there any sense of communication or interaction between characters. His *New York Movie* of 1939 illustrates Hopper's masterly handling of light. The lonely, isolated usherette separated from the auditorium can be seen as a symbol of humanity lost in its individual thoughts. The painting explores the tension between physical reality and our perception of our place in the scheme of things. Hopper himself was, by nature, a reserved and distanced character. His physical appearance had much to do with this. By the age of twelve he was an ungainly six feet tall and was ridiculed by his peers. His understandable embarrassment and resentment caused him to turn his back on his contemporaries and led him into solitude, a state of being that became a major theme in his painting.

Hopper is just as much a painter of the 1920s as, say, the lively and colorful figure of Stuart Davis. Edward Hopper once said of critical examinations of his work, "the loneliness thing is overdone," but loneliness is definitely to be found even in those of his paintings that expressed his passion for architecture and are not peopled. Many of Hopper's paintings provide us with scenes that are endowed with the same poignant symbolism as F. Scott Fitzgerald's "valley of ashes" in *The Great Gatsby*. In the midst of apparent prosperity there will always exist places "where ashes grow like wheat into ridges and hills and grotesque gardens, where ashes take the form of houses and chimneys and rising smoke and, finally, with a transcendent effort, of ash-grey men, who move dimly and already crumbling through the powdery air." You will search in vain for such a scene in the work of Edward Hopper but you will find the same chilly meaning in the first painting of his that you look at.

However, Hopper did not consciously set out to create an art that analytically criticized American society. That task was taken up mainly in the 1930s by the Social Realist painters. Foremost among them was Ben Shahn (1898–1969) who, like John Dos Passos, was particularly inspired by the *Sacco and Vanzetti* case of the late 1920s. Shahn was actually in Europe when the execution took place on August 23, 1927, but, on returning to America in 1929, he began work on a series of paintings depicting the trial and its aftermath. Shahn was born in Lithuania but grew up in an immigrant quarter of New York City where hatred of injustice and distrust of authority were common. At the age of sixteen he was apprenticed to a lithographer from whom he acquired an eye for telling detail. However, his painting relies less on realistic detail than on the devices he absorbed from the work of early German Expressionists. Amongst these devices are the use of oversized hands and heads that forcefully project the characters in his paintings, lending them a poignance and a significance that served his ends as a Social Realist. Shahn once said of the *Sacco and Vanzetti* case: "Ever since I could remember I'd wished that I'd been lucky enough to be alive at a great time—when something big was going on, like the Crucifixion. And suddenly I realized I was. Here I was living through another Crucifixion. Here was something to paint!" Between 1935 and 1938 Shahn took almost 6,000 photographs for the New Deal's Farm Security Administration, documenting the effects of depression on the rural poor. He later used many of these photographs as starting points for paintings.

Engineering Art

Critic Jane Heap, coeditor of the *Little Review,* wanted artists to affiliate themselves with one another and with scientists, engineers, and other constructive professional men of the age. Her hope for works based on a spirit of technological cooperation culminated in the Machine Age Exposition held in Steinway Hall, New York, in spring 1927, considered an ideal, plain setting for the various machines, paintings, and drawings on show. They were all displayed together, rather than with art and technology confined to separate rooms as was historically the case at great expositions. This reflected Jane Heap's conviction that engineers had much to learn from artists, not least basic ideas of artistic sensibility in terms of machine design. As she explained in her contemporaneous article, "Machine-Age Exposition," for the *Little Review* supplement of May 1927, which served as catalogue for the exhibition, she had decided on an exhibition of machines and art and architecture in juxtaposition. The cover was an elegant abstract design by Fernand Léger (1881–1955) and artists and architects represented included John Storrs, Charles Demuth, Louis Lozowick, Hugh Ferriss, Walter Gropius, and Raymond Hood.

The exposition stimulated discussion about Soviet society that was meant to fulfill the true union of arts and technology desired by Jane Heap. However, the exhibition attracted far less attention than the Exposition of Art in Trade, sponsored by Macy's in the first week of May, and which was more attractive because it promised those who attended a consumers' paradise.

It also prompted discussion about Constructivism. Initially a Soviet-inspired art movement, it represented a committed effort by artists to cooperate with industry, that is to use the new resources of industry, notably raw metals, and fashion from them a universal art that would be appreciated by aesthetes and proletariat alike. Among Jane Heap's constructivist heroes was Russian-American painter Louis Lozowick who drew and painted machines as forms of geometric ornament until he discovered how easily other commercial artists could transfer and develop his ornaments into advertising logos, feeding consumer, that is to say, capitalist desires. Dickran Tashjian observes in *The Machine Age in America* how, "Tacitly acknowledging the hegemony of American capitalism, Lozowick suggested that the American revolutionary artist should picture the machine environment 'more as a prognostication than as a fact,' a projection of 'rationalization and economy which must prove allies of the working class in the building of socialism.' " Lozowick shifted emphasis from abstract art to realistic depiction of urban life. In his *High Voltage—cos cob* (1930), he positioned a worker in front of the electric wires he had erected, thereby placing the actual mechanic rather than the engineer or designer in front.

Although Constructivism was a significant political movement in art for a handful of American artists in the 1920s, its political emphasis was successively weakened in the 1930s as there were ever more European styles and movements to stimulate American artists. However, abstract art was increasingly popular among emerging new artists although it was disliked by many radicals and most of the middle class, the potential customers. In fact, abstraction became a central issue for other young artists who lacked opportunities to show their abstract paintings. Rejected by the established art world, in 1936 they formed an association of American Abstract Artists to promote their work. It included Stuart Davis, who was president, Ilya Bolotowsky, Charles Shaw, and Paul Kelpe. In their *Yearbook of 1938* Rosalind Bergelsdorf defended abstract art in general terms, claiming how "the machine guided us to a logical combination of simplicity and functionalism" and that "so-called abstract painting is the expression of art of this age," the age of the machine. The most committed to making works of art from raw materials was Ibram Lassaw (b. 1913) who used sheet metal and steel to fashion biomorphic forms.

One exceptional sculptor made machines work for him and thus transcended the boundaries of his art. Alexander Calder (1898–1976), born into a family of sculptors, moved decisively away from his father's allegorical figures that used equestrian statues, most inappropriately, to symbolize such new forms of energy as electricity, into new, moving forms of sculpture, suggesting a motorized *Universe* (1934). In *Praying Mantis* (1936), Calder drew from his wide range of experiences and used biomorphic shapes, kinetic art, surrealism, and constructivism in his various works. Yet Calder, an American artist whose early career in Paris was significant more for its lack of distinctive achievement than anything else, eventually astounded Europe with his wire toys and metal circus figures. Eventually, he produced the

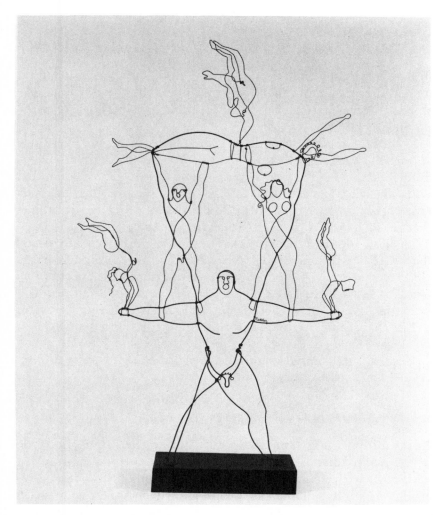

Alexander Calder, *The Brass Family* (1929), brass wire sculpture, 64″ × 41″ × 8½″. (Collection of Whitney Museum of American Art, New York; gift of the artist). The son and grandson of sculptors, Alexander Calder (1898–1976) became himself America's most famous sculptor, noted for his invention of the mobile, a hanging sculpture in motion. He began his professional career as a freelance newspaper artist and sketched both the Ringling Brothers' and the Barnum and Bailey Circuses that remained a continuous source of artistic inspiration for him, as did the city of Paris. *The Brass Family,* in which an outsize athlete balances six other acrobats, demonstrates Calder's irrepressible humor as well as his skill in ink drawings. Indeed, Calder's wire sculptures seem to transform drawn lines into space.

mobile, a hanging sculpture that moved of its own accord and no longer showed its origins in the machine. Thus, as Dickran Tashjian observes, in Calder's hands, "technology became the natural once again."

Ironically, in the 1930s it was three sculptors who were not among the American abstract artists—Charles Biederman, Theodore Roszak, and José de Rivera—who became most identified with constructivist art, itself a form of abstraction. Charles Biederman (1906–   ) used metal and glass as reliefs on paintings that recalled works by Piet Mondrian. Theodore Roszak (1907–81) made sculptures out of steel and bronze, aluminum and plastic that were like futurist architecture. In time, convinced that artists could not work with industry, Roszak abandoned Constructivism. José de Rivera (1904–85) a former machinist who had also been the owner of a tool shop, provided fascinating, graceful shapes that seemed to open and close the space surrounding them. His *Form Synthesis* (1938) of morel metal seemed to anticipate spaceships; his painted aluminum *Red and Black: Double Element* (1938) was both rectilinear and volumetric.

Art in the Great Depression

Realism in painting came to the fore during the depression. One of the major reasons for this shift away from abstraction toward naturalistic representation was the intervention of the federal government with its unparalleled program of wide-scale patronage of the arts. The New Deal encouraged a sense of nationalism radically different from earlier outbursts of xenophobic protectionism. American society was, to a certain extent, united in common misery. The New Deal was a symbol of some hope for the decade. The repercussions of government intervention for American painting were immense. Critical opinion is, as usual, divided over the value of the Federal Art Project and its associated programs and some commentators have emphasized the conservative aspects of its nature, particularly its lack of concern with abstract painting. However, it is undeniable that it sustained many important progressive painters, both realists and modernists, at a time when they may otherwise have been forced to abandon art.

The man who initiated government patronage of the arts in the 1930s was himself a progressive artist and was particularly concerned with mural painting. George Biddle was a member of an influential Philadelphia family and had attended Groton School and Harvard University with Franklin D. Roosevelt. He spurned the career in law that his family expected of him and sailed for France in 1911 where he began his career as a painter. His work always displayed a sensitive social conscience and, in common with the Social Realist painters, he strongly believed that art had not functioned as a positive influence on society for centuries, that it had been, "so to speak, a prostitute, well paid, sleeping in expensive beds, but divorced . . . from our program of life."

On May 9, 1933, Biddle wrote to Roosevelt suggesting that young American painters would support his New Deal and were eager to express the ideals of a social revolution in mural form on the walls of America's public buildings. The inspiration for Biddle's belief came from the experiment sponsored by the Mexican president, Alvaro Obregon, in the 1920s. Public buildings in Mexico City were covered with murals expressing the ideals of the Mexican revolution and the artists had received a small wage from the government for their work. The Mexican muralists created what some critics have considered to be the greatest national school of mural painting since the Italian Renaissance. Their leaders were Diego Rivera, José Clemente Orozco, and David Alfaro Siqueiros. In the late 1920s and early 1930s Orozco and Rivera worked in America and stimulated interest in the mural form. Their presence was particularly beneficial for America's best-known muralist, Thomas Hart Benton. Diego Rivera (1886–1957), the prolific Mexican muralist whose principal subjects were industrial production and political revolution, was one of the very few social artists outside Russia and Germany to devote his career to social art. The range of his art and the extraordinary prestige it enjoys in Mexico were the result of special historical circumstances. The people of Mexico (like those of Russia) were of a partially industrialized generation. Few could read and write. However, they were used to looking at popular devotional art as a prime source of moral instruction.

FDR was enthusiastic about Biddle's proposals and he enlisted the support of Secretary of Labor Frances Perkins, Secretary of the Interior Harold L. Ickes, Assistant Secretary of Agriculture Rexford G. Tugwell, and Eleanor Roosevelt. Yet, despite these impressive governmental supporters, the proposals ran into conservative opposition from an existing artistic agency within the government. The National Commission of Fine Arts had been created by Congress in 1910 and was strongly biased in favor of classical art. Charles Moore had been chairman of the commission since 1915 and he instructed that a long letter be sent to Roosevelt, criticizing Biddle's proposals on the grounds that they were subversive of traditional art. However, in the crisis years of the New Deal the government was open to influence along unorthodox channels and Biddle, along with an artistic ally from the Treasury Department, Edward Bruce, was able to get the project funded through the recently formed relief organization led by Harry Hopkins, the Civil Works Administration (CWA).

The formula that George Biddle and Edward Bruce devised for the administration of the new project was basically that of a central committee in Washington, D.C., with decentralized regional advisory committees each with a regional chairman selected by the central committee. Biddle himself was more concerned with painting than with administration and Bruce eventually became the project's guiding light. As a result, the emphasis on mural painting was expanded to include sculptors and easel painters as well. The Public Works of Art Project (PWAP) was operational by December 1933 when eighty-six artists throughout the sixteen geographic divisions received their first pay checks. Forbes Watson, a former art critic, was appointed technical director for the entire project and became its chief philosopher and spokesman.

However, the PWAP only lasted as long as Harry Hopkin's ill-fated CWA. In using the $400 million allocated to him from Harold Ickes's Public Works Administration (PWA), Hopkins had adopted a policy of administering relief across the board without means tests or other forms of qualified distribution. By early spring of 1934 these unorthodox methods had aroused such strong conservative opposition that Roosevelt was obliged to close down the CWA. This was by no means the end of government patronage of the arts. A major exhibition of PWAP art held at the Corcoran Gallery of Art in Washington, D.C., between April 24 and May 20, 1934, proved to be a success. Five hundred items were chosen as exhibits out of thousands submitted by the regional committees. The organizers were optimistic. The weekend before the opening Forbes Watson proclaimed that the exhibition would be, "the greatest art event in this country since the Armory Show."

While its success did not quite match that of the Armory Show of 1913, the Corcoran exhibition was sufficiently well received to ensure continued government involvement in patronage throughout the decade. Indeed, during the 1930s several government agencies would find themselves competing to employ the best artists available. Edward Bruce continued his involvement in government patronage through the Treasury Relief Art Project (TRAP), created in July, 1935. TRAP was funded with a grant from the recently established Works Progress Administration (WPA) controlled by Harry Hopkins. However, the WPA instituted its own Federal Art Project (FAP) that received fourteen times more money than Bruce's Treasury project and gave aid to ten times the number of artists. The FAP retained the structure of the PWAP and had many important artists on its payroll at one time or another, including some who became leading modern painters in the movement known as Abstract Expressionism: Arshile Gorky (1904–1948), Philip Guston (1930–1980), and Jackson Pollock (1912–1956), for example. Gorky was a painter of Armenian origin who deliberately went through a range of styles— Cubist, Surrealist, and Fauvist—before arriving at his mature style in the 1940s. His painting, *The Artist and His Mother* of 1926–1929, is not typical of that mature style in that it is somewhat naturalistic, but this painting portends something of the sadness and tragedy that overtook Gorky's life in his last years. Between 1946 and 1948 he suffered a major fire at his studio, cancer, marital breakup, and a major car crash in which he broke his neck and damaged his painting arm. In July of 1948 Gorky took his own life.

However, the FAP, despite its sponsorship of modernists such as Gorky, was, on the whole, more committed to realist painting because of its avowed purpose to create a popular art that gave expression to the aspirations and achievements of the American people. The director of the FAP was Holger Cahill whose specific concern was folk art. In fact, the FAP did much to propagate serious painting outside the urban centers, chiefly New York, and was particularly responsible for the rise of the school of painters known as the Regionalists. The Regionalists were undoubtedly disaffected with modernist painting and their ideals concurred with those of the PWAP officials in Westport, Connecticut, who forbade their artists to experiment with "cubism, futurism, and all forms of modernism."

Private sponsors also encouraged American understanding of, and self-expression through, art and wanted people to appreciate modern works. In 1929 the Museum of Modern Art was founded in New York by Lillie P. Bliss, Mrs. Cornelius Sullivan, and Abby Aldrich Rockefeller, as a permanent museum for the best modern works of art produced since the 1880s and to encourage and develop public appreciation of all the visual arts, including film. In 1930 Gertrude Vanderbilt Whitney, sculptor and art collector, founded the Whitney Museum of American Art, firstly in her Greenwich Village studio. She believed that living American artists deserved recognition and encouragement and donated over 600 American works in her possession. During the 1930s the Museum of Modern Art staged two crucial shows that influenced all serious young painters: *Cubism and Abstract Art* (1936) and *Fantastic Art, Dada, Surrealism* (1936–1937). Also, in 1939 the Valentine Gallery exhibited *Guernica* (1937), Picasso's protest at the German bombing and devastation of the defenseless Basque capital on April 27, 1937, in the Spanish Civil War. These exhibitions served to introduce a new generation of American artists to the Cubist revolution of Picasso and Braque.

The Regionalist school of painters, led by John Steuart Curry, Grant Wood, and Thomas Hart Benton, impressed on all their pupils that modernism was useless, unwanted, and decadent, that its techniques were irrelevant to the United States, and that what the American people really wanted was representational art of such American scenes as pasture, field, and harvest. Benton was the most vociferous advocate of this point of view. This was not

Thomas Hart Benton, *People of Chilmark* (Figure Composition) (1921), oil on canvas, 65⅝″ × 77⅝″. (Hirshhorn Museum and Sculpture Garden, Smithsonian Institution, Washington, D.C.). Preeminent regional artist Thomas Hart Benton of Neosho, Missouri, was son and grand-nephew to congressmen and, throughout his youth, his family were discussing the factors that had shaped the Midwest. After an early period of experimentation, he rejected cubism and other modern European styles in favor of the more monumental mural art of the Italian Renaissance, and the easel paintings of El Greco. He wanted to forge an American art that would draw on the history, folklore, and daily life of the United States for subject matter but unfold the themes in stylized compositions dominated by thrusting curved lines.

surprising when we consider that he had begun his career as a modernist, a close friend of Stanton MacDonald Wright, who now turned on his modernist associates with great venom.

Yet much of the criticism of regionalist artists that stressed the conservative aspects of their art is exaggerated and fails to take account of their progressive qualities. Grant Wood (1892–1942) was one of America's foremost regionalist painters and spent most of his life in his native Iowa. He made two journeys to Europe where he was first influenced by Impressionism and later by the meticulous creations of medieval Flemish painters. When he returned to Iowa in the mid-1920s, he concentrated on painting the American scene. However, it was in the 1930s that his art reached its fullest expression and significance, and during this time he supervised most of the government art projects that operated in Iowa. He worked as technical chief on a cooperative mural at the University of Iowa. From the very first day in their workshop (an old swimming pool), Wood found the team of twenty-two painters divided into equal numbers of modernists and realists. Initially, the atmosphere was strained but gave way to a community of feeling that made the completion of the mural project their top priority. At one stage when the PWAP regional quotas were decreased, the twenty-two artists redistributed the incoming pay checks rather than have any artist laid off.

America's leading regionalist was Thomas Hart Benton (1889–1975), much influenced by the work of the Mexican muralists. However, his art evolved independently of them during the 1920s and, like Grant Wood's, reached its fullest expression in the 1930s. During World War I he volunteered for duty and was assigned as an architectural draftsman to the Norfolk Naval Base, Virginia. While studying in a Norfolk lodging house, he came across a nineteenth-century, four-volume history of the United States written by J. A. Spencer and illustrated with engravings. In his professional and technical autobiography, *An American in Art* (1969), he explained the significance of these illustrations for the evolution of his painting of the 1920s and 1930s: "Why could not such subject pictures dealing with the meanings of American history possess aesthetically interesting properties, deliverable along with their meanings? History painting, religious or secular, had occupied a large place in the annals of art. Why not look into it again, I asked, and try to fill the contextual void of my own painting, give it some kind of meaning?" The particular enterprise Benton had in mind was a mural project to be called *History of America*. By 1926 he had completed his first two "chapters" of the American history and had successfully exhibited them at the Architectural League in New York. However, by 1929, when he was invited to create a mural for the New School of Social Research in New York, his concern for history was replaced with a desire to document the contemporary scene. The immediate reason for this change in emphasis was the topical work of José Clemente Orozco who was also creating murals for the New School at the same time as Benton.

Benton himself did little work under government patronage, primarily because he was enjoying success in the private field. Nevertheless, he is closely linked to the art of the 1930s that sought to capture and document American life in all its aspects. The charges of political and artistic conservatism that have been leveled at these Regionalists are largely unfounded. For example, while using traditional artistic techniques, Wood was a New Deal Democrat in his politics, while Benton was a latter-day Populist whose realistic art is hardly conservative in its colorful yet lugubrious depictions of the American scene.

However, the Regionalists were not the only painters to concern themselves with aspects of American life in the 1930s. Jacob Lawrence (b. 1917) grew up in Harlem during the depression and, being black, was naturally aware of the cultural heritage and the hardships of black Americans during the decade. His career began in a settlement house art class that was supported by the FAP and his very first paintings dealt with historical figures who had played important roles in the liberation of slaves: for example, the Haitian Toussaint L'Ouverture and the southerners Frederick Douglass and Harriet Tubman. Between 1940 and 1941 he drew directly on his experience of the depression and created the series of sixty paintings entitled *The Migration of the Negro*. These paintings provide a telling description of the plight of dispossessed blacks in the 1930s. Lawrence has pointed out that this migration was an integral part of his life: "My parents were part of this migration

—on their way North when I was born in Atlantic City in 1917." His use of stark compositions, bright poster colors, and angular, often contorted, human figures, serve to increase the already considerable emotional impact of his subject matter.

Two other leading Social Realists were Philip Evergood (1901–1975) and Jack Levine (b. 1915). Evergood enrolled in the PWAP in 1933 and created his most militant social protest paintings during the next few years. Levine's social protests are often tempered by his ability for comic satire that has made him one of the most durable of all the American painters of this century. Social Realism in painting was essentially an optimistic, socially committed art form and, when Jack Levine spoke of his own painting, he could easily have been talking for his colleagues: "I took my place in the late thirties as part of the general uprising of social consciousness in art and literature. It was part of the feeling that things were the right way; we were all making a point . . . we had a feeling of confidence about our ability to do something about the world." Indeed, such confidence was strengthened by the arrival in America of a kindred European spirit. The Social Realists were deeply indebted to German Expressionists for their manner. In 1933 the leading Expressionist George Grosz (1893–1959) fled from Hitler's Germany and sought asylum in New York. In 1938 he became an American citizen. Grosz's bitter satires were an inspiration for many Social Realists. Other European artists also found at least temporary refuge from fascism in America—Yves Tanguy, Pavel Tchelitchew, Max Ernst, and Salvador Dali—and the weight of their influence became apparent after World War II.

World War II itself was to prove most influential in changing the course of the development of American painting in the twentieth century. The shock of another war after the experience of the war to end all wars proved too much for the American artist and the American art world. Thomas Hart Benton wrote regretfully of the fact that, although he had successfully created a meaningful art in the 1930s, during World War II he saw "most of the meanings, which it took so many years to formulate, disappearing with the dissolution of the world that generated them." Socially concerned artists such as Benton were to be replaced as leaders after the war by the angst-ridden and essentially introspective Abstract Expressionists such as Pollock and Gorky.

Abstract Expressionism

It would be all too tempting and logical enough to conclude that the next major development in art—Abstract Expressionism—was a direct descendant from Cubism, with the shattering of conventional human and other traditional forms and their redesigning. Once one form had been broken, then its shattering or splintering must follow, just as World War II shattered societies almost everywhere but the United States. The years of World War II were not years of artistic sterility. This was the period when Abstract Expressionism was being developed by a handful of artists working in or near New York: Jackson Pollock (1912–1956), Arshile Gorky (1904–1948), Willem de Kooning (b. 1904), and Mark Rothko (1903–1970). Abstract Expressionism was to emerge as the dominant style of the postwar world.

In his *How New York Stole the Idea of Modern Art* (1985) Serge Guilbaut shows how New York intellectuals and artists moved in the late 1930s from popular front interest in the artist's relationship with the masses to a profound sense of alienation and concern for a special audience. Instead of wanting to change society, they became obsessed by the fate of creativity in modern society. In his 1939 essay for *Partisan Review* Clement Greenberg presented the crisis not in terms of society or social justice but in terms of the threat that the mass production of contemporary culture presented to artistic quality. Thus to continue producing painting or writing of high quality in the face of depression and war was, in itself, a radical act. American writers and painters were not immune from those devastating political experiences that had deeply disillusioned the American Left: Stalin's purges and show trials of 1936–1938; the Nazi-Soviet Pact of 1939; the Holocaust of 1941–1945; and the use of the atomic bomb in 1945. Such events forced them to reconsider their position and painters moved to an art form that was apolitical. They began to explore the possibilities of nonrepresentational art. In 1937 Meyer Schapiro had emphasized the humanity of abstract art in an article, "The Nature of

Abstract Art," for the *Marxist Quarterly,* and that abstract art was connected with social experience.

In *Hide-and-Seek* (1940–1942) Pavel Tchelitchev (1898–1957) showed the influence of surrealism in which the central tree surrounded by children's faces can be seen as representing the changing seasons of the year, while the color and composition suggest the internal biological workings of the human body. *The Red Stairway* (1944) shows Ben Shahn's experience in the Office of War Information where he dealt with photographs of bombing in Europe. Here a gleaming red stairway is in marked contrast to its devastated, bombed setting but it leads nowhere for its crippled passenger. The one sign of optimism is a laborer rising from the ground and facing forward, carrying on his back a basket loaded with stones with which to begin rebuilding. Shahn commented on the endless stream of photographs documenting "bombed-out places, so many of which I knew well and cherished. There were the churches destroyed, the villages, the monasteries. . . . I painted Italy as I lamented it, or feared that it might become." Instead of realism, he chose "A symbolism which I might once have considered cryptic" because it "now became the only means by which I could formulate the sense of emptiness and waste that the war gave me, and the sense of the littleness of people trying to live on through the enormity of war."

Faced with the only partly told horrors of the 1940s, art critic and historian Thomas Bender observes how

some painters, Mark Rothko in particular, found possibilities in the universality of primitive and archaic myths. They were able to believe that in speaking to the universal in man they had in fact expanded rather than contracted their connection with the public, even while narrowing their actual audience. By the end of the 40's, these artists thought their work represented not only their private anxiety but the anxiety of the age. They believed its illegibility was the only possible response to media and Government efforts to discuss the bomb in "normal" language and languages.

Of all these gifted, explosive talents, the most widely publicized was Jackson Pollock who studied at the Art Students League under prominent Regionalist Thomas Hart Benton. Benton conveyed his strong sense of vocation and the stature of art to his shy pupil. "You've the stuff, old kid—all you have to do is to keep it up," he is supposed to have told Pollock. From the very beginning, whether his work was regionalist or abstract, Pollock's work showed assured conception, dynamic rhythm and clear touch, and marked contrasts of dark and light. His expressionism was nourished by the work of the Mexican muralists, notably in the nightmarish *Woman* (1930–1933), which many critics see as a private family allegory, with its members surrounding an outsize mother like satellites in a dark sky. His pastoral work, like *Going West* (1934–1938), was nostalgic and melancholy. Yet there were always signs in his loose forms that he would move to abstraction. The New Deal rescued him from penury when he was employed in the FAP of the WPA, joining its painters in 1936 and staying until it was closed down in early 1943. It was his task to paint works for public buildings. He joined an experimental workshop of Alfaro Siquerios in Union Square, New York, where he was stimulated by Siquerios's own experimentation with new materials—spray guns and airbrushes, synthetic paint and lacquers. Pollock also discovered Picasso and his vocabulary of distended, reassembled, and primitive forms.

Since adolescence, Pollock had had a disturbing record of alcoholism and he underwent psychoanalysis with a number of psychiatrists in the period 1937–1943. During this time he made a series of "psychoanalytic drawings" and paintings with awkward limbs and eyes cleverly jumbled. Not only did they serve as therapy but they also served to exercise Pollock's need for the interconversion of form, the transmutation of figures into abstract form, and back again, notably in *White Horizontal* (c. 1938–1941) and *Composition with Masked Forms* (1941). These are fierce, disturbed works, akin to the last terrifying images of Goya or Van Gogh.

Pollock had been working to a breakthrough into major painting, heralded by his participation in a show organized by John Graham at McMillen, Inc., in January 1942, where relatively unknown American artists, such as Willem de Kooning and Lee Krasner, joined more famous ones, such as Stuart Davis and Walt Kuhn, and European notables such as Picasso and Braque. His work was now almost entirely abstract and on a very large scale, incorporating Cubist and Surrealist techniques in three paintings of 1942: *The Moon-Woman, Male and Female,* and *Stenographic Figure.* Elizabeth Frank writes of *Male and Female* that

it is possible to see male and female attributes in each of the figures. Passage yields to passage in an enriched virtuoso vocabulary of spatters, dips, swirls, scumbles, gestures, arabesques, filled-in shapes, and inscribed numbers, hieroglyphics of a painter by calligraphy that, for all its energy, never crowds or squeezes the picture.

As his companion and future wife, Lee Krasner, remembered, he would always continue painting if a recognizable image surfaced because "I choose to veil the imagery." In his *Guardians of the Secret* (1943), he combined a horizontal dog and two vertical figures, a bull and a woman, as "guardians" of his own psyche. He carried the bull imagery into *Pasiphaë* (1943), where the moon goddess of Crete consummates her love for a bull sent to her husband, King Minos.

Pollock moved to ever-larger and more abstract paintings and began pouring and dripping paint onto his canvases now stretched out on the floor, since some were far too large to be supported by an easel. In his *Composition with Pouring II* of 1943 for Peggy Guggenheim, a painting measuring 7' 11¾" by 19' 9½", he used thin vertical lines winding across the canvas in a mix of painting and drawing. In *Night Ceremony* each individual drawn shape exists quite independently in its own space. Sometimes, he returned to clear images as in his Equine series of 1944 that show his fascination with Picasso's horses in his bullfighting paintings. Pollock's *Totem Lesson 1* (1944) and *Totem Lesson 2* (1945) for his second one-man show at Art of This Century in November 1945 achieved complete solutions to the problems of mixing Abstract Expressionism figuration, and a mix of drawings as shapes and as "allover" lines. Clement Greenberg claimed that the show established Pollock "as the strongest painter of his generation." He believed the works were deeply pessimistic. "The only optimism in his smoky turbulent painting comes from his own manifest faith in the efficacy, for him personally, of art." Moreover, "he is not afraid to look ugly—all profoundly original art looks ugly at

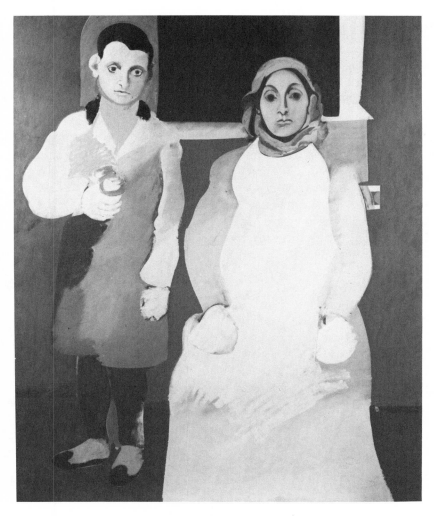

Arshile Gorky, *The Artist and His Mother* (1926–1929), oil, 60″ × 50″.
(Collection of Whitney Museum of American Art, New York; gift of
Julien Levy for Maro and Natasha Gorky in memory of their father).
Armenian artist Arshile Gorky, whose original name was Vosdanig
Manoog Adoian, immigrated to the United States in 1920, and in the
1930s became friendly with abstract artists Stuart Davis and Willem de
Kooning. He set himself the task of translating European modernism
into American modes by retracing the European artistic revolution from
impressionism to cubism and surrealism, generation by generation, in
his own works. In this transitional painting he acknowledges the influence of Picasso, adopting the sort of composition of Picasso's early works.

first." Much the same criticism had been made of cubist art just after the turn of the century.

Abstract Expressionism was the new distinctive American art that allowed New York to supersede Paris as the international center of art, just when American politicians encouraged a high art that would give the United States a new cultural authority, commensurate with its economic, political, and military aims in the postwar world. Clement Greenberg challenged the shopworn idea of the supremacy of Paris and insisted that New York had replaced it. "The conclusion forces itself," he declared, "that the main premises of western art have at last migrated to the United States, along with the center of gravity of industrial power and political power."

American Architecture

Although skyscrapers were first created in the 1870s and 1880s and took definitive form under the expert innovations of Louis Sullivan in the 1890s and 1900s, it was in the 1910s and 1920s that they came to be widely regarded as the most substantive contribution of the United States to modern architecture, representing American determination to excel and turning America's major cities into vertical, man-made canyons.

While modernism in architecture was defined in various sophisticated ways, essential components were the use of modern materials and modern techniques to create a contemporary interior environment and an unqualified modern facade. Thus modernist architects used not only steel, brick, and glass but also aluminum, concrete, and formica in their buildings, many of which in size and spaciousness extolled the power of corporate America. In domestic architecture the aim was to provide homes with the maximum of efficient, cost-effective modern conveniences. Once again, it is the imaginative organizers of the exhibition, *The Machine Age in America,* and the authors of its accompanying catalogue, who help us understand the way modern architecture was an inevitable product of machine age ideas, technology, and images.

At the American Institute of Architects' Convention of 1930

modernist George Howe defined modernism in architecture as essentially technique, functionalism, the use of "modern construction and modern materials to the full, for architectural expression as well as for practical ends." At the time Howe (1886–1955) and his partner William Lescaze (1896–1969) were designing the Philadelphia Savings Fund Society Building, Philadelphia (1928–1932), that drew upon and, indeed, maximized the use of such raw materials and technologies as glass, steel, and electricity in an age where the car also demanded a new sort of building, the garage, to shelter it.

While much concerned with appearances, some architects concentrated on using the machine and its processes to determine the architectural form of their buildings. Here the main influence was all sorts of industrial buildings but, most notably, factories. By the 1910s such industrial architects as Albert Kahn of Detroit had helped create a distinctive American idiom. In 1917 he was commissioned by Henry Ford to create steel frame structures in which some walls were made up of light metal or brick and glass. In his Ohio Steel Foundry Roll and Heavy Machine Shop, Lima, Ohio (1938), Albert Kahn further refined industrial design, emphasizing certain features, such as the sawtooth clerestory and butterfly roofs, while treating the different sections as units within a continuous surface with great luminous spaces in the inside and tall glass walls atop a pediment of light-colored brick on the exterior.

The main schools of architectural style in the 1920s and 1930s were the International and Neoclassical styles, competing idioms that were, nevertheless, simplified in comparison with all previous idioms and much influenced by the starkness of abstract art. While the new buildings were far more mechanically complex on the inside than any previously, they were yet far simpler on the outside.

In their *The International Style* (1932) Philip Johnson and Henry-Russell Hitchcock explained the three principles of the new architecture; architecture as volume rather than mass; regular, rather than axial symmetry as the unit factor in determining design; and the absence of arbitrary, surface ornament. To Johnson and Hitchcock, the International Style did not depend upon function or materials. Walls might look wafer thin yet be composed of thick brick. Nevertheless, the International Style had developed from technology and function. According to Richard Guy Wilson in *The Machine Age in America* (1986), "severity, flat Spartan surfaces, revealed structure, and mechanics as objects became its identifying features; the man-made object in the landscape and white interior its trademarks." Such was the Aluminaire House, Syosset, New York (1931), by A. Lawrence Kochner (1888–1969) and Albert Frey (b. 1903). Made of a light steel and aluminum frame covered by insulated board, tarpaper, and aluminum sheets, it was erected in ten days in 1931.

Architect and architectural artist Hugh Ferriss recognized the energy of massed twisting shapes and his illustrations for his *Metropolis of Tomorrow* are a celebration of towering man-made cliffs lightened by a chiaroscuro of setbacks, dramatic crevices punctuating the grainy texture of the buildings. While Ferris denied that contemporary cities were devoid of humanity and humanizing influences, his sketches are somewhat impersonal with men at the mercy of seemingly obdurate skyscrapers. Modern American cities were, to many, enormous, complex machines—multifaceted and capable of hosting all sorts of activities—yet impervious to many of man's inner needs.

Another crucial architect was Bertram Grosvenor Goodhue (1869–1924), one of the most significant modernists for his building designs that echoed the machine-as-parts approach to automobile design. Thus his most famous building, the Nebraska State Capitol (1920–1931), while retaining such traditional features as tower, dome, and decoration, overall achieved a, then, unique form, a setback tower in which ornament served geometry rather than gratifying it.

A crucial factor influencing skyscraper design was the New York zoning law of 1916, widely copied elsewhere, that limited the height of a building at immediate street level, in order to provide the street with as much light as possible, thereby inspiring architects to introduce setbacks, partly to create ever-higher towers within the letter of the law, partly to achieve greater plasticity of form. A notable example is the New York Telephone Company or Barclay-Vesey Building (1922–1926) by architect Ralph Walker (1889–1973) of the firm of McKenzie, Voorhees, and Gmelin. The site was in the shape of a parallelogram, thus inducing Walker to introduce, through successive designs, a twist between the base of the building and the gothic, art nouveau tower, supported by the raised surrounding setbacks.

The most inventive architect of New York skyscrapers was Raymond Hood (1881–1934) who, between 1922 and his death in 1934, produced a series of dazzling towers. The American Radiator (1924) had a sheath of black brick outside its steel-framed setbacks with a golden gothic tower; the Daily News (1929–1931) played with assertive vertical strips; the McGraw-Hill (1930–1931) alternated dark green horizontal slabs with light green vertical panels and windows.

The Chrysler Building (1930) was conceived primarily as an advertisement. William Van Allen transformed the original design of site developer William Reynolds, eliminating the proposed glass dome, increasing the height to 1,050 feet and seventy-seven stories, and crowning it with a Krupp "KA2" crest of stainless steel with triangular windows lit at night to enhance the effect.

For many, the crowning glory of this period of intense competition between corporations as to which could build the highest skyscraper, and an enduring architectural achievement in its own right, was the Empire State Building, New York (1931), by Shreve, Lamb, and Harmon. Its five-story base gave way to what Paul Goldberger calls "an immensely skillful piece of massing" of 102 stories surmounted by a rounded tower, 1,250 feet above street level. Moreover, its facade mixed granite and limestone of the Stone Age with nickel and aluminum of the machine age.

Radio's most distinctive advertisement was the RCA tower, center of the Rockefeller Center, New York (1932–1940). Widely hailed as a milestone in urban civilization, the Rockefeller Center made its greatest impact through its massive scale and soaring skyscrapers. For the first time a series of skyscrapers were designed as an integral group. In its patterns of building and space, planes and light, the Rockefeller Center was a truly historical achievement. Most of all, it succeeded as glorious advertisement for big business during the depression, a time when few would glorify business in the printed word.

In the course of the 1930s American architects began to achieve a balanced, satisfying synthesis of the various diverse strands of modern architecture—the International Style, setback skyscrapers, and streamlined buildings. The results represented what critic Talbot Hamlin called "a contemporary American Style" in his article of that title for *Pencil Points* of February 1938. These were clean, sparse, neoclassical buildings with conventional proportions and incorporating classical motifs where appropriate. They included the Folger Shakespeare Library, Washington, D.C. (1929–1932) by Paul Cret (1876–1945). This is a white marble building with fluted piers alternating with high narrow windows whose spandrels carry neoclassical sculptured reliefs. Another stripped classical building was the National Airport in Washington, D.C. (1940), built by the PWA and with Howard L. Cheney as consultant architect, a semicircular building with concave entrance and convex glass wall looking upon the landing strip and with immense cylindrical columns.

Chicago became a center for machine housing with such projects as the Battledeck House (1929–1930) by Henry Dubin (1892–1963), so-called because wood was eliminated and because the system of roof and floor of welded steel plate and beams was somewhat like the construction of a ship. George Fred Keck was another architect committed to machine housing, perhaps on account of his background in architectural engineering at the University of Illinois.

For the Century of Progress Exposition he devised a duodecagon House of Tomorrow that could set off an optimum number of new gadgets and materials: General Electric provided appliances, H. W. Howell, the tubular metal furniture, U.S. Gypsum the floors, and Holland Furnace, the air conditioning. Apart from the concrete foundations and floors carried by core steel columns, the house was prefabricated and took only two months to erect. Underlying the design was Keck's assumption that modern life was dependent upon the machine and that the interiors must be adjustable through a sequence of movable, insulation board walls in order to accommodate successive changes in life-style. In the second year of the exposition Keck constructed a second, more refined house, largely prefabricated, the Crystal House, for which all exterior walls were of glass and the only room to be fully enclosed was the kitchen. Other architects who experimented with machine-produced houses included Howard Fisher and Norman Bel Geddes.

In contrast with the more conservative Northeast and Midwest, architects in southern California, such as Richard Neutra and Rudolph Schindler, found their affluent clients welcomed experimental building, partly because they liked to consider themselves part of the avant-garde, partly because of the economic boom and fantasy of Hollywood, partly because the milder climate of California favored more experiments in building. Richard Neutra acknowledged how a new style was being forged by the manufacturers of building materials and specialties, and his work used the technology of construction in a fashion far ahead of any European architect. The Beard House, Altadena, California (1934–1935), was built for William and Melba Beard, respectively a university teacher of engineering and the son of historians Charles and Mary Beard, and his wife, an aviator. The house used hollow steel channels for the walls, open-web steel trusses for the roof, and steel web beams as the base for the concrete floor. The exterior was painted silver gray while the interior had aluminum steel columns, a gray linoleum floor, brown masonite walls, and tubular steel furniture. More dramatic was Neutra's house for film director Josef von Sternberg in the San Fernando Valley (1934–1935) protected by long blank metal walls and a superfluous moat.

Rudolph Schindler (1887–1953) was less successful commercially and artistically than Neutra, partly because he was far less gifted as a publicist, partly because he synthesized a far greater range of influences and, therefore, lacked Neutra's single-minded development. In his Dr. Philip Lovell Beach House, Newport Beach, California (1925–1926), Schindler exploited modern technology; yet the overall effect was deliberately indeterminate, challenging conventional ideas of enclosure. Dissatisfied with Schindler's eclectic style, architect, curator, and critic Philip Johnson refused to allow his work to be exhibited in the MOMA International Style Show. Thus, rejected, Schindler tried to develop new sorts of projects using cheaper materials than steel.

Los Angeles architect Gregory Ain (b. 1908) worked at different times for both Schindler and Neutra and was influenced by

New York Hospital Cornell University Medical College Association Buildings, York Avenue from 68th to 70th Streets, New York, designed by architects Coolidge, Shepley, Bullfinch and Abbott and completed in 1933, is an example of architectural fusion between classical, medieval, and modern styles. (Photo by Irving Underhill, 1932; Library of Congress).

both of them. He wanted to build inexpensive modern housing using, as Schindler planned, cheap modern technology, but with broad, plain surfaces, as Neutra would have wished. Typical of Ain's work was his small, inexpensive Becker House on a hillside in the Silver Lake district of Los Angeles (1938). Made of a wood frame with plywood and stucco, it cost only $3,000 to build. Everything was run on economical lines because of the efficient layout, and Ain's use of open space was broad and subtle. Ain's Dunsimuir Flats, Los Angeles (1937), was another instance of a fully integrated structure using four different building elements to reduce costs, yet, by creating a series of cubes allowing light to enter all major rooms on three sides in each and every room.

Whatever the most ambitious plans of the most progressive architects, mass-produced housing was very expensive in terms of factory tooling and transportation. Moreover, even if a huge volume of production could be achieved in the interest of cutting the cost of individual units, this would not eliminate much of the expense of housing that revolved around costs on site: acquiring land, laying foundations, providing utilities, and meeting local building codes. Yet standardization could be applied to such traditional forms as wooden houses. After World War II mass-produced housing became a practicable proposition and suburbs and towns often built by the Levitt company to specific standards sprung up across the United States.

In February and March 1932 the Museum of Modern Art (MOMA), New York, mounted the International Exhibition of Modern Architecture, which was subsequently shown in another thirty cities and accompanied by a substantial catalog and book. It had three sections: one showed the extent of the International Style; another showed its influence on housing; and the third showed work by nine leaders of the style, including the Americans Richard Neutra, Irving and Monroe Bowman, Raymond Hood, George Howe, and William Lescaze. Maverick architect Frank Lloyd Wright (1869–1959) was also included, although his work was of a very different and romantic order, because his preeminence was widely recognized. The exhibition was jointly planned by Henry-Russell Hitchcock, Philip Johnson, and MOMA's director, Alfred H. Barr, Jr. The emphasis was on a lighter, more volumetric form of building than the rigid setback skyscrapers of the 1920s and one shorn of excessive decoration.

Yet, for all his differences, Frank Lloyd Wright's work was likened to that of architects influenced by the new machines. Critic Richard Guy Wilson comments how the Kaufmann Residence, later known as Fallingwater, in Bear Run, Pennsylvania (1936), the most notable of Wright's organic building designs, is a

machine in the wilderness with its broad, machine-produced, reinforced-concrete decks. Yet *Fallingwater* is tied to the site, part of the waterfall. Rocks push up through the living-room floor, and substantial stone piers carry the machine-like decks. . . . Wright's arguments for, and use of, materials in their nearly natural state—wood with the grain, stone in the rough, and the application of "natural" colors or finishes to the concrete, copper and brick—became a hallmark of organic design. . . .

Wright's fascination with organic shapes also led to his most famous office design of the period, the Johnson Wax Building, Racine, Wisconsin (1938), notable for its twenty-two "Dendiform Shafts," or mushroom, tapering columns, pinned on brass shoes at the bottom and growing outward at the ceiling of gleaming pyrex tubing. They served to divide the office space and enhance it by forming a contrast to the light streaming from the skylight.

Frank Lloyd Wright's professional life was conducted by continuous financial brinkmanship and marred by bouts of ill health, bronchitis, and pneumonia, that drove him to the desert camp at Taliesin West, Arizona. When his clients proved fractious or cowardly, he remonstrated with them. He berated client Alice Birdsall, for whom he had designed the Hollyhock House in California, in 1920, in a rigorous letter of several pages, accusing her of being wayward and headstrong, for going on overseas voyages when she could not cope with building problems.

You had flung my work to clerks who were naturally envious or suspicious. . . . My soul is sore and my mind stiff with this insult. . . . But if . . . in spite of what I have seen to be a disinclination on your part to stand the discipline of steady sustained endeavor . . . if you can break through the obstructions to any understanding with me you have yourself set up and fostered, then I will stand up to my duty to myself and to my work and to you. . . . Whatever its birth pangs [Hollyhock] will take its place as your contribution and mine to the vexed life of our time. What future it will have?—who can say?

Critic Ada Louise Huxtable comments how extraordinary it was that, despite considerable struggles, Wright still managed to produce a body of work, both completed and left at the planning stage, that changed the course of world architecture. Yet his personal vision was swiftly synthesized by avant-garde architects abroad. Indeed, there was much cross-fertilization even between

Wright and immigrant German architect Ludwig Mies van der Rohe who came to America in 1938: "There are some remarkable parallels in the planes and masses of their brick-walled houses. Modernism was fed by many streams, meeting and mingling in a shared vision that the doctrinaire modernist historian has never allowed." Wright's designs were carefully worked out over long periods. Fallingwater had its origins in his Gale House (1910); the Price Tower (1953) of Bartlesville, Oklahoma, had its origins in the 1929 projects of St. Marks-in-the Bouwerie. As Ada Louise Huxtable maintains,

[Wright's] architecture is not about image first and structure after, or a look embellished by some intellectual trimming, as in today's trivializing trends. It is based on the ability to visualize and understand a building simultaneously in every relationship, to see and feel the way its inner and outer forms and spaces are modeled by material, structure and light, and to invest this knowledge with spirit and style.

13

NEW HORIZONS, CLOSED FRONTIERS
America in World Affairs After 1920

THE UNITED States had three overlapping and contesting forms of foreign policy in the 1920s and early 1930s: the rhetoric of isolation with its unfortunate diplomatic impressions of neglect and lassitude upon Britain, France, Germany, and Japan; the sporadically active diplomacy by which the United States tried to resolve international disputes amicably; and commercial penetration of the rest of the world, notably in the matter of oil diplomacy and aviation rivalry, pursued by new multinational companies. The first led to misunderstandings at home and abroad; the second to temporary easing of international tensions; and the third helped lay the foundations for America's rise to globalism in the 1940s.

The shadow of Woodrow Wilson continued to loom over American foreign policy in the 1920s. Statesmen, determined to avoid the sort of controversy surrounding Wilson's handling of foreign affairs, reacted against his policies of intervention and his moralistic rhetoric. The shift in American foreign policy from outright intervention to apparent isolation was accepted, even welcomed, by the public, weary of the war and the political bitterness of 1919 and 1920. Isolationism did not mean withdrawing from economic involvement or political contact with other nations. It meant, rather, a return to the old American insistence on freedom of action, an outright rejection of collective security.

However, the story of America's foreign policy in the 1920s is not quite as isolationist as the myth. Isolationism was more a matter of instinct than of reason. It is certainly true that America enacted a series of measures—the immigration laws of 1921 and 1924 and the high tariffs of 1922 and 1930—that were isolationist. It is also true that America's absence from the League of Nations was a diplomatic handicap for American statesmen. America's commitments in Latin America and its financial loans to the Western powers involved it in negotiations with other nations that could not be conducted formally through the League. Yet we can set against the narrow self-interest of certain policies the altruism of others—such as the proposed reduction of the navy by the agreement of the Washington Conference, President Herbert Hoover's moratorium on war debts, and even the Kellogg Pact.

The economic reasons for American involvement were overwhelming. The United States had emerged stronger than ever from the war. Not only did it still have its superb natural resources and advanced industrial technology but it had also benefited materially from the catastrophe of war. Increased demand for products at home and abroad had stimulated invention and production. Furthermore, the wartime disruption of world trade had enabled American businesses to develop new markets abroad. The financial capital of the world had moved from London to New York. Among the powers, only the United States could expect continued economic progress. In 1920 the United States was producing about 40 percent of the world's coal—far more than twice as much as Britain, its nearest rival; an even greater proportion of the world's pig iron; and almost 70 percent of all crude petroleum. Its wealth in such raw materials as lumber and agricultural crops was prodigious. Despite its deficiency in a few crucial metals (manganese, chromite, and tungsten), rubber, and the crops of coffee, tea, and sugar, it was more nearly self-sufficient than any other country.

Throughout the 1920s the United States consolidated its position as the world's preeminent commercial power. According to the Department of Commerce *Commerce Yearbook of 1930,* it accounted for almost 16 percent of the world's exports, and 12 percent of imports. Its industrial track record was greater still. By the end of the 1920s the value of American industrial production was 46 percent of the world total. As to national income, according to *The United States in the World Economy* (1943), the total for the United States in 1929 was the same as the sum total for twenty-three other leading industrial nations, including Britain, France, Germany, Canada, and Japan.

In finance, the war had reversed the prewar position. In 1914 the United States was a debtor nation with net obligations of $3.7 billion. In 1919 it was a creditor nation owed $12.5 billion by other countries. Of this, $10 billion was in war debts. However, analysis of the figures suggests that in the private sector what was owed to American companies had almost doubled, while what they owed had been almost cut in half. By 1929 additional foreign loans and direct investment had increased private net assets to over $8 billion.

Thus, despite the official rhetoric of its foreign policy, the United States was to play a decisive role in international economic affairs. Through gifts and loans it supported the rehabilitation of Europe, in particular providing France, Germany, and Italy with huge advances to stabilize their currencies. In addition, the United States funded construction in Austria, Poland, and Yugoslavia. American money was also used to fund the digging of oil wells in the Middle East, planting rubber trees in Malaya and the Dutch East Indies and sugar cane in Cuba, and developing public utilities in Tokyo and Shanghai. Furthermore, giant corporations, such as Standard Oil, Ford, General Motors, International Harvester, Singer, and IBM, established various manufacturing companies in China, Europe, and the Caribbean.

The penetration of the rest of the world by American interests was seen most clearly in American pursuit of oil and ascendancy in aviation. In the fields of oil and aviation diplomacy the Americans were hotly pursued by their European former diplomatic allies and current commercial competitors.

International Oil Politics

The seven major oil companies (Exxon, Socal—also known as Chevron—Mobil, Gulf, Texaco, Shell, and BP), sometimes known as the seven sisters, dominated the world of oil from the 1920s onward. They became the first multinational corporations. English investigative journalist Anthony Sampson comments that

Each of them soon developed into an "integrated oil company" controlling not only its own production, but also transportation, distribution and marketing. With their own fleets of tankers, they could soon operate across the world in every sector of the industry, from the "upstream" business of drilling and producing at the oilfields, to the "downstream" activity of distributing and selling at the pumps or the factories. And each company strove, with varying success, to be self-sufficient at both ends, so that their oil could flow into their tankers through their refineries to their filling-stations. It was this world-wide integration, together with their size, which was the common characteristic of these seven.

On the surface, the oil companies were engaged in fierce competition to sell their product, especially as gasoline for motor cars.

Moreover, in the 1920s, the United States was by far the greatest consumer of oil, especially with the dramatic rise in the number of automobiles and the transformation of an entire society based on a superfluity of cheap oil. In the 1920s oilmen and government officials contemplated a world shortage with resources much depleted by the war and the ever-increasing number of automobiles. The director of the United States Geological Survey disclosed how the American oil situation "can best be described as precarious." Disturbed by their realization, American and European oil companies and governments began a scramble for oil, as bitterly contested as the earlier imperialist scramble for colonies. Britain and France tried to turn the Middle East into an Anglo-French oil field from which they planned to exclude the

United States. However, the United States retorted that it was clearly impossible for America to continue to provide the world with oil from its own diminishing supply. Moreover, it had played a decisive part in winning World War I and was thus entitled to a share in world reserves. Consequently, under Harding, the State Department began to support the American oil companies' pursuit of fresh fields. It was, of course, the casual support given the oil companies by the Ohio Gang that led to the Teapot Dome Scandal. Anthony Sampson characterizes the contests: "Ostensibly the [various oil] companies were the boxers in the big fights, and the governments were the seconds, providing encouragement or reproof. This meant that when the fight was most critical, the governments were out of the ring."

On the surface, and to critics of federal policy, it looked as if the State Department were letting the oil companies improvise its own diplomacy. Behind the scenes many diplomats and the secretariat in the State Department deeply distrusted the companies but they were reluctant to create any formal organization to conduct an oleaginous foreign policy. Thus they chose to use the oil companies, as discreetly as possible, to work out foreign policy for them. Government officers wanted to encourage the oil companies' search for fresh fields and began to apply such doctrines as the Open Door to oil, meaning that, in future, the former war allies should not discriminate against one another in the matter of oil supplies.

For their part, Britain and France used their "mandates" of Arab territory acquired from the defunct Ottoman Empire to search for new oil fields. In 1919 at San Remo they revived a prewar oil agreement of 1914 in which Armenian entrepreneur Calouste Gulbenkian had created an oil syndicate, the Turkish Petroleum Company (TPC). It was originally owned by BP, Shell, the Deutsche Bank, and Gulbenkian. The revision gave the Germans' quarter-share to France. When the (initially secret) agreement was discovered, the American ambassador in London protested that Britain was trying to corner the world's share of oil. Britain could argue that, since the United States had never declared war on Turkey, any peace treaty or other agreement with Turkey was beyond its scope. This was technically correct

Modern Brunnhilde. Vivacious aviatrix Amelia Earhart was in the early generation of pioneer pilots who demonstrated the potential of flight. In June 1937 she attempted the first round-the-world flight near the Equator but, after taking off from New Guinea for Howland Island in the Pacific, she and her navigator vanished. A large naval search failed to trace them and, later, rumors abounded that she had not been lost at sea but had been taken in Saipan by the Japanese and been killed. (Library of Congress).

but, perhaps, not the fundamental reason. For its part, America claimed, yet again, that its decisive part in helping Britain and France to win the war merited some compensation. British foreign secretary Lord Curzon said that oil within the British Empire and in Persia amounted to no more than 4.5 percent of world production, while the United States, together with Mexico, accounted for about 82 percent. Nevertheless, after prolonged pressure, Britain was ready to compromise with the United States. In August 1922 Britain offered the United States, first, 12 percent of the TPC and, then, 20 percent, which was accepted. This allowed (initially seven) American oil companies, led by Exxon and Mobil, into the new mandate, later state, of Iraq.

After the small state of Mosul was placed in Iraq under the British mandate, the new government in Iraq signed an agreement, the company was to remain British with a British chairman and would pay Iraq a royalty of 4 gold shillings (about $1 at that time) per ton. The original San Remo concession of 20 percent to Iraq was excluded from the new agreement. This prompted two Iraqi ministers to resign in protest and it remained a continuous source of bitterness with the Iraquis. Gulbenkian not only retained his original 5 percent but also the original clause by which the participants agreed not to seek concessions in the territory of the defunct Ottoman Empire, from Turkey in the north through Jordan, Syria, and Saudi Arabia in the southeast. This was in flat contradiction of the principle of the Open Door but, as the American companies were eager to settle the matter, all partners agreed to the terms in July 1928 at Ostend, Belgium. The TPC was thereafter called the Iraq Petroleum Company (IPC). In fact, none of the participants was exactly sure what had comprised the old Ottoman Empire, which had, after all, been in decline for a hundred years before its final collapse. Calouste Gulbenkian defined what he meant by drawing a line on a map round the territory with a red pencil. The so-called Red Line agreement included all the richest oil-producing areas of the Middle East except Iran and Kuwait. Thus, (initially) five American companies, including Exxon and Mobil, had penetrated the Middle East taking 23.7 percent of the company and the Open Door slammed shut behind them. Drilling began in April 1927 and six months later prospectors struck one of the richest oil fields in the world.

The Iraq Petroleum Company provided the prototype for other joint ventures in the Middle East. Because it included two American and two British companies, it made actual control of production comparatively easy and limited competition. However, it stoked resentment in those advanced countries without their own supply of oil.

In the early 1920s there were only three major contenders in the contest for world oil—the American Exxon, and the European Shell and BP. They now began to draw closer together, lest price-cutting wars should ruin one and all, increasingly convinced by Sir Henri Deterding of Shell's arguments about the dangers of internecine competition. Thus, in 1928, prompted by Walter Teagle of Exxon, the Big Three started a series of secret conferences with the aim of restraining one another from ruinous competition. In August 1928 Sir Henri Deterding rented Achnacarry Castle in the Scottish Highlands where he met with Sir John Cadman (since 1927 chairman of BP) and Walter Teagle (of Exxon). Ostensibly, they were there for trout and grouse. However, as representatives from other oil companies and various oil experts began to augment this select gathering, the British press grew curious about the outcome. The *Sunday Express* of London found the castle "an impenetrable fortress which harbors one of the most interesting groups of silent personalities in the world," whereas "the Scottish lochs themselves are no more communicative than the oil companies." According to Anthony Sampson, the party agreed to divide the world of oil into an international cartel. Their pool association, later known as the Achnacarry agreement, or "As Is," was never implemented in full but its echoes reverberated across the oil world until the 1950s.

In place of "excessive competition" that had led to "tremendous overproduction," it proposed collaboration based on seven principles. In the first, the parties agreed to abide by their present volume of business and to limit any future increases in production in proportion to their existing levels. (Thus, as a mechanism to reduce the possibility of excessive competition, the first principle was obliquely following something like the principle of the 5:5:3 naval agreement in Washington in 1922.) Moreover, according to the third principle "only such facilities [are] to be added as are necessary to supply the public with its increased requirements of petroleum products in the most efficient manner." Underlying the cartel was Deterding's favorite Dutch proverb—*Eendracht maakt macht*—cooperation provides power. Each party knew it could not achieve a global monopoly. Only by cooperation could the companies prosper. Whatever the economic rationale for an international cartel, it was politically insupportable on democratic grounds. Thus it was to be kept secret until 1952. The Achnacarry agreement was a plutocrats' plot to fix prices and generally divide the trade in oil. The basis for the oil cartel was the maintenance of American prices and thus it was especially attuned to the immediate needs of Exxon and Walter Teagle. Anthony Sampson asserts how

The arbiter of the world price of oil was the "Gulf Plus System." To protect American oil, the oil from anywhere else was fixed at the price in the Gulf of Mexico, whence most United States oil was shipped overseas, *plus* the standard freight charges for shipping the oil from the Gulf to its market. While the United States was the only major producing country the system had some justification; but, as American oil was becoming more expensive and threatened by much cheaper oil from Iran or Venezuela, it was a blatant device to keep up prices.

The Achnacarry, or As Is, agreement did not fix rules. It was a statement of intent, agreed first by Exxon, Shell, and BP, and then by fifteen American companies, including the four remaining sisters—Gulf, Socal (or Chevron), Texaco, and Mobil. It did not fix oil absolutely throughout the world because it could not discipline the USSR, but it allowed the largest Western companies to supervise the quota system and create two export associations.

Paradoxically, the Red Line agreement was to lead to an outsider taking the richest prize of all. Ironically, Socal achieved its footholds in two Middle Eastern countries precisely because of its lack of previous involvement. These were, first, Bahrain, and, second, Saudi Arabia, which had the most spectacular oil reserves.

In 1930 the profligate King Ibn Saud was in desperate need of money and his British adviser, Harry St. John Philby, who had left the Colonial Service and converted to Islam, advised him to exploit Saudi Arabia's mineral resources. They had an American geologist Karl Twitchell survey the land but, although he was excited by what he discovered, he failed to rouse Texaco, Exxon, and Gulf. However, Socal, not bound by the Red Line agreement, approached Twitchell, made him an adviser and also promised to pay Philby if he could secure a concession. This he achieved despite the temporary intervention by BP who made a much lower bid. Socal offered the king an immediate loan of £30,000, to be followed by a second loan of £20,000 in eighteen months, and an annual rent of £5,000—all in gold. King and company reached agreement in August 1933 and Philby received an annual salary of £1,000 from Socal. These Arabian oil fields were ready for production in May 1939, an event celebrated by a royal progress to the new oil town and two days of touring and feasting. The king initiated production by turning the valve on the pipeline. He was delighted and soon increased the size of the concession to 444,000 square miles.

The establishment of Socal, a completely American company, not only changed the face of Saudi Arabia irrevocably but also changed the balance of power in the Middle East. At the time of the agreement in 1933 there were no more than fifty Westerners in Jedda, the Saudi capital on the coast, and no American diplomat there at all. Not until 1939 when Bert Fisher, minister to Egypt, was accredited to Saudi Arabia as well, was there an American diplomatic presence. Anthony Sampson remarks that,

On the one hand was a desert kingdom ruled by an absolute monarch with medieval autocracy, with about five million people, many of them nomads. On the other hand were American technologists, as Philby [Saud's adviser] described them, "descending from the skies on their flying carpets with strange devices for probing the bowels of the earth in search of the liquid muck for which the world clamours to keep its insatiable machines alive."

Each new discovery of oil in the Middle East served to weaken still further the authority of the national government in whose territory it was found, as each discovery added to the world glut. In Iran BP retained its monopoly despite the acumen of a formidable ruler, Reza Shah, and it secured a new agreement in 1933 that extended the concession until 1993. In Iraq the IPC consortium made huge profits without giving the government its due return. Between 1934 and 1939 Exxon made a profit of around 52 cents per barrel, double what it paid the Iraqi government. It was said that for an initial investment of $14 million Exxon's share in IPC was worth $130 million by 1937.

American economic penetration of other countries had a profound sociological and cultural impact on them. It was not simply that American cars, bicycles, sewing machines, typewriters, and household goods appeared in ever-greater volume around the world but also that their presence transformed the nature of both European and Asian industries. Competing native companies were obliged to adopt American techniques of mass production and assembly lines. The transformation was most marked in Japan but even the relatively backward industrial system of the U.S.S.R. began to consider new technology called "Fordismus." This led to criticism on both sides of the Atlantic of what Charles Beard, writing for *Harper's* in March 1929 about "The American Invasion of Europe," called "prose against poetry; dollars against sacrifice; calculation against artistic abandon." The debate still continues today. The most significant development, as Beard explained, was that the export of American industrial products, cultural ideas, and customs was remodeling modern societies throughout the world. When American bankers loaned money to foreign countries and their firms, they often retained rights of supervision. This practice was even more pronounced among American corporations investing in foreign factories, assembly plants, or distributing companies.

Of all the American cultural influences, the most insidious and overwhelming was the cinema in which Hollywood dominated the countries of Europe as much as it did the United States. For millions around the world, Hollywood was American civilization. After that, American music and lyrics, especially those in ragtime or jazz, were all-pervasive, whether sung on radio, in theaters, or on disks.

At the same, and for the first, time Europe was being invaded by American tourists *en masse,* at the rate of about 500,000 each year in the 1920s. This was far more than the expatriate writers of the lost generation of Hemingway, Dos Passos, Eliot, Cummings *et al.* who had led the way. Whether on business or pleasure American travelers in Europe, and Asia, began to insist on American cultural standards in a way that was to transform foreign cultures slowly but inexorably. "Can Paris be retaken by the Parisians?" asked the New York *Herald Tribune* of January 24, 1926. "The French claim they cannot walk on the Boulevard St. Germain and hear a word of their native tongue. They claim that the high prices following in the wake of the American visitor are driving them from the best restaurants in Paris. They mourn the days of yesterday and scorn the Americanized Latin Quarter of today."

In view of all these factors, the United States could no more return to its supposed isolation in 1921 than it could have ignored World War I in 1914. Moreover, the coils of commerce set in motion in Cuba and China at the turn of the century were to wind up foreign policy in a way few could have predicted. As the historian of American expansion, Foster Rhea Dulles, concludes, "The United States controlled so much of the world's material wealth and industrial production, so great a proportion of international trade, and such a large share of world capital resources that American policy could not fail to have decisive consequences in every part of the globe."

Despite all these things and increasing press comment on them, the American people in general and their leaders in particular had very little understanding of the changing world that the United States was doing so much to shape. The United States never developed a coordinated economic strategy. If the story of international affairs in the period 1920–1932 is somewhat confused, then the United States's own confusion is partly responsible. These uneasy years and the greater disturbances they led to in the 1930s have led some to call them the years of the lost peace.

Washington Naval Conference

Despite his lack of diplomatic experience, Charles Evans Hughes was an imaginative and persuasive secretary of state (1921–1925). His dignified manner and Jove-like appearance lent style and prestige to any event he attended. However, any controversial proposal in favor of international cooperation from Hughes would have aroused suspicion among certain formidable members of Congress. Wilson's implacable foe, Henry Cabot Lodge of Massachusetts, remained chairman of the Senate Foreign Relations Committee until his death in November 1924 when he was succeeded by William E. Borah of Idaho, whose intransigent isolationism was supported by that of another leading member of the committee, Hiram Johnson of California. Nevertheless, after a Senate resolution that declared the war was over and that the United States reserved rights mentioned in the Treaty of Versailles, Hughes negotiated treaties with Germany, Austria, and Hungary, that were ratified in October 1921.

Having rejected Wilsonian remedies, President Warren Harding was conscious that the Republicans needed to do something "just as good as the League." This was to be the Washington Naval Conference. Peace sentiment in the United States, nurtured by Wilson and frustrated by the turn of events in 1919 and 1920, bridled at the thought of another arms and naval race between the great powers. Even Senator Borah thought that the incipient naval rivalry between America and Japan would end the way of all such rivalries. On December 14, 1920, he tabled a resolution in Congress calling for a reduction in armaments that was in July 1921 opposed by only four members in the House. Moreover, he suggested to Charles E. Hughes that the United States, Britain, and Japan should abstain from further shipbuilding. Hughes had the prestige and personal skill to avoid the sort of partisan antagonism between president and Senate that had so disfigured Wilson's last two years. Furthermore, he was anxious to repair declining American relations with Japan. He feared that Japan, resentful of the Immigration Quota Act of 1921 and antagonized by American economic rivalry in the Far East, might invoke the

The Republicans' attempt "to do something as good as the League" was the Washington Naval Conference of 1921–1922 whose principal achievement was the Five Power Naval Treaty concluded in the Diplomatic Room of the State Department on February 6, 1922, and signed by (from left to right at the table) Augusto Rosso of Italy, H. G. Chilton of Britain, Secretary of State Charles Evans Hughes, André de la Boulaye of France, and Masanao Hanihara of Japan. (Photo by National Photo Company; Library of Congress).

Anglo-Japanese Alliance of 1902 to claim British support against the United States. Britain agreed to a naval conference in Washington because it had no intention of losing American friendship over Japan.

To ensure maximum public support, the Harding administration prepared the ground well in advance. In the first place, the conference would be held in Washington; in the second, the president would not take part himself and the American delegation would consist of Secretary of State Charles Evans Hughes, elder statesman Elihu Root, and, from the Senate Foreign Relations Committee, Henry Cabot Lodge for the Republicans and Oscar W. Underwood for the Democrats. The implication was clear. Had Wilson showed such discretion, the outcome at Paris would have been very different. Moreover, the very fact of the conference, officially the "Conference on the Limitation of Armament," but more widely known as the "Peace Conference," implied that the United States was about to mend its bridges with the other powers.

Ironically, the various tensions between the powers added immeasurably to the success of the conference. On the day before the first session, November 12, 1921, the unknown soldier was buried at Arlington, an ideal ceremonial prelude to the meeting. In his opening address Hughes boldly took the initiative and asked representatives of Britain, Japan, France, Italy, Belgium, the Netherlands, Portugal, and China to sink 1,878,093 tons of capital ships—half the vessels afloat and in dry dock. The total tonnage for battleships and cruisers finally agreed by the powers was:

United States	525,850	to be distributed among 18 ships
Britain	558,950	to be distributed among 20 ships
Japan	301,320	to be distributed among 10 ships
France	221,170	to be distributed among 10 ships
Italy	182,800	to be distributed among 10 ships.

The agreement was simplistically expressed in the ratio 5 : 5 : 3. In addition, the powers accepted Hughes's proposal that no new ships should be built for ten years, and a limit of 35,000 tons to be imposed on new battleships. The conference also provided for restriction of aircraft carriers, normally of no more than 27,000 tons each, whereby Britain and the United States were each allowed 135,000 tons altogether, with Japan allowed 81,000 tons, and Italy and France, 60,000 tons apiece. Britain proposed the outright abolition of submarines but the other powers would not agree. Nevertheless, public opinion demanded some limitation as to submarine tonnage and usage, embodied in a separate five power treaty that lapsed when France refused to ratify it.

The main Five Power Treaty was supposed to last until 1936,

but from December 31, 1934, any country could give two years' notice of withdrawing from it. Japan's determination to secure a bigger ratio was submerged by an agreement with America that neither nation would expand its Pacific naval bases. Hughes knew that Congress would not have approved funds for building up American defenses in Guam and the Philippines. Moreover, he hoped that, if Japan were free from fear of attack, her statesmen would pursue a moderate foreign policy. To this end, and to allay mutual suspicions between the United States, Britain, and Japan, a Four Power Treaty, also signed with France, superseded the 1902 Anglo-Japanese Alliance. The four powers pledged themselves to "respect their rights in relation to their insular possessions in the region of the Pacific Ocean." In addition, a Nine Power Treaty acknowledged the Open Door to China. All nations attending the conference agreed to respect China's sovereignty and integrity. Japan agreed to restore the Shandong Peninsula (taken from Germany) to China and to start withdrawing troops from eastern Siberia. Initially, the powers made half-hearted efforts to abide by their agreements. However, they avoided proper discussion of provisions for enforcement of the naval limitations. Throughout the twenties the U.S. Navy was to be maintained at maximum strength and modernized. Only its overage vessels and those still under construction were scrapped according to the terms of the Washington Conference.

As if recognizing that a successful foreign policy could only be conducted by an expanded and informed civil service, successive presidents and secretaries of state had the State Department reorganized in the course of the 1920s. The diplomatic and consular services were merged and the civil service expanded to administer them, providing increased professional opportunities for career diplomats. Even so, the expansion was probably smaller than the need. According to Graham H. Stuart in *The Department of State* (1949), the State Department's annual budget was about $2 million in the 1920s and its personnel based at home numbered about 600.

Once the Washington Conference was over, public opinion began to lose interest in foreign affairs. Furthermore, isolationist sentiment was nourished by the activities of revisionist historians and pacifists. Revisionist histories of the origins of the war were to have a profound impact on a whole generation and its attitude to foreign affairs. They made particular the grievances expressed in metaphorical terms by the lost generation of war novelists. Both historians and novelists agreed that propaganda had debased language and that in the war the state had become a servile mechanism to malign forces. Revisionism began as an investigation into the causes of World War I and developed into a justification of American isolationism. The most immediate reason for the sudden appearance of revisionist histories about the war was the opening of the archives of the fallen imperial powers of Russia, Germany, and Austria that disclosed the prewar and wartime negotiations of both the Central and Entente powers, and revealed the great disparity between the fraudulent wartime propaganda of the nation states and the ugly reality of backstairs diplomacy.

The first major piece of American revisionist writing was provided by Sidney Bradshaw Fay of Smith College in three articles for the *American Historical Review* in 1920 and 1921, in which he refused to accept government propaganda about the origins of the war. Using Austrian and Russian documents, he derided the war-guilt clause of the Treaty of Versailles. Germany, he argued, had not wanted war and in 1914 had tried to persuade Austria against a declaration of war against Serbia. But Fay did not absolve Germany from blame completely for "in a wider sense, also, Germany is responsible, because one may say that militarism was one of the great causes of the war. . . . And for the growth of militarism in Europe, no country was so much responsible as Germany." Later he repeated his conclusions in *The Origins of the World War* (1928).

The supposed duplicity of Woodrow Wilson in achieving American intervention was a cardinal feature of the argument of *Shall It Be Again?* by J. K. Turner that appeared in 1922. Turner concluded that America had never been in danger of invasion, that Britain was more guilty of violations against American neutrality than Germany and that, in the war of rival imperialism, Wilson was willing to serve the special interests of American businessmen. "The great myth of the world war was Wilson idealism. Our noble President was simply a one hundred per cent American politician. The secret of Wilson is hypocrisy." Moreover, while presidents served Wall Street interests there would always be a danger of getting involved in wars. The real villain was the businessman who wanted to make a fast buck even if it involved plunging America into war. This particular criticism was to bear very bitter fruit in the 1930s. Other leading revisionists were Frederick Bausman, Harry Elmer Barnes, C. Hartley Grattan, Charles A. Beard, and, later, Walter Millis.

A more astute use of prewar and wartime history than these attempts to rewrite the past was made by progressive journalist Walter Lippmann in his influential *Public Opinion* (1922). He summed up the confusion of public and politicians resulting from their bitter experience of international diplomacy and the bombardment of pro-and anti-Wilson propaganda. *Public Opinion* was a pioneer analysis of the way people receive, and are influenced by, news, and the book's general analysis has not been surpassed. The central argument is that democracy is not based on an intelligent, informed, or rational public opinion. People, Lippmann argued, do not react to reality but to their personal view of reality determined by the pictures in their minds that he called "stereotypes." Individuals have their own view of the world—a "pseudo-environment . . . a representation of the environment"—that determines their ideas and opinions. Clemenceau, for example, had gone to the Peace Conference of 1919 determined to wreak vengeance on the Germans because of a stereotyped view of Germany dating back to the Franco-Prussian War.

The impact of the revisionists' moral tracts against Wilson's diplomacy was widespread. Theologian Reinhold Niebuhr, then a young minister working in Detroit, expressed the keen disillusionment of a generation when he set down his own reactions to the revisionist histories in his diary in 1923.

Gradually the whole horrible truth about the war is being revealed. Every new book destroys some further illusion. How can we ever again believe anything when we compare the solemn pretensions of statesmen with the cynically conceived secret treaties. Here was simply a tremendous contest for power between two great alliances of states in which the caprice of statesmen combined with basic economic conflicts to dictate the peculiar form of the alliance. Next time the cards will be shuffled in a different way and the "fellowship in arms" will consist of different fellows.

Many people who shared Niebuhr's great moral outrage had already begun to work for peace in various pacifist societies, both new and old. The term "pacifist," to describe someone who advocates the abolition of war and who will not take part in war, was not coined until 1909. In the following year former steel tycoon Andrew Carnegie gave $10 million in bonds for an organization to "hasten the abolition of international war." This was to be the Carnegie Endowment for International Peace that was led by Nicholas Murray Butler after the war. Hitherto, secular peace societies in America had been principally of this type — organizations committed to educating public and politicians about the horrors of war. But the movement was divided on the issue of American intervention in 1917. Only ardent socialists, social gospel clergymen, and feminists had maintained their opposition, founding such new pacifist societies as the American Union against Militarism. During the twenties the most active were two lobbying societies based in Washington. They were the National Council for the Prevention of War (NCPW) founded in 1921, led by its executive secretary, Frederick Libby, and the Women's International League for Peace and Freedom (WILPF), originally founded by social worker Jane Addams in 1915 but subsequently led by its executive secretary, Dorothy Detzer. In the NCPW Libby managed to bring together pacifists in farming and labor movements and published a monthly magazine, *Peace Action,* that had a circulation of 20,000.

Although revisionist historians and pacifists alike rejected Wilson's diplomacy, they were not isolationists. They wanted greater international cooperation between the nations of the world. American organizations to promote the idea of international cooperation were established on the premise that if people knew more they would understand more. The Foreign Policy Association, founded in 1921, made systematic attempts to inform people about international events. The contemporaneous Council on

Foreign Relations published a quarterly, *Foreign Affairs,* firstly under Archibald Cary Coolidge and later under Hamilton Fish Armstrong. By 1926 there were more than a thousand groups, whether international or isolationist, publishing news on foreign affairs.

Among America's foreign policy makers there remained a residual interest in genuine international cooperation, such as by American membership in the World Court. A World Court in which international law could be enforced and perfected had been discussed by a committee of jurists appointed by the League Council in 1920. It included Elihu Root, the New York corporation lawyer who had served Theodore Roosevelt as both secretary of state and secretary of war. Their recommendations were accepted by the League Assembly that devised a system for electing judges in 1921. Because this Court of International Justice at The Hague was affiliated with the League, it was anathema to some of the American public and to many congressmen. However, on January 26, 1927, the Senate voted 76 to 17 for United States' membership with five reservations. The Senate further stipulated that the reservations had to be accepted individually by all of the court's forty-eight member states. This stance would be interpreted as a way of saying no simply by making the price of membership too high. Of the American reservations one proved quite unacceptable to the other nations—that the United States remain free of any Court decisions given without American assent —although countries on the League Council actually had this privilege. President Calvin Coolidge refused to renegotiate this point and the possibility of American adherence died for the time being.

Economic Affairs

World economic affairs in the twenties were governed by three interrelated problems: reparations demanded of Germany by the victorious European powers; repayments of debts contracted by the Allies from the United States; and the development of American business and its desire for protection from overseas competition.

During the war the United States became a creditor nation. Wartime and postwar loans to friend and foe lent at 5 percent interest had stimulated the American economy and the total debt of $12.5 billion by the early twenties was too large a part of the economy to be overlooked by the government. Three presidents — Wilson, Harding, and Calvin Coolidge—took the attitude that the debts had to be paid in full without reference to other debts and reparations owed to America's debtors. Coolidge's supposed remark, "They hired the money, didn't they?" was much quoted and approved. However, Wilson admitted something that Harding and Coolidge were unwilling to—that only by trade with the United States could Europeans repay their loans.

Nevertheless, by the Fordney-McCumber Act of 1922 Congress raised the average level of duties on imports to a record height. However, the act did allow the president to raise or lower duties by as much as 50 percent but both Harding and Coolidge exercised this prerogative only thirty-seven times and thirty-two of these were upwards. Only on bobwhite quails, mill feed, cresylic acid, phenol, and paint brush handles were the duties lowered. It was on basic commodities of butter, cheese, and pig iron that duties were raised. The Fordney-McCumber tariff was the outcome of a compromise between different bargaining interests in Congress. The *Wall Street Journal* did not mince words in its condemnation calling it "One of the most selfish, short-sighted and extravagant laws of the kind ever enacted." Debts could not be paid without money or surplus products and the act gave Europeans no opportunity of earning dollars to repay their loans. In retaliation, they introduced protective tariffs of their own. Thus the resulting tariff war damaged the United States's foreign trade, persuaded some industrialists to establish plants abroad, and provoked several bankers and manufacturers to doubt the value of protection. Between 1922 and 1929 industrial production within America rose by 50 percent but exports rose only by 38 percent. Because imports rose at a slower rate than exports the United States accumulated a surplus of $11 billion in exports by 1929 and this was to be a contributory cause of the depression.

Administrations might be willing to adopt a flexible approach to the collection of debts, according to the varying abilities of debtor nations to repay loans, but Congress was obdurate. On February 9, 1922, it stipulated that the maximum deadline for repayment would be June 15, 1947, and that the minimum rate of interest would be 4.25 percent. Repayment was to be administered by a World War Foreign Debt Commission. Britain and France took offense at the Debt Funding Act that laid down these provisions. Not only did they consider that they had from the outset borne the highest losses of a common war—human fatality and economic disruption—but they also claimed a close relationship between their own debts and the reparations owed to them by Germany. Nevertheless, in January 1923 Britain and the United States agreed to repayment of Britain's debt of $4.6 billion over a period of 62 years at an average interest of 3.3 percent. The agreement set a precedent and the United States then went on to make similar agreements with fifteen other countries by 1927. France and Italy secured easier terms than Britain. So Britain set about collecting its debt and this entailed finding a way of exacting tribute Germany.

In 1919 John Maynard Keynes, a former British Treasury official, had argued against reparations in his book, *The Economic Consequences of the Peace*. Keynes had been the chief representative of the British Treasury at the Paris Peace Conference. But he had resigned on June 5, 1919, in disgust at the harsh terms of the Treaty of Versailles. He immediately set to work on his great book, paying for the printing himself and negotiating distribution with various publishers such as, in the United States, the new firm of Harcourt, Brace, and Howe. Although, in response to constructive criticism from family and friends, he toned down his personal attacks on politicians, deleting references to Wilson as a fly to Lloyd George's spider, the tenor of his attack was unmistakable. The book became an international best-seller. By April 1920 almost 70,000 copies had been sold in the United States. Readers were roused by Keynes's scornful and passionate denunciation of the failings of Wilson, Clemenceau, and Lloyd George. The heart of the book was a lucid analysis of the problems of reparations. The essential argument was that Europe could only regain its old affluence by restoring Germany to its former economic strength. It was underlined by Keynes's descriptions of a civilization at the point of collapse.

Though their peoples might be stirred, nations did not heed Keynes's arguments. Various countries continued to insist on excessive payments of $33 billion reparations from Germany. The Weimar Republic could not possibly meet these demands but, nevertheless, they were approved by the League on May 5, 1921. Two installments were paid in 1921 but none in 1922. On January 11, 1923, under instructions from French prime minister Raymond Poincaré, French troops occupied the Ruhr to punish Germany for default. German finances, already foundering, were now in chaos and the deutsche mark became worthless. The French army of occupation was withdrawn and Hughes suggested the formation of a European payment commission. In November it was established under the chairmanship of Chicago banker Charles Gates Dawes. Solutions were proposed—and accepted— for the reorganization of German finances.

The Dawes Plan, intended as an interim arrangement, aimed to make Germany solvent and to transfer any surplus of reserves over to the Allies. To stabilize the German currency, Dawes proposed an international loan of $200 million in gold, the reorganization of the Reichsbank under Allied supervision, and a new coinage, the reichsmark, set at 23.8 cents. As to reparations, he proposed payments on a sliding scale, beginning at $250 million and rising over five years to $625 million, with arrangements supervised by a new agent general (S. Parker Gilbert of the House of Morgan) who had to ensure payments were made regularly from a mix of funds, including the international loan, mortgages on principal industries and railroads, and taxes. The new scheme went into operation from September 1, 1924.

In time a new committee headed by New York industrialist Owen D. Young produced final and definitive arrangements, agreed by seventeen nations at The Hague on January 20, 1930. Germany's total liability was now set at $9 billion, with interest at 5.5 percent to be paid over fifty-nine years. Yearly payments were no more than $153 million—much less than the Dawes Plan had proposed. However, they were about the same as the total amount the Allies had agreed to pay the United States in war debts each year.

Germany could only meet its heavy reparations payments by borrowing. Investors, confident of German recovery, supported Germany by buying German securities regularly. The sums loaned by the United States up to July 1, 1931, were not less than $2.6 billion, the sum the United States collected from its Allies in war debts. The connection between German reparations, American loans, and Allied war debts became crystal clear. The United States loaned money to Germany with which it paid reparations to the Allies and they, in turn, repaid some of their debts to the United States. As historian William E. Leuchtenburg has observed in a much quoted sentence, "It would have made equal sense for the United States to take the money out of one Treasury building and put it into another." Far from being Uncle Shylock, the American people were underwriting the entire system of the debts and reparations.

The Young Plan also achieved the final evacuation of the Rhineland in which foreign troops left Coblenz on December 14, 1929, and Mainz on June 30, 1930.

Russo-American relations, embittered by aid given to the White Russian campaign of Admiral Alexander V. Kolchak in Siberia against the Bolsheviks in 1919 and early 1920, were also impeded by United States' insistence on full repayment by communist Russia of czarist debts. Throughout the twenties the United States refused to recognize the Soviet Union. However, Senator Borah argued for recognition after the Communists incorporated the Ukraine, Belorussia, and the Transcaucasian Federation with Russia into the Union of Soviet Socialist Republics (U.S.S.R.) in December 1922, and agreed on a first constitution in January 1924. The proposal was most astonishing coming as it did from Borah, because he was an inveterate isolationist. He was an effective public speaker—usually opposing whatever proposal was being mooted. According to an apocryphal story, Coolidge once met Borah riding through Rock Creek Park and after they had parted he commented, "Must bother the senator to be going in the same direction as the horse!" Borah's arguments for recognition of Russia were pragmatic. Only advantages could follow trade expansion. It had, hitherto, been standard American policy to recognize existing regimes whatever their moral origins. Against this Secretary Hughes argued that little economic gain could be gleaned from closer relations, that investment in a communist country was hazardous if not impossible, and there was no shred of evidence to suggest that countries recognizing the Bolsheviks had fared better economically than those that did not. Moreover, the Bolsheviks had annulled the czars' debts and refused to offer compensation for the confiscation of American property in Russia. This point of view was reaffirmed by Hughes's successors, Frank B. Kellogg (1925–1929) and Henry L. Stimson (1929–1933).

Collective Security, Disarmament, and the League

Between 1921 and 1924 the European powers tried to turn the prescriptions of the Covenant of the League of Nations into a practical program for collective security. The Draft Treaty of Mutual Assistance of 1923 provided the Council of the League, after an outbreak of hostilities, with authority to designate aggressor and victim. Furthermore, it obligated member states to give military support to the victim and take economic sanctions against the aggressor. As a concession and to entice the United States, the treaty said that nations were not obliged to assist the League outside the continent of the initial hostilities. However, Charles Evans Hughes said that since the United States was not a member of the League it could not assent to the proposals. The Geneva Protocol of October 2, 1924, went further than the Draft Treaty with specific proposals for enforcing collective security by sanctions. This, too, was rejected by the United States and, also, by the governments of Britain and the Dominions.

Europe could not be whole until Germany was readmitted to the concert of nations. Gustav Stresemann, chancellor of the Weimar Republic for 100 days in 1923 and, thereafter, foreign minister until his death six years later, attempted to overcome the suspicions of other European powers about the ambitions of Germany. Countering opposition within Germany and hesitation without, Stresemann's strategy was to tie German admission to the League and its Council to a review of territory in Europe. He achieved this in a series of treaties agreed on October 16, 1925, and known later as the Locarno Pact. On September 18, 1926, Germany was admitted to the League and became a permanent member of the Council that now had its numbers raised from ten to fourteen.

British and American delegations to the Peace Conference of 1919 had assured the French that they would together guarantee France's territorial integrity against any future German aggression. But when the United States Senate refused to ratify the Treaty of Versailles the chance of an Anglo-American guarantee also lapsed. In 1927 James T. Shotwell, a professor of Columbia University and associate director of the Carnegie Endowment for International Peace, visited Paris. He persuaded the French foreign minister, Aristide Briand, that he had a practical alternative. This was the Outlawry of War. Rejecting collective security because it was based on force, the American Committee for the Outlawry of War, founded in 1921 by Chicago businessman Salmon O. Levinson, conceived of a new international law prohibiting the use of force between nations.

The Outlawry of War had absolutely no appeal for Presidents Harding and Coolidge nor for Secretaries Hughes and Kellogg. The analogy with the tragicomedy of prohibition was obvious: the scourges of alcoholism and war to be abolished by inadequate legislation. However, Briand did not intend the Outlawry of War to be an empty scabbard. He now proposed a bilateral treaty between France and America. What he really wanted, of course, was the original American guarantee. Neither Coolidge nor Kellogg was deceived. They could not enter into an "entangling alliance" with France. Neither could they ignore the well-organized support for the scheme in America among pacifist societies —especially in the year of Lindbergh's solo flight across the Atlantic to Paris. By comparison with Hughes, Kellogg was an ineffective secretary of state. Perpetually harassed, he was called "Nervous Nellie" by sneering colleagues. Coolidge, on the other hand, was ill-informed about foreign affairs but unwilling to admit it. Yet together president and secretary saw how to outmaneuver Briand with a counterproposal. Senator Borah suggested making the scheme multilateral. Once other leading powers had agreed, the French had to accept the international ban on war that they, themselves, had first proposed. Foster Rhea Dulles observes, "Rarely if ever have moral and ethical factors been played up in such sharp contradiction of reality. The outlawry of war was accepted as the final realization of a historic dream even as the nation refused any sacrifice that might have given that dream substance." On August 27, 1928, the Kellogg-Briand Treaty or Pact of Paris was signed initially by representatives of fifteen nations. The Senate ratified it in jocular, dismissive vein on January 15, 1929, with only a single dissenting vote.

It received a better complement than it deserved in attempts at disarmament. Perhaps the spirit of the pact was responsible for transferring the hesitancy of a naval conference in Geneva in 1927 to more positive declarations in London in 1930. The London Conference from January 21 to April 22, 1930, was attended by the new secretary of state, Henry L. Stimson, and the secretary of the navy, Charles E. Adams. The upshot was a reduction in tonnages leaving the United States with 464,300, Britain with 474,500, and Japan with 272,000. A new provision, Article XXII, forbade submarines to attack without warning or without caring for passengers and crew. The London Treaty was ratified by the Senate by 58 votes to 9. Afterwards it became a matter of pride for the different nations to boast about their flagrant violations, especially with regard to submarines.

There were some signs that the Kellogg Pact was leading to better relations between the powers. In 1929, Britain, France, Italy, and Belgium agreed with Germany in a conference at The Hague to evacuate the Rhineland by the summer of 1930—five years before they were due to do so—and to conclude decisions about reparations. But their calculations were another casualty of the breakdown of the economic order that year.

Air Power

Air power was as significant a new factor in world affairs as oil power and American foreign policy in the 1920s and 1930s had to take account of the fact, especially as the great airlines were drawing their governments into their own empires of the sky. The story has been engagingly told by Anthony Sampson in his *Empires of the Sky* (1984). Leading Republican Wendell Wilkie observed in 1943 how "The modern airplane creates a new geographical dimension. A navigable ocean of air blankets the whole surface of the globe. There are no distant places any longer; the world is small and the world is one. The American people must grasp these new realities if they are to play their essential part in . . . building a world of peace and freedom."

European governments recognized how aviation could be used to tie colonies and other settlements overseas more closely to the homeland. In particular, France wanted to lead the new world of air travel and deploy planes to bind together its empires in Africa and the Far East through its airlines Air Union, (1923), Air Orient (1930), and The Line (1919), and thence a merger of all three as Air France (1933).

By 1934 air travel in Europe was sufficiently popular for Bradshaw's of London to start publication of a monthly *International Air Guide*. Yet, although flights cost only a quarter as much again as a first-class sea voyage and took only half the time, they were too hazardous, unreliable, and fatiguing for most travelers. Long journeys were a bizarre mixture of frivolous luxuries and wearisome discomfort. Thus travelers in the East might be served caviar or lobster and allowed to walk about and admire the view through portholes of flying boats but they were also expected to rise at 4:30 A.M. so that the plane could have an early takeoff.

Different nationalities showed their different characteristics in the air as on the ground. Americans were the most adventurous and informal travelers, accounting for up to 75 percent of passengers on flights from London to Paris. The French showed little interest in comfort for its own sake while the British ascended with all the antiquated snobbery of the officers' mess. Nevertheless, in 1919 a Briton, George Holt Thomas, persuaded six airlines to meet at The Hague to form the International Air Traffic Association (IATA) "with a view to co-operate to mutual advantage in preparing and organising international aerial traffic." By 1929, IATA had twenty-three members and its headquarters at The Hague attempted to standardize timetables and safety systems.

While IATA stoutly maintained it was not a cartel, it followed the pattern of European trade associations that tried to curtail competition.

In 1928 the United States ratified the Havana Air Convention that established the first rules for air traffic in the Americas. Like the convention in Paris in 1919, the Havana convention repudiated the idea of complete freedom of the air and established the principle of air sovereignty. This principle, jealously guarded, limited airplanes far more than ships on the high seas. Nations became concerned that airplanes flying above their territory, whence they could spy, drop bombs, or invade, were more dangerous than ships that were supposed to be able to call at any port they wanted to.

Pan Am and World Affairs

In October 1927 a new airline, Pan American Airways, led by its young executive Juan Trippe, established the first permanent service from the United States to a foreign country. It carried mail from Key West, Florida, to Havana, 100 miles away. It used Fokker F7 trimotor planes and the journey lasted an hour.

Trippe expanded in Latin America. Soon Pan Am joined forces with the Grace trading empire to establish the Panagra airline that flew down the west coast from Ecuador to Peru and Chile and thence across the Andes to Argentina on the east coast. Moreover, he obliged Peter Paul von Bauer to sell his airline SCADTA (Sociedad Colombo Alemana de Transportes Aeros) to him. Trippe's airline was much criticized in Latin America, where it was considered an adjunct to Wall Street and the State Department. By 1929, when he was thirty, Trippe's board included chairman Sonny Whitney, banker Robert Lehman, and diplomat David Bruce, son-in-law to Secretary of the Treasury Andrew Mellon. However, within the United States Pan Am's national profile was above suspicion. It had no domestic land routes to speak of, did not have to compete for passengers, and this, coupled with its overseas monopoly, gave it a dignified image.

During Senate investigations into airline-mail frauds in 1934

Postmaster General Jim Farley disclosed how Juan Trippe had received special favors and how he had concealed Pan Am profits by juggling with accounts in different regions—an early instance of a multinational corporation outfoxing government. Nevertheless, Farley understood that the Pan Am network was essential for American commerce. For his part, Trippe knew how to raise an unwelcome specter—the challenge of foreign airlines to American hegemony of the western hemisphere should Congress decide against Pan Am. Moreover, because Pan Am had not been involved in the way domestic routes were alloted among the airlines, it came through the exposures relatively unscathed.

Juan Trippe also set out to conquer the Pacific, twice the width of the Atlantic but interspersed with numerous islands, large and small, that could provide aircraft with refueling stages. However, the first lap was from the West Coast to Hawaii, a journey of 2,000 miles and longer than the shortest route then established across the Atlantic. By 1935 Pan Am was using Martin flying boats to cover this journey before flying on to China. In 1933 Trippe acquired a half share in the China National Aviation Corporation that flew planes from Shanghai to Canton. The Pacific route was already studded with American naval bases on Honolulu, Midway, Guam, and Manila. However, between Midway and Guam there was only the barren Wake Island, acquired during the War of 1898 but neglected afterward. Trippe petitioned the federal government for a five-year lease of Wake Island. The State Department, already disturbed by Japanese ambitions in the Pacific, was pleased to have an opportunity to extend American naval influence there under the guise of a commercial airline. Accordingly, FDR agreed to place Wake, and other islands, under naval administration that allowed Pan Am access to Wake.

Trippe quickly established airfields and radio stations on various remote islands and thus secured the lucrative airmail contract for the entire route from San Francisco to Canton in October 1935. The first plane, the *China Clipper,* arrived at Manila after sixty hours' flying over seven days and received massive publicity, including issue of a special postage stamp to celebrate the most spectacular of official air routes. In the 1930s American businessmen and diplomats thought the Pacific crossing was a major strategy for the United States to extend American interests in the Far East and to check Japanese expansion.

Trippe encountered British opposition when he wanted to land Pan Am planes in Hong Kong to complete the last lap of the route from Manila to China. However, when he threatened to use the Portuguese island of Macao as an alternative gateway to China, the British colony, fearful of losing trade, agreed to let Pan Am land on the island. Thus Trippe realized his aim of linking Pan Am with his China airline across the Pacific. His empire of the skies was already superseding the empire of the seas and encouraging American interests to encroach on European possessions in the Far East.

Trippe then moved toward Australia which had established a regular service across Asia to Britain by 1934. The obvious staging post en route to Australia and New Zealand was Fiji, a British colony. Trippe was again challenged by a British airline, Imperial Airways, planning a rival route from Vancouver. However, Imperial needed to land on Hawaii and hoped to bargain British landing rights on Hawaii for American landing rights on Fiji. The Americans would not concede Hawaii and Trippe found an alternative for Fiji in the South Pacific in Samoa, the American archipelago that included a magnificent natural harbor of Pago Pago. Moreover, Trippe secured landing rights in New Zealand, simply by threatening (as he had with Hong Kong) to exclude it from his network. Thus Trippe used the ruthless strategy of the early railroad entrepreneurs, demanding rights from whole territories rather than states or single towns.

Nevertheless, there were huge distances between islands in the South Pacific, sometimes called the empty hemisphere, and it proved a most treacherous region. Amelia Earhart disappeared without trace north of New Guinea in July 1937. Then in January 1938, Ed Musick, chief pilot to Pan Am, was killed when his plane, the *Samoa Clipper,* exploded in midair north of Pago Pago. For a time the Pan Am service to New Zealand was suspended but a regular service was resumed by July 1940. In the South Pacific, airlines made neighbors of islands far away from one another. Thus the South Pacific missed out the intervening age of railroad and steamships and yet now moved decisively into the global community.

The North Atlantic was potentially the most lucrative route for cargoes and passengers but in practical terms the most hostile in the 1930s. Its fierce headwinds, lack of any staging post between Canada and Ireland, except the frost-bound Greenland and Iceland to the north or the Azores to the south, made it a far more inhospitable region than the Pacific. Thus Lindbergh's historic solo transatlantic flight of 1927 was followed by prolonged anticlimax: one man might fly the Atlantic but no airplane could then carry mail and passengers for 2,000 miles without a stop. Furthermore, in one sense, air transport was in competition with the easy communication of the telephone, which was far more convenient for most businessmen to use.

Moreover, the North Atlantic proved a diplomatic minefield. Juan Trippe found the Europeans far more intractable about landing rights nearer home than they had been in the Far East. This time Britain and Imperial Airways had a bargaining point, Bermuda, a British island colony 800 miles southwest of New York, the crucial, and only, staging post on the southerly route via the Azores. The upshot was an agreement between Juan Trippe and Pan Am and Sir Eric Geddes of Imperial in 1930 wherein they formed a joint development corporation. As part of its strategy for closing the Atlantic, Britain sought agreement with Canada and Ireland, or Eire, newly independent, in Ottawa in November 1935 by which the three nations would form a joint Atlantic Company, of which Britain would hold 51 percent and Ireland and Canada half each of the remaining 49 percent. Meanwhile, America and Britain agreed to provide one another with reciprocal landing rights. Pan Am's arrangements with various European airlines, including the Dutch KLM company, created in 1924, broke both letter and spirit of the antitrust laws but the government allowed tactful wording in the contracts to conceal what was, in effect, restraint of trade.

Pan Am and Imperial chose Botwood in Newfoundland as their western terminus and Shannon, in Ireland, as their eastern terminus. After a year studying winds and clouds both companies undertook their first survey flights in July 1937. The new Pan Am flying boat, Clipper III, left Botwood in the evening and arrived at Foynes twelve and a half hours later. Yet neither airline had planes that could carry passengers on such a long flight. According to the agreement, Pan Am could not commence regular flights until Imperial was also ready and Imperial was behind Pan Am in research and development. In fact, the Germans were ahead of the Americans and the British. In 1938 Lufthansa flew a fourteen-engine Fokker-Wulf landplane from Berlin to New York in less than twenty-five hours.

Once the British became more engrossed in, first, the threat, and, then, the fact of war, and rapidly expanded the Royal Air Force, Pan Am steadily advanced its transatlantic passenger flights. In May 1939 Pan Am flew the first of the big Boeings, the Yankee Clipper, with twenty-two passengers aboard, from the Marine Terminal, New York (now next to La Guardia Airport), to Lisbon and Marseilles, via the Azores. Anthony Sampson concludes how

The airlines had completed their circumnavigation of the globe and a tireless passenger could now fly round it, with a bit of luck, in ten days —a bewildering change of perspective over the three decades since Blériot had first crossed the English Channel. It was a staggering technical achievement. But the political rhetoric of air transport about bringing peace and understanding was already sounding hollow after warplanes had revealed their destructiveness in Spain and Manchuria. . . . Behind their apparently infinite mobility, the airlines were becoming still more bound by the imperatives of sovereignty and national ambition.

In the 1930s European nations began to sense that aircraft would play a decisive role with lethal potential by dropping bombs in any future war. At a League of Nations disarmament conference in 1932, France, supported by Spain and Belgium, argued for an international air force and civil air service that alone would have the right to own and fly larger planes. Sweden advocated a modified system by which the international organization would simply run airports and supervise national airlines. However, Russia and Germany were opposed to either proposal and other leading countries, such as the United States, Britain, Canada, and Japan, were either skeptical or uninterested. After, first, Germany and, then, other countries began to rearm, French aviation economist Henri Bouche submitted a report to the League of Nations in 1935 that asked, "How could the governments of a mistrustful Europe allow the indefinite development of a powerful means of transport when aircraft sent on peaceful missions over national territories, and to the very heart of those territories, may also carry out their missions?"

In September 1939 Britain, France, and Germany were at war. Pan Am's flights to Europe stopped at Foynes in Ireland or Lisbon in Portugal, since Ireland and Portugal remained neutral. The skies above the Atlantic Ocean were reserved for Pan Am with its Boeing planes. Their supremacy could survive the war.

Latin America and the Good Neighbor Policy

Throughout the twenties American statesmen tried to revise Woodrow Wilson's diplomacy toward Latin America. As we know, in order to discourage revolutions in Latin America and to prevent political adventurers gaining power by assassination, Woodrow Wilson had applied his own special criteria of recognition to new regimes, that of constitutional legitimacy. But his policy had antagonized Latins and created more problems than it solved. In addition, Latins believed that the true motive underlying American interest was economic penetration of their countries, the so-called dollar diplomacy. The United States had superseded Britain as the principal source of capital for development in Latin America. American companies established branches in Latin America, American investors bought Latin-American bonds, and American corporations looked increasingly to Latin America for materials and markets. In certain respects, the two economies of the northern and southern hemispheres were complementary. The United States exported manufactured goods, notably machinery and motor cars, and imported such commodities as rubber, tin, copper, and nitrates, and sugar, bananas, and coffee. However, in other respects, there was a clash of interests. For example, both the United States and Argentina wanted to export their agricultural surplus and were thus in competition for markets. Moreover, the Latin states could not become self-suffi-

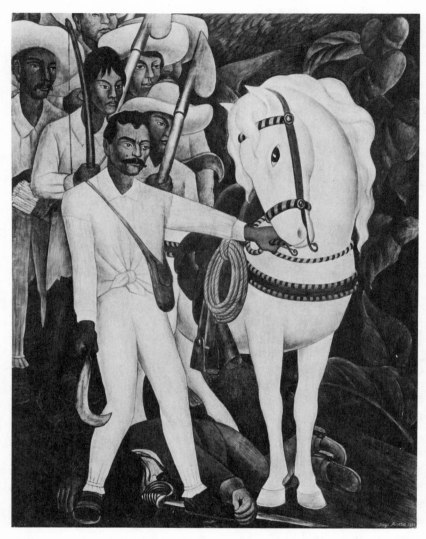

Diego Rivera, *Agrarian Leader Zapata* (1931), fresco 7'9" × 6'2". (Collection, The Museum of Modern Art, New York. Abby Aldrich Rockefeller Fund). The Mexican muralist Diego Rivera exercised a potent influence not only upon his people, who responded to political teaching through paintings and symbols, but also American regional artists such as Thomas Hart Benton and John Steuart Curry who wanted to celebrate pasture and harvest in graphic art that had an immediate impact.

cient economically while they grew ever more dependent on the United States for industrial goods. In addition, they felt more akin in cultural terms to Latin states in Europe than they did to the colossus of the north.

Successive Republican administrations now attempted to repair poor relations by introducing a Good Neighbor policy in Latin America. One sign of this shift was their promotion of more Pan-American conferences. The United States was host to a special conference on Central America in Washington from December 4, 1922, to February 7, 1923. In general, the United States worked for the peaceful settlement of disputes in Latin America and at promoting cooperative efforts in the fields of economics, transportation, and health.

The priority of American foreign policy in the western hemisphere was to maintain security in the Caribbean and in the isthmus between North and South America. The isthmus states were unstable politically and, to protect the Panama Canal, the United States despatched marines whenever and wherever it thought trouble was brewing. However, in the twenties presidents and secretaries of state cared more than ever before about cultivating the good will of these tiny but crucial allies. On April 20, 1921, Harding persuaded the Senate to approve the Treaty of Bogotá of April 6, 1914, by which Colombia was reconciled to the United States over the loss of Panama in 1903. There was method underlying this act of magnanimity. The United States was allowed to expand American operations in the oil fields of Colombia and soon recovered the initial outlay of its grant. Harding and Hughes also persuaded Panama to settle a boundary dispute with Costa Rica in favor of Costa Rica.

Harding also tried to propitiate Mexico and President Álvaro Obregón agreed to modify Mexican restrictions on American business but refused to offer compensation for all American losses in Mexico since 1920 or to agree to guarantee the rights of American nationals in Mexico. Nevertheless, Harding wanted to recognize the new Mexican government and the Bucareli agreements of August 15, 1923, brought to a formal end the hostility engendered by Wilson's policies. In 1924 Coolidge raised the arms embargo on Mexico and allowed American financiers to extend credit to the Mexican government for the purchase of a "few muskets and a few rounds of ammunition."

However, a new Mexican president, Plutarco Elías Calles, was less inclined to friendly relations with the United States than had been Álvaro Obregón. In 1925 the Mexican Congress passed an alien lands law that allowed foreigners to buy land in Mexico on condition that, in this matter, they renounced all rights to protection from foreign governments. It also passed a petroleum law that declared oil deposits were the inalienable and imprescriptible property of Mexico and provided strict laws about concessions to foreigners. Oil companies were ordered to apply for renewal of their rights under the law by January 1, 1927, or else, forfeit them. President Calles estimated that 380 companies, holding 26.83 million acres, assented to the new law while 22 companies, with 1.66 million acres, refused. These included such American interests as Doheny, Sinclair, Standard, and Gulf. Through their press allies they had newspapers circulate accounts that Mexico was adopting revolutionary socialist policies and fomenting communism throughout the western hemisphere. American politicians were not taken in. Borah declared in a speech of May 9, 1927, "The truth is that effort is being made to get this country into a shameless, cowardly little war with Mexico. . . . They talk communism and bolshevism, but what they mean is war."

As a pledge of noninterference, the United States began to withdraw its marines from Latin America and the Caribbean. However, the withdrawal of U.S. Marines from Nicaragua on August 1, 1925, was followed by a most violent civil war beginning on October 25. Coolidge ordered marines to return first in May and, then, in August 1926. He justified his action to Congress on January 10, 1927, on the basis of protecting both the Panama Canal and American investments. But he also sent Henry L. Stimson, a former secretary of war, to Nicaragua to try and persuade the two sides to come to terms. This Stimson achieved in the Peace of Tipitata on May 11, 1927, whereby both sides agreed to a coalition government under Adolfo Díaz until the United States could arrange elections. The election of 1928 was won by a former rebel, José M. Moncada. From February 1931

Stimson, now secretary of state, began to withdraw troops in successive stages.

The civil war in Nicaragua soured Mexican-American relations anew because the two countries supported opposite sides. The new deterioration in relations between the United States and its neighbor prompted what was, perhaps, Coolidge's most inspired decision in foreign policy. In 1927 he appointed Dwight W. Morrow as ambassador to Mexico to succeed the unpopular James R. Sheffield. Morrow had been in Coolidge's class at Amherst College and had an engaging personality. Morrow cleverly defused the situation. To redeem America's image, he had Lindbergh fly to Mexico City where he was received tumultuously. Then Morrow achieved a compromise over subsurface oil rights by persuading the Mexican Supreme Court to declare the most objectionable clauses of the new law unconstitutional. He also induced the Mexican government and the Catholic church, who were at odds over the proposed nationalization of church property, to accept a new accord by which the church withdrew an interdict on certain services in exchange for a government undertaking that it would not attempt the destruction of the church. The tensions between the United States and Mexico that had seemed so important in the early 1920s had dissolved ten years later.

Underlying these various American policies to individual countries was the realization by successive presidents and secretaries that they had to convince Latin America as a whole that the United States neither coveted additional territory nor wanted to interfere in others' internal affairs. Unlike the United States, sixteen Latin-American countries had joined the League of Nations by March 1921. Only Argentina, Ecuador, Mexico, and the Dominican Republic remained outside it. In these circumstances, it is not surprising that the United States eventually recognized the advantages of using the League to mediate in Latin-American disputes. In 1932 and 1933 the State Department twice accepted arbitration by the League, firstly, in the so-called Chaco War between Paraguay and Bolivia about a track of jungle and, secondly, in the war between Peru and Colombia over the village of Leticia. These quarrels made it clear that, no matter how constructive were United States strategies in pursuit of Good Neighbor policies, the machinery to keep the peace in Latin America was unreliable. The conventions on arbitration and conciliation were imperfect vehicles for joint consultation. Nevertheless, the United States could not collaborate effectively with the League while it remained an occasional guest rather than a permanent member.

Hoover and Stimson

When Herbert Hoover became president in March 1929 he was the most widely traveled man to take the office to that time. As secretary of commerce under Harding and Coolidge (1921–1929), Hoover had worked assiduously to secure American investment abroad and diplomatic compromise at home. Between his election and inauguration as president he toured Latin America, the only part of the world he had not previously visited. It seemed here at last was a president better informed on world affairs. Unfortunately, Hoover's crippling limitations of personality that weakened his ability to handle the depression also adversely affected his foreign policy. Moreover, the combination of the cautious new president and his alert, impulsive, and hyperactive secretary of state, Henry L. Stimson, was not harmonious. Stimson was a successful New York lawyer who had previously served as secretary of war under Taft. He admitted he knew little about European affairs but he was willing to act, and to act decisively in crisis.

The system of debts and reparations payments broke down in the wake of the Wall Street Crash. In March 1931 French bankers called in short-term German and Austrian notes. Unable to meet the demands upon it, the Kreditanstalt in Vienna collapsed and this set off a chain reaction. The Weimar Republic defaulted on reparations payments and President Paul von Hindenburg appealed to Hoover. In June 1931 Hoover proposed a one-year moratorium on the payment of international debts and reparations payments. At Lausanne in June 1932 Britain, France, Italy, Japan, and Belgium agreed to reduce the residue of German reparations to $750 million. Cuba alone paid off its American debt in full, $15 million by 1920. Finland, which had contracted a post-war loan of $9 million, was the only country to continue payments after 1935 and to discharge its loan.

Invasion of Manchuria

The Japanese invasion of Manchuria on September 18, 1931, was subsequently recognized as the turning point between peace and war. It symbolized the collapse of attempts to ensure peace, either by arbitration or collective security. It was a climax to Russo-Japanese antagonism since the 1890s. Furthermore, it inaugurated a period of Japanese politics called the *kurai tanima* or dark valley. Like the United States, Japan had emerged from World War I with increased economic and industrial capacity. Japan became a creditor nation and its financial and industrial combines, the *zaibatsu*, did well out of the protracted European struggle. However, Japan could only maintain production by finding additional reserves of raw materials abroad.

Industry, legitimately developed by the Japanese in Manchuria according to treaty, attracted increasing numbers of Chinese settlers north of the Great Wall. Subject to the despotic control of a brigand chief, Zhang Zuolin, Manchuria was not an integral part of China. But after years of confusion following the revolution of 1911 China now seemed ready for reunification. Jiang Jieshi, who was the leader of the conservative wing of the Guomindang or National People's party, established a capital on June 8, 1928, in Beijing. On July 25, 1928, the United States recognized his government. One of Jiang's aims was the recovery of Chinese control of territories leased to foreigners. This policy produced dynamic opposition from the Japanese army determined to resist it. The eventual pretext for the Japanese army's invasion of Manchuria was a minor explosion on the South Manchurian Railway stationed by Japanese soldiers. Their reprisal was an attack on the city of Shenyang and by October 1931 they had begun to bomb cities in southern Manchuria. At this time China was being devastated by floods. Although the Japanese prime minister, Wakatsuki Reijiro, and the foreign minister, Shidehara Kijuro, were indignant at the army's invasion, to save face in public they upheld their country's honor. Thus their envoy to the League, Yoshizawa, enlarged on the vital importance of Manchuria to Japan and the numerous, supposed broken agreements of the Chinese, while world disapproval of the invasion solidified native patriotism among the Japanese people.

The Japanese invasion was an act of flagrant aggression. How did the powers react? The League authorized a Commission of Inquiry headed by Lord Lytton to travel to Manchuria and review the situation. America was represented by General Frank McCoy. Hoover cynically judged European expressions of horror about the invasion as hypocritical. The only distinction between Japan's morals and those of the European imperial powers "was one of timing. The old empires had held the titles longer and thus were more sacrosanct." Nevertheless, he thought that the Japanese had played a dirty game by their "act of rank aggression." "The whole transaction is immoral. The offense against the comity of nations and the affront to the United States is outrageous." For Hoover there were two courses of action, either some form of collective economic sanctions against Japan or diplomatic pressure. He preferred diplomatic pressure because he thought sanctions would lead inevitably to war. His critics said he feared Congress would object to economic boycotts on the grounds that George Washington had never advocated boycotts.

Hoover recalled that William Jennings Bryan had, as Wilson's first secretary of state, used nonrecognition as a diplomatic device in 1915 when Japan made the notorious Twenty-One Demands of China. On November 9, 1931, Hoover suggested to Stimson that he did the same. Prompted by Hoover and urged on by Walter Lippmann, Stimson despatched a note declaring "The United States government . . . cannot admit the legality of any situation de facto" to both China and Japan on January 7, 1932. Acquisition by aggression had no legal validity.

International opposition to Japan did not coalesce. China was left alone to offer what resistance it could. After the first note, Japanese rear admiral Kuichi Shiozawa started a second war within the Great Wall, 200 miles south of Shenyang at Shanghai, on January 28, 1932. Stimson's desire to emphasize nonrecognition then took a different form, an open letter to Senator Borah of

February 23, 1932, in which his view was restated to warn Japan, to encourage China, and to rouse the League. When the Lytton report was published, it exonerated China and condemned Japan. On February 24, 1933, the League accepted the report and refused to recognize Manchuria. On March 27 Japan withdrew from the League. Fighting now extended to south of the Great Wall and, to avert more losses, Jiang Jieshi agreed to a truce on May 31, 1933. In the meantime, the last party cabinet of the thirties in Japan had been brought down after the assassination of the current prime minister, Inukai Tsuyoshi, on May 15, 1932, by a secret association of fanatics, "the League of Blood."

Collective security had fallen apart. The slide to another world war began. The Japanese sought living room. In their search they would enter a room none thought possible, the mushroom of 1945.

14

"WHO IS THIS HITLER, AND WHAT DOES HE WANT?" Isolation and Intervention

To ITALY, Germany, and Japan the League of Nations was a conspiracy of nations, the possessive against the dispossessed. If the Japanese invasion of Manchuria was the turning point between war and peace in the 1930s, the central event was the rise of Germany under the National Socialist, or Nazi, dictatorship of Adolf Hitler. It was his alliance of October 25, 1936, with the National Socialist, or Fascist, dictatorship of Benito Mussolini in Italy, and subsequent pact with Japan of November 25, 1936, that brought the ambitions of the three countries together.

Hitler's foreign policy was expansionist and had two aims. The first was the unification of all German-speaking peoples in Europe in the Third Reich, whether they were minorities within other nations, such as the Sudeten Germans in Czechoslovakia and Germans in Poland, or other entire nations, such as Austria. The second aim was to grasp the hegemony of Europe. Both aims involved undermining the Treaty of Versailles. Yet Hitler's for-

Checkmate at Munich. All were not equal around the round table on September 29, 1938, among Mussolini, Hitler, Dr. P. Schmidt (translator), and Neville Chamberlain. Commenting later on Chamberlain's sacrifice of Czechoslovakia, and his proposed Anglo-German declaration of "peace for our time," little Adolf was supposed to have cheerfully remarked, "He seemed such a nice old gentleman and I thought he was only asking for my autograph." (Bundesarchiv, Koblenz, Germany).

eign policy was improvised and responded to situations as much as it created them. Whether opportunist in the manner of Bismarck's foreign policy—that is to say using situations for the furtherance of a central aim—or not, there was a long-term logic to its success for ten years. The prerequisite of the foreign policy was the rearmament of Germany in defiance of the Treaty of Versailles. Mussolini, who sought the creation of Italian blocs, began as Hitler's tutor in foreign affairs, continued as his accomplice, and declined into his lackey.

The ambitions of Hitler and Mussolini posed crucial strategic, diplomatic, and ethical problems for Britain and France. The Covenant of the League of Nations pledged members to respect one another's integrity and to unite against any agressor. However, states were unwilling to sink their national independence and aspirations in the creation of a multilateral force, or army, for the sake of collective security. Even less successful were attempts at disarmament that were floundering in fall 1933. On October 14, 1933, Germany withdrew from a London conference on disarmament and the following week it left the League. Hitler's policy of rearmament was completed on March 7, 1936, when he sent a token force to reoccupy the Rhineland. Public opinion in Britain would not brook resistance and the government could only renew assurances to France and Belgium guaranteeing their territorial integrity.

For its part in the tragic events that were about to unfold, Italy led a group of so-called "revisionist" powers—Hungary, Bulgaria, and, later, Austria—that also wanted to revise the settlement of 1919. Mussolini dreamed of a new Roman Empire. Italy had two colonies in East Africa, Eritrea and Somaliland, but they were barren, unlike fertile Ethiopia (or Abyssinia) that lay between them and had untapped mineral resources. Italy launched a full-scale invasion of Ethiopia on October 3, 1935, and was able to conclude the war with the decisive battle of Lake Ashangi of March 31 to April 3, 1936, after which the emperor of Ethiopia, Haile Selassie, fled the country. Despite the outrage to the Kellogg Pact and its own Covenant, the League of Nations demurred before briefly imposing economic sanctions against Italy in the form of an oil embargo. Indeed, Britain and France were willing to come to some sort of dishonest compromise with Italy, whereby Ethiopia would be partitioned between Mussolini and Haile Selassie. Neither Britain nor France would bite the bullet of collective security. Here was clear proof that the League lacked teeth.

More damaging to international security was the Spanish Civil War of 1936–1939, which began after a democratically elected but sometimes unstable and disorderly Popular Front government was challenged by a rebellion of right-wing generals led by Francisco Franco on July 17, 1936. The intervention of Italy and Germany on behalf of Franco and of Russia for the Republic transformed the Spanish Civil War into an international issue. Both Britain and France wanted to ignore the problem, principally to prevent its escalation into international war. Thus they undertook not to aid either side in Spain. This time the League was not consulted. It restricted its activities to keeping safe the paintings of the Prado Art Gallery in Madrid.

In the summer of 1937 Britain and France, in protest at the sinking of British, French, and Russian ships carrying food and civilian supplies to the Spanish Republic by "unknown" submarines, which were, in fact, Italian, organized a conference of Mediterranean countries at Nyon. Antisubmarine patrols were set up, a demonstration that a firm line would work. After the fall of Barcelona, the Spanish government's stronghold, in January 1939, many foreign governments extended recognition to Franco's regency and, besides Germany and Italy, these included, on February 27, Britain and France. But the United States delayed recognition until April 3, 1939, after the fall of Madrid in March.

What was true of Franklin Roosevelt's character and temperament in domestic politics was also true of him in foreign affairs. The facts that FDR was raised by a wealthy eastern family and had visited Europe several times, that he had served as assistant secretary of the navy under Woodrow Wilson, and that, as vice-presidential candidate in 1920, he had campaigned for American membership of the League of Nations—all these greatly influenced his foreign policy. At heart he was a committed internationalist and deeply interested in the well-being of Europe. However, the facts that his political education in New York had taught him the necessity of expedience and compromise, that he had had to struggle to overcome the crippling limitations of his poliomyelitis, and that he was temperamentally incapable of adhering to rigid formulas—all these affected the way he would lead America back into the concert of nations and into World War II.

Foreign Relations in the Mid-1930s

When Roosevelt first took office the New Deal subordinated all other issues and throughout his first term he concentrated on domestic policy, leaving his secretary of state, Cordell Hull (1933–

1944), almost in full charge of foreign policy after the abortive London Economic Conference of 1933. Hull had been largely responsible for that part of the Democratic platform of 1932 calling for reciprocal trade agreements and he was too tenacious and persistent a politician to give up the aim of increasing world trade after the setback in London. Hull had sometimes denounced the protective tariff as the "king of evils" and "the largest single underlying cause of the present panic." Thus his critics mimicked his lisp and southern drawl by declaring, "We must eliminate these trade baa-yuhs heah, theah, and ev'ywheah." Hull persuaded Roosevelt and Secretary of Agriculture Henry A. Wallace to seek bipartisan support for a bill to make tariffs the prerogative of the president rather than Congress. By the Reciprocal Trade Agreements Act of June 4, 1934 (renewed in 1937 and 1940), the president was given power to negotiate bilateral concessions with other countries and thence to raise or lower tariff rates by as much as 50 percent, provided other countries made reciprocal arrangements. Within eighteen months agreement had been reached with fourteen countries.

However, Hull went further than the specific terms of the act in order to lower tariff barriers. He turned to the "most favored nation" clause of the old Fordney-McCumber tariff of 1922. This clause enabled him to extend tariff reductions on specific items to all other countries whose duties did not discriminate against America. By 1940 there had been a 61 percent increase of trade with twenty-two countries, compared with only a 38 percent increase with countries not sharing the trade agreements. The acts of 1934, 1937, and 1940 thus reduced the average tariff rates from 40 or 50 percent to 13 percent. However, the value of exports from 1933 to 1939 rose only from $1.7 billion to $3.2 billion, while imports rose from $1.4 billion to $2.3 billion—below the levels of the twenties. Nevertheless, the government had abandoned the openly selfish economic policies of the previous decade. Yet Congress, in an act sponsored by Senator Hiram Johnson of California, and signed by FDR on April 13, 1934, forbade Americans to lend or buy from nations that defaulted on payment of their war debts.

However, some policies, while equally self-serving, were more enlightened and constructive. In 1934 the Roosevelt administration used funds from the RFC and created an Export-Import Bank as another government agency to stimulate foreign trade by offering credits and loans to finance the purchase of American goods. The Export-Import Bank loaned money to European countries so that they could buy American agricultural produce and to Latin-American countries both to stabilize their currencies and to enable them to buy equipment for such projects as road construction.

In the thirties arguments about trade were more propitious than earlier and influenced America's relationship with Russia. In 1930 the U.S.S.R. had bought 36 percent of all American exports of agricultural implements and 50 percent of all tractors; in 1931 it had purchased 65 percent of all machine tools exported. After the rise of the Nazis in Germany and military factions in Japan, both Roosevelt and Joseph Stalin recognized in the other a potential ally. On November 16, 1933, despite opposition from American conservatives, the two nations agreed to resume diplomatic relations. On September 18, 1934, the U.S.S.R. went further and joined the League of Nations. The economic advantages of the new relationship proved disappointing for the United States. Russia was unable to export much, defaulted on its debt agreements, and, in violation of its agreement, continued to foment communist activities in America.

Roosevelt became deeply interested in foreign affairs in 1935. Reforms had achieved modest economic recovery but international relations had begun to deteriorate so badly that they could no longer be ignored. The aggressive acts of Mussolini and Hitler made more urgent the fears first awakened by the Japanese invasion of Manchuria and the collapse of collective security. For fifteen years the issue of American membership of the World Court had hung in the balance of the prevalent isolationism. Now Roosevelt asked the Senate to approved the protocol governing membership that Elihu Root had drawn up in 1929. FDR knew that membership would have little practical effect but it would be an important symbolic gesture. It was not to be. Isolationist sentiment in the country suddenly revealed its latent strength when Father Charles E. Coughlin, the radio priest, and William

Randolph Hearst, owner of the most influential newspaper chain, joining vociferous isolationist Senators Long, Borah, Johnson, and Norris, were able to arouse public opinion against the proposal. American membership of the World Court was rejected by the Senate on January 29, 1935, by 52 votes against to 36 in favor, and with 7 abstentions. For FDR, who had staked his reputation on the issue, the defeat was deeply embarrassing. Defeat of American membership of the World Court marked a turning point in American foreign policy, signifying that a powerful isolationist lobby now threatened to wrest the initiative from the president.

Isolationism

In the 1930s the term "isolationist" had a particular application to those unilateralists or continentalists who wanted the United States to have complete independence of diplomatic action, to avoid what Washington called "entangling alliances," and, most of all, to remain neutral in any war. Isolationists and pacifists agreed that World War I had been a disaster, that a second war would be even worse, and that renewed American intervention would profit only bankers, arms makers, and other industrialists. The cost would be borne by the American people who would lose their lives, their money, and their democratic institutions.

Socially, isolationists were more likely to come from small towns and the countryside in the Midwest than from the great cities of the Northeast, or from the South, and to work as farmers, small businessmen, and manufacturers of light and service industries. Ethnically, they were drawn from the Irish-, German-, and Italian-American blocs.

In Congress their champions included: progressive Republican Senators William E. Borah of Idaho; Hiram Johnson of California, Arthur Capper of Kansas; Gerald P. Nye of North Dakota; Republican Senators Arthur H. Vandenberg of Michigan; Robert A. Taft of Ohio; Republican Congressman Hamilton Fish of New York; progressive Democratic Senator Burton K. Wheeler of Montana; progressive Senators Robert M. La Follette, Jr., of Wisconsin and George W. Norris of Nebraska; and Farm-Labor

Senator Henrik Shipstead of Minnesota. However, it should not be imagined these men all thought and voted consistently or as one. For example, Republican Arthur Capper of Kansas voted for the World Court protocols in 1926 and 1935 while Democratic Burton K. Wheeler of Montana voted for the protocols in 1926 but against them in 1935.

They were, however, crucial allies to FDR in domestic affairs, being committed to the New Deal, and their support was invaluable, especially on the more controversial legislation. It is a political axiom that a wise politician never alienates his support. In short, FDR dared not risk their antagonism in domestic affairs by provoking them on foreign policy, particularly in his second term when he was engaged in adversary politics and when the slide to war was more obvious in Europe and Asia.

Outside Congress, isolationist champions included Governor Philip M. La Follette of Wisconsin; revisionist historian Charles A. Beard; former New Dealers Hugh S. Johnson and George N. Peek; socialist leader Norman Thomas; and, most famous and controversial of all, star aviator Colonel Charles A. Lindbergh. In the mass media they had the voice of press magnate William Randolph Hearst. Their views were also expressed in a whole range of periodicals from the conservative *Scribner's* to the liberal *Christian Century* and *New Republic*.

In convincing the American public that their foreign policy of unilateralism was to be preferred to that of FDR and Hull, isolationists were most fortunate that the slide to war in Europe and Asia could be represented in the syndicated press as the inevitable outcome of a conflict of imperialist rivalries from which the United States would do best to remain aloof. Moreover, as the tragic sequence of events unfolded abroad, the ravages of the Great Depression and a series of domestic crises at home proved of consuming interest to the American people. As historian William Manchester has shown, the preoccupation of Americans with internal events partly explains the slowness of American response to the deterioration in international relations. The actual timing of international crises was partly responsible for confused American reaction to them. Such was the backdrop to the isolationists' campaign to insulate America from war.

The Senate investigation of the munitions industry, led by Republican Senator Gerald P. Nye of North Dakota, and the ensuing four Neutrality Acts of 1935, 1936, 1937, and 1939 represented the high tide of American isolationism in the 1930s.

American demands for the regulation of arms traffic had intensified after the collapse of the Geneva Disarmament Conference in 1933. Dorothy Detzer, executive secretary of the Women's International League for Peace and Freedom, believed that pacifist ideas on restricting the arms traffic would be accepted by the public if an official enquiry were conducted into the munitions industry. Detzer and her ally in the Senate, George W. Norris, persuaded Senator Gerald P. Nye of North Dakota, a humorless zealot of the isolationist cause, that it would be to his advantage to promote such an enquiry. His state had no heavy industry and thus his constituents could not be harmed by any revelation. Moreover, the chair of an important Senate committee could provide him with an ideal base from which to launch his presidential ambitions. On April 12, 1934, the Senate approved Nye's motion calling for a seven-man Senate investigation into the munitions industry of which Nye himself was subsequently chosen as chairman.

The time was ripe. A month earlier H. C. Engelbrecht and F. C. Hanighen had had their sensational article, "Arms and the Men," published in *Fortune* magazine. In asking exactly who had profited from the world war, the authors produced evidence to show that the only financial profits were made by the munitions manufacturers. It was said that the motto of the munitions makers was "When there are wars, prolong them; when there is peace, disturb it." Shortly afterward, Walter Millis added fuel to the fire of economic interpretation of the causes of World War I with his *The Road to War* (1935), a best-seller described as the isolationists' bible.

The Nye committee held its public hearings from September 4, 1934, until February 20, 1936, and during those eighteen months heard evidence from around 200 witnesses and produced a final report of 13,750 pages in thirty-nine volumes. Its star witnesses were the brothers Du Pont (Irénée, Pierre, and Lammot) and J. P. Morgan, Jr., and his senior partners. Newspapers across

America gave somewhat lurid accounts of the hearings, especially the most sensational revelations.

The hearings confirmed the worst suspicions of isolationists and pacifists of double-dealing in aid of arms sales. For instance, a series of letters between Lawrence Y. Spear, a vice-president of Electric Boat, a submarine manufacturer, and Charles Craven, head of the British arms firm Vickers, disclosed the apparently compulsive need of big companies to make profits at the expense of human life. In one letter Spear told Craven, "It is too bad that the pernicious activities of our State Department have put the brake on armaments orders from Peru by forcing the resumption of formal diplomatic relations with Chile." It seemed that countries existed to be cajoled and corrupted by munitions makers whose dupes they were. Nye could sardonically "wonder whether the army or the navy are just organizations of salesmen for private industry, paid for by the American government."

Indeed, some arms sales were supported by the American government. Bernard Baruch, one of Roosevelt's advisers, sent FDR a memorandum on the subject of governmental supervision of arms sales in February 1935 in which he emphasized that the United States had to find ways of maintaining capacity to make arms in peace. This could be done by selling to foreign belligerents:

Governments of industrial countries . . . almost universally . . . encourage the manufacture of lethal weapons for exportation to belligerent countries actively preparing for war, but which have an insufficient munitions industry. . . . This is a method of providing a laboratory to test killing implements and a nucleus for a wartime munitions industry by maintaining an export market for instruments of death. Of course, it is absolutely indefensible. . . .

Historian Charles A. Beard's interpretation of the Nye committee came in a series of articles for the *New Republic* that show a fascination with an economic interpretation of the origins of World War I. In the first article, on March 9, 1936, he said the revelations of the Senate committee made

The files of the newspapers that reported and commented on events look like the superficial scribblings of ten-year-old children. . . . People who imagine that they 'know what is going on' because they read the great metropolitan dailies will find in the Nye records the shallowness and irrelevance of their 'knowledge' gathered from the press in 1914–17.

In a further series of articles for the *New Republic*, Beard made his famous comparison between war and the explosion of a chemical compound, the so-called "devil theory of war." Was the explosion caused by the last ingredient added or did it merely precipitate the explosion in the end? In times of peace men prepared for, and encouraged, the coming of war by their insatiable greed for territory, capital, and profit.

Nye believed he knew the answer and overstated his findings, telling the Senate on January 15, 1935, how he had discovered the existence of a vicious partnership between the federal government and the munitions industry. What Nye considered perhaps "the most important part of the investigation" came in March 1935 when the committee examined the files of American banks relating to loans to European governments in World War I before American intervention. In particular, an announcement by committee member Senator Bennett Champ Clark of Missouri on January 15, 1936, that President Woodrow Wilson and Secretary of State Robert Lansing "had falsified" their knowledge of secret treaties between the Allies caused a minor explosion. Over the next two days Wilson was roundly defended by Tom Connally of Texas and Carter Glass of Virginia on the floor of the Senate. By his angry insistence on Wilson's duplicity, Nye succeeded in uniting somewhat diverse opposition in the Senate to the munitions investigation and thus nothing came immediately of the committee's final recommendations.

However, the damage had been done. The committee had provided the initiative for the Neutrality Acts of 1935, 1936, 1937, and 1939. Much to his subsequent regret, Secretary of State Cordell Hull had acquiesced in the establishment of the committee. In his *Memoirs* he explains how disastrous was the outcome.

The Nye Committee aroused an isolationist sentiment that was to tie the Administration just at the very time when our hands should have been free to place the weight of our influence in the scales where it would count. It tangled our relations with the very nations whom we should have been morally supporting. It stirred the resentment of other nations with whom we had no controls. It confused the minds of our own people as to the real reasons that led us into the First World War. It showed the prospective aggressors in Europe and Asia that our public opinion was pulling a cloak over its head and becoming nationally unconcerned with their designs and that, therefore, they could proceed with fuller confidence.

Naval Construction

In the meantime, FDR, who was distrusted by pacifists and isolationists alike as a big navy man, had begun a program of naval expansion, partly to compete with Japan and partly to satisfy domestic economic needs. In June 1933 he allocated $238 million from public works funds for the construction of thirty-two ships of a total of 120,000 tons. Congress had already provided for five new ships of a total of 17,000 tons. The two programs represented the biggest expansion of the navy since 1916 and, because he knew it would cause controversy at home and abroad, FDR, in his public statements, minimized what was being accomplished. He did the same in 1934 when the Vinson-Trammell naval bill authorized the construction of 102 new ships, taking the replacement of ships to limits set by the Washington and London naval treaties of 1922 and 1930.

The Washington and London naval agreements were, according to different conditions, due to end in December 1936 but FDR wanted to keep the treaty system intact. Japan now sought parity; Britain wanted certain qualitative alterations. If FDR rejected these proposed revisions, he would, in effect, help destroy the treaties; if he accepted them, he would save the treaties but oblige the United States to engage in an extensive program of naval construction in order to assure its security in the Pacific. Whichever he chose, the outcome would be the same—major naval construction in the United States.

Nevertheless, the three powers continued to negotiate naval limitation until January 1936 when the Japanese abandoned a London conference. Their withdrawal allowed FDR to request the largest peacetime naval appropriation ever for the construction of two new battleships and replacements for outmoded destroyers and submarines. On March 25, 1936, the United States, Britain, and France agreed to naval parity.

Neutrality Acts

In America the outcome of fascist adventures abroad and the isolationist sentiment they engendered at home was a series of Neutrality Acts. The pivotal role in shaping the Neutrality Acts was played by Democratic Senator Key Pittman of Nevada, chairman of the Senate Foreign Relations Committee from 1933 to 1940, a most shrewd, if alcoholic, politician, who steered a mid-course between isolationism and internationalism.

The First Neutrality Act was a direct outcome of the imminent Italian war of conquest in Ethiopia and, in its final form, determined by compromises between FDR, Pittman, leading isolationists, and Congressman Sam D. McReynolds of Tennessee, chairman of the House Foreign Affairs Committee. FDR felt deeply divided on the subject. While utterly opposed to the neutrality legislation, he recognized that he dare not jeopardize the New Deal by antagonizing his progressive Republican allies in Congress. In fact, the First Neutrality Act was only passed after a group of isolationist senators, led by Borah, Clark, Nye, Long, and Vandenberg, threatened to institute a filibuster to block ten pieces of domestic legislation unless the administration would agree to accept the First Neutrality Act. FDR gave in to them, partly for the sake of a compromise to limit the life of the act to six months, and partly because he wanted to silence Republican criticism that he was assuming excessive presidential powers. Thus, when he signed the first act on August 31, 1935, he did so with a heavy heart, announcing ruefully, "History is filled with unforseeable situations that call for some flexibility of action. It is conceivable that situations may arise in which the wholly inflexible provisions of Section I of this Act might have exactly the opposite effect from that which was intended. In other words, the inflexible provisions might drag us into war instead of keeping us out."

The First Neutrality Act required the president formally to recognize foreign conflicts and to deny shipments of arms to all belligerents indiscriminately. Thus, when Italy finally invaded Ethiopia in October 1935 Roosevelt invoked the act and ensured federal control of arms sales by the new National Munitions Control Board it had established and from which arms makers had to apply for a license. He also warned businessmen that trade with belligerents would not be protected by the American government. Moreover, American ships were prohibited from carrying arms to a belligerent. The Second Neutrality Act of February 18, 1936, not only extended the terms of the first until May 1, 1937, but also forbade loans or credits to any belligerent and made the president's action obligatory.

But the neutrality acts made no provision for a civil war and the Spanish conflict involved such divisive loyalties within the United States, especially among committed socialists, that Roosevelt and Hull asked Congress for speedy legislation that would uphold the policy of containment established by the European Nonintervention Committee organized by Britain and France, and thus anticipate any pressure from religious, political, and ethnic groups within America on the federal government to choose between Loyalists and Falangists. Whereas American Catholics were torn between loyalty to the Spanish Catholic church, and, thus, to Franco, and dismay at the repression they represented, American Protestants and Jews were not so divided in their support for the Loyalists. At Madison Square Garden they formed a Spanish Ambulance Committee, with Ernest Hemingway as chairman, that sent four ambulances and a medical unit to the Loyalists. Despite the attempt by the State Department to prohibit enlistment in foreign forces, over a thousand Americans died in service to the Loyalists as members of such organizations as the Abraham Lincoln or George Washington battalions among the international brigades serving the Republic.

Hitherto, the State Department had asked American firms for a voluntary embargo to ensure impartiality. On December 24, 1936, Robert Cuse, president of a company dealing in used aircraft, applied for export licenses to sell planes and engines worth almost $3 million to the Spanish Republic. The request was perfectly legal but in conflict with the spirit of official government policy. However, the case prompted the administration to ask Congress to waive the arms embargo for countries fighting civil wars, and this was achieved by an enabling act passed on January 6, 1937, with only one dissenting vote.

The savage bombing of the Basque town of Guernica on April 26, 1937, by German planes, with the indiscriminate killing of 1,654 civilians and wounding of another 889, aroused deep outrage in the United States and renewed discussion about the neutrality acts. It was now impossible to ignore the involvement of Italy and Germany in the war and various pacifist and radical groups began to lobby FDR to apply neutrality provisions to them. Socialist leader Norman Thomas spoke for many when he told FDR on June 29, 1937, that it was both immoral and grossly unfair to deny arms to the Republic while giving them to the technically neutral but active participants, Germany and Italy. As usual, FDR was evasive, sensitive to Catholic opinion in America that supported Franco and knowing he could not count on firm lines from Britain and France. He would only impose an arms embargo on Italy and Germany in response to a general European war. The neutrality acts and FDR's use of them, far from containing aggression, had, if anything, encouraged it.

The Third Neutrality Act of May 1, 1937, was another compromise. The provisions of the 1936 act were extended and included a new measure that allowed belligerents to buy any goods but arms from American firms, provided they paid for them in cash and carried the goods away on foreign ships. The cash-and-carry provisions could be applied by the president with discretion. It was thought that cash-and-carry would help Britain in a war against Germany, by allowing it to take advantage of its navy.

The influence of the revisionist histories on the first three neutrality acts was clear enough. The acts were specifically designed to prevent the "mistakes" of Woodrow Wilson being repeated by FDR. On the assumption that the United States had been drawn in to World War I to protect its foreign loans, Congress forbade war loans. On the premise that the export of arms in 1915 and 1916 had been another cause of intervention, Congress prohibited the export of arms. Because a third cause of intervention had been, supposedly, trade with the Allies, the act of 1937 insisted that if belligerents bought American goods they paid for them with cash and carried them on their own ships. In the belief that the loss of American lives through submarine warfare had contributed to American involvement, Congress forbade Americans to travel on belligerents' ships.

War in China

The slide to world war worsened with the full-scale Japanese invasion of China in 1937. Moreover, the three Axis powers moved closer together. On October 25, 1936, the Berlin-Rome Axis was formed. On November 6, 1937, Italy and Germany signed an Anti-Comintern Pact and on December 12 Italy left the League. Japan had already abrogated the Washington and London disarmament treaties at the end of 1934 and in December 1936 signed an Anti-Comintern Pact with Germany. As we have observed, Japan was deficient in crucial raw materials, especially oil, and the place to obtain them was South East Asia. When fighting broke out between Japanese and Chinese troops near Beijing on July 7, 1937, the prime minister, Prince Fumimaro Konoye, acceded to the demands of his war minister, Hajime Sugiyama, to dispatch reinforcements and escalate an incident into undeclared war. After China had appealed to the League Assembly, a conference opened at Brussels on November 3, 1937, to discuss the Sino-Japanese War. Japan and Germany absented themselves and their part was taken by Italy. Although Russia participated with the United States, Britain, and France, none of the states was willing to take action under the terms of the Nine Power Treaty and the conference was a failure.

The immediate reaction in America was timid. The House rejected Roosevelt's request for funds to defend Guam on July 21, 1937, by 205 votes to 168, mainly on the grounds that Japan should not be provoked. One member, Bruce Barton, author of a best-seller about Jesus, *The Man Nobody Knows,* whether in praise or pique at Margaret Mitchell's even better seller, parodied her title, calling out, "Guam, Guam with the Wind." This, indeed, happened in the week after Pearl Harbor and the recapture of Guam in August 1944 cost almost 8,000 casualties. Yet on August 17, 1937, the United States sent 1,200 marines to Shanghai to safeguard American interests in China.

With the outbreak of war in Asia as well as Europe and Africa, Roosevelt decided to explore the possibility of public support for a discriminatory foreign policy, in place of the neutrality legislation that he criticized for the way it helped aggressor nations. On October 5, 1937, Roosevelt delivered his famous Quarantine Speech in Chicago in which he proposed that the peace-loving nations should contain warlike states, or else aggression could not be checked: "When an epidemic of physical disease starts to spread the community approves and joins in a quarantine of the patients in order to protect the health of the community against the spread of the disease." Judge Samuel I. Rosenman of New York observed "the reaction to the speech was quick and violent—and nearly unanimous. It was condemned as warmongering and sabrerattling."

Events now occurred in such a way as to allow isolationists an opportunity to try and seize the initiative of foreign policy. The bone of contention was the power to declare war. Congressman Louis Ludlow of Indiana had proposed an amendment to the Constitution whereby the president and Congress could not declare war (unless American territory were attacked), without first securing public support in a national referendum. His proposal remained locked in the judiciary committee until the *Panay* incident of December 12, 1937. The *Panay*, an American gunboat on the Yangtze River in China, was attacked and bombed by Japanese planes for reasons never fully explained, despite the suspicion that the unprovoked attack was meant as a test of American nerve. There were three casualties and another eleven sailors were seriously wounded.

Roosevelt and Hull handled a difficult situation with tact and dignity, eventually accepting a Japanese apology and payment of an indemnity of $2.21 million. Nevertheless, the incident stimulated renewed discussions about the danger of the United States getting caught up in foreign wars inadvertently. The controversy over the *Panay*, aggravated by pacifist societies, such as the National Council for the Prevention of War, brought the Ludlow resolution onto the floor of the House. The arguments against the Ludlow amendment were clear enough. If it were adopted, the roles of the president and Senate in foreign affairs would be circumscribed, giving the impression that America could not back up its foreign policy with force, that the American public did not really trust its administration, and leaving wide open the possibility of an enemy victory during the strategic delay whilst a war referendum was held. Moreover, advocates of the Ludlow amendment failed to appreciate that overseas wars could only be sustained by public consent to government policies and that, once public opinion was aroused by government propaganda, it was most unlikely to be deterred from war by some artificially imposed cooling-off period. Nevertheless, it was perhaps a personal letter from FDR to the speaker, William H. Bankhead, that persuaded enough congressmen to defeat the amendment (which would have required a majority of two-thirds) in a vote of 209 against to 188 in favor in the House debate on January 5, 1938.

Checkmate at Munich

Attention was now concentrated on Europe. In January 1938 Roosevelt, still deeply concerned by the turn of events in Europe, proposed to the British prime minister, Neville Chamberlain, that there should be an international conference to discuss territorial possessions and access to raw materials. Chamberlain rejected the proposal: it would undermine Britain's policy of coming to terms with the dictators.

Hitler invited the Austrian chancellor, Kurt von Schuschnigg, to Berchtesgaden to induce him to accept a union of Austria with Germany, or, rather, its incorporation. Schuschnigg refused but resigned on March 11, 1938. On March 12 Hitler and his army entered Austria at Braunar, his birthplace, and on March 13 he took Vienna. From the back benches Winston Churchill warned the House of Commons on March 14 that Europe was "confronted with a programme of aggression, nicely calculated and timed, unfolding stage by stage." After the Anschluss leading psychologist Sigmund Freud was admitted to England without the usual formalities and became a British citizen the next day although the usual practice was to require five years' residence. Like other refugees from Central Europe, his very presence was effective propaganda against the Nazis, especially for their oppression of the Jews. Nazi anti-Semitism, which became a central feature of German policy in 1938, quite undermined arguments in favor of Hitler's foreign policy based on the injury done to Germany at Versailles, Germany's economic rights, and the self-determination of nations.

In response to the growing threat of war, American isolationists now conceded that the United States required a larger navy for the defense of the western hemisphere and Congress voted for the Vinson Naval Act of 1938, which was to expand the navy at a cost of $1 billion. Moreover, FDR was able to rally public opinion behind statements about the territorial integrity of nations in the western hemisphere.

British Prime Minister Neville Chamberlain disliked the uncertainty of foreign policy. He could not rely for safety on treaties and pacts, as the French were determined to, and thus he asked himself what was the alternative but appeasement of Hitler's demands? Not the League, nor an alliance with France, presumed secure behind its defense fortifications, the Maginot Line. Rather, Hitler and Mussolini had to be treated like rational, if unpleasant, statesmen. As English historian A. J. P. Taylor suggests:

The opponents of appeasement . . . often failed to distinguish between "stopping" Hitler and defeating him in a great war. Hitler could be stopped only in areas directly accessible to Anglo-French forces. . . . Austria was the last occasion when direct opposition was possible. Great Britain and France could not have stopped a German invasion of Czechoslovakia. . . . Similarly, they could not stop the German invasion of Poland. They could only begin a general war which brought no aid to the Poles. There were thus two different questions. At first: shall we go to the aid of this country or that? Later: shall we start a general war for the overthrow of Germany as a Great Power? In practice . . . the two questions were always mixed up.

In other words, while Britain and France could defend areas close to them and restrict the conflict, they could not do so in Central Europe, which could only be defended by full-scale military invasion and a general war.

However, in the next crisis Neville Chamberlain took the initiative, believing that Hitler would strike at Czechoslovakia, unless his "grievances" were met in advance. He did not regard Czech independence as a British interest and both he and Hitler disliked Czech alliances with France and Russia.

The rights of 3 million Sudeten Germans, citizens of Czechoslovakia, were guaranteed in name by the League, to whom they could protest against injustice. Rarely had they done so. However, Germany now made claims on their behalf. On September 4, 1938, President Edvard Benes agreed to these demands. But on September 12, 1938, when Hitler spoke to the annual Nazi party rally in Nuremberg, it became clear that the concessions were insufficient. The speech was broadcast live to America by CBS and translated by Kurt Heiman. Historian William Manchester recalls, "Millions of Americans, hearing Hitler for the first time over shortwave, were shaken by the depth of his hatred; on his lips the Teutonic language sounded cruel, dripping with venom." The following day, September 13, there was a revolt in the Sudetenland that the Czech government quelled.

The French government dithered at the prospect of confrontation with Germany, having believed that Hitler would only attack Czechoslovakia if he were certain there would be no Anglo-French opposition. Chamberlain flew to Munich on September 15 and met Hitler at Berchtesgaden where he offered the separation of the Sudeten Germans from the rest of Czechoslovakia: "I didn't care two hoots whether the Sudetens were in the Reich or out of it according to their own wishes." Hitler agreed: "We want no Czechs." However, Edouard Daladier, French prime minister, and Georges Bonnet, his foreign secretary, now argued with Chamberlain on September 18 that Hitler's real aim was the domination of Europe itself. Thus, if Chamberlain believed that Hitler only wanted the unification of all German peoples and was now satisfied, would Britain guarantee the new truncated Czechoslovakia? Chamberlain and three of his Cabinet did so, although they had refused to guarantee the whole state. On September 21 the British and French told the Czech president, Benes, that Czechoslovakia could either capitulate to Hitler's demands or fight alone.

Chamberlain believed the affair was settled and on September 22 again flew to Germany to meet Hitler at Godesberg on the Rhine. However, Hitler now wanted immediate occupation rather than a negotiated transfer of power. Nevertheless, he promised to wait until October 1, 1938, before marching on Czechoslovakia. Chamberlain knew nothing could be done to assist Czechoslovakia but agreed to Mussolini's proposal for a Four Power Conference in Munich. On September 29 Chamberlain met Hitler there and, without much reference to Daladier, the two of them accepted a plan submitted by Mussolini that had actually been prepared by the German foreign office. The Czechs were obliged to agree.

Superficially, it was Mussolini who dominated the Munich conference: he was the only one among Daladier, Hitler, and Chamberlain, who could speak the others' languages. The idea of four incompetent linguists discussing world affairs in cod accents led to a bitter, apocryphal anecdote at Italy's expense. "Remember, if it comes to war," Hitler is supposed to have told Chamberlain in his most gutteral tones, "we shall have Italy on our side this time." More in sorrow than anger, Chamberlain is said to have replied in his most upper-crust accent, "That's only fair. We had to have her last time."

On September 30 Hitler met Chamberlain for the last time and welcomed a statement the prime minister had prepared: "We regard the agreement signed last night and the Anglo-German Naval Agreement as symbolic of the desire of our two peoples never to go to war with one another again." The same evening Chamberlain told cheering crowds in London, "I believe it is peace for our time." (Some later accounts have Chamberlain saying "in our time.") The overwhelming majority of press, public opinion, and Chamberlain's own Conservative party approved, as did the governments of the British Dominions. In fact, it was checkmate. As A. J. P. Taylor says, "The triumph of appeasement also marked its failure. . . . Appeasement had been designed by Chamberlain as the impartial redress of justified grievances. It became a capitulation, a surrender to fear."

From Hitler's point of view, there was also a crucial military consideration to the seizure of Czechoslovakia. The annexation of the Sudetenland by the Reich involved handing over to Hitler the

Nazi artist Josef Plank produced a series of scurrilous but stylish cartoons and posters reviling the United States, Britain, and Russia during the years of the Third Reich. In this cartoon of the Munich crisis and partition of Czechoslovakia, an overpainted nanny, taking mischievous children to the zoo, Benesch (as Czechoslovakia) has his skirt pulled up by such howling brats as Yugoslavia, Romania, and Hungary while the caged Russian bear and conniving Italian ice-cream vendor salivate at the prospect of uproar in Europe. At the end of World War II the Americans confiscated Plank's portfolio and a collection of 250 drawings is now held in the Library of Congress.

powerful fortifications that protected Bohemia and Slovakia, and hence eastern Europe, from invasion by Germany. It was this single achievement, more than any other, that ensured German dominance of Central Europe. A yet more sinister advantage was that Czechoslovakia was comparatively rich in U^{235}, the sort of uranium essential for nuclear fission.

In three stages members of the League had abandoned collective security and common action in the face of aggression. The invasion of Ethiopia was considered by the Council and its members had briefly imposed economic sanctions; the great powers made decisions about the Spanish Civil War through a special Non-Intervention Committee but laid their plans before Council and Assembly; the Czech crisis was never submitted to the League in any form. Winston Churchill's comment was: "Britain and France had to choose between war and dishonour. They chose dishonour. They will have war." Plans for rearmament in Britain were put into effect with great urgency.

Hitler's diplomatic success at Munich encouraged him to intensify his persecution of the Jews. Already the Nuremberg laws of 1935 had divested Jews of their political and civil rights. In November 1938 a new, and even more terrible, wave of persecution began as Nazi gangs attacked Jews and their businesses and synagogues. The streets of German cities were strewn with broken glass, giving the name of *Kristallnacht* to the outrage to humanity. The pretext was the assassination of a German diplomat in Paris by a Jew. In these months hundreds of victims were killed and thousands were transported to concentration camps. While the American press deplored the violence, only the *New Republic,* in its issue of November 23, 1938, urged a revision of the immigration laws to allow the entry of persecuted Jews into the United States. Subsequently, in 1939, Senator Robert Wagner of New York introduced a bill to allow the entry of 200,000 German refugee children above the official quota but, lacking the support of FDR, who was reluctant to press Congress after the failure of the court-packing scheme, the refugee bill expired in committee.

A survey in October 1938 by *Fortune* showed that only 11.6 percent of American public opinion approved of the Munich settlement and that 76.2 percent believed the United States would become involved in a European war. As the editors pointed out, in March, 1937, only 22 percent had thought then that America would get involved in a foreign war.

The Good Neighbor in Latin America

Roosevelt's attempts at a Good Neighbor policy toward Latin America ran into troubled waters when they encountered a mix of Latin-American nationalism, American commercial interests, and the gales of contrary diplomatic doctrine.

Despite their concentration on developments in Europe and the Far East, Roosevelt and Cordell Hull recognized just how significant were Latin-American affairs for the United States. They, and the Senate Foreign Relations Committee, were deeply committed to the Good Neighbor policy and understood exactly how important it was to convince Latins of America's benevolent disinterestedness. Moreover, when it came to Latin America, FDR was exercising his executive role to further his interests elsewhere. As the historian of American isolationism, Wayne S. Cole, explains, "In subtle but increasingly significant ways . . . Roosevelt's policies toward Latin America helped educate the American people in the wisdom and practical benefits of a more active leadership and multilateral peace-keeping role by the United States. It accomplished that from a direction the isolationists were not well prepared to defend." For one thing, FDR's policies toward Latin America were consistent with those advocated by isolationists such as Borah, Nye, and Norris, especially in regard to repudiating dollar diplomacy and the big stick. For another, the administration's policies to defend the western hemisphere from attack from the eastern almost always met with the uniform approval of the American people.

Roosevelt and Hull tried to persuade Latins of America's friendly intentions.

Since 1929 the people of Cuba had been in open revolt against the corrupt dictatorship of Gerardo Machado. The decisive factor in the overthrow of Machado in 1933 was the weight of the army and its pivotal leader, Colonel Fulgencio Batista, who were able to place in power, first, Carlos Manuel de Cespedes, a former diplomat, and, then, Dr. Ramon Grau San Martín, surgeon and professor at the University of Havana. Grau condemned the ascendancy of privileged foreign interests in Cuba and refused to continue the earlier favoritism shown to foreign investors. This policy aroused the indignation of Ambassador Sumner Welles, who advised FDR to intervene with military force under the terms of the Platt amendment of 1901. Instead, FDR simply denied recognition to the Grau regime and sent gunboats to patrol Cuban waters. Of course, the withholding of American recognition precluded Cuba's ability to export sugar to the United States and thus the new, subtle form of pressure threatened Cuba's very economic future. Accordingly, Batista transferred his support to Colonel Carlos Mendieta who was able to seize power in January 1934 and resume more conservative policies toward foreign investors.

Having successfully applied pressure tactics rather than outright force, FDR then abrogated the Platt amendment, retaining only rights to maintain an American naval base at Guantanamo Bay. In May 1934 Congress reduced the tariff on Cuban sugar by 25 percent, and, several months later, reduced the tariff by another 40 percent.

In July 1934 FDR embarked on a goodwill tour of the Caribbean and the Pacific. In Haiti he advanced the withdrawal of American troops from October 1 to August 15, 1934; in Colombia he praised the peaceful resolution in the settlement of the Leticia dispute with Peru; in Panama he promised pacific and just settlement of its differences with the United States. In short, FDR, by his open manner and conciliatory gestures, earned the reputation of being a good neighbor.

In 1935 the State Department reached reciprocal trade agreements with Brazil, Colombia, Haiti, and Honduras and initiated discussions with another nine Latin-American countries. Hull also negotiated a new treaty with Panama, signed on March 2, 1936, by which the United States abandoned its unlimited rights of intervention agreed in 1903, and in which both countries agreed to joint operation and defense of the Panama Canal.

Moreover, FDR and Hull resisted lobbying of Congress by American Catholics, led by the Knights of Columbus, to put pressure on the Mexican government of Làzaro Càrdenas to end its anticlerical policy, if necessary by recalling the U.S. ambassador to Mexico, Josephus Daniels. Neither FDR nor Hull was prepared to jeopardize his reputation of nonintervention in the internal affairs of any Latin-American country, especially over such an emotive and ephemeral issue as religious practices. However, on March 18, 1938, President Cárdenas of Mexico announced the appropriation of the $400 million Mexican oil industry, much of it in foreign hands, because the foreign oil companies had defied the Mexican Supreme Court's decision in a labor dispute. FDR, Josephus Daniels, and the Treasury adviser, Henry Morgenthau, were united in their determination to prevent Cordell Hull and the State Department from sensationalizing the issue and causing an open break with Mexico.

In December 1936 FDR attended the opening of the Inter-American Peace Conference in Buenos Aires, Argentina, where he received a tumultuous public reception. However, Cordell Hull's proposals for a common hemisphere policy on arms and neutrality were shot down by Saavedra Lamas of Argentina who wanted to assert Argentinian supremacy in Latin America. The only U.S. proposal accepted in its original form was that of nonintervention, first put forward at Montevideo, Uruguay, in 1933.

In 1938 and 1939 FDR took action to strengthen the defense of the western hemisphere. In April 1938 he created a Standing Liaison Committee to strengthen military missions to Latin America, establishing firm control over commercial airlines. In November the Joint Army and Navy Board discussed contingency arrangements in case of attack. In 1939 the five so-called Rainbow Plans defined strategy for defending the United States by safeguarding the hemisphere as a whole. Moreover, in December 1938 the American republics attending the Pan American Conference in Lima, Peru, had unanimously adopted a Declaration of Lima, condemning religious and racial prejudice and alien political activity in the western hemisphere. Fear of Nazi infiltration preceded World War II. On January 4, 1939, George C. Stoney advised readers of the *New Republic,* "How the Dictators Woo Argentina."

The Dark Valley of 1939

Roosevelt's annual message to Congress on January 4, 1939, was largely devoted to foreign affairs: "All about us rage undeclared wars—military and economic." Therefore, the United States, without getting involved, should revise its neutrality legislation: "We have learned that when we deliberately try to legislate neutrality, our neutrality laws may operate unevenly and unfairly— may actually give aid to the aggressor and deny it to the victim. The instinct of self-preservation should warn us that we ought not to let that happen any more." Congress continued to oppose any change that indicated the United States would distinguish between aggressor and victim and thereby incur hostility. Yet Gallup public opinion polls of spring and summer 1939 showed 65 percent of Americans favored an economic boycott of Germany and 56 percent wanted a revision of the neutrality laws. For, 51 percent expected a war in Europe and 58 percent expected that the United States would become involved. Thus when the danger of war was greater, fewer Americans feared its inevitably because there was, in early summer 1939, no dramatic crisis such as Munich to focus people's minds on the danger. Yet, although 90 percent said they would fight if America were invaded, only 10 percent said they would do so regardless of invasion.

Despite setbacks, FDR and Hull continued to put pressure on Congress to repeal the neutrality laws. On June 6, 1939, the House Foreign Affairs Committee voted to repeal the arms embargo by only 11 votes to 9. However, seven days later, the committee voted on party lines by 12 votes to 8 to report a new measure, giving the president discretion as to how, where, and when, the law should be applied. On June 29 the House voted by 159 to 157 in favor of an amendment proposed by Congressman John M. Vorys of Ohio, placing an embargo on arms and ammunition but not on other war materiel. This amendment was then incorporated into the main bill of Congressman Sol Bloom of New York that passed the House most narrowly on June 30 by 200 votes to 188.

In the Senate, it fared worse. On July 11 the Foreign Relations

Committee rejected FDR's proposed revision of the neutrality legislation by 12 votes to 11. Originally, the Committee had been divided, with 11 in favor, 10 against, and 2 undecided. The undecided were the Democrats Walter George of Georgia and Guy Gillette of Iowa and both favored repeal. However, because FDR had opposed them in his attempted purge of 1938, the isolationists were able to persuade them to take their revenge by voting against repeal of the neutrality laws.

On July 18, 1939, Roosevelt and Hull invited congressional leaders to discuss European affairs at the White House. Roosevelt predicted war and said he believed France and Britain had only an even chance of survival. He hoped Congress would agree even now to a revision of the neutrality laws in their favor to deter Hitler. However, the most prepossessing senator there, William E. Borah of Idaho, declared, "There's not going to be any war this year. All this hysteria is manufactured and artificial." Brushing aside Hull's references to State Department telegrams, he went on, "I have sources of information in Europe that I regard as more reliable than those of the State Department." He meant newspaper articles. The vice-president, John Nance Garner, is supposed to have advised Roosevelt, "You haven't got the votes and that's all there is to it." Thus, the policy of the United States would continue to be to forbid the sale of munitions to all belligerents, even if there were another European war. The prospect of that war moved closer.

The newly diminished state of Czechoslovakia was divided by ethnic dispute. The Czechs insisted the country was one state, the Slovaks said it was two and, from October 1938, it was spelled Czecho-Slovakia. On March 15, 1939, Slovakia became independent. Hungary claimed the Ukraine district of lower Carpathia. Thus the new president, Hacha, allowed "Czechia" (or Bohemia) to become a German protectorate. The Sudeten territories had not been Hitler's "last territorial demand in Europe," after all. Speaking in Birmingham on March 17, 1939, Neville Chamberlain declared that no one "could possibly have saved Czechoslovakia" but added, "any attempt to dominate the world by force was one which the Democracies must resist." On March 19 he drafted a declaration of resistance to a reported, but nonexistent, German invasion of Romania, which he then invited Russia, France, and Poland to sign. Poland had used the Munich crisis to take Tesin from Czechoslovakia and was negotiating in secret with Germany over Danzig (or Gdansk, the free city created in 1919), and thus refused any proposed alliance with Russia. Yet on March 31 Chamberlain promised Poland a British and French guarantee of its integrity. He had not consulted France. Britain had no way of keeping its bargain with Poland, nor did it advance money or military aid. Hitler called the bluff on April 28 by repudiating Germany's nonaggression pact with Poland of 1934 and an Anglo-German naval agreement of 1935.

Britain and France could not guarantee Poland without the support of Russia. Chamberlain did not trust a Russian alliance but, nevertheless, his government pursued protracted negotiations in Moscow in the spring and summer of 1939. However, on August 23 the foreign ministers of Russia and Germany, Viacheslav Molotov and Joachim von Ribbentrop, signed a Nazi–Soviet Pact in Moscow by which Russia was to stay neutral if Germany went to war. This seemed a prelude to a partition of Poland and on August 25 the Anglo-Polish alliance was signed. A clause by which Danzig was guaranteed as well as Poland was kept secret so that Hitler would not be provoked. The rights of Germans in the free city of Danzig had long been the pretext for German "grievances" against Poland. In reality, Hitler wanted Poland's industrial resources and to recover Germany's ascendancy over Poland lost in 1919. Joseph Kennedy, the American ambassador to Britain, told Cordell Hull that Chamberlain "says the futility of it all is the thing that is frightful; after all they cannot save the Poles." Despite Britain's public assurances, Viscount Halifax, the British foreign secretary, urged Poland to negotiate with Hitler. The Polish foreign minister, Beck, refused to do so and on September 1, 1939, German troops crossed the frontier into Poland.

Chamberlain, Halifax, and Georges Bonnet, the French foreign minister, supported a proposal from Mussolini for another conference. But when Chamberlain reported this to the House of Commons on September 2 the response made it clear that the only British policy could now be an ultimatum delivered to Germany on September 3 and war if it expired without satisfactory assurances. This was what happened. Thus, in the end, Britain and France went to war over a state that they could not defend. World War II had begun. France and the four British dominions of Australia, New Zealand, Canada, and South Africa followed the British declaration of war against Germany with their own. Within eleven days the Nazis had subdued Poland. This was the *blitzkrieg*—lightning war.

While there is no doubt that the prime cause of war was Hitler's aggressive foreign policy, Britain's reluctance to address German aggression earlier was a contributing factor to the terrible crisis. Christopher Andrew shows in *Her Majesty's Secret Service* (1986) how British intelligence officers in the 1930s were incapable of evaluating information about Germany. As a result, the British government was so overwhelmed with alarmist rumors about German intentions and capabilities that it found it impossible to arrive at quick, appropriate, and effective decisions. Thus Neville Chamberlain had made his decision to join staff talks with France in January 1939 on a false intelligence report that Germany was about to invade the Netherlands. He was rushed into guaranteeing the independence of Poland in March 1939 by rumors of German action against Romania. Even more surprisingly, British intelligence failed to realize that a Nazi-Soviet Pact would be signed, a fact that dissident Germans leaked to the United States. Most tragic of all, it concluded that the entire German economy was being overmobilized to such an extent that it must soon crack under the strain of war—an illusion that it took three years of fighting to dispel. It seemed as if British foreign policy was based on Lady Bracknell's dictum to her prospective son-in-law, "Ignorance is like a delicate exotic fruit; touch it, and the bloom is gone. Fortunately in England, at any rate, education produces no effect whatsoever."

Having fought Russia in skirmishes in 1938 and 1939, Japan regarded the Nazi-Soviet Pact as a betrayal by Germany and thus remained neutral at the outset of the European war.

In October 1939 Russian troops occupied eastern Poland. Russia, eager to make sure of the Baltic, also occupied Latvia, Estonia, and Lithuania. Russia demanded that Finland cede, or lease, parts of its territory considered essential to Russian security. Ready to accede to most of the demands, Finland refused a thirty-year lease on the port of Hanko as a Russian naval base and also refused to give up territory across the isthmus of Karelia by Leningrad. On the pretext that Finns had fired across the frontier, Russian armies invaded Finland on November 30 and established an exiled Communist, Kuusinen, as head of the Democratic Republic of Finland. He then acceded to the specific Russian demands. But, buoyed up by what it felt to be the tide of world opinion, Finland protested to the League against Russia on December 2. It was almost as if World War II were not taking place. Whereas Finland wanted the Assembly to persuade Russia to stop fighting, or to provide military and economic aid, the League simply expelled Russia on December 14, 1939, the only time it excluded a member that had broken the Covenant. On March 12, 1940, Finland sued for peace and accepted Russian terms. Once again, Britain and France had paraded their intention of aiding a small victim of aggression and had failed to do anything about it. In France, Daladier's government fell and was replaced by one led by Paul Reynaud.

"Battle of Washington"

Never again would American isolationists hold the dominant position in American politics that was theirs in 1939. But, although they were gradually forced to retreat, they consistently deployed considerable influence against every proposal to involve the United States more directly in world affairs. Responding to the Nazi invasion of Poland, FDR said in his radio "fireside chat" of September 3, "This nation will remain a neutral nation." But, going further than Woodrow Wilson in 1914, he added, "But I cannot ask that every American remain neutral in thought as well."

The cash-and-carry provisions of the 1937 act had expired; the munitions embargo was still in effect. Roosevelt called Congress into special session on September 21 so that the embargo could be replaced by a provision allowing belligerents to purchase munitions and raw materials on a cash-and-carry basis. The administration argued that such a measure would strengthen American neutrality rather than aid Britain and France. However, the real purpose was not in doubt. Germany had increased its own manufacturing capacity and, in seizing Czechoslovakia, had taken over its great munitions works, and thus already possessed military supplies on a scale that neither Britain nor France could match without American support. FDR's aides reported that public opinion was divided and that he could still not count on the votes of nominally loyal congressmen to get the neutrality law revised. FDR decided to compromise and thus, on October 27, 1939, the Senate by 63 votes to 30 and, on November 3, the House by 243 votes to 181, agreed to a revision, permitting the sale of goods to belligerents on the basis of cash-and-carry, provided Congress approved.

The inactive "phony war" of the winter of 1930–1940 lulled Britain and France into a false sense of security. They believed they now had time to make their own arms and thus reduced their orders from the United States. Moreover, since the Johnson act of 1934 had barred countries that defaulted on their loans from borrowing more American money, they decided to conserve their dollar and gold reserves by restricting their purchase of American goods to food, raw materials, aircraft, and machine tools. FDR insisted that Britain and France set up a special Purchasing Mission in the United States that had to operate through the Federal Reserve Board. By exercising such controls, FDR hoped to avoid the Allies' interests clashing with America's own military needs.

In fact, in early 1940 FDR had to fight a "battle of Washington" with his own administration over aid to Britain and France. Secretary of War Henry Woodring opposed Allied purchases of war material and aircraft that interfered with American needs and flatly refused Allied access to secret information necessary to fly the planes they had ordered. FDR became so exasperated that in March he told the War Department that its opposition must end, that leaks to the isolationist press must stop, and that he would transfer any truculent officers to Guam.

However, America was not even prepared for its own national defense, let alone to defend the democracies effectively. In May 1940 the War Department reported that the army could field only 80,000 men and had equipment for fewer than 500,000 combat troops. As to aircraft, America had but 160 pursuit planes, 52 heavy bombers, and only 260 fully trained pilots. This was partly why Air Corps Chief of Staff General Henry ("Hap") Arnold was reluctant to sell aircraft to Britain and France. At their current rate of loss, 100 planes would last only three days, while substantively reducing the number of American planes for self-defense and thus delaying the training of American pilots.

During the 1930s Congress had been miserly about defense appropriations. In May 1940 it could not provide enough. It voted $1.5 billion more for defense—$320 million above what Roosevelt had asked—and then voted another $1.7 billion to expand the regular army from 280,000 to 375,000 men and allowed the president to summon the National Guard for active service.

More ominously, FDR and his closest associates were also preparing the United States for the atomic age.

In a letter delivered to the White House on October 11, 1939, Albert Einstein, the world-famous Jewish physicist, warned FDR that the Germans were working on an atomic bomb and that with this weapon they could conquer the world. Einstein's letter was the outcome of the research and moral courage of distinguished physicists from different countries—Otto Hahn, Niels Bohr, Lise Meitner, James Chadwick, Victor R. Weisskopf, and Edward Teller (who translated the letter from German into English), many of whom had emigrated to the United States. When Niels Bohr arrived in New York from Denmark on January 16, 1939, a telegram awaited him from his Viennese colleagues Lise Meitner and O. R. Frisch, now working in Copenhagen. It explained how, in a recent experiment, they had used TNT and split an atom that had freed 200 million volts of electricity. If uranium could be used, the explosion would be twenty million times greater.

The Meitner-Frisch experiment was repeated at Columbia University by other physicists, including Nobel Prize winner Enrico Fermi of Italy, on January 25, 1939. Discussions at Columbia were open but only briefly reported in the New York press. Bohr told the American Physical Society meeting in Washington that a projectile armed with a fragment of U^{235} bombarded with slow neutrons could produce an explosion that would destroy the

News of the terrors of the German Blitz, or aerial bombardment, of London in fall 1940, which devastated the city and partly damaged St. Paul's Cathedral, helped unite English-speaking peoples across the world in a central purpose of World War II—the elimination of nazism. (British Press Services; Office of War Information; Library of Congress).

District of Columbia. Moreover, it was clear that the Third Reich was committed to the development of such an atomic bomb. Accordingly, Roosevelt was persuaded to enter the atomic race. With the support of pivotal leaders in Congress, FDR secured the necessary funds to start the Manhattan Project, to make an atomic bomb that could be dropped by air.

In the autumn of 1939 Kennedy and Bullitt, America's ambassadors to Britain and France, both consistently predicted that, unless the Allies were given more immediate material aid, they would fall victim to a German assault from the air. At this time FDR expected Germany and Russia to divide Europe between them and then extend their control to Asia Minor and thence the European colonies in Africa and Asia. The United States would be imperiled. Thus, in his State of the Union message on January 5, 1940, he expressed his anxiety in a significant distinction, explaining "there is a vast difference between keeping out of war and pretending that war is none of our business. We do not have to go to war with other nations, but at least we can strive with other nations to encourage the kind of peace that will lighten the troubles of the world, and by so doing help our own nation as well." FDR was anxious to assert, for both domestic and international consumption, that America must play a decisive part in shaping postwar peace. "For it becomes clearer and clearer that the future world will be a shabby and dangerous place to live in —yes, even for Americans to live in—if it is ruled by force in the hands of a few." Moreover, he warned, "I hope we shall have fewer ostriches in our midst. It is not good for the ultimate health of ostriches to bury their heads in the sand."

The degree of sympathy for Europe and support for American intervention varied throughout the United States and depended partly on ethnic origins. According to opinion polls, New York City was more interventionist than any other part; Texas was more anti-German; the South showed itself most ready to fight; the West Coast was more concerned with Japan than Germany. The upper classes were most interventionist: in 1940 more than 66 percent of America's business and intellectual elite wanted increased supplies to be sent to Britain; almost half the people in *Who's Who in America* wanted an immediate declaration of war.

Almost everybody favored increasing military and naval strength. Yet opinion polls indicated an unwillingness to accept the inevitable. In late 1939, after the outbreak of war in Europe, 40 percent thought the United States would become involved. In 1940, after the fall of western Europe, when the likelihood was greater, only 7.7 percent thought so. But one pattern was consistent in these months. To the Gallup question, "Do you think the United States should keep out of war or do everything possible to help England, even at the risk of getting into war outselves?" the public showed increasing acceptance of involvement during 1940. Those willing to take the risk by helping England were 36 percent in May, 50 percent in November, and 60 percent in December.

The *New Republic,* an openly isolationist magazine before the war, underwent a change of attitude that reflected the shift in public opinion. There was a period of transition when it advocated all aid short of war to England and France and supported cash-and-carry legislation before calling on the government to declare war on the Axis. Emphasizing the possibility of Nazi success and the ensuing dangers of Nazi encroachment on the United States, the editors decided on September 6, 1939, that the devil they knew, imperialist Britain and war, was better than the one they had no experience of, Nazi Germany and peace. The *New Republic* accurately assessed the undercurrent of public opinion on February 12, 1940: "You cannot go on day after day and month after month believing with all your heart that one party in a desperate struggle is both dangerous and despicable and must at all costs be defeated, without feeling a sort of moral delinquency in failing to contribute your own strength to the cause." This was the essential point of pundits such as prominent theologian Reinhold Niebuhr and popular columnist Walter Lippmann, who, in various articles and books, showed they, too, were moving from isolationism to interventionism.

Proponents of intervention did not simply keep their own counsel. They mobilized theor forces. The Committee to Defend America by Aiding the Allies was organized in May 1940 by William Allen White with the aim of rousing public opinion to support, first, all aid to Britain short of war, and later, outright intervention. Leading speakers included John McCloy, Robert

Sherwood, and Elizabeth Morrow Cutter, author and mother-in-law to Charles A. Lindbergh. The organization had chapters across the country but was strongest in the East.

In Congress the old guard of the isolationists was changing. Senator William E. Borah died in January 1940. Of the survivors, Senators Hiram Johnson and Arthur Capper were seventy-five years old and no longer had the stamina for a sustained war of words with FDR, while Senator George W. Norris was being drawn increasingly into the Roosevelt camp. The younger men, Nye (who had replaced Borah on the SFRC), Robert La Follette, Clark, and Vandenberg, now led the isolationists in the Senate. Moreover, with the death in November 1940 of Key Pittman, Democratic chairman of the SFRC, and his replacement by Senator Walter F. George, the congressional battle lines had changed once and for all.

Battle of Britain

In April 1940 Germany invaded Denmark and Norway and on May 10 Germany invaded western Europe. At last, Winston Churchill became prime minister of Britain. In a speech with phrases borrowed from Garibaldi and Clemenceau but with an urgency of his own, Churchill told the House of Commons on May 13, 1940, "I have nothing to offer but blood, toil, tears and sweat. You ask, What is your policy? I will say: It is to wage war. . . . You ask, What is our aim? I can answer in one word, victory —victory at all costs." No one foresaw even the immediate cost that entailed placing Britain in pawn to the United States.

Holland capitulated to Germany on May 14, Belgium on May 16. The British army in Europe evacuated the beaches of Dunkirk with such heroism that propaganda almost succeeded in transfiguring the unmitigated disaster into a symbolic victory. Italy then declared war on Britain and France on June 10, 1940. The French government of Paul Reynaud survived the German occupation of Paris on June 14 by two days. In the week when ministers, deputies, and civil servants left the capital, two American films were being shown in cinemas in the Champs Élysées, *Going Places* and *You Can't Take It With You*. This was the philosophy of Renaud's successor, Marshal Philippe Pétain, the eighty-four-year-old hero of Verdun in World War I, who was deter-mined to use the defeat of France to rid his country of the ideolo-gies of the Left. He reached an armistice with Germany on June 22 and established a fascist government, first at Bordeaux and then at the resort of Vichy in southern France that arranged terms of collaboration on October 24. To prevent it falling into German hands, the British government then ordered the scuttling of the French fleet at Mers-el-Kebir (Oran) on July 3, 1940, with consid-erable loss of life. The fall of France was devastating not only for Britain and the rest of Europe but also for the United States, where it was taken as a clear signal that, unless Britain were given substantive material aid, it could not stand alone against the Na-zis, far less turn the tide of the German advance and shield Amer-ica from the greatest military threat ever. Robert Sherwood in *Roosevelt and Hopkins* has said that during the early war Roosevelt was at a loss to know what to do—"a period of terrible, stultify-ing vacuum."

The Battle of Britain of the summer of 1940 began with German attacks on convoys of merchant ships. On August 13 the second part of the battle commenced, with a full-scale German attack on England with bomber aircraft protected by fighters. Provided with 500 new fighters, Air Marshall Hugh Dowding concentrated on the destruction of the bombers. Hence the Germans set out to destroy the fighter bases in the county of Kent and nearly suc-ceeded. Then on September 7 the Germans began to bomb Lon-don, with massive loss of life and the dislocation of society but the Kent airfields were saved. The German Luftwaffe made its last effort on September 15, and then conceded air superiority to the British by withdrawing. Hitler postponed his immediate in-vasion of Britain on September 17. However, the Germans bombed London every night from September 7 to November 2 and then turned to other industrial cities and western ports. The last severe air raid of the so-called "Blitz" came on Birmingham on May 16, 1941. Thereafter, the Luftwaffe prepared to cooperate with the German army in the invasion of Russia that began on June 22, 1941. The conflict with Britain then turned to battle on the seas, essentially Germany's attempt to destroy the convoys carrying

American supplies that reached its first climax between March and July 1941 in the Battle of the Atlantic. That April, 700,000 tons of shipping were sunk.

The artistic metaphor for the physical hurricane and political holocaust of 1938 had been Orson Welles's radio version of *War of the Worlds. The Great Dictator,* Charles Chaplin's film parody of Hitler and Mussolini, which opened in New York on October 15, 1940, served for America as tragicomic comment on the condition of continental Europe. A simple plot has a little Jewish barber returning to his ghetto after World War I to find the whole country, Tomania, dominated by the despot Adenoid Hynkel, with his aids Herring and Garbitch, under the sign of the double cross. When the little fellow is mistaken for Hynkel complications ensue to provide a series of comic and sentimental divertissements. Chaplin could thus play his beloved tramp and caricature Hitler to whom he bore "a coincidental resemblance." The parody is at its peak when Hynkel and his associate, the dictator of Bacteria, Napoloni, allowing Jack Oakie to ridicule Mussolini expansively, debate their apportionment of the globe, a balloon that never quite manages to balance.

Increasing Involvement

American foreign policy from the summer of 1940 to the winter of 1941 developed in response to Germany's conquest of Europe and Japan's conquest of South East Asia in five stages. Three—the destroyers-bases deal, Lend-Lease, and the war at sea—led to the Atlantic Charter signed by Roosevelt and Churchill. The other two—economic restrictions on Japan and intransigent opposition to Japan's territorial claims—led to Pearl Harbor and the full intervention of the United States in the war.

After Italy's declaration of war and the conquest of Holland, Belgium, and France, it was possible for Roosevelt to arouse the American people to the needs of national defense. Roosevelt said at Charlottesville, Virginia, on June 10, 1940, "We will extend to the opponents of force the material resources of this nation and, at the same time, we will harness and speed up the use of those resources in order that we ourselves in the Americas may have equipment and training equal to the task of any emergency and every defense." The next month representatives of the American republics at the Havana Conference in Cuba agreed to take action to prevent any change in the status of the European colonies in the western hemisphere and to consider aggression against any one of them as aggression against them all. This solidarity lasted until Pearl Harbor when Chile refused, temporarily, and Argentina, permanently, to sever their relations with the Axis. Some countries offered the United States military bases, others replaced German military advisers with Americans. The United States increased its purchase of raw materials within the hemisphere and sold its products to the other countries, deprived of European goods, at restricted prices.

In an attempt to widen his base of support Roosevelt appointed two prominent Republicans who had opposed the New Deal, Henry L. Stimson and Frank Knox, as respectively, secretaries of war and navy, on June 19, 1940. They replaced the two most isolationist members of the Cabinet, Henry Woodring and Charles Edison. Knox, the Republican vice-presidential candidate in 1936, favored considerable military expansion, an army of a million men, the strongest air force in the world, and the immediate shipment of late model planes to Britain. Stimson wanted the repeal of all neutrality legislation and the introduction of military conscription. In fact, it was now Harry L. Hopkins who exercised more influence on Roosevelt than either Hull or Welles in this period. Called "Lord Root of the Matter" by Churchill, he had the same sort of position with Roosevelt that House had known with Wilson. Unlike House, he did not pretend to know his chief's mind when he did not and, since his sole aim was to serve, he did not quarrel with the president.

On July 21, 1940, Winston Churchill made a specific plea to Roosevelt for a transference of destroyers from America in exchange for leases of British naval bases. Although Roosevelt had announced all aid short of war in June, he delayed action until the transfer could be presented as an act of defense and accomplished without reference to Congress. The eventual agreement, incorporated in letters exchanged between Cordell Hull and Philip Kerr, Lord Lothian, the British ambassador, on September 2,

1940, gave British bases in Newfoundland and Bermuda to the United States as an outright gift and granted to the United States ninety-nine-year leases on other bases on the Bahamas, Jamaica, St. Lucia, Trinidad, British Guiana, and Antigua in exchange for fifty old American destroyers, built in World War I, now out of commission, and not needed while the British navy controlled the Atlantic. Only nine destroyers entered British service before 1941. The gesture was one of sympathy, rather than support, and afforded by Roosevelt in a calculated and careful maneuver.

However, after the destroyers-bases deal, the United States was not neutral in any real sense of the term. It seemed Roosevelt and Hull believed that total aid short of war would be the best way of avoiding attack or intervention. Joseph Kennedy, former ambassador to the Court of St. James, declared that talk about Britain fighting for democracy was "bunk." John Foster Dulles, a prominent lawyer and later secretary of state, said, "Only hysteria entertains the idea that Germany, Italy or Japan contemplates war upon us."

Election of 1940

The dispute over intervention was exacerbated by the presidential campaign of 1940. The dark horse of the Republicans' campaign was utility tycoon Wendell Willkie of Indiana, president of the Commonwealth and Southern Corporation, who had fought the Tennessee Valley Authority and could thus present himself as a hapless business victim of the encroaching power of the state. He was a liberal and an internationalist. On the radio he was so persuasive that lawyer Oren Root, Jr., was moved to establish the Associated Willkie Clubs of America among his Ivy League associates in order to advance Willkie's campaign. Thus at the Republican National Convention in Philadelphia Willkie took the nomination on the sixth ballot over favorites Thomas E. Dewey of New York and Robert A. Taft of Ohio. Willkie's nomination in preference to some midwestern party regular signaled the start of a new domination of the Republican party by its eastern establishment that would continue for twenty years. The Democrats charged

Willkie with "an electric background, an electric personality and an electric campaign chest."

FDR was as enigmatic over the issue of running for an unprecedented third term as he was about much else. His enemies accused him of being ravenous for unlimited power. His close associates recognized that he was deeply divided as to whether to break the two-term tradition. None of his preferred successors, Hopkins, William O. Douglas, and Robert Jackson, developed any sizable popular following nor did the plausible conservative alternatives, Hull, Garner, and Farley.

The international crisis was the most crucial factor in prompting FDR to decide on his candidacy in May 1940. Ironically, he was supported by a group of leading politicians that included both the proponents and opponents of intervention. Although he chose Chicago as the site of the Democratic National Convention, because he could rely on the local political boss, Ed Kelly, to "pack the galleries," he would not openly campaign for his nomination, seeking instead the fiction of a spontaneous draft. Kelly had his superintendent of sewers rouse delegates for FDR through loudspeakers around the hall. After a dutiful show of reluctance and deference, Roosevelt was nominated by 946 votes on the first ballot. Commented Thomas Gore, former senator from Oklahoma, "You know I have never doubted for one moment since he was nominated in 1932 that he would seek a third term. . . . Caesar thrice refused the kingly crown—but this Caesar, never."

In place of John Nance Garner, FDR chose Secretary of Agriculture Henry A. Wallace as his running mate because Wallace was a committed New Dealer who could carry the Corn Belt and his choice was accepted, reluctantly in some quarters, by the delegates.

FDR was most vulnerable to criticisms that the New Deal had failed to meet America's minimum defense needs, although the wartime economic boom had already begun. Expanded industrial production was providing about 3 million new jobs. Roosevelt retaliated by campaign visits to defense plants and to military and naval sites that served both to demonstrate Democratic preparedness and illustrate his domination of the situation.

In the election FDR took 27,307,819 votes (54.8 percent) to Willkie's 22,321,018 (44.8 percent), and 449 votes in the electoral college to Willkie's 82. Socialist candidate Norman Thomas polled 99,557 votes. Roosevelt had won all but ten states, eight in the Midwest, and Maine and Vermont in the Northeast. Roosevelt won his victory in the cities and it was his decisive pluralities in New York, Chicago, Cleveland, and Milwaukee that gave him the pivotal states of New York, Illinois, Ohio, and Wisconsin. He attracted ethnic groups who had most at stake on his policy of intervention in the war, such as Norwegians, Poles, and Jews.

Because Willkie had, until the eleventh hour, been a committed internationalist, his campaign convinced isolationists they had been deprived of a genuine choice in the election. Against the wishes of Willkie, the Republican National Committee had made anti-intervention broadcasts that declared to mothers, "Don't blame Franklin D. Roosevelt because he sent your son to war—blame yourself because you sent Franklin D. Roosevelt back to the White House." Therefore, taking notice of his advisers, FDR consented to promise, immediately before the election on October 30, 1940, "Your boys are not going to be sent into any foreign wars." Most significant, under pressure from his advisers, FDR had dropped the crucial qualifying phrase, "except in case of attack."

Selective Service and America First

The issue of intervention was debated everywhere and discussion concentrated on peacetime conscription, student dissent, America First, and Lend-Lease.

Most Americans opposed compulsory military service in peace-time—the very idea represented the tyrannies whence their fathers had fled. When FDR courageously raised the issue in a speech on June 10, 1940, he was, perhaps, introducing the most controversial subject ever in an election campaign to that time. However, Willkie supported him. Draft legislation for conscription was introduced in the Senate by Democrat Edward R. Burke of Nebraska and in the House by conservative Republican James

W. Wadsworth, Jr., of New York. It moved comfortably through both houses of Congress between August 27 and September 14 and was signed by the president on September 16, two weeks after the destroyers-bases deal.

The Selective Service Act required the registration of all male citizens and resident aliens between the ages of twenty-one and thirty-five. Those inducted were to serve in the armed forces for twelve months but only either in the United States or in its territories and possessions overseas. On October 16, 1940, 16 million men registered for the draft. Owing to the effective lobbying of the peace churches, led by the Church of the Brethren, the act also provided Civilian Public Service Camps for those who could convince the National Service Board of their deep religious or ethical objection to military or naval service. The Civilian Public Service Camps became an adjunct to the military establishment, and, besides, conscientious objection was a declining phenomenon. Moreover, army doctors rejected almost half the men called for inspection before draft boards and FDR learned why from a national nutrition conference in spring 1941: most suffered from ten years' malnutrition. The census of 1940 disclosed that half of the nation's children came from families with incomes of less than $1,500.

One group, college students, was especially concerned about conscription and how it would affect them. Students throughout America, but particularly those at eastern colleges, indicated that they did not want to fight in another war. The editors of the *New Republic* summed up the way the students were making their protest felt on July 1, 1940:

During the past few months it has become apparent that there is an intellectual gulf between the generations, the post-war and the pre-war. It can be seen almost everywhere but it is especially obvious in the eastern colleges, where the majority of each faculty is already fighting Hitler, while a considerable part of the student body is against military intervention and lukewarm about aiding the Allies. That is the case at Yale, Princeton and Dartmouth, to judge by recent petitions. At Harvard a speaker who advocated help to Britain was booed on Class Day, something that has rarely happened in Harvard history. It would have been inconceivable in 1916.

To Greet the Bomber. A British antiaircraft gunner with gas mask and tin hat is photographed ready to take on the German Luftwaffe and give a vivid impression of the alertness and efficiency of Britain's defenses. People grew accustomed to the ghoulish uniform, and a new generation of science fiction novelists were ready to draw on the strange experiences for alien encounters in fiction of the 1950s. (Office of War Information; Library of Congress).

The attitude of young people was summarized caustically by Arnold Whitridge in the *Atlantic Monthly* of August 1940. His attack on their apathy and "hysterical timidity" initiated a debate between older people who believed that World War II was inevitable and necessary and the young who felt that it was an avoidable fracas. The gist of the article by Whitridge, "Where Do You Stand?" was an indictment of unpatriotic slothful youth when confronted with the task of subduing military dictatorship menacing Europe. The phenomenon was not confined to Ivy League schools. In November 1939 the Jesuit weekly, *America,* published the results of a poll of more than 50,000 students in 182 Catholic colleges and universities. More than a third expected the United States to become involved in the war and nine-tenths of them believed that a second intervention would not lead to a lasting peace. Moreover, they voted fifty to one against intervention.

However, increasingly in the early 1940s, isolationism was synonymous with the America First Committee. Here, it seemed, was where students did stand. America First was founded on September 4, 1940, by two students at Yale, Kingman Brewster, Jr., and R. Douglas Stuart, Jr. Stuart was the son of the Quaker Oats magnate, who arranged for considerable financial backing from Chicago businessmen, led by Robert E. Wood, chairman of Sears Roebuck. The strength of America First lay in its exceptional organization of 450 chapters across the country with a total membership of between 800,000 and 850,000 that drew on support from the rank and file of the National Council for the Prevention of War (NCPW) and the Woman's International League for Peace and Freedom (WILPF). Members included conservative opponents of FDR, college students opposed to the draft, and a few Communists. The big guns were Herbert Hoover, Joseph P. Kennedy, Hugh S. Johnson, and Henry Ford.

It was America First's association with star aviator Charles A. Lindbergh, Jr., that ensured intense and thorough press coverage of its activities. As we have remarked earlier, Lindbergh was always good copy and his visits to Germany in 1930, 1937, and 1938 had been widely reported. During those visits he had inspected German air power and reported his findings back to the U.S. military attaché in Berlin, Major Truman Smith. Lindbergh did not accept the general contemporary pro-British and anti-German interpretation of European affairs. His sympathies for Britain and France had been blunted by what he regarded as their inability to accommodate themselves to the new phenomenon of German air power. He thought American intervention in the war would be a disaster for the United States' economy and that American democracy might not survive it.

America First, knowing Lindbergh's views, wanted to attract him as its principal speaker. He was, quite simply, one of the most popular men in America. However, Lindbergh's popularity was as effervescent as a film star's. He could attract huge audiences—at least 23,000 at Madison Square Garden on May 23, 1941, and at least 40,000 at the Hollywood Bowl on June 20, 1941 —but he could only hope to keep people's sympathy by tapping indefinite fears. Furthermore, Lindbergh was a political novice who failed to realize that his generalizations divided where they were meant to unite. Thus, at Des Moines, Iowa, on September 11, 1941, he told an audience of 8,000 that the interventionists' "ever-increasing efforts to force the United States into the conflict" had been "so successful that, today, our country stands on the verge of war." Further, he identified the "war agitators."

The three most important groups who have been pressing this country toward war are the British, the Jewish, and the Roosevelt Administration. Behind these groups, but of lesser importance, are a number of capitalists, anglophiles, and intellectuals, who believe that their future and the future of mankind, depend upon the domination of the British Empire. Add to these the communistic groups who were opposed to intervention until a few weeks ago, and I believe I have named the major war agitators in this country.

He concluded that these particular groups were trying to involve the United States by advocating increased military preparedness for defense and creating "a series of incidents which would force us into the actual conflict." His designation of the British, the Jews, and the Roosevelt administration as "war agitators" was wide open to the interpretation that he and America First suffered from Anglophobia, anti-Semitism, and selfish conservatism. Of course, Lindbergh meant that, from their own points of view, these "agitators" believed, misguidedly, in the need for American involvement but the Des Moines speech was bitterly attacked by the press, deeply resented by Lindbergh's nominal allies, and, worst of all, praised by the very elements from which America First wished to dissociate itself.

For his part, FDR, by selective use of surveillance and propaganda, managed to give the somewhat erroneous impression that isolationists were narrow-minded, self-serving, and anti-Semitic conservatives. Lindbergh's foolhardiness helped him do so. The reaction to Lindbergh's Des Moines speech was so hostile that widespread support for America First seemed to evaporate almost overnight. In any case, it had already lost the battle against intervention with the passing of lend-lease.

H.R. 1776: Lend-Lease

Roosevelt realised that because Britain had exhausted its cash reserves it could not continue to pay for heavy purchases of materials in the United States without which it could not continue the war. Whilst on a Caribbean cruise recovering from his campaign, Roosevelt received a letter from Winston Churchill explaining the British plight and pleading with him to find a way of providing the necessary additional aid. Britain had less than $2 billion with which to pay orders costing $5 billion. Stimulated by Churchill, Lord Lothian, and the White Committee, Roosevelt proposed Lend-Lease. Roosevelt explained Lend-Lease at a press conference in Washington on December 16, 1940. He introduced it with a parable suggested by Harold Ickes,

Suppose my neighbor's house catches fire, and I have a length of garden hose. If he can take my garden hose and connect it up with his hydrant, I may help him put out the fire. Now what do I do? I don't say to him before that operation, "Neighbor, my garden hose cost me fifteen dollars; you have to pay me fifteen dollars for it." What is the transaction that goes on? I don't want fifteen dollars—I want my garden hose back after the fire is over. All right if it goes through the fire all right, intact, without damage to it, he gives it back to me and thanks me very much for the use of it.

Roosevelt proposed loans of tanks, planes, and ships to Britain without detailed suggestions as to how Britain might repay "in kind" after the war. The argument was sophistical, the appeal unsophisticated. Furthermore, Roosevelt renewed it in his fireside chat of December 29, 1940, when he told the country it was necessary for America to expand its industrial production. For, "We must be the great arsenal of democracy." Mail to the White House was 100 to 1 in favor, while polls of public opinion showed 80 percent who heard the talk direct or read about it approved, while only 12 percent were opposed to FDR's arguments. FDR repeated the argument in his State of the Union address of January 6, 1941, and went further, claiming that victory over the Axis would mean "a world [based] upon four essential human freedoms: freedom of speech and religion and freedom from want and fear."

FDR was swift to counter accusations from America First that he would use the law simply to give away the U.S. navy and convoy supples and to enhance his own powers. He was especially stung by Senator Burton K. Wheeler of Montana's remark that Lend-Lease was "the New Deal's triple A foreign policy; it will plow under every fourth American boy." He described Wheeler's charge as "the most untruthful, [as] the most dastardly, unpatriotic thing that has ever been said. Quote me on that. That really is the rottenest thing that has been said in public life in my generation."

Fortuitously numbered House Resolution 1776, the Lend-Lease bill gave the president power to lend, lease, sell or barter arms, food, or any "defense article," to foreign nations "whose defense the president deems vital to the defense of the United States." Of course, one reason for freeing Lend-Lease entirely from the question of loans was to avoid the sort of controversy attached to Wall Street loans to the Allies in World War I. On March 11, 1941, the Senate approved the bill by 60 votes to 31 and the House did so by 317 votes to 71. Once the president had signed the act, Congress voted an appropriation of $7 billion to implement its terms.

The conception was bold, the accomplishment a bare minimum. Historian Stephen A. Ambrose describes Roosevelt's reluctance to provide strong central control and assesses the conflicting interests of the officials involved: "Some American officials tried to use the new system as a wedge to get American firms into the British Commonwealth market and to force the British to sell their holdings on the American continents, and the Army resisted sending arms needed in the United States to Britain, so that the total amount of goods shipped, in comparison with the need, was small." British imports from the United States increased by only 3 percent in 1941 and the increase was principally in foodstuffs and steel. Most of the American arms obtained were still bought with cash in 1941 and Britain lost most of its remaining dollars. Naturally, Britain could not turn Lend-Lease goods into exports, but exports not made from Lend-Lease materials were cut down so as to avoid an outcry from American manufacturers.

Senator Arthur Vandenberg of Michigan wrote in his diary after the passing of H.R. 1776 that he thought this was the suicide of the Republic: "We have torn up 150 years of traditional foreign policy. We have tossed Washington's Farewell Address into the discard. We have thrown ourselves squarely into the power politics and power wars of Europe, Asia and Africa. We have taken the first step upon a course from which we can never hereafter retreat."

War in the Atlantic

Lend-Lease was no use unless American supplies reached Britain. In February and March 1941 German submarines sank or seized twenty-two ships. Despite the opposition of about half the Senate to the idea of American convoys supporting British freighters across half the Atlantic, Roosevelt announced that the United States's security zone would be extended a thousand miles into the Atlantic from April 11, 1941. The air force was used to patrol the North Atlantic as far as Iceland in order to warn British ships of the presence of German submarines. A majority of the Cabinet favored a declaration of war on Germany. Henry Stimson was concerned that Roosevelt did not follow his victory with the Lend-Lease Act with more positive policy but continued to move with great caution. In this concern he was supported by Secretary of the Navy Frank Knox, Attorney General Robert H. Jackson, and Secretary of the Interior Harold L. Ickes. Stimson tells in his diary for April 25, 1941, how Roosevelt introduced a program for patrolling the western Atlantic and then added defensively, "Well, it's a step forward." Stimson answered, "Well, I hope you will keep on walking, Mr. President. Keep on walking." Clare Booth Luce said Roosevelt's symbolic gesture was not, like Churchill's defiant one, two fingers raised in a V shape, but, rather, a moistened finger held to test the wind.

Unlike Theodore Roosevelt or, for that matter, Winston Churchill, FDR did not believe in war as social therapy, a means of strengthening national fiber. As William Manchester observes, "Divided countries do not win great wars. [FDR] could be a step ahead of the people, perhaps even two steps. But if he ever lost them he would fail them and his oath of office."

Nevertheless, despite FDR's caution, British military staffs had already had secret conversations in Washington with the American combined chiefs from January 29 to March 27, 1941. Britain and the United States were not yet formal allies. However, they were already "associated powers" with a common goal.

Elsewhere, other weaker countries were seeking support from strong allies. By early 1941 Hungary, Bulgaria, and Romania had been conquered by Germany. After making war on them, Italy had failed to subdue Yugoslavia and Greece but, once Germany had launched an offensive on these countries on April 6, 1941, they, too, were made subject to the Axis within three weeks.

In May 1941 the American freighter *Robin Moor* was sunk by Germans in the south Atlantic. Roosevelt declared an "unlimited national emergency," froze all German and Italian assets in the United States and closed their consulates. In June popular support for convoys was 52 percent, according to public opinion polls, and 75 percent approved if it seemed that Britain would not win the war without the security of supplies they provided.

To make the Atlantic patrols more effective, Roosevelt and his advisers decided to secure territories on the edge of the zone. On April 9, 1941, the State Department concluded an agreement with the exiled Danish minister in Washington to occupy the Danish possession of Greenland. In June and July the administration negotiated with Iceland to replace British and Canadian troops stationed there with an American force that landed on July 7. The American patrol ships were given secret orders to extend their duties beyond patrolling rather than allow any hostile force to deflect them from their course.

On June 22, 1941, Hitler repudiated the Nazi-Soviet Pact and invaded Russia. On June 26, 1941, the United States announced that the neutrality laws would not be invoked against Russia because American security was not endangered. But on July 26 Roosevelt sent Hopkins to Moscow to ascertain Stalin's needs and on August 2 promised Russia aid against aggression. On November 7, 1941, Lend-Lease was applied to Russia as well as Britain.

In an attempt to discuss the objectives of Britain and the still technically neutral America in the war, Roosevelt met Churchill at sea in Placentia Bay off Argentia, Newfoundland, from August 9 to 12, 1941. Their meeting had been planned by Harry Hopkins. Intending a complement to Woodrow Wilson's Fourteen Points, the two leaders declared in the Atlantic Charter that their countries sought no new territory in the course of the war; that territorial changes would only be made with reference to the populations involved; that all peoples had the right to choose the form of their government; that all nations had equal right of access to raw materials and trade throughout the world; and that after the war aggressor nations would be forced to disarm until a permanent system of international security was established. In short, the future peace should, as FDR's earlier promise had suggested, give all peoples freedom from want and freedom from fear, and freedom of speech and religion. Roosevelt's recollection of how the United States had treated Woodrow Wilson's scheme for the League of Nations led him to have explicit references to systems of international security deleted. Roosevelt appreciated the tenacity and charm of Churchill and Churchill liked Roosevelt's subtlety and sense of timing.

In response to Churchill's desire that America should declare war, FDR explained that a request to Congress for a declaration of war would simply produce a political debate lasting three months. Instead, according to Churchill's report of August 19, 1941, to his own cabinet, FDR had "said that he would wage war, but not declare it, and that he would become more and more provocative. . . . Everything was to be done to force an 'incident' . . . which would justify him in opening hostilities."

American public opinion was overwhelmingly favorable to the principles of the Atlantic Charter, provided it did not lead to outright intervention in the war. Moreover, isolationist sentiment in Congress was still strong. The occupation of Iceland by 4,000 marines on July 7, 1941, opened debate about the appropriate size and disposition of American forces. The Selective Service Act had allowed for 900,000 draftees for one-year's service in the western hemisphere. Military strategists agreed this was inadequate. However, Congress was reluctant to take the initiative in as unpopular a measure as would be increasing and extending the draft. Therefore, FDR agreed with congressional leaders on July 14 that he would take the responsibility in his strong recommendation to Congress on July 21, warning against the "tragic error" of allowing the "disintegration" of the comparatively modest army. The Senate voted for an extension of service to eighteen months—rather than for the duration of the emergency as FDR had asked—with 45 in favor and 21 senators not voting at all. On August 12 the House agreed by a majority of one, 203 votes in favor of 202 against. That narrow victory was essentially due to the work of Chief of Staff General George C. Marshall from behind the scenes.

On September 4 the United States and Germany began an undeclared naval war after an incident in which the commander of a German submarine U-652 off Iceland sent torpedoes at what he thought was a British destroyer. It was an American, the *Greer*. Describing the attacks on the *Greer* and other ships as "acts of international lawlessness" intended by Germany to destroy freedom of the seas, Roosevelt said in a radio address of September 11, 1941, that American vessels and planes "will no longer wait until Axis submarines lurking under the water, or Axis raiders on the surface of the sea, strike their deadly blow—first."

Had FDR said that the U-boat had fired in self-defense, which was what had really happened, and admitted that Hitler did not intend to attack American ships in the Atlantic, which was what Churchill told his colleagues, he would have had to wait for the imminent collapse of Britain and Russia before getting nationwide support for declared military intervention. Yet here was cause for future unease of a different sort, the manipulation of incident by a president, acting on the basis that the end justifies the means. Historian Robert Dallek observes, somewhat ruefully, "Yet for all the need to mislead the country in its own interest, the President's deviousness also injured the national well-being over the long run. His action in the *Greer* incident created a precedent for manipulation of public opinion which would be repeated by later Presidents in less justifiable circumstances."

In October another destroyer, the *Reuben James,* was sunk off Iceland with the loss of 100 American lives. However, when Roosevelt signed a revision of the neutrality laws on November 17, 1941, permitting the arming of American marine ships and allowing them to carry cargoes to belligerents' ports he was giving assent to an act that was passed by narrow margins in both houses—50 to 37 in the Senate and 212 to 194 in the House—that reflected the still-prevalent division of opinion.

War in the Pacific

In the Pacific, the United States was on a collision course with Japan and it was this that led to its formal entry into World War II.

In December 1938 the Japanese prime minister, Prince Konoye, had announced Japan's ambitious foreign policy for a "Greater East Asia Coprosperity Sphere." From 1938 the State Department issued protests against Japanese interference with American rights in China and the bombing of Chinese civilians. Moreover, Cordell Hull had gone further than the letter of the neutrality laws and asked American bankers not to extend credits to Japan and requested American manufacturers not to sell airplanes and airplane parts to any nation that might attack civilians. American disapproval of Japan's foreign policy culminated in an announcement of July 1939 that the commercial treaty of 1911 would be terminated at the end of the year. The actual sale of goods did not come to an end immediately in January 1941, but within months such exports as gasoline, steel, and scrap iron were made subject to government license.

Japan took full advantage of the fall of France to extend its imperial ambitions to northern Indochina, a French colony comprising the three states of Laos, Cambodia, and Vietnam. Unable to resist Japanese demands for airfields, Vichy France consented to Japanese occupation of Indochina in September 1940. That month Japan concluded the Axis with Germany and Italy by which the three powers were obliged to come to one another's aid if any one of them were attacked. Japan thereby extracted from the others acceptance of its own sphere of influence in South East Asia and the Pacific. Germany hoped the tripartite pact would deter the United States from entering the European War as did Japan for the Sino-Japanese War.

Senator Robert A. Taft of Ohio, who succeeded Vandenberg as Republican spokesman on foreign policy, commenting on opposition within the White House to the Japanese invasion of Vietnam, said no American mother was prepared to let her son be killed in war "for some place with an unpronounceable name in Indochina." Ironically, those who advocated strict neutrality toward Europe did not advance the same arguments toward South East Asia. For example, Senator Burton K. Wheeler of Montana criticized Roosevelt's policy to Europe for its tendency to intervention but supported the stronger line on Japan.

In April 1941 Germany and Japan discussed plans for a projected war on two fronts against America when the Japanese foreign minister, Matsuoka Yosuka, visited Berlin. Joachim von Ribbentrop, the German foreign minister, urged him to commit Japan to an immediate assault on the British protectorate, Singapore. By July 1941 Japan had completed occupation of southern as well as northern Indochina. The United States looked askance at a situation in which the oil, tin, rubber, bauxite, and other resources of South East Asia were controlled by a hostile power and on July 24, 1941, Roosevelt froze all Japanese credits in the United States. When Britain and the Dutch colonial governor in Djakarta in the Netherlands East Indies took similar action, Japan's sources of petroleum dried up. The American ambassador in Tokyo, Joseph Drew, warned Cordell Hull that if America humbled Konoye by its action he would fall and be replaced by a more belligerent prime minister.

Konoye suggested a meeting at sea between himself and Roosevelt at the end of August 1941. Cordell Hull advised the president against discussions without prior agreement on the basic principles underlying any prospective negotiations. This proved impossible and in September an Imperial Conference of cabinet ministers and chiefs of staff met in Tokoyo to consider preparations for war, should talks between Japan and the United States fail.

It was obvious that the United States would not allow Japan to become a great power. Japan had to choose war while it was able to do so. Without war, economic collapse was inevitable and thus, even if Japan lost a war with the United States, there would still be nothing to regret. With the failure of the Japanese ambassador in Washington, Admiral Kichisaburo Nomura, to secure terms with the United States, Prince Konoye was, indeed, humbled as Joseph Drew had predicted. He was succeeded as prime minister, on October 16, by the former war minister, General Hideki Tojo.

Because the Washington ambassador was not a trained diplomat, Tojo sent Saburo Kuruso, a veteran diplomat and once ambassador to Berlin, to assist him in November 1941. He brought an offer of conciliation: Japan would withdraw from Indochina and halt its advance in South East Asia if the United States agreed to Japanese control of China. The American reply on November 26 was equally candid: if Japan withdrew its troops from both China and Indochina America would resume liberal trade with Japan. In this period Winston Churchill, perhaps out of consummate political strategy, appeared content to let the United States negotiate with Japan in a matter affecting not only Britain but also Australia, New Zealand, Malaya, and Hong Kong, as well as Guam, the Philippines, and Hawaii. The last Japanese offer, with a final deadline set at November 29, contained nothing new. Hull originally decided to propose a three-month truce during which limited withdrawal of troops from Indochina would be complemented by limited economic offers from the United States, but when he learned on November 26 of large Japanese convoys moving down the South China coast, he submitted stiff terms leaving no room for compromise.

The outcome of the negotiations was an undeclared attack on American naval bases in Pearl Harbor. The attack, led by the waves of carrier-based Japanese dive-bombers, torpedo planes, and fighters, lasted two hours and demolished the American fleet and air and military installations at Pearl Harbor, Honolulu, and Hawaii. Altogether, 2,403 Americans were killed and another 1,178 wounded. Not only did American intelligence officers, in possession of the Japanese secret code by the decoding system "magic," predict the attack by following telephone conversations between Saburo Kuruso in Washington and Isoroku Yamamoto in Tokyo, but they also made this known to General Walter Short, the army commander in Hawaii, and Admiral Husband E. Kimmel, the naval commander there. Short and Kimmel decided not to put the war plan into operation: their men would become exhausted by being put into a state of constant alert.

As Gordon Prange concludes in his *At Dawn We Slept* (1981) and his associates Donald Goldstein and Katherine V. Dillon conclude in a later edition, *Pearl Harbor: The Verdict of History* (1985), the fundamental causes of the American defeat were the skill, boldness, and luck of the Japanese in planning and carrying out the operation and the inability of American leaders to believe in, and act upon, the idea that the Japanese would dare to make a surprise attack on Pearl Harbor. Those who seek to defend Admiral Husband E. Kimmel, such as Edwin T. Layton in *"And I Was There"* (1985) contend that Kimmel was "shortchanged" by Washington, denied full intelligence information by incompetents in the Navy Department who then tried to cover up their errors. Whatever the failures in Washington, it is also true that Kimmel failed to conduct as much aerial reconnaissance as he might have, and that both army and navy commanders at Pearl failed to coordinate their efforts sufficiently. Thus Gordon W. Prange's emphasis on the states of mind and preconceptions of the principal officers in Washington and Pearl is a more important part of the explanation for the disaster that overtook the United States than any surprise revelation about code-breaking.

An old man in New Jersey asked about the attack answered a reporter, "You got me on that Martian stunt; I had a hunch you'd try again." Senator Gerald P. Nye reacted with the bad grace of a

"A day that will live in infamy." The Japanese air attack on the American naval base at Pearl Harbor, Hawaii, on December 7, 1941, left 2,403 American servicemen and civilians dead and 1,178 others wounded; 149 planes were destroyed; and the battleships *Oklahoma, Tennessee, West Virginia, California,* and *Nevada* were either sunk or damaged beyond repair. Meanwhile, a Japanese air raid on Manila devastated the army's air force in the Philippines. The following day Congress declared war against Japan. (Library of Congress).

small-minded man who saw the desert of political oblivion stretching out before him. "Sounds terribly fishy to me," he told a reporter. However, Senator Burton K. Wheeler was more positive. "The only thing to do now is to lick the hell out of them."

While noting how shocked was FDR, Frances Perkins also recognized that he was relieved to have the decision about war made for him, although he was reluctant to admit this. On December 8, 1941, Roosevelt sent his war message to Congress:

"Yesterday, December 7, 1941—a day which will live in infamy —the United States of America was suddenly and deliberately attacked by naval and air forces of the Empire of Japan." Congress authorized a declaration of war against Japan on December 8. This time there was only one dissenting voice, that of the Quaker pacifist Jeanette Rankin, who had also voted against intervention in 1917.

For three days Hitler's advisers argued against declaration of war on the United States, whatever the terms of the pact with Japan. However, frustrated by setbacks on the Russian campaign and infuriated by American opposition in the Atlantic, Hitler made his declaration of war on December 11.

The most bitter lesson learnt in the wake of Pearl Harbor was that, if America was going to get drawn into others' wars, it would be better to do so on its own terms. Never again would the United States seek to isolate itself from world affairs. Churchill was especially jubilant after Pearl. "Now at this very moment I knew the United States was in the war, up to the neck and in to the death. So we had won after all! . . . Hitler's fate was sealed. Mussolini's fate was sealed. As for the Japanese, they would be ground to powder. . . . No doubt it would take a long time. . . . But there was no more doubt about the end." This was true. The United States was on the eve of an Atomic Age.

SOURCES

ANY HISTORIAN who attempts an interdisciplinary history of a country over a period of twenty or more years immediately puts himself in the debt of others. If he is to be alert in his scholarship, there must be something of Rossini's thieving magpie in his nature. Notwithstanding original research into such papers as those of the NAACP in the Library of Congress, Walter Lippmann at Yale, Jane Addams at Swarthmore College, Norman Thomas in the New York Public Library, and other primary sources, mainly in the Library of Congress—all of which were studied for this volume—the historian will undoubtedly seek interpretations and essential facts from numerous secondary works.

He or she is likely to be moved and captured by a select few. In my case, such writers as Alfred Dupont Chandler, Jr., on industrial corporations and their management, J. K. Galbraith and Milton Friedman on economics, William Leuchtenburg on political and social history, especially in the New Deal period, C. Vann Woodward on the South, Frank Freidel and James MacGregor Burns on Franklin D. Roosevelt, Richard Polenberg and Gaddis Smith on America and World War II, Richard Guy Wilson on the machine age and Gerald Mast on motion pictures, have all had a profound influence upon me. Their very different histories are judiciously written and persuasively argued, and their facts and ideas are represented, and acknowledged, in this work. Similarly, a series of social historians, beginning with Mark Sullivan, Frederick Lewis Allen, and Ray Ginger on the 1920s and 1930s, and continuing with William Manchester for the 1930s and 1940s, provides us with numerous anecdotes, much wit, and a sense of the thrust of popular and cultural history not readily available in more specific political or economic histories. Certain authors like Daniel Snowman on domestic history and Stephen Ambrose on foreign policy are able to sum up their points and present conventional enough material in a fresh way that also makes its mark.

The following bibliography is, like the book itself, intended as a basic guide for anyone new to the history of the United States in the period. It does not include every book or article mentioned in the text, but rather a representative selection of those that we might expect to find in a good university library, such as those of NYU, GWU, or the University of Manchester, England.

Statistics provided in this book on population, immigration, agricultural and industrial production, and election returns are usually taken from the United States Bureau of the Census, *Historical Statistics of the United States,* 2 vols. (Washington, D.C., 1975). A useful abridged version of the bicentennial edition is Ben J. Wattenberg (ed.), *The Statistical History of the United States from Colonial Times to the Present* (New York, 1976). I have taken supplementary factual or statistical information from Richard B. Morris and Jeffrey B. Morris (eds.), *Encyclopedia of American History* (sixth edition, New York, London, etc., 1982). The bibliography is arranged in subsections by chapter, with principal texts placed first in each subsection, and preceded by a list of general works.

BIBLIOGRAPHY

General

Daniel Snowman, *America Since 1920* (revised London, 1978; first published 1968).

William Manchester, *The Glory and the Dream: A Narrative History of America 1932–1972* (New York, 1974; London, 1975).

Ralph F. de Bedts, *Recent American History,* Volume 1 *1933 Through World War II* (Homewood, Ill., London, and Georgetown, Ontario, 1973).

Isabel Leighton, ed. *The Aspirin Age 1919–1941* (New York, 1949).

Jonathan Daniels, *The Time Between the Wars: Armistice to Pearl Harbor* (New York, 1966).

Edmund Wilson, *The American Earthquake: A Documentary of the Twenties and Thirties* (New York, 1979; first published 1971).

Jim Potter, *The American Economy Between the World Wars* (New York, 1974).

Warren I. Susman, *Culture as History: The Transformation of American Society in the Twentieth Century* (New York, 1985).

Chapter 1

A MACHINE AGE

Richard Guy Wilson, Dianne H. Pilgrim, Dickran Tashjian, with the Brooklyn Museum, *The Machine Age in America: 1918–1941* (New York, 1986).

U.S. National Resources Committee, *Technological Trends and National Policy* (Washington, D.C., 1937).

Roger Burlingame, *Engines of Democracy: Inventions and Society in Mature America* (Salem, N.H., 1976; first published 1940).

Stephen Fox, *The Mirror Makers: A History of American Advertising and Its Creators* (New York, 1984).

Chapter 2

THE 1920S

Frederick Lewis Allen, *Only Yesterday: An Informal History of the Nineteen Twenties* (New York, 1931).

Burl Noggle, *Into the Twenties: The United States from Armistice to Normalcy* (Urbana, Ill., 1974).

Paul A. Carter, *The Twenties in America* (New York, 1975; first published 1968).

——, *Another Part of the Twenties* (New York, 1977).

George Soule, *Prosperity Decade: From War to Depression 1917–1930* (New York, 1947).

Ellis W. Hawley, *The Great War and the Search for a Modern Order: A History of the American People and Their Institutions, 1917–1933* (New York, 1979).

J. W. Prothro, *Dollar Decade: Business Ideas in the 1920s* (Westport, Conn.; first published 1954).

Don S. Kirchner, *City and Country: Rural Responses to Urbanization in the 1920s* (Westport, Conn., 1970).

Robert S. Lynd and Helen Merrell, *Middletown* (New York, 1927).

Frank Stricker, "Affluence for Whom?" Another Look at Prosperity and the Working Classes in the 1920s," *Labor History* 24 (Winter 1983): 5–33.

F. May, "Shifting Perspectives on the 1920s," *Mississippi Valley Historical Review* 43 (December 1956): 405–27.

Winthrop Sargeant, "Fifty Years of Women," *Life* 28 (January 2, 1950): 64–67.

SACCO AND VANZETTI

Louis Joughin and Edmund M. Morgan, *The Legacy of Sacco and Vanzetti* (Princeton, N.J., 1976; first published 1948).

John Dos Passos, *Facing the Chair* (New York, 1970; first published 1927).

Francis Russell, *Sacco and Vanzetti: The Case Resolved* (New York, 1986).

William Young and David E. Kaiser, *Postmortem: New Evidence in the Case of Sacco and Vanzetti* (Boston, 1985).

Herbert B. Ehrmann, *The Case That Will Not Die: Commonwealth vs. Sacco and Vanzetti* (Boston, 1969).

NATIONAL PROHIBITION

Andrew Sinclair, *Prohibition: The Era of Excess* (London, 1962).

Charles Merz, *The Dry Decade* (Seattle and Washington, 1970; first published New York, 1930, 1931).

Thomas M. Coffey, *The Long Thirst—Prohibition in America 1920–1933* (New York and London, 1975, 1976).

E. Austin Kerr, *Organized for Prohibition: A New History of the Anti-Saloon League* (New Haven, Conn., 1985).

David E. Kyvig, *Repealing National Prohibition* (Chicago and London, 1979).

J. C. Burnham, "New Perspectives on the Prohibition 'Experiment' of the 1920s," *Journal of Social History* (Fall 1968): 51–67.

CRIME AND THE UNDERWORLD

Fred J. Cook, *The Secret Rulers: Criminal Syndicates and How They Control the U.S. Underworld* (New York, 1966).

Humbert S. Nelli, *The Business of Crime: Italians and Syndicate Crime in the United States* (New York, 1976).

Joseph L. Albini, *The American Mafia—Genesis of a Legend* (New York, 1971).

John Landesco, *Organized Crime in Chicago* (second edition, Chicago, 1968).

Francis A. J. Ianni with Elizabeth Reuss-Ianni, *A Family Business—Kinship and Social Control in Organized Crime* (New York, 1972).

John Kobler, *Capone* (New York, 1971).

Dennis Eisenberg, Uri Dan, and Eli Landau, *Meyer Lansky: Mogul of the Mob* (London and New York, 1979 and 1980).

Mark H. Haller, "Organized Crime in Urban Society: Chicago in the Twentieth Century," *Journal of Social History* (Winter 1971–72: 210–33.

H. L. MENCKEN

Edgar Kemler, *The Irreverent Mr. Mencken* (Boston, 1950).

William Manchester, *Disturber of the Peace: The Life of H. L. Mencken* (New York, 1951).

Charles Angoff, *H. L. Mencken, A Portrait from Memory* (New York, 1956).

THE NEW SOUTH

George Brown Tindall, *The Emergence of the New South 1913–1945* (Baton Rouge, La., 1967).

Ray Ginger, *Six Days or Forever? Tennessee v. John Thomas Scopes* (Chicago, 1969; first published 1958).

Jerry R. Tompkins, *D-Days at Dayton: Reflections on the Scopes Trial* (Baton Rouge, La., 1965).

David M. Chalmers, *Hooded Americanism—The First Century of the Ku Klux Klan 1865–1965* (Garden City, N.Y., 1965).

Kenneth T. Jackson, *The Ku Klux Klan in the City 1915–1930* (New York, 1967).

Charles C. Alexander, *The Ku Klux Klan in the Southwest* (Louisville, Ky., 1965).

Lawrence Levine, *Defender of the Faith: William Jennings Bryan: The Last Decade* (New York and Oxford, 1965).

Charles H. Martin, *The Angelo Herndon Case and Southern Justice* (Baton Rouge, La., 1976).

Wyn Craig Wade, *The Fiery Cross — The Ku Klux Klan in America* (New York, 1987).

Chapter 3

THE REPUBLICAN ASCENDANCY

John D. Hicks, *The Republican Ascendancy 1921–1933* (New York, Evanston, and London, 1960).

Arthur M. Schlesinger, Jr., *The Crisis of the Old Order* (Boston, 1958).

Wesley M. Bagby, *The Road to Normalcy: The Presidential Campaign and Election of 1920* (Baltimore, 1962).

Robert K. Murray, *Warren G. Harding and His Administration* (Minneapolis, 1969).

Burt Noggle, *Teapot Dome: Oil and Politics in the 1920s* (Westport, Conn., 1980; first published 1962).

Claude M. Fuess, *Calvin Coolidge: The Man from Vermont* (Westport, Conn., 1981; first published 1977).

Richard Gid Powers, *Secrecy and Power — The Life of J. Edgar Hoover* (New York, 1987).

David Burner, *The Politics of Provincialism: The Democratic Party in Transition, 1918–1932* (New York, 1968).

Robert K. Murray, *The 103rd Ballot: The Democrats and the Disaster in Madison Square Garden* (New York, 1976).

Paula Elder, *Governor Alfred E. Smith: The Politician as Reformer* (New York, 1982).

Matthew and Hanna Josephson, *Al Smith: Hero of the Cities* (Boston, 1969).

Richard O'Connor, *The First Hurrah: A Biography of Alfred E. Smith* (New York, 1970).

Allan J. Lichtman, *Prejudice and the Old Politics: The Presidential Election of 1928* (Chapel Hill, N.C., 1979).

Richard Lowitt, *George W. Norris: The Persistence of a Progressive 1913–1933* (Champaign, Ill., 1971).

Arthur Link, "Whatever Happened to the Progressive Movement in the 1920s?" *American Historical Review* (July 1959): 833–51.

David Noble, "The New Republic and the Idea of Progress, 1914–1920," *Mississippi Valley Historical Review* 38 (December 1951): 387–402.

Herbert Croly, "The Eclipse of Progressivism," *New Republic* 24 (October 27, 1920): 210–16.

——, "The Outlook for Progressivism in Politics," *New Republic* 41 (December 10, 1924): 60–64.

Charles Merz, "Progressivism, Old and New," *Atlantic Monthly* 132 (July 1923): 102–109.

Allan J. Lichtman, "Critical Election Theory and the Reality of American Presidential Politics, 1916–1940," *American Historical Review* 81 (1976): 317–51.

Chapter 4

THE WALL STREET CRASH

J. K. Galbraith, *The Great Crash–1929* (New York, 1979; first published 1954).

John Brooks, *Once in Golconda: A True Drama of Wall Street 1920–1938* (New York, 1969).

Gordon Thomas and Max Morgan-Witts, *The Day the Bubble Burst* (New York, 1979).

Peter Temin, *Did Monetary Forces Cause the Great Depression?* (New York, 1976).

THE GREAT DEPRESSION

Frederick Lewis Allen, *Since Yesterday: The Nineteen Thirties in America* (New York, 1940).

Broadus Mitchell, *Depression Decade: From New Era Through New Deal, 1929–1941* (New York, 1947).

Lester V. Chandler, *America's Greatest Depression, 1929–41* (New York, 1970).

Studs Terkel, *Hard Times: An Oral History of the Great Depression* (New York, 1970).

Robert S. McElvaine, *Down and Out in the Great Depression: Letters from the Forgotten Man* (Chapel Hill, N.C., 1983).

Leo Ribuffo, *The Old Christian Right: The Protestant Far Right from the Depression to the Cold War* (Philadelphia, 1983).

David Tyack et al., *Public Schools in Hard Times: The Great Depression and Recent Years* (Cambridge, Mass., 1984).

UNEMPLOYMENT

John A. Garraty, *Unemployment in History: Economic Thought and Public Policy* (New York, 1979).

Unemployment in the United States: Hearings before a Subcommittee of the Committee on Labor, House of Representatives, 72d Congress, 1st Session, on H.R. 206, H.R. 6011, H.R. 6066 (Washington, D.C., 1932).

Paul Webbink, "Unemployment in the United States, 1930–1940," *Papers and Proceedings of the American Economic Association* (February 1941).

Federal Aid for Unemployment Relief: Hearings Before a Subcommittee of the Committee on Manufacture, U.S. Senate, 72d Congress, 1st Session, on S. 174, S. 262, and S. 4592; U.S. Senate, 72d Congress, 2d Session, on S. 5125 (Washington, D.C., 1932).

Relief for Unemployed Transients: Hearings before a Subcommittee of the Committee on Manufactures, U.S. Senate, 72d Congress, 2d Session, on S. 5121 (Washington, D.C., 1933).

CONTEMPORARY ARTICLES ON UNEMPLOYMENT

John L. Leary, Jr., "If We Had the Dole," *American Magazine* (December 1931).

George R. Leighton, "And If the Revolution Comes. . . ?" *Harper's Magazine* (March 1932).

Joseph L. Heffernan, "The Hungry City: A Mayor's Experience with Unemployment," *Atlantic Monthly* (May 1932).

George R. Clark, "Beckerstown, 1932: An American Town Faces the Depression," *Harper's Magazine* (October 1932).

Frank A. Vandenlip, "What About the Banks?" *Saturday Evening Post* (November 5, 1932).

Mary Heaton Vorse, "Rebellion in the Cornbelt: American Farmers Beat Their Plowshares into Swords," *Harper's Magazine* (December 1932).

Remley J. Glass, "Gentlemen, the Corn Belt!," *Harper's Magazine* (July 1933).

"A Survey of Unemployed Alumni," *School and Society* (March 10, 1934).

"The Great American Roadside," *Fortune* (September 1934).

THE INCOMPLETE POLITICS OF HERBERT HOOVER

Herbert Hoover, *The Memoirs of Herbert Hoover,* vol. 2, *The Cabinet and the Presidency 1920–1933* (New York and London, 1952).

Martin L. Fansold, *The Presidency of Herbert C. Hoover* (New York, 1985).

Jordan A. Schwarz, *The Inter-Regnum of Despair: Hoover, Congress, and the Depression* (Urbana, Ill., 1970).

Gene Smith, *The Shattered Dream: Herbert Hoover and the Great Depression* (New York, 1970).

Joan H. Wilson, *Herbert Hoover: Forgotten Progressive* (Boston, 1975).

Gilbert Seldes, *The Years of the Locust—America, 1929–1932* (New York, 1973).

Roger Daniels, *The Bonus March: An Episode of the Great Depression* (Westport, Conn., 1971).

Donald Lisio, *The President and Protest: Hoover, Conspiracy and the Bonus Riot* (Columbia, Miss., 1974).

Malcolm Cowley, "The Flight of the Bonus Army," *New Republic* (August 17, 1932).

George Soule, "Are We Going to Have a Revolution?" *Harper's Magazine* (August 1932).

Frank Freidel, *Franklin D. Roosevelt: The Triumph* (New York, 1956).

Chapter 5

FRANKLIN D. ROOSEVELT AND THE NEW DEAL

William E. Leuchtenburg, *Franklin D. Roosevelt and the New Deal 1932–40* (New York, 1963).

Arthur M. Schlesinger, Jr., *The Coming of the New Deal* (Boston, 1958).

———, *The Politics of Upheaval* (Boston, 1960).

James MacGregor Burns, *Roosevelt: The Lion and the Fox* (New York, 1956).

Albert U. Romasco, *The Politics of Recovery: Roosevelt's New Deal* (New York and Oxford, 1983).

Paul Conkin, *The New Deal* (Arlington Heights, Ill., 1975).

Katie Louchlin, ed., *The Making of the New Deal* (Cambridge, Mass., 1983).

Harvard Sitkoff, ed., *Fifty Years Later: The New Deal Evaluated* (New York, 1985).

John Braeman, et al., ed., *The New Deal* (Columbus, Ohio, 1975).

THE NEW DEALERS

Joseph P. Lash, *Eleanor and Franklin: The Story of Their Relationship, Based on Eleanor Roosevelt's Private Papers* (New York, 1971).

William J. Youngs, *Eleanor Roosevelt* (Thorndike, Maine, 1984).

Joan Hoff-Wilson and Marjorie Lightman, ed., *Without Precedent: The Life and Career of Eleanor Roosevelt* (Bloomington, Ind., 1984).

Robert E. Sherwood, *Roosevelt and Hopkins: An Intimate History* (New York, 1948).

Graham White and John Maze, *Harold Ickes of the New Deal* (Cambridge, Mass., 1985).

George Martin, *Madam Secretary, Frances Perkins* (New York, 1977).

John M. Blum, *From the Morgenthau Diaries: Years of Urgency* (Boston, 1964).

Otis L. Graham, Jr., *An Encore for Reform: The Old Progressives and the New Deal* (New York, 1967).

Richard Lowitt, *George W. Norris: The Triumph of a Progressive 1933–34* (Champaign, Ill., 1978).

J. Joseph Huthmacher, *Senator Robert F. Wagner and the Rise of Urban Liberalism* (New York, 1968).

Peter H. Irons, *New Deal Lawyers* (Princeton, N.J., 1982).

Elliott Rosen, *Hoover, Roosevelt, and the Brains Trust* (New York, 1977).

NEW DEAL POLICIES AND PROGRAMS

Raymond Moley, *The First New Deal* (New York, 1966).

Susan Estabrook Kennedy, *The Banking Crisis of 1933* (Lexington, Ky., 1973).

Jordan Schwarz, *1933: Roosevelt's Decision: The United States Leaves the Gold Standard* (New York, 1969).

Jerold S. Auerbach, *Labor and Liberty: The La Follette Committee and the New Deal* (New York, 1966).

Theodore Saloutos, *The American Farmer and the New Deal* (Ames, Iowa, 1982).

Richard S. Kirkendall, *Social Scientists and Farm Policies in the Age of Roosevelt* (Ames, Iowa, 1982; first published 1966).

David E. Conrad, *The Forgotten Farmers: The Story of Sharecropping in the New Deal* (Westport, Conn., 1982; first published 1965).

Sidney Baldwin, *Poverty and Politics: The Rise and Decline of the Farm Security Administration* (Chapel Hill, N.C., 1967).

Betty Lindley and Ernest K. Lindley, *A New Deal for Youth: The Story of the National Youth Administration* (New York, 1938).

Timothy L. McConnell, *The Wagner Housing Act* (Chicago, 1957).

Gilbert Fite, *George N. Peek and the Fight for Farm Parity* (Norman, Okla., 1954).

Richard Polenberg, *Reorganizing Roosevelt's Government: The Controversy over Executive Reorganization* (Cambridge, Mass., 1966).

Bruce Bliven, "Boulder Dam," *New Republic* (December 11, 1935).

J. S. Auerbach, "New Deal, Old Deal, or Raw Deal: Some Thoughts on New Left Historiography," *Journal of Southern History* 25 (February 1969): 18–30.

THE DUST BOWL

R. Douglas Hurt, *The Dust Bowl: An Agricultural and Social History* (Chicago, 1981).

Walter J. Stein, *California and the Dust Bowl Migration* (Westport, Conn., 1973).

Donald Worster, *Dust Bowl: The Southern Plains in the 1930s* (New York, 1979).

F. Barrows Colton, "The Geography of a Hurricane," *National Geographic Magazine* (April 1939).

Chapter 6

ADVERSARY POLITICS

Alan Brinkley, *Voices of Protest: Huey Long, Father Coughlin, and the Great Depression* (New York, 1982).

T. Harry Williams, *Huey Long* (New York, 1969).

Sheldon Marcus, *Father Coughlin* (New York, 1973).

James Patterson, *Congressional Conservatism and the New Deal* (Lexington, Ky., 1967).

Geoffrey S. Smith, *To Save a Nation: American Countersubversives, the New Deal, and the Coming of World War II* (New York, 1973).

Marquis Childs, "They Hate Roosevelt," *Harper's Magazine* (May 1936).

———, "They Still Hate Roosevelt," *New Republic* (January 18, 1939).

NEW DEAL POLICIES

Ellis W. Hawley, *The New Deal and the Problem of Monopoly: A Study in Economic Ambivalence* (Princeton, N.J., 1966).

——, "The New Deal and Business" in John Braeman, Robert H. Bremner, and David Brody, eds., *The New Deal: The National Level* (Columbus, Ohio, 1975).

Chapter 7

WORKERS AND LABOR

James R. Green, *The World of the Worker* (New York, 1980).

David Brody, *Workers in Industrial America: Essays on the Twentieth Century Struggle* (New York, 1980).

Irving Bernstein, *The Lean Years: A History of the American Worker 1920–1933* (New York, 1983).

——, *The Turbulent Years: A History of the American Worker 1933–1941* (Boston, 1970).

——, *A Caring Society: The New Deal, the Worker, and the Great Depression* (New York, 1985).

Herbert R. Northrup, *Organized Labor and the Negro* (New York, 1944).

Matthew Josephson, *Sidney Hillman* (New York, 1952).

John Barnard, *Walter Reuther and the Rise of the Auto Workers* (Boston, 1982).

Sidney Fine, *Sit-Down: The General Motors Strike of 1936–37* (Ann Arbor, Mich., 1969).

——, *Frank Murphy: The Detroit Years* (Ann Arbor, Mich., 1975).

John W. Herever, *Which Side Are You On? The Harlan County Coal Miners 1931–39* (Champaign, Ill., 1978).

Melvyn Dubofsky and Warren Van Tine, *John L. Lewis: A Biography* (New York, 1977).

Melvyn Dubofsky, "Not So 'Turbulent Years': Another Look at the American 1930s," *Amerika Studies–America Studies* 71 (December 1984).

Bruce Bliven, "Sitting down in Flint," *New Republic* (January 27, 1937).

RADICAL MOVEMENTS

David A. Shannon, *The American Socialist Party* (New York, 1955).

Harvey Klehr, *The Heyday of American Communism* (New York, 1984).

Mark Navison, *Communists in Harlem During the Depression* (Champaign, Ill., 1983).

William Swanberg, *Norman Thomas—The Last Idealist* (New York, 1976).

James C. Duram, *Norman Thomas* (New York, 1974).

Harry Fleischman, *Norman Thomas* (New York, 1964).

Bernard K. Johnpoll, *Pacifist's Progress* (Chicago, 1970).

Philip S. Foner, *American Socialism and Black Americans* (Westport, Conn., 1977).

CLASSES AND ETHNIC GROUPS

Richard Polenberg, *One Nation Divisible—Class, Race, and Ethnicity in the United States Since 1938* (Harmondsworth, Middlesex, and New York, 1980), Chapters 1 and 2.

Maurice R. Stein, *The Eclipse of Community* (revised Princeton, N.J., 1972; first published 1960).

Ronald H. Bayor, *Neighbors in Conflict: The Irish, Germans, Jews, and Italians of New York City, 1929–1941* (Baltimore, 1978).

Federal Writers Project in the WPA, *The Italians of New York* (New York, 1938); *The Swedes and Finns in New Jersey* (Bayonne, 1938); *The Armenians in Massachusetts* (Boston, 1937).

Robert and Helen Lynd, *Middletown in Transition* (New York, 1937).

Mark Reisler, *By the Sweat of Their Brow: Mexican Immigrant Labor in the United States 1900–1940* (Westport, Conn., 1976).

Rodolfo Acuna, *Occupied America: A History of Chicanos* (New York, 1980).

Matt S. Meier and Feliciano Rivera, *The Chicanos* (New York, 1972).

WOMEN AND THE FAMILY

Carl Degler, *At Odds: Women and the Family in America from the Revolution to the Present* (New York and Oxford, 1980).

Sheila Rothman, *Woman's Proper Place: A History of Changing Ideals and Practices, 1870 to the Present* (New York, 1980; first published 1978).

Winifred D. Wandersee, *Women's Work and Family Values 1920–1940* (Cambridge, Mass., 1981).

William H. Chafe, *The American Woman: Her Changing Social, Economic, and Political Role* (New York, 1977; first published 1972).

Jacqueline Jones, *Labor of Love, Labor of Sorrow: Black Women, Work, and the Family from Slavery to the Present* (New York, 1985).

J. Stanley Lemons, *The Woman Citizen: Social Feminism in the 1920s* (Champaign, Ill., 1973).

Linda Gordon, *Woman's Body, Woman's Right: A Social History of Birth Control in America* (New York, 1976).

Susan Ware, *Beyond Suffrage: Woman in the New Deal* (Cambridge, Mass., 1982).

——, *Holding Their Own: American Women in the 1930s* (Boston, 1982).

Lois Scharf, *To Work and to Wed: Female Employment, Feminism, and the Great Depression* (Westport, Conn., 1980).

Glen H. Elder, Jr., *Children of the Great Depression: Social Change in Life Experience* (Chicago, 1984; first published 1974).

W. Andrew Achenbaum, *Shades of Gray: Old Age, American Values, and Federal Policies Since 1920* (Boston, 1982).

David H. Fischer, *Growing Old in America* (New York and Oxford, 1978).

INDIANS

David Murray, *Modern Indians: Native Americans in the Twentieth Century* (British Association for American Studies Pamphlets in American Studies 8, 1982).

Mary K. Grafmick, *Sociology of American Indians: A Critical Bibliography* (Bloomington, Ind., 1981).

Edward H. Spicer, *A Short History of the Indians of the United States* (New York, 1969).

Roger L. Nichols and George R. Adams, ed., *The American Indian: Past and Present* (Lexington, Mass., 1971).

Edgar S. Cahn, ed., *Our Brother's Keeper: The Indian in White America* (New York and Cleveland, 1969).

Alan L. Sorkin, *Indians and Federal Aid* (Washington, D.C., 1971).

Margaret Szasz, *Education and the American Indian: The Road to Self-Determination, 1928–1973* (Albuquerque, N.M., 1974).

Wilcomb E. Washburn, *Red Man's Land, White Man's Law: A Study of the Past and Present Status of the American Indian* (New York, 1971).

Kirke Kickingbird and Karen Ducheneaux, *100 Million Acres* (New York, 1973).

Russel L. Barsh and James Y. Henderson, *The Road: Indian Tribes and Political Liberty* (Berkeley and Los Angeles, 1980).

Stan Steiner, *The New Indians* (New York, 1968).

INDIANS AND THE NEW DEAL

John Collier, *From Every Zenith* (Denver, 1963).

Laurence C. Kelly, *The Assault on Assimilation: John Collier and the Origins of Indian Policy Reform* (Albuquerque, N.Mex., 1983).

Kenneth R. Philp, *John Collier's Crusade for Indian Reform* (Tucson, Ariz., 1977).

Donald L. Parman, *The Navajos and the New Deal* (New Haven, Conn., 1976).

Chapter 8

BLACK AMERICA

Lerone Bennett, Jr., *Before the Mayflower: A History of Black America* (Chicago, 1961).

Mary Frances Berry and John W. Blassingame, *Long Memory: The Black Experience in America* (New York, 1982).

L. Franklin Frazier, *The Negro in the United States* (Toronto, 1969; first published 1949, revised 1957).

Benjamin Quarles, *The Negro in the Making of America* (revised New York, 1969; first published 1964).

John White, *Black Leadership in America 1895–1968* (London and New York, 1985).

Joel Williamson, *The Crucible of Race: Black-White Relations in the American South Since Emancipation* (New York, 1984).

BOOKER T. WASHINGTON AND HIS CRITICS

Bernard A. Weisberger, *Booker T. Washington* (New York, 1972).

Louis R. Harlan, *Booker T. Washington: The Making of a Black Leader, 1865–1901* (New York and Oxford, 1972).

——, *Booker T. Washington: The Wizard of Tuskegee, 1901–1915* (New York and Oxford, 1983).

Hugh Hawkins, ed., *Booker T. Washington and His Critics* (Boston, 1974; first published 1962).

W.E.B. DUBOIS

Elliot Rudwick, *W.E.B. DuBois: Propagandist of the Negro Protest* (New York, 1969).

Francis L. Broderick, *W.E.B. DuBois: Negro Leader in a Time of Crisis* (Stanford, Ca., 1966; first published 1959).

Arnold Rampersad, *The Art and Imagination of W.E.B. DuBois* (London, 1976).

Rayford W. Logan, ed., *W.E.B. DuBois: A Profile* (New York, 1971).

E. M. Rudwick, "W.E.B. DuBois in the Role of *Crisis* Editor," *Journal of Negro History* 43 (1958), 214–40.

Mary Law Chafer, "W.E.B. DuBois' Concept of the Racial Problem in the United States," *Journal of Negro History* 41 (1956): 241–58.

MARCUS GARVEY AND THE UNIA

David Cronon, *Black Moses: The Story of Marcus Garvey and the Universal Negro Improvement Association* (Madison, Wis., 1955).

Theodore G. Vincent, *Black Power and the Garvey Movement* (San Francisco, 1972).

Tony Martin, *Race First: The Ideological and Organizational Struggles of Marcus Garvey and the UNIA* (Westport, Conn., 1976).

Robert G. Weisbord, *Ebony Kinship: Africa, Africans, and the Afro-American* (Westport, Conn., 1973).

Leonard E. Barrett, *Soul Force: African Heritage in Afro-American Religion* (New York, 1974).

Alphonso Pinkney, *Red, Black, and Green: Black Nationalism in the United States* (Cambridge, 1976).

Theodore Draper, *The Rediscovery of Black Nationalism* (New York, 1969).

Randall K. Burkett, *Garveyism as a Religious Movement: The Institutionalization of a Black Religion* (London, 1978).

Emory J. Tolbert, *The UNIA and Black Los Angeles: Ideology and Community in the Garvey Movement* (Los Angeles, 1980).

R. H. Brisbane, Jr., "Some New Light on the Garvey Movement," *Journal of Negro History* 36 (1951): 53–62.

C. S. Matthews, "Marcus Garvey Writes from Jamaica on the Mulatto Escape Hatch," *Journal of Negro History* 59 (1974): 170–76.

BLACK CULTURE IN THE NORTH

R. L. Kusmer, *A Ghetto Takes Shape: Black Cleveland, 1870–1930* (Evanston, Ill., 1978).

Gilbert Osofsky, *Harlem: The Making of a Ghetto, 1880–1930* (New York, 1963).

Nathan I. Huggins, *Harlem Renaissance* (New York, 1971).

Jervis Anderson, *Harlem: The Great Black Way, 1900–1950* (London, 1982).

Claude McKay, *Harlem: Negro Metropolis* (New York, 1968; first published 1940).

Roi Ottley, *"New World A-Coming"* (New York, 1968; first published 1943).

James Weldon Johnson, *Black Manhattan* (New York, 1968; first published 1930).

D. J. Hellwig, "Black Meets Black: Afro-American Reactions to West Indian Immigrants in the 1920s," *South Atlantic Quarterly* 77 (1978): 206–24.

Theodore Kornweibel, Jr., *No Crystal Stair: Black Life and the Messenger 1917–1928* (Westport, Conn., 1975).

WHITE OVER BLACK

Gunnar Myrdal, *An American Dilemma* (New York, 1944).

Morton Sosna, *In Search of the Silent South* (New York, 1977).

Charles S. Johnson, *Patterns of Negro Segregation* (New York, 1943).

Dan T. Carter, *Scottsboro: A Tragedy of the American South* (Baton Rouge, La., 1969).

Robert L. Zargrando, *The NAACP Crusade Against Lynching 1909–1950* (Philadelphia, 1980).

——, "The NAACP and a Federal Antilynching Bill, 1934–1940," *Journal of Negro History* 50 (April 1965).

Robert W. Dubay, "Mississippi and the Proposed Federal Anti-Lynching Bills of 1937–1938," *The Southern Quarterly* (October 1968): 73–87.

BLACKS AND THE NEW DEAL

Ralph Bunche, *The Political Status of the Negro in the Age of FDR* (Chicago, 1973).

John B. Kirby, *Black Americans in the Roosevelt Era: Liberalism and Race* (Knoxville, Tenn., 1980).

Nancy J. Weiss, *Farewell to the Party of Lincoln: Black Politics in the Age of FDR* (Princeton, 1983).

Harvard Sitkoff, *A New Deal for Blacks: The Emergence of Civil Rights as a National Issue*, vol. 1, *The Depression Decade* (New York, 1978).

Herbert Garfinkel, *When Negroes March: The March on Washington Movement in the Organizational Politics for FEPC* (Glencoe, Ill., 1959).
William H. Harris, "A. Philip Randolph as a Charismatic Leader, 1925–1941," *Journal of Negro History* 44 (1979): 301–15.

BLACK LITERATURE

Stephen J. Butterfield, *Black Autobiography in America* (Boston, 1975).
Addison Gayle, Jr., *The Way of the New World: The Black Novel in America* (New York, 1976).
Edward Margolies, *Native Sons: A Critical Study of Twentieth Century Black American Authors* (New York, 1968).

Chapter 9

RADIO

Erik Barnouw, *A Tower in Babel: A History of Broadcasting in the United States,* vol. I, *to 1933* (New York, 1966).
——, *The Golden Web: A History of Broadcasting in the United States,* vol. II, *1933–1953* (New York, 1968).
Richard Levinson and William Link, *Stay Tuned* (New York, 1983).
Christopher Sterling and John M. Kitros, *Stay Tuned* (New York, 1978).
Philip T. Rosen, *The Modern Stentors: Radio Broadcasting and the Federal Government 1920–1933* (Westport, Conn., 1980).
Frank Buxton and Bill Owen, *The Big Broadcast 1920–1950* (a revised, expanded edition of *Radio's Golden Age*) (New York, 1972).
Hadley Cantril, *The Invasion from Mars: A Study in the Psychology of Panic, with the Complete Script of the Orson Welles Broadcast* (Princeton, N.J., 1940).
Alexander Kendrick, *Prime Time: The Life of Edward R. Murrow* (Boston, 1969).
Robert Lichello, *Edward R. Murrow: Broadcaster of Courage* (New York, 1972).
Robert Franklin Smith, *Edward R. Murrow — The War Years* (Kalamazoo, Mich., 1978).

Chapter 10

HOLLYWOOD AND THE MOVIES

Gerald Mast, *A Short History of the Movies* (revised New York, 1986; first published 1971).
Paul Michael, ed., *The American Movies Reference Book: The Sound Era* (Englewood Cliffs, N.J., 1970).
Lary May, *Screening Out the Past: The Birth of Mass Culture and the Motion Picture Industry* (revised Chicago, 1983; first published 1980).
Kevin Brownlow, *The Parade's Gone By* (New York, 1968).

Robert Sklar, *Movie-Made America: A Cultural History of American Movies* (New York, 1975).

Andrew Bergman, *We're in the Money: Depression America and Its Films* (New York, 1971).

Eugene Rosow, *Born to Lose: The Gangster Film in America* (New York, 1978).

Raymond Lee and B. C. Van Hecke, *Gangsters and Hoodlums: The Underworld in the Cinema* (New York, 1971).

James Agee, "Comedy's Greatest Era," *Agee on Film* (Boston, 1964), pp. 2–19.

DIRECTORS, MOGULS, AND STARS

Andrew Sarris, *The American Cinema: Directors and Directions, 1929–1968* (New York, 1968).

Iris Barry and Eileen Bowser, *D. W. Griffith: American Film Master* (New York, 1965).

Lillian Gish, *The Movies, Mr. Griffith, and Me* (Englewood Cliffs, N.J., 1969).

Charlie Chaplin, *My Autobiography* (New York, 1964).

David Robinson, *Chaplin: His Life and Art* (New York, 1985).

Isabel Quigley, *Charlie Chaplin: Early Comedies* (New York, 1968).

Mack Sennett, *King of Comedy* (New York, 1954).

Rudi Blesh, *Keaton* (New York, 1966).

Peter Cowie, *The Cinema of Orson Welles* (New York, 1965).

Robert Field, *The Art of Walt Disney* (New York, 1943).

Stephen Farber and Marc Green, *Hollywood Dynasties* (New York, 1984).

Philip French, *The Movie Moguls: An Informal History of the Hollywood Tycoons* (London, 1969; Harmondworth, Middlesex, 1971).

Bob Thomas, *King Cohn* (New York, 1967).

——, *Thalberg: Life and Legend* (New York, 1969).

——, *Astaire: The Man, the Dancer* (New York, 1984).

George Eells and Stanley Musgrove, *Mae West* (New York and London, 1984).

John Grierson, "Directors of the Thirties," *Film: An Anthology* (Berkeley and Los Angeles, 1966).

Chapter 11

THE LOST GENERATION

Alfred Kazin, *On Native Grounds* (New York, 1983; first published 1939).

——, *An American Procession* (New York, 1984).

——, *Starting Out in the Thirties* (New York, 1980).

Robert Crunden, *From Self to Society: Transitions in American Thought, 1919–1941* (Englewood Cliffs, N.J., 1972).

Malcolm Cowley, *Exile's Return: A Literary Odyssey of the 1920s* (Magnolia, Mass., 1983; first published 1934).

Frederick Hoffman, *The Twenties: American Writing in the Postwar Decade* (revised New York, 1965; first published 1962).

Edmund Wilson, *The Twenties* (New York, 1975).

——, *The Thirties* (New York, 1982).

Jerre Mangione, *The Dream and the Deal: The Federal Writers' Project 1935–1943* (New York, 1974).

Richard Wightman Fox, *Reinhold Niebuhr* (New York, 1986).

THE IMPACT OF FREUD

Ernest Jones, *The Life and Work of Sigmund Freud,* 3 vols. (New York, 1953–57; abbreviated edition in one volume edited by Lionel Trilling and Steven Marcus, New York, 1961).

Walter Lippmann, "Freud and the Layman," *New Republic* 2 (April 17, 1915); supp. 9–10.

A. A. Brill, "The Introduction and Development of Freud's Work in the United States," *American Journal of Sociology* 45 (November 1939): 318–25.

MUSIC, MUSICIANS, AND THE PERFORMING ARTS

Stanley Sadie, ed., *New Grove Dictionary of Music and Musicians,* 2 vols. (6th edition, New York and London, 1980).

Paul Oliver, *The Blues Tradition* (New York, 1970).

Marshall Stearns, *The Story of Jazz* (New York, 1956).

Aaron Copland and Vivian Perlis, *Copland: 1900 Through 1942* (New York, 1984).

Joseph Horowitz, *Understanding Toscanini: How He Became an American Culture-God and Helped Create a New Audience for Old Music* (New York, 1987).

Russell Lynes, *The Lively Audience: A History of the Visual and Performing Arts in America, 1890–1950* (New York, 1985).

Jay Gold, ed., *The Swing Era (1936–37: The Movies, Between Vitaphone and Video; 1940–41: How It Was to Be Young Then; 1941–42: Swing as a Way of Life)* (Time-Life Records, New York, 1970).

Charles W. Stein, ed., *American Vaudeville as Seen by Its Contemporaries* (New York, 1984).

Stanley Green, *The Great Clowns of Broadway* (New York, 1984).

Tony Thomas, *That's Dancing* (New York, 1984).

Otis Ferguson, "The Spirit of Jazz," *New Republic* (December 30, 1936).

Richard Hasbany, "Bromidic Parables: The American Musical Theatre during the Second World War," *The Journal of Popular Culture* 6 (Spring 1973).

Timothy B. Donovan, "Oh, What a Beautiful Mornin': The Musical *Oklahoma!* and the Popular Mind in 1943," *Journal of Popular Culture* 8 (Winter 1974).

Chapter 12

PAINTING AND SCULPTURE

Lloyd Goodrich and John Baur, *American Art of Our Century* (New York, 1961).

Sam Hunter, *American Art of the Twentieth Century* (New York, 1972).

Jean Lipman, *What is American in American Art* (New York, 1963).

Jack Burnham, *Beyond Modern Sculpture* (New York, 1963).

Clement Greenberg, *Art and Culture: Critical Essays* (Boston, 1961).

Richard D. McKinzie, *The New Deal for Artists* (Princeton, N.J., 1973).

Serge Guilbaut, translated by Arthur Goldhammer, *How New York Stole the Idea of Modern Art—Abstract Expressionism, Freedom, and the Cold War* (Chicago, 1985).

Susan C. Larsen, "The American Abstract Artists: A Documentary History, 1936–1941," *Archives of American Art Journal* 14 (1974): 2–7.

ARCHITECTURE

Wayne Andrews, *Architecture, Ambition, and Americans* (London, 1984).

John Burchard and Albert Bush-Brown, *The Architecture of America* (Boston, 1961).

William Coles and Henry George Reed, Jr., ed., *Architecture in America: A Battle of Styles* (New York, 1961).

James Fitch, *American Building: The Forces That Shape It* (Boston, 1948).

Talbot Hamlin, *The American Spirit in Architecture* (New Haven, Conn., 1926).

Huson Jackson, *A Guide to New York Architecture, 1650–1952* (New York, 1952).

Charles Jencks, *Modern Movements in Architecture* (second edition, Harmondsworth, Middlesex, and New York, 1985; first published 1973).

Lewis Mumford, *Sticks and Stones: A Study of American Architecture and Civilization* (New York, 1924).

Nikolaus Pevsner, *Pioneers of Modern Design* (New York, 1949).

Vincent Scully, *American Architecture and Urbanism* (New York, 1969).

RAYMOND HOOD AND FRANK LLOYD WRIGHT

Raymond Hood, *Raymond M. Hood* (New York, 1931).

Arthur Norton, *Raymond M. Hood* (New York, 1931).

Frank Lloyd Wright, *An Autobiography* (New York, 1932).

———, *Writings and Buildings* (New York, 1960).

Vincent Scully, *Frank Lloyd Wright* (New York, 1969).

Henry-Russell Hitchcock, *In the Nature of Materials, 1887–1941: The Buildings of Frank Lloyd Wright* (New York, 1942).

Brendon Grill, *Many Masks: A Life of Frank Lloyd Wright* (New York, 1987).

Chapter 13

AMERICA AND WORLD AFFAIRS

Foster Rhea Dulles, *America's Rise to World Power 1898–1954* (New York, 1963; first published 1954).

Richard W. Leopold, *The Growth of American Foreign Policy* (New York, 1962).

Robert H. Ferrell, *American Diplomacy in the Great Depression: Hoover-Stimson Foreign Policy, 1929–1933* (New Haven, Conn., 1957).

———. *Peace in Their Time: The Origins of the Kellogg-Briand Pact* (New York, 1969).

Warren I. Cohen, *The American Revisionists: The Lessons of Intervention in World War I* (Chicago, 1967).

Charles Chatfield, *For Peace and Justice: Pacifism in America 1914–1941* (Knoxville, Tenn., 1971).

Anthony Sampson, *The Seven Sisters* (New York and London, 1976).

———, *Empires of the Sky: The Politics, Contests, and Cartels of World Airlines* (London and New York, 1985).

Merlo Pusey, *Charles Evans Hughes,* 2 vols. (New York, 1951), vol. 2.

Herbert Feis, *The Diplomacy of the Dollar: First Era, 1919–1932* (Baltimore, 1950).

Charles Beard, "The American Invasion of Europe," *Harper's Magazine* 158 (March 1929): 470–79.

LATIN AMERICA AND THE GOOD NEIGHBOR

Bryce Wood, *The Making of the Good Neighbor Policy* (New York, 1961).

———, *The United States and Latin American Wars, 1932–1942* (New York, 1966).

E. David Cronon, *Josephus Daniels in Mexico* (Madison, Wis., 1960).

Chapter 14

ISOLATION AND INTERVENTION

Robert Dalek, *Franklin D. Roosevelt and American Foreign Policy, 1932–1945* (New York and Oxford, 1979).

Wayne S. Cole, *Roosevelt and the Isolationists 1932–1945* (Lincoln, Neb., 1983).

John E. Wiltz, *From Isolation to War, 1931–1941* (Arlington Heights, Ill., 1968).

Julius W. Pratt, *Cordell Hull* (Totowa, N.J., 1964).

Basil Rauch, *Roosevelt: From Munich to Pearl Harbor* (New York, 1975; first published 1950 and 1965).

Walter Johnson, *The Battle Against Isolationism* (New York, 1973; first published 1944).

Warren F. Kimball, *The Most Unsordid Act: Lend-Lease 1939–1941* (Baltimore, 1969).

——. *Franklin D. Roosevelt and the World Crisis 1937–45* (Lexington, Mass., 1974).

T. R. Fehrenbach, *F.D.R.'s Undeclared War* (New York, 1967).

Robert A. Divine, *The Illusion of Neutrality* (Chicago, 1962).

Robert A. Divine, *The Reluctant Belligerent: American Entry into World War II* (New York, 1976; first published 1965).

Gordon W. Prange, *At Dawn We Slept: The Untold Story of Pearl Harbor* (New York, 1981).

Wayne S. Cole, "American Entry in World War II: A Historiographical Appraisal," *Mississippi Valley Historical Review* 43 (March 1957): 575–617.

INDEX